Nutritional Needs of the Preterm Infant

Nutritional Needs of the Preterm Infant
Scientific Basis and Practical Guidelines

Editors

Reginald C. Tsang, M.B.B.S.
Executive Director
The Perinatal Research Institute
Children's Hospital Medical Center
University of Cincinnati Medical Center
Cincinnati, Ohio

Alan Lucas, M.B.B.S.
Head of Infant and Child Nutrition
Medical Research Council, Dunn Nutrition Unit,
    and University Department of Paediatrics
Cambridge, United Kingdom

Ricardo Uauy, M.D., Ph.D.
Professor, Nutrition and Pediatrics
INTA University of Chile
Santiago, Chile;
Senior Research Associate
Retina Foundation of the Southwest
Dallas, Texas

Stanley Zlotkin, M.D., Ph.D.
Associate Professor
Departments of Nutritional Sciences
    and Pediatrics
University of Toronto, Research Institute
    and Division of Clinical Nutrition
The Hospital for Sick Children
Toronto, Canada

WAVERLY EUROPE LTD.
Williams & Wilkins
BALTIMORE · HONG KONG · LONDON · MUNICH
PHILADELPHIA · SYDNEY · TOKYO

Nutritional Needs of the Preterm Infant was produced for Williams & Wilkins by Caduceus Medical Publishers, Inc.

Editorial Director
John Mesevage

Assistant Editor
Beth Beyer

Managing Editor
Carol Verderese

Design Director
Michael McClain

Associate Editor
Doug White

Production Director
Laura Carlson

Copy Editors
Edmund Decker
Laurie Lewis

Publisher
Paul Henrici

Indexer
Margaret Jarpey

Distributed outside of the United States of America by:
Waverly Europe Ltd.
Broadway House
2-6 Fulham Broadway
London SW6 1AA
UK

Printed in the United States of America

Library of Congress Cataloging-in-Publication Data

Nutritional needs of the preterm infant: scientific basis and practical guidelines / editors, Reginald C. Tsang ... [et al.].

    p.   cm.
Sequel to: Vitamin and mineral requirements in preterm infants / edited by Reginald C. Tsang, c1985.
Includes bibliographical references and index.
ISBN 0-683-08425-9
1. Infants (Premature)—Nutrition—Requirements.
2. Infants (Premature)—Nutrition.
I. Tsang, Reginald C. II. Vitamin and mineral requirements in preterm infants.
[DNLM: 1. Infant Nutrition. 2. Infant, Premature. WS 120 N9767]
RJ216.V57 1992
618.92'011—dc20
DNLM/DLC
for Library of Congress

92-49242
CIP

96 97
2 3 4 5

Foreword

BUCKINGHAM PALACE

Ever changing fashions and conflicting health advice on childhood nutrition have resulted in great confusion, amongst both health professionals and parents. There is, however, an underlying agreement that nutrition is a major factor in world health—my own observation of work with children in the least developed countries has made that very clear to me.

Scientists conducting research into nutrition in babies and young children have begun to pay more attention to a critical issue: the possibility that the quality of nutrition in babies is important for health in later life. Clinical researchers have been surprisingly slow to move into this area and yet those involved in the care of animals have appreciated for many years that early nutrition could have profound long-term consequences. In premature babies— born into the world months ahead of time, ill, with poor reserves and with a need for rapid growth—it might be suspected that nutritional care would be of immense importance for the quality of their survival. The chapters in this book, based on careful modern research, indicate that this is indeed so. The lessons learned are potentially of great relevance to all babies, both well and ill, all over the world, and I hope future research will take its lead from some of the exciting new studies on premature infants.

The four editors of this book have aimed to provide a modern international standard of nutritional care for the premature baby. Recommendations have been justified in a series of chapters, each written by a recognized authority. The way this book was put together is most unusual. I understand that each author was assigned two external reviewers, also with international reputations in that area. The chapters were read and assessed by all the editors and other authors. Finally, the authors and editors converged, from numerous countries, and each author in turn "defended" his recommendations in an oral presentation to the others present. The final manuscripts were remodeled following all these inputs. I am told that the whole process, which must be highly unusual if not unique in medical writings, was conducted with good grace and remarkably little acrimony—a commendable (and surprising?) achievement for medical experts!

I would expect this book to be most influential and warmly received and to set a high, and hopefully consistent, international standard of nutritional care for premature babies. I hope also that this book will help stimulate corresponding work on a broader front in childhood nutrition.

Anne

HRH the Princess Royal
Buckingham Palace

Preface

This work, the sequel to the book *Vitamin and Mineral Requirements in Preterm Infants* (Tsang RC, ed. New York: Marcel Dekker, 1985), arose out of many discussions among investigators in the field of neonatal nutrition. Over the last decade, there have been major advances in understanding of the optimal management of low-birthweight infants. Modern neonatal intensive care units can achieve astonishingly high survival rates, >90%, in infants whose birthweights are 1,000 to 1,500 g (Fig. 1). The need to define and meet the nutritional needs of these infants in an optimal way is ever increasing.

Research in the specific area of neonatal nutrition has also progressed significantly in the last decade, and a major work to integrate the findings of investigators around the world appeared timely. Further, there is a great lack of uniformity of nutrition recommendations worldwide, resulting in tremendous disparity of practice, and the production of a confusingly large number of nutrient formulations for use in neonatal intensive care units (see Appendix, Tables A.3 and A.4).

With the sponsorship of the International Union of Nutrition Sciences, an editorial committee comprising Reginald C. Tsang (United States), Stanley Zlotkin (Canada), Alan Lucas (Europe), and Ricardo Uauy (Central and South America) was convened to bring together investigators from different continents to determine if a common approach to nutrition recommendations for the neonatal period could be made.

Twenty-one authors were recruited for this task. They were asked to cover the requirements of individual nutrients for the extremely low-birthweight infant (<1,000 g), the 1,000- to 1,750-g preterm infant, and the postdischarge infant, and to clearly state the specific goal of optimal nutrition for each nutrient. The toxicity and deficiency limits for intake, interactions with other nutrients, and metabolism in specific clinical conditions in the neonate also were to be described. Finally, authors were asked to prepare, when appropriate, a representative case study to bring out practical issues in relation to management of nutrient disorders in the neonatal period.

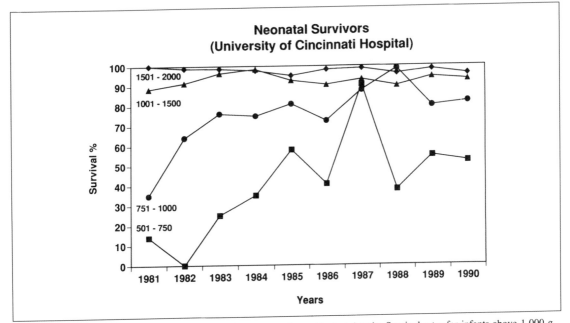

Fig. 1. Dramatic improvements in infant mortality have occurred over the last decade. Survival rates for infants above 1,000 g are now over 90%, and survival rates for infants 751 to 1,000 g approach 80%. (Data from the Perinatal Research Institute, Children's Hospital Medical Center, University of Cincinnati.)

Written with the practicing neonatologist, fellow, registrar, resident, nutritionist, nurse, and pharmacist in mind, this text emphasizes the pragmatic aspects of nutrition and the clinical issues of how to manage a preterm infant's nutrient needs. The key thrust was to produce a text that is *practical and easily accessible,* so that "in the middle of the night" the practitioner could have information readily available for use in his or her management of preterm infants.

In this volume, care has been taken to describe the developmental events that lead to normal fetal growth and the early adaptation to postnatal life. An understanding of these procedures is important to explain the pathologic phenomena that affect the very low-birthweight newborn and to help define the optimal methods of supporting him/her for extrauterine life.

Most neonatal disease processes related to preterm delivery can be explained by immaturity of key organs, leading to unsuccessful adaptation and progressive compromise of specific functions. The occurrence of hyaline membrane disease in babies born before 34 weeks gestation, i.e., before surfactant production is adequate, is an example of developmental pathology; the high prevalence of hypoglycemia in low-birthweight infants represents abnormalities in either storage or mobilization of glycogen.

At birth, the continuous nutrient flux through the placenta is interrupted and the neonate must adapt to intermittent feeds of a product that requires digestion and absorption before entry into circulation. These adaptive responses are integrated and mediated in part by the neuroendocrine system, which acts as a focal point to assure successful adaptation.

The nutritional and metabolic maturational events necessary for extrauterine life include the regulation of substrate flux and metabolism necessary for maintenance and growth needs, and the metabolism and excretion of waste products, including acid, nitrogen, various electrolytes, and minerals. As part of this successful adaptation, the newborn must generate heat and maintain thermal balance independently. Heat production in the neonate is dependent on metabolic thermogenesis rather than muscular activity, i.e., shivering, which does not appear until several months after birth. Successful metabolic adaptation also requires that the neonate be able to mobilize energy reserves (mainly liver glycogen), generate glucose from amino acids and lactate, and regulate fuel supply to key organs by the interaction of various hormones, including insulin, glucagon, cortisol, and catecholamines. Given the wide shifts in oxygenation, cellular metabolism must be able to alternate between aerobic and anaerobic conditions for energy-yielding processes.

This book discusses different approaches to the determination of nutrient requirements in preterm infants. In the term infant, breast milk has traditionally been the "gold standard" for infant nutrition. For the preterm infant, though, human milk has many limitations as a "complete" food. Commonly, for the preterm infant, the intrauterine accretion rate of nutrients becomes the reference point for nutrient needs in the neonatal period. A factorial approach determining the losses and tissue needs for maintenance and growth has been employed and often confirmed by traditional balance or stable isotope studies. Blood concentrations of nutrients serve as another reference point; cord blood values, blood values during a stable growing period, or blood values of the term human milk–fed infant serve as possible references, at least for nutrients that can be easily measured in blood. Functional indices may provide an additional measure of adequacy for some nutrients in the diet. Normal growth has been used as a traditional measure of general nutrient adequacy, often compared to intrauterine growth. However, growth is a fairly gross measure of adequacy of nutrition and more refined measures are usually needed. Urinary excretion of a nutrient may be useful in assessing nutrition status: for example, high urinary excretion of a nutrient, compared with that of term infants, raises suspicion of excess nutrient intake or immature metabolic homeostasis. Nutrient-nutrient interactions may complicate the definition of requirements for specific nutrients: for example, increasing zinc intake may precipitate copper deficiency; iron absorption is likely to be enhanced in the presence of ascorbic acid, and reduced in its absence. From a pragmatic viewpoint, it is sound clinical practice to stay as far away as possible from extremes of nutrient intake—either excessive or deficient, both of which may be associated with pathology. Finally, several follow-up studies have focused, in particular, on the long-term consequences of providing specific nutrients in the neonatal period.

The recommended ranges of intake for nutrients, summarized in the Appendix, Table A.1, are intended as target values applicable to most infants. They do not imply that intakes outside those ranges are associated with deficiency or toxicity, but rather that intakes within the ranges will meet the requirements of most infants within the given birthweight and postnatal stage. It is important for the caregiver at the bedside to identify whether those intakes are adequate or inadequate for a given infant. Intakes need to be adjusted periodically based on physiologic and pathologic conditions specific to each infant (Fig. 2). Preterm infants affected by disease conditions may have an extremely narrow range of acceptable intakes that are not associated with deficiency or toxicity. Tolerance, both clinical and metabolic, needs to be carefully monitored if we are to fulfill the Hippocratic mandate—*primum non nocere*—in this highly vulnerable group of infants.

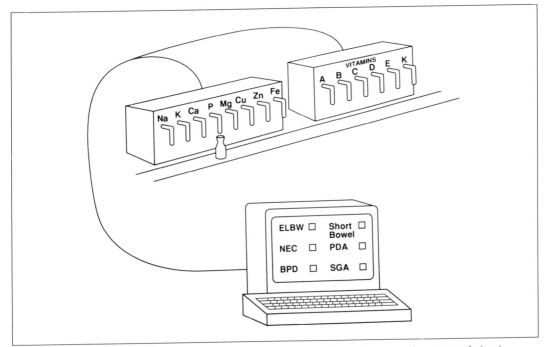

Fig. 2. Future computerized infant-specific nutrient intake? At present, it is possible to formulate parenteral vitamin, mineral and macronutrient mixes utilizing computer-determined nutrient amounts. Can an analogous formulation be applied to enteral nutrition?

To develop a coherent, logical text, a two-day meeting with all of the authors was held. The authors were required to produce manuscripts in advance of the meeting. Then, manuscripts of each chapter were distributed to primary and secondary reviewers prior to the meeting. Reviewers made critical comments on paper and on site. In addition, all other authors were invited to comment on the recommendations. "External" reviewers added their comments by mail and these were integrated into the present text. The names of the reviewers are listed with their respective chapters. The authors' meeting was highly productive and critical, with many mini-sessions conducted during the break times to polish the presentations and gain consensus on the recommendations. The text is indeed a consensus product of all the authors and reviewers.

The editors are particularly indebted to the Mead Johnson Research Center, represented by James W. Hansen, M.D., Ph.D. He worked tirelessly in helping to facilitate the meeting, and he assisted in many of the scientific and administrative details to achieve the goals of this book. Through the generosity of Mead Johnson, the meeting was held in the captivating surroundings of Captiva Island, Florida, which no doubt enhanced the camaraderie and spirit of cooperation among the authors.

The editors also want to thank Renée McKenzie, Sara Stark, Hetty Vankesteren, and Shirley Sizemore for their tremendous assistance in making arrangements for the meeting and in producing the text. Without their efforts this work would not have been possible.

Reginald C. Tsang
Alan Lucas
Ricardo Uauy
Stanley Zlotkin

Contributors and Reviewers

J. Van Aerde, M.D.
The Northern & Central Alberta Perinatal Program,
Edmonton, Alberta, Canada

Billy S. Arant, Jr., M.D.
Professor and Chairman, Department of Pediatrics;
Chattanooga Unit of the University of Tennessee
College of Medicine; Medical Director,
T.C. Thompson Children's Hospital
Medical Center; Chattanooga, Tennessee

Stephanie A. Atkinson, Ph.D.
Associate Professor, Department of Pediatrics;
Coordinator of Nutrition and Metabolism,
McMaster University Children's Hospital,
Hamilton, Ontario, Canada

Stephen Baumgart, M.D.
Professor of Pediatrics, Division of Neonatology,
Jefferson Medical College, Philadelphia, Pennsylvania

Edward F. Bell, M.D.
Professor, Department of Pediatrics,
University of Iowa, Iowa City, Iowa

Margaret C. Cheney, Ph.D.
Chief, Nutrition Evaluation Division, Department of
National Health and Welfare, Ottawa, Ontario, Canada

Andrew T. Costarino, Jr., M.D.
Assistant Professor of Anesthesiology and Pediatrics,
Department of Anesthesiology and Critical Care
Medicine, The University of Pennsylvania School of
Medicine and The Children's Hospital of Philadelphia,
Philadelphia, Pennsylvania

Richard A. Ehrenkranz, M.D.
Professor of Pediatrics and Obstetrics and Gynecology,
Yale University School of Medicine; Clinical Director,
Newborn Special Care Unit, Yale New Haven
Hospital, New Haven, Connecticut

Kenneth J. Falci, Ph.D.
Chief, Regulatory Affairs Staff, Food and Drug
Administration, Washington, District of Columbia

Allan L. Forbes, M.D.
Medical Consultant (Foods and Nutrition),
Rockville, Maryland

Bent Friis-Hansen, M.D.
Professor, Department of Neonatology, Rigshospitalet,
University Hospital, Copenhagen, Denmark

Johan Gentz, M.D., Ph.D.
Head of Department, Department of Pediatrics,
Sach's Children's Hospital, Stockholm, Sweden

Michael R. Gomez, M.D.
Assistant Professor of Pediatrics, Children's
Nutrition Research Center, Baylor College of
Medicine, Houston, Texas

Harry L. Greene, M.D.
Director, Nutritional Science, Bristol-Myers Squibb,
Evansville, Indiana

Frank R. Greer, M.D.
Professor of Pediatrics and Nutritional Sciences,
University of Wisconsin, Madison, Wisconsin

Steven J. Gross, M.D.
Director, Division of Neonatology, Department
of Pediatrics, State University of New York
Health Science Center, Syracuse, New York

Kenneth Hambidge, M.D.
Department of Pediatrics, University of Colorado
Medical Center, Denver, Colorado

Margit Hamosh, Ph.D.
Professor of Pediatrics; Chief, Division of
Developmental Biology and Nutrition,
Georgetown University Children's Medical Center,
Washington, District of Columbia

James W. Hansen, M.D., Ph.D.
Director, Neonatology and Pharmacology,
Mead Johnson Research Center, Bristol-Myers Squibb,
Evansville, Indiana

William W. Hay, Jr., M.D.
Professor of Pediatrics; Director, Neonatal Clinical
Research Center; Director, Training Program in
Neonatal-Perinatal Medicine, University of Colorado
School of Medicine, Denver, Colorado

William C. Heird, M.D.
Professor, Department of Pediatrics,
Children's Nutrition Research Center,
Baylor College of Medicine, Houston, Texas

Sheila M. Innis, Ph.D.
Department of Pediatrics, University of British
Columbia, Vancouver, British Columbia, Canada

C. Lawrence Kien, M.D., Ph.D.
Professor, Department of Pediatrics and Medical
Biochemistry, The Ohio State University
Children's Hospital, Columbus, Ohio

Berthold Koletzko, M.D.
Professor of Pediatrics, Kinderpoliklinik,
Universitat Munchen, Munich, Germany

Winston W.K. Koo, M.B.B.S.
Associate Professor of Pediatrics and Obstetrics
and Gynecology, The University of Tennessee,
Memphis, Tennessee

Bo Lonnerdal, M.D.
Department of Nutrition, University of California,
Davis, California

Alan Lucas, M.B.B.S.
Head of Infant and Child Nutrition,
Medical Research Council, Dunn Nutrition Unit,
and University Department of Paediatrics,
Cambridge, United Kingdom

Jean-L. Micheli, M.D.
Department of Pediatrics, CHUV University Hospital,
Lausanne, Switzerland

Helen Mintz-Hittner, M.D., FACS
Clinical Professor, Departments of Ophthalmology and
Pediatrics, Baylor College of Medicine, Houston, Texas

Donald M. Mock, M.D., Ph.D.
Department of Pediatrics, Division of
Gastroenterology and Nutrition, University
of Iowa Hospital, Iowa City, Iowa

Paul Pencharz, M.B., Ch.B., Ph.D., FRCP(C)
Head, Division of Clinical Nutrition, The Hospital for
Sick Children; Professor, Departments of Paediatrics
and Nutritional Sciences, University of Toronto,
Toronto, Ontario, Canada

Guy Putet, M.D.
Professor of Pediatrics, Claude Bernard University;
Chief, Neonatal Department, Hopital Debrousse,
Lyon, France

Niels C.R. Räihä, M.D.
Professor and Chairman of Pediatrics, Department
of Pediatrics, University of Lund, Malmo, Sweden

R.M. Reifen, M.D.
Research Fellow, Department of Pediatrics,
The Hospital for Sick Children, Toronto, Ontario,
Canada

Pieter J.J. Sauer, M.D.
Professor, Department of Pediatrics,
Sophia Children's Hospital, Rotterdam, Netherlands

Yves Schutz, M.D.
Department of Clinical Physiology, Medical School,
Lausanne, Switzerland

Jacques Senterre, M.D., Ph.D.
Professor and Chairman, Department of Pediatrics,
University Hospital, Liege, Belgium

Jonathan C.L. Shaw, M.D.
Department of Paediatrics, University College
Hospital, London, England

Jayant P. Shenai, M.D.
Associate Professor of Pediatrics;
Director, Newborn Regionalization Program;
Director, Educational Affairs, Vanderbilt University
School of Medicine, Nashville, Tennessee

Laurie J. Smidt, Ph.D., R.D.
Mead Johnson Nutritional Group, Mead Johnson
Research Center, Evansville, Indiana

Patti J. Thureen, M.D.
Assistant Professor of Pediatrics, University of
Colorado Health Sciences Center, Denver, Colorado

Reginald C. Tsang, M.B.B.S.
Executive Director, The Perinatal Research Institute,
Children's Hospital Medical Center,
University of Cincinnati Medical Center,
Cincinnati, Ohio

Ricardo Uauy, M.D., Ph.D.
Professor of Nutrition and Pediatrics, INTA University
of Chile, Santiago, Chile; Senior Research Associate,
Retina Foundation of the Southwest, Dallas, Texas

Joseph Warshaw, M.D.
Professor and Chairman, Department of Pediatrics,
Yale University School of Medicine, New Haven,
Connecticut

Brian A. Wharton, M.D.
Rank Professor of Human Nutrition, University of
Glasgow; Consultant Paediatrician, Royal Hospital
for Sick Children, Glasgow, United Kingdom

Victor Y.H. Yu, M.D., M.Sc., FRACP, FRCP, DCH
Director of Neonatal Intensive Care, Monash Medical
Centre, Clinical Associate Professor of Pediatrics,
Monash University, Victoria, Australia

Stanley Zlotkin, M.D., Ph.D.
Associate Professor, Departments of Nutritional
Sciences and Pediatrics, University of Toronto,
Research Institute and Division of Clinical Nutrition,
Hospital for Sick Children, Toronto, Ontario, Canada

Contents

1. Water as Nutrition

Andrew T. Costarino, Jr.

Stephen Baumgart

Reviewers: Billy S. Arant, Jr., Bent Friis-Hansen, William W. Hay, Jr.

Water is integral to all life functions. It carries nutrients to the body's cells, removes waste products, and makes up the physio-chemical milieu that allows cellular work to occur. Total body water (TBW) volume comprises over 60% of all body matter in the adult, and close to 80% in the newborn.[1,2] The plasma membranes of all of the body's cells establish two large divisions of the TBW: (1) intracellular water (ICW) contained within the cells; and (2) the surrounding extracellular water (ECW), which is subdivided by the capillary endothelium into plasma water and non-plasma water (the interstitial water).[1] The ECW shields the internal cellular compartment from direct interface with the external environment, buffering the effect of sudden changes in water (and solute) concentration. This arrangement requires the organism to have systems that monitor the composition of the ECW, as well as mechanisms that correct both water loss and water gain resulting from contact with the outside world.

Changes in water balance affected by an infant's interaction with his/her environment are impacted by nutrient intake and energy production in a predictable way (Fig. 1.1).[3,4] Fats, carbohydrates, and proteins enter the organism with water and are oxidized to produce energy. Elimination of carbon dioxide, water, nitrogen, fixed acids, and heat as waste products of this metabolism results in water loss. As carbon dioxide is exhaled during respiration, water evaporates passively from the upper respiratory tract. Excess heat required to maintain body temperature is dissipated through skin water loss (sweating and evaporation). Nitrogen wastes and fixed acids eliminated in the urine result in renal water loss. The small amount of water lost from the gastrointestinal tract approximately equals the amount of water gained from oxidation of carbon fuels.

The simple maintenance of cell number and body composition consumes less than half the energy produced by a normal infant.[4-6] Growth requires extra water intake into new tissues. Vigorous activity requires increased intake of fuels and oxygen, and causes variations in heat production and water of oxidation, which in turn increase skin, renal, and respiratory water loss. Thus, growth, activity, and illness, as well as stressful environments, test the water regulatory mechanisms of the infant and may exceed the diminished regulatory capacity of the preterm human.

Regulation of Body Water

Water moves spontaneously from a region of high concentration to one of low concentration. Osmosis is the movement of water down its concentration gradient through the cell's semipermeable membrane. Osmolality is the number of solute particles per kilogram of water solvent, with one osmole constituting one gram molecular weight of a substance. A solution of "pure" water contains 55.5 osmoles of water per kilogram, but when sodium chloride or another solute is added to the solution, the water concentration will be reduced. Since water is the solvent in all body fluids, its concentration is usually expressed conversely; that is, solutions are described by the concentration of their solutes. Thus, solutions with high water concentration have low solute osmolality, and water concentration is "dilute" in solutions with high solute osmolality.

Intracellular Water Regulation

Intracellular water concentration is determined by passive movement of water (solvent), and by active transport of solutes across semipermeable plasma membranes. The driving force for water movement is osmotic pressure generated by the difference in water concentration[7,8] on either side of the cell membrane. Intracellular non-permeable macromolecules (mostly proteins) produce osmotic and electrochemical forces that result in unequal distribution of small molecular weight permeable ions ($Na+$, $Cl-$, and $K+$) inside the cell. This would cause cells to swell with water if not for active transport of $Na+$ (with $Cl-$) out of the cell by the cell membrane ($Na+/K+$ ATPase pump). The $Na+/K+$ ATPase pump is the most important regulator of the ICW,[9,10] and makes the cell effectively impermeable to sodium.

Although cell volume and ICW concentration must be regulated by active ion transport at the cell membrane, the range of osmotic gradient is narrowed by the ECW because internal cellular water space is shielded from direct interface with the external environment, preventing most tissues from sudden and large changes in solute or water concentrations. The ECW environment of the renal medulla where wide variations in the extracellular osmolality occur is an important exception, and requires other mechanisms (production of organic osmolytes) to

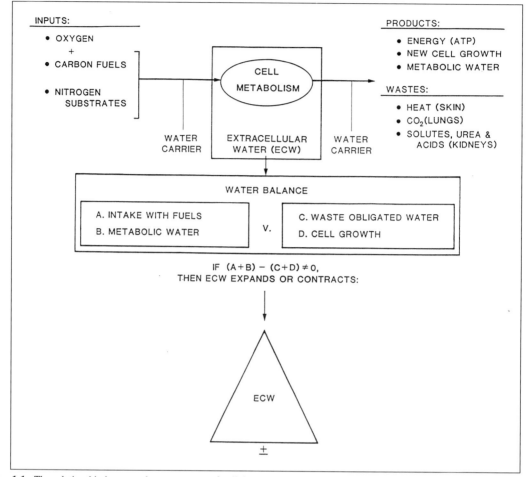

Fig. 1.1. The relationship between the components of cellular metabolism and water balance in the extracellular compartment. (Reproduced, with permission, from Costarino AT, Baumgart S. Neonatal water metabolism. In: Cowett RM, ed. *Principles of perinatal-neonatal metabolism.* New York: Springer-Verlag, 1991:624.)

protect cell size. Additionally, during severe stress when normal mechanisms may fail to maintain normal water concentration in the ECW, some tissues (e.g., brain) can maintain cellular volume through intracellular accumulation of osmolytes.[11,12]

Extracellular Water Regulation

While the ECW limits the range of osmolalities that confront the ICW, a whole-organism system of water volume and concentration regulation is needed to regulate ECW. Changes in water balance associated with an infant's interaction with the environment and energy production are reflected in changes in size of the ECW (Fig. 1.1). The ECW regulatory response should: (1) assure the integrity of the circulation (vascular pressure); and (2) keep the osmolality of the ECW compartment within 3% of the osmolar set point (280 to 290 mOsm).[13,14] Regulation is achieved through changes in heart rate and contractility, vas-

cular tone, renal water excretion, and gastrointestinal intake (thirst). In critically ill newborns, intake is completely controlled by others, making the thirst effector nonfunctional. The system is modulated through hormonal effects on the renal excretion of water and solute, including the renin-angiotensin-aldosterone function, arginine vasopressin, and atrial natriuretic peptide.

The ECW control mechanism functions as follows: an increase in ECW is reflected in an increase in plasma volume, which in turn increases blood flow and pressure. Increased vascular pressure leads to an increase in urinary flow which returns the ECW volume to baseline.[13,15,16] If the perturbation increasing ECW volume lowers plasma osmolality, a dilute urine is produced. Conversely, a decrease in the ECW volume results in decreased cardiac output and glomerular filtration pressure, leading to decreased urinary flow that lasts until intake replenishes the lost volume.

Hypertonicity, which accompanies many low-volume states, stimulates thirst and renal resorption of water.[17] The next section on components of the ECW control system highlights the limitations of the system present in the critically ill and premature infant.

Oncotic and Hydrostatic Pressure The ECW compartment is subdivided into plasma water and interstitial water. A dynamic interaction of oncotic pressure and the hydrostatic pressure generated by the cardiovascular system[18] results in small, but important, differences between these two compartments. These differences allow movement of water from the circulating blood into the surrounding tissues and back again.

Oncotic Pressure. Osmolality of body fluids is affected by the presence of large molecular weight plasma proteins (colloids) that do not pass freely through semipermeable membranes. These proteins are usually ionized at physiologic pH, so they have an associated electromotive force that causes an unequal distribution of the smaller diffusible ions (crystalloids) between body compartments (the Gibbs-Donnan Equilibrium).[7,10,12,19] The increase in osmotic pressure of plasma water compared to the interstitial water due to the colloids (oncotic pressure) is approximately two thirds directly related to the nondiffusible protein particles and one third a result of the difference in diffusible particles. Plasma oncotic pressure is 25 to 28 mm Hg in adults, 15 to 17 mm Hg in term neonates, and sometimes lower in preterm infants with respiratory distress.[20–22]

Hydrostatic Pressure (Starling Relationship). Water movement across an idealized capillary wall was described qualitatively by Starling in 1896,[23] and the formal mathematical treatment of the component forces was presented 40 years ago by Landis and Pappenheimer.[19,23,24]

flow across the capillary ~ [capillary hydrostatic pressure–interstitial hydrostatic pressure]–[plasma oncotic pressure–interstitial oncotic pressure]

The normal balance of these forces results in a small amount of water leaving the plasma at the arterial end of the capillary bed, while much of it re-enters the plasma at the venous end due to the fall in capillary hydrostatic pressure.[7,24] The small amount of fluid that remains in the interstitium is then removed by lymphatic drainage. Disruption of the usual balance of forces within a tissue capillary bed may favor increased movement of fluid volume into the interstitium. The disruption may be caused by: (1) conditions of high plasma hydrostatic pressure; (2) increased vascular permeability; or (3) low plasma oncotic pres-

sure. In these conditions the lymphatic drainage must increase or tissue edema will occur.[7] Since the ability to increase lymphatic drainage varies among the different tissue beds, some organs are more or less prone to develop edema. Other factors affecting lymphatic drainage include: (1) body movement, where lymphatic flow depends in part on tissue movement; (2) lymphatic obstruction due to tissue injury; (3) mechanical factors.

Cardiovascular Contribution to Water Regulation Cardiac flow is proportional to ventricular filling. Therefore, if plasma volume increases, cardiac output rises. The increased blood flow will then increase renal perfusion and urine formation. However, blood pressure rather than flow is most directly correlated with increased urine production,[15,25] and blood pressure is also the prime stimulus to arterial mechanoreceptor afferents of the hormonal modulators in the ECW control system. The systemic vascular resistance, as maintained by the sympathetic nervous system and local metabolic needs, interacts with the direct effect of heart filling in the cardiovascular control of the ECW.[25,26] Term and preterm infants exhibit a blunted response to acute volume loading[27] due to an immature myocardium that has a high content of noncontractile tissue. The immature myocardium may limit the infants' adaptive response to acute loading of the ECW.

Renal Contribution to Water Regulation The kidney's response to an increase in ECW volume is: (1) increasing glomerular filtration rate (GFR), and (2) decreasing tubular resorption of filtered sodium and water. Neonates have renal function that limits the magnitude of their renal response during stress. The number of nephrons in the fetal kidney is only complete at 34 to 36 weeks of gestational age.[28,29] Early in maturation, the glomerular surface area available for filtration is small compared to that in older infants and adults.[30] In addition to structural maturation of the nephron, functional changes occur after birth as blood pressure increases and renal vascular resistance decreases.[31,32] In term infants, GFR increases dramatically during the first postnatal week.[33–36] Glomular filtration continues to rise over the first 2 years of life as nephron maturation is completed.[37] Because of these differences in glomerular function, neonates, particularly the preterm infant, have a narrowed range of renal responses for regulation of the ECW.

The distal nephron can produce a dilute urine even in early gestation.[38] Therefore, any limitation of the fetal or neonatal kidney in excreting excess water is due to the lower GFR rather than limited distal nephron function.[37–40] Conversely, premature infants exhibit a reduced concentrating ability due to: (1) a relatively low interstitial urea concentration[41-44]; (2) an anatomically shortened Loop of Henle[43,45]; and (3) distal tubule and collecting system epithelium that is less responsive to AVP.[29,39,43,46] Decreased ability to concentrate urine renders the preterm infant more vulnerable to ECW contraction and hypertonicity.

Hormonal Contribution to Water Regulation

Renin-Angiotensin-Aldosterone System (RAAS). The RAAS modulates the response of the heart and kidney to ECW contraction. When ECW volume is reduced, a fall in cardiac output and blood pressure lowers GFR.[15,25] The resultant reduction in sodium delivery to the distal nephron leads to increased renin production by the kidney.[26,48,49] Renin cleaves the prohormone, angiotensinogen, forming angiotensin I. Angiotensin converting enzyme (ACE) produced by the vascular endothelium acts on angiotensin I to produce the potent vasoconstricting agent angiotensin II.[49] The primary and secondary effects of angiotensin II stabilize the contracting ECW. The vascular action of angiotensin II raises blood pressure throughout the circulation, and promotes water and salt resorption in the proximal nephron.[50] Additionally, by stimulating the adrenal release of aldosterone, distal nephron sodium resorption is augmented.[50]

The RAAS matures early in gestation, and high hormone levels are present in premature infants, partly due to neonatal renal tubules that have a blunted response to aldosterone.[51,52] With maturation, the physiologic stimuli for all components of the RAAS slowly decrease.[53,54] In critically ill premature infants, respiratory disease, mechanical ventilation, and salt restriction may exaggerate the stimulus for renin angiotensin and aldosterone release.[54-56]

Arginine Vasopressin (AVP). Secretory granules in the supraoptic and paraventricular nuclei of the hypothalamus contain AVP, an antidiuretic hormone. Increased blood osmolality, lowered arterial blood pressure, and other stimuli such as pain trigger the release of this hormone. Arginine vasopressin increases water reabsorption in the collecting duct by increasing cellular concentration of cyclic AMP, which then increases water permeability of the collecting duct cells.[57] Low ECW osmolality is more important than the other stimuli for AVP secretion, suggesting that AVP primarily maintains ECW water concentration rather than ECW volume.[13]

Fetal hypothalamic production and pituitary storage of AVP begin by 11 weeks gestation, and by the end of the second trimester levels are similar to those for term infants.[58-60] Arginine vasopressin release in response to hyperosmolality and hypovolemic hemorrhage in fetal lambs and human neonates indicates that the AVP response to both osmotic and baroreceptor stimulation is functional by mid-gestation.[38,61,62] In the neonate, high plasma AVP levels are associated with parturition but normally fall rapidly during the first 24 hours of life, and continue to decrease during the first week. Gestational age has little effect on this pattern,[60] but factors such as vaginal delivery, birth asphyxia, and meconium aspiration are associated with higher AVP levels,[59,63,64] while maternal anesthetic administration is associated with lower levels.[65] The nonosmotic stimuli for AVP release observed in adult subjects in association with pain, hypoxia, and raised intracranial pressure[13] also seem to be present in the newborn.

The osmolar gradient within the renal interstitium determines the ability of AVP to increase water reabsorption. The highly anabolic state of the infant however, reduces the availability of both urea[41,42,66] and sodium,[66-68] and together with shortened Loops of Henle limit renal medullary solute concentration in the term and premature infant.[41,43,45,66,67] As a result, a neonate's maximum urine osmolality in response to AVP release is less than an adult's.[39,40,60,69] Despite this decreased response, the presence of high levels of AVP in critically ill newborns, in association with stimuli for nonosmotic release, suggests that antidiuretic hormone release (SIADH) may contribute to hyponatremia seen in these infants.[60-71]

Atrial Natriuretic Peptide. Atrial natriuretic peptide (ANP) complements the regulation of ECW concentration by the AVP just described.[72,73] Increase in circulating blood volume with mechanical distortion of the heart's atrial walls results in hormone release, with a rise in circulating plasma levels. The prohormone is cleaved by plasma enzymes to its active form. The principle action of ANP is to promote the renal excretion of water and sodium.[74,75] The duration and action of ANP are probably very short-lived (a few minutes), as demonstrated by acute reduction of ANP levels following ligation of the ductus arteriosus shown in one newborn study.[76]

With transition to extrauterine life, a brisk diuresis of water and salt is observed after the first 1 to 2 days.[77] Measurements of ANP shortly after birth demonstrate strikingly elevated hormone levels coincident with this diuresis. A causal relationship in promoting diuresis in edema states in neonates is suggested by these observations, but not yet proven.[78] If fed a salt-supplemented formula, however, infants persistently maintain elevated ANP plasma concentrations and excrete salt.[79] Atrial natriuretic peptide levels may be high coincident with diuresis in premature babies with respiratory distress syndrome (RDS) but there is no clear renal response to these elevated hormone levels.[80]

Water Balance and Nutrition in the Extrauterine Environment

The water control mechanism outlined in the previous section allows the infant to respond to changes in ECW volume or concentration that occur during interaction with the environment. The ECW losses and gains balance sheet is summarized at the bottom of Figure 1.1. Gains on the left include water intake with fuels, and water of hydration. On the right, the loss includes water necessary to fill new cell volume with growth, and the water required to remove wastes (heat, carbon dioxide and excess solute). In the next section, we elaborate on some of these water balance factors as they relate to the critically ill or premature neonate.

Water Evaporation to the Environment

Evaporative water losses incurred passively from the skin and the upper respiratory tract are not easy to measure. Together they comprise *insensible water loss,* indicating that their volumes are not under strict internal regulatory control. The environment's impact on insensible water loss is important for determining water balance in premature infants, especially in the first days after birth.[81,82] An often cited relationship between infant metabolic rate and insensible water loss suggests that 23% of a mature infant's heat production associated with food digestion and assimilation is dissipated through the evaporation of water from the skin and respiratory tract. Such a relationship may not apply only to the prematurely born baby.[83,84] Transcutaneous evaporation and respiratory water loss in premature infants are not linked to necessary heat dissipation, and may be so large as to endanger infant survival from dehydration and hypothermia. Such insensible losses, therefore, cannot be attributed a fixed proportion of metabolic heat production based on nutrient intake or tissue catabolism.

Insensible Water Loss from the Skin   In the premature infant, transcutaneous evaporation is a passive and unpredictable process where free water is lost in vast quantities from the exposed moist epidermis. Sweat glands secrete little water, since apocrine function and thermal sensory-neural integration are immature well before 34 weeks gestation.[85,86] Recently reported measurements of insensible water loss in premature newborn infants are based on infant weight change assessed either daily or over a period of a few hours. Results are sometimes corrected for the weights of oxygen and carbon dioxide exchange, which may account for 5% to 10% of weight loss.[87-91] These studies differ with regard to subject age and size, environments associated with incubation, and distinction between respiratory and trans-

cutaneous evaporation. Such factors complicate recommendations for fluid replacement.

The transcutaneous evaporimeter is an alternative method for measuring water loss from the premature infant's skin. This method is potentially more applicable in the clinical setting due to its ease of application and replicability compared to more cumbersome, error-prone, and time-consuming measurements of weight change.[92,93] The transcutaneous evaporimeter measures humidity and temperature immediately adjacent to the infant's skin surface using a hollow cylinder probe 1.25 cm in diameter. Transepidermal water evaporation ($g/m^2/h$) is calculated from the temperature and humidity gradient sampled within the cylinder at two discrete distances above the epidermal surface. A higher rate of evaporative water loss is found if the relative humidity and temperature are higher near the surface than below it. This technique has confirmed previous observations on skin water loss (performed under rigidly determined laboratory incubation conditions and using weight loss measurements), and extended them to a large population of premature subjects nursed in more clinically relevant environments.

Much recent work on insensible water loss in infants is the product of an extensive series of studies by Hammerlund, Sedin et al.[92,93] These authors observed transepidermal water losses that were larger for preterm infants than term infants. These studies are important for longitudinal assessment of infants who are making the transition to the extrauterine environment during early postnatal life, and the subsequent development of the epidermal barrier to water evaporation during the first 2 weeks. Extremely high rates of water evaporation, however (10% to 15% of body weight in the first day), confirmed measurements reported previously for very low-birthweight (VLBW) infants.[94] Moreover, these authors described the effect of incubator humidification at 60% relative humidity, which greatly reduced water loss in the most extremely low-birthweight infants. Despite humidification, transepidermal evaporation in these patients was never reduced to the level of the more mature premature population above 28 weeks in gestation. These results support the concept that insensible water loss from the skin of very immature neonates is not a small and fixed proportion of heat produced by the infant, and that metabolic rate alone cannot serve to guide replacement water volumes.

Effect of Incubator Environment on Evaporative Water Loss   The forced-air convection warmed incubator provides an isolated infant enclosure and constitutes the world standard for premature infant warming. Air temperatures may be maintained anywhere from room temperature (25°C), to body temperature (37.5°C), or sometimes above body temperature to assure infant body core warming to 36.5°C to 37.5°C. Most often, the operational temperature within the incubator hood for nurturing low-birthweight neonates ranges 10.0°C above room air temperature, depending on infant and incubator variables. If not artificially humidified (a common practice in the United States used to avoid bacterial contamination of the infant's skin and upper respiratory tract), the warming of room air (with a relative humidity between 50% to 60%) to a level near body temperature results in a significant decrease in relative humidity within the incubator and contributes significantly to insensible water loss. Moreover, turbulence encountered with the circulation of warm, dry air within the incubator hood may further increase evaporative gradients and water loss.[95]

Open-bed platforms with an overhead radiant-heat source are used in many delivery room and intensive care environments to guarantee exogenous warming of critically ill low-birthweight infants while allowing resuscitation and intensive care procedures. These devices maintain the same vapor pressure gradient near the infant's skin as occurs within the dry incubator when air is heated to 36.5°C, and increase evaporation compared to a humidified enclosed environment. Minor air turbulence may also significantly increase evaporation under radiant warmers.[95–98]

Cutaneous water loss is disproportionately higher from VLBW infants weighing under 1 kg than from more mature infants studied.[96,98,99] Two factors may account for this: (1) the immature infant's epidermis is poorly cornified and presents little barrier to passive evaporation from the underlying epithelium, thus yielding a higher rate of transcutaneous passage of water when warmed by radiant heaters; and (2) the VLBW infant's ratio of surface area to body mass (i.e., cutaneously evaporable water mass) is increased in geometric proportion to diminishing patient size.[86,88–92,100]

Several methods have been used to diminish the large water evaporation from the skin of low-birthweight babies who are nursed either under radiant warmers or within dry convection warmed incubators. A variety of clear plastic films and body hoods have been customized in many nurseries to preserve the immature skin's microenvironment (temperature and humidity).[97,101] Each application of these techniques, however, has a unique effect depending on the environment in which it is employed. For example, plastic hoods under radiant heaters may actually attenuate heat delivery from the warming element. The benefits of preserving humidified air near the infant's skin may diminish when ambient humidity is high or when an incubator hood receives humidified medical respiratory gases. Other infant environmental factors influencing insensible water loss include skin blood flow, phototherapy, clothing, ' and artificial skin-like membranes.[90,94,97,100–104] At best, the impact of these factors on predictions of evaporation and prescriptions for rates of replacement are unreliable.

Breathing and Water Balance Evaporation of water from the upper respiratory passages (nasopharynx and trachea) accounts for approximately one third of net insensible water loss.[84,102] At room temperature and moderate relative humidity, the normal neonate at term evaporates free water from these mucosal surfaces at slightly more than 0.5 mL/kg/h.[83] The low-birthweight premature infant, however, may produce somewhat larger (0.8 to 0.9 mL/kg/h) evaporative losses from the upper respiratory passages because, at high respiratory rates, less water is reclaimed by cooling in the nasopharynx during exhalation.[83,102]

An increase in resting ventilation rate may increase evaporation from the respiratory tract two- to threefold if infants breathe air of only moderate temperature and humidity. Cold stress, agitation, or tachypnea with respiratory illness all increase minute ventilation. Nonhumidified incubators may enhance water loss from upper airway passages in premature infants, resulting in evaporation of more than 2.0 mL/kg/h (or more than 50 mL/kg/day). Incubator humidification to 80% relative humidity may be required, particularly for premature babies with respiratory distress, to reduce this rate of evaporation to a more physiologic volume. Endotracheal intubation and mechanical ventilation with warmed gases humidified to >80% relative humidity completely eliminate ventilatory water loss in infants with pulmonary disease, and may result in free water retention relative to room air respiration.[94,105] Water may condense in endotracheal appliances and trickle down into the patient, providing a source of free water intake.[105,106]

Metabolic Water

Metabolic water is the by-product of carbohydrate, lipid, and protein oxidation. Normally, this water of oxidation is less than 5 to 7 mL/kg/day.[83,84] However, in the critically ill or the environmentally stressed premature infant with an accelerated metabolic rate of substrate utilization,[107,108] water of oxidation may increase to as much as 20 mL/kg/day. Stool water loss (usually assumed to balance metabolic water production) is negligible in early life prior to establishing enteral feeding in premature infants.[109] The combined effect of little stool loss, reduced respiratory water loss due to humidified inspired gases, and increased metabolic water may result in a bias toward free water retention in critically ill premature infants.

Water Intake for Nutrition and Cell Growth

The premature neonate progresses from early postnatal transition with a tendency toward negative water balance to a rapid growth and recovery phase in which water balance becomes positive. As hospital discharge approaches, enteral feedings are advanced to promote rapid growth. The baby's protein and caloric energy needs as well as mineral requirements during this time can be met by either human milk or by specially formulated preparations designed for the growing premature infant.

Water content of enteral nutritional intake is inversely proportional to formula concentration and osmolality. The water intake must provide an adequate volume to: (1) assure urine flow for the elimination of urea, fixed acids, and other solutes; (2) match insensible and stool water losses; and (3) provide a small water excess for new tissue formation (both intracellular cellular and extracellular mass), or roughly 0.75 mL of water for each gram of lean tissue mass.[2,110] Fifteen to 20 g/kg/day of new tissue generation (roughly matching normal intrauterine and extrauterine growth rates), is an often cited minimum goal,[111,112] with 65% to 80% of this mass comprised of water (10 to 12 mL/kg/day).

Human milk has a relatively low (albeit efficient) protein content (1.5 g/100 kcal) but a somewhat higher osmolality (40 mOsm/100 kcal) than standard 24 kcal/oz premature infant formulations (protein, 2.4 to 3.0 g/100 kcal, and 21 to 27 mOsm/100 kcal). This difference in osmolar load is due in part to the higher lactose content of human milk or osmotically less-active glucose polymers and fat in premature formulas.[111] It is important that the renal solute load (urea and excess minerals) with any of the enterally replete nutritional formulations ranges between 10 and 30 mOsm/kg/day (while providing 120 to 150 kcal/kg/day).[112,113] A urine osmolality between 100 and 500 mOsm/kg is within the neonate's urine concentrating and diluting capacity, and allows daily solute load excretion with a urine volume of 60 to 120 mL/kg/day.[112,113]

The practice of concentrating premature infant formula fed to babies who have chronic lung disease and persistent pulmonary edema to 27 to 30 kcal/oz (400+ mOsm/kg) in order to limit fluid intake while maximizing caloric ($\geq$150 kcal/kg/day), protein, and mineral intakes may exceed the concentrating capacity of the developing kidney; nitrogen and other solute overload may result. Preliminary investigations are under way to test the application of specialized lipid- and carbohydrate-supplemented formulas. These preparations are designed to meet the hypercaloric substrate demands that have been measured in these patients, while limiting renal solute load and providing enough free water for growth.[114–116]

Clinical Conditions of Perturbed Water Regulation or Balance

As demonstrated in Figure 1.1, water intake with nutrients plus production of metabolic water of oxidation should balance the elimination of water required by solute and carbon dioxide excretion and by evaporation from the skin. During the neonatal period, ECW balance is often perturbed by environment, immature organ function, or disease. Beginning with the transition at birth from the intrauterine to the extrauterine milieu, examples of water perturbations are described here for the baby with RDS, the infant with circulatory failure, the tiny premature infant born at the limit of human viability, and the infant surviving these rigors who experiences rapid growth and recovery.

Transition: Redistribution of Body Water

During intrauterine growth, the relative proportion of water contained in the intracellular compartment expands more rapidly than that of the extracellular fluid volume. At mid-gestation, 85% to 90% of the fetus is water, with one third of the water distributed to ICW and two thirds to ECW.[2,112] By term, these proportions are reversed, and hereafter postnatal growth is characterized more by gradual increases in ICW and nonwater intracellular and interstitial matrix materials.

Profound changes in extracellular and intracellular composition occur during the early transition.[2] Body water is redistributed, and the volume and sodium content of the extracellular space are increased. Heightened blood volume charges the cardiovascular and renal regulatory functions, which flood the neonatal kidney and result in a spontaneous postnatal diuresis.[10,117–119] At the end of the first week of life, nutritional intake accelerates to provide the infant with excess water, essential minerals, and nutrient substrates. A new equilibrium is established between the baby and the extrauterine environment characterized by growth.[2,120]

The ECW expansion that occurs in the first hours to days of life is the result of (1) placental transfusion; (2) resorption of lung fluid; and (3) an efflux of ICW into the ECW compartment.[110,118,121] Then a rebalancing of extracellular volume occurs due to kidney regulation and hormonal modulation of the ECW. Total body water contraction and a urinary diuresis follow. A proportionately greater volume is lost from the ECW space compared to the ICW compartment.[82]

Following birth in premature infants, interstitial volume is rapidly lost as a result of large evaporative losses[94] and a large volume of dilute urine produced by the kidney.[77,119] An increased osmolality of the ECW compartment is also observed over the first 3 to 5 days as serum sodium concentration rises. Contraction in the ICW compartment may occur due to this increase in ECW tonicity.

In critically ill premature neonates, diuresis may be delayed for days, causing severe fluid retention and edema formation. Even if intake of water and salt is restricted,[122-124] peripheral and pulmonary edema may result. Conversely, in infants with high urine-flow rates, excessive administration of fluid to maintain body weight and "chase" diuresis is often difficult, failing to keep pace with both insensible urine water losses. Usually, premature infants recover from acute illness, achieving a "dry" neonatal weight and electrolyte composition. Tissue growth commences thereafter with expansion of cellular mass and the ICW.

Respiratory Distress Syndrome

Premature infants with surfactant deficiency manifest the following physiologic aberrations: diminished lung compliance, high pulmonary vascular and peripheral airways resistances, and atelectasis and abnormal pulmonary lymphatic drainage.[125,126] Frequently, capillary leak and low serum albumin (low oncotic pressure)[121,122] perturb Starling's relationship in the pulmonary microvasculature, promoting fluid transudation into the pulmonary interstitium. Lung water content increases and lung compliance further deteriorates.[126,127] Treatment with high inspired oxygen and positive pressure ventilation may contribute to further fluid accumulation and lung injury.[122]

A delayed or reduced physiologic diuresis occurs during transition in infants with RDS but precedes clearance of pulmonary edema and is associated with improved pulmonary gas exchange.[77,128] The increased urine flow is associated with an increase in GFR and free water clearance.[77,128] Investigators have used medications to stimulate diuresis and improve pulmonary function in babies who have RDS, with mixed results.[129] Diuretic therapy for RDS has not been shown to improve ultimate outcome (more rapid recovery without bronchopulmonary dysplasia).

We favor a modified approach to the maintenance of fluid and electrolyte balance in premature babies with RDS that addresses the disordered physiology.[130] We do not recommend replacement of all predicted fluid losses to artificially maintain body weight within only 5% to 10% of birthweight, (the traditional concept of maintenance). Rather, we permit TBW to contract as much as 15% or more over the first 3 to 5 days, anticipating that the interstitial fluid volume will stabilize in a new, "dry" equilibrium within the pulmonary capillary and interstitium. Fluid restriction during the acute phase of RDS may help prevent later development of pulmonary edema, patent ductus arteriosus with heart failure, and bronchopulmonary dysplasia.[124,131-134]

The Infant with Shock and Edema

Congestive heart failure, oliguric pre-renal or renal failure, and tissue edema with profound capillary leak characterize the asphyxiated premature infant. Water homeostasis is morbidly disrupted in these babies. The goal of parenteral fluid therapy is maintenance of effective circulating blood volume and tissue perfusion, and therapies include blood product transfusion and vasoactive/inotropic pressor agents. Positive-pressure mechanical ventilation with high intrathoracic pressure often complicates these efforts to maintain cardiac output by impeding venous return and compressing the heart.[70] Diuretics may be applied to increase urine flow and preserve renal waste removal.

Anasarca results from disruption of the Starling's hydrostatic and oncotic pressure balance at the tissue vascular and interstitial levels. This condition is made worse by the stimulation of the compensatory mechanisms for maintaining circulating blood volume that causes retention of water and salt.[26] Renin, angiotensin, and aldosterone levels become high, and ADH may be inappropriately secreted.

As deterioration of the circulatory system progresses, congestion of the venous system worsens and arterial vascular tone is lost. Volume depletion acts as an overwhelming regulatory signal to all compensatory systems, and renal fluid retention persists even as pulmonary and peripheral edema worsens and respiratory and circulatory function deteriorates.

The two goals of effective fluid therapy often contradict each other. The first goal is maintenance of the circulating blood volume with intermittent saline, albumin, plasma, or blood transfusions, as guided by central venous and arterial circulation measurement. The second goal is minimization of edema, achieved by restricting maintenance intake (often <60 to 80 mL/kg/day). Electrolyte intake is adjusted accordingly with sodium and potassium restriction. Assiduous calcium phosphorous and magnesium supplementation should also be used.

Minimal amounts of carbohydrate, lipid, and amino acids are provided to prevent or reduce tissue breakdown. But catabolism is usually rampant, and utilization of nutrients for energy and tissue repair is often suppressed. Strict attention to details of acid-base balance, and cardiorespiratory support, often make up the most effective therapy.

The Tiny Baby

Extremely premature infants (weighing 500 to 800 g at <25 to 26 weeks gestation) are born with essentially no barrier to transcutaneous evaporation. Moreover, the ratio of body surface area to body water volume is geometrically higher than in more mature prematures. Extremely high rates of water loss (e.g., 5 to 7 mL/kg/h), produce a hyperosmolar extracellular compartment characterized by hypernatremia, hyperglycemia, and hyperkalemia. The intracellular compartment eventually participates as well, and intracellular dehydration may occur. Intracellular dehydration has been implicated in neurologic injuries frequently encountered in this group of tiny babies.[130,135]

Paradoxically, urine flow with a high fractional excretion of sodium is maintained (e.g., 2 to 4 mL/kg/h) in spite of rapid dehydration of the ICW and ECW. Blood pressure and peripheral perfusion may also be maintained until shock and cardiac dysrhythmias suddenly occur.

Alternatively, replacing free water in excess of 180 to 200 mL/kg/day to prevent dehydration and electrolyte abnormalities may cause inadvertent fluid and/or dextrose overload, leading to patent ductus arteriosus, pulmonary edema, sudden congestive heart failure, and intraventricular hemorrhage.[123,136-138] Fluid therapy should be targeted to prevent excessive dehydration during the first 48 to 72 hours of life. By restricting sodium intake and giving the least amount of intravenous water volume necessary to maintain serum sodium concentrations below 150 mmol/L, these targets can be achieved.[130,139] This therapy permits the ECW to contract isotonically, thus preventing hypertonic dehydration with ICW dehydration.

A variety of plastic shields have been advocated for these infants to reduce transcutaneous water loss and simplify the estimation of free water replacement.[96] Placing these infants into warmed and humidified incubators to control free water loss by reducing the evaporation gradient near the skin may also be helpful. However, limitation of this tactic to only the first week of care is advised to avoid water-borne bacterial contamination.[140]

The Growing Premature Infant with High Water Concentration in the Extracellular Water (Late Hyponatremia of Prematurity)

Occasionally, clinically healthy infants growing on enteral feedings are found to be mildly or moderately hyponatremic with serum sodium concentrations between 124 to 130 mmol/L. Most commonly, this clinical presentation occurs at 2 to 6 weeks of age following premature birth at 26 to 30 weeks of gestation. Cardiorespiratory failure is resolved, phototherapy for hyperbilirubinemia is complete, the infant is beginning feedings, and sometimes methylxanthine therapy is being initiated for apnea.

Hyponatremia in the healthy, growing premature infant was first noted in the early 1970s.[141,142] This syndrome has been called "late hyponatremia of prematurity."[143,144] The pathogenesis of this syndrome is incompletely understood, but in contrast to most hyponatremic states, it is probably not a result of water excess. Rather, a relative lack of sodium intake has been provided to keep pace with renal sodium loss and new tissue growth.[67,68,145] Glomerular filtration and urinary flow have increased with advancing postconceptional age and, although tubular function is maturing, distal tubular delivery of sodium is increasing at a rate greater than the infant can accommodate. As a result, urinary sodium loss remains high. Levels of plasma renin activity, aldosterone, and AVP are also high in these infants.[68,69,141,142,145] These children will exhibit a positive sodium balance.[68,141,145]

All of these observations suggest that growth and limited renal function combine with inadequate sodium intake, previous losses, and other clinical factors to create the presentation just described. The patient has recovered from the immediate stresses of prematurity; the skin is cornified, the radiant warmer bed is no longer needed for emergency access, and phototherapy is completed. As a result, large insensible water losses that parallel or exceed sodium loss during the first days of the infant's life are dramatically reduced. While enteral nutrition may be sufficient to sustain an anabolic state, intolerance to feeding or fear of bowel injury motivates beginning with a relatively dilute formulation. Theophylline administration may further increase sodium losses.[146,147] Since new tissue growth, particularly bone, requires that the infant incorporate sodium at a rate of 1.2 mmol/kg/day,[120,82] growth results in further loss of sodium from the ECW. Resolution is usually spontaneous as postconceptional age approaches term and water-regulatory mechanisms reach maturity.

Fluid Management Recommendations (See Table 1.1)

Phase 1: Transition

Shortly after birth and during the first week of life, the VLBW infant's skin is an insufficient barrier to massive insensible water loss as detailed in the previous section. Water evaporation from the interstitial space exceeds the rate of sodium and chloride excretion by the neonate's kidney in response to the expanded extracellular fluid volume acquired in utero from the placental circulation and from the sodium and water transport mechanisms geared to ensure prenatal growth. The preterm infant is therefore predisposed to hypernatremic (>145 to 150 mmol/L) contraction of the ECW. Although fractional excretion of sodium by the preterm infant's kidney is high (3% to 10%), it may represent response to fluid and salt overload during the first 3 to 5 days of transition to extrauterine life.

Phase 2: Stabilization

By days 10 to 14 of life, the preterm neonate has contracted ECW and salt volume up to 10% to 20% in the most extreme cases. A fall in urine volume formation to <1 to 2 mL/kg/h, and in fractional excretion of sodium to 1% to 3% of the filtered sodium load may be observed. Urine flow is maintained as long as effective circulating vascular volume is adequate. Strict fluid or salt restriction, while appropriate early in the transitional phase of fluid maintenance therapy for such babies, may be determined after the first week of life. Aldosterone levels remain high to conserve body salt and water volume at this stage of development, but fractional sodium excretion as low as <3% is not sufficient to maintain serum sodium concentrations >125 to 130 mmol/L. Hyponatremia at this point may represent a relative sodium depletion due to the ICW sodium restriction as well as due to the neonate's kidney immaturity.

Phase 2 fluid therapy must maintain electrolyte and water balance by liberalizing both water volume and salt administration after the transitional phase (Table 1.1). Our recommendations for fluid therapy during the stabilization phase (≤10 to 14 days) are placed with two principles in mind: (1) insensible water loss from the skin has dramatically decreased with maturation and cornification of the epidermal layer, and (2) electrolyte repletion of normal renal losses (1 to 3 mmol/kg/day variously of potassium, chloride, and sodium) must be supplemented. Therefore, a relative water restriction remains in effect; protein, carbohydrate, and lipid administration are advanced within these narrow limits of water replacement, avoiding catabolism, and sodium intake is liberalized. Weight gain is a therapeutic priority.

Phase 3: Established Growth

After the first 2 weeks of transition and stabilization, new tissue growth is the primary goal. Nutritional substrate administration (including water and salt) should therefore commence. The neonate's kidney function is now adequate enough to tolerate the usual environmental stress within the limits of this more liberal therapy. At this juncture, the demands of caloric supply beyond maintenance energy requirements and of protein repletion to heal damaged tissues and sustain catch-up growth require water intake volume in excess of 150 to 200 mL/kg/day, the amount necessary to carry an excess of nutrients into the body. Sodium, potassium, and chloride requirements are easily met within this liberalized volume. Supplemental electrolytes of 3 to 4 mmol/L must be provided to: (1) replete early losses from restriction during transition, and (2) provide for new tissue growth (particularly bone). Fortunately, most preterm infants recovering during this phase of development

Table 1.1. Recommendations for Water and Electrolyte Administration in Preterm Newborn Infants

Goals:
1. *Expect weight loss* during first 3–5 days of life.
2. *Maintain normal serum electrolyte concentrations:*

Sodium	135–145	mmol/L
Potassium	3.5–5.0	mmol/L
Chloride	98–108	mmol/L

3. *Avoid oliguria* <0.5-1.0 mL/kg/h for 8–12 hours.

Phase 1: TRANSITION* during the first 3–5 days of life is characterized by: (1) large transcutaneous water evaporation, and (2) renal diuresis of a large surfeit of extracellular salt and water.

Birthweight (grams)	Expected Weight Loss (%)	Water Intake[†] (mL/kg/day)	Sodium Intake[‡] (mmol/kg/day)	Chloride Intake (mmol/kg/day)	Potassium Intake (mmol/kg/day)
<1,000	15–20	90–140	0.0	0.0	0.0
1,000–1,500	10–15	80–120	0.0	0.0	0.0

*The end of transition is recognized by: (1) Urine volume <1.0 mL/kg/h, and urine osmolality > serum osmolality; (2) Fractional excretion of sodium diminishes from >3% to ≤1%; and (3) Urine specific gravity above 1.012.

[†]Water intake volume should be 10–20% less, with humidified incubator or artificial plastic shielding placed over the infant to conserve insensible water evaporation.

[‡]Often 0.5–1.5 mmol/kg/day sodium is administered to these infants inadvertently with transfusions, medications, and line infusions.

Table 1.1. *(continued)*

PHASE 2: STABILIZATION at euvolemic weight for ≤ 10–14 days. Weight gain is not a priority as parenteral and enteral nutrition are cautiously advanced. Transcutaneous water evaporation is diminishing as the neonatal epidermis cornifies.

Birthweight (grams)	Weight Change (%)	Water Intake (mL/kg/day)	Sodium Intake‡ (mmol/kg/day)	Chloride Intake (mmol/kg/day)	Potassium Intake (mmol/kg/day)
<1,000	0	80–120	2.0–3.0	2.0	1.0–2.0
1,000–1,500	0	80–100	2.0–3.0	2.0	1.0–2.0

PHASE 3: ESTABLISHED GROWTH past 2 weeks of postnatal life in all weight categories to match intrauterine growth rate is the objective. Oral enteral intake is eventually ad libitum.

Weight gain (g/kg/day)	Parenteral Volume (mL/kg/day)	Enteral Volume (mL/kg/day)	Sodium Intake (mmol/kg/day)	Chloride Intake (mmol/kg/day)	Potassium Intake (mmol/kg/day)
15–20	140–160	150–200	3.0–5.0	3.0–5.0	2.0–3.0

achieve an independence of prescribed formula intakes, and will eventually self-regulate on demand feeding regimens.

References

1. Edelman IS, Liebman J. Anatomy of body electrolytes. *Am J Med* 1959;27:256–277.
2. Friis-Hansen B. Body water compartments in children. *Pediatrics* 1961;28:169–181.
3. Dahlstrom H. Basal metabolism and extracellular fluid. *Acta Physio Scand* 1950;21 (suppl 71):5–80.
4. Wedgewood RJ, Bass DE, Klincis JA, Kleeman CR, Quinn M. Relationship of body composition to basal metabolic rate in normal man. *J Appl Physiol* 1953;6:317–334.
5. Astrup J. Energy-requiring cell functions in the ischemic brain. *J Neurosurg* 1982;56:282–497.
6. Valtin H. *Renal function: mechanisms preserving fluid and solute balance in health.* Boston: Little Brown, 1973:28.
7. Michel CC. Fluid movements through capillary walls. In: Renkin EM, Michel CC, eds. *Handbook of physiology,* section II, vol. II. Bethesda, Md: American Physiologic Society 1984:chap 9.
8. Guyton AC. *Textbook of medical physiology,* 6th ed. Philadelphia: WB Saunders, 1981:339.
9. MacKnight ADC, Leaf A. Regulation of cellular volume. *Physiol Review* 1977;57:510–573.
10. Linshaw M. Selected aspects of cell volume control in renal cortical and medullary tissue. *Pediatr Nephrol* 1991;5:653–665.
11. Trachtman H, Barbour R, Sturman JA, Finburg L. Taurine and osmoregulation: taurine is a cerebral osmoprotective molecule in chronic hypernatremic dehydration. *Pediatr Res* 1988;23:35–39.
12. Trachtman H. Cell volume regulation: a review of cerebral adaptive mechanisms and implications for clinical treatment of osmolal disturbances. *Pediatr Nephrol* 1991;5:743–750.
13. Robertson GL, Berl T. Water metabolism. In: Brenner BM, Rector FC, eds. *The kidney.* Philadelphia: WB Saunders, 1986:385–431.
14. Andersson B. Regulation of body fluids. *Annu Rev Physiol* 1977;39:185–200.
15. Guyton AC, Scanlon LJ, Armstrong GG. Effects of pressoreceptor reflex and cushing reflex on urinary output. *Fed Proc* 1952;11:61–62.
16. Barr PA, Bailey PE, Sumners J, Cassady G. Relation between arterial blood pressure and blood volume and effect of infused albumin in sick preterm infants. *Pediatrics* 1977;60:282–289.
17. Mann JFE, Johnson AK, Gantten D, et al. Thirst and the reninangiotensin system. *Kidney Int* 1987;32 (suppl 21):527–534.
18. Landis EM, Pappenheimer JR. Exchange of substances through capillary walls. In: *Handbook of physiology.* Circulation Section 2, Vol. 2, Washington, DC: American Physiologic Society, 1963:961–1034.
19. Webster HL. Colloid osmotic pressure: Theoretical aspects and background. *Clin Perinatol* 1982;9:505–521.
20. Kero P, Korvenranta H, Alamaakala P, et al. Colloid osmotic pressure of cord blood in relation to neonatal outcome and mode of delivery. *Acta Paediatr Scand.* 1983;305 (suppl):88–91.
21. Bhat R, Javed S, Malalis L, Vidyasagar D. Colloid osmotic pressure in healthy and sick neonates. *Crit Care Med* 1981;9:563–567.
22. Sola A, Gregory GA. Colloid osmotic pressure of normal newborns and premature infants. *Crit Care Med* 1981;9:568–572.
23. Starling EH. On the absorption of fluid from the connective tissue spaces. *J Physiol (Lond) 1896;19:312–326.*

24. Pappenheimer JR, Soto-Rivera. Effective osmotic pressure of the plasma proteins and other quantities associated with capillary circulation in the hind limb of cats and dogs. *Am J Physiol* 1948;152:471–491.

25. Shapiro MD, Nicholls KM, Groves BM, Kluge R, Chung HM, Bichet DG, Schrier RW. Interrelationship between cardiac output and vascular resistance as determinants of effective arterial blood volume in cirrhotic patients. *Kidney Int* 1985;206–211.

26. Schrier RW. Pathogenesis of sodium and water retension in high output and low output cardiac failure, nephrotic syndrome, cirrhosis, and pregnancy. *N Engl J Med* 1988;319 (pt 1):1065–1071.

27. Baylen BG, Ogata H, Ikeganim M, Jacobs H, Jobes A, Emmonouildes GC. Left ventricular performance and contractility before and after volume infusion: a comparative study in preterm and full-term newborns. *Circulation* 1986;73:1042–1049.

28. Robillard JE, Matson JR, Sessions C, et al. Maturational changes in the fetal glomerular filtration rate. *Am J Obstet Gynecol* 1975;122:601–606.

29. Robillard JE, Matson JR, Sessions C, et al. Developmental aspects of renal tubular reabsorption of water in the lamb fetus. *Pediatr Res* 1979;13:1172–1176.

30. Knutson DW, Chisu F, Bennett CM, et al. Estimation of relative glomerular capillary surface area in normal and hypertrophic rat kidneys. *Kidney Int* 1978;14:437.

31. Ichikawa I, Maddox DA, Brenner BM. Maturational development of glomerular ultrafiltration in the rat. *Am J Physiol* 1979;236:F465–471.

32. Gruskin AB, Edelman CM Jr, Yuan S. Maturational changes in renal blood flow in piglets. *Pediatr Res* 1970;4:7–13.

33. Fawer CL, Torrado A, Guigmard JP. Maturation of renal function in full-term and premature neonates. *Helv Paediatr Acta* 1979;34:11–21.

34. Aperia A, Broberger O, Elinder G, et al. Postnatal development of renal function in pre-term and full-term infants. *Acta Paediatr Scand* 1981;70:183–187.

35. Guignard JP, Torrado A, Mazouni SM, Gautier E. Renal function in respiratory distress syndrome. *J Pediatr* 1976;88:845–850.

36. Reitel H, Scopes J. Rates of creatinine clearance in babies less than one week of age. *Arch Dis Child* 1973;48:717–720.

37. Spitzer A. Renal physiology and function development. In: Edelman CM, Jr, ed. *The kidney and urinary tract.* Boston: Little Brown, 1978: Vol 1:25–128.

38. Leake RD, Zakanddin S, Trygstad CW, et al. The effects of large-volume intravenous fluid infusion on neonatal renal function. *J Pediatr* 1976;89:968–972.

39. Robillard J, Weitzman RE. Development aspects of the fetal renal response to exogenous arginine vasopression. *Am J Physiol* 1980;238:F407–F414.

40. Robillard JE, Nakamura KT. Hormonal regulation of renal function during development. *Biol Neonate* 1988;53:201–211.

41. Edelman CM, Wolfish NM. Dietary influence on renal maturation in preterm infants. *Pediatr Res* 1968;2:421.

42. Edelman CM, Barnett HL, Stark H. Effect of urea on concentration of urinary nonurea solute in premature infants. *J Appl Physiol* 1966;21:1021–1025.

43. Edelman CM, Barnett HL. Role of kidney in water metabolism in young infants. *J Pediatr* 1960;56:154–179.

44. Edelman CM, Trompkon V, Barnett HL. Renal concentrating ability in newborn infants. *Fed Proc* 1959;18:49.

45. Speller AM, Moffat DB. Tubulo-vascular relationships in the developing kidney. *J Anat* 1977;123:487–500.

46. Imbert-Teboul M, Chabardes D, Cligue A, et al. Ontogenesis of hormone-dependent adenylate cyclase in isolated rat nephron segments. *Am J Physiol* 1984;247:F316–25.

47. Laragh JH. Atrial natriuretic hormone, the renin-aldosterone axis, and blood pressure-electrolyte homeostasis. *N Engl J Med* 1985;313:1330–1340.

48. Mills IH. Renal regulation of sodium excretion. *Annu Rev Med* 1970; 21:75–98.

49. Laragh JH, Sealey JE. The renin-angiotension-aldosterone hormonal system of sodium, potassium and blood pressure homeostasis. In: Orloff J, Berliner RN, eds. *Handbook of physiology.* Washington, DC; American Physiological Society, 1973:831–908.

50. Johnson MD, Malvin RL. Stimulation of renal sodium reabsorption by angiotension II. *Am J Physiol* 1977; 232(2):F298–F306.

51. Aperia A, Broberger O, Jerin P, et al. Sodium excretion in relation to sodium intake and aldosterone excretion in newborn and preterm infants. *Acta Paediatr Scand* 1979; 68:813–817.

52. Haycock GB, Aperia A. Salt and the newborn kidney. *Pediatr Nephrol* 1991; 5:65–70.

53. Spitzer A. The role of the kidney in sodium homeostasis during maturation. *Kidney Int* 1982; 21:539–545.

54. Pipkin FB, Phil D, Smales ORC. A study of factors affecting blood pressure and angiotensin II in newborn infants. *J Pediatr* 1977; 91:113–119.

55. Godard C, Geering JM, Geering K, Vallotton MB. Plasma renin activity related to sodium balance, renal function and urinary vasopressin in the newborn infant. *Pediatr Res* 1979; 13:742–745.

56. Mattioli L, Zakheim M, Mullis K, Molteni A. Angiotensin-I converting enzyme activity in idiopathic respiratory distress syndrome of the newborn infant and in experimental alveolar hypoxia in mice. *J Pediatr* 1975;87:97–101.

57. Grantham JJ, Burg MB. Effect of vasopressin and cyclic amp on permeability of isolated collecting tubules. *Am J Physiol* 1966; 211:255–259.

58. Schubert F, George JM, Rao MB Vasopressin and oxytocin content of human fetal brain at different stages of gestation. *Brain Res* 1981; 213:111–117.

59. Chard T, Hudson CN, Edwards CRW, Boyd NRH. Release of oxytocin and vasopressin by the human foetus during labour. *Nature* 1971; 234:352–353.

60. Wiriyathian S, Rosenfeld CR, Arant BS, Porter JC, Faucher DJ, Engle W. Urinary arginine vasopressin: pat tern of excretion in the neonatal period. *Pediatr Res* 1986; 20:103–108.

61. Weitzman RE, Fisher DE, Robillard JE, et al. Arginine vasopressin response to an osmotic stimulus in the fetal sheep. *Pediatr Res* 1978;12:35–38.

62. Robillard JE, Weitzman RE, Fisher DE, Smith FG. The dynamics of vasopressin release and blood volume regulation during fetal hemorrhage in the lamb fetus. *Pediatr Res* 1979;13:606–610.

63. Rees L, Forsling ML, and Brook CGD. Vasopressin concentrations in the neonatal period. *Clin Endocrinol* 1980;12:357–362.

64. Hadeed AJ, Leake RD, Weitzman RE, Fisher DA. Possible mechanisms of high blood levels of vasopressin during the neonatal period. *J Pediatr* 1979;94:805–808.

65. Pohjavuori M. Obstetric determinants of plasma vasopressin concentrations and renin activity at birth. *J Pediatr* 1983;103:966–968.

66. Svenningsen NW, Aronson AS. Postnatal development of renal concentration capacity as estimated by DDAVP-test in normal and asphyxiated neonates. *Biol Neonate* 1974;25:230–241.

67. Kovacs L, Sulyok E, Lichardus B, Mihajlovskij N, Bircak J. Renal response to arginine vasopressin in premature infants with late hyponatraemia. *Arch Dis Child* 1986;61:1030–1032.

68. Sulyok E, Kovacs L, Lichardus B, Michajlovskij N, Lehotska V, Nemethova V, Varga L, Ertl T. Late hyponatremia in premature infants: role of aldosterone and arginine vasopressin. *J Pediatr* 1985;106:990–994.

69. Rees L, Brook GD, Shaw JCL, Forsling ML. Hyponatremia in the first week of life in preterm infants. *Arch Dis Child* 1984;59 (pt I):414–422.

70. Leslie GI, Philips JB, Work J, Ram S, Cassady G. The effect of assisted ventilation on creatinine clearance and hormonal control of electrolyte balance in very low birth weight infants. *Pediatr Res* 1986;20:447–452.

71. Weinberg JA, Weitzman RE, Zakauddin S, Leake RD. Inappropriate secretion of antidiuretic hormone in a premature infant. *Pediatrics* 1977;90:111–114.

72. Sagnella GA, MacGregor GA. Cardiac peptides and the control of sodium excretion. *Nature* 1984;309:666–667.

73. Blaine EH. Emergence of a new cardiovascular control system: atrial natriuretic factor. *Clin Exp Theory Pract* 1985;A7 (pts 5&6):887.

74. Seymour AA. Renal and systemic effects of atrial natriuretic factor. *Clin Exp Theory Pract* 1985;A7(pts 5&6):887.

75. Richards AM, Ikram H, Yanckle TG, et al. Renal, hemodynamic, and hormonal effects of human alpha atrial natriuretic peptide in healthy volunteers. *Lancet* 1985; 1:545–548

76. Andersson S, Tikkanen I, Pesonen E, Meretoja O, Hynynen M, Fyhrquist F. Atrial natriuretic peptide in patent ductus arteriosus. *Pediatr Res* 1987;21:396–398.

77. Costarino AT, Baumgart S, Norman ME, Polin RA. Renal adaptation to extrauterine life in patients with respiratory distress syndrome. *Am J Dis Child* 1985; 139:1060–1063.

78. Kojuma T, Hirata Y, Fukuda Y, Iwase S, Kobayashi Y. Plasma atrial natriuretic peptide and spontaneous diuresis in sick neonates. *Arch Dis Child* 1987;62:667–670.

79. Tulassay T, Rascher W, Seyberth HW, Lang RE, Toth M, Sulyok E. The role of atrial natriuretic peptide in sodium homeostasis in premature infants. *J Pediatr* 1986; 109:1023–1027.

80. Rozycki HJ, Baumgart S. Atrial natriuretic factor and postnatal diuresis in respiratory distress syndrome. *Arch Dis Child* 1991;66:43–47.

81. Cheek DB, Talbert JI. Extracellular volume (and sodium) and body water in infants. In: Cheek DB, ed. *Human growth: body composition, cell growth, energy and intelligence.* Philadelphia: Lea & Febiger; 1968:117–134.

82. Arant BS. Adaptation of the infant to an external milieu. In: Gruskin AB, Norman ME, eds. *Pediatric nephrology. Proceedings of the fifth international pediatric nephrology symposium, 1980.* The Hague: Martinus Nijhoff; 1981:261–272.

83. Sinclair JC. Metabolic rate and temperature control. In: Smith CA, Nelson NM, eds. *The physiology of the newborn infant,* 4th ed. Springfield, IL: Charles Thomas; 1976:354–415.

84. Winters RW. Maintenance fluid therapy. In: *The body fluids in pediatrics.* Boston: Little Brown, 1973:113–133.

85. Bruck K. Heat production and temperature regulation. In: Stave U, ed. *Perinatal physiology.* New York: Plenum Medical Publishing, 1987:455.

86. Brück K. Neonatal thermal regulation. In: Polin RA, Fox WW, eds. *Fetal and neonatal physiology.* Philadelphia: WB Saunders; 1992:488–514.

87. Fanaroff, AA, Ward M, Gruber HS, et al. Insensible water loss in low birthweight infants. *Pediatrics* 1972; 50:236–245.

88. Williams PR, Oh W. Effects of radiant warmer on insensible water loss in newborn infants. *Am J Dis Child* 1974;128:511–514.

89. Baumgart S, Engle WD, Fox WW, et al. Radiant warmer power and body size as determinants of insensible water loss in the critically ill neonate. *Pediatr Res* 1981; 15:1,495–1,499.

90. Hey EN, Katz G. Evaporative water loss in the newborn baby. *J Physiol (Lond)* 1969;200:605–619.

91. Wu PYK, Hodgman JE. Insensible water loss in preterm infants: changes with postnatal development and nonionizing radiant energy. *Pediatrics* 1974;54:704–712.

92. Hammarlund K, Sedin G. Transepidermal water loss in newborn infants. *Acta Paediatr Scand.* 1983;72 (pt VIII): 721–728.

93. Sedin G, Hammarlund K, Nilsson GE, et al. Measurements of transepidermal water loss in newborn infants. *Clin Perinatol* 1985;12:79–96.

94. Baumgart S, Langman CB, Sosulski R, et al. Fluid, electrolyte, and glucose maintenance in the very low birthweight infant. *Clin Pediatr (Phila)* 1982;21:199–206.

95. Okken A, Blijhan C, Franz W, et al. Effects of forced convection of heated air on insensible water loss and heat loss in preterm infants in incubators. *J Pediatr* 1982; 101:108–112.

96. Wheldon AE, Rutter N. The heat balance of small babies nursed in incubators and under radiant warmers. *Early Hum Dev* 1982;6:131–143.

97. Baumgart S, Engle WD, Fox WW, et al. Effect of heat shielding on convection and evaporation, and radiant heat transfer in the premature infant. *J Pediatr* 1981;99: 948–956.

98. Baumgart S. Radiant energy and insensible water loss in the premature newborn infant nursed under a radiant warmer. *Clin Perinatol* 1982;9:483–503.

99. Baumgart S. Partitioning of heat losses and gains in premature newborn infants under radiant warmers. *Pediatrics* 1985;75:89–99.

100. Bell EF, Neidich Ga, Cashore WJ, et al. Combined effect of radiant warmer and phototherapy on insensible water loss in low-birthweight infants. *J Pediatr* 1979;94:810–813.

101. Baumgart S, Fox WW, Polin RA. Physiologic implications of two different heat shields for infants under radiant warmers. *J Pediatr* 1982;100:787–790.

102. Sulyok E, Jequier E, Prod'hom LS. Respiratory contribution to the thermal balance of the newborn infant under various ambient conditions. *Pediatrics* 1973;51:641–650.

103. Engle WD, Baumgart S, Schwartz JG, et al. Combined effect of radiant warmer power and phototherapy on insensible water loss in the critically ill neonate. *Am J Dis Child* 1981;135:516–520.

104. Knauth A, Gordin MS, McNelis W, Baumgart S. A semipermeable polyurethane membrane as an artificial skin in the premature neonate. *Pediatrics* 1989;83:945–950.

105. Sosulski R, Baumgart S. Respiratory water loss and heat balance in incubated premature infants receiving humidified air. *J Pediatr* 1983;103:307–310.

106. Rosenfield WN, Linshaw M, Fox HA. Water intoxication: a complication of nebulization with nasal CPAP. *J Pediatr* 1976;89:113–114.

107. Weinstein MR, Oh W. Oxygen consumption in infants with bronchopulmonary dysplasia. *J Pediatr* 1981;99: 958–961.

108. Kurzner SI, Garg M, Bautista B, Sargen CW, Bowman CM, Keens TG. Growth failure in bronchopulmonary

dysplasia: elevated metabolic rates and pulmonary mechanics. *J Pediatr* 1988;112:73–80.

109. Jhaveri M, Kumar SP. Passage of the first stool in very low birthweight infants. *Pediatrics* 1987;79:1005–1007.

110. MacLaurin JC. Changes in body water distribution during the first two weeks of life. *Arch Dis Child* 1966;41:286–291.

111. Tsang RC, Nichols EL, eds. *Nutrition during infancy.* Philadelphia: CV Mosby, 1988:418–424.

112. Bell EF, Oh WH. Calculation of maintenance requirements of water and electrolytes. *Clin Perinatol* 1978;6:141–150.

113. Brans YW, Cassady G. Intrauterine growth and maturation in relation to fetal deprivation. In: Gruenwald P, ed. *The placenta and its maternal supply line.* London: Medical and Technical Publishing, 1975:307–334.

114. Baumgart S, Pereira GR, Stallings VA, Henstenburg JA. High fat formula for infants with bronchopulmonary dysplasia: metabolic rate and respiration. *Pediatr Res* 1990;27:280A.

115. Pereira GR, Baumgart S, Corcoran L, Butler S, Ellis L, Hamosh M. High fat formula for infants with bronchopulmonary dysplasia: balance and nutritional studies. *Pediatr Res* 1990;27:287A.

116. Baumgart S, Pereira GR, Bennett MJ. Dicarboxylic aciduria in premature bpd babies fed long-chain triglyceride enriched high fat formula vs special-care formula with polycose. *Pediatr Res* 1991;29:291A.

117. Costarino AT, Baumgart S. Controversies in fluid and electrolyte therapy for the premature infant. *Clin Perinatol* 1988;15:863–878.

118. Cassady G. Effect of caesarian section on neonatal body water spaces. *N Engl J Med* 1971;285:887–891.

119. Lorenz JM, Kleinman LI, Kotagal UR. Water balance in very low birthweight infants: relationship to water and sodium intake and effect on outcome. *J Pediatr* 1982;101:423–432.

120. Strauss J. Fluid and electrolyte composition of the fetus and newborn. *Pediatr Clin North Am* 1966;13:1077–1102.

121. Ertyl T, Sulyok E, Bodis J, Csaba IF. Plasma prolactin levels in full-term newborn infants with idiopathic edema: response to furosemide. *Biol Neonate* 1986;49:15–20.

122. Brown ER, Stark A, Sosenko I, et al. Bronchopulmonary dysplasia: possible relationships to pulmonary edema. *J Pediatr* 1978;92:982–984.

123. Bell EF, Warburton D, Stonestreet BS, et al. Effect of fluid administration on the development of symptomatic patent ductus arteriosus and congestive heart failure in premature infants. *N Engl J Med* 1980;302:598–604.

124. Spitzer AR, Fox WW, Delavoria-Papadopoulos M. Maximum diuresis: a factor in predicting recovery for respiratory distress syndrome and the development of bronchopulmonary dysplasia. *J Pediatr* 1981;98:476–479.

125. Bland RD. Edema formation in the newborn lung. *Clin Perinatol* 1982;9:593–611.

126. Lauweryns JM, Claessens S, Boussauw L. The pulmonary lymphatics in neonatal hyaline membrane disease. *Pediatrics* 1968;41:917–930.

127. Jefferies AL, Coates G, O'Brodovich H. Pulmonary epithelial permeability in hyaline membrane disease. *N Engl J Med* 1984;31:1075–1080.

128. Rees L, Shaw JCL, Brook GD, Forsling ML. Hyponatremia in the first week of life in preterm infants. *Arch Dis Child* 1984;59 (pt II):423–429.

129. Green TP, Thompson TR, Johnson DE, et al. Diuresis and pulmonary function in premature infants with respiratory distress syndrome. *J Pediatr* 1983;103:618–623.

130. Costarino AT, Baumgart S. Modern fluid and electrolyte management of the critically ill premature infant. *Pediatr Clin North Am* 1986;33:153–178.

131. Cornblath M, Forbes AE, Pildes RS, et al. A controlled study of early fluid administration on survival of low birthweight infants. *Pediatrics* 1966;38:547–554.

132. Spahr RC, Klein AM, Brown DR, et al. Fluid administration and bronchopulmonary dysplasia. *Am J Dis Child* 1980;134:958–960.

133. Gersony WM, Peckham GJ, Ellison RC, Miettinen OS, Nadas AS. Effects of indomethacin in premature infants with patent ductus arteriosus: results of a national collaborative study. *J Pediatr* 1983;102:895–906.

134. Palta M, Gabbert D, Weinstein MR, Peters ME. Multivariate assessment of traditional risk factors for chronic lung disease in very low birth weight neonates. *J Pediatr* 1991;285–292.

135. Finberg L. Dangers to infants caused by changes in osmolal concentration. *Pediatrics* 1967;40:1031–1034.

136. Brown ER, Stack A, Sosentio I, Lawson EE, Avery ME. Bronchopulmonary dysplasia: possible relationships to pulmonary edema. *J Pediatr* 1978;92:982–984.

137. Spitzer AR, Fox WW, Delavoria-Papadopoulos M. Maximum diuresis: a factor in predicting recovery for respiratory distress syndrome and the development of bronchopulmonary dysplasia. *J Pediatr* 1981;98:476–479.

138. McDonald MM, Koops BL, Johnson ML, et al. Timing and antecedents of intracranial hemorrhage. *Pediatrics* 1984;74:32–36.

139. Costarino AT, Gruskay J, Corcoran L, Polin RA, Baumgart S. Sodium restriction vs daily maintenance replacement in very low birthweight infants, a randomized and blinded therapeutic trial. *J Pediatr* 1992;120:99–106.

140. Harpin A, Rutter N. Humidification of incubators. *Arch Dis Child* 1985;60:219–224.

141. Sulyok E. The relationship between electrolyte and acid base balance in premature infants during early postnatal life. *Biol Neonate* 1971;95:227–237.

142. Honour JW, Shackleton CHL, Valman HB. Sodium homeostasis in preterm infants. *Lancet* 1974;2:1147.

143. Day RL, Radde IC, Balfe JW, et al. Electrolyte abnormalities in very low birthweight infants. *Pediatr Res* 1976;10:522–526.

144. Roy RN, Chance CW, Radde IC, et al. Late hyponatremia in very low birthweight infants (1.3 kg). *Pediatr Res* 1976;10:526–531.

145. Sulyok E, Nemeth M, Teny IF, et al. Relationship between maturity, electrolyte balance, and the function ofrenin-angiotension-aldosterone system in newborn infants. *Biol Neonate.* 1979;35:60–65.

146. Gouyon JB, Guignard JP. Renal effects of theophylline and caffeine in newborn rabbits. *Pediatr Res* 1987;21:615–618.

147. Harkavy KL, Scanlon JW, Jose P. The effects of theophylline on renal function in the premature newborn. *Biol Neonate* 1979;35:126–130.

2. Energy

Guy Putet

Reviewers: Sheila M. Innis, C. Lawrence Kien, Pieter J.J. Sauer, J. Van Aerde

It is not possible to define energy requirements for very low-birthweight (VLBW) infants without defining ''optimal'' growth for these infants. In the absence of a model for determining quantitative and qualitative optimal growth for preterm infants during their extrauterine life, two facts should be considered. First, growth velocity in the human is higher at 25 or 30 weeks than at 40 or more postconceptional weeks. If no growth or poor growth is achieved during this period of maximal growth capacity because of inadequate nutrition, adequate catch-up growth may be impossible whatever the amount and quality of nutrient intake. After very premature birth, weight loss occurs (opinions conflict regarding whether this initial weight loss is mainly due to fluid loss or to tissue loss caused by catabolism) and may persist for several days, followed by weight stabilization and then growth. To take advantage of this unique period of remarkable growth capacity, energy and nutrient intake should be sufficient to reinstate as soon as possible the premature infant on a growth curve similar to the intrauterine one for length, head circumference, and weight gain. It may even be necessary to increase energy and nutrient intake to above-average values in order to allow catch-up growth if needed.

Second, the amount of energy stored during growth will vary according to weight gain composition (qualitative aspect of growth). Considering that 9 kcal are stored in 1 g of fat deposited, fat deposition may represent much energy stored with a small impact on weight gain. For an equivalent weight gain of 20 g/kg/day, a weight gain composition of 40% fat (i.e., 8 g of fat) will represent 72 kcal deposited, while a weight gain composition of 20% fat (i.e., 4 g of fat) will represent only 36 kcal. Thus estimated energy requirements will depend greatly on the type of growth considered most desirable for preterm infants: fat deposition similar to that of the fetus[1] (Fig. 2.1) (14% of weight gain between 32 and 36 weeks) or of the term infant[2] (30% to 40% of weight gain), or in between, taking into account that fat deposition may be a necessary adaptation to extrauterine life.

Keeping in mind these preliminary remarks, it is generally accepted that achieving a quantitative postnatal growth that reinstates the premature infant on his or her intrauterine growth curve for length, weight, and head circumference is a reasonable estimate of adequate growth, at least for the period of time lasting until 36 to 38 postconceptional weeks. The qualitative aspect will be discussed in the section on Energy Stored. After 40 weeks, adequate growth may be qualitatively and quantitatively similar to that of the term infant fed human milk.

Most of the data on energy requirements of VLBW infants have been obtained in healthy well-growing infants. Published data on sick infants, either during the first days of life or during chronic disease, are rare, and estimation of energy intake required during these periods is much more difficult to assess.

Energy and Energy Expenditure Measurements

Energy

The chemical energy produced during oxidation of nutrients is the only available source of energy for man and animals. Energy liberated during these reactions cannot be used directly and must be converted into an appropriate chemical form, mostly adenosine-5-triphosphate (ATP). Later, when hydrolyzed to adenosine-5-diphosphate (ADP), ATP will provide the energy necessary for activities such as muscular contraction and synthesis of new molecules.

To understand the methodology used to estimate energy expenditure measurement,[3-5] it is important to consider the classic relationship between the liberation of energy during nutrient oxidation and during oxygen consumption. For instance, glucose oxidation will consume oxygen and produce carbon dioxide, water, and energy:

$$C_6H_{12}O_6 + 6O_2 \rightarrow 6CO_2 + 6H_2O - 673 \text{ kcal}$$

Heat liberated by the oxidation of one molecule of glucose is -673 kcal (the minus sign indicates that heat is liberated). The respiratory quotient (RQ), which is the ratio between the volume of CO_2 produced and the volume of O_2 consumed ($VCO_2:VO_2$) and which varies according to the type of nutrient oxidized, equals 1 with glucose and other carbohydrates. The heat produced by 1 g of glucose is 673:180 (with 180 indicating the molecular weight of glucose), or 3.74 kcal/g, and the heat liberated by 1 L of oxygen consumed during this reaction is 673:(6 x 22.4), or 5.01 kcal/L of oxygen (22.4 = conversion

15

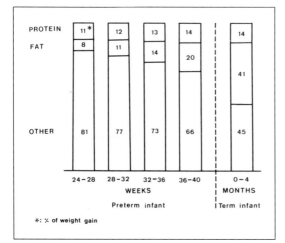

Fig. 2.1. Composition of weight gain of reference fetus from 24 to 40 postconceptional weeks (adapted from Ziegler et al.[1]). For comparison, weight gain composition of the male reference infant during the first 4 months of life is indicated. (Adapted from Fomon.[2])

factor of 1 mol of gas to liters under standard conditions of pressure, temperature, and humidity).

Table 2.1 summarizes these classic parameters for glucose, palmitate (representing fat), and protein.

These parameters may vary according to the type of carbohydrate, fat, and protein oxidized.

Energy Expenditure Measurements

The equation in the previous section shows that energy expenditure can be estimated by measuring either heat liberated (*direct calorimetry*), or the amount of O_2 consumed and CO_2 produced (*indirect calorimetry*) and by applying adequate values for the caloric equivalent of the liter of O_2 consumed (see Table 2.1). Recently, indirect calorimetry has been more widely used, as it may be applied over longer periods while preserving adequate access to the neonate for routine care. In addition, it allows estimation of the type of nutrient oxidized from the RQ.[3-7] Both techniques have some restrictions, though, mostly because of the inconvenience and difficulties of use over prolonged periods (days).

Recently, the *doubly labeled water technique* has provided another promising way of estimating energy expenditure. Water is produced during nutrient oxidation and its production rate is proportional to energy expenditure. When water, labeled with ^2H (deuterium) and ^{18}O, is administered orally to a subject, it distributes quickly in the body water. The loss of

Table 2.1. Energy Balance Data for the Three Main Types of Nutrients*

	Glucose (180)[†]	Palmitate (256.4)[†]	Protein (88)[†]
(a) Heat liberated (kcal)			
per mol oxidized	673	2,398	475
per gram oxidized	3.74	9.3	5.4
(b) O_2 consumed			
(mol)	66	23	5.1
(liters)	134	515	114
(c) CO_2 produced			
(mol)	66	16	4.1
(liters)	134	358	92
(d) Number of ATP[‡] produced[§]			
(mol)	36	129	23
ATP Cost:			
Energy kcal/mol of ATP (a/d)	18.7	18.3	20.7
O_2 L/mol (b/d)	3.72	3.99	4.96
CO_2 L/mol (c/d)	3.72	2.77	4.00
Respiratory quotient (c/b)	1	0.7	0.81
Energy equivalent of (or produced by)			
one liter of oxygen oxidized (kcal/L)	5.02	4.66	4.17

*Adapted from Ferrannini.[5]

[†]Molecular weight. Molecular weight and caloric values may vary according to the type of carbohydrate, fat, and protein oxidized.

[‡]ATP= adenosine-5-triphosphate.

[§]Biologically available.

isotopes from the body is then monitored over several days. The ^2H disappearance rate is proportional to the water output; the ^{18}O disappearance rate is faster than that for ^2H and has a rate constant proportional to water output plus CO_2 production (there is a quick equilibration of $^{18}O_2$ between the body water and bicarbonate pools). The difference between disappearance rates of ^{18}O and ^2H is proportional to total CO_2 production. Energy expenditure can be calculated from CO_2 production if the RQ of the subject is known or approximated. The great advantage of this method is that total energy expenditure can be estimated noninvasively over long periods in free-living subjects, including premature infants.[8,9] This method requires a water pool of fairly constant size, however, something which cannot be expected in the sick, very small preterm infant.

Energy Requirements in Growing Very Low-Birthweight Infants

Estimation of the energy requirements of the growing preterm infant requires knowledge of the outcome of the energy given. This is shown in the classic energy (E) balance equation:

$$E\ intake = E\ excreted + E\ stored + E\ expended$$

Energy *intake* or *gross energy* is the energy provided by food. Energy *excreted* occurs mainly in the feces and to a small extent in the urine. The difference between E intake and E excreted is the *metabolizable* energy. (Metabolizable energy is often confused with *absorbed* energy, which is the difference between energy intake and energy excreted in the stools and does not take into account energy which may be lost in urine. In practice, both values are similar.) Energy *stored* is the energy laid down in newly formed tissue (mainly as fat and protein); energy *expended* comprises the energy used for resting metabolism, thermoregulation, and the activity and synthesis of new tissue.

Each term of this equation can be estimated in the preterm infant using methods such as indirect calorimetry and nutrient balance measurements. From such measurements and accurate anthropometry data, weight gain composition can be estimated, as explained in Figure 2.2.

Complete energy balances, including nutrient balances and concomitant energy expenditure measurements, have been performed in VLBW infants, most of them healthy growing infants. Table 2.2 presents most of the studies[11-20] in which both techniques were performed. Few nutrient balances have been performed during the first 2 weeks[21] or in sick infants. These published data allow reasonable estimation of the level of each term of the energy balance equation in preterm infants.

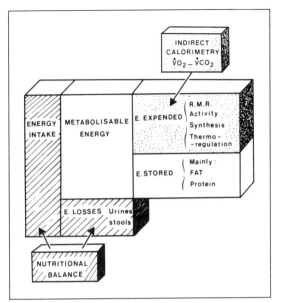

Fig. 2.2. The classic energy balance equation (energy intake = energy excreted + energy stored + energy expended) is represented in this figure. Metabolizable energy (energy intake − energy excreted or lost in urine and feces) is the only energy available to the cells and can be either expended or stored. In a growing preterm infant the amount of energy that is laid down consists mainly of fat and protein (glycogen deposition is very low in this stable anabolic situation, accounting for <1% of body weight,[10] and for this reason will not be considered in calculations). Nutritional balance allows precise measurement of the amount of energy absorbed (metabolizable). Energy expenditure measurement (by indirect calorimetry) performed over several hours gives estimations of the total energy expenditure; total energy storage will be the difference between metabolizable energy minus total energy expenditure. Knowing the amount of protein stored (estimated by nitrogen balance [nitrogen retained × 6.25]), the energy stored as protein can be calculated (amount of protein stored × caloric equivalent of the protein) and subtracted from the total amount of energy stored. The resulting nonprotein energy storage consists mainly of fat, the amount of which can be easily calculated (nonprotein energy stored divided by caloric equivalent of fat: 9.3 kcal/g). If weight gain is accurately known (through precise and repeated anthropometric measurements), the weight gain composition made up mainly of water, fat, and protein can be estimated.

Energy Excretion

Energy excretion is mainly due to fat and protein losses via the feces (and to a small extent due to urinary urea excretion), the major factor being the long-chain saturated fatty acid malabsorption of the VLBW infant. From published data,[11-20,22,23] an average retention of 85% to 90% of the energy intake may be expected by 2 to 3 weeks of age (90% in Table 2.2); few data are available for infants weighing <1,000 g or during the first and second weeks of life. However, according to the data of Atkinson et al., an

Table 2.2. Energy Balances Reported in Literature where Both Nutrient Balances and Energy Expenditure Were Measured along with Adequate Anthropometry Data in Preterm Infants (adapted from 223 balances)

			At Birth		At Study		Gains		
Reference	Number of Studies*	Type of Milk†	Weight (g)	Gestational Age (wks)	Postnatal Age (days)	Gestational Age (wks)	Weight (g/kg/day)	Length (cm/wk)	Head Circumference (cm/wk)
Schulze et al.[11]	8	F	1,448	31	15	33	14.4	—	—
	5	F	1,436	31	15	33	16.8	—	—
	6	F	1,502	32	19	34.7	21.7	—	—
Catzeflis et al.[12]	10	HM or F	1,223	30	26	33.7	15.4	0.81	0.94
Whyte et al.[13]	8	HM	1,320	30	—	320−33	15.2	0.86	1.1
	19	F	1,250	30	—	32−33	16.9	0.95	0.9
Reichman et al.[14]	15	HM	1,160	30.3	21	33.3	15.2	0.98	0.76
	22	F	1,155	29.3	21	32.3	16.8	1.02	0.94
Putet et al.[15]	6	HM	1,318	30.5	21	33.2	13.6	1.0	1.0
	6	F	1,302	29.9	29	33.3	22.1	1.4	1.1
	5	HM	1,318	30.5	45	36	15.6	1.0	1.0
	6	F	1,302	29.9	46	36	19.6	1.4	1.1
Putet et al.[16]	8	HM	1,315	30	31	34.4	15.3	1.1	1.0
	8	HM	1,391	29.9	33	34.6	17.1	1.2	1.2
Whyte et al.[17]	15	F	1,380	31	15−25	—	21.2	1.3	1.1
	15	F	1,380	31	15−25	—	21.8	1.1	1.1
Kashyap et al.[18]	12	HM	1,381	31.1	~18	—	16.5	0.91	1.0
	8	HM	1,435	30.5	~22	—	20.5	1.3	1.2
	12	HM	1,266	30.7	~22	—	18.2	1.1	0.9
Roberts, Lucas[19]	10	HM	1,353	30.6	27	34.4	14.0	—	—
	10	F	1,379	30.2	25	33.7	19.4	—	—
Freymond et al.[20]	9	F	1,740	33	21	36	16.6	—	—
Mean			1,352	30.6			17.5		
±SD			124	0.8			2.7		

*Number of energy balances performed.

†F = formula (usually preterm formula); HM = human milk (pooled human milk or human milk supplemented with protein or energy or both).

energy absorption of around 80% may be expected during this early postnatal period.[21]

Energy Expenditure

Energy expenditure includes energy for resting metabolism, activity, thermoregulation, and synthesis of new tissue. Most of the information available on energy expenditure has been derived from indirect calorimetry measurements performed in a thermoneutral environment over several hours, knowing that measurements performed over 8 to 12 hours may be representative of total energy expenditure over 24 hours.[24−26]

Components of Energy Expenditure The usual comparative measurement in the neonate is *resting*

energy expenditure, or resting metabolic rate (RMR), since measurement of the so-called basal metabolic rate (BMR), which requires at least a 12-hour fast, cannot ethically be performed in the preterm infant. Resting metabolic rate differs from BMR in that it includes BMR together with a part of energy used for growth (see following). On average, RMR estimations vary from 45 to 60 kcal/kg/day; lower values have been reported,[27] though, especially during the first week of life. Resting metabolic rate rises during the first week of life [28−30] due partly to an increase in energy intake, and is higher in small-for-gestational-age (SGA) than in average-for-gestational-age (AGA) infants.[30,31]

Activity has been shown to increase energy expenditure two- to threefold over short periods. Estima-

Protein (g/kg/day)			Energy (kcal/kg/day)				Energy Stored as Fat (g/kg/day[§])
Intake	Absorbed	Stored	Intake[‡]	Metabolizable (% of Intake)[‡]	Expended	Stored	
2.2		1.6	113	106 (94%)	60	47	4.1
3.6		2.6	115	104 (90%)	58	46	3.3
3.5		2.6	149	137 (92%)	69	69	5.9
3.0	2.6	1.8	114	99 (88%)	58	41	3.4
2.6	2.2	1.6	127	108 (85%)	53	55	4.9
2.6	2.3	1.7	126	111 (87%)	58	53	4.7
3.0	2.6	2.0	111	100 (90%)	56	44	3.6
3.2	2.6	1.9	149	130 (87%)	63	68	6.1
2.5	2.1	1.6	103	87 (84%)	46	40	3.4
3.1	2.8	2.3	126	118 (94%)	57	60	5.1
2.4	2.0	1.5	107	102 (94%)	52	50	4.5
3.1	2.9	2.1	130	123 (94%)	63	59	5.1
2.5	2.1	1.6	107	95 (88%)	49	47	4.1
3.9	3.0	2.0	106	91 (86%)	58	33	2.3
3.2	—	2.1	134	123 (92%)	63	60	5.2
3.2	—	2.1	133	120 (90%)	63	57	4.9
2.4	—	—	128	121 (94%)	59	62	5.6
3.2	—	—	130	123 (95%)	61	62	5.3
2.8	—	—	122	113 (93%)	62	51	4.4
2.1	—	1.4	92	83 (90%)	52	31	2.5
3.6	—	2.6	154	130 (84%)	63	67	5.7
3.3	3.0	2.0	123	110 (90%)	68	42	3.2
3.0		2.0	123	111 (90%)	58	52	4.4
0.8		0.4	16	15 (3%)	7	11	1.1

[‡]Referred to as total energy (nonprotein and protein energy) intake.
[§]Calculated as described in the legend for Figure 2.2.

tions over 24 hours are more difficult to achieve. Activity cost has been estimated at 3.6 kcal/kg/day by Freymond,[20] 4.3 kcal/kg/day by Reichman,[29] and 7.4 kcal/kg/day by Sauer,[32] but higher estimations, 13 to 19 kcal/kg/day, have been reported by Brooke.[33]

It is likely that during studies, handling of the infants is decreased in comparison with normal nursing conditions (Yeh[34] has estimated nursing procedures to amount to approximately 2% to 12% of the total daily energy expenditure). A total activity cost of 5 to 10 kcal/kg/day is a reasonable estimate.

In VLBW infants, energy lost in *thermoregulation* should be minimized with careful adherence to standard methods for maintaining a thermoneutral environment.[35] However, it has been shown that temper-

ature instability is frequent during nursing procedures.[36] Moreover, nurses' estimation of the thermal environment might be erroneous, and an increase in energy expenditure of 7 to 8 kcal/kg/day may be achieved in infants maintained just below the thermoneutral range.[37] Thermal losses might also increase when a sick preterm infant is handled frequently, or when a stable growing infant is bathed or nursed. Great importance must be given to thermal losses because they, more than any of the other components of energy expenditure, can be controlled by adequate nursing.

The *energy cost of growth* includes energy utilized for the *synthesis* of new tissues and the *energy stored* in these new tissues. The estimation of energy uti-

Table 2.3. 24-Hour Energy Expenditure Measurements in Premature Infants

Reference	Number of Measurements	At Birth Weight (g)	At Birth Gestational Age (wks)	At Study Weight (g)	At Study Postnatal Age (days)	Weight Gain (g/kg/day)	Total Energy Intake (g/kg/day)	Energy Expenditure (kcal/kg/day)
Bell et al.[24]	9	1,260	30.6	1,510	20	—	101	60
Schulze et al.[26]	12	1,228	29.6	1,463	34	—	102–150	67
Putet[39]	7	1,323	31	1,760	34	18	116	62
Freymond et al.[20]	9	1,740	33	—	21	16.6	122	68
Roberts et al.[25]	4	1,591	30.5	1,695	22	14	—	56

lized for synthesis in preterm infants is controversial, and published values demonstrate great variability: 0.26,[32] 0.55,[27] 0.67,[29] and 1.2[12] kcal/g of weight gain (4.8, 6.2, 11.3, and 18 kcal/kg/day, respectively). Hommes,[38] using Atkinson's metabolic price system, estimated the energy needs for synthesis at 0.3 kcal/g of weight gain in term infants. These discrepancies relate in part to the fact that the composition of weight gain is not similar in all studies (the cost of deposition of 1 g of protein is not equal to the cost of deposition of 1 g of fat). It is difficult to provide a more precise estimation of energy required for synthesis, and an average of 10 kcal/kg/day is acceptable in view of these data and of total energy expenditure measurements obtained in these infants. The amount of energy stored in new tissues is discussed later.

Total Energy Expenditure Estimation In Table 2.3 are listed some of the few 24-hour energy expenditure measurements published.[20,24–26,39] These data, which range from 56 to 68 kcal/kg/day, are in accordance with the numerous data on energy expenditure measured over shorter periods (see Table 2.2) and show that at around 34 weeks gestational age and 3 to 4 weeks postnatal age, most of the well-growing preterm infants have a total energy expenditure of around 60 kcal/kg/day; these values may be lower at a lower gestational age and at a lower postnatal age. It can be accepted that most of the well-growing VLBW infants have a total energy expenditure of 50 to 70 kcal/kg/day.

Energy Stored

Calculations of fat and protein accretion during fetal growth are available from several studies.[1,10] For a mean weight gain of 15 g/kg/day, a value of 20 to 30 kcal/kg may be estimated to be stored every day during the last trimester.

During postnatal growth, energy and protein metabolism are tightly linked with respect to growth and quality of growth. Nonprotein energy storage, mainly in the form of fat, will be influenced both by the absolute energy intake and by the protein:energy ratio as shown in Figure 2.3. This figure shows that for a similar weight gain, nonprotein energy stored as fat may vary from 22[16] to 57[14] kcal/kg/day. Thus, for a similar growth, energy requirement may vary widely according to the weight gain composition. Figure 2.4 shows the composition of weight gain in preterm infants orally fed *different amounts of energy* but a

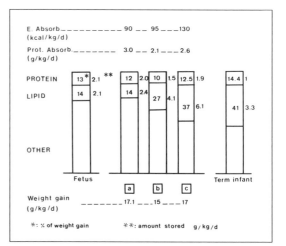

Fig. 2.3. Weight gain composition of the fetus (32 to 36 weeks)[1] and of the term infant (0 to 4 months)[2] compared with those of VLBW infants fed pooled human milk (HM) (b),[16] protein-supplemented pooled HM (a),[16] and a preterm formula (c)[14] (the amounts of protein and energy [E] absorbed and weight gain composition have been measured as indicated in Figure 2.2). Comparison of these published data shows that: feeding pooled HM (b) results in a lower protein and higher fat storage that in the fetus[16]; increasing only the amount of protein intake (a) results in a higher protein retention, lower fat storage, and weight gain composition more similar to that of the fetus[16]; and inversely, an increase in the amount of energy absorbed (c) results mainly in an increase in fat storage. At this level of absorbed energy, weight gain composition is similar to what is seen in the normally growing full-term infant during the first months of life.[2]

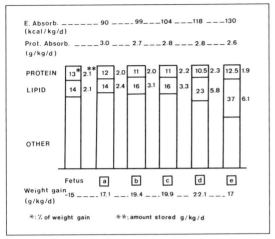

Fig. 2.4. Weight gain composition of the fetus (at 32 to 36 weeks[1]) and of VLBW infants of similar gestational age fed different types of milk:
—pooled human milk enriched with protein: a[16]
—pooled human milk enriched with protein and energy: b (Putet, unpublished data)
—various preterm formula: c (Putet, unpublished data), d[15], e[14]

The amount of nutrients absorbed has been measured by nutrient balance. Weight gain composition has been calculated according to the method explained in Figure 2.2. The amount of absorbed protein provided by these different regimens is similar. It appears that an increase in absorbed energy results mainly in a higher fat storage, as is especially seen with d and e. This increase in fat storage is not associated with an obvious effect on weight gain.

similar amount of protein; these data are compared with fetal weight gain composition between 32 and 36 weeks. According to these studies, and *at this level of protein intake,* most of the calories given above 118 kcal/kg/day (of absorbed energy or metabolizable energy) are deposited directly as fat with little effect on weight gain. Indeed, energy stored as fat increases from 30 kcal/kg/day (16% of weight gain) at an intake of 104 kcal/kg/day up to 57 kcal/kg/day (37% of weight gain) at a metabolizable energy intake of 130 kcal/kg/day. This increase in fat storage is not followed by obvious weight gain. Figure 2.5 shows that for a *given amount of energy absorbed, an increase in protein intake* (within reasonable range) will influence growth and fat deposition.

It is not known whether it is "better" to have a weight gain composition with either 15% as fat (similar to the fetus) or with 40% as fat (as in the term infant). However, it is important to consider that, at term, a prematurely born infant growing with 40% weight gain as fat would have at least twice (around 800 g) the amount of fat of a newborn term infant. Few studies have addressed this point nor its long-term consequences, and the results of those that have are not entirely consistent: Agras et al.[40] have found

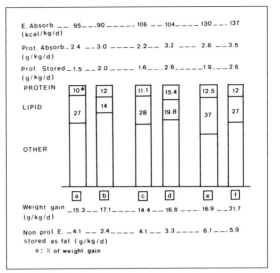

Fig. 2.5. Weight gain composition of VLBW infants fed three levels of metabolizable energy intake (around 95, 105, and 130 kcal/kg/day) with low or high protein intake. (The amounts of protein and energy absorbed and weight gain composition have been measured as indicated in Figure 2.2.) At each level of metabolizable energy intake, an increase in protein intake is followed by an increase in weight gain and a decrease in fat storage (a,b[16]; c,d[11]; e[14]; f[11]).

that greater adiposity at birth was a predictive factor of greater fatness at 6 years of age; De Gamarra et al.[41] have shown that preterm infants, subjected to rapid growth during the neonatal period, with 20% of weight gain as fat, experienced "normalization" of adiposity within the first 2 years of life; Cooper et al.,[42] comparing three types of feeding (human milk, standard formula, and preterm formula) which produced wide differences in skinfold increase during the neonatal period, did not find differences in growth parameters at 3 years of age. A fat deposition of 20% (up to 25%) of weight gain is probably a reasonable goal, but there are no long-term experimental data to justify the rationality of this weight gain composition.

Energy Intake Recommendations for Enteral Feeding in Growing Very Low-Birthweight Infants

From all the above data and assuming (a) a weight gain of 18 to 20 g/kg/day, (b) a protein retention of 2 g/kg/day, and (c) a fat retention of 20% to 25% of weight gain, a total energy intake of 120 kcal/kg/day can be recommended in growing VLBW infants. In order to achieve these requirements, human milk has to be supplemented at least with protein (see Chapter 3) and with energy (if a large volume of milk intake is not wanted). Formulas have to contain a well-absorbed fat blend (see Chapter 5) and care has to be taken that there is no nutrient loss during tube feeding.[43] Energy intake above 120 kcal/kg/day (up to 130 kcal/kg/day) is rarely necessary when energy absorption is above 85%.

These recommendations can be compared with published data reported in Table 2.4 where weight gain, protein retention, and energy balance data were available.

The same recommendations seem to be valuable for the group of VLBW infants weighing <1,000 g at birth.

Small-for-Gestational-Age Infants

Although many neonatal units empirically provide higher calorie and protein intakes to SGA infants, nutritional recommendations[44-46] do not usually differentiate between the needs of SGA and AGA VLBW infants. Higher total energy expenditure (5% to 10%, or around 5 kcal/kg/day) is usually reported in SGA infants when compared to AGA infants.[47-50] Term SGA infants given high-energy formulas showed marginally better weight gain and head growth than those receiving standard formula.[51] Gill et al.[52] showed that SGA VLBW infants had a higher growth rate than AGA infants (although the difference was not significant) during the first weeks of life, but the exact amounts of energy and protein intake received in each group were not reported. When complete data on energy intake, protein balance, and weight gain are available,[47-50] it appears that weight gain is not statistically different between AGA and SGA infants receiving similar energy intake and having the same protein retention. As in AGA preterm infants, an increase in both energy and protein intakes may lead to higher growth (see Chapter 3); this may be beneficial in SGA infants for optimal catch-up growth.

Transitional Period

Weight loss that follows birth is due both to water loss and to inadequate energy intake, although opinions differ on the respective importance of water and body solid losses.[53-55] In fact, during these first days, body weight may not be the optimal tool to estimate the level of energy intake needed to maintain or increase body solid mass, as it is possible that growth, in the sense of the formation of new tissues, may go on even if the infant is still losing weight through water loss. Also, during the first days of life, increase in energy intake is usually limited by difficulties in giving adequate enteral volume, especially in sick infants, and parenteral feeding is often limited by glucose intolerance.

The minimal caloric intake to be given in order to avoid catabolism and to induce growth is difficult to estimate. From published data, Brooke[56] estimated total daily energy expenditure at 39 kcal/kg for in-

Table 2.4. Energy Requirement Estimations

	ESPGAN* Recommendations	Adapted from Published Data[†]	Personal Data[‡]		
			HM	PF	Total
Energy expended (kcal/kg/day)	85	58±7	55	62	59
Energy excreted (kcal/kg/day)	20	12±5	13	8	11
Energy stored (kcal/kg/day)	25	52±11	38	51	44
Energy intake (kcal/kg/day)	130	123±16	106	121	113
Metabolizable energy intake (kcal/kg/day)	110	111±15	94	114	103
Weight gain (g/kg/day)	15	17.5±2.7	18.7	20.6	19.6

*According to the Committee on Nutrition of the Preterm Infant, the European Society of Paediatric Gastroenterology and Nutrition (ESPGAN).[43,45]

†From published data quoted in Table 2.1 (223 published nutritional balances have been reviewed; 206 have adequate data with energy expenditure measurements performed, most of them done around 32 to 34 weeks gestational age; few are available below 32 weeks gestational age at the time of the study). These numbers are not recommendations.

‡From personal data:
HM = Human milk–fed infants (pooled HM, protein-supplemented pooled HM, protein- and energy-supplemented HM); n = 40; weight gain = 18.7 g/kg/day; protein intake = 3.2 g/kg/day; protein retention = 1.9 g/kg/day.
PF = Preterm formulas; n = 35; weight gain = 20.6 g/kg/day; protein intake = 3 g/kg/day; protein retention = 2.1 g/kg/day.

fants <1,000 g and at 41 kcal/kg for infants from 1,000 to 1,500 g during the first week of life, and at 49 and 48 kcal/kg/day, respectively, during the second week of life. In current clinical practice weight gain is observed most often at energy intakes higher than in Brooke's estimates. We collected data on weight and total energy intake (intravenous and oral energy intakes were calculated from the amount of nutrients given, applying the adequate caloric equivalent for each nutrient class) in 21 VLBW infants <1,200 g at birth, most of them being ventilated for respiratory distress (Fig. 2.6). Weight gain became apparent when calculated energy intake was above 80 kcal/kg/day. Knowing that at 1 week of age half the energy intake was given enterically (pooled human milk) and assuming that 80% of the enteric energy intake was absorbed, one can estimate that 70 to 75 kcal/kg/day was necessary for weight gain to occur. Similar data were published by Gill et al.[52] showing that, in VLBW infants born at 23 to 29 weeks gestation, growth occurred once energy intake reached 80 kcal/kg/day. In that study the lowest weight was seen for all age groups on the sixth day of life while mean caloric intake ranged from 55 to 60 kcal/kg/day

during the first week. These values correlate with data published during total parenteral nutrition which showed that body fat oxidation occurs when total caloric intake is below 70 kcal/kg/day, demonstrating the need for extra calories to cover energy expenditure.[57,58] Recently, Bauer et al.[53] showed that minimal postnatal weight gain was achieved in very premature infants (birthweight 810 to 1,310 g, gestational age 26 to 30 weeks) while they were receiving 57 kcal/kg/day both enterally and parenterally. They pointed out that at this level of caloric intake and at a nitrogen intake of 378 mg/kg/day there was no sign of catabolism and that nitrogen balance was positive. From total body water measurement (deuterium oxide), they observed that the postnatal weight loss reflected total water loss rather than body solid losses. These data are consistent with a study performed in 2- to 5-day-old VLBW infants on total parenteral nutrition showing that, with a nonprotein energy intake of 53 kcal/kg/day and a nitrogen intake of 400 mg/kg/day, no weight gain but positive nitrogen balance was obtained.[59] It was also pointed out by Bauer[53] that extreme attention was given to keep the infants in a strict thermoneutral environment and that they were all ventilated for respiratory distress and sedated with phenobarbitone. Under these conditions, total daily energy expenditure was estimated by Bauer to be within the published values of 40 to 50 kcal/kg/day.[56] It is important to realize that different clinical conditions (thermal stress, increase in insensible water loss, work of breathing during respiratory distress, sepsis) would certainly increase energy expenditure and thus the amount of energy to be given. This underlines the need for optimal nursing conditions during the first weeks of life.

Thus, during this transitional period, effort should be made to provide as soon as possible sufficient calories to cover energy expenditure, which has to be kept at the lowest level possible by adequate nursing. Body weight alone is not the perfect tool to judge the level of energy intake necessary to avoid catabolism, but in practice, clinicians have to rely on this parameter. According to the above-quoted studies, a total energy intake of 60 to 70 kcal/kg/day may be the minimal amount of energy that should be given, as soon as it can be tolerated (along with adequate protein intake). Further increase in energy intake to achieve adequate growth should be done as quickly as possible, according to infant tolerance.

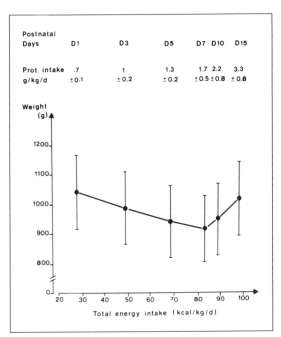

Fig. 2.6. Evolution of weight (g) in 21 premature infants <1,200 g at birth during the first 2 weeks of life fed both orally (pooled human milk) and intravenously. Weight gain started after day 7 when infants received above 80 kcal/kg/day (if 80% of the oral energy intake is absorbed, one can estimate that 70 to 75 kcal/kg/day is needed for weight gain to occur—see text). Protein intake is indicated at the top of the figure, as well as the postnatal day on which the measurement was performed. In this study it is important to note that protein intake was low.

The Sick Neonate

Little information is available on energy expenditure in sick VLBW infants during the acute phase of disease. In sick preterm infants receiving ventilatory support for respiratory disease, published values for total energy expenditure measurements range from 45 to 60 kcal/kg/day.[60-63] Richardson et al.[60] reported a decrease in oxygen consumption from 8.3 mL/kg/min (around 58 kcal/kg/day) on day 1 down to 5.3 mL/min (around 38 kcal/kg/day) on day 4; this decrease was in part imputed to a reduction in high evaporative heat losses. Such a decrease was not observed by other authors. The level of energy expenditure does not seem to be associated with severity of disease.[60,62] It is generally thought that the higher respiratory rate and greater work of breathing contribute to increased energy expenditure, but adequate ventilatory support in sedated infants may limit this increase.[53] As none of these studies involved healthy control subjects, and knowing the great variability between reported data in well infants,[56] it is difficult to estimate to what extent energy expenditure is increased in these sick infants. Thus, during the acute phase of a disease, it seems reasonable to recommend an energy intake at least equal to that recommended for well infants. The real challenge is to provide the needed calories, because metabolic disturbances or gastrointestinal intolerance are often observed in acute and unstable clinical situations. Although some authors suggest that there is an increase in energy expenditure, there are no definite data showing the need for or advantage of increasing the energy intake.

More data on energy expenditure are available in chronically sick infants especially those with bronchopulmonary dysplasia (BPD). Growth failure is a major problem in these infants, but little is known about its cause. One explanation is that these infants have increased energy expenditure because of higher mechanical breathing work,[64,65] but chronic hypoxia, poor nutritional intake, poor gastrointestinal absorption, or psychological problems are other possible causes. Most recent studies[64-68] show an increase in energy expenditure of around 15% to 30% (10 to 20 kcal/kg/day). The difficulties of oxygen consumption measurements in infants receiving oxygen have been discussed by Kalhan and Denne,[69] who estimate the magnitude of these reported increases is perhaps too high, and ask for further studies before recommending high caloric supplemented feeding. It is important to note that Kurzner et al.[65] found no difference in energy expenditure between control subjects and normally growing BPD infants at 6 months of age, but showed a higher energy expenditure in BPD infants with growth failure. Yeh et al.[66] found that infants with BPD received relatively fewer calories than control infants, while their energy expenditure was higher; in that study, absorbed energy represented 93% of energy intake in both BPD and control infants, demonstrating no impairment in nutrient absorption. Recently, Billeaud et al.[67] demonstrated that the increase in oxygen consumption was present early in the disease process and was correlated with the severity of the respiratory condition. In fact, the reasons for growth failure in chronically sick infants are not fully understood, and energy is certainly only one of the factors involved. As precise data on energy balance are lacking in these infants, recommendations on the level of energy intake are difficult to make. At the very least, energy intake has to be at the same level as that recommended for well infants, and fulfilling this level is often difficult in these sick infants. The apparent increase in their energy expenditure is an argument to raise the energy intake by 10% to 20%, but the need for such an increase is not truly documented by current published data.

Energy Intake during Total Parenteral Nutrition

Data from Zlotkin et al.[70] presented in Table 2.5 indicate that during total parenteral nutrition (TPN), as well as during enteral nutrition, growth is the result of an adequate balance between energy and protein in-

---

Table 2.5. Influence of Nonprotein Energy Intake and Protein Intake on Weight Gain and Protein Retention during Total Parenteral Nutrition

	Group A	Group B	Group C	Group D
Total energy intake (kcal/kg/day)	62	96	101	94
Nonprotein energy intake (kcal/kg/day)	50	80	80	83
Protein intake (g/kg/day)	3.1	3.0	3.9	2.0
Protein retention (g/kg/day)	1.6	2.0	2.7	1.1
Weight gain (g/kg/day)	2.2	16.2	15.6	5.2

*A nonprotein intake energy of 80 kcal/kg/day, along with a protein intake of 3 g/kg/day, provides acceptable growth (group B). At a lower protein intake (group D) or at a lower nonprotein energy intake (group A) weight gain is less. Further increase in protein intake (group C) with similar nonprotein energy intake has no influence on weight gain. Growth is the result of an adequate balance between energy and protein intakes. (Adapted from Zlotkin et al.[70])

take. A nonprotein energy intake of 80 kcal/kg/day and a protein intake of 3 g/kg/day are necessary to achieve a growth rate of 16 g/kg/day in premature infants with a mean gestational age of 29.2 weeks. With a nonprotein intake of 63 to 67 kcal/kg/day and a protein intake of 2.6 g/kg/day, a lower weight gain of 13.6 g/kg/day was obtained by Piedboeuf et al.[71] Almost no growth is achieved with a nonprotein energy intake of 50 to 55 kcal/kg/day and a protein intake of 2.5 to 3 g/kg/day,[59] but a positive nitrogen balance occurs. It has been shown that when nonprotein energy is given in excess of 70 kcal/kg/day intravenously as glucose and amino acids, preterm and term infants have no net endogenous fat oxidation[57,58,72]; this indicates that the energy supply exceeds total energy expenditure and that further increase in energy intake will be stored as fat.

In the study by Zlotkin et al.[70] (Table 2.5), it should be noted that when the energy content of the protein intake is taken into account (3 g/kg/day), the total energy intake reaches approximately 96 to 106 kcal/kg/day (energy equivalent of 1 g of protein = 5.4 kcal) and this level of energy is very similar to the metabolizable (absorbed) energy intake necessary for adequate growth during enteral feeding (Table 2.2). This is also similar to the total energy requirement of the fetus (who may be considered as a model of parenteral nutrition) estimated at 100 kcal/kg/day by Sparks et al.[73]

Thus, a nonprotein energy intake of 80 to 90 kcal/kg/day is accepted to be a rational estimate of the energy requirements for preterm infants during TPN. With a concomitant amino acid intake of 3 g/kg/day, a weight gain approximating the intrauterine rate is usually obtained. Greater energy intake may lead to a greater rate of weight gain, but it is likely that this additional weight gain will be mostly fat deposition as seen during enteral nutrition. There are not enough published data on TPN in preterm infants to warrant further discussion at this time.

Nonprotein energy can be given as glucose alone or as glucose and intravenous fat. Indirect calorimetry data and isotopic studies show that during glucose-lipid mixture infusion, fat oxidation may be impaired if high-energy intake is given simultaneously as glucose.[58,72] Indeed, fat utilization as a source of energy (i.e., oxidation) will depend mainly on glucose intake.[39,58,72,73] At 80 kcal/kg/day, with 25% of energy as fat (2 g) and 75% as glucose (around 16 g), 20% to 30% of the calories oxidized are expected to be derived from fat oxidation. At 100 kcal/kg/day, with 75% of energy as glucose (20 g/kg/day), the percentage of calories derived from fat will be lower[58,72] (Fig. 2.7). Thus, above a certain level of glucose intake (the level at which glucose will provide almost all of the calories needed), fat oxidation will not contribute greatly to energy expenditure, but will be

mostly deposited.[39,58] These results are consistent with a study in older children by Bresson et al.[74] showing that fat utilization as a source of energy (i.e., fat oxidation) is inversely related to the amount of glucose oxidized for the coverage of energy expenditure. Several studies in adults and children have shown that increasing intravenous glucose load augments energy expenditure, carbon dioxide production, and oxygen consumption.[71,75-77] It is important to be reminded that any increase in energy intake (given either enterally or parenterally) is followed by such augmentations, especially when energy intake is increased into the positive energy balance range and fuel storage begins.[75] The difference between a glucose and a glucose-fat diet is presumably accounted for by the different precursors (glucose or fat) of triglyceride synthesis; these changes are more pronounced when glucose is the predominant nutrient.[76]

Future Research

Future clinical research on energy metabolism is expected to provide information on:

—Energy expenditure during the first 2 weeks of life (transitional period), especially in sick infants.
—Energy balance and energy requirements for chronically sick newborn infants with BPD.
—Growth of SGA infants, including energy requirements, optimal protein:energy ratio, and growth factors.
—Nutrient tolerance during the first days of life in infants <1,000 g.

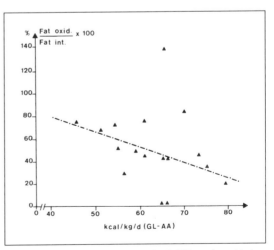

Fig. 2.7. Influence of the glucose load (GL) on fat oxidation during total parenteral nutrition in preterm and term infants (solid triangles). Fat oxidation decreases as glucose intake increases (amino acid [AA] intake was stable at around 2 to 2.5 g/kg/day and represented around 10 kcal/kg/day in this study). Above 80 kcal/kg/day infused as glucose, the amount of fat oxidized would be minimal. (Adapted from Putet et al.[58])

CASE STUDY

A male SGA VLBW infant was born at 28 weeks gestation, weighing 700 g to a primiparous mother aged 26. Apgar score was 7 at 3 minutes. He had no respiratory distress and was transferred to the neonatal unit and placed in a servocontrol single-walled incubator set to keep his abdominal skin temperature at 36.8°C. Room temperature was 26°C. During the first day only intravenous infusion was given. Oral alimentation was started the second day at 20 mL/kg/day and then further increased daily to 160 mL/kg/day. Intravenous supplementation was stopped when the baby received 120 mL/kg/day enterally. Milk was given by continuous infusion using a syringe pump put on the isolette. At first, half-strength preterm formula was given, replaced during the second week of life by his mother's milk. Birthweight was regained at day 19. From day 19 to day 25 weight gain was 13 g/kg/day. Feeding volume was increased to 180 mL/kg/day. During the following 2 weeks, weight gain was around 14 g/kg/day.

Commentary. In this well SGA preterm infant without any medical problem, a growth rate of 14 g/kg/day can be considered poor, as this will not allow for catch-up growth. Human milk alone is clearly not ideal nutrition. Energy (as well as protein) has to be added in order to increase caloric density to around 70 to 80 kcal/dL (it is not desirable to increase caloric density above 80 kcal/dL); thus, at 160 mL/kg/day, gross energy intake will, theoretically, reach 110 to 130 kcal/kg/day. Increasing energy intake to 120 to 130 kcal/kg/day may be necessary if a weight gain of 18 to 20 g/kg/day is desired.

Supplemental energy may be supplied as medium-chain triglycerides (MCTs) and/or dextrin maltose. Adding MCT directly to the milk is not the best solution, though, as it has been shown that adherence of medium-chain fatty acids to the feeding tube during gavage feeding may be followed by a loss of energy within the tube.[78] Positioning the syringe is also important, as a part of human milk fat will remain within a horizontal syringe; care should thus be taken to have the syringe put in a vertical position. It is also better if the syringe is left below the level of the baby: because of its low density, fat will naturally stay in the upper position of the tube and deposit; this phenomenon will not occur if the syringe and tubing are below the baby's body level. Energy supplementation alone is not ideal and protein should be added as well. Utilization of a human milk fortifier is preferable in this situation, as protein (and minerals) as well as energy will be simultaneously given (see Chapter 3).

Thermal environment is another important point to be considered: an abdominal skin temperature of 36.5°C is certainly low, and rectal (or axillary) temperature has to be assessed and kept at around 37°C. A higher skin temperature (36.8° to 36.9°) should be aimed for, and a kind of heat shield (or double-walled incubator) would allow a better thermal environment and decrease energy expenditure for thermoregulation.

In this situation, great care has to be taken to provide adequate energy, protein, and other nutrients necessary for growth (and for catch-up growth). Furthermore, one has to be sure that nutrients will reach the infant and not stay within the syringe or the tubing system.

References

1. Ziegler EE, O'Donnell A, Nelson SE, Fomon SJ. Body composition of the reference fetus. *Growth* 1976;40:329–341.
2. Fomon SJ. Body composition of the male reference infant during the first year of life. *Pediatrics* 1967;40:863–870.
3. Frayn KN. Calculation of substrate oxidation rates in vivo from gaseous exchange. *J Appl Physiol* 1983;53(2):628–634.
4. Jequier E, Acheson K, Schutz Y. Assessment of energy expenditure and fuel utilization in man. *Ann Rev Nutr* 1987;7:187–208.
5. Ferrannini E. The theoretical bases of indirect calorimetry: a review. *Metabolism* 1988;37:287–301.
6. Elia M, Liversey G. Theory and validity of indirect calorimetry during net lipid synthesis. *Am J Clin Nutr* 1988;47:591–607.
7. Liversey G, Elia M. Estimation of energy expenditure, net carbohydrate utilization and net fat oxidation and synthesis by indirect calorimetry: evaluation of errors with special reference to the detailed composition of fuels. *Am J Clin Nutr* 1988;47:608–628.
8. Jones PJH, Winthrop AL, Schoeller DA, et al. Validation of doubly labeled water for assessing energy expenditure in infants. *Pediatr Res* 1987;21:242–246.
9. Roberts SB, Coward WA, Norhia V, Schlingenseipen KH, Lucas A. Comparison of the doubly labeled water ($^2H^{18}O$) method with indirect calorimetry and a nutrient-balance study for simultaneous determination of energy expenditure, water intake, and metabolizable energy intake in premature infants. *Am J Clin Nutr* 1986;44:315–322.
10. Widdowson EM. Growth and composition of the fetus and newborn. *Biology of Gestation* 1968;2:1–49.
11. Schulze KF, Stefanski M, Masterson J, et al. Energy expenditure, energy balance, and composition of weight gain in low-birthweight infants fed diets of different protein and energy content. *J Pediatr* 1987;110:753–759.
12. Catzeflis C, Schutz Y, Micheli JL, Welsch C, Arnaud MJ, Jequier E. Whole body protein synthesis and energy expenditure in very low-birthweight infants. *Pediatr Res* 1985;19:679–687.
13. Whyte RK, Haslam R, Vlainic C, et al. Energy balance and nitrogen balance in growing low-birthweight infants fed human milk or formula. *Pediatr Res* 1983;17:891–898.
14. Reichman B, Chessex P, Verellen G, et al. Dietary composition and macronutrient storage in preterm infants. *Pediatrics* 1983;72:322–328.
15. Putet G, Senterre J, Rigo J, Salle B. Nutrient balance, energy utilization, and composition of weight gain in very low-birthweight infants fed pooled human milk or a preterm formula. *J Pediatr* 1984;105:79–85.
16. Putet G, Rigo J, Salle B, Senterre J. Supplementation of pooled human milk with casein hydrolysate: energy and nitrogen balance and weight gain composition in very low-birthweight infants. *Pediatr Res* 1987;21:458–461.
17. Whyte RK, Campbell D, Stanhope R, et al. Energy balance in low-birthweight infants fed formula of high or low medium-chain triglyceride content. *J Pediatr* 1986;108:964–971.
18. Kashyap S, Schulze KF, Forsyth M, Dell RB, Ramakrishnan R, Heird WC. Growth, nutrient retention, and metabolic response of low-birthweight infants fed supplemented and unsupplemented preterm human milk. *Am J Clin Nutr* 1990;52:254–262.

19. Roberts SB, Lucas A. Energetic efficiency and nutrient accretion in preterm infants fed extremes of dietary intake. *Clin Nutr* 1987;416:105–113.

20. Freymond D, Schutz Y, Decombaz J, Micheli JL, Jequier E. Energy balance, physical activity and thermogenic effect of feeding in premature infants. *Pediatr Res* 1986;20:638–645.

21. Atkinson SA, Bryan HM, Anderson GH. Human milk feeding in premature infants: protein, fat, and carbohydrate balances in the first two weeks of life. *J Pediatr* 1981; 99:617–624.

22. Shanler RJ, Garza C, Nichols BL. Fortified mother's milk for very low-birthweight infants: results of growth and nutrient balance studies. *J Pediatr* 1985;107:437–445.

23. De Curtis M, Brooke OG. Energy and nitrogen balances in very low-birthweight infants. *Arch Dis Child* 1987; 62:830–832.

24. Bell EF, Rios FR, Wilmoth PK. Estimation of 24-hour energy expenditure from shorter measurement periods in premature infants. *Pediatr Res* 1986;20:646–649.

25. Roberts SB, Murgatroyd PR, Crisp JA, Nohria V, Schlingenseipen K-H, Lucas A. Long-term variation in oxygen consumption rate in preterm infants. *Biol Neonate* 1987; 52:1–8.

26. Schulze KF, Stefanski M, Masterson J, et al. An analysis of the variability in estimates of bioenergetic variables in preterm infants. *Pediatr Res* 1986;20:422–427.

27. Gudinchet F, Schutz Y, Micheli JL, Stettler E, Jequier E. Metabolic cost of growth in the very low-birthweight infants. *Pediatr Res* 1982;16:1025–1030.

28. Sinclair JC. Energy balance of the newborn. In: Sinclair JC, eds. *Temperature regulation and energy metabolism in the newborn.* New York: Grune Stratton, 1978; 187–204.

29. Reichman BL, Chessex P, Putet G, et al. Partition of energy metabolism and energy cost of growth in the very low-birthweight infant. *Pediatrics* 1982;69:446–451.

30. Hill JR, Robinson DC. Oxygen consumption in normally grown, small for date and large for date newborn infants. *J Physiol* 1968;199:685–703.

31. Bhakoo ON, Scopes JW. Minimal rates of oxygen consumption in small for date babies during the first week of life. *Arch Dis Child* 1974;49:583–585.

32. Sauer PJJ, Dane HJ, Wisser HKA. Longitudinal studies on metabolic rate, heat loss, and energy cost of growth in low-birthweight infants. *Pediatr Res* 1984;18:254–259.

33. Brooke OG, Alvear J, Arnold M. Energy retention, energy expenditure, and growth in healthy immature infants. *Pediatr Res* 1979; 13:215–220.

34. Yeh TF, Lilien LD, Leu ST, Pildes RS. Increased O_2 consumption and energy loss in premature infants following medical care procedures. *Biol Neonate* 1984;46:157–162.

35. Hey E. Thermal neutrality. *Br Med Bull* 1975;31:69–74.

36. Mok Q, Bass CA, Ducker DA, McIntosh N. Temperature instability during nursing procedures in preterm neonates. *Arch Dis Child* 1991;66:783–786.

37. Glass L, Silverman WA, Sinclair JC. Effects of the thermal environment on cold resistance and growth of small infants after the first week of life. *Pediatrics* 1968;41: 1033–1046.

38. Hommes FA. The energy requirement for growth—a reevaluation. *Nutr Metab* 1980;24:110–113.

39. Putet G. Lipids as an energy source for the premature and full-term neonate. In: Polin RA, Fox WW, eds. *Fetal and neonatal physiology.* Philadelphia: WB Saunders, 1992: 326–328.

40. Agras WS, Kraemer HC, Berkowitz RI, Hommer LD. Influence of early feeding style on adiposity at 6 years of age. *J Pediatr* 1990;116:805–809.

41. De Gamarra ME, Schutz Y, Catzeflis C, et al. Composition of weight gain during the neonatal period and longitudinal growth follow-up in premature babies. *Biol Neonate* 1987;52:181–187.

42. Cooper PA, Rothberg A, Davies VA, Horn J, Vogelman L. Three-year growth and developmental follow-up of very low-birthweight infants fed own mother's milk, a premature formula, or one of two standard formulas. *J Pediatr Gastroenterol Nutr* 1989;8:348–354.

43. Brooke OG, Barley J. Loss of energy during continuous infusion of breast milk. *Arch Dis Child* 1978;53:344–345.

44. Committee on Nutrition of the Preterm Infant, European Society of Paediatric Gastroenterology and Nutrition. Nutrition and feeding of preterm infants. *Acta Paediatr Scand* 1987;336(suppl):1–14.

45. Committee on Nutrition, American Academy of Pediatrics. Nutritional needs of low-birthweight infants. *Pediatrics* 1985;75:976–986.

46. Committee on Nutrition of the Preterm Infant, European Society of Paediatric Gastroenterology and Nutrition. *Nutrition and feeding of preterm infants.* Oxford, UK: Blackwell Scientific Publications; 1987.

47. Cauderay M, Schutz Y, Micheli JL, Calame A, Jequier E. Energy-nitrogen balances and protein turnover in small and appropriate for gestational age low-birthweight infants. *Eur J Clin Nutr* 1988;42:125–136.

48. Chessex P, Reichman B, Verellen G, et al. Metabolic consequences of intrauterine growth retardation in very low-birthweight infants. *Pediatr Res* 1984;18:709–713.

49. Sulkers EJ, Goudoever JB, Leunisse C, Wattimena JLD, Sauer PJJ. Comparison of two preterm formulas with or without addition of medium-chain triglycerides (MCTs). I: Effects on nitrogen and fat balance and body composition changes. *J Pediatr Gastroenterol Nutr* 1992;15:34–41.

50. Pencharz PB, Masson M, Desgrandes F, Papageorgiou A. Total body protein turnover in human premature neonates: effects of birthweight, intrauterine nutritional status, and diet. *Clin Sci* 1981;61:207–215.

51. Brooke OG, Kinzey JM. High energy feeding in small for gestation infants. *Arch Dis Child* 1985;60:42–46.

52. Gill A, Yu VYH, Bajuk B, Astbury J. Postnatal growth in infants born before 30 weeks gestation. *Arch Dis Child* 1986;61:549–553.

53. Bauer K, Bovermann G, Roithmaier A, Götz M, Prölss A, Versmold HT. Body composition, nutrition, and fluid balance during the first two weeks of life in preterm neonates weighing less than 1500 grams. *J Pediatr* 1991;118:615–620.

54. Shaffer SG, Bradt SK, Hall RT. Postnatal changes in total water and extracellular volume in the preterm infant with respiratory distress syndrome. *J Pediatr* 1986;109:509–514.

55. Wagen AVD, Okken A, Zweens J, Zijlstra G. Composition of postnatal weight loss and subsequent weight gain in small for dates newborn infants. *Acta Paediatr Scand* 1985;74:57–61.

56. Brooke OG. Energy expenditure in the fetus and neonate: sources of variability. *Acta Paediatr Scand* 1985; 319(suppl):128–134.

57. Putet G, Heim T, Smith J, Swyer P. Substrate utilization during isocaloric, isovolemic parenteral nutrition with glucose, amino-acid and fat emulsion [Abstract]. *Pediatr Res* 1978;12:440.

58. Putet G, Verellen G, Heim T, Smith JM, Swyer PR. Energy intake and substrate utilization during total parenteral nutrition in newborn. In: Westorp IC, Socters PB, eds. *Clinical nutrition.* New York: Churchill Livingstone, 1982;63–70.

59. Anderson TL, Muttart CR, Bieber MA, Nicholson JF, Heird WC. A controlled trial of glucose versus glucose and amino acids in premature infants. *J Pediatr* 1979;94:947–951.

60. Richardson P, Bose CL, Bucciarelli RL, Carlstrom JR. Oxygen consumption of infants with respiratory distress syndrome. *Biol Neonate* 1984;46:53–56.

61. Lucas A, Nohria U, Roberts SB. Measurement of carbon dioxide production rate in sick ventilated premature infants. *Biol Neonate* 1987;51:138–143.

62. Hazan J, Chessex P, Piedboeuf B, Bourgeois M, Bard H, Long W. Energy expenditure during synthetic surfactant replacement therapy for neonatal respiratory distress syndrome. *J Pediatr* 1992;120:529–533.

63. Mayfield SR. Technical and clinical testing of a computerized indirect calorimeter for use in mechanically ventilated neonates. *Am J Clin Nutr* 1991;54:30–34.

64. Weinstein MR, Oh W. Oxygen consumption in infants with bronchopulmonary dysplasia. *J Pediatr* 1981;99: 958–959.

65. Kurzner SI, Garg M, Bautista B, Sargent CW, Bowman CH, Keens TG. Growth failure in bronchopulmonary dysplasia: elevated metabolic rates and pulmonary mechanics. *J Pediatr* 1988;112:73–80.

66. Yeh TF, McClenan DA, Ajayi OA, Pildes RS. Metabolic rate and energy balance in infants with bronchopulmonary dysplasia. *J Pediatr* 1989;114:448–451.

67. Billeaud C, Piedboeuf B, Chessex P. Energy expenditure and severity of respiratory disease in very low-birthweight infants receiving long-term ventilatory support. *J Pediatr* 1992;120:461–464.

68. Yunis KA, Oh W. Effects of intravenous glucose loading on oxygen consumption, carbon dioxide production, and resting energy expenditure in infants with bronchopulmonary dysplasia. *J Pediatr* 1989;115:127–132.

69. Kalhan SC, Denne SC. Energy consumption in infants with bronchopulmonary dysplasia. *J Pediatr* 1990;116: 662–664.

70. Zlotkin SH, Bryan MH, Anderson GH. Intravenous nitrogen and energy intakes required to duplicate in utero nitrogen accretion in prematurely born human infants. *J Pediatr* 1981;99:115–120.

71. Piedboeuf B, Chessex P, Hazan J, Pineault M, Laurie JC. Total parenteral nutrition in the newborn infant: energy substrate and respiratory gas exchange. *J Pediatr* 1991; 118:97–102.

72. Heim T, Putet G, Verellen G, et al. Energy cost of intravenous alimentation in the newborn infant. In: Stern L, Salle B, Friss-Hansen B, eds. *Intensive care in the newborn*. New York: Masson, 1981; 3:219–239.

73. Sparks JW, Girard JR, Battaglia FC. An estimate of the caloric requirements of the human fetus. *Biol Neonate* 1980;38:113–119.

74. Bresson JL. Narcy P, Putet G, Ricour C, Sachs C, Rey J. Energy substrate utilization in infants receiving total parenteral nutrition with different glucose to fat ratios. *Pediatr Res* 1989;25:645–648.

75. Heymsfield SB, Erbland M, Casper K, et al. Enteral nutritional support. *Clin Chest Med* 1986;7:41–67.

76. Askanazi J, Rosenbaum S, Hyman A, Silverberg P, Milic-Emili J, Kinney J. Respiratory changes induced by the large loads of total parenteral nutrition. JAMA 1980;14:1444–1447.

77. Van Aerde JEE, Sauer PJJ, Pencharz PB, Smith JM, Swyer PR. Effect of replacing glucose with lipid on the energy metabolism of newborn infants. *Clin Sci* 1989; 76:581–588.

78. Mehta NR, Hamosh M, Bitman J, Wood DL. Adherence of medium-chain fatty acids to feeding tubes of premature infants fed formula fortified with medium-chain triglyceride. *J Pediatr Gastroenterol Nutr* 1988;7:307–308.

3. Protein

Jean-L. Micheli

Yves Schutz

Reviewers: William W. Hay, Jr., William C. Heird, Paul Pencharz, Niels C.R. Räihä

The major difficulty in evaluating protein needs of the preterm infant is the lack of generally accepted goals for feeding such infants. For practical purposes, the goals chosen here for assessing appropriate protein supply are: (1) a protein gain that approximates the in utero protein gain of a normal fetus of the same postconceptional age (Fig. 3.1, Table 3.1); and (2) long-term statural growth and psychomotor development (Table 3.2) within the physiologic ranges for normal term infants of the same corrected (postconceptional) age.

Protein Gain and Changes in Lean Body Mass during Intrauterine and Postnatal Growth

As far as protein gain is concerned, we have no better model for the growing preterm infant than the growing fetus of the same gestational age. Measurements of body composition in preterm infants are of major importance and represent the basis for estimating protein needs. The total protein content of a 26-week-old fetus weighing 1,000 g must increase by about five times to reach the values observed in a term infant of 3,500 g. There is a concomitant increase in serum protein concentration and a decrease in the hydration of lean tissue from 86% at 26 weeks to 80% at term.[1-3]

Measurements of the fetal body composition at sequential gestational ages have been published by Widdowson[1] and Ziegler[3]; similarly, Fomon et al.[4] have compiled normative data on body composition for the term baby. We have restricted our analysis to the period from 22 weeks gestational age to 6 months of age.

Figure 3.1 shows the pattern of change in lean body mass and fat during growth. Lean mass is a heterogeneous compartment, composed essentially of water, protein, glycogen, and minerals. The protein content of the lean body mass increases with gestational age.[1,3] There is rapid growth in both fat-free weight and fat weight during the intrauterine period. At 22 weeks the fetus has approximately 99% of lean mass and 1% of fat compared with 86% and 14%, respectively, at 40 weeks.

Physiology

Relationship between Protein Gain and Protein Intake

The simplest physiological issue related to protein metabolism and growth is determining how much of the daily protein intake is incorporated into the lean tissues (protein gain). This can be done using the nitrogen balance technique. Nitrogen balance is the difference between nitrogen intake and nitrogen excretion. In spite of several potential sources of variability with this method,[5-7] study results have been relatively consistent (Fig. 3.1), and this method is the most extensively used for evaluating in vivo protein metabolism (Table 3.1).

The nitrogen balance technique takes into account only nitrogen eliminated in the urine and feces. Nitrogen losses from skin and sweat are quantitatively small, 20–25 mg/kg/day,[3] and difficult to measure in babies.[8,9] Once the nitrogen balance (N) is calculated, the protein gain can be obtained using the formula: gram N $\times$ 6.25 = gram of protein.

The mean values from a number of neonatal studies relating protein gain to intake are shown in Figure 3.1. The daily protein gain increases linearly between approximately 2 and 4 g/kg/day (Table 3.1). Above this level, the effect on protein gain appears to diminish. It should be noted, however, that newborns with the highest protein exhibited altered plasma aminograms.[10-14] Thus, even if it were possible to achieve further protein gain by exceeding an intake of 4 g/kg/day, it would be undesirable due to the concomitant noxious metabolic consequences.

Coefficient of Protein Utilization

The relationship between protein intake and protein gain provides an index of the efficiency with which metabolizable protein intake can be channeled to tissue growth. This ratio of protein gain to intake is sometimes called the coefficient of protein utilization or the efficiency of protein gain. Many factors are known to affect protein utilization: (*a*) nutritional factors, i.e., the biological value of protein in-

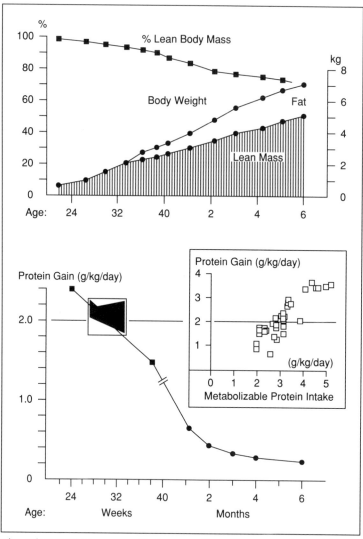

Fig. 3.1. Top, Intrauterine and postnatal time course of body composition with respect to lean weight and fat weight. Bottom inset, The protein gain is linearly related to protein intake over a range of net protein intakes extending from 2 to 4 g/kg/day. Each ☐ represents the mean values for protein intake and protein gain of a group of newborns described in Table 3.1. Bottom, Intrauterine and postnatal time course of protein gain. The hatched area between 27 and 35 weeks and around 2.0 g/kg/day represents the target protein gain for preterm infants, approximating the in utero protein gain of a fetus of the same postconceptional age. (Adapted from Widdowson,[1] Fomon et al.,[4] Ziegler,[3] Reichman et al.[44])

gested,[15,16] the energy:protein ratio,[6,7,17-19] and the nutritional status; (b) physiological factors, e.g., individual variations, catch-up growth in small-for-gestational-age (SGA) infants[20-26]; (c) endocrine factors, including insulin-like growth factors[27,28]; and (d) pathological factors, e.g., sepsis and other disease states.[29]

In "healthy" preterm infants, the efficiency of protein gain has been fairly well established at a mean value of 0.7 (70%). The mean (±SD) of the published values is 0.72 (± 0.08) for 331 infants ranging in gestational age from 29 to 35 weeks and in

birthweight from 1,080 to 1,730 g (Table 3.1 summarizes the results of 36 studies). This means that 70% of the absorbed amino acids are laid down as protein in the tissues and the remaining 30% are oxidized and excreted. According to the above-mentioned studies, this coefficient seems to be independent from gestational age (Table 3.3).

Since the synthesis of protein molecules entails a considerable amount of energy, the protein-energy interaction as well as the in vivo contribution of protein gain to the energy expenditure during rapid growth need to be briefly discussed.

Table 3.1. Overview of Protein Metabolism Data Obtained "at the Bedside" in Very Low-Birthweight Infants

Reference		n	Gestational Age (weeks)	Birthweight (g)	Age at Study (days)	Weight Gain	Net Protein Intake (g/kg/day)	Protein Gain (g/kg/day)	Protein Synthesis* (g/kg/day)	Metabolizable Energy Intake (kcal/kg/day)	% Protein Gain Optimal†
Anderson et al.[114]		7	32	1,532	1–5	−2.0	2.50	1.11	—	57	
Bhatia et al.[115]	a)	7	33	1,480	—	18.9	2.34	—	—	117	
	b)	8	31	1,336	—	19.7	2.79	—	—	120	
	c)	8	32	1,335	—	20.9	3.42	—	—	118	+
De Benoist et al.[53]		7	31	1,733	36	14.7	2.61	1.91	11.3	116	+
Brooke et al.[71]	a)	11	32	1,436	20	15.8	2.93	1.63	—	105	
	b)	10	32	1,436	20	21.5	3.30	2.01	—	122	
	c)	11	32	1,436	20	15.3	1.91	1.15	—	113	
	d)	5	32	1,436	20	13.7	3.18	1.75	—	106	
Catzeflis et al.[8]		10	30	1,220	26	15.0	2.65	1.76	11.2	90	+
Cavderay et al.[20]	SGA‡	8	35	1,520	18	17.8	2.90	2.00	7.7	110	+
	AGA§	11	32	1,560	20	18.3	3.00	2.10	9.7	108	+
Chessex et al.[23]	SGA	6	33	1,120	26	19.4	2.20	1.6	—	126	+
	AGA	13	29	1,155	21	16.8	2.65	1.90	—	130	
Darling et al.[116]	a)	5	—	1,450	25	16.4	3.30	3.0	—	140	
	b)	5	—	1,450	25	13.2	3.10	2.50	—	143	
	c)	5	—	1,450	25	13.7	4.10	3.19	—	146	
Duffy et al.[15]	a)	6	30	1,197	5–7	—	2.70	1.16	8.8	90	
	b)	6	29	1,165	5–7	—	2.5	0.78	7.5	66	
	c)	6	30	1,394	5–7	—	2.90	1.78	8.9	96	
	d)	6	30	1,289	5–7	—	2.80	1.34	6.8	70	
Duffy et al.[37]	a)	12	36	2,251	14	—	2.75	1.21	8.7	85	
	b)	12	36	2,251	30	—	2.67	1.53	12.6	111	
Freymond et al.[117]		9	33	1,740	21	16.6	2.95	2.12	—	110	+
Kashyap et al.[118]	a)	9	32	1,469	15	13.9	2.01	1.57	—	100	
	b)	9	32	1,453	19	18.3	3.26	2.64	—	100	
	c)	9	31	1,394	21	22.0	3.15	2.65	—	130	

continued

Table 3.1. *(continued)*

Reference		n	Gestational Age (weeks)	Birthweight (g)	Age at Study (days)	Weight Gain	Net Protein Intake	Protein Gain	Protein Synthesis*	Metabolizable Energy Intake (kcal/kg/day)	% Protein Gain Optimal†
							(g/kg/day)				
Kashyap et al.[119]	a)	14	31	1,381	—	16.5	2.22	1.72	—	129	
	b)	13	31	1,140	—	20.5	2.88	2.25	—	131	
	c)	15	31	1,320	—	18.2	2.53	1.96	—	119	+
Nissim et al.[57]		8	30	1,246	18	14.9	1.92	1.51	8.4	72	
Pencharz et al.[26]	AGA>1,500g	10	33	1,361	15	15.1	4.3	3.07	13.6	152	
	AGA<1,500g	10	26	1,082	41	17.9	4.4	3.06	15.2	139	
	SGA>1,500g	10	37	1,350	9	17.7	4.7	3.06	19.1	147	
	SGA<1,500g	10	35	1,142	20	21.9	4.9	3.14	17.4	157	
Putet et al.[43]	a)	6	31	1,318	21	13.6	2.13	1.65	—	87	
	b)	6	31	"	45	15.6	2.00	1.49	—	102	
	c)	5	30	1,302	29	22.1	2.89	2.33	—	117	+
	d)	6	30	"	46	19.6	2.86	2.10	—	123	
Schutze et al.[120]	a)	8	31	1,448	15	14.4	2.02	1.63	—	106	
	b)	5	32	1,436	19	16.8	3.24	2.59	—	106	
	c)	6	32	1,502	19	21.7	3.15	2.83	—	137	
Reichmann et al.[44]		13	29	1,155	21	16.8	2.64	1.92	—	130	+
Whyte et al.[46]		15	31	1,380	15	21.5	2.63	2.10	—	122	+
Whyte et al.[47]	a)	9	30	1,320	12	15.2	2.22	1.61	—	106	
	b)	19	30	1,250	16	16.9	2.26	1.70	—	111	
Zlotkin et al.[6,7]	a)	6	29	—	19	1.5	4.03	1.71	—	53	
	b)	5	29	—	19	15.6	3.97	2.76	—	70	+
	c)	6	29	—	19	2.2	3.06	1.54	—	50	
	d)	8	29	—	19	16.2	3.00	1.96	—	70	
	e)	5	29	—	19	—	2.40	0.94	—	60	

*Protein synthesis measured via stable isotopes

†Plus sign (+) indicates that protein gain approximates the in utero gain ± 5%

‡SGA indicates small for gestational age

§AGA indicates appropriate for gestational age

Summary and conclusions: (1) Protein metabolism in vivo has been studied over a wide range of protein intakes. (2) An "optimal" protein gain can be achieved by different sets of protein-energy intakes. (3) The protein synthesis/gain ratio decreases with gestational age.

Table 3.2. Effect of Early Diet on Developmental Outcome*

	Bayley Psychomotor and Developmental Indices at 18 Months			
	Mental		Motor	
Intakes During the First 4 Weeks				
g protein/kg/day	2.6	3.6	2.6	3.6
% protein energy	8.5	10	8.5	10
Small for gestation (n = 42)	90±4	101±5	81±4	104±4
Appropriate for gestation (n = 72)	94±3	97±3	86±2	96±3
Pooled infants (n = 114)	93±3	99±3[†]	84±2	99±2[‡]

*Adapted from Lucas et al.[107]

[†] $p < 0.05$

[‡] $p < 0.01$

Summary and conclusion: A difference in protein-energy supply over a short postnatal period had major consequences for later development. This suggests that the first weeks may be critical for nutrition.

Protein-Energy Interaction

Protein gain is not only related to protein intake but also to energy intake.[6,7,18,19,30–36] Therefore, rapid growth is a situation in which protein-energy interrelationships are of special relevance. The effects of protein intake and the effects of energy intake on protein gain cannot be considered independently. Protein and energy are supplied concurrently, and it is reasonable to assume that there is an optimal range of protein-energy intake for each newborn.

Undesirable consequences have been observed when this range is not achieved. If energy intake is deficient, endogenous protein is used as an energy source and the nitrogen balance becomes negative. When energy intake reaches a suboptimal level (metabolizable energy approximately 50 to 90 kcal/kg/day), the newborn is in a very sensitive range of protein-energy interaction. An increase, either in energy intake or in protein intake, will result in an increase in nitrogen retention (Fig. 3.2).

Similarly, if protein intake is suboptimal, then increasing energy intake will spare protein for lean tissue gain. Situations of suboptimal protein-energy supply are frequently met in neonatal intensive care situations and have been repeatedly investigated.[6,7,15,37,38] If there is a surfeit of energy for a given protein intake, the protein gain plateaus and there is no further positive effect of increasing energy intake.

Metabolic Cost of Protein Gain
The energy required for protein deposition can be partitioned into the energy content of the gained protein, i.e., retained or stored energy (4 kcal/g protein), and the extra energy expenditure[39–41] associated with the formation of new protein, i.e., metabolic cost of protein gain. The latter can be estimated either at bedside, by correlating the results of nitrogen balance to measurements of energy expenditure, or, theoretically, on the basis of the energy equivalent of adenosine triphosphate (ATP).

In vivo studies have shown a linear relation between energy expenditure and protein gain. From the slope of the regression line one can infer that the metabolic cost of protein gain is approximately 10 kcal/g.[20,42–47] A theoretical approach can also be used to estimate the cost of protein gain in a growing baby.[48,49] The incorporation of 1 mol amino acids into protein requires 6 mol ATP. With an average value of 18 kcal energy released per mol ATP,[50] 108 kcal (6 × 18) are needed to incorporate 1 mol amino acids into protein. Assuming that 1 mol of an average amino acid is about 110 g, the theoretical cost of protein gain is approximately 1 kcal/g.

The striking discrepancy between this result (1 kcal/g) and the in vivo data (approximately 10 kcal/g) obtained at bedside warrants reexamination of the theory. The theoretical, or "static," approach makes the incorrect assumption that protein gain during growth is equal to the amount of protein synthesized. It does not reflect the dynamics of protein turnover, where protein gain results from the difference between protein synthesis and breakdown and each gram of protein gain needs five to six times more protein to be synthesized.

Protein Turnover

Stable Isotope Techniques and Protein Turnover
The dynamic aspect of protein metabolism has been studied by using nonradioactive, stable ^{15}N- or ^{13}C-labeled amino acids as biological markers.[5,8,15,20,25,26,51–68] Whole-body protein synthesis and protein

Table 3.3. Protein Metabolism in Preterm Infants Achieving "Optimal" Protein Gains*

Reference	n	Gestational Age (weeks)	Birthweight (g)	% Protein Energy† B	Weight Gain	Net Protein Intake	Protein Gain	Metabolizable Energy Intake (kcal/kg/day)	Protein Gain to Protein Intake Ratio A
						(g/kg/day)			
29 weeks									
Reichmann et al.[44]	13	29	1,155	8.1	16.8	2.64	1.92	130	.73
Chessex et al.[23]	13	29	1,155	8.1	16.8	2.64	1.92	130	.73
30 weeks									
Putet et al.[43]	6	30	1,302	9.3	19.6	2.86	2.10	123	.73
31 weeks									
De Benoit et al.[53]	7	31	1,733	9.0	14.7	2.61	1.91	116	.73
Kashyap et al.[118]	15	31	1,320	8.5	18.2	2.53	1.96	119	.77
Whyte et al.[47]	15	31	1,380	8.6	21.5	2.63	2.10	122	.79
32 weeks									
Brooke et al.[69]	10	32	1,436	12.1	21.5	3.30	2.01	122	.61
Cauderay et al.[20]	11	32	1,560	11.1	18.3	3.00	2.10	108	.70
≥33 weeks									
Freymond et al.[117]	9	33	1,740	10.7	16.6	2.95	2.12	110	.72
Cauderay et al.[20]	8	35	1,520	10.5	17.6	2.90	2.00	110	.69

*"Optimal" protein gain approximates the in utero gain ± 5%. Synthesis measured via stable isotopes.

†% protein energy = 100 × net protein intake × 4/metabolizable energy intake

Summary and conclusions: (A) It appears from the studies achieving "optimal" protein gains that the protein gain to metabolizable protein intake ratio (protein utilization coefficient) is independent from gestational age. (B) The gestational age-related change in the % of protein energy needed to achieve an "optimal" protein gain can be explained by the effect of postconceptional age on protein turnover (see Table 3.1).

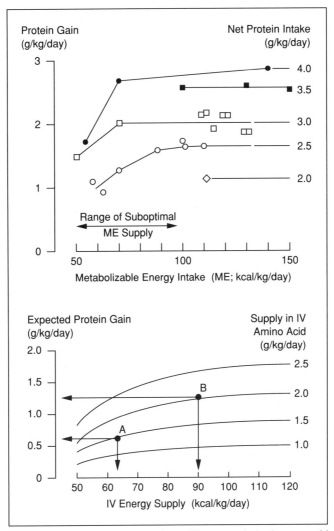

Fig. 3.2. Top, Effect of increasing energy intake on protein gain at different protein intakes grouped into 5 categories: 2.0 (◇), 2.5 (○), 3 (□), 3.5 (■), and 4 (●) g/kg/day. Each symbol represents the mean value of a group of preterm infants described in Table 3.1. In the range of "suboptimal metabolizable energy supply" (50–90 kcal/kg/day), protein gain can be improved by increasing energy intakes, whereas above 100 kcal/kg/day there is no further positive effect on protein gain. (Adapted from references 1, 2, 9, 22, 24, 47, 49, 52, 53, 63, 64, 72, 79, 88, 111, 113, 123, 125). Bottom, An extrapolation from the data shown in top part of figure to two clinical situations, A and B: in A, a preterm infant is receiving 1.5 g/kg/day IV amino acid and 60 to 65 kcal/kg/day; his expected protein gain would be around 0.6 g/kg/day. In B, the infant receives 2.0 g/kg/day IV amino acid and 90 kcal/kg/day; his expected protein gain would be around 1.2 g/kg/day.

breakdown in very low-birthweight (VLBW) preterm infants reared on either human milk,[56,63] milk formula,[8,58] or total parenteral nutrition[15,37,38] were found to be elevated compared with that of older infants.[8] Since the formation of peptide bonds is a high-energy process, simultaneous determination of the rate of protein synthesis and the rate of energy expenditure is of interest. Two methods, stable isotopes and indirect calorimetry, are generally well accepted.[5,39,69–73] A stable isotope enrichment technique used for in vivo assessment of protein turnover is summarized in the following example[35]:

Constant doses of ^{15}N-labeled glycine were added to each meal of a preterm infant, requiring feeding every 3 hours by intragastric tube. This represents an ideal situation for measuring protein turnover. The infant's urinary excretion of ^{15}N-labeled urea increased shortly after the experiment began. Within 48 to 60 hours, the enrichment of ^{15}N in urinary urea seemed to reach a plateau. This plateau, according to the model of Picou and Taylor-Roberts,[35] allowed the computation of the nitrogen flux through the amino acid pool, the rate of protein synthesis, and the rate of protein breakdown.

Table 3.4. Protein Absorption and Concentration of Protein in Gained Tissues*

Gestational age (weeks)	≤27	28–30	31–33
Body weight (g)	700–1,000	1,001–1,500	>1,500
Net protein[†] to gross protein intake ratio	0.82	0.85	0.88
% protein in gained weight	9.8	10.4	11.3

*Adapted from references 3, 8, 20, 22, 23, 43, 73, 121, 115, 117, 123, 124.

[†]Net protein intake = gross intake − fecal losses

Conclusions: In parallel with gestational age, there is: (1) a slight increase in the rate of protein absorption, and (2) an increase of the protein content in the composition of weight gain.

Ratio of Protein Synthesis to Protein Gain

The rate of protein synthesis in the preterm baby greatly exceeds that required for net protein gain (10 g/kg/day for synthesis versus 2 g/kg/day for gain). With respect to energy utilization, the excess protein synthesis would appear to be a wasteful mechanism.[65–67] However, it has been suggested that this "futile cycling" is a positive adaptation. For example, in case of suboptimal supply of protein and calories, the protein gain decreases in parallel with a decrease in protein synthesis and breakdown and a concomitant reduction in energy needs.[40] This dynamic mechanism of protein turnover may also be viewed as a physiologic phenomenon that allows fast remodeling of body protein during rapid growth.[26]

Cellular and Molecular Aspects

All in vivo tracer studies of whole protein metabolism[8,15,20,35,53] support the conclusion that the more rapid the expected growth and expected protein gain the higher the rates of protein synthesis and breakdown. This means that the net intracellular production of protein must be sensitively adjusted through regulated changes in the rates of protein synthesis and breakdown.

As surprising as it may seem in view of recent breakthroughs in molecular biology, the mechanisms and functions of selective intracellular protein breakdown are still poorly understood. Thus the regulating links between synthesis and breakdown remain obscure. It has been shown recently that, under normal metabolic conditions, protein breakdown does not occur in the lysosomes but in the extralysosomal compartment.[74] In this compartment, indiscriminate proteolysis is prevented by a requirement for an ATP-dependent conjugation of target proteins.[75] This seems to be one major pathway for selective protein breakdown in vivo. Since the key genes regulating protein breakdown have been cloned, there is hope that information at the molecular level will soon be provided to answer clinical questions regarding situations of growth and nongrowth, as well as the metabolic responses of "sick" neonates to stress.[74,75]

Effect of Protein Intake

In a wide range of protein intake, any increase will elicit a proportionate increase in protein gain and protein synthesis (Table 3.1). In order to make valid interstudy comparisons and to avoid the confounding effect of different protein intakes, protein synthesis should be considered together with the protein synthesis:gain ratio. The interstudy variability is much narrower for the protein synthesis:gain ratio (4.6 to 6.5) than for the rate of protein synthesis per se (8 to 19 g/kg/day).

Effect of Postconceptional Age on Protein Turnover

A significant inverse relationship was observed between postconceptional age and the protein synthesis:gain ratio. Thus, the more immature an infant is, the higher the rate of protein turnover.[20,57,76] This relationship is also apparent in the interstudy comparison previously mentioned (Table 3.1). Similar studies of animal fetuses demonstrate that the rate of protein synthesis per unit body weight decreases throughout gestation.[77,78] It appears that besides energy and protein intakes, postconceptional (or postmenstrual) age plays a major role in the regulation of whole-body protein metabolism.

This age-related effect may influence the optimal amount of protein energy given to infants below 27 gestational weeks (Tables 3.4 and 3.5).

Nutritional Status

It has been observed that the protein turnover, synthesis, and breakdown rates are higher during catch-up growth in SGA infants than in normally grown infants of the same gestational age.[26,59] These observations are consistent with the studies on the rate of protein turnover in malnourished infants during and after completion of refeeding.[35,79]

On the other hand, when the protein turnover of a group of SGA infants was compared with that of a group of identically fed preterm infants of the same birthweight, the former had the lower values and the

Table 3.5. Estimation of the Protein Requirement

Factorial approach[3]

	g/kg/day		
Gestational age (weeks)	≤ 27	28–30	31–33
Body weight (g)	700–1,000	1,001–1,500	> 1500
Requirement	3.71	3.72	3.17
Advisable intake	4.0	4.0	3.5

American guidelines[99,100]

	g/kg/day	
Gestational age (weeks)	26–28	29–31
Body weight (g)	800–1,200	1,200–1,800
Advisable intake	4.0	3.5

European guidelines[106]

	g/kg/day	
Gestational age (weeks)	28–32	
Body weight (g)	1,001–1,800	
	upper limit	lower limit
Advisable intake	3.6	2.9

Metabolic approach (Table 3.3)

	g/kg/day
Gestational age (weeks)	29–35
Body weight (g)	1,100–1,750
Gross intake (=advisable intake)	3.70–3.10
Net intake	3.20–2.64
Protein gain	2.12–1.92

Neurodevelopmental approach[107,122]

	g/kg/day
Gestational age (weeks)	31–32
Body weight (g)	1,300
Advisable intake	3.80–3.60

Present recommendation

	g/kg/day	
Gestational age (weeks)	≤ 27	28–34
Body weight (g)	≤1,000	1,000–1,750
Gross intake (=advisable intake)	3.8–3.6	3.6–3.0

better protein synthesis:gain ratio.[20] This may explain why SGA infants have a faster rate of postnatal growth than identically fed, normally grown preterm infants.[80]

Route of Feeding
It has been well established that the growth of the intestinal tract in the neonate is dependent on enteral feeding. Infants who are fed intravenously have protein turnover rates approximately two thirds lower than levels observed when the same infants are fed enterally.[37,38] This difference appears to hold whether ^{15}N-labeled urea or ammonia is used as the end product.[61,62] The significantly lower turnover in the intravenously fed infants cannot be completely explained on the basis of differences in protein-energy intakes and probably reflects differences in visceral protein metabolism.[37,61]

Type of Feeding
Although at one time it had been suggested that the protein turnover in breast-fed infants was higher than that of formula-fed infants,[58] this has not been confirmed.[63]

Other studies have questioned whether the level of nonprotein energy in intravenously fed infants might specifically affect steps in protein metabolism. The results showed that increasing nonprotein energy intake led to improvement in protein gain.[15]

Another question under study is whether the balance of carbohydrate to lipid might affect the protein metabolism of the neonate. In a recent study, intravenously fed infants received either all their nonprotein energy from glucose or two thirds from glucose and one third from lipid. No differences were shown in nitrogen balance or in protein turnover.[63]

Table 3.6. Comparisons of Plasma Concentrations of Eight Essential Amino Acids*

	Fetus[†]	Term[‡]	Preterm[§]	Reference Concentrations in Healthy Term Breast-Fed Infants[81] (μmol/L)
	(% ranges of mean specific amino acid value measured in preterm infants)			
Phenylalanine	158–360	125–216	60–140	22–71
Valine	140–330	110–190	83–117	88–222
Lysine	150–290	67–108	75–125	80–231
Threonine	142–267	58–108	75–125	34–168
Histidine	133–240	117–175	50–150	34–119
Methionine	92–234	92–200	75–125	22–50
Leucine	83–192	92–167	83–117	53–169
Isoleucine	83–175	83–167	83–117	26–93

*Adapted from Polberger et al.[84,89,90]

[†]*Fetus* indicates fetal blood taken at amnioscopy.

[‡]*Term* indicates breast-fed term infants.

[§]*Preterm* indicates very low-birthweight, preterm infants (n = 14; 26–32 weeks; 900–1,500g birthweight) fed protein-enriched human milk (3.6 g/kg/day; 127 kcal/kg/day).

Link between Potential Toxicity of Protein and Amino Acid and Biochemical Immaturity of the Preterm Infant

Premature infants have incomplete development of several amino acid metabolic pathways.[11–13,81] This biochemical immaturity substantially narrows the margin between an adequate protein intake and the possible adverse effects of a deficiency or an excess. Many of the amino acids previously thought to be nonessential, e.g., cysteine, taurine, and glycine, may be essential for the immature organism and must be supplied by the diet.[56,82–85] In cases of excessive protein intake, incomplete amino acid catabolism may result in elevated plasma concentration of amino acids, hydrogen ion, and ammonia.[12,86] It is still a matter of debate whether these metabolic changes are harmful[84,87,88]; indeed, similar values have been found in fetal blood at fetoscopy and from the umbilical cord at birth.[88,89]

At least three different "gold standards" against which to assess plasma amino acid responses to feeding have been proposed for the prematurely born infant: (1) the amino acid concentrations of the midtrimester fetal blood; (2) that of rapidly growing preterm infants receiving their own mother's milk; and (3) that of healthy breast-fed term infants.[81,88,90–94] In general, the blood amino acid levels of preterm infants fed either preterm milk or protein-enriched human milk fall within the broad range of plasma amino acid levels reported for breast-fed term infants (Table 3.6).

Methods for Determining If Protein Needs of "Healthy" Preterm Infants Are Met

Weight Gain. While this fundamental expression of growth is nonspecific and provides no information on changes in body composition, it remains the cornerstone of growth assessment.[95] Length gain is less susceptible to the confounding effects of changing body composition and should be a better estimate of gain in lean body mass.[96,97] However, the practical limitation is that measurements of length, unless they are taken over long observation periods, are difficult to perform reproducibly.

More Specific Indicators. These include serum concentrations of albumin, total protein, prealbumin, and retinol-binding protein.[5] The usefulness of these serum biochemical parameters for determining the adequacy of protein intake is severely limited by difficulties in interpretation. Severe deficiencies are easily classified as abnormal but borderline values are not.[98] However, inadequate or excessive protein intakes can be detected by measurement of urea concentrations in serum and/or urine; the latter obviates blood sampling.[91]

Physiologic Approach. This method appears to be the most sensible at present: an adequate protein intake results in rates of weight gain and protein gain approximating the in utero growth. Protein intake must be considered in conjunction with energy intake, since the energy cost of growth is mainly dependent upon the protein metabolism. To illustrate this point, 10 metabolic studies were selected on the basis that the rates of protein gain measured in them were very similar to intrauterine values (Table 3.3). Interestingly, this effect was obtained within a relatively narrow range of protein and energy intakes. The weight gains of the infants studied as well as the composition of their weight gains were different, however, as evidenced by various energy densities (retained energy/unit weight). The highest energy and the lowest protein intakes led to the greatest fat deposition. The highest protein and lowest energy intakes had the opposite effect.

Comparison between the measurements shown in Table 3.1 and the estimated values of the American Academy of Pediatrics[99,100] strongly illustrates the fact that "healthy" low-birthweight infants can accommodate various levels of protein intakes provided the energy level is not limiting.

Amino Acid Profile in Plasma. These values (Table 3.6) and the coefficient of protein utilization can help assess the type of protein most suitable for growth. Premature infants fed whey:casein protein ratios of 60:40 (similar to that of breast milk) have reasonably well balanced plasma amino acids[90,101] and a coefficient of protein utilization (protein gain:intake) of 0.7, as shown in the inset of Figure 3.1. Higher proportions of casein cannot be handled with the same efficiency, as evidenced by the development of metabolic acidosis and higher plasma tyrosine and phenylalanine concentrations reported with whey-casein formulas with 18:82 ratios.[99,100,102–104]

The major proteins supplied in enteral nutrition to preterm infants stem either from human milk (70% human whey, 30% human casein) or from bovine milk (60% or 18% bovine whey, 40% or 82% bovine casein). Bovine casein proteins are particularly rich in phenylalanine and tyrosine; so infants fed formulas in which bovine casein predominates typically have higher concentrations of plasma phenylalanine and tyrosine than do infants fed human milk or formulas in which bovine whey predominates. Conversely, infants fed bovine whey-predominant formulas have higher plasma threonine concentrations than those fed either bovine casein-predominant formulas or human milk.[11–13,19,105] Bovine whey proteins are very rich in threonine compared with bovine casein proteins or human milk whey proteins. At present, it is difficult to know whether this has major implications in the protein metabolism of preterm infants.

Foods for the Stable Growing Period

Human Milk

The protein content of mature human milk is about 1.2 g/dL or 0.35 g/oz (1.8 g/100 kcal) when expressed as total nitrogen × 6.25; about 25% of the total nitrogen is nonprotein nitrogen. Because all human milk proteins are not always fully absorbed from the gut, the nutritionally available amount of protein may be even less than expected.[14] The protein content of colostrum (first 5 days postpartum) is 2.3 g/dL and that of transitional human milk (6 to 10 days postpartum) 1.6 g/dL. It has been reported that the milk of women delivering prematurely contains approximately 20% more nitrogen than the milk of mothers delivering at term. However, the higher nitrogen content decreases rapidly, and after the first 14 days there is no or only a minimal difference between the former and the latter. The whey proteins represent more than 70% of the total proteins in human milk.[106] Human milk from milk banks is inadequate for VLBW preterm infants and results not only in failure to thrive but also in delayed psychomotor development.[107] Human milk from milk banks can be enriched with protein components of human milk.[34,88,108]

Bovine Milk–Based Formula

Formulas designed for VLBW infants have a higher protein content, 1.8 to 2.4 g/dL (0.53 to 0.71 g/oz), and a higher energy density, 75 to 85 kcal/dL (22 to 25 kcal/oz), than the formulas generally used for term infants. They provide about 2.2 to 3.2 g of protein per 100 kcal.[106,108,109]

Own Mother's Milk

The amount of human bank milk with 1.2 g of protein per dL, or 0.35 g/oz, necessary to provide 3.0 g/kg/day to a preterm infant, is 250 mL/kg/day, but such high intakes are not commonly used. Intakes of 185 to 200 mL/kg/day of their own mother's fresh milk are not unusual in moderately low-birthweight preterm infants (around 1,500 g) and may be considered an "ideal" intake. The amino acid profile of such infants has been proposed as a gold standard.[94] However, when the infant's mother's milk is not available in such large quantities, or if it is heat treated, the situation ceases to be ideal.

In early life, when protective factors of the infant's own mother's milk may be of great value, it is advantageous to provide the mother's own fresh preterm milk, especially if the infant is very immature with a very low birthweight (<1,000 g). Soon after this critical period for survival is over, the metabolic needs for growth and development have to be matched. For that to occur, it is necessary to either enrich the mother's milk or introduce a preterm formula. Considering the practical difficulties in assuring availability of fresh preterm human milk, preterm formulas are used in the majority of cases.

Parenteral Amino Acids

The optimal concentration and composition of parenteral amino acids for preterm infants is unknown.

Table 3.7. Protein and Fluid Supply during the Transitional Period of the First Postnatal Days in 1,000- to 1,750-g Preterm Infants*

Postnatal days	1	2	3	4	5	6	7
Total fluids (mL/kg)	80	100	120	140	160		
Enteral feeding preterm formula (mL/kg) or enriched mother's milk	20	40	60	80	100	140	160
Enteral protein (g/kg)	.45	.9	1.3	1.8	2.2	3.1	3.5
Parenteral fluids (mL/kg)	60	60	60	60	60	stop	
Amino acid (g/kg) if < 1250 g	.5	.5	.5	.5	.5		
Total protein (g/kg), enteral + parenteral	.95	1.4	1.8	2.2	2.7		
Modify intakes if:	unexplained metabolic acidosis (check ammonia, reduce protein intake, investigate metabolism); weight loss >10% of birthweight (increase fluids, watch glucosuria); infant on a ventilator (fluid reduction around 20 mL/kg); weight gain instead of weight loss during the first 3–4 postnatal days (fluid reduction around 20 mL/kg); as long as body weight < birthweight, take the latter as reference for calculations.						
Preterm formula[†]	2.2 g protein/dL (0.65 g protein/oz); 75 kcal/dL (22 kcal/oz); 2.9 g protein/100 kcal.						
Enriched mother's milk[†]	2.1 g protein/dL (0.61 g protein/oz); 85 kcal/dL (25 kcal/oz); 2.45 g protein/100 kcal.						

*Amounts must be modified according to individual need.
[†]Approximate values.

However, the current amino acid formulations come close to meeting their needs as far as can be observed on the basis of growth, nitrogen retention, plasma amino acid profile, and acid-base status. From recent reviews of the subject,[81,110] one can conclude that preterm infants receiving total parenteral nutrition require more than 70 nonprotein kcal/kg/day and more than 2.5 g/kg/day of amino acid to achieve acceptable (albeit not optimal) protein gain. Parenteral amino acids are used not only for total parenteral nutrition in preterm infants who cannot be fed enterally, but also as an adjunct to enteral feeding during the first postnatal days (Tables 3.7 and 3.8).

Preterm Infants Weighing from 1,000 to 1,750 g

Due to the progress in perinatal medicine, a number of preterm infants weighing from 1,000 to 1,750 g are considered "healthy." They have been thoroughly investigated, and their protein requirements have been defined through different approaches (Table 3.5). A practical example of supplying these infants with protein is given in Table 3.7.

Preterm Infants Weighing <1,000 g

In most neonatal units, the number of very immature infants weighing <1,000 g is steadily increasing. By combining the information given by the factorial approach with data from the few metabolic studies undertaken thus far, a range of advisable protein intake is provided in Table 3.5. A practical example of supplying these infants with protein appears in Table 3.8. Protein is increased in daily increments from 0 to around 3.6 or 3.8 g/kg/day during the first 14 days. Similarly, the energy supply increases from 35 to 130 kcal/kg/day over the same period. The time period of the protein-energy supply can be shortened or lengthened according to the clinical situation.

Table 3.8. Protein and Fluid Supply during the Transitional Period of the First Postnatal Days in Extremely Low-Birthweight Infants of <1,000 g*

Postnatal days	1	2	3	4	5	6	7	8	9	10	11	12	13	14
Total fluids (mL/kg)	80	100	120	140	160	160	160	160	160	160	160	160	160	160
Enteral feeding preterm formula (mL/kg) or enriched mother's milk	—	10	20	30	40	50	60	70	80	90	100	120	140	160
Enteral protein (g/kg)	—	.25	.5	.75	1.0	1.2	1.4	1.7	1.9	2.2	2.4	2.9	3.4	3.8
Parenteral fluids (mL/kg)	80	90	100	110	120	110	100	90	80	70	60	40	20	stop
Amino acid (g/kg)	.5	.75	1.0	1.25	1.5	1.5	1.5	1.5	1.5	1.2	1.0	.5	—	
Total protein (g/kg), enteral + parenteral	.5	1.0	1.5	2.0	2.5	2.7	2.9	3.2	3.4	3.4	3.4	3.4	3.4	3.4

Modify intakes if: unexplained metabolic acidosis (check ammonia, reduce protein intake, investigate metabolism); weight loss >10% of birthweight (increase fluids, watch glucosuria); infant on a ventilator (fluid reduction around 20 mL/kg); weight gain instead of weight loss during the first 3–4 postnatal days (fluid reduction around 20 mL/kg); as long as body weight < birthweight, take the latter as reference for calculations.

Preterm formula[†] 2.4 g protein/dL (0.7 g protein/oz); 85 kcal/dL (25 kcal/oz); 2.8 g protein/100 kcal.

Enriched mother's milk[†] 2.1 g protein/dL (0.61 g protein/oz); 85 kcal/dL (25 kcal/oz); 2.45 g protein/100 kcal.

*Amounts must be modified according to individual needs.
[†]Approximate values.

41

Clinical Conditions Affecting Protein Requirements

Protein Requirements of "Sick," Nongrowing, Very Low-Birthweight Infants

Clinicians are commonly faced with life-threatening illnesses that severely stress the infant, preventing growth even when all nutrients are provided. The goal of nutritional management is limited to a nitrogen balance close to equilibrium. From a pragmatic standpoint, administering protein at the level of about 1.0 to 1.5 g/kg/day in the form of intravenous amino acids would be a defensible approach.[5,32] This amount may be too high in some critically ill neonates, however. Another approach stems from physiologic studies in stable, growing preterm infants.[15,40,111] The aim is to define "minimal intakes" in protein and energy which would prevent net protein loss by keeping protein synthesis and breakdown in balance. An extrapolation of the regression lines of protein gain versus intake[40,112] shows that a protein intake of 0.5 g/kg/day projects to a slowing down of protein turnover to zero protein gain. Whether these findings are relevant to the situation of the unstable, nongrowing preterm infant is not yet known.

A reasonable compromise between these two strategies is to start with minimal protein intakes of 0.5 g/kg/day and increase the intake gradually if the sick neonate seems free of adverse effects (Fig. 3.2). As long as the infant is critically ill, the intake should not go beyond the "pragmatic limit" of 1.0 to 1.5 g/kg/day. It is reasonable to expect that an intake of this order will maintain the infant at zero protein gain, wherein net synthesis of protein equals protein breakdown.

Protein Requirements of Small-for-Gestational-Age, Very Low-Birthweight Infants

Neither the American nor the European recommendations[99,100,106] differentiate SGA from appropriate-for-gestational-age (AGA), low-birthweight infants. In fact, in many neonatal units, SGA infants receive higher protein and energy intakes than AGA infants in order to facilitate their catch-up growth.[113]

Published studies comparing the protein metabolism of a group of SGA infants with that of a group of AGA infants[23,26] used feeding schedules that were not the same in both groups. Thus, the clinical question of whether SGA infants should be fed differently from AGA infants was not answered. A study comparing a group of AGA infants to a group of SGA infants under the same feeding conditions showed that the latter had a slower rate of protein turnover,[20] indicating that for the same gain of protein, the rates of synthesis and breakdown are lower in SGA infants than in AGA infants. Being more mature in a number of physiological and biochemical systems,[11-13] SGA in-

fants have a lower protein synthesis:gain ratio than AGA infants of the same birthweight and are thus able to handle protein more efficiently. They may be able to tolerate higher protein intakes without adverse effects. However, even during catch-up growth, there is no conclusive evidence that protein intakes beyond the recommended values are beneficial.

Future Research

Future clinically oriented research on protein metabolism is expected to provide data on:
—In vivo protein metabolism in very immature (<27 weeks) preterm infants of less than 1,000 g birthweight.
—The link between early postnatal feeding, protein metabolism, and later neurodevelopmental outcome.
—The factors limiting protein gain and growth in "sick" preterm infants.
—"Ideal" protein:energy ratios at different gestational ages.

CASE STUDY

A 980-g female infant was delivered at 29 gestational weeks. The mother, a 36-year-old primipara, had been hospitalized since the 24th postmenstrual week and treated for severe pregnancy-induced hypertension. The fetal monitoring was within the normal range up to delivery, when signs of intrauterine hypoxia appeared suddenly, prompting an emergency cesarean section. Resuscitating the infant required mask and bag ventilation followed by elective nasotracheal intubation because of respiratory distress. At 2 hours of life, she appeared to be clinically stable: She was ventilated with an FiO_2 of 0.6; blood gases were within normal range.

Questions and Answers

Q. How and what should this infant be fed during the early transitional period?
A. Intravenous (IV) maintenance was begun as soon as possible after birth. The solution, 60 mL over the first 24 hours, contained 10% glucose. At 24 hours of age, parenteral fluids were increased to 70 mL/24 h, amino acid (0.5 g) was added to the IV solution, and enteral nasogastric tube feeding was started with 10 × 1mL/24 h (10 feedings of 1 mL each in a 24-hour period) preterm formula (protein, 0.24 g/24 h). Enteral and parenteral feeding was increased in daily increments according to Table 3.8: at 4 days of age parenteral fluids were at 90 mL/24 h, with 1.0 g amino acid; and the infant received 10 × 3mL/24 h preterm formula (0.72 g protein). She had lost 95 g of body weight. Her respiratory condition had improved, and extubation was planned for the next day.

Q. How should this infant be fed during the first day after extubation?
A. On the fifth postnatal day the infant was extubated. Enteral feeding was stopped in order to prevent broncho-

aspiration. A moderate fluid restriction was decided: parenteral fluids were set at 120 mL/24 h. Amino acid (2.2 g) was added to the IV solution in order to maintain a positive nitrogen balance. The next day, the infant was doing well except for mild clinical and echographic signs of a patent ductus arteriosus with a moderate degree of left to right shunting. Nothing was changed in her infusion. It was decided to cautiously reintroduce enteral feeding.

Q. How should the enteral feeding be resumed?
A. Over the next 14 days, enteral feeding of preterm formula was gradually increased from 10 × 1 mL/24 h to 8 × 20 mL/24 h; concomitantly, the parenteral solution of amino acid was tapered off according to Table 3.8. On day 21 she had regained her birthweight and was fully enterally fed with 160 mL/kg preterm formula (protein intake, 3.8 g/kg/day). Her crown-heel length increased from 36 cm at birth to 38 cm at 21 days.

References

1. Widdowson EM. Changes in body composition during growth. In: Davis JA, Dobbing J. *Scientific foundation of paediatrics*. 2nd ed. Heinemann Medical Books Ltd; London, 1981.
2. Widdowson EM. Protein needs during infancy. In: Fomons SJ, Heird WC, eds. *Energy and protein needs during infancy*. Orlando: Academic Press, 1986.
3. Ziegler EE. Protein requirements of preterm infants. In: Foman SJ, Heird WC, eds. *Energy and protein needs during infancy*. Orlando: Academic Press; 1986.
4. Fomon SJ, Haschke F, Ziegler EE, Nelson SE. Body composition of reference children from birth to age 10 years. *Am J Clin Nutr* 1982; 35:1169–1175.
5. Yudkoff M, Nissim I. Methods for determining the protein requirement of infants. *Clin Perinatol* 1986;13: 123–132.
6. Zlotkin SH, Bryan MH, Anderson GH. Intravenous nitrogen and energy intakes required to duplicate in utero nitrogen accretion in prematurely born human infants. *J Pediatr* 1981; 99:115–120.
7. Zlotkin SH. Protein-energy interactions in humans. In: Foman SJ, Heird WC, eds. *Energy and protein needs during infancy*. Orlando: Academic Press; 1986.
8. Catzeflis C, Schutz Y, Micheli JL, Welsch C, Amaud MJ, Jéquier E. Whole body protein synthesis and energy expenditure in very low birth weight infants. *Pediatr Res* 1985; 19:679–687.
9. Fenton TR, McMillan DD, Sauve RS. Nutrition and growth analysis of very low birth weight infants. *Pediatrics* 1990; 86:378–383.
10. Benevenga NJ, Steele RD. Adverse effects of excessive consumption of amino acids. *Annu Rev Nutr* 1984; 4:157–161.
11. Räihä NCR. Biochemical basis for nutrition management of preterm infants. *Pediatrics* 1974; 53:147–156.
12. Räihä NCR, Heinoven K, Rassin DK, Gaull GE. Milk protein quantity and quality in low-birthweight infants: metabolic responses and effects on growth. *Pediatrics* 1976; 57:659–674.
13. Räihä NCR. Protein in the nutrition of the preterm infant: biochemical and nutritional considerations. *Adv Nutr Res* 1980;3:173–206.
14. Räihä NCR. New perspectives in the nutrition of very low birthweight infants. In: Domenech E, Castro R, Ormazabal C, Mendez A, Moran J, eds. *Neonatal nutrition and metabolism*. Barcelona: Editiones Cientificas y Technicas; 1991.
15. Duffy B, Gunn T, Collinge J, Pencharz P. The effect of varying protein quality and energy intake on the nitrogen metabolism of parenterally fed very low birthweight (<1600 g) infants. *Pediatr Res* 1981; 15:1040–1044.
16. Millward DJ, Rivers JPW. The nutritional role of indispensable amino acids and the metabolic basis for their requirements. *Eur J Clin Nutr* 1987; 42:367–393.
17. Pencharz PB, Steffee WP, Cochran W, Rand W, Scrimshaw NS, Young VR. Protein metabolism in human neonates: nitrogen balance studies, estimated obligatory N losses and whole body N turnover. *Clin Sci Mol Med* 1977; 52:485–98.
18. Senterre J, Voyer M, Putet G, Rigo J. Nitrogen, fat and mineral balance studies in preterm infants fed bank human milk, a human milk formula, or a low birthweight infant formula. In: Baum D, ed. *Human milk processing, fractionation, and the nutrition of the low birthweight baby*. Nestlé Nutrition Workshop Series. NY: Raven Press; 1983; 3:102–111.
19. Senterre J, Rigo J. Nutritional requirements of low birthweight infants. In: Gracey M, Falkner F, eds. *Nutritional needs and assessment of normal growth*. Nestlé Nutrition Workshop Series, New York: Raven Press; 1985; 7:45–49.
20. Cauderay M, Schutz Y, Micheli JL, Calame A, Jequier E. Energy-nitrogen balances and protein turnover in small and appropriate for gestational age low birthweight infants. *Eur J Clin Nutr* 1988; 42:125–136.
21. Chessex P, Reichman BL, Verellen GJE, et al. Influence of postnatal age, energy intake, and weight gain on energy metabolism in the very low-birthweight infant. *J Pediatr* 1981; 99:761–776.
22. Chessex P, Reichman BL, Verellen GJE, Smith JM, Heim T, Swyer PR. Quality of growth in premature infants fed their own mother's milk. *J Pediatr* 1983; 102:107–112.
23. Chessex P, Reichmann B, Verellen G, et al. Metabolic consequences of intrauterine growth retardation in very low birthweight infants. *Pediatr Res* 1984; 18:709–713.
24. Chessex P, Gagne G, Pineault M, Vaucher J, Bisaillon S, Brisson G. Metabolic and clinical consequences of changing from high-glucose to high-fat regimens in parenterally fed newborn infants. *J Pediatr* 1989; 115:992–997.
25. Pencharz PB, Masson M, Desgranges F, Papageorgiou A. Total-body protein turnover in human premature neonates: effects of birth weight, intra-uterine nutritional status and diet. *Clin Sci* 1981; 61:207–215.
26. Pencharz PB, Parsons H, Motil K, Duffy B. Total body protein turnover and growth in children: is it a futile cycle? *Med Hypoth* 1981; 7:155–160.
27. Adams SO, Nissley SP, Handwerger S, Rechler MM. Developmental patterns of insulin-like growth factor I and II synthesis and regulation in rat fibroblasts. *Nature* 1983; 302:150–153.
28. Schoenle EJ, Haselbacher GK, Briner J, et al. Elevated concentration of IGF II in brain tissue from an infant with macrencephaly. *J Pediatr* 1986; 108:737–740.
29. Wannemacher RW. Key role of various individual amino acids in host response to infection. *Am J Clin Nutr* 1977; 30:1269–1280.
30. Cooke RJ, Perrin F, Moore J, Paule C, Ruckman K. Nutrient balance studies in the preterm infant: crossover and parallel studies as methods of experimental design. *J Pediatr Gastroenterol Nutr* 1988; 7:718–722.
31. De Curtis M, Senterre J, Rigo J, Putet G. Carbohydrate derived energy and gross energy absorption in preterm infants fed human milk or formula. *Arch Dis Child* 1986; 61:867–870.
32. Easton LB, Halata MS, Dweck HS. Parenteral nutrition in the newborn: a practical guide. *Pediatr Clin North Am* 1982; 29:1171–1190.

33. Gudinchet F, Schutz Y, Micheli JL, Stettler E, Jéquier E. Metabolic cost of growth in very low-birthweight infants. *Pediatr Res* 1982; 16:1025–1030.

34. Moro G, Minoli I, Heininger J, Cohen M, Gaull G, Räihä N. Relationship between protein and energy in the feeding of preterm infants during the first month of life. *Acta Paediatr Scand* 1984; 73:49–54.

35. Picou D, Taylor-Roberts T. The measurement of total protein synthesis and catabolism and nitrogen turnover in infants in different nutritional states and receiving different amounts of dietary protein. *Clin Sci* 1969;36:283–296.

36. Polberger S, Axelsson I, Räihä N. Growth of very low birth weight infants on varying amounts of human milk protein. *Pediatr Res* 1989; 25:414–419.

37. Duffy B, Pencharz P. The effect of feeding route (IV or oral) on the protein metabolism of the neonate. *Am J Clin Nutr* 1986; 43:108–111.

38. Duffy B, Pencharz P. The effects of surgery on the nitrogen metabolism of parenterally fed human neonates. *Pediatr Res* 1986; 20:32–35.

39. Elia M, Livesey G. Theory and validity of indirect calorimetry during net lipid synthesis. *Am J Clin Nutr* 1988; 47:591–607.

40. Micheli JL, Schutz Y. Protein metabolism and postnatal growth in very low birthweight infants. *Biol Neonate* 1987;52 (suppl 1):25–40.

41. Schutz Y. Estimates of the energy cost of growth in young children. *Int J Vitamin Nutr Res* 1979;20(suppl): 113–124.

42. Meurling S, Arturson G, Zaar B, Eriksson G. Energy, fat and nitrogen balance in healthy newborn infants during the first week after birth. *Acta Chir Scand* 1981; 147: 487–495.

43. Putet G, Senterre J, Rigo J, Salle B. Nutrient balance, energy utilization, and composition of weight gain in very-low-birth-weight infants fed pooled human milk or a preterm formula. *J Pediatr* 1984; 105:79–85.

44. Reichman B, Chessex P, Putet G, et al. Diet, fat accretion, and growth in premature infants. *N Engl J Med* 1981; 305:1495–1500.

45. Reichman BL, Chessex P, Putet G, et al. Partition of energy metabolism and energy cost of growth in the very low-birth-weight infant. *Pediatrics* 1982; 69:446.

46. Whyte RK, Haslam R, Vlainic C, et al. Energy balance and nitrogen balance in growing low birthweight infants fed human milk or formula. *Pediatr Res* 1983;17: 891–898.

47. Whyte RK, Campbell D, Stanhope R, Bayley HS, Sinclair JC. Energy balance in low birth weight infants fed formula of high or low medium-chain triglyceride content. *J Pediatr* 1986; 108:964–971.

48. Hommes FA, Drost YM, Geraets WXM, Reijenga MA. The energy requirement for growth: An application of Atkinson's metabolic price system. *Pediatr Res* 1975;9: 51–55.

49. Hommes FA. The energy requirement for growth, a re-evaluation. *Nutr Metab* 1980; 24:110–113.

50. Flatt JP. The biochemistry of energy expenditure. In: Bray L, ed. *Recent advances in obesity research*. London: Libbey; 1980; 2:211–229.

51. Nicholson JF. Rate of protein synthesis in premature infants. *Pediatr Res* 1970; 4:389–397.

52. Bier DM, Young VR. Assessment of whole-body protein-nitrogen kinetics in the human infant. In: Fomon SJ, Heird WC, eds. *Energy and protein needs during infancy*. Orlando: Academic Press; 1986.

53. De Benoist B, Abdulrazzak Y, Brooke OG, Hallyday D, Millward D. The measurement of whole body protein turnover in the preterm infant with intragastric infusion of L-[1–13C] leucine and sampling of the urinary leucine pool. *Clin Sci* 1984; 66:155–164.

54. Heine W, Richter C, Plath C, et al. Evaluation of different ^{15}N-tracer substances for calculation of whole body protein parameters in infants. *J Pediatr Gastroenterol Nutr* 1983; 2:599–605.

55. Heine W, Wutzke KD, Mix M. Protein nitrogen utilization in short bowel syndrome as measured with ^{15}N-labelled yeast protein. In: Chapman TE, Berger, R, Reijngoud DJ, Okken A, eds. *Stable isotopes in paediatric nutritional and metabolic research*. Andover, UK: Intercept; 1990.

56. Jackson AA, Shaw JCL, Barber A, Golden MHN. Nitrogen metabolism in preterm infants fed human donor breast milk: the possible essentiality of glycine. *Pediatr Res* 1981; 15:1454–1461.

57. Nissim I, Yudkoff M, Pereira G, Segal S. Effects of conceptual age and dietary intake on protein metabolism in premature infants. *J Pediatr Gastroent Nutr* 1983;2: 507–516.

58. Pencharz PB, Fairi L, Papageorgiou A. The effect of human milk and low protein formulae on the rates of total body protein turnover and urinary 3-methylhistidine excretion of preterm infants. *Clin Sci* 1983; 64:611–616.

59. Pencharz PB, Masson M, Desgranges F, Papageorgiou A. The effects of post-natal age on the whole body protein metabolism and the urinary 3-methyl histidine excretion of premature infants. *Nutr Res* 1984;4:9–19.

60. Pencharz PB. The 1987 Borden Award Lecture: protein metabolism in premature human infants. *Can J Physiol Pharmacol* 1988; 66:1247–1252.

61. Pencharz PB, Beesley J, Sauer P, et al. A comparison of the estimates of whole-body protein turnover in parenterally fed neonates obtained using three different end products. *Can J Physiol Pharmacol* 1988; 67:624–628.

62. Pencharz PB, Clarke R, Archibald EH, Vaisman N. The effect of a weight-reducing diet on the nitrogen metabolism of obese adolescents. *Can J Physiol Pharmacol* 1988; 66:1469–1474.

63. Pencharz PB, Beesley J, Sauer P, et al. Total-body protein turnover in parenterally fed neonates: effects of energy source studied by using [^{15}N] glycine and [1-^{13}C] leucine 1–3. *Am J Clin Nutr* 1989; 50:1395–400.

64. Pencharz PB, Clarke R, Papageorgiou A, Farri L. A reappraisal of protein turnover values in neonates fed human milk or formula. *Can J Physiol Pharmacol* 1989; 67:282–286.

65. Young VR, Steffee WP, Pencharz PB, Winterer JC, Scrimshaw NS. Total human body protein synthesis in relation to protein requirements at various ages. *Nature* 1975; 253:192–193.

66. Young VR, Munro HN. N^t-methylhistidine (3-methylhistidine) and muscle protein turnover: an overview. *Fed Proc* 1978; 37:2291–2300.

67. Young VR., Kinetics of human amino acid metabolism: nutritional implications and some lessons: 1987 McCollum Award Lecture. *Am J Clin Nutr* 1987; 46:709–725.

68. Waterlow JC, Garlick PJ, Millward DJ. *Protein turnover in mammalian tissues and in the whole body*. Amsterdam: Elsevier, 1978.

69. Brooke OG, Alvear J, Arnold M. Energy retention, energy expenditure, and growth in healthy immature infants. *Pediatr Res* 1979; 13:215–220.

70. Brooke OG. Energy balance and metabolic rate in preterm infants fed with standard and high-energy formulas. *Br J Nutr* 1980; 44:13.

71. Brooke OG, Wood C, Barley J. Energy balance, nitrogen balance, and growth in preterm infants fed expressed breast milk, a premature infant formula, and two low-solute adapted formulae. *Arch Dis Child* 1982;57:898–904.

72. Brooke, OG. Energy expenditure in the fetus and neonate: sources of variability. *Acta Paediatr Scand* 1985; 319 (suppl):128–134.

73. Brooke OG. Nutritional requirements of low and very low birthweight infants. *Rev Nutr* 1987; 7:91–116.

74. Pontremoli S, Melloni E. Extralysosomal protein degradation. *Annu Rev Biochem* 1986; 55:455–481.

75. Rogers S, Wells R, Rechsteiner M. Amino acid sequences common to rapidly degraded proteins: the PEST hypothesis. *Science* 1986; 234:364–369.

76. Golden M, Waterlow JC, Picou D. The relationship between dietary intake, weight change, nitrogen balance and protein turnover in man. *Am J Clin Nutr* 1977; 30:1345–1348.

77. Meer PR, Peterson RG, Bonds DR, Meschia G, Battaglia FG. Rates of protein synthesis and turnover in fetal life. *Am J Physiol* 1981; 240:E320–E324.

78. Morton AJ, Goldspink F. Changes in protein turnover in rat uterus during pregnancy. *Am J Physiol* 1986; 250:E114–E120.

79. Spady DW, Payne PR, Picou D, Waterlow JC. Energy balance during recovery from malnutrition. *Am J Clin Nutr* 1976; 29:1073–1078.

80. Micheli JL, Schutz Y, Cauderay M, Calame A, Jéquier E. Catch-up growth in small for date, low birthweight infants. *Dev Physiopathol Clin* 1990; 1:97–108.

81. Hanning RM, Zlotkin SH. Amino acid and protein needs of the neonate: effects of excess and deficiency. *Semin Perinatol* 1989; 13:131–141.

82. Gaull GE, Sturman JA, Räihä NCR. Development of mammalian sulfur metabolism: absence of cystathionase in human fetal tissues. *Pediatr Res* 1972; 6:538–547.

83. Gaull GE, Rasin DK, Räihä NCR, Heinonen K. Milk protein quality and quantity in low-birth-weight infants. III. Effects of sulfur amino acids in plasma and urine. *J Pediatr* 1977; 90:348–355.

84. Polberger S, Axelsson I, Räihä N. Amino acid concentrations in plasma and urine in very low birth weight infants fed non-protein-enriched or human milk protein-enriched human milk. *Pediatrics* 1990; 86:909–915.

85. Rassin DK, Gaull GE, Jäervenpää AA, Räihä NCR. Feeding the low birthweight infant: effect of taurine and cholesterol supplementation on amino acids and cholesterol. *Pediatrics* 1983; 71:179–186.

86. Svenningsen NW, Lindroth M, Lindquist B. Growth in relation to protein intake of low birth weight infants. *Early Hum Dev* 1982; 6:47–58.

87. Borch-Johnsen K, Mandroup-Poulsen T, Zachau-Christiansen B, et al. Relation between breast-feeding and incidence rates of insulin-dependent diabetes mellitus. *Lancet* 1984; 10:1083–6.

88. Polberger S, Fex GA, Axelsson I, Räihä N. Eleven plasma proteins as indicators of protein nutritional status in very low birth weight infants. *Pediatrics* 1990; 86:916–921.

89. McIntosh N, Rodeck CH, Heath R. Plasma amino acids of the mid trimester human fetus. *Biol Neonate* 1984; 45:218–224.

90. Polberger S. *Fortified human milk for very low birth weight infants: effects on growth and metabolism.* [Thesis]. Lund, Sweden: University of Lund, 1990.

91. Polberger S, Axelsson I, Räihä N. Urinary and serum urea as indicators of protein metabolism in very low birthweight infants fed varying human milk protein intakes. *Acta Paediatr Scand* 1990; 79:737–742.

92. Atkinson SA, Bryan MH, Anderson GH. Human milk: difference in nitrogen concentration in milk from mothers of term and premature infants. *J Pediatr* 1978; 93:67–69.

93. Atkinson SA, Bryan MH, Anderson GH. Human milk feeding in premature infants: protein, fat, and carbohydrate balances in the first two weeks of life. *J Pediatr* 1981; 99:617.

94. Atkinson SA, Hanning RM. Amino acid metabolism and requirements of the premature infant: does human milk feeding represent the "gold standard"? In: Atkinson SA, Lonnerdal B, eds. *Protein and non-protein nitrogen in human milk*. Boca Raton, FL: CRC Press; 1989.

95. Shaffer SG, Quimiro CL, Anderson JV, Hall RT. Postnatal weight changes in low birth weight infants. *Pediatrics* 1987; 79:702–705.

96. Prader A, Largo R, Walli R, Fanconi A. Schweizerische Wachstumskurven von der 28: Schwangerschaftswoche bis zum 18. Lebensjahr. *Helv Paediatr Acta* 1980; 45 (suppl):32–44.

97. Etter HR. Die körperliche Entwicklung früh und termingeborener Kinder in den ersten vier Lebensjahren [Thesis]. Zurich: University of Zürich, 1986.

98. Davidson M, Levine SZ, Bauer CH, Dann M. Feeding studies in low birth weight infants: a relationship of dietary protein, fat and electrolytes to rates of weight gain, clinical courses and serum chemical concentrations. *J Pediatr* 1967; 70:695–713.

99. American Academy of Pediatrics Committee on Nutrition. Nutritional needs of low-birthweight infants. *Pediatrics*. 1985; 75:976–986.

100. Committee on Nutrition, American Academy of Pediatrics. *Pediatric nutrition handbook*. 2nd ed. American Academy of Pediatrics; Elk Grove Village, IL: 1985.

101. Gaull GE, Wright CE. Proteins and growth modulators in human milk. In: Foman SJ, Heird WC, eds. *Energy and protein needs during infancy*. Orlando, FL: Academic Press; 1986.

102. Axelsson IE, Ivarsson SA, Räihä NC. Protein intake in early infancy: effects on plasama amino acid concentrations, insulin metabolism, and growth. *Pediatr Res* 1989; 26:614–617.

103. De Curtis M, De Curtis D, Ciccimarra F. Nutritional requirements of preterm infants. *World Rev Nutr Diet* 1989; 58:33–60.

104. Gross SJ. Growth and biochemical response of preterm infants fed human milk or modified infant formula. *N Engl J Med* 1983; 308:237–241.

105. Denne SC, Kalhan SC. Leucine metabolism in human newborns. *Am J Physiol* 1987; 253:E608–615.

106. Committee on Nutrition of the Preterm Infant, European Society of Paediatric Gastroenterology and Nutrition. *Nutrition and feeding of preterm infants*. Oxford, UK: Blackwell Scientific Publications; 1987.

107. Lucas A, Morley R, Cole TJ, et al. Early diet in preterm babies and developmental status at 18 months. *Lancet* 1990; 335:1477–1481.

108. Fomon SJ, Thomas LN, Filer LJ, Ziegler EE, Leonard MT. Food consumption and growth of normal infants fed milk-based formulas. *Acta Paediat Scand* 1971; 223 (suppl):1–36.

109. Moro GE, Minoli I, Fulconis F, Clementi M, Räihä NCR. Growth and metabolic responses in low-birth-weight infants fed human milk fortified with human milk protein or with a bovine milk protein preparation. *J Pediatr Gastroenterol Nutr* 1991; 13:150–154.

110. Clark D, Henderson M, Smith M, Dear P. Plasma amino acid concentrations in parenterally fed preterm infants. *Arch Dis Child* 1989; 64:939–942.

111. Micheli JL, Schutz Y, Jéquier E. Protein metabolism in newborns. In: Polin RA, Fox WW, eds. *Textbook of neonatal and fetal medicine: physiology and pathophysiology*. Philadelphia: Grune & Stratton, 1991.

112. Georgieff MK, Mills MM, Zempel CE, Chang PN. Catch-up growth, muscle and fat accretion, and body pro-

portionality of infants one year after newborn intensive care. *J Pediatr* 1989; 114:288–292.

113. Ashworth A, Millward DJ. Catch-up growth in children. *Nutr Rev* 1986; 44:157–163.

114. Anderson TL, Muttart CR, Bieber MA, Nicholson JF, Heird WC. A controlled trial of glucose versus glucose and amino acids in premature infants. *J Pediatr* 1979; 94:947–951.

115. Bhatia J, Rassin DK. Feeding the premature infant after hospital discharge: growth and biochemical responses. *J Pediatr* 1991; 118:515–519.

116. Darling P, Lepage G, Tremblay P, Collet S, Kien LC, Roy C. Protein quality and quantity in preterm infants receiving the same energy intake. *Am J Dis Child* 1985; 139:186–190.

117. Freymond D, Schutz Y, Decombaz J, Micheli JL, Jéquier E. Energy balance, physical activity, and thermogenic effect of feeding in premature infants. *Pediatr Res* 1986; 20:638–645.

118. Kashyap S, Forsyth M, Zucker C, Ramakrishnan R, Dell RB, Heird WC. Effects of varying protein and energy intakes on growth and metabolic response in low birth weight infants. *J Pediatr* 1986; 108:955–963.

119. Kashyap S, Schulze K, Forsyth M, Dell RB, Ramakrishnan R, Heird WC. Growth, nutrient retention, and metabolic response of low-birthweight infants fed supplemented and unsupplemented preterm human milk. *Am J Clin Nutr* 1990; 52:254–262.

120. Schulze KF, Stefanski M, Masterson J, et al. Energy expenditure, energy balance, and composition of weight gain in low birthweight infants fed diets of different protein and energy content. *J Pediatr* 1987; 110:753–759.

4. Carbohydrates*

C. Lawrence Kien

Reviewers: Johan Gentz, Guy Putet

Carbohydrate constitutes approximately 40% of the energy intake of infants ingesting human milk or bovine milk–based formulas. This chapter will consider how dietary carbohydrate is utilized and will discuss the nutritional significance of the quantity and type of sugar present in the diet or administered intravenously. In the fed state, glucose is an important, if not the sole, source of energy metabolism for brain and other nervous tissue, red blood cells, the renal medulla, and the retina.[1-4] The high proportion of carbohydrate energy to total energy present in human milk (41%) contrasts with the much smaller proportion (5% to 15%) in milks from species such as the rat, dog, guinea pig, pig, and rabbit.[2] It is tempting to speculate that this difference relates to the large size of the human brain and the large relative size of the infant brain, but such reasoning fails to explain all of the inter-species differences in the carbohydrate content of milk.[2]

Carbohydrate intake, either through the gastrointestinal tract or via parenteral means, has potential clinical significance by virtue of these important biological effects: improved nutritional status and function of the intestine and colon via the stimulatory effects of short-chain fatty acids on cell proliferation and ion absorption[5,6]; stimulation of insulin secretion with its attendant effects on urinary sodium excretion (antinatriuresis), metabolism and growth (inhibition of muscle protein degradation)[7-13]; stimulation of peripheral deiodination of thyroxine to triiodothyronine[14-16]; enhanced metabolic response to growth hormone[17]; increased calcium absorption[18-21]; and increased respiratory quotient (RQ), i.e., the relative proportion of carbon dioxide generated, per mole of adenosine triphosphate (ATP) produced (or oxygen consumed).[22] Carbohydrate is therefore essential to the overall health of the gastrointestinal tract and the fulfillment of energy requirements.

As outlined in Table 4.1, controversy and research have focused on lactose digestion and fermentation and the possible association of lactose intake with necrotizing enterocolitis (NEC)[5,6]; the facilitating role of hydrolyzed lactose on calcium absorption[18-20]; mechanisms for glucose intolerance and hypoglycemia[1,23-31]; the recommended percentage of carbohydrate calories in high caloric density formulas fed to infants with bronchopulmonary dysplasia (BPD)[32-34]; and the role of insulin as a therapeutic agent in infants with hyperglycemia.[23,35-37] Figure 4.1 schematically depicts the various sites of carbohydrate assimilation and summarizes the physiologic implications of many of these issues.

Physiology

Fetal Metabolism

Both parturition and stress associated with respiratory disease and infection can affect the hormonal milieu in the preterm infant, which may differ drastically from that present in the fetus of comparable postconceptional age. One could thus argue that studies of fetal carbohydrate metabolism might be of greater relevance to issues of nutrition and pregnancy than to

*Supported in part by NIH Grant HD19773.

Table 4.1. Controversial Aspects of Carbohydrate Nutrition in the Preterm Infant

Area of Controversy

Relative rate of lactose hydrolysis in the small intestine versus assimilation in the colon[5,74,77,174]

Lactose and fermentation causing necrotizing enterocolitis[6]

Lactose facilitating calcium absorption[18-21]

Mechanisms for hyper- and hypoglycemia[1,23-31]

Excessive carbohydrate intake increasing respiratory quotient in patients with bronchopulmonary dysplasia[32-34,167,172]

Insulin treatment in preterm infants with glucose intolerance[23,35-37]

the management of the preterm infant. Nevertheless, a brief review of carbohydrate production, utilization, and storage of fetal life, as well as the hormonal modifiers of these processes, is warranted to provide insight into the "metabolic background" of the preterm newborn. Readers desiring more detail should refer to the excellent reviews of this subject listed in the reference section at the end of this chapter.

In the fetal sheep, glucose and glucose-derived lactate are utilized at a rate approximately 65% of oxygen consumption.[25] The lamb brain accounts for only 15% to 20% of fetal glucose consumption versus approximately 75% for the larger, human brain.[25] Fetal glucose utilization is controlled by fetal plasma glucose concentration independent of insulin; but at constant glucose concentration, insulin increases fetal glucose uptake and oxidation.[30,38] Fetal glucose supply and circulating concentration are primarily affected by maternal glucose concentration,[25,30,39] since maternal peptide hormones, including insulin, cannot cross the placenta.[39,40] Apparently, uterine blood flow, within usual physiologic limits, has little effect on fetal glucose uptake from the placenta.[25] Insulin is probably not a factor either, even though there are insulin receptors on the maternal side of the placenta.[25,30] During maternal fasting or hypoglycemia, fetal glucose oxidation decreases and leucine oxidation increases.[25,38,41] The fetal human brain utilizes ketones, as indicated by the presence of hepatic ketogenesis at 10 weeks gestation.[28] Further, offspring of mothers who were ketotic during pregnancy may be at increased risk for cognitive and psychomotor delay at 3 to 5 years of age.[28] Gluconeogenesis, particularly in the unstressed fetus, is minimal until just prior to the end of gestation.[30,38,42,43] The most important source of glycogen to the fetus is probably the liver because it contains most of the glucose-6-phosphatase activity.[30] However, hepatic glycogen formation is minimal prior to the third trimester; therefore, the preterm infant may be born with minimal glycogen stores.[28,43,44]

Human pancreatic β cells synthesize and store insulin and proinsulin by 10 to 11 weeks gestation, and insulin is detectable in the fetal circulation by 12 weeks.[28,40,43,45] The insulin secretory response is apparently blunted during early gestation, though circulating insulin concentration and insulin receptors, and thus sensitivity to insulin, increase during the third trimester.[44] In fetal sheep, acute suppression of insulin secretion with somatostatin does not affect glucose utilization, but chronic insulin deficiency has more pronounced effects.[38] Although present in the human anterior pituitary gland by 15 weeks of gestation,[46] growth hormone does not appear to have significant effects on fetal growth; for example, anencephalic infants or those with congenital absence of the pituitary are normal size for gestation.[40] Thyroid hormone also does not seem to be critical for normal human fetal growth, since infants having hypothyroidism at birth are normally grown. In contrast, insulin is a major stimulus of fetal growth.[28,30,40,41] Infants born of diabetic mothers (IDM) and infants with hyperinsulinemia from other causes (Beckwith-Wiedemann syndrome or nesidioblastosis) tend to be large and obese, while infants with hypoinsulinemia (e.g., congenital diabetes mellitus) are usually growth-retarded.[28,40,45]

As reviewed in more detail below, insulin has a number of effects on protein metabolism that are apt to promote growth. Insulin-like growth factor I (IGF I) is a peptide hormone, resembling proinsulin in structure, which has important anabolic activity with

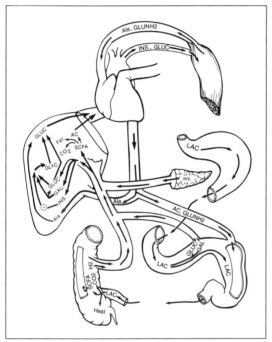

Fig. 4.1. Schematic diagram showing some of the major physiologic considerations related to carbohydrate nutrition in the preterm infant. Lactose (LAC) is hydrolyzed in the small intestine to glucose (GLUC) and galactose (GAL), which are absorbed and transported to the liver where GAL is almost totally converted to GLUC and either of the sugars can be retained as glycogen. Lactose escaping hydrolysis can be fermented in the colon to short-chain fatty acids (SCFA) and various gases. The SCFA are absorbed in the colon and are either utilized as energy substrates there or transported to the liver where propionate and butyrate, but not acetate (AC), are almost totally removed. Insulin (INS) secreted in response to GLUC absorption inhibits muscle protein breakdown. Glutamine (GLUNH2) and AC may be important effectors of intestinal cell proliferation. Alanine (ALA) produced in muscle may be generated in excess under conditions of either hyperglycemia or hypoglycemia and will serve as a substrate for gluconeogenesis.

respect to skeletal growth and muscle development.[40] It is synthesized in the liver and secreted into the circulation (in response to growth hormone, for example), as well as being produced within certain target tissues such as muscle. Insulin apparently can substitute for IGF I in stimulating fetal limb-bud cell growth.[40] In addition, insulin may be necessary for normal expression of IGF I mRNA,[47] although it is unclear whether insulin enhances blood IGF I concentrations and cartilage growth activity primarily by direct effects on IGF I or via indirect effects on substrate utilization.[40]

Glucagon-containing cells appear in the human fetal pancreas by 8 to 10 weeks gestation and reach a peak by 17 to 20 weeks. Glucagon, which does not cross the placenta, is present in the plasma by 12 to 15 weeks of gestation, reaching post-absorptive adult concentrations by 40 weeks.[28,38,43,48] Glucagon secretion in the fetus appears to be unaffected by acute changes in blood glucose concentration, but chronic maternal fasting (e.g., 4 days in rats and 9 to 11 days in sheep) does affect increased fetal glucagon secretion.[43] In the fetal rat or sheep, an infusion of catecholamines that produces circulating concentrations typical of stress, labor, or hypoxia also causes a rise in blood glucagon; this effect may be blocked by propranolol.[38] The number and affinity of glucagon receptors remain below adult levels during fetal life, and thus there is insensitivity to glucagon in the fetus. In the rat fetus, glucagon, at pharmacological but not physiologic doses, will increase plasma glucose and cause a decrease in liver glycogen as well as the premature appearance of cytosolic phosphoenolpyruvic acid carboxykinase (PEPCK), a gluconeogenic enzyme.[38]

Digestion, Absorption, and Fermentation of Carbohydrate

Carbohydrates in Human Milk and Preterm Infant Formulas
Lactose is the sole carbohydrate in human milk. The lactose content of mature human milk has been reported as 6.8 g/dL, or 9.1 g/100 kcal (0.022 g/kJ),[49] and 7.4 g/dL.[50] The carbohydrate content of preterm human milk can also be calculated from the nitrogen, fat, and total energy content of milk obtained during the first month after term and preterm delivery[51] using data on the heat of combustion of protein, fat, and lactose.[52] The calculated values for lactose concentration are 6.99 g/dL after 26 to 31 weeks gestation and 6.24 g/dL after 32 to 36 weeks gestation. These values could be slight underestimates since it was assumed in the calculation that all the nitrogen was protein. Using similar assumptions, the calculated value for lactose concentration in term human milk is 7.37 g/dL, which is close to previous estimates (presumably based on direct analysis of lactose concentration).[50] In preterm infant for-

mulas, lactose and glucose polymers each constitute approximately 50% of the carbohydrate content. The total carbohydrate concentration, although varying from lot to lot, is about 8.5 g/dL in the concentrated form of the formulas, i.e., 0.8 kcal/mL. (See Appendix, Table A.3, for g/100 kcal carbohydrate values of several commercial formulas.) The glucose polymers (oligomers) of these formulas are mostly medium length (approximately five glucose units) and are prepared from partially hydrolyzed corn starch.[53]

Fetal Development Carbohydrate digestion, including fetal enzyme development, was recently reviewed in detail.[5] Lactose is hydrolyzed in the small intestine by β-D-galactosidase (lactase) present on the brush border at the villus tip. Sucrase-isomaltase, present both at the mid-zone of the villus and at its tip, hydrolyzes sucrose and maltose (disaccharide of two glucose molecules released during glucose-polymer digestion).[5] Starch or glucose polymers can be digested by salivary and pancreatic amylase, α-amylase present in human milk, and intestinal mucosal hydrolases.[5] Intestinal sucrase-isomaltase and maltase activities rise slowly from 10 to 26 weeks, and then rise more rapidly; by 34 weeks, the activities are 70% those of term infants.[54] Intestinal lactase is detectable as early as 12 weeks but accumulates more slowly so that by 34 weeks, the activities are only 30% those of term infants; by 35 to 38 weeks, however, concentrations reach the level of approximately 70% those of term infants.[54] The presence of amylase in fetal pancreas is controversial.[5,55-57] Data on monosaccharide absorption in the fetus are scarce.[5] In the human fetus, glucose transport is more developed in the jejunum than in the ileum, and it appears that the capacity for jejunum transport of glucose is present at 10 weeks and increases substantially from 10 weeks to about 16 to 19 weeks. The time when glucose transport reaches "term" levels is not clear.[5,58,59]

Postnatal Development of Capacity to Digest and Absorb Carbohydrates Pancreatic amylase does not seem essential to the digestion of starch or glucose polymer in newborn infants. Apparently, salivary amylase and mucosal α-glucosidases are sufficient for glucose polymer digestion.[5,52,53,60] The blood glucose and insulin responses of preterm infants fed test doses of glucose polymers are similar to those of term infants.[53] Glucose absorption capacity in preterm infants is about three fourths that in term infants. It seems to increase during the first 3 weeks of life, but declines somewhat after that.[5,59]

Despite evidence of low fetal lactase activity[54,61-63] controversy exists over the extent to which lactose fed to preterm infants is hydrolyzed to glucose and galactose (digestion) or is fermented (Table 4.2). Certain types of data favor the concept that, postnatally, preterm infants acquire a relatively effi-

Table 4.2.   Evidence for and against Efficient* Lactose Hydrolysis to Glucose and Galactose in the Small Intestine

<table>
<tr><td align="center">Evidence Favoring Efficient Lactose Hydrolysis</td></tr>
</table>

Weight gain, absence of diarrhea, and minimal excretion of carbohydrate energy on formulas containing lactose as sole carbohydrate[52,64–67]

Rise in blood glucose after lactose ingestion[68–70]

Measurement of urine lactose/lactulose ratio (decreased appearance of lactose in urine shortly after birth implies improved absorption)[71]

Measurement of colonic H_2 absorption (previous estimates of lactose fermentation based on H_2 concentration may be too high)[77]

Tracer studies of lactose digestion[174]

<table>
<tr><td align="center">Evidence against Efficient Lactose Hydrolysis</td></tr>
</table>

Low fetal lactase activity[54,61–63]

Increased breath H_2 concentration with increased lactose intake[64,73,74]

Diarrhea and metabolic acidosis with "added lactose" formula[72]

Measurements of whole body acetate production and fecal acetate excretion (imply high fermentation rate); correlate with breath H_2 concentration or lactose intake[78,79]

*"Efficient" defined as $\geq 80\%$ of lactose hydrolyzed in the small intestine as might be estimated from breath H_2 or tracer studies. Clinical observations and tolerance tests do not provide quantitative data.

cient capacity to hydrolyze lactose in the small intestine (e.g., $\geq 80\%$ digested at that site) at an earlier developmental stage than do infants in utero. Preterm infants (<32 weeks gestation) ingesting human milk or formulas containing lactose as the sole carbohydrate do seem to thrive. They excrete in the feces only minimal energy derived from lactose, and generally do not exhibit osmotic diarrhea.[52,64–67] Also, lactose tolerance tests in preterm infants indicate that blood glucose concentration rises equally after meals containing lactose, glucose, and glucose polymers.[68–70] While it is impossible to determine without a tracer to what extent compensatory increased hepatic output can maintain blood glucose concentration during such tolerance tests, the results do suggest that glucose is either absorbed or produced in response to the lactose-containing meal. Moreover, recent dual stable tracer studies in a few premature infants suggest that in vivo hydrolysis (digestion) of lactose may be efficient.[71]

Lactulose, a disaccharide of galactose and fructose, cannot be digested by mammalian enzymes in the gut; therefore, it quantitatively reaches the colon where a small percentage is absorbed intact and excreted in the urine.[72] The excretion of this compound in the urine is thought to be a marker for the nonspecific absorption of carbohydrate in the colon. Lactose reaching the colon also may be absorbed intact. Thus, measurements of the ratio of urine lactose to lactulose in preterm infants fed both sugars in a constant ratio are thought to provide insight into

how much lactose escapes intestinal digestion. Such studies suggest that intestinal lactase activity becomes almost completely efficient shortly after birth.[72] On the other hand, one study comparing "added lactose" to "added sucrose" formulas showed that added lactose produced a relative increase in the incidence of diarrhea and metabolic acidosis during the first week of life.[73]

Studies of breath hydrogen concentration further support the view that lactose is not efficiently hydrolyzed in the small intestine in the preterm infant and instead reaches the colon, where it undergoes extensive fermentation.[64,74,75] Breath hydrogen concentration correlates, too, with lactose intake in preterm infants.[64,75] These findings are consistent with the hypothesis that a significant proportion of dietary lactose reaches the colon in the preterm infant.[52,64,75] In older children, measurement of breath hydrogen concentration appears to be a sensitive (75% to 94%), if not very specific (41% to 59%), indicator of abnormal small intestinal histology, deficient intestinal lactase activity, and symptomatology resulting from milk ingestion.[76]

The relationship between the rate of fermentation of lactose in preterm infants and the actual hydrogen production rate is apt to be complex.[77] There is a broad range of estimates of the percent of dietary lactose not hydrolyzed and reaching the colon: 66% to 100%, assuming adult colon absorption rates of hydrogen[75]; or 12% to 19% based on actual measurements of absorption in six infants.[78] One is thus led to question the biological relevance of high breath hydrogen concentration in preterm infants as an index of the capacity for lactose hydrolysis. It is of interest, though, that lactose intake and breath hydrogen concentration in the preterm infant correlate with the whole body rate of production of acetate (a prominent metabolite of carbohydrate fermentation) as well as its fecal excretion, providing additional indirect evidence that increased lactose intake is associated with, if not causally related to, increased colonic fermentative activity.[79,80]

Effects of Colonic Fermentation of Carbohydrate
When carbohydrate is not fully digested in the small intestine, it will be fermented in the colon to short-chain fatty acids (SCFAs), such as acetate, propionate, and butyrate; lactate, and various gases, including carbon dioxide, methane, and hydrogen.[64,75,77,79-85] Using a tracer technique that takes into account colonic fermentation, we[80] have estimated that the body production of acetate, the most abundant SCFA resulting from fermentation, is approximately equal to that seen in ruminants (23 to 70 μmol/kg/min). Most of the SCFAs and a certain percentage of the gases are absorbed in the colon.[5] Short-chain fatty acids produced in the colon from carbohydrate fermentation may be very important to maintaining the nutriture and function of both the colon and the intestine[86-91] in lactose-fed preterm infants and in older children and adults ingesting fiber, starch, and other carbohydrates incompletely hydrolyzed in the small intestine. Hepatic gluconeogenesis from lactate is stimulated by acetate and butyrate and inhibited by propionate[92-95]; thus, measurement of glucose concentration changes after a lactose meal could be a misleading indication of how much glucose or galactose from lactose is actually absorbed. However, recent studies of adult humans suggest that oral acetate administered at a rate thought to be consistent with the colonic production of acetate on a high-fiber diet (approximately 14 μmol/kg/min) does not affect hepatic glucose output (HGO).[96]

Despite the putative benefits of lactose fermentation, bacterial metabolism of hexose units to acetate and other SCFA may have negative effects on energy balance and protein nutrition, even if fecal excretion of carbohydrate energy is minimal.[52,64-66] If, for example, the secretion of insulin, an important effector of normal growth and protein accretion, were decreased because of diversion of hexose to fatty acids in the colon, the efficiency of utilization of dietary amino acids for protein synthesis might be impaired. Moreover, the quality and quantity of growth, and perhaps even brain development,[97-101] might be affected. Our preliminary estimates of colonic acetate production in preterm infants suggest that 24% to 74% of dietary lactose could be converted to acetate.[79]

While colonic fermentation of lactose prevents loss of energy via fecal excretion,[52,65,66,102] there may be considerable (approximately 30%) loss of potential adenosine triphosphate (ATP) when lactose is fermented to acetate (bypassing the energy-yielding biochemical pathway from glucose to acetyl-CoA).[52,103]

There is controversy over whether lactose fermentation enhances the risk of NEC[6] or could lead to clinically significant D-lactic acidosis.[5,6] Although some studies have shown that NEC develops more frequently in infants with higher breath hydrogen concentrations or with positive reducing substances in the feces,[104-108] these observations may simply reflect a higher incidence of NEC in preterm infants with a history of more aggressive feeding, perhaps characterized by rapid advances in feeding.[6,109] While studies linking fermentative activity and gas production to NEC are cogent, it is not at all clear that carbohydrate fermentation in the colon has primary relevance to this devastating problem.[6,110-112]

Summary Fetal lactase activity and breath hydrogen studies suggest that lactose digestion is inefficient, while clinical observations and assessment of weight gain suggest efficient lactose assimilation. Whether lactose is fully digested in the small intestine versus being assimilated via fermentation may be of clinical significance. Enhanced calcium absorption by lactose appears to depend on adequate intestinal hydrolysis of lactose.[18-20] Moreover, while colonic fermentation of lactose or other carbohydrates may be considered a beneficial and normal mechanism for maintaining the colonic and intestinal nutriture, the possible relationship of this process to NEC remains a matter of concern.

Postnatal Carbohydrate Metabolism and Hormonal Responses
At birth, separation of the fetus from the maternal blood supply is associated with a fall in the infant's blood glucose concentration from about 70 to 80 mg/dL (3.9 to 4.4 mmol/L) to around 40 to 50 mg/dL, necessitating increased HGO (glycogenolysis and gluconeogenesis from lactate and amino acids).[2,25,42] This metabolic response includes increases in the activities of the enzymes involved in both glycogenolysis and gluconeogenesis and normally is effected in part by a hormonal surge (particularly a rise in glucagon secretion) concomitant with parturition.[38,43]

Effects of Insulin and Glucagon on Carbohydrate Metabolism In addition to its effects on enhancement of cellular glucose uptake, stimulation of glycogen synthesis, and inhibition of glycogenolysis, insulin directly impacts protein metabolism and growth, which in turn affect fetal growth. Whole body and muscle protein turnover and leucine oxidation are affected favorably by insulin treatment[9-13,113] and unfavorably by diabetes or insulin withdrawal in diabetes.[13]

Insulin may be a major regulator of fetal growth.[30,41] During fasting or in patients or animals with protein-energy malnutrition, circulating concentrations of IGF I are decreased.[114,115] A potent anabolic hormone, insulin may be a direct stimulator of other growth factors necessary for normal growth[47,116-119] and appears to be necessary for normal expression of IGF I mRNA.[47] Hypoinsulinemia in conditions such as juvenile onset diabetes mellitus is associated with poor growth and short stature, especially in the absence of adequate insulin therapy.[120, 121] Thus, a normal circulating concentration of insulin may be necessary for optimal growth in preterm infants. It is of interest, too, that cyclic, adenosine monophosphate-mediated processes of surfactant synthesis and release are inhibited by insulin.[44]

Glucagon affects carbohydrate metabolism by enhancing glycogenolysis and gluconeogenesis. It increases the mRNA for PEPCK, an important enzyme of gluconeogenesis. Insulin deficiency also causes premature appearance of PEPCK.

Changes in the Secretion of Insulin and Other Hormones in the Neonatal Period Shortly after birth, the plasma insulin concentration falls and the epinephrine and glucagon concentrations rise.[25,38,42,43,48] The first feeding is associated with a rise in plasma insulin, but the glucagon concentration does not change.[122] Continuous versus bolus feeding of formula results in higher preprandial plasma concentrations of insulin in preterm infants.[123] The C-peptide:insulin ratio is lower in preterm infants compared with term infants, possibly indicating decreased hepatic extraction of insulin.[45] Also, compared with term newborns or adults, there appears to be higher insulin binding to red blood cells in preterm infants. The relevance of this finding to muscle and other targeted cells is unclear, however.[45] Insulin secretion in preterm infants is less responsive to intravenous or oral glucose than in term infants.[24] Likewise, compared with adults, glucagon secretion in newborns does not decrease as readily in response to glucose, insulin, or somatostatin[124]; and glucagon secretion in the preterm infant is less responsive to glucose than in the term infant.[125]

Birth and enteral feeding per se induce complex responses from a number of other hormones, including pancreatic glucagon, enteroglucagon, growth hormone, gastrin, motilin, neurotensin, and gastric inhibitory polypeptide (GIP).[46,123,126-131] Delays in the initiation of enteral feeding seem to affect, in particular, the basal plasma concentrations of pancreatic glucagon and enteroglucagon.[129] Continuous feeding of preterm infants induces higher preprandial levels of GIP and gastrin than bolus feeding.[123] Compared with human milk, a formula containing lactose, glucose, and maltodextrins in approximately equal proportions resulted in an earlier rise (from cord-blood levels) in preprandial plasma GIP, with a significantly higher level observed at 10 days of age. Insulin levels were not different in the two groups, however.[132] Diet protein and intravenous amino acids seem to potentiate insulin secretion.[133,134]

The effects of lipid administration on glucose metabolism are also noteworthy. Medium-chain triglyceride (MCT) feeding in preterm and term infants increases blood glucose concentrations and stimulates HGO.[135-137] Similarly, administration of intravenous fat emulsion to preterm infants causes an increase in blood glucose concentration.[138,139] The mechanism for these effects of lipid administration is not clear. In fasted, hypoglycemic newborn rats, MCT administration stimulates gluconeogenesis.[38] When hypoglycemia was induced by inhibition of long-chain fatty acid oxidation through pharmacological inhibition of carnitine acyltransferases, the effect was overcome by treatment with MCT, which bypassed the inhibition.[38] Fatty acid oxidation increases the supply of both acetyl-CoA, an obligate activator of mitochondrial pyruvate carboxylase, and nicotinamide adenine dinucleotide (which shifts the equilibrium between glyceraldehyde 3-phosphate and 1,3-diphosphoglyceric acid in the direction of glyceraldehyde 3-phosphate, thus favoring gluconeogenesis).[30,38] Using a stable isotope technique, Bougneres,[137] in a brief report, noted an increase in glucose production in neonates in the post-absorptive state who were fed MCT. He also attributed this result to the effect of intrahepatic fatty acid oxidation. But other investigators have offered alternative hypotheses. Thiebaud et al.[140] showed that intravenous lipid infusions in adult volunteers caused a decrease in glucose uptake, which was in turn associated with a decrease in both oxidative and nonoxidative uptake. They[140] also showed that moderate lipid infusions (equivalent to 2 to 4 g/kg/day) had significant effects on glucose metabolism, a finding that is of clinical interest since some studies in neonates[138] have used much higher lipid infusion rates (e.g., 6 to 12 g/kg/day). Yunis et al.,[139] studying preterm infants, also reported that lipid infusion caused an elevation in blood glucose concentration without affecting HGO, concluding that peripheral glucose utilization was impaired by lipid infusion. Whatever the mechanism for these effects of lipid on glucose metabolism, it appears that efficient fatty acid utilization may be necessary for maintaining normal glucose homeostasis in the preterm neonate.[137] Administration of intravenous lipid may impair glucose tolerance in the parenterally fed preterm infant, but the feeding of lipid supplements (e.g., MCT) may have a role in future management of recurrent hypoglycemia in such infants.

Hepatic Glucose Output and Glucose Oxidation

Both glycogenolysis and gluconeogenesis from amino acids contribute to HGO.[141] At steady state glucose concentrations, the rate of peripheral glucose utilization can be equated to HGO, normalized for plasma glucose concentration. Glucose utilization is proportional to brain weight, and normally is high in newborn infants compared with adults; in infants with diminished brain mass, the rate is closer to that in adults.[38] Several groups have estimated HGO in both term infants and average- or small-for-gestational-age preterm infants.[136,142-151] In preterm infants, intravenous glucose infusion rates (GIR) of less than about 8 mg/kg/min (0.044 mmol/kg/min, 11.5 g/kg/day) are not sufficient to suppress HGO in all infants.[142,143,147,149-151] Adult subjects demonstrate virtually total suppression of HGO at a GIR of 3.2 mg/kg/min.[142] One may conclude from these various studies that insulin secretion, or perhaps hepatic sensitivity to insulin, may be impaired in the preterm neonate; perhaps this insulin resistance is mediated by counter-regulatory hormones secreted in response to stress (e.g., infection) or hypoxemia.[25,124,142,147,152-155] The effect of enteral feeding on HGO has not been studied. On the one hand, via the effects of GIP,[156] the insulin secretory response to enteral feeding might be enhanced compared with intravenous administration of glucose. On the other, if lactose digestion were defective and lactose-derived glucose were diverted to fermentation pathways, there might be reduced insulin secretion with its attendant effects on HGO and protein metabolism.[9-13]

If exogenous glucose is not oxidized, it may be converted to glycogen or fat (particularly in the liver). The metabolism of glucose to fat not only wastes energy, but it also results in excessive carbon dioxide production (the biochemical pathway from glucose to fat is associated with an RQ considerably above 1). In a preterm infant with ventilatory insufficiency, the excretion of this excessive carbon dioxide may present a clinical problem. A few studies have specifically addressed the inter-relationships of the glucose oxidation rate, energy expenditure, and carbon dioxide production. Sauer et al.[154] showed that increased glucose intake was associated with increased glucose oxidation rate in a group of newborn term and preterm infants. They observed a linear relationship between glucose oxidation and glucose intake at GIRs of 10 to 24 g/kg/day, but fat synthesis from glucose appeared to increase as the GIR increased.[154,157] In older infants, a GIR >12.6 mg/kg/min (17.9 g/kg/day) was not associated with

increased glucose oxidation.[158] Thus, increasing the GIR to >18 g/kg/day may not yield increased ATP (e.g., to be used for synthetic processes and growth), but may result only in excessive carbon dioxide production and perhaps steatosis of the liver. Bresson et al.[159] compared two isocaloric, isonitrogenous regimes for total parenteral nutrition which differed with respect to the source of nonprotein calories: glucose only (28.5 g/kg/day) or fat (5.5 g/kg/day) plus glucose (13.9 g/kg/day). The two regimens resulted in similar rates of oxygen consumption, but the lipid-containing regimen was associated with a lower rate of carbon dioxide production and a higher net rate of protein synthesis, again suggesting that excessive glucose intake may not be oxidized for energy but instead stored as fat. Thus, in considering the source of nonprotein energy in parenteral nutrition, not only is it necessary to consider the effects of lipid on lung function and bilirubin binding and the nutritional requirements for fatty acids, but also the capacity of the infant for utilizing glucose as an energy source. Therapeutic manipulations designed to increase carbohydrate intake (e.g., insulin) may not necessarily augment protein accretion. A higher rate of adipose tissue accretion is not necessarily disadvantageous in the preterm infant who has undergone a period of hypocaloric feeding because of illness, but the more immediate goals of parenteral feeding may be to enhance protein accretion (e.g., in the accessory muscles of respiration). Greater understanding of the metabolic consequences of various feeding regimens is needed.

Galactose

Galactose represents 50% of the monosaccharide present in lactose and thus is an important energy source in milk and an important metabolite of small intestinal digestion of lactose. Except for the inborn error, galactosemia, it seems that pediatric research has placed little emphasis on this important nutrient. After digestion of lactose by lactase, glucose and galactose are readily absorbed via the same carrier mechanism.[160] The fate of galactose in the enterocyte is not entirely understood, but it is assumed that more than 90% of the absorbed glucose and galactose reaches the portal vein.[160] The systemic concentration of galactose in normal infants is generally quite low (<30 mg/L). The liver removes most of the dietary galactose on first pass principally by converting it to glucose or glycogen.[30,160-163] It appears that galactose does not directly stimulate insulin secretion, but through conversion to glucose and via stimulation of GIP by enterally administered galactose, feeding this sugar may ultimately result in some insulin secretion. The response is thought to be slightly less than that for glucose, however.[30,160,164,165] Experimental galactose feeding, compared with glucose, seems to result in a preferential utilization of galactose for glycogen synthesis[160,162-165] and attenuated HGO.[165] Also, a 50% substitution of galactose for glucose in a parenteral infusion in preterm infants resulted in a lower blood glucose concentration, the elimination of glucosuria, and an increase in the carbohydrate infusion rate.[160,166] Thus, theoretically, it is possible that galactose administration either parenterally or as a component of lactose could have comparative advantages, relative to glucose infusion or glucose polymer feeding, respectively, in terms of suppression of HGO, control of hyperglycemia, and increased glycogen synthesis. However, it is unclear whether the hypothetical outcome of reduced insulin secretion would necessarily be advantageous. Moreover, questions remain about the safety of unphysiological doses of galactose due to suppressing effects on hepatic ATP levels.[162]

Selected Clinical Problems Associated with Carbohydrate Metabolism

Hyperglycemia

The definition of "clinically significant hyperglycemia" varies from center to center and study to study; upper-limit cut-offs indicating the need for reduced glucose infusion or insulin therapy include plasma glucose concentration >125 to 240 mg/dL (6.94 to 13.32 mmol/L) and/or urine glucose concentration >250 to 500 mg/dL (13.88 to 27.76 mmol/L).[1,23,35-37] On a practical basis, however, intervention for "hyperglycemia" depends on individual circumstances related to clinical progress (e.g., weight gain and fluid status). Hyperglycemia, with associated glucosuria and secondary limitation of carbohydrate energy intake, is common in preterm infants during intravenous infusion of glucose or parenteral nutrition.[1,25,166] Causes for hyperglycemia include inadequate insulin secretion, failure of glucose (via insulin secretion) to suppress HGO, and peripheral insulin resistance.[23,24] Besides prematurity per se, precipitating factors include high circulating levels of counter-regulatory hormones and the clinical conditions associated with such hormonal stimulation— e.g., intrauterine stress and growth retardation, sepsis, theophylline therapy, hypoxemia, and surgical stress.[1,25,26] Preterm infants usually have a relatively low renal threshold for glucose excretion which readily results in hyperglycemia-induced glucosuria.[166] Reduction in intravenous glucose infusion and insulin therapy are the only treatments currently employed.

Insulin therapy in preterm infants may be appropriate when: lipid infusion (as an alternative source of energy) is not feasible (e.g., because of high serum indirect bilirubin concentration); energy intake and growth have been severely restricted for 1 to 2 weeks (e.g., due to fluid restriction); the infant is thought to be hypermetabolic and/or already wasted (e.g., small-for-gestational-age infants or infants who have been severely ill). There have been several reports of retrospective analyses and clinical trials indicating that insulin therapy may be used successfully to treat severe hyperglycemia in preterm infants.[23,35-37] As shown by Collins et al.[37] in a controlled clinical trial, insulin therapy for plasma glucose >180 mg/dL (9.9 mmol/L) at birth in preterm infants 24 to 28 weeks gestation resulted in a 52% increase in the GIR, a 45% increase in nonprotein energy intake, and a 150% increase in weight gain over approximately 7 to 21 days of therapy. This report[37] also showed that insulin therapy, under very controlled study conditions, can be relatively safe in preterm infants: only 4 of 1,848 glucose determinations in the subjects receiving insulin were <40 mg/dL (2.2 mmol/L), and no clinical signs were associated with these episodes, which were easily treated with suspension of the insulin infusion.

Collins et al.[37] describe in detail a reasonable approach to infusing insulin, although insulin therapy is not the only option for managing the above-mentioned conditions. In theory, insulin is an important growth hormone and may suppress muscle proteolysis leading to greater lean tissue accretion.[167] Infants who develop hyperglycemia on relatively low parenteral glucose intakes may be stressed (e.g., with infection). One of the putative positive outcomes of insulin therapy in stressed patients could relate to insulin's stimulation of sodium/potassium pumps in muscle and its inhibition of glutamine efflux resulting in diminished muscle wasting.[168] Suppression of muscle proteolysis[167] is not necessarily a desirable outcome, however; one must bear in mind that glutamine, produced in muscle, is an important substrate both for intestine and for the immune system.[169] Even suppression of muscle proteolysis may not benefit the infected neonate suffering from temporary glucose intolerance. In addition, important unresolved questions remain about the effect of insulin therapy on growth and body composition (particularly protein accretion) in the preterm infant and about whether increased glucose utilization by insulin-sensitive tissues might deprive the brain of this important substrate.[37,166] One must consider, in particular, whether increased glucose intake is efficiently oxidized. As mentioned in the section Hepatic Glucose Output and Glucose Oxidation, glucose infused beyond the limit of oxidation may be converted to fat, especially in the liver, and this process, in addition to being inefficient from the standpoint of energy utilization, generates excessive carbon dioxide.[154,157-159,170,171] If the increased glucose uptake (and normalization of plasma glucose concentrations) induced by insulin therapy does not result in efficient generation of ATP, improved fat rather than protein accretion could result. Still, increased fat mass is not necessarily an adverse outcome if the infant is extremely preterm and born with limited fat reserves (and thus limited skin insulatory capacity).

The findings of Collins et al.[37] are intriguing and provocative, indicating that insulin therapy can be safe in a research setting. However, pending further study, this therapeutic approach should be considered strictly investigational, largely because of the obvious distinction between administering insulin to preterm infants for the purpose of increasing glucose energy intake and treating patients with diabetes mellitus who would otherwise suffer life-threatening ketoacidosis and protein wasting. Finally, one must caution against using insulin as just another modality of "nutritional support" in light of the numerous adverse outcomes associated with hyperinsulinism in utero, particularly in IDMs.

Hypoglycemia and the Infant of the Diabetic Mother

The definition of hypoglycemia tends to be based on statistical considerations related to the population being studied or on the risk of adverse clinical outcomes.[1,28] Thus, hypoglycemia has been defined statistically as plasma or serum glucose concentration ≤25 mg/dL (1.39 mmol/L) in sick preterm infants, <40 mg/dL (2.2 mmol/L) in well preterm infants, ≤35 mg/dL (1.94 mmol/L) in term infants ≤72 hours of age, and ≤45 mg/dL (2.50 mmol/L) in term infants >72 hours of age.[1] However defined, hypoglycemia may not be statistically associated with an increased risk of such acute "signs of hypoglycemia" as apnea, vomiting, jitteriness, and convulsions.[1,172] In the newborn, causes of hypoglycemia and the conditions associated with these causes include: (1) hyperinsulinemia: IDM, nesidioblastosis, islet cell adenoma, hemolytic disease of the newborn, exchange transfusion, Beckwith-Wiedemann Syndrome, maternal drug treatment (e.g., chlorpropamide, β-sympathomimetic tocolytic therapy, and benzothiazides); (2) deficient HGO: preterm birth, small for gestational age, asphyxia, cold stress, and sepsis; (3) lack of glycogen stores: preterm birth, small for gestational age; perinatal stress, glycogen storage disease (types 1, 3, and 4); (4) genetic defects in gluconeogenesis (e.g., glucose 6-phosphatatase deficiency; (5) impaired secretion of glucagon and catecholamines in response to hypoglycemia: IDM.[1,27–31]

Since there is poor correlation between the presence of signs and chemical hypoglycemia, therapy of hypoglycemia with glucose infusions, glucagon, steroids, or diazoxide should be based primarily on low plasma glucose concentration, e.g., <35 to 45 mg/dL

(1.9 to 2.5 mmol/L).[1,27,28] Details regarding the acute diagnostic workup and management of hypoglycemia in the newborn can be found in various review articles.[1,27,28] The use of glucose infusions and pharmacological treatment are discussed in the Recommendations section. One should bear in mind that MCT feeding may have a role in the treatment of infants with hypoglycemia since this will stimulate HGO.[38,135,136] Also, since galactose does not seem to directly stimulate insulin secretion and since its carbon skeleton is preferentially incorporated into glycogen (Fig. 4.1), an argument could be made that, theoretically, feeding this sugar in the form of lactose could have an advantageous effect in infants with hyperinsulinemia. Preferential synthesis of glycogen would not be beneficial in glycogen storage disease, however.

Mortality risk is increased in the IDM, and in addition to hypoglycemia, there are many clinical problems associated with the IDM syndrome, including macrosomia, congenital anomalies, metabolic abnormalities such as hypocalcemia and hypomagnesmia, hematologic abnormalities such as hyperbilirubinemia and polycythemia, increased risk for respiratory distress syndrome and deficient surfactant synthesis, and impaired postnatal growth and development.[1,27] In the IDM, it may be difficult to distinguish the effects of hypoglycemia per se from other factors (e.g., congenital anomalies) in the causation of developmental problems.[1] However, moderate hypoglycemia, defined as <46.8 mg/dL (2.6 mmol/L), was found in 433 of 661 preterm infants, and when this condition persisted for ≥5 days, there was increased risk for mental and motor impairment at 18 months of age.[172]

Bronchopulmonary Dysplasia

Infants with BPD may suffer acute protein-energy malnutrition and growth retardation in association with insufficient voluntary formula intake, fluid restriction, increased energy expenditure, and, possibly, ill-defined metabolic abnormalities which perhaps limit protein accretion in sick patients at any age.[32–34,168,173] The effects of nutrient intake on respiration are complex and involve more than just the relationship between protein accretion and respiratory muscle mass. For example, protein and amino acids tend to enhance the ventilatory response to carbon dioxide while carbohydrate intake may increase the RQ, i.e., the amount of carbon dioxide produced per amount of oxygen consumed (and thus per amount of ATP generated). An increase in the RQ could result in a disproportionate rise in carbohydrate production in a patient with ventilatory insufficiency, which in turn could lead to hypercarbia and reduced ventilatory effort.[174] In sick adult patients, glucose oxidation may be limited, and high rates of infusion of parenteral glucose can result in increased RQ, inefficient utilization of glucose for energy production, and increased hepatic fat synthesis.[170] Substitution of fat for carbohydrate in the nutritional support of patients with BPD could, then, have beneficial effects, as has been shown in adult patients with ventilatory insufficiency.[22,157] However, as mentioned above, insulin appears to be a very important anabolic hormone in states of health and illness, and it is not yet clear whether some infants with growth problems and BPD would benefit from specialized feedings with a lower carbohydrate content.

Suggestions for Future Research

There are several issues related to carbohydrate nutrition in the preterm infant that need to be addressed via clinical research: delineation of the capacity for small intestinal hydrolysis of lactose and its relationship to development; determination of the sites, small intestine versus colon, for carbohydrate fermentation in the preterm infant; the effects of insulin infusion in glucose intolerant infants on glucose oxidation, protein accretion, and body composition; and the relative level of carbohydrate that should be fed to infants with BPD. There is also a need for more expansive research into developmental aspects of carbohydrate nutrition and metabolism in the fetus and newborn. Such research could be carried out in animal models that in some cases would complement human studies.

The suggestion that feeding lactose, as opposed to glucose polymers, might have therapeutic benefit in infants with hyperinsulinemia should spur investigation of the metabolic fate of the galactose carbon skeleton, focusing on the rate at which dietary galactose-derived glucose appears in the peripheral circulation. At present, we have developed a dual stable isotope method for quantifying the rate of appearance of lactose-derived glucose into the peripheral circulation in relative terms.[71] Its use together with similar isotope models may provide insight into the capacity for intestinal lactose hydrolysis and glucose absorption at various postconceptional ages, the metabolic fate of galactose, and the nature of lactose absorption in the neonatal colon.[175]

Recommendations

Parenteral Nutrition

From the standpoint of carbohydrate intake, the two goals of parenteral feeding are (1) euglycemia and (2) optimal growth and body composition. If fluid, lipid, or glucose intolerance prevents these, preservation of lean body mass becomes the main objective. The "optimal" body composition and rate of growth in preterm infants is, of course, a matter of continued debate. While intrauterine weight and length gain are often achievable in healthy preterm infants receiving enteral feeding, fat accretion as a percentage of weight gain is frequently greater in these infants, although higher protein intakes as a percentage of calories seem to promote fat accretion rates similar to that of the fetus.[176-178] Presumably, glucose—as opposed to fat—if fully oxidized, would promote insulin secretion and protein anabolism on this basis, as well as provide energy for biosynthesis. If, on the other hand, glucose is not readily oxidized at high intakes—especially in sick preterm infants, for whom parenteral nutrition is particularly important—this fuel source would not be used optimally for energy, but instead would be converted to fat, especially in the liver, with an attendant increase in the RQ.[170,171] As already indicated, this dilemma has yet to be completely resolved. Available data[158,159] suggest that in older infants, the parenteral GIR should probably not exceed 18 g/kg/day and fat should be used to provide the remaining portion of the nonprotein energy requirement.[158] It may be necessary, though, to limit intake of presently available intravenous lipid emulsions to 3 g/kg/day for metabolic reasons (see Chapter 5) or because the indirect bilirubin or serum triglyceride is elevated; GIR may also need to be limited because of glucose intolerance. Recommendations that discriminate between preterm infants of various postconceptional age groups are unavailable due to lack of data. There has been some intriguing research involving the use of parenteral galactose,[160,166] but this remains an experimental consideration. Glucose should be the source of carbohydrate for routine parenteral nutrition.

In summary, for preterm infants in both birth-weight categories (<750 g and >750 g), the minimum glucose intake in infants receiving total parenteral nutrition is approximately 4 to 8 mg/kg/min, or the amount required to suppress HGO. The maximum GIR generally should not exceed 12.6 mg/kg/min.

Enteral Feeding

The goals of enteral feeding will be similar to those for parenteral feeding, with the addition of preventing or limiting gastric or abdominal distention, diarrhea, or lower gastrointestinal bleeding, and, of course, specific signs of NEC (e.g., pneumatosis intestinalis). Rapid progression of enteral feeding should probably be avoided, but there is no convincing evidence that the composition of the carbohydrate source (lactose versus other sugars) affects the risk of NEC.[6,109] Despite the importance of carbohydrate and wide agreement that some lactose intake may be beneficial,[50] there are no precise requirements for carbohydrate, glucose, and galactose with respect to the preterm infant. The level of carbohydrate present in mature human milk or bovine milk formulas is accepted as sufficient to support glucose needs as well as normal growth and development.[49] One might speculate that in preterm infants receiving total enteral nutrition, carbohydrate intake should be adequate to suppress gluconeogenesis, but there is no clear evidence even for this premise. Moreover, HGO in enterally fed infants will be determined both by the rate of entry of dietary hexose (especially glucose) reaching the liver and by insulin secretion. Thus, glucose homeostatis in preterm infants may be regulated in part by digestion and absorption of carbohydrates. It should be noted, however, that HGO has not been assessed in enterally fed preterm infants.

In the absence of specific information on carbohydrate requirements, one must conclude that either human milk, probably supplemented with minerals and protein,[177,178] or preterm infant formulas, containing mixtures of glucose polymer and lactose, are ideal from the standpoint of available feedings. Some lactose in the feeding is recommended both for teleological reasons and because if hydrolyzed, it may promote calcium absorption[18-21,50]; there is, however, no scientific basis for giving a precise minimum lactose intake for healthy preterm infants. Likewise, there is no strict recommendation for a maximum lactose intake in preterm infants without confirmed signs of lactose intolerance, except as dictated by energy, protein, and fat needs.

Specific minimum and maximum guidelines can be derived based on an estimated energy requirement of 120 kcal/kg/day, and the lactose concentration (g/100 kcal) of preterm human milk or preterm infant formulas available in various parts of the world (see Appendix, Table A.3). The guideline for minimum lactose intake would then correspond to the ingestion of Enfamil Premature Formula Special (Mead Johnson, Canada, 4.0 g/100 kcal): 4.8 g/kg/day. There is no particular basis for suggesting that this intake of lactose is inadequate. The intake of lactose associated with the other Mead Johnson, Ross, and Wyeth preterm infant formulas available in North America would be 4.8 to 5.5, 6.4, and 6.4 g/kg/day, respectively. There is no guideline for minimum intake of glucose polymer, but maximum glucose oligomer (polymer) intake would correspond to the ingestion of 8.4 g/kg/day of the Enfamil Premature Formula Special (7.0 g/100 kcal). The guideline for maximum lactose intake would depend in part on gestational age at birth, since the composition of human milk seems to vary depending on this factor. For infants with birthweights <750 g, the highest lactose intakes would be found in those ingesting human milk (approximately 9.3 g/100 kcal) or the PreNan formula (Nestle, 8.7 g/100 kcal) in the amount of

11.2 or 10.4 g/kg/day, respectively. For infants with birthweights >750 g, the highest lactose intake would be derived from the ingestion of human milk (9.8 g/100 kcal) in the amount of 11.8 g/kg/day.

These guidelines are appropriate for preterm infants at all stages of postnatal development: transitional (1 to 5 days of age), late transitional (6 days to 2 weeks), stable (2 weeks to term), and postdischarge (until 4 to 6 months). In this author's experience, enteral feeding prior to the late transitional period, especially in infants with birthweights <1,000 g, is likely to be minimal for various clinical reasons. In the early days of life, cardiorespiratory status and fluid tolerance as well as gross assessment of gastrointestinal function, especially gastric emptying, will be the most important factors governing the progression of enteral feedings—not the amount or source of carbohydrate per se. Occasionally, hypoglycemia may mandate reliance on parenteral glucose intake.

Lactose-free formulas should be used only for definite clinical indications, such as suspected protein allergy or watery diarrhea (associated with other signs of lactose intolerance). If possible, protein allergy should be documented by challenge, depending on the clinical picture. In the preterm infant, it is difficult to document lactose malabsorption except by formula manipulation, since stools often contain reducing substances, and breath hydrogen concentrations are high in lactose-fed infants without diarrhea.[64] The preterm infant must be considered at risk for lactose malabsorption, though, if watery stools are observed. Failure to increase blood glucose concentration associated with formula feeding could be a useful criterion for lactose intolerance, but clear guidelines are not available; moreover, coexistent abnormalities of HGO could obscure the interpretation of blood glucose measurement as an index of digestion. Our own work is too preliminary to determine if a stable isotope test will be a practical method for determining lactose digestibility.

Hypoglycemia

The possible benefits of feeding hypoglycemic infants MCTs and the theoretical advantages of feeding hyperinsulinemic infants lactose were discussed above. Treatment for hypoglycemia has been recommended when the plasma glucose is <35 to 45 mg/dL (1.9 to 2.5 mmol/L).[27,28] Although some endocrinologists recommend treating only infants with hypoglycemia fitting the definitions provided in the section Hypoglycemia and the Infant of the Diabetic Mother (e.g., plasma glucose concentration, ≤25 mg/dL) in the preterm infant, it seems reasonable to begin expectant treatment of infants at somewhat higher plasma glucose concentrations in view of the data indicating an association between developmental defects in infants with prolonged (≥5 days) periods of plasma glucose concentration <46.8 mg/dL (2.6 mmol/L).[172] Also, since there may be a lag between discovery of hypoglycemia and initiation of treatment, it seems reasonable to maintain a target range for initiating treatment of hypoglycemia that exceeds the statistical level of abnormality. Once the decision to specifically treat is made, glucose should be infused at a concentration of 10 to 15 g/dL (0.56 to 0.83 mol/L) at an initial rate sufficient to provide approximately 4 to 6 mg/kg/min (.022 to .033 mmol/kg/min). Larger infusion rates (e.g., 10 to 12 mg/kg/min) may be required in infants with hyperinsulinemia. Although intravenous glucose should be the treatment of choice,[27] if this is insufficient to correct hypoglycemia or if intravenous access is not readily available, glucagon (30 to 300 μg/kg/IM dose), diazoxide (10 to 15 mg/kg/day), and steroids (hydrocortisone 5 mg/kg/day or prednisone 2 mg/kg/day) also have been used to treat severe hypoglycemia.[1] A long-acting analog of somatostatin, octreotide acetate (Sandostatin®, Sandoz Pharmaceuticals Corp, East Hanover, NJ) is particularly useful in treating infants with hyperinsulinism. In cases of severe, recurrent, or intractable hypoglycemia, endocrinology consultation is recommended in order to initiate thorough diagnostic investigation.

Hyperglycemia

As reviewed above, there are too many important unanswered questions about the effect of insulin in the nondiabetic, preterm infant to warrant its routine use for the sole purpose of effecting greater rates of growth (via higher energy intake).[37] A more cautious approach may be to substitute parenteral glucose with lipid if possible.

CASE STUDY _____

A preterm infant girl was born at 34 weeks gestation (1,425 g). Enteral feedings, consisting of supplemented human milk, were started on day 4 of life. At age 14 days, she underwent surgical ligation of a patent ductus arteriosus, and from day 14 to 21, she was fed mainly by total parenteral nutrition and received systemic ampicillin and gentamicin. Complete enteral feeding with human milk was resumed on day 26 (weight: 1,370 g; energy intake: 117 kcal/kg/day). She exhibited loose stools from day 26 to 32. Breath hydrogen concentration was measured on day 26 for suspected lactose intolerance; the average value between feedings was only 7 ppm. On day 32, when the stool frequency and consistency appeared normal, the comparable breath hydrogen concentration was 66 ppm (weight: 1,530 g; 131 kcal/kg/day). It is likely that changes in stool pattern in this infant ("loose stools") were a consequence of un-

fermented lactose in the colon: relative lack of lactose fermentation was evidenced by the low breath hydrogen concentration. One can speculate that disruption of normal enteral feeding, and perhaps also antibiotic therapy, were associated with a reduction of colon bacteria flora capable of fermenting, and thus salvaging, undigested lactose reaching the colon. Presumably, as feeding progressed and the bacterial flora re-established itself in the colon, undigested lactose was fermented to absorbable SCFAs. Increased fermentation activity was evidenced by higher breath hydrogen concentration at 32 days versus 26 days.

Although our recent preliminary work suggests that more than 80% of dietary lactose is hydrolyzed to glucose and galactose by 34 weeks postconceptional age, it is probable that some lactose reached the colon in this infant. This case illustrates that in preterm infants, high breath hydrogen concentration does not necessarily indicate clinical intolerance to lactose, and in fact, the inverse may be true. The case illustrates, too, that mild diarrhea in preterm infants, particularly when it occurs in the context of recent introduction of enteral feeding, does not always necessitate a change in feeding. In this infant, in spite of loose stools, persistent and progressive feeding of human milk was associated with weight gain and eventual normalization of stool frequency.

Acknowledgments

The work described in this paper was supported in part by NIH Grant HD 19773 and the Children's Hospital Research Foundation. The author appreciates the thoughtful comments of Dr. Guy Putet regarding the possible clinical role of lipid in glucose homeostatis in the preterm infant.

References

1. Cowett RM. Pathophysiology, diagnosis, and management of glucose homeostatis in the neonate. *Curr Prob Pediatr* 1985;15:1–47.
2. Ferre P, Decaux JF, Issad T, Girard J. Changes in energy metabolism during the suckling and weaning period in the newborn. *Reprod Nutr Dev* 1986;26:619–631.
3. Cremer JE. Substrate utilization and brain development. *J Cerebral Blood Flow Metab* 1982;2:394–407.
4. Doyle LW, Nahmias C, Firnau G, Kenyon DB, Garnett ES, Sinclair JC. Regional cerebral glucose metabolism of newborn infants measured by positron emission tomography. *Devel Med Child Neurol* 1983;25:143–151.
5. Kien CL, Heitlinger LA, Li BU, Murray RD. Digestion, absorption, and fermentation of carbohydrates. *Semin Perinatol* 1989;13:78–87.
6. Kien CL. Colonic fermentation of carbohydrate in the premature infant: possible relevance to necrotizing enterocolitis. *J Pediatr* 1990;117:S52–S58.
7. Rocchini AP, Key J, Bondie D, et al. The effect of weight loss on the sensitivity of blood pressure to sodium in obese adolescents. *N Engl J Med* 1989;321:580–585.
8. DeHaven J, Sherwin R, Hendler R, Felig P. Nitrogen and sodium balance and sympathetic-nervous-system activity in obese subjects treated with a low-calorie protein or mixed diet. *N Engl J Med* (1980;302:477–482.
9. Fukagawa NK, Minaker KL, Rowe JW, et al. Insulin-mediated reduction of whole body protein breakdown:

dose-response effects on leucine metabolism in post-absorptive men. *J Clin Invest* 1985;76:2306–2311.

10. Abumrad NN, Jefferson LS, Rannels SR, Williams PE, Cherrington AD, Lacy WW. Role of insulin in the regulation of leucine kinetics in the conscious dog. *J Clin Invest* 1981;70:1031–1041.

11. Flakoll PJ, Kulaylat M, Frexes-Steed M, et al. Amino acids augment insulin's suppression of whole body proteolysis. *Am J Physiol* 1989;257:E839–E847.

12. Millward DJ, Odedra B, Bates PC. The role of insulin, corticosterone and other factors in the acute recovery of muscle protein synthesis on refeeding food-deprived rats. *Biochem J* 1983;216:583–587.

13. McNurlan MA, Garlick PJ. Influence of nutrient intake on protein turnover. *Diabetes/Metab Rev* 1989;5:165–189.

14. Balsam A, Ingbar SH. The influence of fasting, diabetes, and several pharmacological agents on the pathways of thyroxine metabolism in rat liver. *J Clin Invest* 1978;62:415–424.

15. Azizi F. Effect of dietary composition on fasting-induced changes in serum thyroid hormones and thyrotropin. *Metabolism* 1978;27:935–942.

16. Otten MH, Hennemann G, Docter R, Visser TJ. The role of dietary fat in peripheral thyroid hormone metabolism. *Metabolism* 1980;29:930–935.

17. Snyder DK, Clemmons DR, Underwood LE. Dietary carbohydrate content determines responsiveness to growth hormone in energy-restricted humans. *J Clin Endocrinol Metab* 1989;69:745–752.

18. Ziegler EE, Fomon SJ. Lactose enhances mineral absorption in infancy. *J Pediatr Gastroenterol Nutr* 1983;2:288–294.

19. Wirth FH, Numerof B, Pleban P, Neylan MJ. Effect of lactose on mineral absorption in preterm infants. *J Pediatr* 1990;117:283–287.

20. Griessen M, Speich PV, Infante F, et al. Effect of absorbable and nonabsorbable sugars on intestinal calcium absorption in humans. *Gastroenterology* 1989;96:864–872.

21. Griessen M, Cochet B, Infante F, et al. Calcium absorption from milk in lactase-deficient subjects. *Am J Clin Nutr* 1989;49:377–384.

22. Askanazi J, Rosenbaum SH, Hyman AI, Silverberg PA, Milic-Emili J, Kinney JM. Respiratory changes induced by the large glucose loads of total parenteral nutrition. *JAMA* 1980;243:1444.

23. Kanarek KS, Santeiro ML, Malone JI. Continuous infusion of insulin in hyperglycemic low-birth weight infants receiving parenteral nutrition with and without lipid emulsion. *JPEN* 1991;15:417–420.

24. King RA, Smith RM, Dahlenburg GW. Long term postnatal development of insulin secretion in early premature infants. *Early Hum Dev* 1986;13:285–294.

25. Hay WW, Sparks JW. Placental, fetal, and neonatal carbohydrate metabolism. *Clin Obstet Gynecol* 1985;28:473–485.

26. Anand KJS, Hickey PR, Hansen DD. Hormonal-metabolic stress responses in neonates undergoing cardiac surgery. *Anesthesiology* 1990;73:661–670.

27. Tsang RC, Ballard J, Braun C. The infant of the diabetic mother: today and tomorrow. *Clin Obstet Gynecol* 1981;24:125–147.

28. Ogata ES. Carbohydrate metabolism in the fetus and neonate and altered neonatal glucoregulation. *Pediatr Clin North Am* 1986;33:25–45.

29. Kalhan SC, Savin SM, Adam PAJ. Attenuated glucose production rate in newborn infants of insulin dependent diabetic mothers. *N Engl J Med* 1977;296:375–376.

30. Hay WW. Fetal and neonatal glucose homeostatis and their relation to the small for gestational age infant. *Semin Perinatol* 1984;8:101–116.

31. Mehta A, Wootton R, Cheng KN, Penfold P, Halliday D, Stacey TE. Effect of diazoxide or glucagon on hepatic glucose production rate during extreme neonatal hypoglycaemia. *Arch Dis Child* 1987;62:924–930.

32. Yeh TF, McClenan DA, Ajayi OA, Pildes RS. Metabolic rate and energy balance in infants with bronchopulmonary dysplasia. *J Pediatr* 1989;114:448–451.

33. Kurzner SI, Garg M, Bautista DB, Sargent CW, Bowman CM, Keens TG. Growth failure in bronchopulmonary dysplasia: elevated metabolic rates and pulmonary mechanics. *J Pediatr* 1988;112:73–80.

34. Yunis K, Oh W. Effects of intravenous glucose loading on oxygen consumption, carbon dioxide production, and resting energy expenditure in infants with bronchopulmonary dysplasia. *J Pediatr* 1989;115:127–132.

35. Vaucher YE, Walson PD, Morrow G III. Continuous insulin infusion in hyperglycemic, very low birth weight infants. *J Pediatr Gastroenterol Nutr* 1982;1:211–217.

36. Binder ND, Raschko PK, Benda GI, Reynolds JW. Insulin infusion with parenteral nutrition in extremely low birth weight infants with hyperglycemia. *J Pediatr* 1989;114:273–280.

37. Collins JW, Hoppe M, Brown K, Edidin DV, Padbury J, Ogata ES. A controlled trial of insulin infusion and parenteral nutrition in extremely low birth weight infants with glucose intolerance. *J Pediatr* 1991;118:921–927.

38. Girard J. Control of fetal and neonatal glucose metabolism by pancreatic hormones. *Clin Endocrin Metab* 1989;3:817–836.

39. Economides DL, Proudler A, Nicolaides KH. Plasma insulin in appropriate- and small-for-gestational-age fetuses. *Am J Obstet Gynecol* 1989;160:1091–1094.

40. Underwood LE, D'ercole AJ. Insulin and insulin-like growth factors/somatomedins in fetal and neonatal development. *Clin Endocrinol Metab* 1984;13:69–89.

41. Liechty EA, Denne SC, Lemons JA, Kien CL. Effects of glucose infusion on leucine transamination and oxidation in the ovine fetus. *Pediatr Res* 1991;30:423–429.

42. Townsend SF, Rudolph CD, Wood CE, Rudolph AM. Perinatal onset of hepatic gluconeogenesis in the lamb. *J Devel Physiol* 1989;12:329–335.

43. Ktorza A, Bihoreau MT, Nurjhan N, Picon L, Girard J. Insulin and glucagon during the perinatal period: secretion and metabolic effects on the liver. *Biol Neonate* 1985;48:204–220.

44. Sperling MA, Ganguli S, Leslie N, Landt K. Fetal-perinatal catecholamine secretion: role in perinatal glucose homeostatis. *Am J Physiol* 1984;247:E69–E74.

45. Knip M, Puukka R, Lautala P, Leppilampi M, Puukka M. Basal insulin secretion and erythrocyte insulin binding in preterm and term newborn infants. *Biol Neonate* 1983;43:172–180.

46. Adrian TE, Lucas A, Bloom SR, Aynsley-Green A. Growth hormone response to feeding in term and preterm neonates. *Acta Paediatr Scand* 1983;72:251–254.

47. Murphy LJ. Impaired estrogen-induced uterine insulin-like growth factor-I gene expression in the streptozotocin diabetic rat. *Diabetologia* 1988;31:842–847.

48. Grasso S, Fallucca F, Romeo MG, Distefano G, Sciullo E, Reitano G. Glucagon and insulin secretion in low birthweight preterm infants. *Acta Paediatr Scand* 1990;79:280–285.

49. Fomon SJ, Filer LJ. Milks and formulas. In: Fomon SJ, ed. *Infant nutrition*. 2nd ed. Philadelphia: WB Saunders, 1974:359–407.

50. Committee on Nutrition of the Preterm Infant, European Society of Paediatric Gastroenterology and Nutrition. *Nu-*

trition and feeding of preterm infants. Oxford, UK: Blackwell Scientific Publications, 1987.

51. Lepage G, Collet S, Bougle D, et al. The composition of preterm milk in relation to the degree of prematurity. *Am J Clin Nutr* 1984;40:1042–1049.

52. Kien CL, Sumners JE, Stetina JS, Heimler R, Grausz JP. A method for assessing carbohydrate energy absorption and its application to premature infants. *Am J Clin Nutr* 1982;36:910–916.

53. Williams PR. Comparison of glucose tolerance and insulin response of full-term and preterm infants fed glucose polymers. In: Sauls HS, Benson JD, eds. *Meeting nutritional goals for low-birth-weight infants*. Proceedings of the Second Ross Clinical Research Conference. Columbus, OH: Ross Laboratories, 1982:87–89.

54. Antonowicz I, Lebenthal E. Developmental pattern of small intestinal enterokinase and disaccharidase activities in the human fetus. *Gastroenterology* 1977;72:1299–1303.

55. Keene, MFL, Hewer EE. Digestive enzymes of the human fetus. *Lancet* 1929;1:767–769.

56. Track NS, Creutzfeldt C, Bockermann M. Enzymatic, functional and ultrastructural development of the exocrine pancreas. *Comp Biochem Physiol* 1975;51:95–100.

57. Davis MM, Hodes ME, Munsick RA. Pancreatic amylase expression in human development. *Hybridoma* 1986;5:137–145.

58. Jirsova V, Koldovsky O, Heringova A. The development of the functions of the small intestine of the human fetus. *Biol Neonate* 1965;9:44–49.

59. McNeish AS, Mayne A, Ducker DA, Hughes CA. Development of D-glucose absorption in the perinatal period. *J Pediatr Gastroenterol Nutr* 1983;2 (suppl):S222–S226.

60. Tucker NT, Hodge C, Choi T, Lee P, Prihoda TJ, Lebenthal E. Postprandial glucose and insulin responses to glucose polymers by premature infants. *Biol Neonate* 1987;52:198–204.

61. Auricchio S, Rubino A, Murset G. Intestinal glycosidase activities in the human embryo, fetus, and newborn. *Pediatrics* 1963;35:944–954.

62. Antonowicz I, Chang SK, Grand RJ. Development and distribution of lysosomal enzymes and disaccharidases in human fetal intestine. *Gastroenterology* 1974;67:51–58.

63. Mobassaleh M, Montgomery RK, Biller JA, Grand RJ. Development of carbohydrate absorption in the fetus and neonate. *Pediatrics* 1985;75:160–166.

64. Kien CL, Liechty EA, Myerberg DZ, Mullett MD. Dietary carbohydrate assimilation in the premature infant: evidence for a nutritionally significant bacterial ecosystem in the colon. *Am J Clin Nutr* 1987;46:456–460.

65. Kien CL, Liechty EA, Mullett MD. Effects of lactose intake on nutritional status in premature infants. *J Pediatr* 1990;116:446–449.

66. Kien CL, Kepner J, Grotjohn KA, Gilbert MM, McClead RE. Efficient assimilation of lactose carbon in premature infants. *J Pediatr Gastroenterol Nutr* 1992;15:253–259.

67. Murray RD, Boutton TW, Klein PD, Gilbert M, Paule CL MacLean WC Jr. Comparative absorption of 13C-glucose and 13C-lactose by premature infants. *Am J Clin Nutr* 1990;51:59–66.

68. Cicco R, Holzman IR, Brown DR, Becker DJ. Glucose polymer tolerance in premature infants. *Pediatrics* 1981;67:498–501.

69. Boellner SW, Beard AG, Panos TC. Impairment of intestinal hydrolysis of lactose in newborn infants. *Pediatrics* 1965;36:542–549.

70. Jarrett EC, Holman GH. Lactose absorption in the premature infant. *Arch Dis Child* 1966;41:525–527.

71. Kien CL, Ault K, McClead RE. In vivo estimation of lactose hydrolysis in premature infants using a dual stable tracer technique. *Am J Physiol* 1992;263(*Endocrinol Metab* 26):E1002–E1009.

72. Weaver LT, Laker MF, Nelson R. Neonatal intestinal lactase activity. *Arch Dis Child* 1986;61:896–899.

73. Fosbrooke AS, Wharton BA. "Added lactose" and "added sucrose" cow's milk formulae in nutrition of low birthweight babies. *Arch Dis Child* 1975;50:409–418.

74. Kien CL, Liechty EA, Myerberg DZ, Mullett MD. Effects in premature infants of normalizing breath H_2 concentrations with CO_2: increased H_2 concentration and reduced interaliquot variation. *J Pediatr Gastroenterol Nutr* 1987;6:286–289.

75. MacLean WC Jr, Fink BB. Lactose malabsorption by premature infants: magnitude and clinical significance. *J Pediatr* 1980;97:383–388.

76. Hyams JS, Stafford RJ, Grand RJ, Watkins JB. Correlation of lactose breath hydrogen test, intestinal morphology, and lactase activity in young children. *J Pediatr* 1980;97:609–612.

77. Florent C, Flourie B, Leblond A, et al. Influence of chronic lactulose ingestion on the colonic metabolism of lactulose in man (an in vivo study). *J Clin Invest* 1985;75:608–613.

78. Modler S, Kerner JA Jr, Castillo RO, Vreman HJ, Stevenson DK. Relationship between breath and total body hydrogen excretion rates in neonates. *J Pediatr Gastroenterol Nutr* 1988;7:554–558.

79. Kien CL, Liechty EA, Mullett MD. Contribution of low molecular weight compounds to the fecal excretion of carbohydrate energy in premature infants. *Gastroenterology* 1990;99:165–174.

80. Kien CL, Kepner J, Grotjohn K, Ault K, McClead RE. Stable isotope model for estimating colonic acetate production in premature infants. *Gastroenterology* 1991;102:1458–1466.

81. Murray RD, McClung HJ, Li BUK. Short-chain fatty acid profile in the colon of newborn piglets using fecal water analysis. *Pediatr Res* 1987;22:720–724.

82. Saunders DR, Wiggins HS. Conservation of mannitol, lactulose, and raffinose by the human colon. *Am J Physiol* 1981;241:G397–G402.

83. Ruppin H, Bar-Meir S, Soergel KH, et al. Absorption of short-chain fatty acids by the colon. *Gastroenterology* 1980;78:1500–1507.

84. Garcia J, Smith FR, Cucinell SA. Urinary D-lactate excretion in infants with necrotizing enterocolitis. *J Pediatr* 1984;104:268–270.

85. Levitt MD. Production and excretion of hydrogen gas in man. *N Engl J Med* 1969;281:122–127.

86. Koruda MJ, Rolandelli RH, Settle RG, Zimmaro DM, Rombeau JL. Effect of parenteral nutrition supplemented with short-chain fatty acids on adaptation to massive small bowel resection. *Gastroenterology* 1988;95:715–720.

87. Roediger WEW. Utilization of nutrients by isolated epithelial cells of the rat colon. *Gasteoenterology* 1982;83:424–429.

88. Sakata T, Yajima T. Influence of short chain fatty acids on the epithelial cell division of the digestive tract. *Q J Exp Physiol* 1984;69:639–648.

89. Harig JM, Soergel KH, Komorowski RA, Wood CM. Treatment of diversion colitis with short-chain-fatty acid irrigation. *N Engl J Med* 1989;320:23–28.

90. Kripke SA, Fox AD, Berman JM, Settle RG, Rombeau JL. Stimulation of intestinal mucosal growth with intra-

colonic infusion of short-chain fatty acids. *JPEN* 1989; 13:109–116.

91. Argenzio RA, Miller N, von Engelhardt W. Effect of volatile fatty acids on water and ion absorption from the goat colon. *Am J Physiol* 1975;229:997–1002.

92. Anderson JW, Bridges SR. Short-chain fatty acid fermentation products of plant fiber affect glucose metabolism of isolated rat hepatocytes (41958). *Proc Soc Exp Biol Med* 1984;177:372–376.

93. Whitton PD, Rodrigues LM, Hems DA. Stimulation by acetate of gluconeogenesis in hepatocyte suspensions. *FEBS Lett* 1979;98:85–87.

94. Chan TM, Freedland RA. The effect of propionate on the metabolism of pyruvate and lactate in the perfused rat liver. *Biochem J* 1972;127:539–543.

95. Blair JB, Cook DE, Lardy HA. Interaction of propionate and lactate in the perfused rat liver: effects of glucagon and oleate. *J Biol Chem* 1973;248:3608–3614.

96. Scheppach W, Wiggins HS, Halliday D, et al. Effect of gut-derived acetate on glucose turnover in man. *Clin Sci* 1988;75:363–370.

97. Winick M. Malnutrition and brain development. *J Pediatr* 1969;74:667–679.

98. Rush D, Stein Z, Susser M. A randomized controlled trial of prenatal nutritional supplementation in New York City. *Pediatrics* 1980;65:683–697.

99. Vuori L, Christiansen N, Clement J, Mora JO, Wagner M, Herrera MG. Nutritional supplementation and the outcome of pregnancy, II: visual habituation at 15 days. *Am J Clin Nutr* 1979;32:463–469.

100. Lucas A, Morley R, Cole TJ, et al. Early diet in preterm babies and developmental status at 18 months. *Lancet* 1990;335:1477–1481.

101. Lucas A, Morley R, Cole TJ, et al. Early diet in preterm babies and developmental status in infancy. *Arch Dis Child* 1989;64:1570–1578.

102. Murray RD, Boutton TW, Klein PD, Gilbert M, Paule CL, MacLean WC. Comparative absorption of [13C]glucose and [13C]lactose by premature infants. *Am J Clin Nutr* 1990;51:59–66.

103. Grossklaus R. Energy gap? *Nutr Res* 1983;3:595–604.

104. Book LS, Herbst JJ, Atherton SO, Jung AL. Necrotizing entercolitis in low-birth-weight infants fed an elemental formula. *J Pediatr* 1975;87:602–605.

105. Book LS, Herbst JJ, Jung AL. Carbohydrate malabsorption in necrotizing enterocolitis. *Pediatrics* 1976;57: 201–204.

106. Kirschner BS, Lahr C, Lahr D, Madden J, Rosenberg IH. Detection of increased breath hydrogen in infants with necrotizing enterocolitis [Abstract]. *Gastroenterology.* 1977;72:A-57/1080.

107. Cheu HW, Brown DR, Rowe MI. Breath hydrogen excretion as a screening test for the early diagnosis of necrotizing enterocolitis. *Am J Dis Child* 1989;143:156–159.

108. Godoy G, Philips J, Price J, et al. Breath hydrogen in premature infants [Abstract]. *Pediatr Res* 1985;19:342A.

109. Uauy RD, Fanaroff AA, Korones SB, Phillips EA, Phillips JB, Wright LL. Necrotizing enterocolitis in very low birth weight infants: biodemographic and clinical correlates. *J Pediatr* 1991;119:630–638.

110. Perman JA, Waters LA, Harrison MR, Yee ES, Heldt GP. Breath hydrogen reflects canine intestinal ischemia. *Pediatr Res* 1981;15:1229–1233.

111. Clark DA, Thompson JE, Weiner LB, McMillan JA, Schneider AJ, Rokahr JE. Necrotizing enterocolitis: intraluminal biochemistry in human neonates and a rabbit model. *Pediatr Res* 1985;19:919–921.

112. Clark DA, Miller MJS. Intraluminal pathogenesis of necrotizing enterocolitis: a hypothetical model. *J Pediatr* 1990;117:S64–S67.

113. Fulks RM, Li JB, Goldberg AL. Effects of insulin, glucose, and amino acids on protein turnover in rat diaphragm. *J Biol Chem* 1975;250:290–298.

114. Clemmons DR, Underwood LE, Dickerson RN, et al. Use of plasma somatomedin-C/insulin-like growth factor I measurements to monitor the response to nutritional repletion in malnourished patients. *Am J Clin Nutr* 1985;41:191–198.

115. Soliman AT, Hassan AEHI, Aref MK, Hintz RL, Rosenfeld RG, Rogol AD. Serum insulin-like growth factors I and II concentrations and growth hormone and insulin responses to arginine infusion in children with protein-energy malnutrition before and after nutritional rehabilitation. *Pediatr Res* 1986;20:1122–1130.

116. Mabry CC. Permanent growth impairment due to early deprivation of insulin in juvenile onset diabetes mellitus [Abstract]. *Pediatr Res* 1979;13:478.

117. Heinze E, Beischer W, Teller WM. Insulin secretion in growth hormone deficient children and the effect of the sulfonyluria drug glebenclamide on linear growth. *Eur J Pediatr* 1978;128:41–48.

118. Farber S. Pancreatic function and disease in early life. *Virchows Arch Pathol Anat* 1944;37:238–250.

119. Larrson Y. The islets of Langerhans in pancreatic fibrosis. *Pediatrics* 1958;21:893–902.

120. Yalow RS, Block H, Vilazon M, Berson SA. Comparison of plasma insulin levels following administration of tolbutamide and glucose. *Diabetes* 1960;9:356–362.

121. Varsano-Aharon N, Echemendia E, Yalow RS, Berson SA. Early insulin response to glucose and tolbutamide in maturity-onset diabetes. *Metabolism* 1970;19:409–417.

122. Aynsley-Green A. Plasma hormone concentrations during enteral and parenteral nutrition in the human newborn. *J Pediatr Gastroenterol Nutr* 1983;2:S108–S112.

123. Aynsley-Green A, Adrian TE, Bloom SR. Feeding and the development of enteroinsular hormone secretion in the preterm infant: effects of continuous gastric infusions of human milk compared with intermittent boluses. *Acta Paediatr Scand* 1982;71:379–383.

124. Hetenyi G, Cowan JS. Glucoregulation in the newborn. *Can J Physiol Pharmacol* 1980;58:879–888.

125. Grasso S, Fallucca F, Mazzone D, Giangrande L, Romeo MG, Reitano G. Inhibition of glucagon secretion in the human newborn by glucose infusion. *Diabetes* 1983; 32:489–492.

126. Lucas A, Boyes S, Bloom SR, Anysley-Green A. Metabolic and endocrine responses to a milk feed in six-day-old term infants: differences between breast and cow's milk formula feeding. *Acta Paediatr Scand* 1981;70:195–200.

127. Lucas A, Bloom SR, Aynsley-Green A. Metabolic and endocrine events at the time of the first feed of human milk in preterm and term infants. *Arch Dis Child* 1991;53: 731–736.

128. Aynsley-Green A, Bloom SR, Williamson DH, Turner RC. Endocrine and metabolic response in the human newborn to first feed of breast milk. *Arch Dis Child* 1977; 52:291–295.

129. Lucas A, Bloom SR, Aynsley-Green A. Metabolic and endocrine consequences of depriving preterm infants of enteral nutrition. *Acta Paediatr Scand* 1983;72:245–249.

130. Aynsley-Green A, Lucas A, Bloom SR. The effect of feeds of differing composition on entero-insular hormone secretion in the first hours of life in human neonates. *Acta Paediatr Scand* 1979;68:265–270.

131. Lucas A, Blackburn AM, Aynsley-Green A, Sarson DL, Adrian TE, Bloom SR. Breast vs bottle: endocrine responses are different with formula feedings. *Lancet* 1980; 1:1267–1269.

132. Calvert SA, Soltesz G, Jenkins PA, et al. Feeding premature infants with human milk or preterm milk formula. *Biol Neonate* 1985;47:189–198.

133. Zetterstrom R, Ginsburg BE, Lindblad BS, Persson B. Relation between protein intake, plasma valine, and insulin secretion during early infancy. *Klin Padiat* 1985; 197:371–374.

134. Androikou S, Hanning I. Parenteral nutrition effect on serum insulin in the preterm infant. *Pediatrics* 1987; 80:693–697.

135. Sann L, Divry P, Lasne Y, Ruitton A. Effect of oral lipid administration on glucose homeostatis in small-for-gestational-age infants. *Acta Paediatr Scand* 1982; 71: 923–927.

136. Bougneres PF, Castano L, Rocchicioli F, Pham GH, Leluyer B, Ferre P. Medium-chain fatty acids increase glucose production in normal and low birth weight newborns. *Am J Physiol* 1989;256:E692–E697.

137. Bougneres PE. Influence de l'oxydation de substrats lipidiques sur la production neonatale de glucose. *Ann Pediatr (Paris)* 1988;35:449.

138. Vileisis RA, Cowett RM, Oh W. Glycemic response to lipid infusion in the premature neonate. *J Pediatr* 1982; 100:108–112.

139. Yunis KA, Kalhan S, Oh W, Cowett RM. Mechanism of glucose perturbation following intravenous fat infusion in the low birthweight infant. *Pediatr Res* 1989;25:299A.

140. Thiebaud D, DeFronzo RA, Jacot E, et al. Effect of long chain triglyceride infusion on glucose metabolism in man. *Metabolism* 1982;31:1128–1136.

141. Wolfe RR, Jahoor F, Hartl WH. Protein and amino acid metabolism after injury. *Diabetes/Metab Rev* 1989;5: 149–164.

142. Cowett RM, Oh W, Schwartz R. Persistent glucose production during glucose infusion in the neonate. *J Clin Invest* 1983;71:467–475.

143. Lafeber HN, Sulkers EJ, Chapman TE, Sauer PJJ. Glucose production and oxidation in preterm infants during total parenteral nutrition. *Pediatr Res* 1990;28:153–157.

144. Kalhan SC, Bier DM, Savin SM, Adam PA. Estimation of glucose turnover and 13C recycling in the human newborn by simultaneous [1-13C] glucose and [6,6-2H2] glucose tracers. *J Clin Endocrinol Metab* 1980;50:456–460.

145. Bier DM, Leake RD, Haymond MW, et al. Measurement of "true" glucose production rates in infancy and childhood with 6,6-dideuteroglucose. *Diabetes* 1977;26: 1016–1023.

146. Denne SC, Kalhan SC. Glucose carbon recycling and oxidation in human newborns. *Am J Physiol* 1986;251: E71–E77.

147. Kalhan SC, Oliven A, King KC, Lucero C. Role of glucose in the regulation of endogenous glucose production in the human newborn. *Pediatr Res* 1986;20:49–52.

148. Kalhan SC, Savin SM, Adam PA. Measurement of glucose turnover in the human newborn with glucose 1-13C. *J Clin Endocrinol Metab* 1976;43:704–707.

149. Zarlengo KM, Battaglia FC, Fennessey P, Hay WW. Relationship between glucose utilization rate and glucose concentration in preterm infants. *Biol Neonate* 1986; 49:181–189.

150. Cowett RM, Susa JB, Oh W, Schwartz R. Glucose kinetics in glucose-infused small for gestational age infants. *Pediatr Res* 1984;18:74–79.

151. Cowett RM, Andersen GE, Maguire CA, Oh W. Ontogeny of glucose homeostatis in low birth weight infants. *J Pediatr* 1988;112:462–465.

152. King KC, Tserng K, Kalhan SC. Regulation of glucose production in newborn infants of diabetic mothers. *Pediatr Res* 1982;16:608–612.

153. Knip M, Akerblom HK. Plasma C-peptide and insulin in neonates, infants, and children. *J Pediatr* 1981;99: 103–105.

154. Sauer PJJ, Van Aerde JEE, Pencharz PB, Smith JM, Swyer PR. Glucose oxidation rates in newborn infants measured with indirect calorimetry and [U-13C] glucose. *Clin Sci* 1986;70:587–593.

155. Goldman SL, Hirata T. Attenuated response to insulin in very low birthweight infants. *Pediatr Res* 1980;14: 50–53.

156. King KC, Oliven A, Kalhan SC. Functional enteroinsular axis in full-term newborn infants. *Pediatr Res* 1989;25: 490–495.

157. Van Aerde JEE, Sauer PJJ, Pencharz PB, Smith JM, Swyer PR. Effect of replacing glucose with lipid on the energy metabolism of newborn infants. *Clin Sci* 1989;76: 581–588.

158. Bresson JL, Narcy P, Putet G, Ricour C, Sachs C, Rey J. Energy substrate utilization in infants receiving total parenteral nutrition with different glucose to fat ratios. *Pediatr Res* 1989;25:645–648.

159. Bresson JL, Bader B, Rocchiccioli F, et al. Protein-metabolism kinetics and energy-substrate utilization in infants fed parenteral solutions with different glucose-fat ratios. *Am J Clin Nutr* 1991;54:370–376.

160. Kliegman RM, Sparks JW. Perinatal galactose metabolism. *J Pediatr* 1985;107:831–841.

161. Kaempf JW, Li H-Q, Groothuis JR, Battaglia FC, Zerbe GO, Sparks JW. Galactose, glucose, and lactate concentrations in the portal venous and arterial circulations of newborn lambs after nursing. *Pediatr Res* 1988;23: 598–602.

162. Kliegman RM, Morton S. Sequential intrahepatic metabolic effects of enteric galactose alimentation in newborn rats. *Pediatr Res* 1988;24:302–307.

163. Kunst C, Kliegman R, Trindade C. The glucose-galactose paradox in neonatal murine hepatic glycogen synthesis. *Am J Physiol* 1989;257:E697–E703.

164. Kliegman RM, Miettinen EL, Kalhan SC, Adam PAJ. The effect of enteric galactose on neonatal canine carbohydrate metabolism. *Metabolism* 1981;30:1109–1118.

165. Kliegman RM, Miettinen EL, Morton S. Potential role of galactokinase in neonatal carbohydrate assimilation. *Science* 1983;220:302–304.

166. Sparks JW, Avery GB, Fletcher AB, Simmons MA, Glinsmann WH. Parenteral galactose therapy in the glucose-intolerant premature infant. *Pediatrics* 1982;100: 255–259.

167. Fukagawa NK, Minaker KL, Rowe JW, et al. Insulin-mediated reduction of whole body protein breakdown. *J Clin Invest* 1985;76:2306–2311.

168. Rennie MJ, Babij P, Taylor PM, et al. Characteristics of a glutamine carrier in skeletal muscle have important consequences for nitrogen loss in injury, infection, and chronic disease. *Lancet* 1986;2:1008–1012.

169. Lacey JM, Wilmore DW. Is glutamine a conditionally essential amino acid? *Nutr Rev* 1990;48:297–309.

170. Wolfe RR, O'Donnell TF Jr, Stone MD, Richmond DA, Burke JF. Investigation of factors determining the optimal glucose infusion rate in total parenteral nutrition. *Metabolism* 1980;29:892–900.

171. Wolfe RR, Durkot MJ, Allsop JR, Burke JF. Glucose metabolism in severely burned patients. *Metabolism* 1979;28:1031.

172. Lucas A, Morley R, Cole TJ. Adverse neurodevelopmental outcome of moderate neonatal hypoglycaemia. *Br Med J* 1988;297:1304–1308.

173. Wilmore DW. Catabolic illness: strategies for enhancing recovery. *N Engl J Med* 1991;325:695–702.

174. Askanazi J, Weissman C, Rosenbaum SH, Hyman AI, Milic-Emili J, Kinney JM. Nutrition and the respiratory system. *Crit Care Med* 1982;10:163–172.

175. Murray RD, Ailabouni AH, Powers PA, et al. Absorption of lactose from the colon of the newborn piglet. *Am J Physiol* 1991;261:G1–G8.

176. Schulze KF, Stefanski M, Masterson J, et al. Energy expenditure, energy balance, and composition of weight gain in low birth weight infants fed diets of different protein and energy content. *J Pediatr* 1987;110:753–759.

177. Kashyap S, Schulze KF, Forsyth M, Dell RB, Ramakrishnan R, Heird WC. Growth, nutrient retention, and metabolic response of low-birth-weight infants fed supplemented and unsupplemented preterm human milk. *Am J Clin Nutr* 1990;52:254–262.

178. Putet G, Rigo J, Salle B, Senterre J. Supplementation of pooled human milk with casein hydrolysate: energy and nitrogen balance and weight gain composition in very low birth weight infants. *Pediatr Res* 1987;21:458–461.

5. Fat

Sheila M. Innis

Reviewers: Steven J. Gross, Margit Hamosh, Berthold Koletzko, Ricardo Uauy

The fat and essential fatty acid requirements of premature infants remain a subject of considerable uncertainty, with current recommendations based largely on the composition of human milk rather than on scientific data regarding infant needs. This may be appropriate, because intakes of energy sufficient for optimal growth cannot normally be achieved unless significant amounts of fat are included in the parenteral and enteral diet, and because lipid metabolism is more analogous to the breast-fed term infant than to the fetus in utero. Of further relevance, greater metabolic efficiency is achieved if dietary fat rather than carbohydrate is used as the source of fatty acid for assimilation in growing adipose tissue.

Mammalian cells lack the enzymatic ability to insert a double bond at the n-6 or n-3 position of a fatty acid carbon chain; thus a source of n-6 and n-3 fatty acids is essential in the diet. The n-6 and n-3 fatty acids recognized as essential dietary nutrients are the parent C18 fatty acids of each series—that is, linoleic acid (18:2n-6) and linolenic acid (18:3n-3).[1] Dietary linoleic acid (18:2n-6) and linolenic acid (18:3n-3) may be further metabolized to longer chain, more unsaturated fatty acids, of which arachidonic acid (20:4n-6) and docosahexaenoic acid (22:6n-3) are known to be essential for normal growth and development (Fig. 5.1). Fatty acids are important components of the phospholipids which make up the structural matrix of all cell and subcellular membranes. The composition of membrane lipid is known to determine membrane functions such as hormone receptor activity, transmembrane transport, and membrane enzyme activities. In addition, di-homolinolenic acid (20:3n-6), arachidonic acid (20:4n-6), and eicosapentaenoic acid (20:5n-3) are precursors for synthesis of highly active oxygenated metabolites, leukotrienes, thromboxanes, prostaglandins, and prostacyclins, collectively known as eicosanoids. These eicosanoids, particularly those derived from arachidonic acid (20:4n-6), are important modulators and mediators of a variety of physiological and developmental processes such as patency of the ductus arteriosus, platelet-vessel wall interactions, and renal function.[2] Deficiency of linoleic acid (18:2n-6) and/or linolenic acid (18:3n-3) in animals during brain development is known to result in long-term problems in learning[1,3-6] and visual function,[3,7-9] which may be irreversible in later life even if a fatty acid–

sufficient diet is provided.[1,7] These problems are related to reduced amounts of arachidonic acid (20:4n-6) and docosahexaenoic acid (22:6n-3) in the brain and retina.[1,3-9] The goal of fatty acid nutrition in the premature infant is the support of normal pathways of eicosanoid metabolism and optimum levels of metabolically essential n-6 and n-3 fatty acids in membranes of the central nervous system (CNS), as well as other organs.

The fat requirements of premature infants thus encompass:

1. The amount of fat needed to ensure adequate energy for optimum utilization of diet protein and weight gain. This includes oxidization of fat to supply the energy costs of basal metabolic functions and new tissue synthesis, as well as fatty acids for storage in adipose tissue triglycerides.

2. The amount of n-6 and n-3 essential fatty acids required for optimum fatty acid composition and function of growing tissues and for normal eicosanoid synthesis. This represents only a small proportion of the recommended and usual percentage of total energy from fat in human milk or formula diets.

Scientific data to allow estimation of requirements for total fat or specific fatty acids in individuals or variance among individuals are not available. The tissue levels of the various n-6 and n-3 fatty acids that provide optimum metabolic and physiological function during growth and development also are not known. Recommendations for total fat, and for the essential n-6 and n-3 fatty acids given here for premature infants <1,750 g are, therefore, based on review of in utero fat accretion, the fat content and composition of human milk, and biochemical and functional studies relating to essential fatty acid requirements of infants and other species.

I agree that there is no scientific basis for simply deducing infant nutrient requirements from the average composition of human milk. Moreover, absorption and metabolism of individual nutrients are not necessarily the same when the nutrients are supplied with human milk as when they are supplied with formulas. However, in those areas where we do not yet have sufficient data on the actual nutrient require-

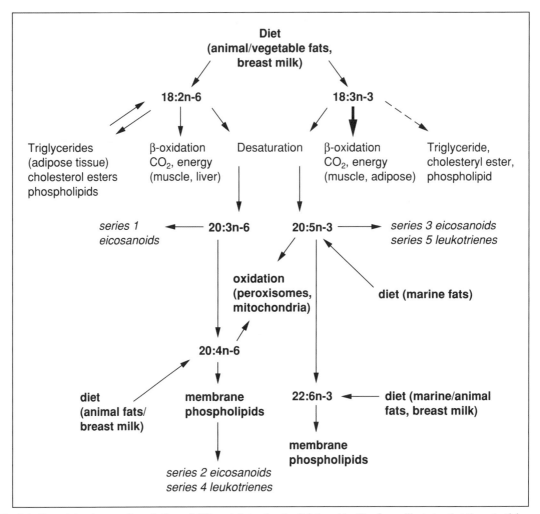

Fig. 5.1. Potential pathways of metabolism of different diet n-6 and n-3 fatty acids. The figure illustrates that the potential metabolic pathways of linoleic acid (18:2n-6) and linolenic acid (18:3n-3) are oxidation for energy, direct acylation into tissue lipids, and desaturation to arachidonic acid (20:4n-6) and docosahexaenoic acid (22:6n-3), respectively. Because of the "loss" of linoleic acid (18:2n-6) and linolenic acid (18:3n-3) to oxidation and tissue storage, the conversion of 18:2n-6 to 20:4n-6 and of 18:3n-3 to 22:6n-3 is not 1:1. Consequently, dietary linoleic acid (18:2n-6) and linolenic acid (18:3n-3) are not quantitatively equivalent to dietary arachidonic acid (20:4n-6) and docosahexaenoic acid (22:6n-3), and factors for "losses" (oxidation/acylation) must be used when considering 18:2n-6 and 18:3n-3 as the only dietary essential fatty acids.

ments of infants, human milk composition may give us some guidance on dimensions of acceptable intakes. Breastfeeding has allowed mankind to survive and develop reasonably well for many generations. (B. Koletzko)

Physiology

Fatty Acid Nomenclature and Metabolism

Most fatty acids in the diet are supplied in triglycerides, with small amounts also obtained from phospholipids and cholesterol esters. The usual fatty acid nomenclature, as used here, gives the number of car-

bon atoms followed by a colon, then the number of unsaturated bonds in the fatty acid chain; for example, 16:0 (palmitic acid, 16 carbons: no double bonds). The notation n is used to designate the position of the first double bond from the methyl terminus, and the notation $\triangle$ to indicate the position from the carboxyl terminal at which a double bond is inserted. The carbon chain length (C) and number of double bonds influence the absorption and subsequent metabolism of the fatty acids. Of particular importance, the greater solubility in water of C8:0 (caprylic acid) and C10:0 (capric acid), known as medium-chain fatty acids (MCFA), compared to fatty acids of C14 or more—for example, 16:0 (palmitic acid) and 18:1 (oleic acid)—results in several important differences in physical and biochemical properties. C12:0 (lauric acid) has an intermediate position, sharing the properties of both MCFA and of longer chain fatty acids.

Saturated fatty acids, and unsaturated fatty acids of the n-9 and n-7 series, can be synthesized de novo from acetyl CoA. Further metabolism of the dietary essential fatty acids, linoleic acid (18:2n-6) and linolenic acid (18:3n-3), occurs by alternating desaturation (insertion of double bonds) and elongation (addition of two carbon units) of the carbon chain. The result is a series of more highly unsaturated, longer chain fatty acids (Fig. 5.1) of which arachidonic acid (20:4n-6) from linoleic acid (18:2n-6) and docosahexaenoic acid (22:6n-3) from linolenic acid (18:3n-3) are of particular metabolic importance. The n-6 and n-3 fatty acids are not interconvertible either in the body or in their essential metabolic functions.

The clinical sequelae of essential fatty acid deficiency (deficiency of both linoleic acid [18:2n-6] and linolenic acid [18:3n-3]), especially the skin lesions, are well-known. Many of the metabolic functions of the n-6 and n-3 fatty acids, particularly those related to CNS function, are poorly understood. The roles of arachidonic acid (20:4n-6), as the precursor of series 2 eicosanoids and series 4 leukotrienes[2], and of docosahexaenoic acid (22:6n-3) in normal visual processes[7] are, however, well-known. Linoleic acid (18:2n-6), but not linolenic acid (18:3n-3), also seems to have independent essential metabolic roles, perhaps related to normal triglyceride and cholesterol metabolism, in addition to providing substrate for synthesis of arachidonic acid (20:4n-6).[1]

The biochemistry and metabolism of the essential fatty acids is complex, involving differences in metabolism and competition among the various n-6 and n-3 fatty acids. The desaturase enzymes are known to show substrate preference in the order n-3>n-6>n-9, and are inhibited by products of either the n-6 or n-3 fatty acid series.[1] Consequently, the rate of desaturation of linoleic acid (18:2n-6) to arachidonic acid (20:4n-6) and of linolenic acid (18:3n-3) to docosahexaenoic acid (22:6n-3) depends on the quantities of linoleic acid (18:2n-6) and linolenic acid (18:3n-3) substrate and preformed arachidonic acid (20:4n-6) and/or docosahexaenoic acid (22:6n-3) in the diet.

Eicosapentaenoic acid (20:5n-3), which is found predominantly in fish oils, also inhibits synthesis of arachidonic acid (20:4n-6). This is due to inhibition of the desaturation of linoleic acid (18:2n-6) to arachidonic acid (20:4n-6). Eicosapentaenoic acid also replaces arachidonic acid in tissue structural lipids.[10] Normal regulatory control of tissue arachidonic acid (20:4n-6) may be lost if inappropriately high amounts of eicosapentaenoic acid (20:5n-3) are fed, or if the milk or formula diet contains a high ratio of

22:6n-3 and 20:5n-3 to 20:4n-6.[1] This has important implications, because the effects of series 3 prostanoids and series 5 leukotrienes derived from eicosapentaenoic acid (20:5n-3) are often antagonistic to or different from the physiological effects of cyclooxygenase and lipoxygenase products from arachidonic acid (20:4n-6).[2,10]

In addition to desaturation (microsomal), linoleic acid (18:2n-6) and linolenic acid (18:3n-3) are readily oxidized in the mitochondria for energy (Fig. 5.1). Linoleic acid is also incorporated into adipose tissue triglycerides in amounts related to the quantity provided in the infant's diet.[11] In contrast, arachidonic acid (20:4n-6) and docosahexaenoic acid (22:6n-3) are preferentially incorporated into structural phospholipids, rather than being oxidized, or acylated into storage lipids. Oxidation of C20 and C22 polyunsaturated fatty acids is also different, and may involve initial chain shortening and retroconversion in the peroxisomes, prior to mitochondrial β-oxidation.[12] These differences in oxidation and acylation probably explain why dietary linoleic acid (18:2n-6) and linolenic acid (18:3n-3) have less "biological activity" as a source of membrane components than dietary arachidonic acid (20:4n-6) and docosahexaenoic acid (22:6n-3). Factors to equate dietary linoleic acid (18:2n-6) and linolenic acid (18:3n-3) with dietary arachidonic acid (20:4n-6) and docosahexaenoic acid (22:6n-3) (that is, to account for losses due to oxidation) are not yet available. Useful analogies are retinol equivalents, used to equate the lower activity of carotenes with preformed vitamin A, and tocopherol equivalents, used to equate α with γ and other tocopherols. Best estimates at this time suggest that dietary eicosapentaenoic acid (20:5n-3) and docosahexaenoic acid (22:6n-3) are about four times more "active" than linolenic acid (18:3n-3).[1]

In summary, the ability of premature infants to synthesize arachidonic acid (20:4n-6) from linoleic acid (18:2n-6) and docosahexaenoic acid (22:6n-3) from linolenic acid (18:3n-3) depends on adequate energy and the amount of linoleic acid (18:2n-6) and linolenic acid (18:3n-3), as well as endogenous desaturase enzyme activities. There is no direct information on the desaturase enzyme activity of preterm or term infants. It is reasonable to expect, however, that in infants in whom the energy supply is below maintenance requirements, diet linoleic acid (18:2n-6) and linolenic acid (18:3n-3) will be oxidized for energy and will not be available for desaturation to arachidonic acid (20:4n-6) and docosahexaenoic acid (22:6n-3). In these infants, or in infants in whom endogenous desaturase enzyme activity is low, arachidonic acid (20:4n-6) and docosahexaenoic acid (22:6n-3) can be regarded as "conditionally essential" dietary nutrients.

Essential Fatty Acid Deficiency

Substrate affinity of the desaturase enzymes in the order of n-3>n-6>n-9 effectively limits desaturation of significant amounts of oleic acid (18:1n-9) to eicosatrienoic (20:3n-9) as long as there is a dietary intake of linoleic acid (18:2n-6) or linolenic acid (18:3n-3). Analyses of the proportion of eicosatrienoic acid (20:3n-9) in the plasma lipids is, therefore, a useful diagnostic index of essential fatty acid deficiency, particularly when considered in relation to the amount of arachidonic acid (20:4n-6). The ratio of 20:3n-9 to 20:4n-6 (known as the triene:tetraene ratio) in plasma lipids is usually <0.1 in healthy adults, children, and breast-fed infants, but increases to >0.4 in essential fatty acid deficiency.[13]

For the ratio of 20:3n-9 to 20:4n-6, the Food and Agriculture Organization (FAO) of the United Nations[14] suggested an even lower threshold value of >0.2 as an indicator of essential fatty acid deficiency. (B. Koletzko)

This increase in the triene:tetraene ratio is explained by increased synthesis of eicosatrienoic acid (20:3n-9) from oleic acid (18:1n-9) and decreased synthesis of arachidonic acid (20:4n-6) resulting from inadequate intake or absorption of linoleic acid (18:2n-6). Because desaturation of oleic acid (18:1n-9) to eicosatrienoic acid (20:3n-9) is inhibited by either linoleic acid (18:2n-6) or linolenic acid (18:3n-3), measurement of the triene:tetraene ratio is useful only for the diagnosis of inadequate total polyunsaturated fat intake or absorption. It is not of value for diagnosing a deficiency of only n-6 fatty acids or of only n-3 fatty acids, and it is not useful for judgments on the quality of the n-6 and n-3 fatty acid supply to the infant.

Dietary intakes of 1% to 2% kcal from linoleic acid (18:2n-6) maintain normal triene:tetraene ratios and avoid clinical signs of essential fatty acid deficiency in infants.[15-17] It is unlikely that such low intakes are compatible with adequate assimilation of arachidonic acid (20:4n-6) and docosahexaenoic acid (22:6n-3) in the rapidly growing structural membranes of premature infants. While this can be assessed in other species by tissue analysis, there are no accepted biochemical measures—other than the triene:tetraene ratio—of tissue n-6 or n-3 fatty acid status and membrane function in the human infant.

Essential Fatty Acid Requirements during Perinatal Development

Several approaches have been used to estimate the requirements of premature infants for n-6 and n-3 fatty acids. These include extrapolations from fetal autopsy tissue analyses, usual intakes provided by human milk, biochemical and functional evaluations of infants fed human milk or formulas, and studies in other species. There is no direct evidence on the desaturase enzyme capacity of the developing human. Consequently, determining whether dietary linoleic acid (18:2n-6) and linolenic acid (18:3n-3) can supply the metabolic requirements of premature infants for arachidonic acid (20:4n-6) and docosahexaenoic acid (22:6n-3) at present depends largely on circumstantial evidence.

Tissue Accretion It is theoretically possible to predict the tissue requirement for n-6 and n-3 fatty acids from a knowledge of the quantity of these fatty acids deposited in tissues at various stages of development. Dietary requirements may then be extrapolated from the amounts needed for tissue growth if factors are available to account for losses in absorption, oxidation to energy, and incorporation into adipose triglycerides. If the arachidonic acid (20:4n-6) and docosahexaenoic acid (22:6n-3) needed for membrane growth are provided as linoleic acid (18:2n-6) and linolenic acid (18:3n-3), then an estimate of the efficiency of conversion (bioequivalence) must be included.

It is known that large amounts of arachidonic acid (20:4n-6) and docosahexaenoic acid (22:6n-3) are deposited in the developing brain and liver during the third trimester of gestation,[18-20] but about 70% to 78% of the total n-6 and n-3 fatty acids accumulated by the fetus are accounted for by deposition in adipose tissue.[18] For example, third-trimester weekly rates of accumulation have been estimated as follows: approximately 2.6 g n-6 fatty acid and 0.37 g n-3 fatty acids for adipose tissue; approximately 0.044 g n-6 and 0.022 g n-3 fatty acid for the brain; and approximately 0.014 g n-6 and 0.004 g n-3 fatty acid for the liver.[18-20] Information has not yet been published to show that adipose triglyceride n-6 and n-3 fatty acids are of functional significance, or that such a "reserve" would be available to the brain after birth, unless there is mobilization of the reserve because of energy deficit leading to tissue lipolysis.

Fetal liver, brain,[19,20] and adipose tissue[21] growth seems to follow a sigmoidal (S-shaped) curve rather than a linear course during the last trimester. Calculations of average daily or weekly rates of fatty acid accretion that assume linear growth may, therefore, underestimate the tissue requirements of infants born prior to 33 weeks gestation. In summary, estimation of dietary n-6 and n-3 fatty acid requirements of infants <1,750 g from current knowledge of in utero accretion is not possible, due to uncertainty regarding the need to support in utero rates of adipose tissue n-6 and n-3 fatty acid assimilation, the question of how to extrapolate from periods of limited tissue data and possible nonlinear organ growth, and a lack of factors to account for losses in n-6 and n-3 fatty acids during absorption or to oxidation.

Human Milk It is known that the composition of developing tissue lipids depends on the dietary fat composition. The fat composition of human milk, however, varies widely depending on the mother's diet, as well as other factors.[22] Consequently, infant dietary or tissue requirements for particular fatty acids cannot be derived from knowledge of the amounts supplied by human milk. If used as the model for infant feeding, the fatty acids supplied by average mature human milk can be assumed to provide in excess of the true requirement of the infant for any fatty acid.

It is correct that to a certain extent maternal diet does influence lipid composition of human milk. In addition to diet, however, the C20 and C22 n-6 and n-3 fatty acid contents of milk are regulated by metabolic processes. The content of these fatty acids in milk is little affected by varied self-selected diets in different geographic regions.[23] Even women who consume diets very low in preformed C20 and C22 n-6 fatty acids (e.g., rural African, vegetarians) maintain high levels in milk. It is tempting to speculate that metabolic regulation of milk C20 and C22 polyunsaturated fatty acids may serve to protect the breast-fed infant by providing a relatively constant supply of these biologically active compounds. (B. Koletzko)

There is no published biochemical evidence of a metabolic process to control the content of C20 and C22 n-6 or n-3 fatty acids in human milk. Fatty acid analysis of human milk does not provide evidence for such regulated processes.

The C20 and C22 n-3 long-chain polyunsaturated fatty acids (LCPs), particularly docosahexaenoic acid (22:6n-3), are clearly influenced by the amount of these fatty acids in the maternal diet. The data given in Table 5.1 for the fatty acid composition of human milk from different regions of the world clearly show this. Sanders and Reddy[24] recently published further analyses of human milk from women following vegan, vegetarian, and omnivorous diets in the United Kingdom. They reported 0.14% 22:6n-3 fatty acids in the milk from the vegans and 0.37% in the milk from the omnivorous women. Milk from racial groups with a fairly high intake of fish—as, for example, women from the Malay peninsula (Table 5.1)[25]—has about 0.9% 22:6n-3, while the milk from extreme populations such as the Canadian Inuit has 1.4% 22:6ω-3.[26] In my opinion this gives strong evidence of the effect of maternal diet on milk n-3 LCP

and does not suggest metabolic regulation by the mammary gland.

The question of the relationship between maternal diet and mammary gland control of the arachidonic acid content of milk remains open. Studies of extreme ranges of intake of 20:4n-6 are more difficult and have not been published. Reported values for 20:4n-6 do vary by two- to threefold (Table 5.1),[24] but this may be explained by analytical differences rather than true differences in the milk.

Although scientists are at liberty to speculate, the available data do not provide scientific evidence to substantiate the suggestion "that metabolic regulation of milk C20 and C22 polyunsaturated fatty acids may serve to protect the breast-fed infant by providing a relatively constant supply of these biologically active compounds." (S. Innis)

Several approaches can be taken: (1) recommend similar levels of all fatty acids, with the intent of mimicking the tissue fatty acid composition of the breast-fed infant; (2) assume that linoleic acid (18:2n-6) and linolenic acid (18:3n-3) are the only essential dietary fatty acids, and extrapolate an amount equal to the total n-6 and n-3 fatty acids in human milk, which includes factors to account for higher bioactivity of the human milk C20 and C22 n-6 and n-3 fatty acids; or (3) assume that linoleic acid (18:2n-6) and linolenic acid (18:3n-3), as well as arachidonic acid (20:4n-6) and docosahexaenoic acid (22:6n-3), are essential nutrients, and recommend intakes of all n-6 and n-3 fatty acids similar to the amounts provided by human milk. The latter two approaches assume that the saturated and monounsaturated fatty acids are not important and have no effect on the metabolism of n-6 and n-3 fatty acids. There is no published information to show any deleterious effects to growth or development in infants fed formulas containing much less palmitic acid (16:0) and oleic acid (18:1) than are in human milk. It is not correct, however, to assume these fatty acids are insignificant to normal lipid metabolism.

Some representative published analyses for North American, European, and Asian human milk from women following diets typical of their cultures[25,27,28] and of Canadian women delivering at 28 to 33 weeks gestation[17] are in Table 5.1, and are used as the basis for estimation of possible appropriate intakes for infants in energy balance. The average amounts of linoleic acid (18:2n-6) and linolenic acid (18:3n-3) provided by human milk—assuming 50% of the energy in the milk is from fat—are about 6.0% and 0.32%, respectively, of total dietary energy, with the lowest amounts being about 4.4% kcal for linoleic acid (18:2n-6) and 0.15% kcal for linolenic acid

Table 5.1. Fatty Acid Composition of Term and Preterm Human Milk from Different Populations*

Fatty Acid	Germany[28]	USA[27]	Chinese[25]	Malay[25]	Indian[25]	Canada[18]
Saturate						
monounsaturates						
16:0 (palmitic)	21.8	22.2	22.0	26.9	25.8	18.2
18:0 (stearic)	8.2	7.8	5.2	4.1	5.0	5.8
18:1n-9 (oleic)	34.3	36.3	33.8	30.8	30.7	35.5
N-6 series						
18:2n-6 (linoleic)	10.8	15.2	17.0	8.8	10.7	11.3
18:3n-6	0.16	0.13	tr.	tr.	tr.	0.03
20:3n-6	0.26	0.41	0.51	0.27	0.40	0.37
20:4n-6 (arachidonic)	0.36	0.57	0.64	0.47	0.57	0.54
22:4n-6	0.08	0.11	0.21	0.13	0.13	0.13
22:5n-6	n.d.	0.04	n.r.	n.r.	n.r.	0.07
N-3 series						
18:3n-3 (linolenic)	0.81	0.87	0.38	0.30	0.33	1.11
20:5n-3 (eicosapentaenoic)	0.04	n.r.	n.r.	n.r.	n.r.	0.13
22:5n-3	0.17	0.10	0.21	0.21	0.19	0.13
22:6n-3 (docosahexaenoic)	0.22	0.18	0.71	0.90	0.90	0.30
Total n-6 fatty acids	11.66	16.46	18.36	9.67	11.8	12.44
Total n-6 desaturation products (20 + 22n-6)	0.86	1.26	1.36	0.87	1.1	1.14
Total n-3	1.24	1.15	1.30	1.41	1.42	1.72
Total n-3 desaturation products (20 + 22n-3)	0.43	0.28	0.91	1.11	1.09	0.56
18:2n-6/18:3n-3 ratio	13.3	17.5	44.7	29.3	32.4	10.2

*Values are given only for major fatty acids (cis isomers) with 16 or more carbons. Tr. = trace; n.d. = not detected; n.r. = not reported. The data are adapted from the references shown and represent mature breast milk from women delivering at term gestation (22–24) or 28–33 weeks gestation.[18] The fatty acids are given as a percent of the total and defined using common nomenclature to give the number of carbon atoms in the fatty acid: number of double bonds and the fatty acid series (n-9, 6, or 3). Common and systematic names for fatty acids are included in parentheses for reference.

(18:3n-3). Human milk supplies significant amounts of C20 and C22 fatty acids, which are more effective in supporting tissue arachidonic acid (20:4n-6) and docosahexaenoic acid (22:6n-3) accretion than similar amounts of dietary linoleic acid (18:2n-6) or linolenic acid (18:3n-3), respectively.[1] Docosahexaenoic acid (22:6n-3) seems to be particularly high in milks with a low linolenic acid (18:3n-3) of <0.4% fatty acids. The average amount of linolenic acid (18:3n-3) in the milk samples (Table 5.1) containing the lower levels of docosahexaenoic acid (22:6n-3) is about 0.46% of total dietary energy. Using a best estimate of 4:1 to account for difference in bioactivity of the carbon chain 18, 20, and 22 fatty acids, the percentages of 18:2n-6 and 18:3n-3 fatty acid "equivalents," as calculated from the milks in Table 5.1, range for linoleic acid (18:2n-6) from 12.3% to 22.4% and for linolenic acid (18:3n-3) from 1.0% to 6.6% (6.1% to 11.2% kcal 18:2n-6 and 1.0% to 3.3% kcal 18:3n-3). Using this approach, an acceptable intake for infants receiving no dietary C20 or C22 n-6 or n-3 fatty acids is 0.68 g linoleic acid (18:2n-6) per 100 kcal and 0.11 g linolenic acid (18:3n-3) per 100 kcal. These estimates are based on assumptions of equivalence factors for precursor-product relationships. The validity of the factors used, or the approach under varying precursor and product intakes, has not yet been demonstrated.

It is an interesting hypothesis that human milk contents of α-linolenic acid (18:3n-3) and its metabolite docosahexaenoic acid (22:6n-3) could be inversely related in order to compensate for low levels of each other, but analytical data do not show any relation between the two fatty acids in human milk.[29] (B. Koletzko)

In order to test the possibility that there is an inverse relationship between 18:3n-3 and 22:6n-3 in milk, samples with ranges in content of both 18:3n-3 and 22:6n-3 must be considered, such as those described in Table 5.1. The samples Dr. Koletzko has analyzed and referenced seem fairly homogeneous, and by his own statements do not vary in n-3 LCP content. Therefore, Dr. Koletzko should not expect to find an inverse relationship to 18:3n-3 within his data set. (S. Innis)

It is possible that high dietary intakes of linolenic acid (18:3n-3) could limit the desaturation of linoleic acid (18:2n-6) to arachidonic acid (20:4n-6). This competitive interaction, however, seems to be significant in vivo only when the dietary intake of linoleic acid (18:2n-6) is very low or the intake of linolenic acid (18:3n-3) very high.[1] Ratios of linoleic acid (18:2n-6) to linolenic acid (18:3n-3) in human milk range from about 10:1 to over 45:1 (Table 5.1). Soybean oils usually have a linoleic acid (18:2n-6) to linolenic acid (18:3n-3) ratio of about 5:1, have been studied extensively, and do not lower arachidonic acid (20:4n-6) levels in developing tissues when compared to corn or safflower oils with ratios in excess of 50:1.[1,3-9] Thus, in the absence of more definitive data, it is recommended that the ratio of 18:2n-6 to 18:3n-3 be at least 5:1.

If it is assumed that arachidonic acid (20:4n-6) and docosahexaenoic acid (22:6n-3) are essential nutrients for the human infant, recommendation for intakes must consider the usual balance of C20 and C22 n-6 and n-3 in milk and recognize that endogenous desaturases are inhibited by these fatty acids. Using human milk as the model, an appropriate composition for formulas providing C20 and C22 fatty acids is 4.0% to 5.0% kcal 18:2n-6, 0.5% kcal C20 and C22 n-6 fatty acids, 0.5% kcal 18:3n-3, and 0.25% kcal C20 and C22 n-3 fatty acids. Breast milk contains very low levels of eicosapentaenoic acid (20:5n-3); therefore, the predominant n-3 fatty acid should be docosahexaenoic acid (22:6n-3), not eicosapentaenoic acid (20:5n-3). In addition, the ratio of arachidonic acid (20:4n-6) to eicosapentaenoic acid (20:5n-3) should never be less than 1:1, because eicosapentaenoic acid (20:5n-3) inhibits and competes with the metabolism of arachidonic acid (20:4n-6), and docosahexaenoic acid (22:6n-3) levels in milk are always several times higher than eicosapentaenoic acid (20:5n-3) levels.

Biochemical and Functional Studies in Infants Fed Formula and Human Milk Biochemical studies on infant fatty acid requirements have relied on comparative measures of plasma and red blood cell (RBC) fatty acids.[1] How these measures relate to the accumulation of n-6 and/or n-3 fatty acids in developing organs is uncertain. Fetal plasma phospholipids characteristically contain little linoleic acid (18:2n-6). Low plasma levels of linoleic acid, however, represent a goal that is neither achievable nor appropriate for the enterally or parenterally fed preterm infant. The RBC phosphatidylethanolamine (a phospholipid found predominantly on the inner surface of the RBC membrane) has high amounts of arachidonic acid (20:4n-6) and docosahexaenoic acid (22:6n-3), which usually remain at about 22% to 26% and 8% to 9% total fatty acids, respectively, during the last trimester of gestation and first months after birth in term breast-fed infants.[1] Maintenance of RBC arachidonic acid (20:4n-6) and docosahexaenoic acid (22:6n-3) at levels equivalent to those in utero is a reasonable goal for the lipid nutrition of premature infants <1,750 g.

The RBC phosphatidylethanolamine docosahexaenoic acid (22:6n-3) decreases rapidly in preterm infants receiving parenteral or enteral feeds of <100 kcal/kg/day.[1] A similar rapid decline occurs in arachidonic acid (20:4n-6), but is of greater magnitude in the plasma and RBC phosphatidylcholine than in the RBC phosphatidylethanolamine.[1] It is not clear if the energy deficit during early postnatal life, delay after birth before start of significant lipid infusion, or inappropriate composition of parenteral lipid emulsions is to blame for the decline in arachidonic acid (20:4n-6) and docosahexaenoic acid (22:6n-3). However, many small premature infants are clearly depleted in arachidonic acid (20:4n-6) and docosahexaenoic acid (22:6n-3) by the time full-volume enteral feedings are successfully established, and may have higher requirements both for repletion and to support subsequent rapid rates of tissue growth. Indeed, it has been shown that 120 kcal/kg/day of expressed preterm human milk does not restore 20:4n-6 or 22:6n-3 to in utero levels in preterm infants of about 2 to 3 weeks postnatal age.[9] In this regard, theoretical calculations based on fetal tissue analyses have also projected that 200 mL/kg/day of preterm milk may not meet the tissue needs of a 1,300 g infant growing at 17 g/day if accretion in adipose tissue is included, unless n-6 and n-3 fatty acids are spared from oxidation.[18]

The data and calculations of Clandinin et al.[18] do allow the conclusion that feeding 200 mL of human milk provides quantities of n-6 and n-3 LCPs with 20 and 22 carbon atoms sufficient to cover the needs for their accretion in neural and liver tissues at intra-uterine rates. These authors also estimated that the LCP supplied with human milk would not cover an additional extrauterine LCP deposition in adipose tissue at the high intrauterine accretion rates, but there is no reason to believe that such a high LCP accretion would or should occur in infants growing ex utero. The fatty acid composition of adipose tissue reflects the composition of fat intake. Replacement of the preferential placental LCP supply by postnatal feeding of diets rich in linoleic acid markedly increases linoleic acid and decreases LCP contents in adipose tissue at any gestational age.[18] If this is taken into account, the LCP supply of full human milk feeding can be expected to suffice for the tissue needs of growing premature infants. (B. Koletzko)

To my knowledge there is no valid scientific data for preferential placental LCP transfer as yet. Fatty acids are released into the fetal circulation as free fatty acids, then transferred to the fetal liver where they may be oxidized, incorporated into various lipids, or into lipoprotein lipids for secretion back into the fetal circulation. Comparative analysis of lipoprotein phospholipid fatty acids in maternal compared to fetal (infant cord) blood clearly cannot be construed as a measure of selectivity of placental transfer. The studies on placental perfusion have raised, in discussion of their own data, the possibility that the high amounts of 20:4n-6 in phospholipid found in the placental perfusate were due to placental membrane damage, resulting from the perfusion.[30] The placenta is not known to secrete lipoproteins or phospholipids into the fetal circulation.[31]

Clandinin et al.[18] do not provide data to show that diets rich in linoleic acid increase linoleic acid content and decrease LCP content of adipose tissue at any age. The autopsy data of Clandinin regarding fetus and infants of varying age provided no nutritional history for any of the samples analyzed, nor data for adipose tissue of preterm infants who had been fed formulas or human milk.

The question of whether or not full volume feeding with human milk fulfills the requirements of very preterm infants for LCP is an open question. There is no scientific data to either support or refute this. Given that other chapters in this text affirm that human milk provides inadequate levels of protein, calcium, phosphorus, and other nutrients, I suggest that it is prudent to maintain an open mind on the adequacy of milk fatty acids for preterm infants until further data become available. (S. Innis)

Levels of RBC docosahexaenoic acid (22:6n-3) remain fairly constant in human milk–fed infants <1,750 g who are in energy balance, but decline in infants fed vegetable-oil formulas providing linolenic acid (18:3n-3) but no docosahexaenoic acid (22:6n-3).[32–34] The decline is rapid, and is associated with overt differences in electroretinograph recordings of retinal function, when formula with <0.37% kcal linolenic acid (18:3n-3) are fed.[32,33] Plasma and RBC levels of docosahexaenoic acid (22:6n-3), and visual functional development, seem to be similar over at least the first month of full-volume feeding in preterm infants fed human milk or formulas with ≥1% kcal linolenic acid (18:3n-3).[32,34] Addition of small amounts of marine fish oil, supplying 0.25% kcal or more eicosapentaenoic acid (20:5n-3) plus docosahexanoic acid (22:6n-3),[34–36] restores the RBC phosphatidylethanolamine docosahexaenoic acid (22:6n-3) to in utero levels[1] but exacerbates the poor arachidonic acid (20:4n-6) status.[36] This is reasonably explained by the well-known inhibition of linoleic acid (18:2n-6) desaturation by long-chain n-3 fatty acids, and competitive interaction between arachidonic acid (20:4n-6) and eicosapentaenoic acid (20:5n-3) for incorporation into membrane lipids.[10] Visual acuity, assessed by forced preferential looking[37] or electroretinograph recordings of reversed-pattern visual evoked potentials,[34] is better in infants fed marine oil–supplemented rather than unsupplemented formula. However, the circulating lipid arachidonic acid (20:4n-6) in preterm infants is positively related to growth and cognition through 1 year corrected postnatal age.[38] The problems in growth and cognition do not become significant for several months after hospital discharge. Some published data indicate that addition of small amounts of arachidonic acid (20:4n-6) to a formula increases the plasma arachidonic acid (20:4n-6) of preterm infants of about 33 to 34 weeks gestational age.[39] Long-term functional studies demonstrating benefit to growth and development, or safety of such formulas, are not yet available.

Based on a considered review of the available knowledge, the Committee on Nutrition of the European Society of Paediatric Gastroenterology and Nutrition (ESPGAN) recently published a comment covering different aspects of the content and composition of lipids in European infant formulas.[40] It was recommended that all types of formula (infant formulas, formulas for low-birthweight infants, and follow-on formulas) contain linoleic acid in the range of 4.5% to 10.8% of energy content. The lower limit of linoleic acid intake is similar to that recommended now by Dr. Innis. In addition, an upper limit was set because of concerns about potential untoward effects of excessive polyunsaturated fatty acid intakes. It was also recommended that all European formulas contain α-linolenic acid; but rather than defining a min-

imal absolute concentration, the Committee recommended a linoleic/α-linolenic acid ratio ranging from 5:1 to 15:1. Dr. Innis agrees with the lower limit of this range. The ESPGAN Committee set the upper limit not only in view of conceivable interference of a very high linoleic/α-linolenic acid ratio with n-3 fatty acid metabolism, but also to guarantee a certain minimum of α-linolenic acid intakes. Dr. Innis's interpretation is that the minimal α-linolenic acid intake covered by this recommendation would be 0.5%. In fact, if a manufacturer would choose to combine the lowest extreme of recommended linoleic acid content (4.5% of energy) with the highest extreme of the recommended ratio (15% of energy), this would result in a α-linolenic acid supply of only 0.3% of energy. However, this is unlikely for practical reasons, and if median values of both ranges are combined, the resulting α-linolenic acid intake is 0.8% of kcal, which is similar to the value suggested now by Dr. Innis. (B. Koletzko)

My recommendation is based not on an interpretation of the ESPGAN recommendations but on a review of the same literature and work in other species (see preceding text). (S. Innis)

The ESPGAN Committee also considered it desirable to enrich formulas for low-birthweight infants "with metabolites of both linoleic and α-linolenic acids approximating levels typical of human milk (n-6 LCP 1%, n-3 LCP 0.3% of total fatty acids)." It was emphasized that in low-birthweight infant formulas, the "supplementation of metabolites of linoleic and α-linolenic acids should aim at achieving an LCP status in the infant similar to that of infants at birth, or infants fed human milk." The use of formulas supplying only n-3 LCP or high proportions of eicosapentaenoic acid (C20:5n-3), as provided by conventional fish oils, was discouraged. No definite recommendation was made for LCP supplementation of infant formulas, i.e., formulas for infants born at full term. This comment is in favor of enriching low-birthweight infant formulas with LCP, but it is not contradictory to the need of further research in the area and it does not endorse a final recommendation for routine feeding of all infants. (B. Koletzko)

Extrapolation from Other Species The young of several other species, including nonhuman primates, accumulate large amounts of arachidonic acid (20:4n-6) and docosahexaenoic acid (22:6n-3) in the CNS when fed diets or formulas providing linoleic acid (18:2n-6) and linolenic acid (18:3n-3) but no arachidonic acid (20:4n-6) or docosahexaenoic acid (22:6n-3).[1,3-6,8,9,41] Intakes of ≥0.7% kcal linolenic acid (18:3n-3) or 0.4% kcal eicosapentaenoic acid

(20:5n-3) and docosahexaenoic acid (22:6n-3) support normal deposition of docosahexaenoic acid (22:6n-3) in developing CNS of term-gestation nonhuman primates, piglets, and rodents.[1,42] Reduced levels of arachidonic acid (20:4n-6) are found in the liver and plasma, but not the brain, when eicosapentaenoic acid (20:5n-3) and docosahexaenoic acid (22:6n-3) are used as the source of n-3 fatty acids in formulas without arachidonic acid (20:4n-6).[1,42] Visual function, assessed by forced preferential looking or electroretinograph recordings, is impaired when diets provide <0.1% kcal linolenic acid (18:3n-3).[3,8,9] Maximum assimilation of arachidonic acid (20:4n-6) in the brain is attained with approximately 5% kcal linoleic acid (18:2n-6),[1,3,40,42] although, as in infants, plasma arachidonic acid (20:4n-6) remains lower in formula- than in milk-fed animals.[1]

Summary Definitive information on the fatty acid requirements of preterm infants <1,750 g, or on their tissue desaturase activity, is not available. Based on the composition of human milk, changes in blood lipid fatty acids of preterm infants in energy balance, and studies of other species, the recommended minimum intake for all infants fed formulas without C20 or C22 fatty acids is 4% to 5% kcal linoleic acid (18:2n-6) and 1% kcal linolenic acid (18:3n-3). It seems probable that arachidonic acid (20:4n-6) and docosahexaenoic acid (22:6n-3) are conditionally essential nutrients for infants <1,750 g fed on current premature infant formulas. The recommended intake for these infants is 4% to 5% kcal linoleic acid (18:2n-6), 0.5% kcal linolenic acid (18:3n-3), 0.5% kcal C20 and C22 n-6 fatty acids, and 0.25% kcal C20 and C22 n-3 fatty acids. The C20 and C22 n-3 fatty acids should be given predominantly as docosahexaenoic acid (22:6n-3) and should be fed only if a source of arachidonic acid (20:4n-6) in approximately similar amounts is also provided. The long-term safety and efficacy of feeds (other than human milk) with these fatty acids have not been demonstrated and need to be evaluated before recommendations for routine feeding of formulas supplemented with C20 and C22 fatty acids can be endorsed. Information from several laboratories has provided what seems to be conclusive evidence that neither docosahexaenoic acid (22:6n-3) nor arachidonic acid (20:4n-6) are essential dietary nutrients for normal CNS growth of term gestation animals in positive energy balance. Although similar information is not available for the human, there is at present no scientific evidence to consider it essential to include a source of C20 and C22 n-6 or n-3 fatty acids in term infant formulas.

The European Society of Paediatric Gastroenterology and Nutrition Committee on Nutrition recently recommended 4.5% kcal linoleic acid (18:2n-6),

0.5% kcal linolenic acid (18:3n-3), and a linoleic acid to linolenic acid ratio of 5:1 to 15:1.[40] The Committee also considered it desirable to provide 1% kcal C20 and C22 n-6 fatty acids and 0.5% kcal C20 and C22 n-3 fatty acids in formula for low-birthweight infants. Based on review of the same literature, and detailed work in other species,[1,43] it seems possible that formulas with 0.5% kcal 18:3n-3 but no longer chain n-3 fatty acid may not meet the n-3 fatty acid requirements of the infant. It is recommended here, therefore, that infants should be fed with formulas containing 1% kcal 18:3n-3. Although there is concurrence that the ratio of linoleic acid to linolenic acid in formula should not fall below 5:1, there seems to be no valid way to extrapolate an upper limit for this ratio from human milk. Many human milks have linoleic acid to linolenic acid ratios in excess of 15:1 (for example, the Chinese milk described in Table 5.1 has a 18:2n-6 to 18:3n-3 ratio of over 40:1).[25]

The recommendation from the European Committee regarding addition of longer chain n-6 and n-3 fatty acids to formula for low-birthweight infants seems to be based on a 21-day feeding study.[37] Reduced growth and psychomotor development of preterm infants, evident only several months later, has been reported to result from addition of long-chain n-3 fatty acids to their formula.[36,7] Data on immune or other functions related to eicosanoid metabolism following long-chain fatty acid modification of formulas have not been published. Studies on formulas with C20 and 22n-6 and n-3 fatty acids are, however, in progress and should provide the necessary information on long-term growth and development in the near future. In light of the absence of long-term safety and efficacy data, and the possibility of harmful effects,[36,44] the conclusion here is that there is insufficient scientific data to endorse a recommendation for routine feeding of infants with formula containing C20 and C22 n-6 and/or n-3 fatty acids.

Enteral Feeding

Physiology of Fat Digestion, Absorption, and Metabolism

Composition of Human Milk Lipids Fat is the most variable macronutrient in human milk, varying with the stage of lactation, diurnally, and within a feed.[22] The fat content of mature, expressed human milk is usually about 3.5 to 4.5 g/dL, representing 40% to 55% milk kcal. Both the fat content and caloric density are often much lower in the first 1 to 2 weeks postpartum.[45] Although the caloric density of milk from women delivering prematurely is usually similar to that of women delivering at term, the fat content may be lower.[45] Consequently, extrapolations of infant fatty acid requirements based on the

fat density of term human milk may project that the essential fatty acid supply from some preterm milk is inadequate.

Fat is secreted into milk as globules containing a core of triglycerides, representing approximately 98% of the total fat in milk. During secretion the triglyceride becomes enveloped by the apical part of the phospholipid-rich plasma membrane of the mammary gland epithelial cell.[46] The resulting trimolecular surface layer of phospholipids accounts for about 1% of the total lipids in milk, but can be calculated to contain less than 10% of the arachidonic acid (20:4n-6) and docosahexaenoic acid (22:6n-3). Small amounts of cholesterol and protein are also present in the globule membrane. The cholesterol content of human milk is 20 mg/dL, approximately one third of it esterified to a fatty acid.[22]

Milk fatty acids are derived from synthesis in the mammary alveolar cells and by uptake from plasma. The fatty acid composition of mature human milk from women delivering prematurely is not particularly different from that of women giving birth at term[47] (Table 5.1). Due to a mammary specific enzyme (thioesterase II), fatty acids synthesized in the mammary cells are generally of shorter carbon-chain length (C10 to C14) than the longer chain (C16 to C20) fatty acids taken up from the plasma. Medium-chain fatty acids (MCFA) are minor components of milk, usually representing <2% total fatty acids.[22] Fatty acids of mammary origin (12:0 and 14:0) are somewhat higher in milk from women who follow high-carbohydrate rather than high-fat diets,[48] presumably reflecting a higher contribution of fatty acids from mammary synthesis. Typical human milk from North American or European women who follow usual mixed diets contains 20% to 25% palmitic acid (16:0), 30% to 38% oleic acid (18:1n-9), 7% to 18% linoleic acid (18:2n-6), and 0.5% to 1.0% linolenic acid (18:3n-3)[22](Table 5.1). The desaturation-elongation products of linoleic acid (18:2n-6), including 20:3n-6, arachidonic acid (20:4n-6), and 22:4n-6, usually account for about 1% fatty acids, with another 0.5% to 1% present as the n-3 series, 18:4n-3, eicosapentaenoic acid (20:5n-3), 22:5n-3, and docosahexaenoic acid (22:6n-3).

The palmitic acid (C16:0) content of human milk is fairly constant at approximately 20% to 25% human milk fatty acids, with 70% or more of the palmitic acid (16:0) esterified to the center position (sn-2) of the three-carbon unit of glycerol.[22] This structure has significant implications for the digestion and absorption of saturated fatty acids, as well as divalent cations, from human milk. This aspect is discussed further in subsequent sections on the digestion and absorption of breast milk and formula fats.

Large differences are found in milk fat oleic acid (18:1n-9) and linoleic acid (18:2n-6) and in the n-3 fatty acids eicosapentaenoic acid (20:5n-3) and docosahexaenoic acid (22:6n-3), depending on the type of vegetable fat and the amount of marine fat in the mother's diet. For example, human milk fatty acids of vegan and vegetarian women have been reported to contain as much as 32%[49] and 29%[50] linoleic acid (18:2n-6), respectively. Levels of docosahexaenoic acid (22:6n-3) ranging from 0.2% to 1.4% human milk fatty acids have been reported and seem to be related to the mother's dietary intake of docosahexaenoic acid (22:6n-3) from animal tissues, particularly fish[26,51] (Table 5.1). The predominant long-chain n-3 fatty acid in human milk is docosahexaenoic acid (22:6n-3), even when the mother consumes large amounts of eicosapentaenoic acid (20:5n-3) from marine oils. Levels of arachidonic acid (20:4n-6) are fairly constant despite wide variations in milk linoleic acid (18:2n-6) or high maternal marine oil intakes, and are usually one to two times higher than levels of docosahexaenoic acid (22:6n-3).[26,49-52]

Composition of Infant Formula Lipids   The fat in many commercial infant formulas is a blend of one or more vegetable oils held in dispersion with plant lecithin, sometimes with the aid of mono- and diglycerides. Palmitic acid is predominantly esterified to the sn-1,3 position of vegetable oil triglycerides, leading to release of free palmitic acid (16:0) following intraluminal hydrolysis of the sn-1,3 ester linkages by pancreatic colipase-dependent lipase. The coefficiency of absorption of free palmitic acid (16:0), as well as of free stearic acid (18:0), is low and further complicated by formation of soaps with calcium or other divalent cations.[53] This process can lead to fecal loss of both fat and minerals. To avoid these problems, infant formulas often contain medium-chain triglyceride (MCT) or coconut oils as a source of nonessential-fat calories, and avoid oils containing significant amounts of palmitic acid (16:0) or stearic acid (18:0). Oleo oils are used in some products to give a similar saturated and monounsaturated fatty acid content to human milk. Although oleo oil has about 26% palmitic acid (16:0) and 19% stearic acid (18:0), about 82% and 86%, respectively, of these are found at the sn-1,3 ester linkages (glycerol carbon atoms) of the oleo triglycerides.[22]

Formulas for preterm infants often include 20% to 50% of the fat blend as MCT oils. These oils usually replace coconut oil (predominantly 12:0 and 14:0), rather than the polyunsaturated oils in formulas designed for infants >1,750 g. Medium-chain triglyceride oils are semi-synthetic oils prepared from coconut oil to contain predominantly saturated MCFA — 8:0 (caprylic acid) and 10:0 (capric acid), with smaller amounts of 6:0 (caproic acid) and 12:0 (lauric acid). Commercial MCT oils in North America usually contain about 68% 8:0 and 24% 10:0, while European versions may contain higher proportions of 10:0.

In summary, the fat in infant formulas differs from that in human milk in the following important ways: (1) formulas based on vegetable or oleo triglycerides provide variable oleic acid (18:1n-9), linoleic acid (18:2n-6), and linolenic acid (18:3n-3), depending on the fat blend used, and do not provide significant amounts of arachidonic acid (20:4n-6), docosahexaenoic acid (22:6n-3), or cholesterol; and (2) the proportions and type of saturated fat differ; if palmitic acid (16:0) is present, the unique characteristics of the milk triglyceride fatty acid configuration with palmitic acid (16:0) predominantly esterified, the sn-2 linkage (center glycerol carbon atom) is not reproduced. The fat blend and fatty acid composition of typical North American preterm infant formula are given in Table 5.2.

Digestion and Absorption of Human Milk Lipids and Formula Lipids   The process of fat digestion and absorption can be divided into: (1) the luminal phase involving solubilization and hydrolysis of the fat; (2) the mucosal phase that involves re-esterification of fatty acids and secretion into the lymphatics in chylomicrons, or release of unesterified fatty acids into the portal venous system; and (3) uptake of the unesterified fatty acid or chylomicron triglyceride into the tissues.

Luminal Phase.   Triglyceride hydrolysis in adults is generally considered the result of colipase-dependent lipase in the upper intestine.[54] This enzyme has a specificity for the sn-1,3 ester bonds, giving rise to two free fatty acids and sn-2 monoglycerides. The free fatty acid and sn-2 monoglyceride products become solubilized in the aqueous portion of the intestine by micellar concentrations of bile salts and are absorbed as components of mixed micelles into the intestinal mucosal cells.[54] Colipase-dependent pancreatic lipase activity, the bile salt pool, and intraluminal bile salt concentrations are low in newborn infants.[55-58] The infant, however, has several alternate mechanisms that together overcome the relative deficiency in pancreatic lipase activity and bile salts and provide for efficient fat absorption.

Triglyceride hydrolysis in infants fed fresh human milk is the result of the combined action of bile salt–stimulated lipase, produced in the mammary gland and secreted in milk, and the endogenous lingual and gastric (gastric) lipases and colipase-dependent lipase.[55-58] The major preduodenal enzyme acting in the stomach of infants is gastric lipase.[59,60] The milk fat globule, due to its surface layer of phospholipid, cholesterol, and protein, is relatively resistant to colipase-dependent pancreatic lipase or bile salt–stimulated lipase.[61-63] The hydrophobic nature of the gastric lipase, however, allows the enzyme to penetrate to the core of the milk fat globule and initiate hydrolysis without disrupting the membrane. Gastric

Table 5.2. Fat Blends and Approximate Fatty Acid Composition of Commonly Used North American Preterm Formulas and of Intravenous Lipid Triglycerides*

	Preterm Formula			Parenteral Lipid (Soybean oil)
	1	2	3	
Fat blend				
MCT	+	+	+	
Coconut oil	+	+	+	
Soy oil	+	+	+	+
Oleo oil			+	
High oleic safflower oil			+	
Fatty acids (% total)				
8:0 (caprylic)	30	38	8.2	—
10:0 (capric)	12	14.8	4.3	—
12:0 (lauric)	9.4	9.4	14.6	—
14:0 (myristic)	3.6	3.6	5.6	—
16:0 (palmitic)	5.9	4.9	10.3	11
18:0 (stearic)	2.4	1.9	5.1	4
18:1 (oleic)	11.2	8.8	34.2	22
18:2n-6 (linoleic)	22.0	16.4	14.3	54
18:3n-3 (linolenic)	3.1	2.3	1.2	8
20:4n-6 (arachidonic)	—	—	—	—
22:5n-3 (eicosapentaenoic)	—	—	—	—
22:6n-3 (docosahexaenoic)	—	—	—	—

*The fatty acids are given using common nomenclature with the common or systematic name in brackets.
— indicates the amount present is ≤0.1%.

lipase, from the chief cells of the gastric mucosa, has functional specificity for the sn-3 ester bond of triglyceride, giving rise to free fatty acids and sn-1,2 diglycerides.[64] However, the enzymes have a relatively low specific activity, are rapidly inactivated by pancreatic proteases in the presence of bile salts, and are very sensitive to inhibition by product-free fatty acids, at least in in vitro studies.[57,65] It seems unlikely, therefore, that gastric lipase is of major quantitative importance to total fat absorption or contributes to fat hydrolysis in the intestine.[56] The initial partial hydrolysis, however, is critically important because the free fatty acids released by gastric lipase induce binding between the colipase-lipase complex and the milk fat globules, thus eliminating the resistance of the globule to hydrolysis.[65–68] Gastric lipase is present from about 26 weeks of gestation.[55,69] It seems possible, therefore, that limited gastric lipase activity could result in inability to hydrolyze human milk fat in some very small premature infants of <26 weeks gestation.

In infants fed formulas, gastric lipase and colipase-dependent pancreatic lipase hydrolyze about two thirds of the triglyceride fatty acids, with the final products being free fatty acids and sn-2 monoglycerides. Additional hydrolysis of milk fat may occur in infants fed fresh human milk, due to the action of the milk bile salt–stimulated lipase.[55] This enzyme has no positional specificity and can hydrolyze the sn-2 monoglyceride left by pancreatic lipase[56,57] when mixed with bile salts. This lipase is present in milk from about 26 weeks gestation, has a pH optimum of 7 to 9, and hydrolyzes a wide variety of triglycerides to free fatty acids and glycerol in the presence of bile salts.[55,69] The importance of this additional hydrolysis is uncertain. Free fatty acids (unesterified fatty acids) are more soluble than monoglycerides in the vesicular phase of the aqueous intraluminal contents, thus possibly improving net fat absorption in infants with low intraluminal bile salt concentrations.[56] On the other hand, the sn-2 monoglyceride products of colipase-dependent lipase activity are micellarized and absorbed more readily than free fatty acids.[54]

Little is known about the development of other endogenous enzymes involved in fat hydrolysis. Phospholipase A_2, which hydrolyzes fatty acids from phospholipids, has an absolute requirement for bile salts.[58] Pancreatic carboxylic ester hydrolase seems to be functionally similar to bile salt–stimulated lipase, and has been thought to be important to hydrolysis of long-chain polyunsaturated fatty acids such as arachidonic acid (20:4n-6), from triglycerides.[70] The known low activity of colipase-dependent lipase in the newborn[55-58] suggests that the activity of other pancreatic enzymes of fat hydrolysis such as phospholipase A_2, cholesterol esterase, and carboxylic ester hydrolase may also be limiting. Whether this has significance to hydrolysis and absorption of triglycerides or phospholipid arachidonic acid (20:4n-6) and docosahexaenoic acid (22:6n-3) from human milk or artificial infant diets has yet to be explored.

The coefficient of fat absorption in preterm infants depends on gastrointestinal maturity, the fat composition of the formula fed, and any storage or processing of expressed human milk. The coefficiency of absorption of fat from fresh human milk in preterm infants <1,500 g is 90% to 95%, similar to that in term gestation infants.[71-73] Total fat absorption is lower (approximately 85% to 92%) from formulas that do not contain significant amounts of MCT oil.[55] The higher absorption of fat from human milk may be explained by the additional activity of the milk bile salt–stimulated lipase, the *sn*-2 palmitic acid configuration of the milk triglycerides, and the structure of the milk fat globule.

The efficiency of absorption of oleic acid (18:1) and linoleic acid (18:2n-6) from polyunsaturated vegetable oil triglycerides is high (>90%).[53] The coefficiency of absorption of myristic acid (14:0), palmitic acid (16:0), and stearic acid (18:0), however, is much lower (approximately 89%, 75%, and 62%, respectively).[53] In contrast, MCT oils and their MCFA hydrolysis products do not need to be solubilized to mixed micelles for absorption. This allows for almost 100% absorption of 8:0 (caprylic acid) and 10:0 (capric acid), even in the presence of low lipase activities and intraluminal bile salt concentrations, and leads to high total fat absorption in very small infants fed formulas made from MCT oils and unsaturated vegetable oils.

Pasteurization (63°C) of expressed human milk leads to inactivation of the milk bile salt–stimulated lipase.[74] The reduction in the coefficient of fat absorption to 75% to 90% in infants fed heat-treated milk[73] may be explained by inactivation of the milk lipase, as well as possible changes in the milk fat globule structure. Although the total lipid content of human milk does not change during frozen storage, there is a gradual loss of triglyceride and increase in free fatty acids during storage for >48h at −11°C.[75] Lipolysis seems to be greatest for oleic acid (18:1), linoleic acid (18:2n-6), and arachidonic acid

(20:4n-6), but may be limited by storage at −70°C.[75]

Several studies have shown that the formula content of palmitic acid (16:0) and stearic acid (18:0) may influence the efficiency of fat as well as mineral absorption. This finding seems to be explained by the formation of insoluble soaps of calcium and magnesium with free 16:0 and 18:0, as well as 14:0, in the stomach or intestine.[53,76] Thus, supplementation with calcium resulted in a reduction in fat absorption of approximately 10% from frozen human milk or preterm infant formula containing 16:0 and 18:0 from oleo oils.[77] Analyses of fecal fatty acids showed the effect was primarily on 16:0 and 18:0 rather than monounsaturated, n-6, or n-3 fatty acids. Other studies suggest that the fat and mineral malabsorption is predominantly the result of fat malabsorption, not the amount of calcium in the formula.[53] The importance of providing 16:0 esterified to the *sn*-2 linkage of infant formula fats is evident. It also seems that advantages in total fat and mineral absorption conferred by feeding fresh human milk are lost if the milk is processed.

Mucosal Phase. The route of transport of absorbed fat is determined by absorption as free fatty acids or *sn*-2 monoglycerides, the polarity of the fatty acids, and specificity of fatty acid–binding proteins involved in mucosal triglyceride reassembly. Medium-chain triglycerides incorporated directly into mucosal cells are hydrolyzed by mucosal lipase, then transported predominantly via the portal system. The division of MCFA to transport as unesterified, albumin-bound fatty acids via the portal venous route, and of fatty acids of carbon chain length 14 and longer to transport in chylomicron triglyceride via the lymphatics is not complete. Physiologically significant amounts of saturated and unsaturated fatty acids, including linoleic acid (18:2n-6) and linolenic acid (18:3n-3), are transported via the portal pathway,[78] and MCFA are found in chylomicron triglycerides.[79] Approximately 75% of the fatty acids absorbed in the *sn*-2 position as monoglycerides are conserved during reassembly of the triglyceride, whereas fatty acids originating from the *sn*-1,3 positions are re-esterified at random[80] and secreted as components of chylomicron. Indeed, lymphatic transport of MCFA has been shown to be greater for MCFA absorbed as *sn*-2 monoglycerides than for MCFA located on the *sn*-1,3 position of the diet fat.[81]

Metabolism of Absorbed Lipid. Hydrolysis of the triglyceride constituents of intestinal chylomicrons and hepatic very low-density lipoprotein (VLDL) is the result of lipoprotein lipase activity released from adipose tissue, muscle, and possibly other tissues to the capillary endothelium. Compared to the lipoprotein lipase activity in infants born at term, lipoprotein lipase activity seems to be lower in infants <28 weeks gestation but not different in infants >32 weeks gestation.[82] Whether the relative deficiency of lipase activity in very small infants <28 weeks gestation is due to immaturity of lipoprotein lipase enzyme synthesis, or to limited adipose tissue (i.e., the major site of fat deposition), is not clear. The small adipose mass of infants <1,000 g, however, has possible implications for the metabolism of products of triglyceride hydrolysis. Theoretically, limited capacity for adipose tissue assimilation of free fatty acids could result in uptake by the liver, then resecretion as VLDL triglyceride.

Studies in the 1970s indicated that when compared to longer chain fatty acids, MCT oils increased energy absorption and retention, weight gain, calcium absorption, and nitrogen retention in preterm infants.[83-85] Improved fat absorption in the presence of low lipase activity and intraluminal bile salt concentrations, together with assumed advantages related to rapid, portal venous transport of the albumin-bound MCFA to the liver, carnitine-independent transport into the mitochondria, and subsequent oxidation that is more rapid than for longer chain fatty acids—these are commonly cited reasons for including significant quantities of MCT oils in preterm infant formulas. Contemporary studies have not found that MCT oils improve energy or nitrogen balance, or weight gain in preterm infants.[85-88] Evidence has been published to show that MCFA are not completely oxidized, that their metabolism involves extrahepatic tissues and carnitine, and that when infants are fed at 40% to 50% fat blend, as in some preterm formulas, metabolism exceeds the capacity for normal mitochondrial fatty acid β-oxidation.[89-94]

Although it is generally assumed that all dietary MCFA are oxidized, recent studies using stable isotope methodology have estimated only 32% to 64% C8:0 was oxidized by preterm infants of birthweight <1,600 g.[92] Analyses of adipose tissue fatty acids with methods to limit losses during extraction or high-temperature gas-liquid chromatography have also shown that MCFA, and particularly C12:0, are incorporated into adipose tissues of preterm infants in amounts related to the formula content.[95] Feeding MCT oils, rather than long-chain fatty acids, to young rodents results in diminished fat deposition and adipose tissue cellularity.[96] Whether this finding can be construed as beneficial is debatable.

The increased urinary ω-oxidation products of fat (dicarboxylic acids) and elevated plasma ketones that occur in infants fed >10% kcal (20% of fat) MCT oils[87,88,90,94] clearly show that high intakes of MCT oils overwhelm the capacity for normal mitochondrial oxidation for energy. Small amounts of dicarboxylic acids, primarily of adipic (C6), suberic (C8), and sebacic (C10) acid, are found in the urine of normal breast-fed infants. These represent the products of fatty acid ω-oxidation involving cytochrome P-450 of the endoplasmic reticulum and cytosolic dehydrogenase. Dicarboxylic acid excretion is not significantly increased by 5% MCT oils in the formula fat,[89] but increases linearly with increasing MCT oils up to 50% formula fat blend.[90,91,93,97] The increase in dicarboxylic acid excretion is largely the result of a marked increase in C10. Concentrations 200-fold above normal have been reported for infants fed formula with 40% fat as MCT oils.[90] The total amount of energy lost to the urine is low, and there is at present no evidence that the significant production of dicarboxylic acid caused by MCT feeding has any deleterious effect on growth or development of infants <1,750 g, except in infants with a congenital defect in MCFA dehydrogenase activity.

The mild degree of ketonemia induced by formula with MCT is of uncertain benefit. Ketone body synthesis results when the rate of formation of acetyl CoA from fat oxidation exceeds the capacity for entry to the tricarboxylic acid cycle. Undoubtedly, ketone bodies can be used by the developing brain for energy,[98,99] and as a substrate for synthesis of myelin cholesterol and fatty acids.[100,101] However, adenosine triphosphate is required for uptake of ketone bodies into the brain, and glucose and fatty acid, which can both be oxidized by the developing brain, should not be limited in the appropriately nourished preterm infant. An argument for including large amounts of MCT in formulas in order to provide ketones for the brain of preterm infants is not convincing at present.

The European Society of Paediatric Gastroenterology and Nutrition Committee on Nutrition has suggested that the amount of MCT oil in formulas for low-birthweight infants should not exceed 40% of the total fat.[40] The increase in plasma ketones and urinary dicarboxylic acid excretion is linearly related to the amount of MCT oil in the formula fed.[97] The scientific rationale for selecting 40% MCT rather than 30%, 50%, or some other value as the upper limit for MCT oil in infant formulas is not clear.

In Europe the maximal recommended content of MCT oils in low-birthweight infant formulas is 40%, while the use in infant formulas and follow-on formulas is discouraged.[40] The maximum contents of lauric acid (C12:0) and myristic oils (C14:0), which are found in high concentrations in coconut oil, are 15% each.[102]

The choice of the ESPGAN Committee to select 40% as the upper limit of MCT is influenced by some degree of subjective judgment, as are the choices of particular numbers by Dr. Innis in this chapter, and by the published data that MCT contents higher than

40% are of little advantage with respect to fat absorption.[103] (B. Koletzko)

Choices of particular numbers have to be made when there is no scientific data, and only subjective judgment. In North America, there are preterm infant formulas with 40% and 50% MCT. There is no scientific data to state that a formula with 50% MCT is better or worse than a formula with 40% MCT. Therefore, in my opinion it is inappropriate to select 40% MCT, which has the practical effect also of placing the products of one company outside of the recommendations. (S. Innis)

Plasma cholesterol concentrations, particularly of LDL cholesterol, are lower in infants fed formula rather than human milk. This may be related to the higher cholesterol and saturated fatty acid content of human milk. The role of cholesterol in human milk is still a subject of considerable uncertainty, and there is no convincing evidence that low-cholesterol diets result in either deficiency or long-term metabolic changes related to altered cholesterol metabolism or atherosclerosis in the human. It is also unlikely that placental transfer is a significant source of the cholesterol deposited in growing fetal tissue membranes during the last trimester of gestation. Therefore, recommendation is not made for the addition of cholesterol to formulas for feeding infants <1,750 g.

Summary of Recommendations for Fat and Fatty Acid Intakes of Enterally Fed Premature Infants

Recommendations for fat intakes for preterm infants include considerations of the need to provide adequate energy while maintaining safe intakes of protein,[104] of the greater metabolic efficiency of providing fat rather than carbohydrate for growth of adipose tissue, and of the preterm infant's lipid and energy metabolism, which is more similar to that of the term infant than to that of the fetus. Placental fat transfer involves release of unesterified fatty acid (free fatty acids) from the placenta into the fetal circulation. Triglyceride-rich lipoproteins from the intestine (chylomicron) and liver (VLDL) are either low or absent from the fetal circulation.[31] After birth, enteral and parenteral feedings both initiate chylomicron and VLDL production. There are no scientific data relating functional aspects of growth and development to the requirement of individuals or of groups of preterm infants for fat as a source of energy at the levels found in human milk. Practically, it is unlikely that adequate energy can be provided with fat intakes of <36 kcal/kg/day (approximately 30% kcal). In the absence of other scientific

data, the recommended intake of fat for enterally fed preterm infants <1,750 g, more mature infants, and term infants is 40% to 55% kcal (4.4 to 6.0 g/100 kcal), which is the usual amount provided by mature, term human milk. This amount is equal to the previous recommendation from the European Society of Paediatric Gastroenterology and Nutrition Committee on Nutrition for a fat content of 4.4 to 6.0 g/100 kcal in infant formulas.[40] The Committee has also recommended 4.0 to 6.0 g fat/100 kcal for European follow-up formulas.[40]

Although it is reasonable to assume that LCP requirements depend on gestational age and/or body weight and are influenced by food intake, there are no hard data to support the limits chosen here—fat intake <1,750 g and energy intake of 100 kcal/kg/day—as threshold criteria for the need of dietary preformed LCP. (B. Koletzko)

Advantages to fat absorption conferred by the milk lipase and triglyceride structure and the presence of arachidonic acid (20:4n-6) and docosahexaenoic acid (22:6n-3) in a ratio of about 1–2:1 in human milk supports use of the mother's expressed human milk for the nutrition of infants <1,750 g. To avoid reduced fat absorption resulting from lipase inactivation and/or loss of the globule or triglyceride structure during pasteurization or lyophilization, fresh rather than processed expressed milk should be fed. Prolonged frozen storage at temperatures above −20°C should be avoided to limit release of free fatty acids from milk triglycerides.

No clear advantage to growth and development, or intermediary metabolism, is conferred by feeding preterm infants MCT oils in amounts exceeding the small amounts (1% kcal) in human milk. However, palmitic acid (16:0) and stearic acid (18:0), and to some extent myristic acid (14:0), are likely to limit fat and mineral absorption if provided on the sn-1,3 ester linkages of triglycerides, as in oleo, palm oil, or other vegetable oils. Although these oils may provide a saturated fat content similiar to that of human milk, they do not provide analogous digestion and absorption and are not necessarily acceptable alternatives to MCT oils.

Based on the usual composition of human milk, clinical studies, and work in other species, the recommended intake is 4% to 5% kcal linoleic acid (18:2n-6) and 1.0% kcal linolenic acid (18:3n-3) for infants <1,750 g and older infants fed formulas with no arachidonic acid (20:4n-6) or docosahexaenoic acid (22:6n-3). Infants in negative energy balance are unlikely to utilize linoleic acid (18:2n-6) or linolenic acid (18:3n-3) for desaturation. Tissue requirements may also be increased in infants who have received several days or weeks of parenteral nutrition, because of the need to replete depleted tissue levels. Consequently, arachidonic acid (20:4n-6) and docosahexaenoic acid (22:6n-3) may be considered conditionally essential nutrients for infants <1,750 g who experience delay or difficulty in maintaining full enteral feeding >100 kcal/kg/day. The recommended intake of C20 and C22 n-3 fatty acids for these infants is 0.25% kcal. Levels of eicosapentaenoic acid (20:5n-3) are very low in human milk, and eicosapentaenoic acid (20:5n-3) is known to reduce arachidonic acid (20:4n-6) synthesis and incorporation into membrane lipids, inhibit triglyceride synthesis and secretion from the liver, and alter numerous biochemical and physiological pathways related to prostanoid and leukotriene metabolism. Therefore, it is recommended that eicosapentaenoic acid (20:5n-3) not be used as a source of n-3 fatty acids for routine nutrition of preterm infants, outside the context of carefully controlled clinical trials. The preferred long-chain n-3 fatty acid is docosahexaenoic acid (22:6n-3), and when fed, it should be provided with a source of arachidonic acid (20:4n-6) to give a ratio of the C20 and C22 n-6 to n-3 fatty acids of approximately 1:1. Although recommended intakes for C20 and C22 n-6 and n-3 fatty acids are given here, and although suggested intakes have been previously published by the European Society of Paediatric Gastroenterology and Nutrition Committee on Nutrition,[40] the long-term safety and efficacy of potential oil sources of these fatty acids in infant nutrition have not been demonstrated. Therefore, until this information is published, these recommendations are considered theoretical rather than practical. In addition, it is strongly recommended that fish oils high in eicosapentaenoic acid (20:5n-3) not be fed to infants <1,750 g without a diet source of arachidonic acid (20:4n-6).

Parenteral Nutrition with Intravenous Lipids

Metabolism of Intravenous Lipids

Intravenous (IV) lipid emulsions provide high-calorie, isotonic solutions of linoleic acid (18:2n-6) and linolenic acid (18:3n-3), as well as other fatty acids, which can be given through peripheral lines. The most widely available commercial products are prepared from soybean oil triglycerides emulsified with egg yolk or soy phospholipids. Typical soybean oil contains about 45% to 55% linoleic acid (18:2n-6) and 6% to 9% linolenic acid (18:3n-3), but very little saturated or monounsaturated fat (Table 5.2), quite unlike the composition of human milk (Table 5.1) or mixed adult diets. Concerns over the effect of these emulsions on the composition of fatty acids deposited in the developing tissues of very small infants are justified. Alternative, more physio-logical fat blends, however, are not yet available for clinical practice.

Intravenous lipid particles are similar in size to chylomicrons, and hydrolysis of their triglyceride core is accomplished by endogenous lipase activity similar to that of chylomicron and VLDL. Thus, the rate of infused triglyceride clearance is determined by the available lipase activity, with the uptake of unesterified fatty acid products related to the adipose tissue mass and/or fatty acid oxidation in muscle. Heparin releases hepatic lipase and lipoprotein lipase from the capillary endothelium into the circulation, and when given as a continuous low-dose infusion (5 U/h), maintains a relatively constant and significantly lower circulating triglyceride concentration than repeated heparin bolus infusion.[82] However, the increase in serum free fatty acids is also higher.[82] Uncertainty regarding potential accumulation of free fatty acids in excess of muscle or adipose tissue clearance does not allow a recommendation for the use of heparin to be given at this time.

Adequate clearance of up to 2 g lipid per kg per day is found in most infants >28 weeks gestation and of up to 3 g lipid per kg per day in most infants >32 weeks gestation. About 30% of infants 27 to 32 weeks gestation develop serum lipid concentrations >100 mg/dL with lipid infusions between 2 and 3 g/kg/day.[20] The lower post-heparin lipolytic activity in preterm infants <28 weeks gestation or 1,000 g in weight[82] may explain the higher triglyceride concentrations often encountered in these infants. Limited adipose tissue or muscle mass in infants <1,000 g could also limit free fatty acid clearance, leading to uptake by the liver with secretion as VLDL triglyceride, thus contributing to the hypertriglyceridemia. Trauma and infection are also associated with a decrease in lipolytic activity. Consequently, serum lipid concentrations need to be monitored more closely in infants <1,000 g or 28 weeks gestation, and infected or traumatized infants, and the lipid infusion preferably adjusted to maintain the serum triglyceride concentration at ≤200 mg/dL.

Lipolysis of the emulsion triglyceride core, without uptake of free fatty acids by adipose tissue or muscle, is of concern because of possible displacement of bilirubin from albumin. This displacement depends on the relative concentrations of albumin, bilirubin, and unesterified fatty acid.[105,106] Accumulation of free fatty acid sufficient to result in clinical problems is unlikely, because generation of free bilirubin does not occur until the molar ratio of free fatty acid to albumin exceeds 6.[107] Recent studies have shown that infusion of 1 g IV lipid per kg per day to infants with a mean birthweight of 1.35 kg from the first morning after the infants were 24 hours old did result in a significant rise in free bilirubin in association with increased free fatty acids.[108] However, at no time and for no infant did the measured free fatty acid:albumin ratio remotely approach the range at which there may be some measurable risk of bilirubin encephalopathy.[108] No reports of an increased incidence of kernicterus due to IV fat infusion in preterm infants have been published. A precautionary approach may be taken for infants with bilirubin concentrations >12 mg/dL. In these infants, fat infusion should be limited to the amount needed to prevent essential fatty acid deficiency (0.5 to 1.0 g/kg/day, or >2% kcal requirement from linoleic acid [18:2n-6]).

Concerns over potential effects of IV lipids on pulmonary function in very small infants seem to have been resolved. Early reports of fat accumulation in alveolar macrophages, lung arteries, or capillaries of infants who had received IV lipid have been explained as postmortem artifacts that are present with similar frequency in tissues of infants with no history of IV lipid.[109,110] Measures of pulmonary function or oxygenation have also showed no causal relationship to the elevation of plasma triglycerides due to IV fat infusion.[111,112] However, use of IV lipids should be restricted to the amount needed to support essential fatty acid requirements (0.5 to 1.0 g/kg/day) in infants with severe compromise in oxygenation (i.e., FiO_2 >0.60), because of the concern over an increased pulmonary artery pressure.

The dyslipoproteinemia, usually with hypercholesterolemia and hyperphospholipidemia,[113,114] caused by IV fat infusion is well known. This occurs even in the absence of elevated triglycerides and is largely the result of accumulation of abnormal particles of free cholesterol and phospholipid, generally known as Lp X.[113] Clearance probably involves the usual lipoprotein receptors, as well as the reticular endothelial system. The accumulation of plasma lipoprotein cholesterol appears to be explained by the excess phospholipid emulsifier (mesophase phospholipid) in IV lipid emulsion products which, when infused, has an effect similar to infusion of phospholipid liposomes. The net effect is active mobilization of free cholesterol from cell membranes, leading to marked hypercholesterolemia and increased endogenous cholesterol synthesis.[115] The phospholipid:triglyceride ratio of the product determines the extent of hypercholesterolemia and hyperphospholipidemia.[115-117] Thus, problems of hypercholesterolemia and hyperphospholipidemia are substantially lower when vegetable oil triglyceride emulsions of 200 (20%) mg/dL are infused rather than triglyceride emulsions of 100 (10%) mg/dL, when both have similar concentrations of phospholipid.[114] In Europe, 20% and 30% soybean oil emulsions are available. As long as the emulsion has a phospholipid:triglyceride ratio not higher than the standard 10% emulsion, these products may be good alternatives to the conventional 10% emulsions.

Emulsions containing mixtures of MCT with soy or other vegetable oils are receiving increasing attention.[117,118] Emulsification is achieved with egg phospholipid, in a similar triglyceride:phospholipid ratio to conventional emulsions. Dyslipoproteinemia with lipid accumulation in the LDL region of plasma is not improved.[117] Infused MCT, however, are cleared rapidly,[117] offering potential advantage if endogenous lipoprotein lipase activity is low, as in infants <28 weeks gestation, or in infants with sepsis or trauma. Studies of parenterally fed septic rats have not confirmed a benefit of mixed MCT–long-chain fatty acid emulsions. Further, the margin between safety and toxicity was narrow in these studies, leading to greater mortality in previously starved animals infused with MCT–long-chain fatty acid emulsions compared with 100% long-chain fatty acid emulsions.[118] While questions remain concerning potential metabolic benefit, it is clear that MCT do not offer the advantages of a more physiological fat blend for the IV feeding of infants <1,750 g.

Fat Administration and Requirements

Even short delays in addition of fat to the IV diet of preterm infants leads to biochemical essential fatty acid deficiency, evident as a rise in the plasma triene:tetraene ratio within 72 hours after birth.[119] These changes extend to the lung[120] and most likely to other organs as well. The clinical implications of short-term essential fatty acid deficiency are not well understood. However, essential fatty acid deficiency is known to interfere with normal lung surfactant synthesis,[104] possibly further impairing pulmonary function in infants already at risk for respiratory problems. Abnormalities in platelet function, which could have implications for clinical bleeding, have also been described.[121] Essential fatty acid deficiency is avoided by infusions of 0.5 to 1.0 g lipid per kg per day.[122,123]

The absence of an elevated triene:tetraene ratio does not provide assurance of adequate formation of arachidonic acid (20:4n-6) and/or docosahexaenoic acid (22:6n-3) in very small infants. If the total kcal supply is less than approximately 80 kcal/kg/day, it is likely that linoleic acid (18:2n-6) and linolenic acid (18:3n-3) will be oxidized to provide energy for essential metabolic and physiological functions, rather than being desaturated.[1] Negative energy balance is also accompanied by mobilization of limited tissue n-6 and n-3 fatty acids,[120] further compromising tissue status. The duration of parenteral nutrition with inadequate energy for anabolic metabolism is an important criterion in determining the extent of arachidonic acid (20:4n-6) and docosahexaenoic acid (22:6n-3) depletion. Since it is important to preserve functional and anatomical development of the CNS, parenteral lipid must be fed with sufficient energy intake to allow prompt postnatal resumption of growth and utilization of fatty acids for essential functions rather than energy. In order to facilitate this, lipid infusion from a 20% emulsion should preferably proceed from the first 1 to 2 days after birth, increasing as tolerated in increments of 0.5 g/day to 3.0 g/day unless contraindicated.

Summary of Recommendations for Parenterally Fed Infants

There is no reason to consider that the tissue requirements, and thus the recommended intakes, of linoleic acid (18:2n-6), linolenic acid (18:3n-3), and the C20 and C22 n-6 and n-3 fatty acids, for infants <1,750 g fed parenterally are different than infants fed enterally with formula or human milk. The fatty acid composition of available parenteral lipid emulsions, however, is neither physiological nor likely to support an appropriate fatty acid composition in developing infant tissues. Problems of dyslipoproteinemia are also well known. Therefore, parenteral lipid emulsions should be infused with the objectives of preventing essential fatty acid deficiency (0.5 to 1.0 g/kg/day) and providing energy adequate to allow prompt resumption of growth and to expedite the transition to full-volume enteral feeding.

Infusion of IV lipid, using a 20% long-chain fatty acid emulsion, should commence within 24 hours of birth for infants >28 weeks gestation and >1,000 g. Information on the safety and efficacy of commencing lipid infusion within 24 hours of birth in very preterm infants, however, has not yet been published. Until this is available, a prudent clinical approach may be to delay administration of IV lipid to very small infants until the second to third day of life. Ten percent triglyceride emulsions with a phospholipid:triglyceride ratio equivalent to the standard 20% emulsions (a ratio of <0.6), should be equivalent. The dose should be increased, as tolerated, in increments of 0.5 g every 2 to 3 days to a maximum of 3 g/kg/day. In all cases, the triglyceride infusion dose should be adjusted to maintain a serum lipid <200 mg/dL. Monitoring triglyceride clearance should be by enzymatic assay of plasma or serum triglyceride, or by light scattering (turbidometry) to determine if the infused lipid particles are adequately cleared. Glycerol is used in the IV lipid emulsion products to achieve isotonicity. Because standard assays for plasma or serum triglycerides are based on assay of the quantity of glycerol released after hydrolysis of triglyceride, glycerol infused with the lipid emulsions may cause erroneous triglyceride results if procedures are not available for preliminary oxidation of free glycerol, prior to the triglyceride assays. Infants <28 weeks gestation or <1,000 g may have low lipase activity or limited adipose mass for clearance of free

fatty acids. A more cautious approach should be taken with assessment of serum lipid clearance in these infants throughout the infusion period. Lipid clearance should also be monitored in all other infants as the infusion approaches and exceeds 2 g/kg/day. In infants with serum bilirubin concentrations above 12 mg/dL, with sepsis, or in whom there is a severe compromise in oxygenation, the lipid infusion should be restricted to 0.5 to 1.0 g/kg/day, sufficient to prevent essential fatty acid deficiency.

Carnitine

The need to provide a source of carnitine for parenterally fed infants is not yet clear. Arguments for this are based on information that led to inclusion of carnitine in soy protein and semi-elemental formulas, as well as a few published studies on carnitine supplementation during parenteral nutrition of preterm infants.

The most well-known function of carnitine is in facilitating transport of long-chain fatty acids through the mitochondrial membrane, which would otherwise be impermeable to them.[124] This function gives carnitine an essential role in oxidation of fatty acids for energy, particularly in heart and skeletal muscle, and in ketogenesis in the liver. The precursor of carnitine, γ-butyrobetaine, is synthesized in the kidney from the essential amino acids lysine and methionine, then hydroxylated to form carnitine in the liver. The activity of γ-butyrobetaine hydroxylase is much lower in infant than adult liver, increasing from about 12% of usual adult values during the first months of life to 100% of adult activity by 15 years of age.[124] Studies conducted prior to routine addition of carnitine to soy-protein or protein hydrolysate formulas found that plasma carnitine concentrations decreased over prolonged feeding,[125] whereas blood carnitine levels were maintained and urinary carnitine increased with age in small preterm infants fed their mothers' milk.[126] This, together with the very low tissue carnitine contents,[127–129] and limited ability of preterm and term infants to produce ketone bodies even in the presence of hypoglycemia,[130] suggests a need for dietary carnitine. Despite these considerations, there does not seem to be any definitive evidence of metabolic or physiologic benefit following carnitine supplementation in infants.

Several studies have shown that plasma and tissue carnitine and ketone body concentrations are low in preterm infants receiving parenteral lipid without carnitine,[131–135] and that supplementation of approximately 10 mg L-carnitine per kg per day increases fat oxidation, as indicated by decreased serum-plasma free fatty acid concentrations and increased ketogenesis.[135] The latter findings, however, are not always reproducible.[135,136] Higher doses of carnitine seem to have pharmacological effects leading to increased protein and fat oxidation, with loss of potential metabolic energy. For example, supplementation with 48 mg L-carnitine per kg per day (about 300 μmol/kg/day) increased the metabolic rate, decreased fat and protein accretion, and prolonged the time to regain birthweight in preterm infants receiving parenteral nutrition with lipid.[137]

The carnitine content of milk is approximately 9 to 10 μmol/dL in the first 2 weeks postpartum, decreases to approximately 6 μmol/dL in mature milk, and is not different in milk from women delivering prematurely. Similar amounts are now provided by all formulas, either as a component of the bovine milk protein, or by supplementation of soy protein or semi-elemental products prepared from hydrolysates of bovine milk protein.[138] The European Society of Paediatric Gastroenterology and Nutrition Committee on Nutrition recently recommended that infant formulas contain at least 7.5 μmol/100 kcal.[39] Calculations based on intrauterine carnitine accretion have predicted tissue accretion of carnitine equivalent to approximately 13 μmol/day.[125]

In summary, it is recognized that carnitine plays an essential role in metabolism and is provided in human milk in amounts that should cover the needs of the infant <1,750 g for in utero rates of tissue accretion, but may have undesirable effects if given in high doses. There seems to be no convincing evidence of metabolic or physiologic benefit in preterm infants following addition of carnitine to their parenteral lipid infusions. However, if parenterally nourished infants are supplemented with carnitine, approximately 15 μmol/100 kcal, which is similar to the amount provided by human milk and enough to support in utero rates of tissue accretion, seems appropriate.

References

1. Innis SM. Essential fatty acids in growth and development. *Prog Lipid Res* 1991;30:39–103.
2. Seyberth HW, Kuhl PG. The role of eicosanoids in paediatrics. *Eur J Pediatr* 1988;147:341–349.
3. Bourre JM, Francois M, Youyou A, Dumont O, Piciotti M, Pascal G, Durand G. The effects of dietary α-linolenic acid on the composition of nerve membranes, enzymatic activity, amplitude of electrophysiological parameters, resistance to poisons and performance of learning tasks in rats. *J Nutr* 1989;119:1880–1892.
4. Lamptey MS, Walker BL. Physical and neurological development of the progeny of female rats fed an essential fatty acid-deficient diet during pregnancy and/or lactation. *J Nutr* 1978;108:351–357.
5. Lamptey MS, Walker BL. Learning behaviour and brain lipid composition in rats subjected to essential fatty acid deficiency during pregnancy, lactation and growth. *J Nutr* 1978;108:358–367.
6. Yamamoto N, Saitoh M, Moriuchi A, Nomura M, Okuyama H. Effect of dietary linolenate/linoleate balance on brain lipid compositions and learning ability of rats. *J Lipid Res* 1987;28:144–151.
7. Connor WE, Neuringer M. The effects of n-3 fatty acid deficiency and repletion upon the fatty acid composition and function of the brain and retina. In: Karnovsky ML, Leaf A, Bolis LC, eds. *Biological Membranes: Aberrations in Membrane Structure and Function.* New York: AR Liss Inc.; 1988:275–294.
8. Neuringer M, Connor WE, Lin DS, Barstad L, Luck S. Biochemical and functional effects of prenatal and postnatal ω3 fatty acid deficiency on retina and brain in rhesus monkeys. *Proc Natl Acad Sci USA* 1986;83:4021–4025.
9. Neuringer M, Connor WE, Van Petten C, Barstad L. Dietary omega-3 fatty acid deficiency and visual loss in infant rhesus monkeys. *J Clin Invest* 1984;73:272–276.
10. Kinsella JE, Lokesh B, Stone RA. Dietary n-3 fatty acids and eicosanoids. *Am J Clin Nutr* 1990;51:1–28.
11. Widdowson EM, Dauncey MJ, Gairdner DMT, Jonxis JHP, Pelikan-Filipkova M. Body fat of British and Dutch infants. *Br Med J* 1975;i:653–655.
12. Norum KR, Christiansen EN, Christopherson BO, Brenner J. In: Bergroesen AJ, Crawford M, eds. *The role of fats in human nutrition.* 2nd ed. San Diego: Academic Press Inc; 1989;117–149.
13. Holman RT. The ratio of trienoic:tetraenoic acids in tissue lipids as a measure of essential fatty acid requirement. *J Nutr* 1970;60:405–410.
14. Food and Agriculture Organization of the United Nations. *Dietary fats and oils in human nutrition.* Rome: FAO Publications Division, 1980.
15. Hansen AE, Wiese HF, Boelsche AN, Haggard ME, Adam DJD, Davis H. Role of linoleic acid in infant nutrition. *Pediatrics* 1963;II:171–192.
16. Holman RT, Caster WO, Wiese HF. The essential fatty acid requirement of infants and the assessment of their dietary intake of linoleate by serum fatty acid analysis. *Am J Clin Nutr* 1964;14:70–75.
17. Paulsrud JR, Pensler L, Whitten CF, Stewart S, Holman RT. Essential fatty acid deficiency in infants induced by fat-free intravenous feeding. *Am J Clin Nutr* 1972;25:897–904.
18. Clandinin MT, Chappell JE, Heim T, Swyer PR, Chance GW. Fatty acid utilization in perinatal de novo synthesis of tissues. *Early Hum Dev* 1981;5:355–366.
19. Clandinin MT, Chappell JE, Heim T, Swyer PR, Chance GW. Fatty acid accretion in fetal and neonatal liver: implications for fatty acid requirements. *Early Hum Dev* 1981;5:7–14.
20. Clandinin MT, Chappell JE, Leong S, Heim T, Swyer PR, Chance GW. Intrauterine fatty acid accretion rates in human brain: implications for fatty acid requirements. *Early Hum Dev* 1980;4(pt 2):121–129.
21. Filler RM. Nutrition in the premature infant. In: Falkner F, Kretchmer N, Rossi E, eds. *Modern problems in paediatrics.* Basel, Switzerland: S Karger; 1975:50–157.
22. Jensen RG. Lipids in human milk-composition and fat-soluble vitamins. In: Lebenthal E, ed. *Textbook of gastroenterology and nutrition in infancy.* 2nd ed. New York: 1989, Raven Press Ltd; 157–208.
23. Koletzko B, Thiel I, Abiedun PO. The fatty acid composition of human milk in Europe and Africa. *J Pediatr* 1992;120:S62–S70.
24. Sanders TAB, Reddy S. The influence of a vegetarian diet on the fatty acid composition of human milk and the essential fatty acid status of the infant. *J Pediatr* 1992:120:S71–S77.

25. Kneebone GM, Kneebone R, Gibson RA. Fatty acid composition of breast milk from three racial groups from Penang, Malaysia. *Am J Clin Nutr* 1985;41:765–769.

26. Innis SM, Kuhnlein HV. Long chain ω-3 fatty acids in breast milk of Inuit women consuming traditional foods. *Early Hum Dev* 1988;18:185–189.

27. Bitman J, Hamosh M, Wood DL, Freed LM, Hamosh P. Lipid composition of milk from mothers with cystic fibrosis. *Pediatrics* 1987;80:927–932.

28. Koletzko B, Mrotzek M, Bremer HJ. Fatty acid composition of mature human milk in Germany. *Am J Clin Nutr* 1988;47:954–959.

29. Koletzko B, Thiel I, Springer S. Lipids in human milk: a model for infant formulae? *Eur J Clin Nutr* 1993. In press.

30. Kühn DC, Crawford M. Placental essential fatty acid transport and prostaglandin synthesis. *Prog Lipid Res* 1986;25:345–353.

31. Coleman RA. The role of the placenta in lipid metabolism and transport. *Semin Perinatol* 1989;13:180–191.

32. Innis SM, Foote KD, MacKinnon MJ, King DJ. Plasma and red blood cell fatty acids of low birthweight infants fed their mother's expressed breast milk or preterm-infant formula. *Am J Clin Nutr* 1990;51:994–1000.

33. Carlson SE, Rhodes PG, Ferguson MG. Docosahexaenoic acid status of preterm infants at birth and following feeding with human milk or formula. *Am J Clin Nutr* 1986;44:798–804.

34. Uauy RD, Birch DG, Birch EE, Tyson JE, Hoffman DR. Effect of omega-3 fatty acids on retinal function of very low birth weight neonates. *Pediatr Res* 1990;28:485–492.

35. Carlson SE, Rhodes PG, Rao VS, Goldgar DE. Effect of fish oil supplementation on the n-3 fatty acid content of red blood cell membranes in preterm infants. *Pediatr Res* 1987;21:507–510.

36. Carlson S, Cooke RJ, Rhodes PG, Peeples JM, Werkman SH, Tolley EA. Long-term feeding of formulas high in linolenic acid and marine oil to very low birth weight infants: phospholipid fatty acids. *Pediatr Res* 1991;30:404–412.

37. Carlson S, Cooke R, Werkman S, Peeples J. Docosahexaenoate (DHA) and eicosapentaenoate (EPA) supplementation of preterm infants: effects on phospholipid DHA and visual acuity [Abstract]. *FASEB J* 1989;3:A1056.

38. Cooke RJ, Carlson SE, Werkman SH, Tolley EA. First year growth of preterm infants fed standard compared to marine oil (n-3) supplementation of formula [Abstract]. FASEB J 1992;5:A1072.

39. Koletzko B, Schmidt E, Bremer HJ, Haug M, Harzer G. Effects of dietary long-chain polyunsaturated fatty acids on the essential fatty acid status of premature infants. *Eur J Pediatr* 1989;148:669–675.

40. Committee on Nutrition, European Society of Paediatric Gastroenterology and Nutrition. Comment on the content and composition of lipids in infant formulas. *Acta Paediatr Scand* 1991;80:887–896.

41. Hrboticky N, MacKinnon MJ, Innis SM. Effect of vegetable oil formula rich in linoleic acid on tissue fatty acid accretion in the brain, liver, plasma and erythrocytes of infant piglets. *Am J Clin Nutr* 1990;51:173–182.

42. Arbuckle LD, Rioux FM, MacKinnon MJ, Hrboticky N, Innis SM. Response of (n-3) and (n-6) fatty acids in brain, liver and plasma of piglets fed formula to increasing, but low, levels of fish oil supplementation. *J Nutr* 1991;121:1536–1547.

43. Innis SM. Effect of different milk or formula diets on brain, liver and blood omega-6 and omega-3 fatty acids.

Proc. 3rd International Congress on Essential Fatty Acids and Eicosanoids [Monograph]. *Am Oil Chem Soc* 1992. In press.

44. Carlson SE. Lipid requirements of very low birthweight infants for optimal growth and development. In: Dobbing J, ed. *Lipids, learning and the brain: fats in infant formula*. 103rd Ross Conference on Pediatric Research. In press.

45. Butte NF, Garza C, Johnson CA, Smith EO, Nichols BL. Longitudinal changes in milk composition of mothers delivering preterm and term infants. *Early Hum Dev* 1984;9:153–162.

46. Neville MC. The physiological basis of milk secretion. *Ann NY Acad Sci.* 1990;586:1–11.

47. Bitman J, Wood DL, Hamosh M, Hamosh P, Mehta NR. Comparison of the lipid composition of breast milk from mothers of term and preterm infants. *Am J Clin Nutr.* 1983;38:300–312.

48. Hachey DL, Silber GH, Wong WW, Garza C. Human lactation. II: Endogenous fatty acid synthesis by the mammary gland. *Pediat Res* 1989;25:63–68.

49. Sanders TAB, Ellis FR, Dickerson JWT. Studies of vegans: the fatty acid composition of plasma choline phosphoglycerides, erythrocytes, adipose tissue, and breast milk, and some indicators of susceptibility to ischemic heart disease in vegans and omnivore controls. *Am J Clin Nutr* 1978;31:805–813.

50. Specker BL, Wey HE, Miller D. Differences in fatty acid composition of human milk in vegetarian and nonvegetarian women: long-term effect of diet. *J Pediatr Gastroenterol* 1987;6:7764–7768.

51. Harris WS, Connor WE, Lindsey S. Will dietary ω-3 fatty acids change the composition of human milk? *Am J Clin Nutr* 1984;40:780–785.

52. Gibson RA, Kneebone GM. A lack of correlation between linoleate and arachidonate in human breast milk. *Lipids* 1984;19:469–471.

53. Jensen C, Buist NRM, Wilson T. Absorption of individual fatty acids from long chain or medium chain triglycerides in very small infants. *Am J Clin Nutr* 1988;43:745–751.

54. Carey MC, Small DM, Bliss CM. Lipid digestion and absorption. *Annu Rev Physiol* 1983;45:651–677.

55. Hamosh M. Lipid metabolism in premature infants. *Biol Neonate* 1987;52:50–64.

56. Hernell O, Blackberg L, Bernbäck S. Digestion of human milk fat in early infancy. *Acta Paediatr Scand* 1989;351:57–62.

57. Hernell O, Blackberg L, Bernbäck S. Digestion and absorption of human milk lipids. In: Linblad BS, ed. *Perinatal nutrition*. San Diego: Academic Press, Inc.; 1988:259–272.

58. Watkins JB. Physiology of fat absorption. In: Grand RJ, Sutphen JL, Dietz WH, eds. *Pediatric nutrition: theory and practice*. Stoneham, MA Butterworth; 1987:127–137.

59. DeNigris SJ, Hamosh M, Kasbekar DK, Lee TC, Hamosh P. Lingual and gastric lipases: species differences in the origin of prepancreatic digestive lipases and in the localization of gastric lipase. *Biochim Biophys Acta* 1988;959:38–45.

60. Moreau H, Gargouri Y, Lecat D, Junien JL, Verger R. Screening of preduodenal lipases in several mammals. *Biochim Biophys Acta* 1988;959:247–252.

61. Cohen M, Morgan RG, Hofmann AF. Lipolytic activity of human gastric and duodenal juice against medium and long chain triglycerides. *Gastroenterology* 1971;60:1–15.

62. Plucinski TM, Hamosh M, Hamosh P. Fat digestion in rat: role of lingual lipase. *Am J Physiol* 1979;237:E541–547.

63. Iverson SJ, Kirk CL, Hamosh M, Newsome J. Milk lipid digestion in the neonatal dog: the combined actions of gastric and bile salt stimulated lipases. *Biochim Biophys Acta* 1991;1083:109–119.

64. Patton JS, Rigler MW, Liao TH, Hamosh P, Hamosh M. Hydrolysis of triacylglycerol emulsions by lingual lipase. A microscopic study. *Biochim Biophys Acta* 1982;712:400–407.

65. Bernbäck S, Blackberg L, Hernell O. Fatty acids generated by gastric lipase promote human milk triacylglycerol digestion by pancreatic colipase-dependent lipase. *Biochim Biophys Acta* 1989;1001:286–293.

66. Borgström B. Importance of phospholipids, pancreatic; phospholipase A2, and fatty acid for the digestion of dietary fat: in vitro experiments with the porcine enzymes. *Gastroenterology* 1980;78:954–962.

67. Gargouri Y, Pieroni G, Rivière C, Lowe PA, Saunière JF, Sarda L, Verger R. Importance of human gastric lipase for intestinal lipolysis: an in vitro study. *Biochim Biophys Acta* 1986;879:419–423.

68. Larsson A, Erlanson-Albertsson G. Effect of phosphatidylcholine and free fatty acids on the activity of pancreatic lipase-colipase. *Biochim Biophys Acta* 1986;876:543–550.

69. Hamosh M. In: Tsang RC, Nichols BL, eds. *Nutrition in infancy*. Philadelphia: Hanley & Belfus; 1988:133–159.

70. Chen Q, Sternby B, Nilsson A. Hydrolysis of triacylglycerol arachidonic and linoleic acid ester bonds by human pancreatic lipase and carboxylester lipase. *Biochim Biophys Acta* 1989;1004:372–386.

71. Katz L, Hamilton JR. Fat absorption in infants of birth weight less than 1300 g. *J Pediatr* 1974;85:608–614.

72. Rey J, Schmitz J, Amedee-Menesme O. Fat absorption in low birthweight infants. *Acta Paediatr Scand* 1982;296 (suppl):81–84.

73. Soderhjelm L. Fat absorption studies in children. 1. Influence of heat treatment on milk fat retention by premature infants. *Acta Paediatr Scand* 1952;41:207–221.

74. Hernell O, Blackberg L, Fredrikson B, Olivecrona T. Bile salt-stimulated lipase in human milk and lipid digestion during the neonatal period. In: Lebenthal E, ed. *Textbook of gastroenterology and nutrition in infancy*. New York: Raven Press; 1981:465–472.

75. Lavine M, Clark RM. Changing patterns of free fatty acids in breast milk during storage. *J Pediatr Gastroenterol Nutr* 1987;6:769–774.

76. Tantibhedyangkul P, Hashim SA. Medium-chain triglyceride feeding in premature infants: effects on calcium and magnesium absorption. *Pediatrics* 1979;61:537–545.

77. Chappell JE, Clandinin MT, Kearney-Volpe C, Reichman B, Swyer PW. Fatty acid balance studies in premature infants fed human milk or formula: effect of calcium supplementation. *J Pediatr* 1986;108:439–447.

78. McDonald GB, Weidman M. Partitioning of polar fatty acids into lymph and portal vein after intestinal absorption in the rat. *J Exp Physiol* 1987;72:153–159.

79. Swift LL, Hill JO, Peters JC, Greene HL, Medium-chain fatty acids: evidence for incorporation into chylomicron triglycerides in humans. *Am J Clin Nutr* 1990;52:834–836.

80. Akesson B, Gronowitz S, Herslof B, Ohlson R. Absorption of synthetic, stereochemically defined acylglycerols in the rat. *Lipids* 1978;13:338–343.

81. Ikeda I, Tomari Y, Sugano M, Watanabe S, Nagata J. Lymphatic absorption of structured glycerides containing medium-chain fatty acids and linoleic acid, and their effect on cholesterol absorption in rats. *Lipids* 1991;26:369–373.

82. Hamosh M and Hamosh P. Lipoprotein lipase, hepatic lipase, and their role in lipid clearing during total parenteral nutrition. In: Lebenthal E, ed. *Total parenteral nutrition: indications, utilization, complications, and pathophysiological considerations*. New York: Raven Press; 1986:29–58.

83. Roy CC, Ste-Marie M, Chartrand L, Weber A, Bard H, Doray B. Correction of the malabsorption of the preterm infant with medium chain triglyceride formula. *J Pediatr* 1975;86:446–450.

84. Tantibhedyangkul P, Hashim SA. Medium chain triglyceride feeding in premature infants. Effects on fat and nitrogen metabolism. *Pediatrics* 1975;55:359–70.

85. Tantibhedyangkul P, Hashim SA. Clinical and physiologic aspects of medium chain triglycerides: alleviation of steatorrhea in premature infants. *Bull NY Acad Med* 1971;47:17–33.

86. Huston, RK, Reynolds JW, Jensen C, Buist NRM. Nutrient and mineral retention and vitamin D absorption in low birthweight infants: effect of medium chain triglycerides. *Pediatrics* 1983;72:44–48.

87. Okamoto E, Muttart CR, Zucker CL, Heird WC. Use of medium chain triglycerides in feeding the low birthweight infant. *Am J Dis Child* 1982;136:428–431.

88. Whyte RK, Campbell D, Stanhope R, Bayley HS, Sinclair, JC. Energy balance in low birthweight infants fed formula of high or low medium chain triglyceride content. *J Pediatr* 1986;108:964–971.

89. Dupont C, Rocchiccioli F, Bougneres PF. Urinary excretion of dicarboxylic acids in term newborns fed with 5% medium-chain-triglycerides-enriched formula. *J Pediatr Gastroenterol Nutr* 1987;6:313–314.

90. Henderson MJ, Dear PRF. Dicarboxylic aciduria and medium chain triglyceride supplemented milk. *Arch Dis Child* 1986;61:610–611.

91. Shigematsu Y, Momoi T Sudo M, Suzuki Y. (ω-1)-Hydroxymonocarboxylic acids in urine of infants fed medium-chain triglycerides. *Clin Chem* 1981;27:1661–1664.

92. Sulkers EJ, Lafeber HN, Sauer PJJ. Quantitation of oxidation of medium-chain triglycerides in preterm infants. *Pediatr Res* 1989;26:294–297.

93. Whyte RK, Whelan D, Hill R, McClorry S. Excretion of dicarboxylic acids and w-1-hydroxy fatty acids by low birthweight infants fed with medium-chain triglycerides *Pediatr Res* 1986;20:122–125.

94. Rössle C, Carpentier YA, Richelle M, et al. Medium-chain triglycerides induce alterations in carnitine metabolism. *Am J Physiol* 1990;258:E940–E947.

95. Sarda P, Lepage G, Roy CC, Chessex P. Storage of medium chain triglycerides in adipose tissue of orally fed infants. *Am J Clin Nutr* 1987;45:399–405.

96. Hashim SA, Tantibhedyangkul P. Medium chain triglyceride in early life: effects on growth of adipose tissue. *Lipids*. 1987;22:429–434.

97. Ponder DL. Medium chain triglycerides and urinary dicarboxylic acids in newborns. *JPEN* 1991;93–94.

98. Kraus H. Developmental changes of cerebral ketone body utilization in human infants. *Hoppe-Seyler's Z Physiol Chem* 1974;355:164–170.

99. Settergren G, Lindblad BS, Persson B. Cerebral blood flow and exchange of oxygen, glucose, ketone bodies, lactate, pyruvate and amino acids in infants. *Acta Paediatr Scand* 1976;65:345–353.

100. Edmond J, Korsak RA, Morrow JW, Torok-Both G, Catlin DH. Dietary cholesterol and the origin of cholesterol in the brain of developing rats. *J Nutr* 1991;121:1323–1330.

101. Bossi E, Kohler E, Herschkowitz N. Utilization of D-β-hydroxybutyrate and oleate as alternate energy fuels in

brain cell cultures of newborn mice after hypoxia at different glucose concentrations. *Pediatr Res* 1989;26:478–481.

102. Commission directive on infant formulas and follow-on formulas, May 14, 1991 (91/321/91). *Office J Eur Comm* 1991; 4.7.

103. Committee on Nutrition of the Preterm Infant, European Society of Paediatric Gastroenterology and Nutrition. *Nutrition and feeding of preterm infants*. Oxford, UK: Blackwell Scientific Publications; 1987.

104. Herin P, Zetterstrom, R. Studies on renal response to various protein intakes in preterm infants. *Acta Paediatr Scand* 1987;76:447–452.

105. Jocobsen J. Binding of bilirubin to human serum albumin. *FEBS Lett* 1969;5:112.

106. Starinsky R, Shafir E. Displacement of albumin-bound bilirubin by free fatty acids: implications for neonatal hyperbilirubinemia. *Clin Chim Acta* 1970;29:311.

107. Andrew G, Chan G, Schiff D. Lipid metabolism in the neonate. II. The effect of intralipid on bilirubin binding in vitro and in vivo. *J Pediatr* 1976;61:694.

108. Gutcher GR, Farrell PM. Intravenous infusion of lipid for the prevention of essential fatty acid deficiency in premature infants. *Am J Clin Nutr* 1991;54:1024–1028.

109. Andersen GE, Hertel J, Tygstrup I. Pulmonary fat accumulation in preterm infants. *Lancet* 1981;2:441.

110. Paust H, Schroder H, Park W. Intravascular fat accumulation in the very-low-birthweight infant. *J Pediatr* 1983;103:668–669.

111. Pereira GR, Fox WW, Stanley CA. Decreased oxygenation and hyperlipemia during intravenous fat infusion in premature infants. *Pediatrics*. 1980;66:26–30.

112. Adamkin DH, Gelke KN, Wilkerson SA. The influence of intravenous therapy on tracheal effluent phospholipids and oxygenation in severe respiratory distress syndrome. *J Pediatr* 1985;106:122–124.

113. Griffin EA, Bryan MH, Angel A. Variations in intralipid tolerance in newborn infants. *Pediatr Res* 1983;17:478–487.

114. Haumont D, Deckelbaum, RJ, Richelle M, Dahlan W, Coussaert E, Bihain B, Carpentier YA. Plasma lipid and plasma lipoprotein concentrations in low birth weight infants given parenteral nutrition with twenty or ten percent lipid emulsion. *J Pediatr* 1989;115:787–93.

115. Hamilton JJ, Innis SM. Influence of intralipid on plasma cholesterol and lathosterol levels of preterm (23–32 wk gestation) infants. *Pediatr Res* 1992;31:396–400.

116. Hajri T, Ferezou J, Lutton C. Effects of intravenous infusions of commercial fat emulsions (intralipid 10 or 20%) on rat plasma lipoproteins: phospholipids in excess are the main precursors of lipoprotein-X-like particles. *Biochim Biophys Acta* 1990;1047:121–130.

117. Hailer S, Wolfram G, Zollner N. Changes in serum lipoproteins in humans following the infusion of a fat emulsion containing medium- and long-chain triglycerides. *Eur J Clin Invest* 1987;17:402–407.

118. Stein TP, Fried RC, Torosian MJ, Leskiw MD, Schluter MD, Settle RG, Buzby GP. Comparison of glucose, LCT and LCT plus MCT as calorie sources for parenterally nourished septic rats. *Am J Physiol* 1986;250:E312–E318.

119. Foote KD, MacKinnon MJ, Innis SM. Effect of early introduction of formula versus fat free parenteral nutrition on essential fatty acid status of preterm infants. *Am J Clin Nutr* 1991;54:93–97.

120. Friedman Z, Rosenberg A. Abnormal lung surfactant related to essential fatty acid deficiency in a neonate. *Pediatrics* 1979;76:447–452.

121. Friedman Z, Lambeth EL Jr, Stahlman MT, Oates JA. Platelet dysfunction in the neonate with essential fatty acid deficiency. *J Pediatr* 1977;90:439–443.

122. Cooke RJ, Zee P, Yeh Y-Y. Safflower oil emulsion administration during parenteral nutrition in preterm infant. 1. Effect on essential fatty acid status. *J Pediatr Gastroenterol Nutr* 1985;4:799–803.

123. Cooke RJ, Yeh Y-Y, Gibson D, Debo D, Bell GL. Soybean oil emulsion administration during parenteral nutrition in the preterm infant: effect on essential fatty acid, lipid and glucose metabolism. *J Pediatr* 1987;111:767–773.

124. Borum PR. Carnitine. *Annu Rev Nutr* 1983;3:233–259.

125. Novak M, Wieser PB, Buch M, Hahn P. Acetylcarnitine and free carnitine in body fluids before and after birth. *Pediatr Res* 1979;13:10–15.

126. Cederblad G, Svenningsen H. Plasma carnitine and breast milk carnitine intake in premature infants. *J Pediatr Gastroenterol Nutr* 1986;5:616–621.

127. Penn D, Ludwigs B, Schmidt-Sommerfeld E, Pascu F. Effects of gestational age and nutrition on tissue carnitine concentrations in infants. *Biol Neonate* 1985;47:130–135.

128. Shenai JP, Borum PR, Mohan P, Donlevy SC. Carnitine status at birth of newborn infants of varying gestation. *Pediatr Res* 1983;17:579–582.

129. Shenai JP, Borum PR. Tissue carnitine reserves of newborn infants. *Pediatr Res* 1984;18:679–681.

130. Sann L, Divry P, Cartier B, Vianey-Land C, Maire I. Ketogenesis in hypoglycaemic neonates. Study of carnitine and dicarboxylic acids in neonatal hypoglycaemia. *Biol Neonate* 1987;52:80–85.

131. Penn D, Schmidt-Sommerfeld E, Wolf H. Carnitine deficiency in premature infants receiving total parenteral nutrition. *Early Hum Dev* 1980;4:23–34.

132. Schiff D, Chan G, Seccombe D, Hahn P. Plasma carnitine levels during intravenous feeding of the neonate. *J Pediatr* 1979;95:1043–1046.

133. Penn D, Ludwig B, Schmidt-Sommerfeld E, Pascu F. Effect of nutrition on tissue carnitine concentrations in infants of different gestational ages. *Biol Neonate* 1985;47:130–135.

134. Schmidt-Sommerfeld E, Penn D, Wolf H. Carnitine blood concentrations and fat utilization in parenterally alimented premature newborn infants. Deficiency in premature infants receiving total parenteral nutrition: effect of L-carnitine supplementation. *J Pediatr* 1982;100:260–264.

135. Schmidt-Sommerfeld E, Penn D. Carnitine and total parenteral nutrition of the neonate. *Biol Neonate* 1990;58:81–88.

136. Larrson LE, Olegard R, Ljung A, Rubensson A, Cederblad G. Parenteral nutrition in preterm neonates with and without carnitine supplementation. *Acta Anaesthesiol Scand* 1990;34:501–505.

137. Sulkers EJ, Lafeber HN, Degenhart, HJ, Przyrembel H, Schlotzer E, Sauer PJJ. Effects of high carnitine supplementation on substrate utilization in low-birth-weight infants receiving total parenteral nutrition. *Am J Clin Nutr* 1990;52:889–894.

138. Penn D, Dolderer M., Schmidt-Sommerfeld E. Carnitine concentrations in the milk of different species and infant formulas. *Biol Neonate* 1987;52:70–79.

6. Vitamin A

Jayant P. Shenai

Reviewers: Harry L. Greene, Frank R. Greer, Joseph Warshaw

Vitamin A is a fat-soluble micronutrient recognized since 1912 as a constituent of the diet that is essential for the promotion of growth.[1,2] The vitamin A compounds (retinoids) are present in three natural forms: retinol, retinaldehyde, and retinoic acid. Retinol (vitamin A alcohol) is a dietary component present in the form of retinyl esters in food sources of animal origin and is also formed in vivo from its precursor, β-carotene, which is present in food sources of plant origin. The chemical structure of all-*trans*-retinol was first described in 1931[3] and that of β-carotene in 1930.[4] Retinyl esters are derived from esterification of retinol and constitute the principal storage forms of vitamin A; the major retinyl esters found in animal and human tissues are retinyl palmitate and stearate and, to a lesser extent, oleate and linoleate. Retinaldehyde, also called retinal, is derived from reversible oxidation of retinol and, in combination with various lipoproteins, forms the visual pigment of the retina.[5] The photoisomerization of retinaldehyde is necessary for vision.[6] Retinoic acid is derived from further, irreversible oxidation of retinaldehyde in the tissues[7] and is considered to be the active metabolite of vitamin A in functions related to growth, differentiation, and transformation.[8]

Vitamin A is transported in plasma as retinol bound to a specific carrier protein, retinol-binding protein (RBP). The isolation and partial characterization of RBP was first reported in 1968.[9] The human RBP molecule consists of a polypeptide chain of about 180 amino acid residues; it has a molecular weight of approximately 21,000 and a single binding site for one molecule of retinol.[10,11] Retinol-binding protein is synthesized in the liver and secreted into the plasma as the retinol-RBP complex.[12] In plasma, the retinol-RBP complex interacts with another protein, transthyretin (previously called prealbumin), and circulates as a 1:1 molar RBP-transthyretin complex.[12] The transthyretin molecule is a stable, symmetrical tetramer composed of four identical subunits and has a molecular weight of approximately 55,000.[13]

The role of vitamin A in the promotion of growth and differentiation of epithelial tissues makes it an important nutrient during development in the perinatal period. This chapter focuses on the role of vitamin A in the nutritional management of the preterm infant and specifically examines its influence on lung injury and healing.

Physiology

Intrauterine Vitamin A Acquisition

Vitamin A is transferred from the mother to the fetus, particularly in late gestation, in most animal species.[14-20] Although the precise mechanisms of intrauterine transfer are undefined, the transplacental transport of maternal retinol-RBP complex appears to be the predominant source of vitamin A for the fetus in early gestation. In late gestation, RBP synthesized by the fetal liver appears to be involved in extracting vitamin A from the placental circulation. Swallowed amniotic fluid containing vitamin A[21,22] and transfer of maternal lipoproteins containing retinyl esters[18] are other possible sources of vitamin A for the fetus.

The transplacental transport of vitamin A in humans has been studied by examining paired samples of maternal blood and fetal or cord blood obtained at various gestational ages.[23-27] The ratio of maternal to fetal concentration of plasma vitamin A in healthy human pregnancies is approximately 2:1. In conditions in which the maternal vitamin A status is marginal or deficient, the fetal plasma vitamin A concentrations are often maintained within normal limits and may exceed maternal plasma vitamin A concentrations.[23,28,29] In studies involving maternal vitamin A supplementation, the cord blood vitamin A concentrations have been found to be similar to those seen in unsupplemented controls.[23,30,31] Thus, fetal plasma vitamin A concentrations appear to be maintained within a normal range despite variations in the maternal vitamin A status and intake. The precise regulatory mechanisms by which this homeostasis is achieved remain unclear. Nor is it known whether such mechanisms can compensate successfully for extreme conditions of maternal vitamin A deprivation or excess.

Vitamin A Absorption

Dietary retinyl esters are processed by a complex but coordinated series of physical and chemical events in the bowel lumen.[32] These events include dispersion and emulsification of retinyl esters in the stomach, their hydrolysis in the intestinal lumen by pancreatic and other enzymes, and solubilization of retinol (derived from retinyl ester hydrolysis) with bile salts in mixed micelles. These intraluminal events facilitate uptake of vitamin A by the enteral mucosal cells (Fig. 6.1). Retinol within the mucosal cells is largely reesterified with long-chain fatty acids. The retinyl esters are then incorporated, together with other lipids and apolipoproteins, into chylomicron particles. The chylomicrons are secreted by the enteral mucosal cells into the intestinal lacteals and enter the plasma compartment through the intestinal lymphatics, largely via the thoracic duct. Retinyl esters found in the lymph chylomicron are almost entirely retained in the particle during its processing to a chylomicron remnant. The chylomicron remnants and the retinyl esters are almost completely removed from the circulation by the liver.

The reesterification of retinol in the enteral mucosal cells and its subsequent absorption into the lymph are influenced by a specific carrier protein called cellular retinol-binding protein type two (CRBP II). The CRBP II molecule consists of a polypeptide chain with a molecular weight of approximately 16,000. In the adult rat, CRBP II is present almost exclusively in the absorptive cells of the small intestine.[33,34] Its concentration in the small intestine appears to be age related; it is low in immature fetuses relative to mature newborns and adults.[33] A similar gut-specific CRBP II recently has been shown to be present in the human small intestine.[35] Its localization in the mature, villus-associated enterocytes of the jejunum suggests that this protein may play an important role in vitamin A absorption in the gut. Its role possibly may be to receive newly absorbed retinol and present it to an enzyme for the obligatory esterification before incorporation into chylomicrons. The development of this protein during fetal and neonatal life in humans has not been studied. It is possible that the lower concentrations of this protein in the small intestine of preterm neonates relative to mature term infants may result in differences in vitamin A absorption by these infants.

Vitamin A Storage

As much as 90% of the total body reserve of vitamin A is stored in the liver in adults of most animal species.[32] The normal liver vitamin A concentration in healthy human adults ranges from 100 to 300 μg/g.[36] The liver vitamin A concentration in children varies with age, being lower in infancy than in later childhood, adolescence, and young adulthood.[37,38] A liver vitamin A concentration <40 μg/g is considered indicative of low vitamin A reserve, and a concentration <20 μg/g is considered indicative of a deficiency.[37-39]

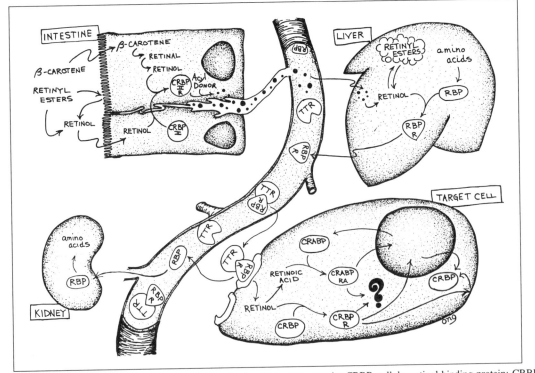

Fig. 6.1. Physiology of vitamin A. CRABP, cellular retinoic acid-binding protein; CRBP, cellular retinol-binding protein; CRBP II, cellular retinol-binding protein type two; R, retinol; RA, retinoic acid; RBP, retinol-binding protein; TTR, transthyretin. (Adapted, with permission, from Ong DE. Vitamin A-binding proteins. *Nutr Rev* 1985; 43: 225–232, and ILSI North America.)

The liver vitamin A reserve at birth was studied in a group of preterm infants (n=25) who died within 24 hours after birth, before changes in vitamin A status could be induced by postnatal events.[40] The mean (±SD) liver vitamin A concentration was 30 ± 13 μg/g (range, 2 to 49 μg/g). A high percentage of preterm infants in this study, 76%, had values of liver vitamin A <40 μg/g; approximately 37% of those infants had values <20 μg/g. Other authors[38,41-43] have published similar values for liver vitamin A concentrations. These studies have shown that preterm infants are born with low liver reserves of vitamin A. The ability of these infants to offset an inadequate vitamin A intake in the postnatal period is therefore limited.

Although the liver is the principal storage site for vitamin A, other organs, including the developing lung, are capable of storing vitamin A.[44,45] The ontogeny of vitamin A storage in fetal and neonatal lungs was examined in the rat, and significant vitamin A storage was found to occur in the last third of prenatal life.[46] Depletion of these stores, which begins before birth and continues into the early postnatal period, suggests that the developing lung may be dependent on these local vitamin A stores during active growth and differentiation. The utilization of vitamin A stores in the developing lung appears to be independent of the liver stores of vitamin A. Whether the developing lung of humans is capable of vitamin A uptake, esterification, and storage remains undetermined.

Because significant vitamin A storage occurs in the fetal rat lung near term, prematurely born animals deprived of adequate stores in their lungs may be susceptible to the adverse effects of vitamin A deficiency. The possibility of augmenting fetal lung vitamin A stores by maternal administration of vitamin A was examined in the perinatal rat.[47] This study showed that a prompt, sustained increase in fetal lung stores of vitamin A is possible after prenatal administration of a large intragastric dose of vitamin A to the mother. The possibility that administration of vitamin A to human mothers with imminent preterm deliveries might augment the lung vitamin A stores of their newborn infants remains unexplored. The precise dosage of maternal vitamin A supplementation and its effect on lung disease in the neonate also remain undetermined.

Vitamin A Metabolism

Vitamin A is distributed to the target tissues in the form of retinol-RBP complex bound to transthyretin (Fig. 6.1). The cellular uptake of vitamin A is dependent upon a specific membrane receptor that recognizes RBP. This receptor, which has not been fully characterized, has been demonstrated in vitro by studies with isolated cells[48] and in vivo by autoradiographic studies with ^{125}I-labeled RBP.[49] After delivery of vitamin A to the plasma membranes, RBP is returned to the circulation and is in part eliminated by the kidney and in part reused for vitamin A delivery.[50] The mechanisms involved in the processing of transthyretin are not known.

The movement of vitamin A within the tissue cells involves two intracellular vitamin A-binding proteins, cellular retinol-binding protein (CRBP) and cellular retinoic acid-binding protein (CRABP).[51-53] The CRBP molecule consists of a polypeptide chain with a molecular weight of approximately 14,600 and a single binding site for one molecule of all-*trans*-retinol. Cellular retinol-binding protein plays a role in the transfer of retinol from the plasma membrane to specific binding sites for retinol within the nucleus on some component of chromatin.[54] The CRABP molecule also consists of a polypeptide chain with a molecular weight of approximately 14,600 and a single binding site for one molecule of all-*trans*-retinoic acid. Given the apparent absence of a plasma delivery system specific for retinoic acid, it seems likely that the retinoic acid within the cell is mostly derived from oxidation of retinol occurring within the cell. Cellular retinoic acid-binding protein may be involved in an interaction of retinoic acid within the cell nucleus.[55,56] The precise mechanisms by which both retinol and retinoic acid influence nuclear metabolism, regulate genomic expression, and induce orderly differentiation of tissues remain under investigation.

Vitamin A Excretion

The excretory end products of vitamin A metabolism are largely derived from retinoic acid.[57] Retinoic acid is partly excreted in the ester form of β-glucuronide via the biliary system and is subject to reabsorption in the gut.[58] The enterohepatic circulation of retinoic acid serves to conserve this biologically active form of vitamin A. The rest of the retinoic acid is largely excreted in the urine in the form of oxidation products.[59]

Although several metabolites of vitamin A have been identified in the blood, tissue, and urine, none has proved to be an accurate indicator of the rate of utilization of vitamin A.[60] These metabolites have not been systematically studied in the preterm infant.

Vitamin A and Preterm Infant Feedings

Enteral Feeding

The vitamin A value of a diet is expressed in International Units (IU) or Retinol Equivalents (RE).[61] One IU of vitamin A is equivalent to 0.3 μg of preformed retinol; 1 RE of vitamin A is equivalent to 1.0 μg of retinol.

Human Milk The vitamin A content of human milk is variable and is influenced by several factors, such as age, parity, and socioeconomic status of the mother; postpartum age; and the volume and fat content of the milk. The vitamin A concentration of colostrum is high (>331 IU/dL or >99 μg/dL). The concentration of vitamin A in human milk decreases gradually in the first few months of lactation.[62-65] The vitamin A concentration of mature human milk ranges from 110 to 257 IU/dL (33 to 77 μg/dL).[62,63, 65-68]

The milk of mothers giving birth prematurely differs in composition from that of mothers delivering at term gestation. The vitamin A concentration of preterm milk is lower than that of term milk in early lactation, but it becomes higher than that of term milk about the second week of lactation.[68-70] At approximately 35 days postpartum age, the vitamin A concentration of preterm milk ranges from 277 to 333 IU/dL (83 to 100 μg/dL).[69-70] Assuming that the vitamin A concentration of preterm milk is approximately 300 IU/dL (90 μg/dL), the vitamin A intake of a preterm infant on full enteral feeding of its own mother's milk at a conventional rate of 150 mL/kg/day is estimated to be 450 IU/kg/day (135 μg/kg/day), or approximately 450 IU/100 kcal/day (135 μg/100 kcal/day).

More than 90% of the vitamin A in human milk is in the form of retinyl esters contained in the core of the milk fat globules.[71] The composition of retinyl esters is dependent on the fatty acid composition of the milk lipids. Less than 10% of the vitamin A in human milk is present as free retinol.[67,72-74] Thus, the efficiency of utilization of vitamin A in a preterm neonate fed human milk depends largely on the ability of the infant's gastrointestinal tract to process retinyl esters.

Infant Formulas and Multivitamin Supplements
Various infant formulas designed to meet the nutritional needs of a preterm infant are commercially available. The vitamin A content of these formulas varies from 240 to 972 IU/dL (72 to 292 μg/dL). The intake of vitamin A for a preterm infant on full enteral feeding of one of these infant formulas at a conventional rate of 150 mL/kg/day ranges from 360 to 1,456 IU/kg/day (108 to 437 μg/kg/day), or approximately 300 to 1,215 IU/100 kcal/day (90 to 365 μg/100 kcal/day).

Preterm infants on full enteral feeding often are given multivitamin supplements. The vitamin A content of a typical multivitamin supplement is 1,500 IU/mL (450 μg/mL). The vitamin A intake of a preterm infant on full enteral feeding thus can be increased by 1,500 IU/day (450 μg/day) with administration of a daily dose of 1 mL of a multivitamin supplement.

Most of the vitamin A in the infant formulas and multivitamin supplements is in the form of retinyl esters. Thus, the efficiency of utilization of vitamin A in a preterm neonate fed an infant formula with or without multivitamin supplementation depends largely on the ability of the infant's gastrointestinal tract to process retinyl esters.

Carotene The carotene content of human milk is variable and is influenced largely by the maternal dietary carotene intake.[62,66,67] Only about 15% to 25% of the total carotene in human milk is present as β-carotene, the precursor of vitamin A; the remainder is present largely in the form of lycopene or lutein, which has no vitamin A activity.[66,71] The β-carotene content of infant formulas is also limited, ranging from 0 to 25 IU/dL (0 to 15 μg/dL). The contribution of β-carotene to the vitamin A intake of a preterm infant therefore appears to be small.

Digestion and Absorption Several factors can influence the ability of a preterm infant to digest and absorb enterally administered vitamin A. Transpyloric infusion is often used to feed preterm infants, particularly those requiring mechanical ventilation or continuous distending airway pressure. Bypassing the stomach, which is inherent with this method of feeding, may preclude intragastric dispersion and emulsification of dietary fat and retinyl esters. Absorption of dietary fat has been shown to be less efficient in preterm infants fed transpylorically compared with those fed by the gastric route.[75]

Pancreatic lipase activity is markedly low at birth and in the early postnatal period.[76] Likewise, the intraluminal bile acid concentrations and the bile acid pool size are low in newborn infants.[77,78] Immature development of these enzymes in preterm infants may contribute to inefficient digestion and absorption of both dietary fat and retinyl esters.

The absorption of vitamin A by the enteral route is inefficient in preterm infants but improves as gastrointestinal function matures.[79-83] Several strategies to improve the enteral absorption of vitamin A in preterm infants have a reasonable basis:

1. The presence of a bile salt–stimulated lipase in human milk enhances hydrolysis of retinyl esters and may account for the increased bioavailability of vitamin A in infants fed human milk.[84, 85] The use of fresh unprocessed human milk for feeding may result in more complete utilization of dietary vitamin A in preterm infants.

2. The vitamin A content of human milk from mothers delivering at term can be increased by maternal dietary supplementation with 50,000 IU (15,000 μg) or more of preformed vitamin A.[63,64,86] Whether this strategy is applicable or desirable in mothers delivering prematurely is unknown. The precise dosage of supplemental vitamin A and the optimal timing and duration of supplementation are also unknown.

3. Enhancement of enteral fat absorption may facilitate absorption of all fat-soluble vitamins, including vitamin A. Preterm infants fed longchain triglyceride diets are prone to fat malabsorption because of inadequate duodenal lipase and bile acid activity.[87,88] Substitution of a diet containing a high proportion of medium-chain triglycerides may alleviate the steatorrhea.[89] Preterm neonates fed an infant formula containing a high proportion of medium-chain triglycerides have a mean ($\pm$SD) coefficient of fat absorption as high as 92.5% $\pm$ 2.8%.[90] The efficiency of vitamin A absorption in infants fed such a formula remains unknown.

4. The vitamin A intake of a preterm infant on full enteral feeding can be increased with enteral administration of a multivitamin supplement. A study in preterm infants, however, failed to show significant improvement in the vitamin A status of formula-fed infants with supplementation.[91] The optimal amount and chemical form of vitamin A in supplemental preparations are unknown.

Parenteral Nutrition

Preterm infants who experience difficulties with enteral feeding are often sustained exclusively with intravenous nutrition for prolonged periods. A protein-dextrose solution and a lipid emulsion are commonly used for intravenous nutrition. Various nutrients, including vitamins, are generally administered through the protein-dextrose solution. The vitamin A concentration of the protein-dextrose solution is estimated to be 930 IU/dL (279 µg/dL). A newborn infant on total parenteral nutrition receiving the protein-dextrose solution at a conventional rate of 120 to 135 mL/kg/day is therefore expected to receive a vitamin A intake ranging from 1,116 to 1,256 IU/kg/day (335 to 377 µg/kg/day), or approximately 988 to 1,013 IU/100 kcal/day (296 to 304 µg/100 kcal/day).

However, vitamin A is subject to photodegradation,[92] and it binds to intravenous tubing[93]—potential sources of loss of the vitamin in transit from the solution bottle to the infant. The efficiency of vitamin A administration in a parenteral nutrition solution has been studied in an in vitro system.[94] If the expected delivery of vitamin A, based on a constant infusion rate and a fixed vitamin A concentration in the parenteral nutrition solution, was expressed as 100%, then the mean ($\pm$SD) loss of vitamin A from photodegradation in this study was 16% $\pm$ 9%, and the loss from adsorption to intravenous tubing was 59% $\pm$9%. The net loss ranged from 62% to 89%, suggesting that even under optimal conditions, no more than 38% of the expected amount of vitamin A was actually delivered through the parenteral route. Gillis et al.[95] have made similar observations. Using the above estimates for losses, the vitamin A intake of a newborn infant on total parenteral nutrition receiving the protein-dextrose solution at the conventional rate of 120 to 135 mL/kg/day is calculated to range from 424 to 477 IU/kg/day (127 to 143 µg/kg/day), or approximately 375 to 385 IU/100 kcal/day (113 to 116 µg/100 kcal/day).

Thus, the intravenous administration of vitamin A is inefficient because of substantial photodegradative and adsorptive losses of the vitamin. Until such losses can be substantially reduced or eliminated, either through development of new intravenous tubing material or through improved administration of fat-soluble vitamins in the lipid emulsion,[96] alternative methods of vitamin A administration, such as by intramuscular route, may be necessary to optimize the vitamin A status of a newborn infant on long-term parenteral nutrition.

Vitamin A Deficiency

Vitamin A influences orderly growth and differentiation of epithelial cells, and its deficiency affects various organ systems, including the lung.[97] The characteristic histopathologic changes in the respiratory system generally precede consequences of vitamin A deficiency involving the genitourinary system, eye, and skin.[97] Vitamin A deficiency results in a predictable sequence of progressive changes in the epithelial lining of pulmonary conducting airways.[97–99] These changes consist of necrotizing tracheobronchitis in early stages of the deficiency and squamous metaplasia in more advanced stages. The pathophysiologic consequences of these changes include the following: (1) loss of normal secretions of goblet cells and of other secretory cells; (2) loss of normal water homeostasis across the tracheobronchial epithelium; (3) loss of cilia and resultant predisposition to recurrent atelectasis and airway infection; and (4) narrowing of the lumen and loss of distensibility of airways, with resultant increase in airway resistance and the work of breathing. The histopathologic changes seen in vitamin A deficiency are reversible with restoration of normal vitamin A status.[100,101]

Preterm infants, who are susceptible to acute, subacute, and chronic lung injury, are at risk for the development of a form of chronic lung disease called bronchopulmonary dysplasia (BPD).[102] The diagnosis of BPD is based on the triad of supplemental oxygen need, respiratory symptoms, and characteristic chest radiograph abnormalities that persist beyond 28 days postnatal age.[103] The histopathologic changes seen in BPD consist of necrotizing tracheobronchitis in the early stages and squamous metaplasia in more advanced stages of the disease. The changes in human infants with BPD and those in animals with vitamin A deficiency are remarkably similar. The clinical manifestations that are typically seen in infants with BPD and in children with vitamin A deficiency, such as recurrent atelectasis and airway infection, can be explained by the functional alterations caused by the histopathologic changes in the lung and tracheobronchial tree.

The development of BPD in preterm infants is believed to be influenced by lung immaturity, by factors promoting injury, and by factors inhibiting healing of tissues of the lung and tracheobronchial tree.[102] Preterm infants are susceptible to repeated lung injury from such insults as hyaline membrane disease, prolonged and high inspired oxygen concentrations, barotrauma from mechanical ventilation, and secondary infection with prolonged tracheal intubation, all occurring against the background of lung immaturity.[104] It has been hypothesized that if injury occurred in the presence of vitamin A deficiency, normal healing would not occur, and lung disease would worsen. The role of vitamin A in influencing orderly differentiation of regenerating airways could have a favorable effect on the healing process, resulting in reduced pulmonary morbidity.[105] To test this hypothesis, three clinical studies[106–108] have been performed to evaluate vitamin A status and its influence on lung disease in preterm infants.

Vitamin A Status at Birth

The vitamin A status at birth of infants of various gestational ages was studied by examining cord blood samples obtained at delivery.[106] The mean plasma vitamin A concentration at birth was significantly lower in preterm infants than in term infants (Table 6.1). A high percentage of preterm infants in this study, 82%, had values of plasma vitamin A below 20 µg/dL (0.70 µmol/L), the level considered to be indicative of vitamin A deficiency.[61] Brandt et al.[109] have published similar values for cord blood concentrations of vitamin A.

The mean plasma RBP concentration at birth was also significantly lower in preterm infants than in term infants (Table 6.1).[106] A high percentage of preterm infants in this study, 77%, had plasma RBP values below 3.0 mg/dL (1.43 µmol/L), which is considered indicative of vitamin A deficiency.[110] The normal plasma RBP concentration (mean ± SD) in healthy human adults is 4.6 ± 1.0 mg/dL (2.20 ± 0.48 µmol/L),[111] and the concentrations in children are approximately 60% of the adult values.[25] Bhatia and Ziegler[112] have published values for cord blood concentrations of RBP similar to those seen in Table 6.1.

The plasma retinol/RBP molar ratio is calculated from the values of plasma concentrations of vitamin A and RBP, assuming that the molecular weights of retinol and RBP are 286 and 21,000, respectively.[113] In vitamin A-sufficient individuals, RBP is saturated with vitamin A in plasma and, consequently, the plasma retinol/RBP molar ratio is approximately 1.0.[111] The reported mean plasma retinol/RBP molar ratio in healthy adults is 0.82,[25] whereas the mean ratio at birth is 0.51 in term neonates[27,106] and only 0.39 in preterm neonates.[106]

These studies show that most preterm infants are born with low plasma concentrations of vitamin A and RBP and have low plasma retinol/RBP molar ratios. It is likely that these infants are vitamin A-deficient because delivery at an early gestational age has deprived them of transplacental vitamin A supply.

Vitamin A Status and Supplementation in Bronchopulmonary Dysplasia

A prospective study[107] compared the vitamin A status of two groups of preterm infants, one with clinical and radiographic evidence of BPD (n = 10) and the other, the controls, with no significant lung disease (n = 8). All weighed less than 1,500 g at birth and were born before 32 weeks gestational age. The mean plasma vitamin A concentrations of infants with BPD were significantly lower than those of controls at four sampling times in the first postnatal month (Table

Table 6.1. Plasma Vitamin A and Retinol-Binding Protein (RBP) at Birth in Neonates*

Group	Gestation (weeks)	Birthweight (g)	Vitamin A (µg/dL [µmol/L])	RBP (mg/dL [µmol/L])
Term (n = 32)	37–42	2,600–4,080	23.9±10.2[†] [0.84±0.36]	3.6±1.1[†] [1.72±0.53]
Preterm (n = 39)	24–36	570–2,640	16.0±6.2[†] [0.56±0.22]	2.8±1.2[†] [1.34±0.57]
p			<0.001	<0.001

*Data from Shenai et al.[106]
[†]Mean ±SD.

Table 6.2. Relationship of Plasma Vitamin A and Lung Disease in Neonates*

Group	Postnatal Age (days)			
	4	14	21	28
Bronchopulmonary dysplasia (BPD)	13.3±6.0[†] [0.47±0.21]	12.0±3.9[†] [0.42±0.14]	10.6±6.3[†] [0.37±0.22]	10.3±8.7[†] [0.36±0.30]
No BPD	23.3±13.1[†] [0.82±0.46]	29.3±9.9[†] [1.03±0.35]	18.1±8.3[†] [0.63±0.29]	18.9±6.7[†] [0.66±0.23]
p	<0.05	<0.001	<0.05	<0.05

*Data from Shenai et al.[107]
[†]Plasma vitamin A concentrations (mean ± SD) in μg/dL [μmol/L].

6.2). In contrast to controls, the infants with BPD showed a substantial decline in plasma vitamin A concentrations; the lowest plasma vitamin A concentrations were measured at 3 to 5 weeks and were markedly below the optimal level. During the phase of declining plasma vitamin A concentrations, the average vitamin A intake was <700 IU/kg/day (<210 μg/kg/day); the mode of feeding was predominantly intravenous. Although a gradual increase in plasma vitamin A concentrations was seen in most of these infants during the subsequent 4-week period, 88% of individual plasma vitamin A values remained below 20 μg/dL during the 8-week period of postnatal observation. During this phase of increasing plasma vitamin A concentrations, the average vitamin A intake exceeded 1,500 IU/kg/day (>450 μg/kg/day), and the mode of feeding was predominantly enteral. This study showed that most preterm infants with BPD manifest clinical, biochemical, and histopathologic evidence of vitamin A deficiency. Hustead et al.[114] found a similar association between vitamin A deficiency and BPD in preterm infants.

A randomized, blinded, controlled clinical trial[108] determined whether vitamin A supplementation from early postnatal life could reduce the morbidity associated with BPD in preterm infants. The study involved 40 preterm infants (700 to 1,300 g birthweight, 26 to 30 weeks gestational age) who required supplemental oxygen and mechanical ventilation for at least 72 hours after birth. The infants were given either supplemental vitamin A (2,000 IU or 600 μg retinyl palmitate) intramuscularly or 0.9% saline solution on postnatal day 4 and on alternate days thereafter, for a total of 14 injections over 28 days. The study groups were comparable in gestational maturity, clinical characteristics, initial lung disease, and vitamin A status at entry into the trial. Vitamin A administration resulted in significantly higher mean plasma concentra-

tions of vitamin A and RBP (Fig. 6.2). Compared with controls, fewer infants given vitamin A supplementation developed BPD or required supplemental oxygen, mechanical ventilation, and intensive care (Table 6.3). Airway infection and retinopathy of prematurity also were less frequent in the vitamin A group. The lower incidence of retinopathy of prematurity in vi-

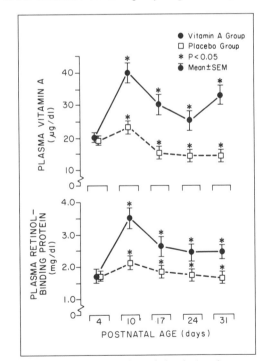

Fig. 6.2. Plasma concentrations of vitamin A and retinol-binding protein in a controlled trial of vitamin A supplementation in 40 preterm infants. Values on postnatal day 4 are before vitamin A supplementation and were comparable in the two study groups. At all subsequent determinations, mean values were significantly higher in the vitamin A group. (Reproduced, with permission, from Shenai et al.[108])

Table 6.3. Clinical Outcome of Neonates in Vitamin A Supplementation Trial*

| Outcome | Study Group | | p |
	Vitamin A (n = 20)	Control (n = 20)	
Incidence of bronchopulmonary dysplasia n(%)	9/20 (45)	17/20 (85)	<0.008
Supplemental oxygen (days)	44.5 ± 24.2[†]	63.8 ± 26.6[†]	<0.026
Mechanical ventilation (days)	17.9 ± 15.7[†]	28.1 ± 12.2[†]	<0.032
Intensive care (days)	62.8 ± 16.2[†]	78.9 ± 23.3[†]	<0.020
Airway infection n(%)	4/19 (21)	11/20 (55)	<0.029
Retinopathy of prematurity n(%)	5/19 (26)	12/20 (60)	<0.034

*Data from Shenai et al.[108]
[†]Mean ± SD.

tamin A-treated infants might have been related to their reduced exposure to prolonged, high concentrations of supplemental oxygen. This study showed that vitamin A supplementation resulting in a total vitamin A intake between 1,500 and 2,800 IU/kg/day (450 to 840 μg/kg/day) not only improves the vitamin A status of preterm infants but also appears to promote regenerative healing from lung injury, as evidenced by the decreased incidence and morbidity of BPD. Additional studies will be important in assessing this therapeutic approach in the management of preterm infants at risk for BPD.

Other Possible Roles for Vitamin A

Vitamin A Status in Other Neonatal Disorders

The potential role of vitamin A in influencing orderly differentiation of regenerating tissues could have a favorable effect on the healing process in other neonatal disorders associated with tissue injury. Necrotizing enterocolitis is believed to be the response of the immature gastrointestinal system to potentially injurious factors such as hypoxia or ischemia, microbial infection, and enteral substrate-induced injury.[115] Retinopathy of prematurity is a proliferative disorder of newly formed blood vessels in the retina that is thought to be initiated by injury to vascular endothelium from potentially noxious agents such as oxygen radicals.[116] A systematic evaluation of vitamin A sta-

tus in prevention and management of these disorders is warranted.

Vitamin A Status and Immune Function

Vitamin A may be required for optimal maintenance and function of the immune system.[117] Vitamin A deficiency is associated with increased susceptibility to infectious disease in both human populations and experimental models. The immunopotentiating effects of vitamin A have been supported by animal studies that demonstrate enhanced humoral and cell-mediated immunity in response to vitamin A treatment. Vitamin A supplementation has been shown to be beneficial in reducing mortality and morbidity from infectious diseases in children in areas where vitamin A deficiency is prevalent.[118–120] The role of vitamin A in prevention of infections in preterm infants with immature immune systems and resultant increased susceptibility to infections has not been systematically evaluated.

Vitamin A Toxicity

Hypervitaminosis A may result from acute intoxication or from chronic ingestion of vitamin A. Administration of a single large dose of vitamin A in excess of 100,000 IU (30,000 μg) may cause acute intoxication in infants.[61] The clinical manifestations of acute hypervitaminosis A include symptoms and signs of increased

Table 6.4. Recommendations for Vitamin A Intake in the Newborn Infant*

Transitional Period (0–2 weeks)

Bodyweight (g)	Intake(IU/kg/day)
>2,500	333
1,751–2,500	700
1,000–1,750	700–1,500
<1,000	1,500

Stable Period (2 weeks–term)

Lung Disease[†]	Intake (IU/kg/day)
No	700–1,500
Yes	1,500–2,800

Postdischarge Period (term–6 months)

Lung Disease[†]	Intake (IU/kg/day)
No	167–333
Yes	?

*Based on Underwood,[61] Shenai et al.,[107,108,128] and FAO/WHO.[127]
†Supplemental oxygen need, respiratory symptoms, and chest radiographic abnormalities.[103]

intracranial pressure. Long-term ingestion of vitamin A in excess of 25,000 IU/day (7,500 µg/day) may cause chronic intoxication in children and adults.[61,121,122] The clinical manifestations of chronic hypervitaminosis A include symptoms and signs of increased intracranial pressure, bone and joint pains, and mucocutaneous lesions; hepatomegaly and hepatic injury, hypercalcemia, and hematologic abnormalities are sometimes seen.[123] The radiographic findings in infants younger than 6 months of age include widened metaphyses, especially of the distal ulna, and radiolucent zones in the radius proximal to the metaphysis.[124] Cortical hyperostosis of multiple long bones and soft tissue changes are typically seen in infants older than 6 months.[124] In hypervitaminosis A, the plasma vitamin A concentrations are generally in excess of 100 µg/dL, and the ratio of retinyl ester to free retinol in plasma is elevated, but the plasma RBP concentrations usually remain normal.[125]

Hypervitaminosis A is reversible with restriction of vitamin A intake. Infusion of 2-hydroxypropyl-β-cyclodextrin as a means of solubilizing retinoids and enhancing their urinary excretion has been used occasionally as adjunctive therapy.[126]

Whether the threshold for acute and chronic hypervitaminosis A is lower in neonates compared to older infants and children is not known. The diagnosis is made by careful physical examination and search for evidence of increased intracranial pressure, bone and joint abnormalities, and mucocutaneous lesions. Periodic monitoring of blood chemistry profiles, including liver function tests and hematologic indexes, and serial measurements of plasma concentrations of vitamin A and RBP are important. Ultrasonographic scanning of the brain to detect intracranial hemorrhage and assessment of intracranial pressure by noninvasive methods such as fontanelle tonometry are also useful.

Recommendations

Dietary Intake

The recommended dietary intake of vitamin A for term newborn infants is 100 RE/kg/day or approximately 333 IU/kg/day.[127] This recommendation may not be appropriate for preterm neonates, particularly those with lung disease or other evidence of tissue injury. In preterm infants, a vitamin A intake <700 IU/kg/day (<210 µg/kg/day) is associated with a marked decline in plasma vitamin A concentrations.[107] Normalization of plasma concentrations of vitamin A and RBP in preterm infants is possible with a vitamin A intake above 1,500 IU/kg/day (>450 µg/kg/day).[108,128] Lack of clinical and biochemical evidence of toxicity in studies of vitamin A-supplemented infants and maintenance of their plasma vitamin A concentrations below 80 µg/dL suggest that a total vitamin A intake in the range of 1,500 to 2,800 IU/kg/day (450 to 840 µg/kg/day) is safe for preterm infants.[108,128] If the ideal energy intake in a preterm infant is 120 kcal/kg/day, then the desirable vitamin A intake is estimated to be 1,250 to 2,333 IU/100 kcal/day (375 to 700 µg/100 kcal/day). Recommendations for vitamin A intake in the newborn infant are outlined in Table 6.4.

Vitamin A Supplementation

Preterm neonates at risk for BPD are predisposed to vitamin A deficiency,[38,40–43,106,107,109,114] but vitamin A supplementation from early postnatal life may reduce the morbidity associated with BPD.[108,128] These observations have led to a protocol of vitamin A supplementation for certain infants hospitalized at Vanderbilt Medical Center. According to this protocol, all infants meeting the following criteria are eligible for supplementation: (1) birthweight <1,300 g; (2) gestational age <31 weeks; (3) appropriate growth for gestational age; (4) no major congenital anomalies; and (5) need for supplemental oxygen (FiO$_2$ >0.3) and mechanical ventilation for at least 24 hours after birth. These criteria are similar to those proposed by Bancalari et al.[129] to prospectively identify infants at risk for BPD. In addition to routine vitamin A intake from parenteral and enteral sources, these infants are given 2,000 IU (600 µg) retinyl palmitate by intramuscular injection on postnatal day 1 and on alternate days thereafter, for a total of 14 injections over 28 days until full enteral feeding is established (i.e., when energy intake by the enteral route exceeds 75% of the total energy intake and when enteral multivitamin supplementation is initiated). Plasma concentrations of vitamin A are monitored before the first dose of supplemental vitamin A and at weekly intervals throughout the period of supplementation. The dose of supplemental vitamin A is adjusted on the basis of these serial plasma vitamin A concentrations. All infants are monitored for evidence of toxicity. Correlations between vitamin A status and pulmonary outcome are examined to determine the effect of vitamin A supplementation on lung disease and associated morbidity.

Further studies confirming the beneficial effects of vitamin A supplementation are warranted before these guidelines can be recommended for general use in preterm infants.

Assessment of Vitamin A Status

Assessment of the vitamin A status of a preterm infant includes estimation of vitamin A intake, measurement of plasma concentrations of vitamin A and RBP, and calculation of plasma retinol/RBP molar ratio. The cumulative vitamin A intake by all routes (intravenous, intramuscular, and enteral) in any 1-week period can be calculated to determine the average daily intake of vitamin A (IU/kg/day) during that week. The plasma vitamin A concentration can be determined by the fluorometric method,[130] and the plasma RBP concentration can be determined either by quantitative radial immunodiffusion or by enzyme-linked immunosorbent assay.[131] The plasma retinol/RBP molar ratio is calculated from the plasma concentrations of vitamin A and RBP.[113]

The plasma RBP response to vitamin A administration recently was shown to be a useful test for assessing functional vitamin A status of a preterm infant.[128] This test is based on the varied response of RBP secretion from the liver into the plasma after vitamin A administration in animals with varying degrees of vitamin A sufficiency.[132,133] The plasma RBP response test consists of measurement of plasma RBP concentrations in sequentially obtained blood samples just before (baseline) and 1, 3, and 6 hours after an intramuscular injection of vitamin A (2,000 IU or 600 μg retinyl palmitate per kg bodyweight). The dose of vitamin A used in this test is based on previous observations about vitamin A supplementation in preterm infants.[108] The timing of blood samples is based on kinetic studies of RBP secretion in rats[133] and in human adults.[134] The percent increase in the plasma RBP concentration

from baseline (△-RBP) is calculated by the following equation:

$$\triangle\text{-RBP (\%)} = (\text{RBP [maximum]} - \text{RBP [baseline])/RBP (baseline)} \times 100.$$

Zero, the lowest △-RBP value, is assigned if there is no change or if there is a decrease in the plasma RBP concentration from the baseline value.

The plasma RBP response test was evaluated in 24 preterm infants at risk for BPD who were studied shortly after birth and again after a 28-day period of vitamin A supplementation.[128] On postnatal day 1, the △-RBP value was high (mean ± SD, 61% ±37%), and the plasma vitamin A and RBP concentrations were low; these findings were indicative of vitamin A deficiency. Supplemental vitamin A improved the vitamin A status of all infants, as shown by low △-RBP values (mean ± SD, 8% ± 9%) and normal plasma vitamin A and RBP concentrations on postnatal day 28. The 12 infants with a diagnosis of BPD had a higher mean △-RBP on postnatal day 28 than the infants without BPD (13% ± 10% vs 3% ±3%, p <0.01). This suggested persistent functional vitamin A deficiency despite supplementation in infants with lung disease. The individual △-RBP values on postnatal day 28 were 8% or higher in most infants with BPD and less than 8% in all infants without BPD.

This study showed that the plasma RBP response test is a useful indicator of the functional vitamin A status of a preterm infant. The test is simple to perform and is clinically applicable. More importantly, the test provides information that may be used to identify infants with persistent functional vitamin A deficiency despite supplementation and, possibly, with increased risk for BPD. Additional studies will be necessary in assessing the value of this diagnostic approach in the management of preterm infants at risk for BPD.

Loerch et al.[135] described a relative dose response test, in which the increase in plasma vitamin A concentration 5 hours after an oral dose of retinyl acetate was correlated with liver vitamin A stores in rats. This relative dose response test has been evaluated in adults with alcoholic hepatic cirrhosis,[136] adults undergoing abdominal surgery,[137] and children having liver biopsy.[138] A variation of the relative dose response test has been performed in preterm infants to determine their vitamin A status at discharge from the hospital.[139] However, no studies have reported correlations between the relative dose response test and pulmonary outcome in preterm infants.

Acknowledgments

This work was supported by Research Grants HL 14214 and HD 09195 from the National Institutes of Health.

The author gratefully acknowledges Mildred T. Stahlman, M.D., for her advice and encouragement, and Frank Chytil, Ph.D., for his sharing of expertise on vitamin A metabolism.

References

1. Hopkins FG. Feeding experiments illustrating the importance of accessory factors in normal dietaries. *J Physiol* 1912; 44:425–460.

2. McCollum EV, Davis M. The influence of certain vegetable fats on growth. *J Biol Chem* 1915;21: 179–182.

3. Karrer P, Morf R, Schopp K. Vitamin A from fish oils (I) and (II). *Helv Chim Acta* 1931;14:1431–1436.

4. Karrer P, Helfenstein A, Wehrli H. The coloring materials of plants, XVIII: further contribution to the constitution of the carotenoids. *Helv Chim Acta* 1930; 13:87–88.

5. Hubbard R. The molecular weight of rhodopsin and the nature of the rhodopsin-digitonin complex. *J Gen Physiol* 1954; 37:381–399.

6. Wald G. Molecular basis of visual excitations. *Science* 1968; 162:230–239.

7. Emerick RJ, Zile M, DeLuca HF. Formation of retinoic acid from retinol in the rat. *Biochem J* 1967;102: 606–611.

8. Robert AB, Sporn MB. Cellular biology and biochemistry of the retinoids. In: Sporn MB, Roberts AB, Goodman DS, eds. *The retinoids*. Orlando, FL: Academic Press, 1984; 2:209–286.

9. Kanai M, Raz A, Goodman DS. Retinol-binding protein: the transport protein for vitamin A in human plasma. *J Clin Invest* 1968; 47:2025–2044.

10. Raz A, Shiratori T, Goodman DS. Studies on the protein-protein and protein-ligand interactions involved in retinol transport in plasma. *J Biol Chem* 1970;245: 1903–1912.

11. Rask L, Anundi H, Bohme J, et al. Structural and functional studies of vitamin A-binding proteins. *Ann NY Acad Sci* 1981; 359:79–90.

12. Goodman DS. Plasma retinol-binding protein. In: Sporn MB, Roberts AB, Goodman DS, eds. *The retinoids*. Orlando, FL: Academic Press, 1984; 2:41–88.

13. Kanda Y, Goodman DS, Canfield RE, Morgan FJ. The amino acid sequence of human plasma prealbumin. *J Biol Chem* 1974; 249:6796–6805.

14. Moore T. Vitamin A transfer from mother to offspring in mice and rats. *Int J Vitamin Nutr Res* 1971;41: 301–306.

15. Branstetter RF, Tucker RE, Mitchell GE Jr, Boling JA, Bradley NW. Vitamin A transfer from cows to calves. *Int J Vitamin Nutr Res* 1973; 43:142–146.

16. Mitchell GE Jr, Rattray PV, Hutton JB. Vitamin A alcohol and vitamin A palmitate transfer from ewes to lambs. *Int J Vitamin Nutr Res* 1975; 45:299–304.

17. Takahashi YI, Smith JE, Goodman DS. Vitamin A and retinol-binding protein metabolism during fetal development in the rat. *Am J Physiol* 1977;233:E263–E272.

18. Ismadi SD, Olson JA. Dynamics of the fetal distribution and transfer of vitamin A between rat fetuses and their mother. *Int J Vitamin Nutr Res* 1982; 52:112–119.

19. Donoghue S, Richardson DW, Sklan D, Kronfeld DS. Placental transport of retinol in sheep. *J Nutr* 1982; 112:2197–2203.

20. Vahlquist A, Nilsson S. Vitamin A transfer to the fetus and to the amniotic fluid in rhesus monkey (*Macaca mulatta*). *Ann Nutr Metab* 1984; 28:321–333.

21. Wallingford JC, Milunsky A, Underwood BA. Vitamin A and retinol-binding protein in amniotic fluid. *Am J Clin Nutr* 1983; 38:377–381.

22. Sklan D, Shalit I, Lasebnik N, Spirer Z, Weisman Y. Retinol transport proteins and concentrations in human amniotic fluid, placenta, and fetal and maternal sera. *Br J Nutr* 1985; 54:577–583.

23. Lund CJ, Kimble MS. Plasma vitamin A and carotene of the newborn infant with consideration of fetal-maternal relationships. *Am J Obstet Gynecol* 1943; 46:207–221.

24. Baker H, Thompson FO, Langer AD, Munves A, DeAngelis ED, Kaminetzky HA. Vitamin profile of 174 mothers and newborns at parturition. *Am J Clin Nutr* 1975; 28:59–65.

25. Vahlquist A, Rask L, Peterson PA, Berg T. The concentrations of retinol-binding protein, prealbumin, and transferrin in sera of newly delivered mothers and children of various ages. *Scand J Clin Lab Invest* 1975; 35:569–575.

26. Baker H, Thind IS, Frank O, DeAngelis B, Caterini H, Louria DB. Vitamin levels in low-birth-weight newborn infants and their mothers. *J Obstet Gynecol* 1977; 129:521–524.

27. Jansson L, Nilsson B. Serum retinol and retinol-binding protein in mothers and infants at delivery. *Biol Neonate* 1983; 43:269–271.

28. Venkatachalam PS, Belavady B, Gopalan C. Studies on vitamin A nutritional status of mothers and infants in poor communities in India. *Trop Pediatr* 1962; 61:262–268.

29. Butte NF, Calloway DH. Proteins, vitamin A, carotene, folacin, ferritin and zinc in Navajo maternal and cord blood. *Biol Neonate* 1982; 41:273–278.

30. Lewis JM, Bodansky O, Lillienfeld MCC, Schneider H. Supplements of vitamin A and of carotene during pregnancy: their effect on the levels of vitamin A and carotene in the blood of mother and of newborn infant. *Am J Dis Child* 1947; 73:143–150.

31. Barnes AC. The placental metabolism of vitamin A. *Am J Obstet Gynecol* 1951; 61:368–372.

32. Goodman DS, Blaner WS. Biosynthesis, absorption, and hepatic metabolism of retinol. In: Sporn MB, Roberts AB, Goodman DS, eds. *The retinoids*. Orlando, FL: Academic Press, 1984; 2:1–39.

33. Ong DE. A novel retinol-binding protein from rat: purification and partial characterization. *J Biol Chem* 1984; 259:1476–1482.

34. Crow JA, Ong DE. Cell-specific immunohistochemical localization of a cellular retinol-binding protein (type two) in the small intestine of rat. *Proc Natl Acad Sci USA* 1985; 82:4707–4711.

35. Ong DE, Page DL. Cellular retinol-binding protein (type two) is abundant in human small intestine. *J Lipid Res* 1987; 28:739–745.

36. Pearson WN. Blood and urinary vitamin levels as potential indices of body stores. *Am J Clin Nutr* 1967; 20:514–525.

37. Huque T. A survey of human liver reserves of retinol in London. *Br J Nutr* 1982; 47:165–172.

38. Olson JA, Gunning DB, Tilton RA. Liver concentrations of vitamin A and carotenoids, as a function of age and other parameters, of American children who died of various causes. *Am J Clin Nutr* 1984; 39:903–910.

39. Olson JA. Evaluation of vitamin A status in children. *World Rev Nutr Diet* 1978; 31:130–134.

40. Shenai JP, Chytil F, Stahlman MT. Liver vitamin A reserves of very low birth weight neonates. *Pediatr Res* 1985; 19:892–893.

41. Iyengar L, Apte SV. Nutrient stores in human foetal livers. *Br J Nutr* 1972; 27:313–317.

42. Olson JA. Liver vitamin A reserves of neonates, preschool children and adults dying of various causes in Salvador, Brazil. *Arch Latinoam Nutr* 1979; 26:992–997.

43. Montreewasuwat N, Olson JA. Serum and liver concentrations of vitamin A in Thai fetuses as a function of gestational age. *Am J Clin Nutr* 1979; 32:601–606.

44. Goodman DS, Huang HS, Shiratori T. Tissue distribution and metabolism of newly absorbed vitamin A in the rat. *J Lipid Res* 1965; 6:390–396.

45. Zachman RD, Kakkad B, Chytil F. Perinatal rat lung retinol (vitamin A) and retinyl palmitate. *Pediatr Res* 1984; 18:1297–1299.

46. Shenai JP, Chytil F. Vitamin A storage in lungs during perinatal development in the rat. *Biol Neonate* 1990; 57:126–132.

47. Shenai JP, Chytil F. Effect of maternal vitamin-A administration on fetal lung vitamin-A stores in the perinatal rat. *Biol Neonate* 1990; 58:318–325.

48. Rask L, Peterson PA. In vitro uptake of vitamin A from the retinol-binding plasma protein to mucosal epithelial cells from the monkey's small intestine. *J Biol Chem* 1976; 251:6360–6366.

49. Bok D, Heller J. Transport of retinol from the blood to the retina: an autoradiographic study of the pigment epithelial cell surface receptor for plasma retinol-binding protein. *Exp Eye Res* 1976; 22:395–402.

50. Glover J, Jay C, White GH. Distribution of retinol-binding protein in tissues. *Vitamin Horm* 1974;32:215–235.

51. Bashor MM, Toft DO, Chytil F. In vitro binding of retinol to rat-tissue components. *Proc Natl Acad Sci USA* 1973; 70:3483–3487.

52. Ong DE, Chytil F. Retinoic acid binding protein in the rat tissue. *J Biol Chem* 1975; 250:6113–6117.

53. Chytil F, Ong DE. Cellular retinol- and retinoic acid-binding proteins in vitamin A action. *Fed Proc* 1979; 38:2510–2514.

54. Liau G, Ong DE, Chytil F. Interaction of the retinol/cellular retinol-binding protein complex with isolated nuclei and nuclear compounds. *J Cell Biol* 1981; 91:63–68.

55. Wiggert B, Russel P, Lewis M, Chader G. Differential binding to soluble nuclear receptors and effects on cell viability of retinol and retinoic acid in cultured retinoblastoma cells. *Biochem Biophys Res Commun* 1977;79: 218–225.

56. Jetten AM, Jetten MER. Possible role of retinoic acid-binding protein in retinoid stimulation of embryonal carcinoma cell differentiation. *Nature* (London) 1979; 278:180–182.

57. Sundaresan PR, Sundaresan GM. Studies on the urinary metabolites of retinoic acid in the rat. *Int J Vitamin Nutr Res* 1973; 43:61–69.

58. Dunagin PE Jr, Meadows EH Jr, Olson JA. Retinoyl beta-glucuronic acid: a major metabolite of vitamin A in rat. *Science* 1965; 148:86–87.

59. Zile MH, Inhorn RC, DeLuca HF. The biological activity of 5,6-epoxyretinoic acid. *J Nutr* 1980; 110:2225–2230.

60. Sundaresan PR, Bhagavan HN. Metabolic studies on retinoic acid in the rat. *Biochem J* 1971; 122:1–4.

61. Underwood BA. Vitamin A in animal and human nutrition. In: Sporn MB, Roberts AB, Goodman DS, eds. *The retinoids*. Orlando, FL: Academic Press, 1984;1: 281–392.

62. Lesher M, Brody JK, Williams HH, Macy IG. Human milk studies, XXVI: vitamin A and carotenoid contents of colostrum and mature human milk. *Am J Dis Child* 1945; 70:182–192.

63. Hrubetz MC, Deuel HJ Jr, Hanley BJ. Studies on carotenoid metabolism, V: The effects of a high vitamin A

64. Ajans ZA, Sarrif A, Husbands M. Influence of vitamin A on human colostrum and early milk. *Am J Clin Nutr* 1965; 17:139–142.

65. Tarjan R, Kramer M, Szoke K, Lindner K, Szarras T, Dworachak E. The effect of different factors on the composition of human milk during lactation. *Nutr Dieta* 1965; 7:136–154.

66. Chanda R, Owen EC, Cramond B. The composition of human milk with special reference to the relation between phosphorus partition and phosphatase and to the partition of certain vitamins. *Br J Nutr* 1951; 5:228–242.

67. Gebre-Medhin M, Vahlquist A, Hofvander Y, Uppsall L, Valquist B. Breast milk composition in Ethiopian and Swedish mothers: I, vitamin A and β-carotene. *Am J Clin Nutr* 1976; 29:441–451.

68. Thomas MR, Pearsons MH, Demkowicz IM, Chan IM, Lewis CG. Vitamin A and vitamin E concentration of the milk from mothers of preterm infants and milk of mothers of full term infants. *Acta Vitaminol Enzymol* 1981; 3:135–144.

69. Chappell JE, Francis T, Clandinin MT. Vitamin A and E content of human milk at early stages of lactation. *Early Hum Dev* 1985; 11:157–167.

70. Vaisman N, Mogilner BM, Sklan D. Vitamin A and E content of preterm and term milk. *Nutr Res* 1985;5: 931–935.

71. Thompson SY, Kon SK, Mawson EH. The application of chromatography to the study of the carotenoids of human and cow's milk. *Biochem J* 1942; 36:17–18.

72. Parrish DB, Wise GH, Hughes JS. The state of vitamin A in colostrum and in milk. *J Biol Chem* 1947;167: 673–678.

73. Fujita A, Kimura K. An improved micromethod for fractional determination of vitamin A alcohol and ester and the changes in both types of vitamin A in blood plasma, milk and liver after loading with both types of the vitamin and β-carotene. *J Vitaminol* 1960; 6:6–15.

74. Valhquist A, Nilsson S. Mechanisms for vitamin A transfer from blood to milk in rhesus monkeys. *J Nutr* 1979; 109:1456–1463.

75. Roy RN, Pollinitz RP, Hamilton JR, Chance GW. Impaired assimilation of nasojejunal feeds in healthy low-birth-weight newborn infants. *J Pediatr* 1977;90: 431–434.

76. Lebenthal E, Lee PC. Development of functional response in human exocrine pancreas. *Pediatrics* 1980; 66:556–560.

77. Norman A, Strandvik B, Ojamae O. Bile acids and pancreatic enzymes during absorption in the newborn. *Acta Paediatr Scand* 1972; 61:571–576.

78. Watkins JB, Ingall D, Szczepanik P, Klein PD, Lester R. Bile-salt metabolism in the newborn: measurement of pool size and synthesis by stable isotope technic. *N Engl J Med* 1973; 288:431–434.

79. Henley TH, Dann M, Golden WRC. Reserves, absorption and plasma levels of vitamin A in premature infants. *Am J Dis Child* 1944; 68:257–264.

80. Lewis JM, Bodansky O, Birmingham J, Cohlan SQ. Comparative absorption, excretion, and storage of oily and aqueous preparations of vitamin A. *J Pediatr* 1947; 31:496–508.

81. Sobel AE, Besman L, Kramer B. Vitamin A absorption in the newborn. *Am J Dis Child* 1949; 77:576–591.

82. Kahan J. The vitamin A absorption test, I: studies on children and adults without disorders in the alimentary tract. *Scand J Gastroenterol* 1969; 4:313–324.

83. Norman A, Strandvik B, Zetterstrom R. Test-meal in the diagnosis of malabsorption in infancy: tolerance tests using simultaneous oral administration of glucose, d-xylose, cream and vitamin A. *Acta Paediatr Scand* 1971; 60:165–172.

84. Hernell O, Gebre-Medhin M, Olivecrona T. Breast milk composition in Ethiopian and Swedish mothers, IV: Milk lipases. *Am J Clin Nutr* 1977; 30:508–511.

85. Fredrikzon B, Hernell O, Blackberg L, Olivecrona T. Bile salt-stimulated lipase in human milk: evidence of activity in vivo and of a role in the digestion of milk retinol esters. *Pediatr Res* 1978; 12:1048–1052.

86. Lesher M, Robinson A, Brody JK, Williams HW, Macy IG. Metabolism of women during the reproductive cycle, XVI: the effect of multivitamin supplements on the secretion of vitamin A in human milk. *J Am Diet Assoc* 1948; 24:12–16.

87. Zoppi G, Andreotti G, Pajno-Ferrara F, Njai DM, Gaburro D. Exocrine pancreas function in premature and full term neonates. *Pediatr Res* 1972; 6:880–886.

88. Signer E, Murphy GM, Edkins S, Anderson CM. Role of bile salts in fat metabolism of premature infants. *Arch Dis Child* 1974; 49:174–180.

89. Roy CC, Ste-Marie M, Chartrand L, Weber A, Bard H, Doray B. Correction of the malabsorption of the preterm infant with a medium-chain triglyceride formula. *J Pediatr* 1975; 86:446–450.

90. Shenai JP, Reynolds JW, Babson SG. Nutritional balance studies in very-low-birth-weight infants: enhanced nutrient retention rates by an experimental formula. *Pediatrics* 1980; 66:233–248.

91. Woodruff CW, Latham CB, James EP, Hewett JE. Vitamin A status of preterm infants: the influence of feeding and vitamin supplements. *Am J Clin Nutr* 1986;44:384–389.

92. Howard L, Chu R, Feman S, Mintz H, Ovesen L, Wolf B. Vitamin A deficiency from long-term parenteral nutrition. *Ann Intern Med* 1980; 93:576–577.

93. Hartline JV, Zachman RD. Vitamin A delivery in total parenteral nutrition solution. *Pediatrics* 1976; 58:448–451.

94. Shenai JP, Stahlman MT, Chytil F. Vitamin A delivery from parenteral alimentation solution. *J Pediatr* 1981; 99:661–663.

95. Gillis J, Jones G, Pencharz P. Delivery of vitamins A, D, and E in total parenteral nutrition solutions. *J Parenteral Enteral Nutr* 1983; 7:11–14.

96. Greene HL, Phillips BL, Franck L, et al. Persistently low blood retinol levels during and after parenteral feeding of very low birth weight infants: examination of losses into intravenous administration sets and a method of prevention by addition to a lipid emulsion. *Pediatrics* 1987; 79:894–900.

97. Wolbach SB, Howe PR. Tissue changes following deprivation of fat-soluble vitamin A. *J Exp Med* 1925:42:753–777.

98. Wong YC, Buck RC. An electron microscopic study of metaplasia of the rat tracheal epithelium in vitamin A deficiency. *Lab Invest* 1971; 24:55–66.

99. McDowell EM, Keenan KP, Huang M. Effects of vitamin A-deprivation on hamster tracheal epithelium: a quantitative morphologic study. *Virchows Arch Pathol* 1984; 45:197–219.

100. Wolbach SB, Howe PR. Epithelial repair in recovery from vitamin A deficiency. *J Exp Med* 1933; 57:511–526.

101. McDowell EM, Keenan KP, Huang M. Restoration of mucociliary tracheal epithelium following deprivation of vitamin A: a quantitative morphologic study. *Virchows Arch Pathol* 1984; 45:221–240.

102. Northway WH Jr, Rosan RC, Porter DY. Pulmonary disease following respirator therapy of hyaline-membrane disease: bronchopulmonary dysplasia. *N Engl J Med* 1967; 276:357–368.

103. Hazinski TA. Bronchopulmonary dysplasia. In: Chernick V, Kendig Jr EL, eds. *Disorders of the respiratory tract in children*. Philadelphia: WB Saunders, 1990: 300–320.

104. Stahlman MT, Cheatham W, Gray ME. The role of air dissection in bronchopulmonary dysplasia. *J Pediatr* 1979; 95:878–882.

105. Stahlman MT, Shenai JP, Gray ME, Sundell HW, Kennedy K, Chytil F. Lung differentiation and repair in relation to vitamin A status. In: BS Lindblad, BS, ed. *Perinatal nutrition*. Bristol Myers Nutrition Symposia. San Diego, CA: Academic Press, 1988; 1:117–123.

106. Shenai JP, Chytil F, Jhaveri A, Stahlman MT. Plasma vitamin A and retinol-binding protein in premature and term neonates. *J Pediatr* 1981; 99:302–305.

107. Shenai JP, Chytil F, Stahlman MT. Vitamin A status of neonates with bronchopulmonary dysplasia. *Pediatr Res* 1985; 19:185–188.

108. Shenai JP, Kennedy KA, Chytil F, Stahlman MT. Clinical trial of vitamin A supplementation in infants susceptible to bronchopulmonary dysplasia. *J Pediatr* 1987;111: 269–277.

109. Brandt RB, Mueller DG, Schroeder JR, et al. Serum vitamin A in premature and term neonates. *J Pediatr* 1978; 92:101–104.

110. Vahlquist A, Sjolund K, Norden A, Peterson PA, Stigmar G, Johansson B. Plasma vitamin A transport and visual dark adaptation in diseases of the intestine and liver. *Scand J Clin Lab Invest* 1978; 38:301–308.

111. Smith FR, Goodman DS. The effects of diseases of liver, thyroid, and kidneys on the transport of vitamin A in human plasma. *J Clin Invest* 1971; 50:2426–2436.

112. Bhatia J, Ziegler EE. Retinol-binding protein and prealbumin in cord blood of term and preterm infants. *Early Hum Dev* 1983; 8:129–133.

113. Smith JE, Goodman DS. Retinol-binding protein and the regulation of vitamin A transport. *Fed Proc* 1979; 38:2504–2509.

114. Hustead VA, Gutcher GA, Anderson SA, Zachman RD. Relationship of vitamin A (retinol) status to lung disease in the preterm infant. *J Pediatr* 1984; 105:610–615.

115. Kliegman RM, Fanaroff AA. Necrotizing enterocolitis. *N Engl J Med* 1984; 310:1093–1103.

116. Flynn JT. Retinopathy of prematurity. *Pediatr Clin N Am* 1987; 34:1487–1516.

117. Nauss KM. Influence of vitamin A status on the immune system. In: Bauernfeind JC, ed. *Vitamin A deficiency and its control*. Orlando, FL: Academic Press, 1986: 207–243.

118. Sommer A, Tarwotjo I, Djunaedi E, et al. Impact of vitamin A supplementation on childhood mortality: a randomized controlled community trial. *Lancet* 1986;1:1169–1173.

119. Hussey GD, Klein M. A randomized, controlled trial of vitamin A in children with severe measles. *N Engl J Med* 1990; 323:160–164.

120. Rahamthullah L, Underwood BA, Thulasiraj RD, et al. Reduced mortality among children in southern India receiving a small weekly dose of vitamin A. *N Engl J Med* 1990; 323:929–935.

121. Mahoney CP, Margolis MT, Knauss TA, Labbe RF. Chronic vitamin A intoxication in infants fed chicken liver. *Pediatrics* 1980; 65:893–896.

122. Farris WA, Erdman JW Jr. Protracted hypervitaminosis A following long-term, low-level intake. *JAMA* 1982;247: 1317–1318.

123. Goodman DS. Vitamin A and retinoids in health and disease. *N Engl J Med* 1984; 310:1023–1031.

124. Persson B, Tunell R, Ekengren K. Chronic vitamin A intoxication during the first half year of life: description of 5 cases. *Acta Paediatr Scand* 1965; 54:49–60.

125. Smith FR, Goodman DS. Vitamin A transport in human vitamin A toxicity. *N Engl J Med* 1976; 294:805–808.

126. Carpenter TO, Pettifor JM, Russell RM, et al. Severe hypervitaminosis A in siblings: evidence of variable tolerance to retinol intake. *J Pediatr* 1987; 111:507–512.

127. Food and Agriculture Organization/World Health Organization. Requirements of vitamin A, thiamine, riboflavin and niacin: report of a Joint FAO/WHO Expert Group. Geneva: FAO/WHO. 1967; 362.

128. Shenai JP, Rush MG, Stahlman MT, Chytil F. Plasma retinol-binding protein response to vitamin A administration in infants susceptible to bronchopulmonary dysplasia. *J Pediatr* 1990; 116:607–614.

129. Bancalari E, Abdenour GE, Feller R, Gannon J. Bronchopulmonary dysplasia: clinical presentation. *J Pediatr* 1979; 95:819–823.

130. Thompson JN, Erdody P, Brien R, Murray TK. Fluorometric determination of vitamin A in human blood and liver. *Biochem Med* 1971; 5:67–89.

131. Monji N, Bosin E. Use of enzyme-linked immunosorbent assay technique for quantitation of serum retinol-binding protein. *Meth Enzymol* 1986; 123:85–92.

132. Muto Y, Smith JE, Milch PO, Goodman DS. Regulation of retinol-binding protein metabolism by vitamin A status in the rat. *J Biol Chem* 1972; 247:2542–2550.

133. Smith JE, Muto Y, Milch PO, Goodman DS. The effects of chylomicron vitamin A on the metabolism of retinol-binding protein in the rat. *J Biol Chem* 1973;248: 1544–1549.

134. Vahlquist A, Peterson PA, Wibell L. Metabolism of the vitamin A transporting protein complex, I: turnover studies in normal persons and in patients with chronic renal failure. *Eur J Clin Invest* 1973; 3:352–362.

135. Loerch JD, Underwood BA, Lewis KC. Response of plasma levels of vitamin A to a dose of vitamin A as an indicator of hepatic vitamin A reserves in rats. *J Nutr* 1979; 109:778–786.

136. Mobarhan S, Russell RM, Underwood BA, Wallingford J, Matheieson RD, Al-Midani H. Evaluation of the relative dose response test for vitamin A nutriture in cirrhotics. *Am J Clin Nutr* 1981; 34:2264–2270.

137. Amedee-Manesme O, Anderson D, Olson JA. Relation of the relative dose response test to liver concentrations of vitamin A in generally well-nourished surgical patients. *Am J Clin Nutr* 1984; 39:898–902.

138. Amedee-Manesme O, Mourey MS, Hanck A, Therasse J. Vitamin A relative dose response test: validation by intravenous injection in children with liver disease. *Am J Clin Nutr* 1987; 46:286–289.

139. Woodruff CW, Latham CB, Mactier H, Hewett JE. Vitamin A status of preterm infants: correlation between plasma retinol concentration and retinol dose response. *Am J Clin Nutr* 1987; 46:985–988.

7. Vitamin E

Steven J. Gross

Reviewers: Richard A. Ehrenkranz, Sheila M. Innis, Helen Mintz-Hittner

Vitamin E was discovered in 1922 when Evans and Bishop demonstrated the existence of a fat-soluble dietary factor that was required for reproduction in rats.[1] Animals deficient in vitamin E ovulated and conceived normally, but fetal death and reabsorption often followed. A pure form of vitamin E was isolated from wheat-germ oil in 1936 and named α-tocopherol from the Greek noun *tocos* meaning childbirth and the verb *phero* meaning to bear. The suffix -ol was added to indicate that the substance was an alcohol.[2]

Animal models exist to support the role of vitamin E in maintaining health in a wide variety of organ systems. Disorders as diverse as encephalomalacia in chicks and necrotizing myopathy in monkeys and minks result from vitamin E deficiency. Attempts to find human correlates of these animal disorders have met with limited success. Vitamin E deficiency does not readily occur in adult humans, because of large tissue stores of the vitamin and its wide distribution in vegetable and animal dietary products.[3,4] However, vitamin E deficiency has been described in association with severe fat malabsorption syndromes and in preterm neonates.[5]

Vitamin E is the generic term for a number of tocopherol compounds. There are eight naturally occurring compounds with characteristic antioxidant activity. The most active of these compounds is α-tocopherol, which accounts for greater than 90% of vitamin E present in human tissues.[6] While the d stereoisomer of α-tocopherol is the only naturally occurring form, the most commonly used pharmacologic forms of α-tocopherol contain both the d and l stereoisomers. These pharmacologic forms have considerably less activity (approximately 75%) than the pure d form. The only other vitamers of importance in infant nutrition are β- and γ-tocopherol; these compounds respectively possess 33% and 10% of the activity of α-tocopherol.[7] Once extracted, the naturally occurring free alcohol form of α-tocopherol has a limited shelf-life due to its interaction with oxygen. Therefore, commercially derived forms of vitamin E are esterified to the acetate or succinate forms. Since each of these forms of vitamin E has different biologic activity, preparations have been standardized to International Units (IU) where 1.0 IU is equivalent to the activity of 1.0 mg of d,l-α-tocopherol acetate.

Table 7.1 compares the activities of the tocopherol compounds that are available.

Physiology

The known physiologic role of vitamin E in humans is as a biologic antioxidant. Vitamin E acts by inhibiting the naturally occurring peroxidation of polyunsaturated fatty acids (PUFA) present in the lipid layers of cell membranes. This inhibition is accomplished by the vitamin's ability to scavenge free radicals that are generated during the univalent reduction of molecular oxygen and normal activity of oxidative enzymes. Peroxidation begins when a hydrogen atom escapes from one of the carbons of a double bond, "unmasking" a highly reactive intermediate that can interact with free oxygen (Fig. 7.1). The lipid free radical formed interacts with another PUFA side chain and creates stable lipid hydroperoxides and more lipid free radicals. This process can repeat as a potentially endless chain reaction.[8] Tappel identified vitamin E as a chain-breaking antioxidant because of its ability to readily substitute for oxygen in this reaction by donating a stabilizing hydrogen ion to the "lipid free radical."[8] In the process of inhibiting fatty acid peroxidation, the α-tocopherol is oxidized to α-tocopherol quinone, which is excreted in the urine (Fig. 7.1).

Vitamin E Status at Birth

The total body content of tocopherol in the human fetus increases from about 1 mg at 5 months gestation to approximately 20 mg at term.[9] The increase in tocopherol during gestation is paralleled by an increase in total body fat.[9] Blood concentrations of tocopherol in preterm and term infants at birth average less than half the value of normal adults of 1.05 ±0.27 mg/dL and are only 20% to 30% of corresponding maternal levels.[10–13] Furthermore, increasing maternal blood tocopherol levels by administration of large doses of vitamin E (100 to 900 mg/day) during the last weeks of pregnancy results in minimal increase in cord blood levels.[14, 15] These data led to the assumption that the placenta acts as a natural barrier to the passage of vitamin E from the mother to the fetus.[12]

Table 7.1. Biologic Activity of Vitamin E Compounds*

		IU/mg
d,l	α-tocopherol acetate	1.00
d,l	α-tocopherol	1.10
d	α-tocopherol acetate	1.36
d	α-tocopherol	1.49
d,l	α-tocopherol succinate	0.89
d	α-tocopherol succinate	1.21

*Reproduced, with permission, from Slagle TA, Gross SJ.[31]

It is now known that the concentrations of vitamin E in both mother's and infant's blood are related to their different tissue lipid contents. When expressed as a ratio to lipid, the amount of α-tocopherol in blood, as well as the total body vitamin E content, are similar for neonates and adults.[16] From these data, it is suggested that low blood levels of α-tocopherol may not represent a deficiency state.

Absorption

Free tocopherols are absorbed by passive diffusion from the mid-portion of the small intestine and taken via chylomicrons into the gastrointestinal lymphatics. Esterified forms of vitamin E are completely hydrolyzed prior to absorption. This hydrolysis requires the presence of both bile salts and pancreatic esterases.

Vitamin E enters the venous circulation from the lymph and is carried by nonspecific low-density lipoproteins to body tissues, where it is incorporated into cell membranes. At the tissue level, vitamin E isomers are concentrated where there is an abundance of fatty acids; thus, tissue concentrations of the vitamin are related to the lipid content of specific organs. Adipose tissue, liver, and skeletal muscle represent the major storage depots.[17] These "stores," however, are not readily mobilized during times of deficiency.[7]

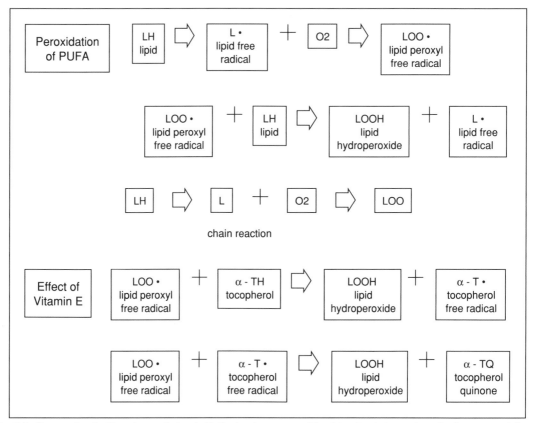

Fig. 7.1. Suggested antioxidant theory of vitamin E. During the process of breaking the chain reaction of polyunsaturated fatty acid (PUFA) peroxidation, the α-tocopherol donates a stabilizing hydrogen ion to the lipid free radical and is itself oxidized to tocopherol quinone. (Reproduced, with permission, from Slagle TA, Gross SJ.[31])

Table 7.2. Factors Affecting Tocopherol Absorption in Neonates*

Factor	Effect on Absorption
1. Gestational age	Absorption is decreased in infants <32 weeks gestational age.[18]
2. Fat absorption	Fat malabsorption states (e.g., cystic fibrosis and cholestasis) are associated with evidence of vitamin E deficiency.[19, 20]
3. Presence of lipoproteins	Abetalipoproteinemia is associated with low serum vitamin E levels.[21]
4. Nutritional source	Tocopherol absorption is greater from human milk than from formula.[22, 23]
5. Amount ingested	Percent absorption decreases as amount ingested increases.[7, 24]
6. Preparation given	Absorption is better with water-miscible than with fat-soluble forms.[25]

*Reproduced, with permission, from Slagle TA, Gross SJ.[31]

Intestinal absorption of vitamin E by the neonate is variable and influenced by multiple factors (Table 7.2). Most important among these factors are the infant's gestational age, the components of the diet, and the preparation of vitamin E given.

Nutritional Interactions
It is well known that the amount of vitamin E required to prevent lipid peroxidation is dependent upon the dietary intake of fat, particularly the intake of PUFA.[26] Diets with high concentrations of PUFA result in corresponding changes in the PUFA content of cell membranes, which therefore exhibit a greater susceptibility to fatty acid peroxidation and increase the requirements for vitamin E. Iron administration may increase the need for vitamin E, since it catalyzes the oxidation of cell lipids through the generation of free radicals, and interferes with vitamin E absorption by increasing its destruction in the gut.[7] Williams et al.[27] characterized the interaction of these three dietary factors (vitamin E, PUFA, and iron) in determining the vitamin E status in preterm infants. In their study, infants fed a formula high in PUFA (32% linoleic acid) demonstrated a greater degree of red-cell hemolysis and a lower serum tocopherol concentration than did infants who received a low PUFA formula (13% linoleic acid). Additionally, infants who received supplemental iron (2 mg/kg/day) in the formula rich in linoleic acid had significantly lower blood hemoglobin contents and higher reticulocyte counts than did infants in the other dietary groups.[27]

An interrelationship between vitamin E and selenium-dependent glutathione peroxidase has been found in animal species. Administration of one antioxidant (vitamin E or selenium) may protect against deficiency of the other nutrient. A similar interaction between tocopherol and selenium in infant nutrition is uncertain.[7]

Assessment of Status
The assessment of vitamin E status in neonates depends upon the biochemical analysis of tocopherol in blood. Until recently, determinations of total tocopherols were performed by colorimetric procedures. These procedures were technically difficult, required large amounts of blood, and were imprecise because of interference caused by carotene.[17,28] High-performance liquid chromatography has eliminated these problems and allows the separation and quantitation of the alpha, beta, and gamma isomers of tocopherol.

The influence of circulating lipids on tocopherol concentration makes it preferable to express plasma α-tocopherol concentration as a ratio to B-lipoprotein, cholesterol, or total lipid.[29] Another indicator of vitamin E status is the red blood cell tocopherol concentration, a reflection of general tissue stores.[30] Additionally, a functional measure of tissue antioxidant activity, such as the degree of erythrocyte hemolysis in dilute hydrogen peroxide, although nonspecific, is useful.

Vitamin E deficiency is most practically defined by a ratio of serum α-tocopherol to total lipid that is <0.8 mg/g and erythrocyte hemolysis >10% in hydrogen peroxide.[31]

Requirements

The vitamin E requirements for preterm infants depend upon the clinical objective or outcome desired for the nutrient. The proposed clinical effects of tocopherol in the newborn can be divided into two categories: (1) *physiologic effects* that include the prevention of hemolytic anemia,[32] and possibly the facilitation of normal heme synthesis[33] and normal phagocytosis,[34] and (2) *pharmacologic effects* that may include protection against bronchopulmonary dysplasia,[35] retinopathy of prematurity,[36] and intraventricular hemorrhage.[37] While the physiologic effects of vitamin E result from the prevention or correction of a deficient state, pharmacologic effects presumably result from elevated plasma or tissue concentrations.[38]

Physiologic Needs

Advisable Enteral Intakes for Preterm Infants

The American Academy of Pediatrics Committee on Nutrition recommends that formulas designed for preterm infants meet minimum vitamin E requirements of 0.7 IU/100 kcal and 1.0 IU/g of linoleic acid.[39] The vitamin E and linoleic acid compositions of human milk and formulas currently used for preterm infants are summarized in Table 7.3. In the United States, three commercial formulas designed for preterm infants provide sufficient vitamin E to meet the requirements set forth by the Committee on Nutrition. In addition, because of limited tissue stores of tocopherol at birth, poor absorption of dietary fats, and rapid postnatal growth, the Committee suggests that preterm infants receive 5 to 25 IU of supplemental oral vitamin E per day.[39] Others do not consider such routine supplementation to be essential.[40]

Milk produced in the early postpartum period by mothers of preterm infants is particularly well suited to meet the vitamin E needs of the low-birthweight infant. The concentration of α-tocopherol and ratio of α-tocopherol to linoleic acid decrease with progressing lactation; however, even after 6 weeks postpartum, they remain twofold higher than those of milk produced in the mature stage of lactation (>3 months postpartum) by mothers of term infants. Maternal tocopherol intake does not appear to have a major influence on the vitamin E content of breast milk. The addition of 50 mg/day of vitamin E to the diet of nursing mothers for 1 week has not resulted in an increase in vitamin E content of milk.[41]

Preterm infants fed human milk, particularly those fed their own mother's milk, maintain vitamin E sufficiency. In a recent study, Gross et al.[22] compared the vitamin E status of 36 infants with birthweight <1,500 g fed one of three diets from birth to 6 weeks; all infants received routine multivitamin supplementation providing 4.1 mg/day of d α-tocopherol succinate (5 IU). The results of this study are summarized in Table 7.4. After 6 weeks, infants fed "preterm milk" had a higher mean serum concentration of α-tocopherol (1.80 ± 0.18 mg/dL) than did similar infants fed mature human milk (1.38 ± 0.20 mg/dL) or premature infant formula (1.15 ± 0.20 mg/dL) (p <.001). Ratios of serum vitamin E/total lipid (mg/g) at 6 weeks were also significantly higher in infants fed preterm milk (3.06 ± 0.26) than in those fed formula (2.81 ± 0.67). The addition of iron (2 mg/kg/day) to all three diets resulted in significantly lower serum vitamin E concentrations; however, only in the group fed formula was there evidence of vitamin E deficiency. All infants fed human milk (with or without iron supplementation) were vitamin E sufficient by the criteria proposed above. However, the majority of infants fed the proprietary formula with iron supplementation had evidence of tocopherol deficiency (serum vitamin E to total lipid ratio <0.8). The formula utilized in the above study provided 1.95 mg of α-tocopherol per 100 kcal and an α-tocopherol:PUFA ratio of 1.54. These amounts are considerably lower than those provided by current formulas designed for preterm infants (Table 7.3).

Table 7.3. Tocopherol Content and E:PUFA Ratio of Milks Fed to Preterm Infants*

Type of Milk	α-tocopherol content[†]		E:PUFA[‡]
	mg/100 kcal	IU/100 kcal	
Human Milk[§][22]			
Postpartum week 1	1.3	1.9	2.0
Postpartum week 2	1.1	1.6	1.3
Postpartum week 4	0.6	0.9	0.7
Enfamil Premature 67 kcal/dL (Mead Johnson)	4.6	4.6	2.9
Similac Special Care 67 kcal/dL (Ross)	4.0	4.0	3.8
SMA Preemie 67 kcal/dL (Wyeth)	2.2	2.2	3.0

*Reproduced, with permission, from Slagle TA, Gross SJ.[31]
[†]Human milk contains d-α-tocopherol (1 mg = 1.49 IU); proprietary formulas contain d,l-α-tocopherol acetate (1 mg = 1 IU).
[‡]E:PUFA ratios calculated as mg d-α-tocopherol per g linoleic acid.
[§]Human milk obtained from mothers delivering preterm infants; analyses performed on pooled weekly collections from 40 to 80 mothers.

Table 7.4. Comparison of Vitamin E Status in Preterm Infants Fed Human Milks or Infant Formula*

Serum Values	Milks with No Iron Supplementation			Milks with Iron Supplementation		
	Preterm Milk	Mature Milk	Infant Formula	Preterm Milk	Mature Milk	Infant Formula
Vitamin E (mg/dL)						
Day 1	0.50 ± 0.08	0.40 ± 0.04	0.62 ± 0.04	0.37 ± 0.07	0.38 ± 0.08	0.36 ± 0.07
Week 6[†]	1.80 ± 0.18	1.38 ± 0.20	1.15 ± 0.20	1.52 ± 0.17	1.04 ± 0.12	0.45 ± 0.09
Vitamin E/lipid (mg/g)						
Day 1	1.00 ± 0.15	0.83 ± 0.10	1.32 ± 0.10	0.79 ± 0.10	0.70 ± 0.12	0.71 ± 0.09
Week 6[‡]	3.06 ± 0.26	2.38 ± 0.30	2.81 ± 0.67	3.16 ± 0.43	2.14 ± 0.44	0.79 ± 0.16

*Data from Gross et al[22]; values represent mean $\pm$ SEM; all groups comprised of 6 infants. (Reproduced, with permission, from Slagle TA, Gross SJ.[31])
[†]Preterm milk vs. formula, $p < 0.0001$; mature milk vs. formula, $p < 0.02$; preterm milk vs. mature milk, $p < 0.01$. Milks without iron vs. milks with iron, $p < 0.05$.
[‡]Preterm milk vs. formula, $p < 0.001$; mature milk vs. formula, $p < 0.05$.

From the above data, it is suggested that a supplement of 5 IU of vitamin E is adequate for human milk–fed infants. It is also possible that no additional vitamin E beyond that provided by breast milk is needed, but this remains to be clarified. The appropriate supplement for infants fed currently available formulas has not been well studied; pending further data, 5 to 25 IU/day would seem reasonable.

Parenteral Needs for Preterm Infants Requirements for vitamin E for parenterally nourished infants are not well defined. Toxicity has been associated with intravenous vitamin E administration as well as with the use of pharmacologic doses of vitamin E resulting in serum levels >3.0 mg/dL (see the section on Toxicity).

Studies to date are preliminary. For infants with a birthweight of 1,000 to 1,500 g, a dose of 4.6 mg/day of d,l-α-tocopherol acetate seems appropriate. In 19 infants (mean birthweight 1,270 g) studied by Phillips el al.,[42] the mean serum α-tocopherol concentration increased from 0.33 ± 0.03 mg/dL prior to vitamin supplementation to 1.44 ± 0.10 mg/dL after 48 hours. Weekly monitoring of serum vitamin concentrations during 4 weeks of parenteral nutrition showed mean concentrations between 1.5 and 2.0 mg/dL. Only four (21%) infants had α-tocopherol levels <1 mg/dL at any time during supplementation and only one (5%) infant had a level >2.5 mg/dL.[42] Concomitant oral supplementation in such infants is not necessary, and resulted in serum α-tocopherol concentrations >3.0 mg/dL.[43]

For smaller preterm infants with birthweight $<1,000$ g, a dose of 4.6 mg/day of α-tocopherol may be excessive.[42, 44, 45] Three days of supplementation with this dose resulted in a mean serum α-tocopherol concentration of 2.4 mg/dL in 16 infants of birthweight 450 to 980 g; 5 of the 16 (31%) infants had serum vitamin E levels above 3.5 mg/dL.[42] Similarly, DeVito et al.[44] reported a mean serum vitamin E concentration of 3.68 ± 0.85 mg/dL within 2 weeks of initiating supplementation with 4.5 mg/day in six infants with birthweight <900 g. A much lower dose of 2.1 mg/day d,l-α-tocopherol acetate was found to be inadequate, since 7 of 16 (44%) similar infants never achieved a serum α-tocopherol level >1.0 mg/dL during 4 weeks of supplementation.[42] The best results were found by Amorde-Spalding et al.[46] with an intermediate dose of 3.5 mg/day of d,l-α-tocopherol acetate. One hundred and ten infants (100%) with birthweights $<1,000$ g demonstrated a mean plasma α-tocopherol concentration of 1.52 ± 0.70 mg/dL after 7 days of supplementation; all infants were vitamin E sufficient and only two had concentrations above 3.0 mg/dL. Alternately, a dose of 2.8 mg/kg/day was found to be satisfactory by Baeckert et al.[47] In their study, seven infants (100%) with birthweights between 450 and 1,360 g demonstrated a mean plasma α-tocopherol concentration of 2.44 ± 0.13 mg/dL after 4 weeks of supplementation; none of the infants had levels above 3.0 mg/dL. Unlike previous studies in which vitamins were administered in glucose-amino acid solutions, in the latter study the vitamin supplementation was added to the lipid. Determination of what, if any, effect the mode of administration has on vitamin delivery requires further study.

M.V.I. Pediatric (Astra Pharmaceutical) was the parenteral vitamin supplement used in the above studies and is the currently available parenteral supplement for infants and children. This preparation contains 7 IU of d,l-α-tocopherol acetate per 5 mL vial. Based on the limited data available, two thirds of a vial of M.V.I. Pediatric per day (providing 4.6 mg/day of α-tocopherol acetate) should maintain vitamin E sufficiency for preterm infants of 1,000 to 1,500 g birthweight. A smaller dose of 50% of a vial of M.V.I. Pediatric per day (providing 3.5 mg/day of α-tocopherol acetate) would be most appropriate for preterm infants with a birthweight <1,000 g. Alternately, a dose of 40% of a vial of M.V.I. Pediatric per kg per day (providing 2.8 mg/kg/day of α-tocopherol acetate) would be acceptable. These recommendations are based on the assumption that optimal blood concentrations of vitamin E are between 1 and 2 mg/dL[48,49] and that optimal blood concentrations are equivalent to optimal body nutrient status. Several conditions, however, may change blood concentrations without significantly altering the body content of the vitamin. Thus, recommendations for intravenous vitamin E needs based on results of blood concentrations are only initial steps toward optimizing the vitamin E intake for preterm infants receiving parenteral nutrition.[47]

Postdischarge Needs Vitamin E status was assessed in 51 preterm infants (birthweight 620 to 1,520 g) during hospitalization and for 1 year following discharge by Rönnholm et al.[50] All infants were fed human milk during hospitalization and maternal milk or infant formula (containing α-tocopherol 1.0 mg/dL) after discharge. Supplemental oral vitamin E was begun at 1.6 mg/day on day 3 and increased to 10 mg/day by 2 weeks; the latter dose was continued until infants were 12 weeks of age. Maintenance iron (3 to 4 mg/kg/day) was supplied up to age 15 months. Plasma vitamin E concentrations steadily increased from 0.3 mg/dL at birth to approximately 1.5 mg/dL at 12 weeks of age. Subsequently, after vitamin E supplementation was discontinued, plasma vitamin E levels showed a steady decline, reaching a mean concentration of <0.8 mg/dL at 15 months. A subgroup of infants received intramuscular vitamin E (20 mg/kg/day) during the first 3 days of life. This supplementation resulted in a significant increase in plasma α-tocopherol concentration by 2 weeks of age, but no long-lasting change in concentration after oral supplementation was discontinued. These findings suggest that some small preterm infants may need vitamin E supplementation after hospital discharge.

Pharmacologic Needs
The use of vitamin E for prevention and/or treatment of oxidant-induced injury to potentially susceptible tissues including retinopathy of prematurity (ROP), bronchopulmonary dysplasia (BPD), and intraventricular hemorrhage (IVH) will be briefly discussed. Since this topic falls outside the primary nutritional focus of this chapter, the reader is referred to several reviews.[35, 36, 51]

Randomized controlled trials of vitamin E supplementation for the prevention[52–58] or treatment[58] of ROP have been reported. Routes of administration of vitamin E have included oral[52,56] as well as parenteral followed by oral.[53–55,57,58] A wide range of serum tocopherol concentrations have been targeted, from physiologic (1 to 1.5 mg/dL)[52] to concentrations as high as 4 to 5 mg/dL.[53–55,58] While one study demonstrated a reduction in the incidence of ROP in vitamin E–treated infants[58] and one study demonstrated a modest decrease in the severity of disease in affected infants,[52] most studies have reported no reduction in either risk of ROP or in the severity of disease.[53–57] These studies have been well summarized by Law et al.[51]

An initial report that vitamin E supplementation reduced the incidence of BPD[59] has not been confirmed.[35] One reason for the discrepancy between results of earlier and more recent studies could be that the increased use of human milk and more appropriate infant formulas have resulted in less vitamin E deficiency in infants who do not receive pharmacologic treatment.

Preliminary data suggest that vitamin E supplementation can reduce the incidence of IVH in preterm infants if given within the first 12 hours of life.[37, 60–62] These trials showed no reduction in hemorrhage confined to the germinal matrix and no significant reduction in parenchymal hemorrhage. One of the studies[62] demonstrated a 50% reduction in hemorrhage for infants of 501 to 750 g birthweight, but not for those of 751 to 1,000 g birthweight. Chiswick et al.[61] postulate that the protective effect of vitamin E is based on its ability to trap free radicals generated during ischemic injury of the subependymal layer and thus limit tissue damage and the magnitude of hemorrhage on reperfusion. Additional study is necessary to establish the optimal dosage, timing, and target population.[62]

Deficiency

Human tocopherol deficiency has been recognized in two groups of patients: (1) children with prolonged and severe fat malabsorption secondary to biliary atresia, cystic fibrosis, or abetalipoproteinemia who may manifest a syndrome of progressive sensory and motor neuropathy that becomes apparent late in the first decade of life,[20,21] and (2) preterm infants who present with hemolytic anemia at 1 or 2 months of age.

In 1967, Oski and Barness[32] first described the syndrome of vitamin E deficiency in 11 premature infants. These infants presented between 6 and 11 weeks of age with anemia (mean hemoglobin, 7.6 ±1.1 g/dL), elevated reticulocyte count (8.2% ±2.9%), and a striking increase in sensitivity of the erythrocytes to hemolysis in hydrogen peroxide (80% ± 14%). All of these infants had deficient serum vitamin E concentrations (<0.41 mg/dL). These findings have been confirmed by others[63-65] with the manifestations expanded to include peripheral edema and thrombocytosis. All clinical and hematologic abnormalities were corrected after the initiation of oral vitamin E therapy.

It was soon recognized that this syndrome was associated with the ingestion of formulas that were high in polyunsaturated fatty acids and low in vitamin E. After the interrelationships of dietary PUFA, α-tocopherol, and iron were clarified,[27] infant formulas utilized for feeding preterm infants were modified appropriately. The disappearance of this syndrome soon followed.

Toxicity

A wide range of toxicities associated with vitamin E administration have been reported. These have primarily followed the pharmacologic usage of tocopherol. The mildest of these are local, transitory reactions including erythema, edema, and soft tissue calcification at the site of intramuscular injection.[66,67] The most devastating toxicity has been the syndrome of pulmonary deterioration, thrombocytopenia, and liver and renal failure in very low-birth-weight (VLBW) infants, which was associated with the use of a parenteral d,l-α-tocopherol acetate in polysorbate vehicle (E-Ferol).[68] A total of 38 reported deaths prompted the removal of E-Ferol from the market only 6 months after it was released. A retrospective analysis of this tragedy found mortality related to decreasing birthweight as well as increasing cumulative dose of E-Ferol.[69] Toxicologic studies suggest that the emulsifiers, polysorbates 80 and 20, were responsible for the major toxicologic effects.[69]

Other important side effects have been identified following pharmacologic vitamin E usage. Johnson et al.[70] reported that VLBW infants given parenteral and oral tocopherol from birth in an effort to maintain serum tocopherol concentrations at 5 mg/dL had a 2.7-fold increase in the occurrence of sepsis or necrotizing enterocolitis. The authors postulate that high serum concentrations of vitamin E may decrease the oxygen-dependent killing ability of cells. In another study, Finer et al.[71] found a twofold increase in the incidence of necrotizing enterocolitis in VLBW infants who received pharmacologic doses

of oral vitamin E. Although not routinely measured, serum vitamin E concentrations prior to the development of disease were obtained in nine of these infants; the mean level in this group was 3.1 mg/dL and only one of these infants had a serum level >3.5 mg/dL. This finding raises the possibility that other properties of the oral formulation (e.g., the osmolality or vehicle rather than the serum concentration) might be responsible for the toxicity. These data highlight the extreme caution that must be exercised before treating any infant with pharmacologic doses of a vitamin for which efficacy has not been proven.

Recommendations

The preterm infant's own mother's milk is a good source of α-tocopherol; a supplement of no more than 5 IU/day oral vitamin E is needed for human milk–fed infants. Formulas designed for preterm infants should provide a minimum of 0.7 IU (0.7 mg d,l-α-tocopherol acetate) per 100 kcal and at least 1.0 IU of vitamin E per g linoleic acid. It is not clear how much additional vitamin supplementation is necessary for infants fed currently available formulas, since these formulas exceed minimum requirements by two- to threefold. The American Academy of Pediatrics Committee on Nutrition recommends that preterm infants receive a supplement of 5 to 25 IU/day oral vitamin E.

Preterm infants receiving parenteral nutrition should receive supplemental vitamin E. M.V.I. Pediatric contains 7 IU of vitamin E per 5 mL vial; two thirds of a vial is appropriate for infants with birthweight >1,000 g, while 50% of a vial is recommended for infants with birthweight <1,000 g.

Recommendations for the pharmacologic use of vitamin E to modify the incidence or severity of ROP, BPD, or IVH are not warranted at this time.

CASE STUDY

A male infant is born at 28 weeks gestation weighing 1,050 g. He suffers from severe respiratory distress, requiring mechanical ventilation for the first week of life. Enteral feeds are started on day 7 of life with proprietary formula. During the next 3 weeks, the infant has recurrent episodes of abdominal distention necessitating temporary discontinuance of enteral feeds on three occasions. He receives dextrose and electrolyte fluids intravenously.

At 4 weeks of age, the infant is tolerating 15 cc of formula (110 cc/kg/day) every 3 hours. He is receiving no iron or vitamin supplements. Routine laboratory testing reveals a hematocrit of 24% and a reticulocyte count of 10%. What is the cause of this infant's anemia?

In light of the fact that the infant has received no vitamin supplementation and has had poor enteral intake, vitamin E deficiency should be considered.

Further studies reveal a peripheral blood smear showing red blood cell fragments and moderate poikilocytes, a serum tocopherol concentration of 0.3 mg/dL, and a serum tocopherol to total lipid ratio of 0.5. Erythrocyte hemolysis in hydrogen peroxide is 30%.

This infant subsequently begins oral tocopherol supplementation (25 U/kg/day), resulting in resolution of his hemolytic anemia. Three weeks later, hematocrit is 32% and reticulocyte count is 3%.

References

1. Evans HM, Bishop KS. On the existence of a hitherto unrecognized dietary factor essential for reproduction. *Science* 1922;56:650–651.
2. Evans HM, Emerson OH, Emerson GA. The isolation from wheat germ oil of an alcohol, α-tocopherol, having properties of vitamin E. *J Biol Chem* 1936;113:319–322.
3. Bieri JG, Farrell PM. Vitamin E. *Vitam Horm* 1976; 34:37–75.
4. Bunnell RH, Keating J, Quaresimo A, et al. Alpha-tocopherol content of foods. *Am J Clin Nutr* 1965; 17:1–10.
5. Ehrenkranz RA. Vitamin E and the neonate. *Am J Dis Child* 1980;134:1157–1166.
6. Mandel HG, Cohn VA. Fat-soluble vitamins. In: Gilman AG, Goodman LS, Gilman A, eds. *The pharmacologic basis of therapeutics*. New York: MacMillan 1975:1172.
7. Farrell PM, Zachman RD, Gutcher GR. Fat-soluble vitamins A, E, and K in the premature infant. In: Tsang R, ed. *Vitamin and mineral requirements in preterm infants*. New York: Marcel Dekker 1985:63–98.
8. Tappel AL. Vitamin E as the biologic lipid antioxidant. *Vitam Horm* 1962;20:493–510.
9. Dju MY, Mason KE, Filer LI. Vitamin E (tocopherol) in human fetuses and placentae. *Etudes Neonatales* 1952;1: 49–62.
10. Baker H, Frank O, Thomson AD, et al. Vitamin profile of 174 mothers and newborns at parturition. *Am J Clin Nutr* 1975;28:59–65.
11. Leonard PJ, Doyle E, Harrington W. Levels of vitamin E in the plasma of newborn infants and of the mothers. *Am J Clin Nutr* 1972;25:480–484.
12. Straumfjord JV, Quaife ML. Vitamin E levels in maternal and fetal blood plasma. *Proc Soc Exp Biol Med* 1946; 61:369–371.
13. Tateno M, Ohshima A. The relationship between serum vitamin E levels in the perinatal period and the birth weight of the neonate. *Acta Obstet Gynaecol Jap* 1973;20: 177–181.
14. Cruz, CS, Wimberley PD, Johansen K, Friis-Hansen B. The effect of vitamin E on erythrocyte hemolysis and lipid peroxidation in newborn premature infants. *Acta Paediatr Scand* 1983;72:823–826.
15. Mino M, Nishimo H. Fetal and maternal relationship in serum vitamin E level. *J Nutr Sci Vitaminol* 1973;19: 475–482.
16. Karp WB, Robertson AF. Vitamin E in neonatology. *Adv Pediatr* 1986;33:127–147.
17. Machlin L, ed. Handbook of vitamins. In: *Nutritional biochemical and clinical aspects*. New York: Marcel Dekker, 1984:99–145.
18. Melhorn DK, Gross S. Vitamin E-dependent anemia in the premature infant. II. Relationships between gestational age and absorption of vitamin E. *J Pediatr* 1971;79:581–588.
19. Filer LI, Wright SW, Manning MP, Mason KE. Absorption of α-tocopherol and tocopherol esters by premature and full term infants and children in health and disease. *Pediatrics* 1951;8:328–339.
20. Sokol RJ, Heubi JE, Iannaccone ST, et al. Vitamin E deficiency with normal serum vitamin E concentration in children with chronic cholestasis. *N Engl J Med* 1984; 310:1209–1212.
21. Muller DP, Lloyd JK, Wolff OH. Vitamin E and neurologic function: abetalipoproteinemia and other disorders of fat absorption. *CIBA Foundation Symposium* 1983;101: 106–117.
22. Gross SJ, Gabriel E. Vitamin E status in preterm infants fed human milk or infant formula. *J Pediatr* 1985;106:635–639.
23. Wright SW, Filer LJ, Mason KE. Vitamin E blood levels in premature and full term infants. *Pediatrics* 1951;7: 386–392.
24. Lambert GH, Papp LA, Paton JB. Megadoses of vitamin E in oxygen-dependent premature newborn infants. *J Perinatol* 1985;5:44–47.
25. Gross S, Melhorn DK. Vitamin E-dependent anemia in the premature infant. III. Comparative hemoglobin, vitamin E, and erythrocyte phospholipid responses following absorption of either water-soluble or fat-soluble d-alpha tocopherol. *J Pediatr* 1974;85:753–759.
26. Witting LA. Vitamin E-polyunsaturated lipid relationship in diet and tissue. *Am J Clin Nutr* 1974;27:952–959.
27. Williams ML, Shott RJ, O'Neal PL, Oski FA. Role of dietary iron and fat on vitamin E deficiency anemia in infancy. *N Engl J Med* 1975;292:887–890.
28. Scott ML. Vitamin E. In: DeLuca HL, ed. *The fat-soluble vitamins*. New York: Plenum Press; 1978:133–210.
29. Horwitt MK. Interrelations between vitamin E and polyunsaturated fatty acids in adult men. *Vitam Horm* 1962; 20:541–559.
30. Duc G, Tuchschmid P. The use and abuse of vitamin E in the newborn. In: Cucinotta G, Mazzaglia E, Orzalesi M, eds. *Proceedings of the International Symposium of Neonatology.* 1986;255–278.
31. Slagle TA, Gross SJ. Vitamin E. In: Tsang RC, Nichols BL, eds. *Nutrition during infancy*. Philadelphia: Hanley and Belfus, 1988:277–287.
32. Oski FA, Barness LA. Vitamin E deficiency: a previously unrecognized cause of hemolytic anemia in the premature infant. *J Pediatr.* 1967;70:211–220.
33. Nair PP, Murty HS, Caasi PI, Brooks SK, Quartner J. Vitamin E: regulation of the biosynthesis of porphyrins and heme. *J Agr Food Chem* 1972;20:476–480.
34. Baehner RI, Boxer LA. Role of membrane vitamin E and cytoplasmic glutathione in the regulation of phagocytic functions of neutrophils and monocytes. *Am J Pediatr Hematol Oncol* 1979;1:71–76.
35. Bell, EF. Prevention of bronchopulmonary dysplasia: vitamin E and other antioxidants. In: Farrell PM, Taussig LM, eds. *Bronchopulmonary dysplasia and related chronic respiratory disorder.* Report of the Ninetieth Ross Conference on Pediatric Research, 1986; 77–82.
36. Phelps DL. Vitamin E and retinopathy of prematurity. In: Silverman W, Flynn J, eds: *Contemporary issues in fetal and neonatal medicine: retinopathy of prematurity.* Boston: Blackwell, 1985:181–205.
37. Chiswick ML, Johnson M, Woodhall L, et al. Protective effect of vitamin E (dl-alpha-tocopherol) against intraventricular hemorrhage in premature babies. *Br Med J* 1983;287:81–84.
38. Bell EF, Filer LJ. The role of vitamin E in the nutrition of premature infants. *Am J Clin Nutr* 1981;34: 414–422.
39. Committee on Nutrition, American Academy of Pediatrics. Nutritional needs for low-birth-weight infants. *Pediatrics* 1985;75:976–986.

40. Committee on Nutrition of the Preterm Infant, European Society of Paediatric Gastroenterology and Nutrition. Nutrition and feeding of preterm infants. *Acta Paediatr Scand* 1987;336(suppl):1–14.

41. Haug M, Laubach C, Burke M, Harzer G. Vitamin E in human milk from mothers of preterm and term infants. *J Pediatr Gastroenterol Nutr* 1987;6:605–609.

42. Phillips B, Franck LS, Greene HL. Vitamin E levels in premature infants during and after intravenous multivitamin supplementation. *Pediatrics* 1987;80:680–683.

43. Greene HL, Moore C, Phillips B, et al. Evaluation of a pediatric multiple vitamin preparation for total parenteral nutrition. II. Blood levels of vitamin A, D, and E. *Pediatrics* 1986;77:539–547.

44. DeVito V, Reynolds JW, Benda GI, Carlson C. Serum vitamin E levels in very low-birth weight infants receiving vitamin E in parenteral nutrition solutions. *J PEN* 1986; 10:63–65.

45. Etches PC, Koo WWK. Parenteral vitamins A, D, and E for premature infants. *J Perinatol* 1988;8(2):93–95.

46. Amorde-Spalding K, D'Harlingue AE, Phillips BL, et al. Tocopherol levels in infants ≤1,000 grams receiving M.V.I. Pediatric. *Pediatrics* 1992;90:992–994.

47. Baeckert PA, Greene HL, Fritz I, Oelberg DG, Adcock EW. Vitamin concentrations in very low birth weight infants given vitamins intravenously in a lipid emulsion: measurement of vitamins A, D, and E and riboflavin. *J Pediatr* 1988;113:1057–1065.

48. Greene HL, Hambidge KM, Schanler R, Tsang RC. Guidelines for the use of vitamins, trace elements, calcium, magnesium, and phosphorus in infants and children receiving total parenteral nutrition: report of the Subcommittee on Pediatric Parenteral Nutrient Requirements from the Committee on Clinical Practice Issues of the American Society for Clinical Nutrition. *Am J Clin Nutr* 1988;48: 1324–1342.

49. Poland R: Vitamin E: What should we do? [Letter]. *Pediatrics* 1986;77:787–788.

50. Rönnholm KAR, Dostälovä L, Siimes MA: Vitamin E supplementation in very-low-birth-weight infants: long term follow-up at two different levels of vitamin E supplementation. *Am J Clin Nutr* 1989;49:121–126.

51. Law MR, Wijewardene K, Wald NJ. Is routine vitamin E administration justified in very low-birthweight infants? *Dev Med Child Neurol* 1990;32:442–450.

52. Hittner HM, Godio LB, Rudolph AJ, et al. Retrolental fibroplasia: efficiency of vitamin E in a double-blind clinical study of preterm infants. *N Engl J Med* 1981; 305:1365–1371.

53. Finer NN, Schindler RF, Grant G, et al. Effect of intramuscular vitamin E on frequency and severity of retrolental fibroplasia. *Lancet* 1982;1:1087–1091.

54. Puklin JE, Simon RM, Ehrenkranz RA. Influence on retrolental fibroplasia of intramuscular vitamin E administration during respiratory distress syndrome. *Ophthalmology* 1982;89:96–102.

55. Schaffer DB, Johnson L, Quinn GE, et al. Vitamin E and retinopathy of prematurity: follow-up at one year. *Ophthalmology* 1985;92:1005–1011.

56. Watts JL, Milner RA, McCormick AQ. Failure of vitamin E to prevent RLF. *Clinical and Investigative Medicine* 1985;8:A176.

57. Phelps DL, Rosenbaum AL, Isenberg SJ, Leake RD, Dorey FJ. Tocopherol efficacy and safety for preventing retinopathy of prematurity: a randomized controlled double masked trial. *Pediatrics* 1987;79:489–500.

58. Johnson L, Quinn GE, Abbasi S, et al. Effect of sustained pharmacologic vitamin E levels on incidence and severity of retinopathy of prematurity: a controlled clinical trial. *J Pediatr* 1989;114:827–838.

59. Ehrenkranz RA, Bonta BW, Ablow RC, Warshaw JB. Amelioration of bronchopulmonary dysplasia after vitamin E administration: a preliminary report. *N Engl J Med* 1978;299:564–569.

60. Speer ME, Blifeld C, Rudolph A, et al. Intraventricular hemorrhage and vitamin E in the very-low-birth-weight infant: evidence for efficacy of early intramuscular vitamin E administration. *Pediatrics* 1984;74:1107–1112.

61. Chiswick M, Gladman G, Sinha S, et al. Vitamin E supplementation and periventricular hemorrhage in the newborn. *Am J Clin Nutr* 1991;53:370S–372S.

62. Fish WH, Cohen M, Franzek D, et al. Effect of intramuscular vitamin E on mortality and intracranial hemorrhage in neonates of 1,000 grams or less. *Pediatrics* 1990; 85:578–584.

63. Hassan H, Hashim SA, Van Itallie TB, Sebrell WH. Syndrome in premature infants associated with low plasma vitamin E levels and high polyunsaturated fatty acid diet. *Am J Clin Nutr* 1966;19:147–157.

64. Ritchie JH, Fish MB, McMasters V, Grossman M. Edema and hemolytic anemia in premature infants: a vitamin E deficiency syndrome. *N Engl J Med* 1968;279:1185–1190.

65. Lo SS, Frank D, Hitzig WH. Vitamin E and hemolytic anemia in premature infants. *Arch Dis Child* 1973;48: 360–365.

66. Barak M, Herschkowitz S, Montag J. Soft tissue calcification: a complication of vitamin E injection. *Pediatrics* 1986;77:382–385.

67. Graeber JE, Williams ML, Oski FA. The use of intramuscular vitamin E in the premature infant: optimal dose and iron interaction. *J Pediatr* 1978;90:282–284.

68. Lorch V, Murphy D, Hoersten L, et al. Unusual syndrome among premature infants: association with a new intravenous vitamin E product. *Pediatrics* 1985;75:598–602.

69. Arrowsmith JB, Faich GA, Tomita DK, et al. Morbidity and mortality among low birth weight infants exposed to an intravenous vitamin E product, E-Ferol. *Pediatrics* 1989;83:244–249.

70. Johnson L, Bowen F, Abbasi S, et al. Relationship of prolonged pharmacologic serum levels of vitamin E to incidence of sepsis and encrotizing enterocolitis in infants with birth weight 1,500 grams or less. *Pediatrics* 1985; 75:619–638.

71. Finer NN, Peters KL, Hayek Z, Merkel CL. Vitamin E and necrotizing enterocolitis. *Pediatrics* 1984;73:387–393.

8. Vitamin K

Frank R. Greer

Reviewers: Steven J. Gross, Jayant P. Shenai

As a nutrient for both the preterm infant and the newborn infant, vitamin K enjoys a special status. It is the only vitamin or mineral routinely administered in large quantities at the time of birth in many developed countries. Furthermore, it is perhaps the only nutrient whose concentration in cord blood is not reliably detectable by present assay techniques at any gestational age. The vitamin K concentration of human milk is very low, and for the breastfeeding infant, a deficiency state has been described. Thus, there is not at present a true "gold standard" for assessing the nutritional needs of this vitamin in infants.

Physiology

There are two known forms of vitamin K: (1) vitamin K_1, or phylloquinone, which is the plant form of the vitamin, and (2) vitamin K_2, a series of vitamin K compounds with unsaturated side chains synthesized by bacteria and referred to as menaquinones.

Vitamin K functions post-ribosomally as a cofactor in the metabolic conversion of intracellular precursors of vitamin K–dependent proteins to active forms. The coagulation factors II (prothrombin), VII, IX, and X were the first of these proteins to be described. All vitamin K–dependent proteins contain glutamyl ("glu") residues which are converted to gamma-carboxy glutamyl ("gla") residues by a microsomal vitamin K–dependent carboxylase (Fig. 8.1). The detailed molecular role of vitamin K in this conversion reaction has not been determined. It is hypothesized that it removes the hydrogen of a "glu" residue as a proton from the vitamin K–dependent protein, leaving a carbanion that is attacked by a free CO_2 molecule to form a "gla" residue[1] (Fig. 8.1). Because "glu" is a weak calcium chelator and "gla" a much stronger one, the vitamin K–dependent conversion significantly increases the calcium-binding capacity of a protein. The precursor of the vitamin K–dependent protein prothrombin contains 10 "glu" residues. It is thought that if eight or more of these residues are converted from "glu" to "gla" residues, prothrombin is physiologically active.[2]

In addition to coagulation factors II, VII, IX, and X, other vitamin K–dependent proteins in plasma include proteins C, S, and Z.[3] Vitamin K–dependent proteins have also been identified in the liver, kidneys, spleen, lungs, uterus, placenta, pancreas, thyroid, thymus, testes, skin, and bones.[4] To date, the only tissues in which they have not been identified are brain, muscle, and tendon. Outside the coagulation system, significant "gla"-containing proteins include those of the skeleton (osteocalcin or bone "gla" protein, as well as matrix "gla" protein) and kidney (renal "gla" protein). The most widely studied of these proteins are the skeletal "gla" proteins, though their mechanism of action and exact function are unclear.[5]

There is no specific information available about the physiology of vitamin K in the premature infant. In general, vitamin K is absorbed from the intestine into the lymphatic system, requiring the presence of bile salts, pancreatic secretions, and chylomicron formation.[6] No specific carrier proteins are known. In rats, phylloquinone absorption appears to be an energy-dependent process from the proximal portion of the small intestine.[7] In contrast, menaquinone absorption has been found to be a passive, non-carrier-mediated process from both the large and small intestines.[8,9] In newborn infants it has been estimated that 29% of an oral dose of phylloquinone is absorbed from the intestine.[10] In the adult man, 19% to 20% of a parenteral dose of 1 mg of vitamin K is excreted in the urine within 3 days and 34% to 38% is excreted in the feces via the bile.[11-13] There is little information about degradation products of phylloquinone and menaquinones in humans, though some major products of phylloquinone metabolism have been identified.[14] The importance of the enterohepatic circulation in humans is unknown.

Absorption of vitamin K may be inhibited by mineral oil[15] and by high dietary intakes of vitamins A[16] and E.[17-19] Vitamin K deficiency has been observed in subjects with impaired fat absorption secondary to obstructive jaundice, pancreatic insufficiency (cystic fibrosis), and adult celiac disease.[19,20]

After parenteral injection of vitamin K in the rat, phylloquinone is rapidly concentrated in the liver but has a short half-life (17 hours) consistent with the minimal long-term storage capacity of this organ.[21] In pigs and dogs, both phylloquinone and menaquinone (presumably of bacterial origin) are detected in the liver.[22] In the adult man it has been demonstrated with labelled phylloquinone that the total body pool of vitamin K is replaced approximately every 2.5 hours.[23] Hepatic concentrations of vitamin K_1 and vitamin K_2 in 11 human livers (8 infants and 3 adults)

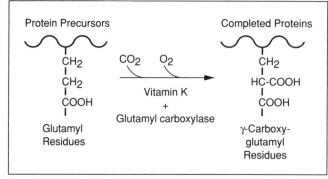

Fig. 8.1. Vitamin K functions as a cofactor with the microsomal enzyme glutamyl carboxylase to convert glutamyl residues ("glu" residues) to γ-carboxy-glutamic acid residues ("gla" residues) on precursor proteins (i.e., prothrombin).

have recently been reported.[24] Relatively small amounts of vitamin K have been found in the liver at any age compared to other fat-soluble vitamins. Vitamin K_1 was the predominant form, with much smaller concentrations of vitamin K_2, suggesting that infants may be largely dependent on phylloquinone for vitamin K–dependent clotting-factor synthesis.

Sources of Vitamin K

There are several potential sources of vitamin K for the newborn infant. However, the vitamin K content of cord blood is largely unmeasurable by current methods.[25] It also has been demonstrated that fairly large doses of maternal vitamin K do not significantly alter cord blood concentrations of phylloquinone.[26,27] Thus, transport from mother to fetus across the placenta is not thought to be a significant source of vitamin K to the newborn. In the United States and other developed countries, the major source is the prophylactic dose given intramuscularly at time of birth. Likewise, in premature infants receiving total parenteral nutrition (TPN), relatively large amounts of phylloquinone are found in the multivitamins now included in these solutions. For human milk–fed premature or full-term infants, the vitamin K content of human milk is very low (<2.0 ng/mL) despite estimated maternal intakes of phylloquinone exceeding the Recommended Dietary Allowance (RDA) of 1 μg/kg/day.[28] The phylloquinone intake of breast-fed infants during the first 6 months of lactation ranges from 0.075 ± 0.026 μg/kg/day to 0.125 ± 0.082 μg/kg/day, much less than the RDA. On the other hand, infants fed standard formula average intakes of 7 to 9 μg/kg/day[28] in formula fortified with 55 ng/mL of phylloquinone.

A possible source of vitamin K in the premature infant is the synthesis of menaquinones by bacterial flora in the gastrointestinal tract. At this time it is not known whether or not this is a significant source of vitamin K, since vitamin K_2 is not reliably measur-

able in infant serum. It is known that the intestinal bacterial flora commonly found in breast-fed infants do not synthesize menaquinones, unlike the gram-negative organisms frequently associated with the intestinal flora of formula-fed infants.[29] In fact, fecal menaquinone concentrations have been reported to be higher in the first week of life in formula-fed infants compared to breast-fed infants.[30] However, in rat liver, the ability of menaquinones to function as a carboxylase substrate for the synthesis of coagulation factors has been questioned.[31]

Early, Immediate Needs of the Fetus and Premature Infant

Why is the cord concentration of phylloquinone nearly unmeasurable at all gestational ages? Why are the fetus, newborn, and particularly the breast-feeding infant placed at risk for hemorrhagic disease? Does "vitamin K deficiency" confer an advantage to these subjects, counterbalancing the disadvantages of low vitamin K and delayed maturation of the coagulation system? The answers to these questions remain unknown, though it has recently been reported that high or "normal" levels of phylloquinone may potentiate mutagenic or carcinogenic events in mice[32,33] as well as fetal sheep leukocytes.[34] From these observations it has been hypothesized that low plasma concentrations of phylloquinone may confer a biological advantage by reducing the risk of mutagenic events during the rapid cell proliferation that occurs in both the fetus and fast-growing premature infant.

Another issue in the premature infant is whether the risk of periventricular-intraventricular hemorrhage in the fetus/newborn is potentiated by very low serum concentrations of phylloquinone. Will large amounts of maternal phylloquinone protect the premature infant from periventricular-intraventricular hemorrhage? (See discussion that follows.) Do large prophylactic amounts of maternal phylloquinone cross the placenta from mother to fetus? In a recent study, 78 women at 35 weeks gestation but in preterm labor were randomized to receive either 10 mg of phylloquinone intramuscularly or no treatment.[35] If delivery did not occur within 4 days, the dose was repeated in the treated group. Women whose pregnancies continued beyond 8 days received 20 mg of phylloquinone orally per day until delivery or 34 weeks gestation. The median maternal plasma vitamin K concentration was significantly higher in treated than in untreated subjects (11.59 versus 0.102 ng/mL, $p<.001$). The median cord plasma concentration of phylloquinone was 0.024 ng/mL in the treated group and 0.010ng/mL in the controls ($p<.046$). There was no correlation between cord plasma vitamin K concentrations and gestational age or duration of maternal phylloquinone supplementation.[35]

Vitamin K–dependent clotting factors differ very little in preterm and full-term infants at time of birth, being 30% to 60% of those in adult normals.[36,37] In addition, intramuscular injection of vitamin K shortly after birth does not dramatically affect coagulation or concentrations of coagulation factors,[38,39] despite much higher infant serum concentrations of phylloquinone than can be achieved by maternal phylloquinone supplements prior to delivery. In any event, the immediate oral administration to or injection of relatively large quantities of phylloquinone (0.5 to 1.0 mg) into the preterm infant would provide for all immediate phylloquinone needs. Serum concentrations of phylloquinone after oral supplements (2 mg) of phylloquinone rise up to 100 times the adult normal level in low-birthweight infants by 12 hours.[10] In full-term infants, serum phylloquinone concentrations also rise dramatically after oral supplementation of phylloquinone.[40] The serum half-life is approximately 30 hours. Following the intramuscular injection of vitamin K_1, serum concentrations increase a thousand times to $>1,000$ ng/mL[39,41] by 12 hours post-injection. In breast-feeding infants 5 days after a 1 mg intramuscular injection of phylloquinone, serum concentrations remain 10 times higher than adult normals.[30]

Transitional Needs of Premature Infants

The serum phylloquinone concentration in low-birthweight infants remains five times the adult normal concentration 8 days after a 2 mg oral dose.[10] For the premature infant who has progressed to formula feedings by this time, no additional vitamin K is necessary, as formula is generally fortified with phylloquinone (approximately 55 ng/mL in the United States). Regarding the human milk–fed premature infant during transition from birth to establishment of full caloric intake, initial supplements of phylloquinone are probably adequate, though there are no long-term studies of the vitamin K status of preterm infants fed human milk. We do know that the phylloquinone concentration of human milk is very low at all stages of lactation, generally <2.0 ng/mL.[28]

The extremely low-birthweight premature infant ($<1,000$ g) is likely to receive an extended period of parenteral nutrition after birth. Parenteral nutrition solutions in the United States are now generally supplemented with multivitamins containing 200 μg of phylloquinone per 5 mL (M.V.I. Pediatric, Astra Pharmaceutical). Generally, these infants receive less than a full vial. Two milliliters of a vial would provide 80 μg of phylloquinone, and as doses of 70 to 130 μg/day in the preterm infant have not been associated with bleeding disorders, this would seem adequate.[42] Prior to the availability of these intravenous vitamin solutions for pediatric patients, it was common practice to give weekly injections of 0.5 to 1.0 mg of phylloquinone to premature infants. Serum phylloquinone concentrations in preterm infants within 24 hours of these injections were 100 times or more than the normal adult concentration of 1 ng/mL (Greer FR, Khayata S. 1987. Unpublished data).

Needs of Growing Premature Infants

For the growing premature infant, all standard formulas (containing at least 55 ng/mL) would supply a relatively large amount of vitamin K. However, for the exclusively human milk–fed preterm infant, there is no information on long-term vitamin K status. Currently available oral multivitamin solutions do not contain phylloquinone. Oral supplements (20 mg) of phylloquinone for breast-feeding mothers will greatly increase the vitamin K concentration of human milk (up to 130 ng/mL 12 hours after the dose), but these supplements are not recommended for breast-feeding mothers.[28] Hemorrhagic disease generally does not occur in full-term breast-fed infants who received 1 mg of phylloquinone at birth, despite very low serum phylloquinone concentrations during the first 6 months of life.[28] This type of disease rarely occurs in growing premature infants, and reported cases generally have many other complicating factors.[43]

Vitamin K Deficiency

Hemorrhagic Disease of the Newborn
Though vitamin K deficiency in the newborn presenting as neonatal hemorrhage is currently not a major concern in the United States, it remains a worldwide health problem in areas where prophylactic vitamin K is not administered at birth. Hemorrhagic disease of the newborn was recognized early on as a disease of

breast-fed infants. The first large series of cases was published nearly a century ago, when it was speculated that the disease was of an infectious etiology.[44] It was not until the mid-twentieth century that this disease was further studied, at which time the incidence among breast-feeding full-term infants was estimated to range as low as 1 in 400 to as high as 1.7 per 100.[45,46] It was also noted at this time that the disease usually occurred in breast-fed infants who did not receive prophylactic vitamin K.

Several forms of newborn hemorrhagic disease attributed to vitamin K deficiency are described in the literature. In the "classic" disorder, hemorrhage occurs between 2 and 10 days of life and intracranial hemorrhage is uncommon. The disease is usually hallmarked by generalized ecchymoses or gastrointestinal hemorrhage. Bleeding from the circumcision site or umbilical cord stump also occurs frequently. The most common form of hemorrhagic disease reported in the world literature is the "late onset" type which presents after 2 weeks of age. In a recent review of 89 cases of hemorrhagic disease in the newborn, 80 of the reported cases were of this late onset type.[47] Sixty-six of these 80 infants experienced intracranial hemorrhage, a very common feature of late onset disease. The reported mortality rate was 17% and the morbidity rate was undoubtedly much higher, though it was not documented in all reports. It is of interest that 76 of these 80 infants were breast-fed exclusively and did not receive prophylactic vitamin K at birth. Only six infants were reported to have been breast-fed and also to have received prophylactic vitamin K at birth.

A less common form of hemorrhagic disease of the newborn is that associated with maternal anticonvulsant therapy during pregnancy.[48] Only 2 of the 89 cases just referred to were of this type. Although infants respond to vitamin K administration, our understanding of the role of anticonvulsants in this hemorrhagic disorder is very limited.

Periventricular-Intraventricular Hemorrhage

Periventricular-intraventricular hemorrhage (PIVH) has been a long-standing problem in premature infants, particularly in those with a birthweight <1,500 g. Studies have associated PIVH with coagulation defects in preterm infants.[49–54] However, not until recently has maternal vitamin K administration been studied as prophylaxis for PIVH,[55] thus assuming a clinical "deficiency state" in the fetus and preterm infant. These studies have taken place despite the fact that phylloquinone is transported very poorly across the placenta, and that the balance of previous studies have shown minimal effects of intramuscular vitamin K injections on coagulation factors in premature or full-term infants.

To date, three studies have utilized prophylactic maternal phylloquinone administration to prevent PIVH in infants.[56–58] In the first of these studies, 53 mothers in preterm labor and their infants (mean gestational age 30 weeks, mean birthweight <1,000 g) were placed into one of two groups.[56] Mothers in the vitamin K group received 10 mg of phylloquinone intramuscularly every 5 days until delivery. Although there was less infant PIVH in the vitamin K group, the subjects were not randomized appropriately; significantly more infants were placed in the control group (33 versus 20). The control group also had a higher percentage of male infants, more severe respiratory disease, and a higher incidence of indomethacin therapy. The vitamin K group, on the other hand, had a significantly higher incidence of maternal antenatal steroid administration. Furthermore, only a single cranial ultrasound was done on each infant in the first few days of life. In the second study, 100 mothers with preterm labor and their infants (mean gestational age <30 weeks, mean birthweight <1,130 g) were randomized.[57] Mothers in the vitamin K group received 10 mg intramuscularly every 5 days until delivery. This study also found significantly less PIVH among infants in the vitamin K group than the control group, but did not include any cranial ultrasounds after 3 days of life. The study was also confounded by the use of antenatal steroids as well as phenobarbital, with the vitamin K group receiving more of each drug than the controls. In the third and most recent study, 103 mothers in preterm labor and their infants were also randomized.[58] The vitamin K group received 10 mg intramuscularly. If delivery did not occur by 4 days, mothers then received 20 mg/day orally until delivery. These investigators found no differences in the incidence of PIVH between the two groups, and all infants had cranial ultrasounds through 14 days of age. This study was not confounded by the use of antenatal steroids or phenobarbital, though infants were larger (mean birthweight <1,525 g and mean gestational age <33 weeks) than in the previous two studies. Additionally, prothrombin time (PT) and partial thromboplastin time (PTT), as well as concentrations of coagulation factors II, VII, and IX, did not differ between the two groups of infants. Median cord plasma phylloquinone concentrations were only slightly higher in the vitamin K group compared to the control group (0.024 versus 0.010 ng/mL, $p = 0.046$, normal adult values being 0.5 to 1.0 ng/mL). Thus, the data to date would not consistently support the conclusion that PIVH in premature infants was secondary to a vitamin K deficiency state. It is also clear that many cases of PIVH occur in infants 3 or more days after receiving the customary prophylactic dose of phylloquinone at birth.

Assessment of Vitamin K Deficiency

Historically speaking, the assessment of vitamin K deficiency has been a difficult task. It is estimated that there must be more than a 50% decrease in the concentrations of coagulation factors before a significant decrease in PT occurs.[59] However, two recent technological advances have improved our ability to directly assess the vitamin K status of the newborn. The first of these was the development of a sensitive and reliable assay for measuring phylloquinone. Since it was first described in 1982,[25] this assay has been further modified.[60] This technology has allowed measurement of phylloquinone in infant plasma, stools, and liver, as well as human milk. It is also possible to estimate phylloquinone intake by measuring phylloquinone concentrations in food.

The second important development in the technology of vitamin K assessment was the description of an abnormal protein induced by vitamin K absence or deficiency (PIVKA). Though the presence of this abnormal protein was first suspected in 1963,[61] development of assays has been relatively recent. The molecular basis of abnormal prothrombin is secondary to the absence of phylloquinone, needed as an essential cofactor to the liver enzyme glutamyl carboxylase which normally converts the "glu" residues to "gla" residues of the prothrombin molecule. The recognition of this abnormal prothrombin (characterized by an excess of "glu" or acarboxylated residues) has resulted in speculation about its usefulness as a biochemical marker for clinical or subclinical vitamin K deficiency. While many terms have been used in the literature for this abnormal protein (des-gamma-carboxy-prothrombin, hypocarboxyprothrombin, a-carboxyprothrombin), PIVKA-II will be used here to designate the PIVKA associated with prothrombin (the second factor in the coagulation scheme).

It should be noted that PIVKA-II is a very heterogenous molecule. It consists of a pool of partially carboxylated prothrombin as well as some completely uncarboxylated prothrombin at the gamma sites.[1] The number of acarboxylated sites (up to 10) per individual prothrombin molecule and the specific sites involved remain areas of investigation). Likewise, the degree of physiological activity may vary with the number of uncarboxylated gamma sites on the molecule. Recently, a preparation lacking 20% of the gamma-carboxylated sites, primarily at the more carboxy-terminal sites of the molecule, has been demonstrated to have nearly normal physiological activity.[2]

Since the first attempt to detect PIVKA-II in cord blood of newborn infants,[62] numerous subsequent efforts using a variety of methods have reported detection rates of PIVKA-II in cord blood ranging from 0% to 89%. The discrepancies among these reports reflect the various assay techniques used to measure PIVKA-II, which fall into one of four basic methodologies.

One of these methods, cross-immunoelectrophoresis (CIE), is based on the separation of PIVKA-II from physiologic prothrombin by its different calcium-binding affinities using gel electrophoresis.[63] Most reports have failed to detect PIVKA-II in cord blood or have detected it at a very low rate (<5% of samples). However, if this method is used in exclusively breast-fed infants receiving no vitamin K supplements, a dramatic increase in PIVKA-II detection rate occurs at 5 to 7 days compared to cord blood.[63–66] This marked elevation in PIVKA-II detection rate (to approximately 50%) corresponds with the peak incidence of early hemorrhagic disease of the newborn.

Another technique for measuring PIVKA-II is the so-called "ratio method" that utilizes both physiological activation of prothrombin and a variety of nonphysiological activators of prothrombin such as snake venom and bacterial endotoxins. The nonphysiological conditions activate both normal prothrombin and PIVKA-II, which make up "total" plasma prothrombin. Thus, if PIVKA-II is present, the ratio of thrombin generated by physiological activation to total thrombin activation is decreased. Both normal and below-normal mean ratios as compared to adult normal plasma values have been reported.[62,67,68] In one study of infants with and without vitamin K prophylaxis during the first 5 days of life, the most marked decrease in the ratio occurred in those infants not receiving vitamin K prophylaxis.[69]

A third technique for measuring PIVKA-II is the so-called absorption method. It involves precipitation of the physiologically active prothrombin with any of a number of insoluble salts, followed by measurement of the remaining PIVKA-II using methods detecting total prothrombin as discussed previously. This method has been used only to detect PIVKA-II in cord blood.[70–73]

The fourth method for detecting PIVKA-II utilizes "specific" PIVKA-II antibody. The principle of this method is the preparation of a murine monoclonal antibody.[74] This method has been applied to PIVKA-II measurements in cord blood and infants 4 to 6 weeks of age. The utilization of the murine antibody by different investigators in a number of countries has consistently found detection rates of PIVKA-II in cord blood of approximately 20%.[74–76] As expected, the PIVKA-II detection rate on days 4 and 5 of life was also decreased dramatically by vitamin K prophylaxis.[74,77] Unexpected was the finding in four infants of significant PIVKA-II concentrations on day 5 of life, which were unchanged from those measured in cord blood despite vitamin K prophylaxis.[74] In a similar observation, detectable PIVKA-II was found in 5 out of 61 breast-fed infants who received vitamin K at birth.[76] At 4 to 6 weeks of life, there is also a difference in PIVKA-II detection rates between studies done in Holland and Japan (3.3% versus 12.9%).[76,78] Additionally, newborn oral vitamin K supplements did not significantly alter PIVKA-II detection rates of Japanese infants at 4 to 6 weeks.[77,79]

The relevance of using PIVKA-II detectability as a definition of vitamin K deficiency has been questioned, because PIVKA-II has been detected in infants in both cord blood and again at day 5 of life despite receiving vitamin K prophylaxis at birth.[74] Since PIVKA-II detectability may occur despite normal or elevated plasma concentrations of phylloquinone, PIVKA-II is not useful at present as a screen for subclinical vitamin K deficiency in preterm or full-term infants. Interpretations of results would require simultaneous measurements of serum phylloquinone and phylloquinone intakes in infants in a variety of clinical situations. Until more extensive investigations are completed, the use of PIVKA-II is limited to research purposes. It is anticipated that research in the next decade will focus on the role of PIVKA for the diagnosis of vitamin K deficiency before overt hemorrhagic disease occurs.

Toxicity

Little information regarding vitamin K toxicity in humans is available. There seems to be little or no toxicity from the currently available forms, other than occasional anaphylaxis.[80] In the 1950s, however, menadione (a synthetic form of vitamin K no longer used in medicine) administration for vitamin K prophylaxis in newborn infants was associated with hyperbilirubinemia, presumably secondary to increased red cell hemolysis and decreased protein binding of bilirubin.[81,82] This problem was compounded by the practice of administering large doses of menadione (72 mg) to mothers in premature labor.[82] When phylloquinone became available for newborn prophylaxis and much smaller doses were utilized, this problem was eliminated.

Future Research

Vitamin K research in the newborn is still a wide-open field. Little specific information regarding the premature infant exists. At the present time, very large doses of vitamin K are given to these infants both for initial prophylaxis and in TPN solutions. Research is needed to determine the physiological requirements.

There is great need for more research in detecting vitamin K deficiency in clinical situations where there is no overt hemorrhage. Much work remains to be done in developing assays for the various circulating proteins induced by absence of vitamin K.

Recommendations

The current RDA of vitamin K for infants, children, and adults is 1 μg/kg/day.[83] Infants on vitamin K–fortified formula exceed the RDA; there is no information to suggest that this amount is harmful, even though serum concentrations of phylloquinone are much higher in formula-fed infants compared to breast-fed infants or the adult normal population. In human milk–fed infants, phylloquinone serum concentrations and vitamin K intakes are extremely low as long as diets are exclusively human milk. However, at the present time there are insufficient data to recommend further supplementation of these infants beyond the prophylactic dose received in the immediate newborn period.

For premature infants on TPN, phylloquinone should continue to be supplemented. For infants receiving daily multivitamins containing vitamin K (M.V.I. Pediatric contains 200 μg/5 mL) in the TPN solutions, no additional supplements are needed. For premature infants <1,000 g, one half-dose (100 μg with M.V.I. Pediatric) should supply sufficient vitamin K. However, only 10 μg/kg/day would seem to be more than adequate for these infants and would approximate the vitamin K intake of infants fed fortified formula, which is known to prevent hemorrhage disease of the newborn. There are no commercially available parenteral vitamins that deliver this decreased amount of vitamin K.

In the immediate newborn period, it seems prudent to continue 1 mg of phylloquinone intramuscularly or 2 mg by mouth to all infants with a birthweight >1,000 g as recommended by the American Academy of Pediatrics. For infants with a birthweight <1,000 g, 0.3 mg/kg intramuscularly would be sufficient. If vitamin K is to be given very early and to absolutely assure that the dose is received in full, it would seem best to administer phylloquinone intramuscularly, when feasible, to preterm infants at birth. This initial prophylactic dose of vitamin K should be sufficient to maintain premature infants through the transition period (first 2 weeks of life).

During the periods of stabilization and post-hospital discharge up to 6 months, fortified formulas will supply 7 to 9 μg/kg/day of vitamin K. No additional supplements are necessary. For exclusively human milk–fed premature infants during this stable period, additional supplements of vitamin K to achieve at least the amount of vitamin K received by formula-fed infants (7 to 9 μg/kg/day) would seem to be indicated. Additional supplements of phylloquinone may be necessary in older premature infants who are in other special situations (prolonged antibiotic therapy, malabsorptive states, etc.).

CASE STUDY

A 3-week-old 2.5-kg male infant with seizures is brought by ambulance to the emergency room. Past medical history documented that the infant was born at home to an Amish family at 34 weeks gestation with a birthweight of 2,000 g. The history also revealed that there was some blood oozing from the umbilical cord stump between days 3 and 5 of life, and that the infant had been exclusively breast-fed since birth. No prophylactic vitamin K had been given in the neonatal period.

Questions and Answers

Q. Relative to vitamin K, what diagnoses should be considered in this infant?
A. Cord stump oozing of blood is indicative of early hemorrhagic disease of the newborn. The seizures may be secondary to the intracranial hemorrhage of late hemorrhagic disease.

Q. What should be included in the diagnostic workup to rule out vitamin K deficiency?
A. Coagulation studies (PT, PTT) and a CAT scan or ultrasound of the head. Serum should be obtained for a subsequent assay for vitamin K concentration.

Q. What is the immediate treatment for this infant?
A. Along with appropriate anticonvulsant therapy, a parenteral dose of vitamin K is indicated (after blood for diagnostic studies is obtained).

References

1. Suttie JW. Vitamin K-dependent carboxylase. *Annu Rev Biochem* 1985; 54:459–477.
2. Liska DJ, Suttie JW. Location of gamma-carboxyglutamyl residues in partially carboxylated prothrombin preparations. *Biochem* 1988; 27:8636–8641.
3. Dahlback B. Interaction between complement component C4b-binding protein and the vitamin K-dependent protein S. *Scand J Clin Lab Invest* 1985; 45(suppl 177):33–41.
4. Vermeer C. D-carboxyglutamate-containing proteins and the vitamin K dependent carboxylase. *Biochem J* 1990; 266:625–636.
5. Price PA. Role of vitamin-K-dependent proteins in bone metabolism. *Annu Rev Nutr* 1988; 8:565–584.
6. Blomstrand R, Forsgren L. Vitamin K_1 ^{3}H in man. Its intestinal absorption and transport in the thoracic duct lymph. *Int J Vit Forschung* 1968; 38:45–64.
7. Hollander D, Rim E, Muralidhara KS. Vitamin K_1 intestinal absorption in vivo: influence of luminal contents on transport. *Am J Physiol* 1977; 232:E69–E74.
8. Hollander D, Muralidhara KS, Rim E. Colonic absorption of bacterially synthesized vitamin K_2 in the rat. *Am J Physiol* 1976; 230:251–255.
9. Hollander D, Rim E. Vitamin K_2 absorption by rat everted small intestinal sacs. *Am J Physiol* 1976; 231:415–419.
10. Sann L, Leclercq M, Guillaumand M, Trouyez R, Bethenod M, Bourgeay-Causse M. Serum vitamin K_1 concentrations after oral administration of vitamin K_1 in low birth weight infants. *J Pediatr* 1985; 107:608–611.
11. Shearer MJ, Barkhan P, Webster GR. Absorption and excretion of an oral dose of tritiated vitamin K_1 in man. *Brit J Haematol* 1970; 18:297–308.
12. Shearer MJ, Mallinson CN, Webster GR, Barkham P. Clearance from plasma and excretion in urine, faeces, and bile of an intravenous dose of tritiated vitamin K_1 in man. *Brit J Haematol*. 1972; 22:579–588.
13. Shearer MJ, Barkhan P. Studies on the metabolites of phylloquinone (vitamin K_1) in the urine of man. *Biochem Biophys Acta* 1973; 297:300–312.
14. Suttie JW. Vitamin K. In: Diplock AT, ed. *Fat soluble vitamins: their biochemistry and applications*. Lancaster, PA: Technomic Publishing; 1985:225–311.
15. Elliot MC, Isaacs B, Ivy AC. Production of "prothrombin deficiency" and response to vitamin A, D, and K. *Proc Soc Exp Biol Med* 1940; 43:240–245.
16. Doisy EA, Matschiner JT. In: Morton RA, ed. *Fat soluble vitamins*. Oxford, UK: Pergamon Press, 1970:293.
17. Corrigan JJ, Ulfers LL. Effect of vitamin E on prothrombin levels in warfarin-induced vitamin K deficiency. *Am J Clin Nutr* 1981; 34:1701–1705.
18. Rao GH, Mason KE. Antisterility and antivitamin K activity of d-α-tocopherol hydroquinone in the vitamin E–deficient female rat. *J Nutr* 1975; 105:495–498.
19. Corrigan JJ, Taussig LM, Beckerman R, Wagner JS. Factor II (prothrombin) coagulant activity and immunoreactive protein. Detection of vitamin K deficiency and liver disease in patients with cystic fibrosis. *J Pediatr* 1981; 99:254–257.
20. Shearer MJ, McBurney A, Barkhan P. Studies on the absorption and metabolism of phylloquinone (vitamin K_1) in man. *Vitamins and Hormones* 1974; 32:513–542.
21. Thierry MJ, Hermodson MA, Suttie JW. Vitamin K and warfarin distribution and metabolism in the warfarin-resistant rat. *Am J Physiol* 1970; 219:854–859.
22. Duello TJ, Matschiner JT. Characterization of vitamin K from pig liver and dog liver. *Arch Biochem Biophys* 1971; 144:330–338.
23. Bjornson TD, Meffin PG, Swezey SE, Blaschke TF. Disposition and turnover of vitamin K_1 in man. In: Suttie JW, ed. *Vitamin K metabolism and vitamin K-dependent proteins*. Baltimore: University Park Press; 1980:328–332.
24. Khayata S, Kindberg C, Greer FR, Suttie JW. Vitamin K_1 and K_2 in infant human liver. *J Pediatr Gastroenterol Nutr* 1989; 8:304–307.
25. Shearer MJ, Barkhan P, Rahim S, Stimmler L. Plasma vitamin K_1 in mother and their newborn babies. *Lancet* 1982; II:460–463.
26. Von Kries R, Shearer M, McCarthy PT, Haug M, Harger G, Gobel U. Vitamin K_1 content of maternal milk: influence of the stage of lactation, lipid composition and vitamin K_1 supplements given to the mother. *Pediatric Research* 1987; 22:513–517.
27. Tamura T, Takasaki K, Yanaihara T, Marugama M, Nakayama T. Effect of vitamin K administration to the mother on prevention of vitamin K deficiency in the neonate. *Acta Obst Gynaec Jpn* 1986; 38:880–886.
28. Greer FR, Marshall S, Cherry J, Suttie JW. Vitamin K status of lactating mothers, human milk and breast-feeding infants. *Pediatrics* 1991; 88:751–756.
29. Bentley R, Meganathan R. Biosynthesis of vitamin K (menaquinones) in bacteria. *Microbiol Rev* 1982; 46:241.

30. Greer FR, Mummah-Schendel LL, Marshall S, Suttie JW. Vitamin K_1 (phylloquinone) and vitamin K_2 (menaquinone) status in newborns during the first week of life. *Pediatrics* 1988; 81:137–140.

31. Uchida K, Komeno T. Relationships between dietary and intestinal vitamin K_1 clotting factor levels, plasma vitamin K_1 and urinary gla. In: Suttie JW, ed. *Current advances in vitamin K research*. New York: Elsevier Science Publishing, 1988:477–492.

32. Israels LG, Allman DJ, Israels ED. Vitamin K_1 as a modulator of benzo(a)pyrene metabolism as measured by in vitro metabolite formation and in vivo ANA-adduct formation. *Int J Biochem* 1985; 17:1263–1266.

33. Israels LG, Walls GA, Allman DJ, Friesen E, Israels ED. Vitamin K as a regulator of benzo(a)pyrene metabolism, mutagenesis and carcinogenesis. *J Clin Invest* 1983; 71:1130–1140.

34. Israels LG, Friesen E, Jansen AH, Israels ED. Vitamin K_1 increases sister chromatid exchange in vitro in human leukocytes and in-vivo in fetal sheep cells: a possible role for "vitamin K deficiency" in the fetus. *Pediatr Res* 1987; 22:405–408.

35. Kazzi NJ, Ilagan NB, Liang KC, Kazzi GM, Grietsell LA, Brans YW. Placental transfer of vitamin K_1 in preterm pregnancy. *Obstet Gynecol* 1990; 75:334–337.

36. Andrew M, Paes B, Milner R, Johnston M, Mitchel L, Tollefsen DM, Castle V, Powers P. Development of the human coagulation system in the healthy premature infant. *Blood* 1988;72:1651–1657.

37. Andrew M, Paes B, Milner R, Johnston M, Mitchel L, Tollefsen DM, Powers P. Development of the human coagulation system in the full-term infant. *Blood* 1987; 70:1 65–172.

38. Pietersma-de Bruyn ALJM, Haard PMM, Van Beunis MH, Hamulyak K, Kuijpers JC. Vitamin K levels and coagulation factors in healthy term newborns till 4 weeks after birth. *Haemostasis* 1990; 20:8–14.

39. Goldschmidt B, Kisrakoi C, Teglas E, Verbengi M, es Kovacs I. Vitamin K_1 serum-concentration and vitamin K-dependent clotting factors in newborn infants after intramuscular or oral prophylactic vitamin K_1. *Orvosi Hetilap* 1990; 131:1297–1300.

40. Sann L, Leclercq M, Bourgeois J, Frederick A. Pharmokinetics of vitamin K_1 in newborn infants. *Pediatr Res* 1983; 17:155A.

41. McNinch AW, Upton C, Samuels M, Shearer MJ, McCarthy PT, Tripp JH, L'Orme R. Plasma concentrations after oral or parenteral vitamin K_1 in neonates. *Arch Dis Child* 1985; 60:814–818.

42. Greene HL, Hambidge M, Schanler R, Tsang RC. Guidelines for the use of vitamins, trace elements, calcium, magnesium and phosphorus in infants and children receiving total parenteral nutrition: a report of the sub-committee on Pediatric Nutritional Requirements from the Committee on Clinical Practice Issues of the American Society for Clinical Nutrition. *Am J Clin Nutr* 1988; 48:1324–1342.

43. Morgan SK. Vitamin K in bleeding infants. *J S C Med Assoc* 1969; 65:5–6.

44. Townsend CW. The haemorrhagic disease of the newborn. *Arch Pediatr* 1894; 11:559–565.

45. Sutherland JM, Glueck HI, Gleser G. Hemorrhagic disease of the newborn. *Am J Dis Child* 1967;113:524–533.

46. Keenan, WI, Jewett T, Glueck H. Role of feeding and vitamin K in hypoprothrombinemia of the newborn. *Am J Dis Child* 1971; 121:271–277.

47. Greer FR, Suttie JW. Vitamin K and the newborn. In: Tsang RC, Nichols BL, eds. *Nutrition during infancy*. Philadelphia: Hanley and Belfus, 1988: 289–297.

48. Srinivasan G, Seeler RA, Tiruvury A, Pildes RS. Maternal anticonvulsant therapy and hemorrhagic diseases of the newborn. *Obstet Gynecol* 1982; 59:250–252.

49. Gray OP, Ackerman A, Fraser AJ. Intracranial haemorrhage and clotting defects in low-birth-weight infants. *Lancet* 1968; I: 545–548.

50. Cole VA, Durbin M, Olaffson A, Reynolds EOR, Rivers RPA, Smith JF. Pathogenesis of intraventricular haemorrhage in newborn infants. *Arch Dis Child* 1974; 49: 722–728.

51. Setzer ES, Webb IB, Wassenaar JW, Reeder JD, Mehta PS, Eitzman DV. Platelet dysfunction and coagulopathy in intraventricular hemorrhage in the premature infant. *J Pediatr* 1982; 100:599–605.

52. McDonald MM, Johnson ML, Rumack CM, Koops BL, Guggenheim MA, Babb C, Hathaway WE. Role of coagulopathy in newborn intracranial hemorrhage. *Pediatrics* 1984; 74:26–31.

53. Beverley DW, Chance GW, Inwood MJ, Schaus M, O'Keefe B. Intraventricular haemorrhage and haemostasis defects. *Arch Dis Child* 1984; 59:444–448.

54. Van de Bor M, Van Bel F, Lineman R, Ruys JH. Perinatal factors and periventricular-intraventricular hemorrhage in preterm infants. *Am J Dis Child* 1986; 140: 1125–1130.

55. Ment LR, Ehrenkranz RA, Duncan CC. Intraventricular hemorrhage of the preterm neonate: prevention studies. *Semin Perinatol* 1988; 12:359–372.

56. Pomerance JJ, Teal JG, Gogolok JF, Brown S, Stewart ME. Maternally administered antenatal vitamin K_1: effect on neonatal prothrombin activity, partial thromboplastin time, and intraventricular hemorrhage. *Obstet Gynecol* 1987; 70:235–241.

57. Morales WJ, Angel JL, O'Brien WF, Knuppel RA, Marsalis F. The use of antenatal vitamin K in the prevention of early neonatal intraventricular hemorrhage. *Am J Obstet Gynecol* 1988; 159:774–779.

58. Kazzi NJ, Ilagan NB, Liang KC, Kazzi GM, Poland RL, Grietsel LA, Fujii Y, Brans YW. Maternal administration of vitamin K does not improve coagulation profile of preterm infants. *Pediatrics* 1989; 84:1045–1050.

59. Hathaway WE, Bonnar J. *Perinatal coagulation*. New York: Grune & Stratton, 1978:53.

60. Haroon Y, Bacon DS, Sadowski JA. Liquid-chromatographic determination of vitamin K_1 in plasma, with fluorometric detection. *Clin Chem* 1986; 32:1925–1929.

61. Hemker HC, Vellkamp JJ, Hensen A, Loeliger EA. Nature of prothrombin biosynthesis: pre-prothrombinaemina in vitamin K-deficiency. *Nature* 1963; 200:589.

62. Van Doorm JM, Muller AD, Hemker HC. Heparin-like inhibitor, not vitamin K deficiency, in the newborn. *Lancet* 1977; I:852–853.

63. Ganrot PO, Nilehn JE. Plasma prothrombin during treatment with Dicumarol II. Demonstration of an abnormal prothrombin fraction. *Scand J Clin Lab Invest* 1968; 22:23–28.

64. Von Kries, Göbel U, Maase B. Vitamin K deficiency in the newborn [letter]. *Lancet* 1985; II:728–729.

65. Von Kries R, Becker A, Göbel U. Vitamin K in the newborn: influence of nutritional factors on acarboxyprothrombin detectability and factor II and VII clotting activity. *Eur J Pediatr* 1987; 146:123–127.

66. Von Kries R, Kreppel S, Becker A, Tangermann R. Göbel U. Acarboxyprothrombin activity after oral prophylactic vitamin K. *Arch Dis Child* 1987; 62:938–940.

67. Malia RG, Preston FE, Mitchel VE. Evidence against vitamin K defiency in normal neonates. *Thromb Haemost* 1980; 44:159–60.

68. Corrigan JJ, Krye JJ. Factor II (prothrombin) level in cord blood: correlation of coagulant activity with immunoreactive protein. *J Pediatr* 1980; 97:979–983.

69. Schettini F, DeMattia D, Mantone A. Preprothrombin and prothrombin in full-term newborns. *Haemostasis* 1972/1973; 1:271–278.

70. Atkinson PM, Bradlow BA, Moulineaux JD, Walker NP. Acarboxy-prothrombin in cord plasma from normal neonates. *J Pediatr Gastroenterol Nutr* 1984; 3:450–453.

71. Bloch CA, Rothberg AD, Bradlow BA. Mother-infant prothrombin precursor status at birth. *J Pediatr Gastroenterol Nutr* 1984; 3:101–103.

72. Shapiro AD, Jacobson LL, Armon ME, Manco-Johnson MJ, Hulac P, Lane PA, Hathaway WE. Vitamin K deficiency in the newborn infant: prevalance and perinatal risk factors. *J Pediatr* 1986; 109:675–680.

73. Francis JL. A rapid and simple micromethod for the specific determination of decarboxylated prothrombin. *Med Lab Sci* 1988; 45:69–73.

74. Motohara K, Endo F, Matsuda I. Effect of vitamin K administration on acarboxyprothrombin (PIVKA-II) levels in newborns. *Lancet* 1985; II:242–244.

75. Von Kries R, Shearer MJ, Widdershoven J, Göbel U. Comparison of des-gamma-carboxy-prothrombin and plasma vitamin K₁ in newborns and their mothers [abstract]. *Thromb Haemost* 1989; 62:287.

76. Widdershoven J, Lambert W, Motohara K, Monnens L, deLeenbeer A, Matsuda I, Endo F. Plasma concentrations of vitamin K₁ and PIVKA-II in bottle-fed and breast-fed infants with and without vitamin K prophylaxis at birth. *Eur J Pediatr* 1988; 148:139–142.

77. Motohara K, Takayi S, Endo F, Kiyoto Y, Matsuda I. Oral supplementation of vitamin K for pregnant women and effects on levels of plasma vitamin K and PIVKA-II in the neonate. *J Pediatr Gastroenterol Nutr* 1990; 11:32–36.

78. Motohara K, Endo F, Mutsuda I. Vitamin K deficiency in breast-fed infants at one month of age. *J Pediatr Gastroenterol Nutr* 1986; 5:931–933.

79. Motohara K, Endo F, Matsuda I. Screening for late neonatal vitamin K deficency by acarboxyprothrombin in dried blood spots. *Arch Dis Child* 1987; 62:370–375.

80. Anderson TH, Hindsholm KB, Fallingborg J. Severe complication to phytomenadione after intramuscular injection in women in labor. *Acta Obstet Gynecol Scand* 1989; 68:381–382.

81. Meyer TC, Angus J. The effect of large doses of "Synkavit" in the newborn. *Arch Dis Child* 1956; 31:212–215.

82. Lucey JF, Dolan RG. Hyperbilirubinemia of newborn infants associated with the parenteral administration of a vitamin K analogue to the mothers. *Pediatrics* 1959; 23:553–560.

83. Food and Nutrition Board Commission on Life Sciences National Research Council. *Recommended dietary allowances*. 10th ed. Washington, DC: National Academy Press, 1989: 111.

9. Water-Soluble Vitamins: C, B₁, B₂, B₆, Niacin, Pantothenic Acid, and Biotin

Harry L. Greene

Laurie J. Smidt

Reviewers: William C. Heird, Jean-L. Micheli, Donald M. Mock

The estimation of recommended vitamin intake for infants is based mainly on the vitamin content of human milk and the average milk intake of thriving term infants[1] (Table 9.1). One flaw in this concept is that the vitamin content of human milk varies considerably between individuals and changes substantially over the course of lactation. For example, vitamins A and E decrease during lactation, while thiamine and vitamin B_6 increase (Fig. 9.1). Over 3 months of lactation, the amount of vitamin B_6 in human milk may increase fourfold. This relatively new information adds to the difficulty of extrapolating appropriate recommendations for the extremely low-birthweight infant where little precise information exists. More precise estimates of vitamin needs, derived from blood and urine analyses in response to specific vitamin intake dose response data, have not

been deemed critical since vitamin deficiency or toxicity is rare in term infants receiving vitamin intakes approximating the average amounts consumed during breast-feeding. (Exceptions are vitamins D and K, and appropriate supplementation of these vitamins has been incorporated into most neonatal programs.) Nevertheless, recent observations indicate that special considerations must be brought to bear when assessing vitamin requirements for infants delivered prematurely. The reasons for this include: (1) immaturity of the organ systems involved in assimilation and conservation of vitamins; (2) low tissue stores of vitamins; and (3) an increased tendency for disease conditions including systemic infection, which may further alter the usual patterns of vitamin assimilation and metabolism. These complicating factors are particularly apt

Table 9.1. Vitamin Content of Human Milk and Commercial Infant Formulas

Vitamins	Human Milk[50] (U/100 kcal)	Standard Milk-Based Formulas* (U/100 kcal)	Preterm Formulas† (U/100 kcal)
C, mg	5.6	8.1–9	8.6–37
Thiamine, μg	29	78–100	100–250
Riboflavin, μg	49	150	160–620
B₆, μg	28	60–63	60–250
Niacin, mg	0.21	0.75–1.25	0.75–5
Biotin, μg	0.56	2.2–4.4	2–37
Pantothenic acid, μg	250	315–470	450–1,900
B₁₂, μg	0.07	0.2–0.25	0.3–0.55
Folate, μg	6.9	7.5–15.6	12.5–37
A, μg	93	90–93	90–360
D, μg	0.08	1.5–1.58	1.5–6.8
E, mg	0.32	1.4–3.1	1.9–4.6
K, μg	0.29	8–8.6	8.6–13

*Enfamil (Mead Johnson & Co, Evansville, Ind), Similac (Ross Laboratories, Columbus, Ohio), SMA (Wyeth Laboratories, Philadelphia, Penn).

†Enfamil Premature (Mead Johnson), Similac Special Care (Ross), SMA Preemie (Wyeth).

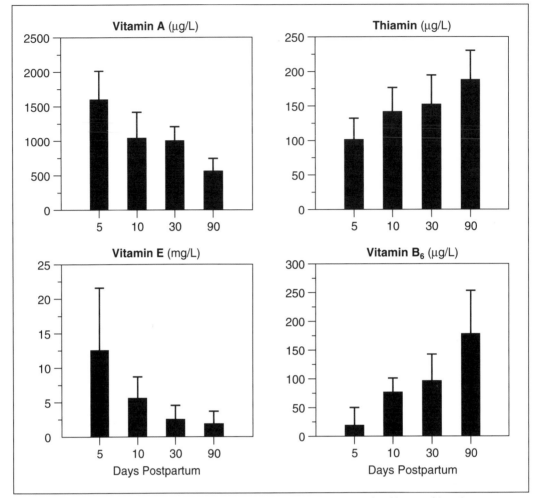

Fig. 9.1. Concentrations of vitamins A, E, thiamine, and B_6 in human milk during the first 90 days of lactation.

to occur when infants are delivered prior to 32 weeks gestation.

The purpose of this chapter is to draw attention to the special considerations inherent in meeting the nutritional needs of this group of infants, and to review the published data that suggest specific differences between the needs of term and preterm infants. Finally, these data will be used to formulate an estimate of vitamin intakes for very low-birthweight (VLBW) infants which should prevent deficiency and avoid the potential for toxicity.

Special Considerations for Estimating Vitamin Needs of Very Low-Birthweight Infants

Vitamin Delivery
Nutritional management of the VLBW infant (<32 weeks gestation with weight <1,500 g) often requires

initial treatment with total parenteral nutrition (TPN) before "weaning" to specially formulated preterm infant formulas or breast milk with nutritional fortifiers. The relationship between intravenous and oral vitamin needs therefore needs to be addressed.

Two major differences exist between intravenous and orally administered vitamins. First, in the intravenous mode, the daily doses of vitamins are infused continuously over 24 hours. Second, the infusions are given systemically rather than via the portal vein which is purported to increase renal losses. These differences led the American Medical Association's Nutrition Advisory Group (NAG) to speculate that renal clearance of water-soluble vitamins would be greater during TPN compared with oral administration. Thus, the adult and pediatric recommended intake during TPN is between 50% and 100% higher than the established oral recommendations.[2] This postulated difference between oral and intravenous

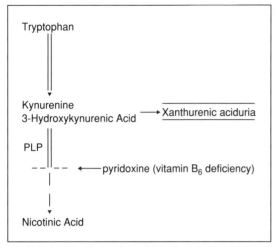

Fig. 9.2. Pyridoxal phosphate (PLP)–dependent stage of synthesis of nicotinic acid from tryptophan. Pyridoxine deficiency causes decreased conversion of 3-hydroxykynurenic acid to nicotinic acid. Thus, with an increase in dietary tryptophan, there is increased excretion of xanthurenic acid.

needs has not been established quantitatively; the determination of renal losses of vitamins is mandatory in future studies in order to interpret the plasma response to specific doses of water-soluble vitamins. Of further concern is that some of the vitamins present in the multiple-vitamin mixture degrade during storage and after being mixed with the TPN solution. Therefore, in order to provide the level of vitamins indicated by the manufacturer's label, there is generally a 10% to 25% increase in vitamin content over the label claim. Research comparing oral versus intravenous intakes must include actual measurements of vitamin concentration in the intravenous or enteral formula mixture.

Vitamin Measurements

Historically, vitamin nutriture has been reflected by the vitamin content of blood together with urinary losses. Vitamin deficiency has been determined by measurements of vitamin-requiring enzymes in red blood cells, or in some instances, by a decrease in urinary excretion of the vitamin. In the case of erythrocyte enzyme measurements, transketolase (reflecting vitamin B_1), glutathione reductase (reflecting vitamin B_2), or glutamic-oxaloacetic transaminase (reflecting vitamin B_6) activities are measured initially and again with the vitamin cofactor added (activity coefficient). Although there are some problems with interpretation of these types of assays in malnourished individuals, an increase in the activity coefficient after addition of the vitamin cofactor usually indicates a deficiency in the test vitamin. Another method of evaluating vitamin nutriture is to measure the urinary excretion of a metabolite normally cleared by a specific vitamin-requiring enzyme. In the case of vitamin B_6, a measured dose of tryptophan (which requires B_6 for further metabolism) is given and the efficiency of its metabolism is determined by urinary excretion of xanthurenic acid. Since the activity of the pyridoxine-requiring enzyme necessary for metabolism of 3-hydroxykynurenic acid is reduced in vitamin B_6 deficiency, an excessive excretion of xanthurenic acid is indicative of vitamin B_6 deficiency, as presented in Figure 9.2.

Although coefficients of erythrocyte-enzyme activity have been described as "normal" in VLBW infants receiving TPN, interpretation of this finding has been questioned since such infants often require multiple erythrocyte transfusions of vitamin-containing cells from donor blood. Additionally, the erythrocyte-enzyme assay has not been validated to detect deficiency states in this population of VLBW infants. Therefore, it seems most appropriate to develop

Table 9.2. Recommended Vitamin Methods for Use in Future Studies of VLBW Infants

Vitamin	Method
Vitamin C	Colorimetric
Vitamin B_1	HPLC*
Vitamin B_2	HPLC
Vitamin B_3 (niacin)	Microbiological
Vitamin B_6	HPLC
Biotin	Microbiological
Sodium pantothenate	HPLC
	Microbiological

*HPLC indicates high-performance liquid chromatography.

mathematical modeling using quantitative measurements in blood (plasma and erythrocyte) coupled with urinary losses of the vitamin metabolites. Newer methods of vitamin measurements have been developed which provide an accurate determination of the water-soluble vitamins as well as several of their active cofactors. A summary of these methods is listed in Table 9.2.

Goals for Blood Concentrations

Standards for VLBW infant blood concentrations are difficult to determine since the "normal" state of this group of infants is ill-defined and blood concentrations in infants exclusively fed human milk are not available. For this reason, the cord blood concentrations of VLBW infants are used as standards to indicate safe and effective concentrations.

Blood Sampling and Processing

The collection, storage, and measurement of vitamins require special consideration because of photoreactive and stability problems. For example, riboflavin is photoreactive and pyridoxal phosphate tends to degrade to pyridoxic acid over time. The following procedures are recommended to minimize the risks of vitamin loss during sample collection, preparation, and storage.

The typical sample size is 0.8 to 1.0 mL collected by either needle stick or capillary sampling. Blood is collected in a glass container at 4°C and protected from light. Within 12 hours of collection, the blood is centrifuged for 5 minutes at 5,000 g. The plasma is removed and stored in a 2.2 mL microcentrifuge tube (Costar™, Cambridge, Mass). The red blood cells are washed twice with cold (4°C) normal saline and stored for future measurement. Both samples are stored at $-70°C$ until vitamin determinations are performed. Mailed samples are packed with frozen carbon dioxide. Urine samples are collected without preservative over a 12- to 24-hour period and frozen at $-70°C$ for storage. Samples are shipped packed with frozen carbon dioxide.

Vitamin Doses for Very Low-Birthweight Infants

General Considerations

The water-soluble vitamins C, B_1, B_2, Niacin, B_6, pantothenate, and biotin share a number of features. First, they act as cofactors for several important enzymatic reactions, and deficiencies can be related to abnormal substrate utilization.[3] Second, since they are water soluble, excess intakes are usually excreted by the kidney; marginal nutriture normally results in maximum tubular reabsorption of any filtered vitamins to reduce further losses. Third, during periods of rapid growth, metabolic demands imply an increase in exogenous vitamin needs. Fourth, the placenta actively transports most water-soluble vitamins against a concentration gradient to the fetus. These features indicate a continued need for exogenous vitamins shortly after birth in order to maintain adequate growth.

The apparent increased vitamin need during early development is further complicated by the inability to easily recognize clinical signs of deficiency for any one vitamin. That is, the marked immaturity of the VLBW infant coupled with the increased tendency for infection and metabolic disturbances preclude the characteristic signs of vitamin deficiency. Even more challenging is the suggestion that normal metabolism may be adversely affected by the 10- to 100-fold fluctuations in circulating serum concentrations of riboflavin, pyridoxic acid, and thiamine that may occur with current management protocols using parenteral multivitamins.[4-6]

Because data concerning metabolism and blood concentrations during TPN and oral feedings are unique for each vitamin, they will be discussed in separate sections below.

Considerations for Gestational and Postnatal Age

The data available on vitamin B_2 and vitamin B_6 are relatively sparse but suggest that low renal excretion plays a major role in blood vitamin concentrations. With an intravenous vitamin B_2 intake of 0.66 mg/kg/day, the extremely low-birthweight infant (<750 g) demonstrates a substantial reduction in urinary output and a progressive increase in vitamins B_2 and B_6 concentrations during the first 3 weeks. By the fourth week, urinary excretion increases, with a gradual decline in blood concentrations of vitamins over the next 2 weeks. Similar changes in blood and urine concentrations are seen with larger VLBW infants except that by the second week, urinary excretion increases while blood concentrations are usually less elevated. This finding suggests that by the time most infants are "weaned" to formulas, excessive vitamin intakes are more likely to be excreted. By the postconception (postmenstrual) age of 32 weeks, the recommended intakes prescribed in Table 9.3 may result in moderately increased concentrations compared with those of cord blood. The same per kilogram dose given to newborns 27 to 30 weeks gestation would be expected to yield higher blood concentrations. During the early transition period of 2 to 4 weeks, then, a lower dose of water-soluble vitamins may be more appropriate. This hypothesis has not been fully evaluated, however, and thus cannot be recommended at this time.

Table 9.3. Suggested Target Intakes for Infants Weighing <1,500 g*

Vitamin	Oral			Parenteral*[13]	RDA[‖]
	Formula U/100 kcal	Content[†] U/kg/day	Supplement[‡§] U/kg/day	U/kg/day	0–6 months U/day
C, mg	15–20	18–24	15	15–25	30
Thiamine (B$_1$), μg	150–200	180–240	150	200–350	300
Riboflavin (B$_2$), μg	200–300	250–360	200	150–200	400
Pyridoxine (B$_6$), μg	125–175	150–210	150	150–200	300
Niacin (B$_3$), mg	3.0–4.0	3.6–4.8	2.5	4.0–6.8	5.0
Biotin, μg[¶]	3.0–5.0	3.6–6.0	5.0	5.0–8.0	10
Pantothenate, mg[¶]	1.0–1.5	1.2–1.7	1.0	1.0–2.0	2.0

*Unit doses suggested for all infants <1,500 kg. Infants weighing more than 1,500 g should receive the RDA. If receiving total parenteral nutrition, the lower dose/kg is suggested, whereas larger infants (1,250–1,500 g) may receive the maximum dose listed in the second column under Parenteral.

[†]Units per kg/day assuming 150 mL of 24 kcal/30 mL formula.

[‡]Units if Poly-Vi-Sol (Mead Johnson Nutritionals) is given at 2/3 mL.

[§]Suggested supplement for infants receiving exclusively human milk. The total vitamin intake can be calculated using Table 9.1.

[‖]Recommended Daily Allowances.[2]

[¶]Estimated safe and adequate daily dietary intake.

Vitamin C

Biochemistry and Metabolism

Vitamin C, or ascorbic acid, is involved in a number of metabolic roles that we are aware of, with proposed involvement in several more. The known roles for ascorbic acid are: (1) promoting hydroxylation of the amino acids proline and lysine during collagen synthesis[4,5]; (2) activating the catabolism of tyrosine, as well as stimulating the production of norepinephrine from dopamine, and the serotonin precursor 5-hydroxytryptamine from tryptophan[4]; and (3) enhancing iron absorption from the gastrointestinal tract, inhibiting copper uptake, and aiding in the conversion of folic acid to folinic acid, as well as limiting the oxidation of folic acid.[6]

Ascorbic acid is produced from glucose by most animals; however, humans, other primates, elephants, fruit-eating bats, guinea pigs, and the red-breasted bulbul bird cannot synthesize ascorbate and therefore require it in the diet. The L-isomer is the biologically active form and circulates in both reduced and oxidized dehydro- forms. Ascorbic acid is present in all tissues and is transported into the cell against a concentration gradient through a saturable, carrier-mediated, energy-requiring process.[7,8] Highest contents of ascorbic acid are found in the adrenal glands, leukocytes, brain, liver, and spleen, and average 40 to 50 times plasma concentrations. Human milk contains the vitamin at levels exceeding those of

plasma. There is no true storage of ascorbic acid. In a healthy adult, the estimated body pool of ascorbic acid is 1,500 mg and is metabolized at 3% per day. After 60 days on a deficient diet, near deficiency levels are reached in the adult, with clinical symptoms following shortly if the deficient diet persists. The size of the ascorbic acid pool in infants and children is unknown, but deficiency probably occurs more quickly.

Fetal, preterm, and term gestation neonate blood concentrations of ascorbic acid are greater than maternal levels, and there appears to be an active placental transport process operational to a maximum concentration of 114 μmol/L.[8] Since glucose competes with ascorbic acid for placental transport, maternal hyperglycemia may decrease the supply of ascorbic acid to the developing fetus.[9]

Ascorbic acid is excreted in the urine, with one quarter as the unchanged vitamin under conditions of normal intake. The remainder is in the form of inactive metabolites, of which oxalate comprises the majority.

Measurement

The most common method of measurement in use today is the 2,4-dinitro-phenylhydrazine method, which detects both the reduced and dehydroascorbic acid forms of the vitamin. Acceptable plasma concentrations by this technique are greater than 34 μmol/L, while levels less than 11.4 μmol/L are usually associated with the development of clinical signs of deficiency.

Deficiency

Both human milk and proprietary infant formulas are good sources of vitamin C; bovine milk is a poor source. Scurvy is the clinical syndrome resulting from ascorbic acid deficiency and is similar in many respects to the bone changes seen with copper deficiency.[10,11] The infantile form may develop within 6 to 12 months in infants fed bovine milk exclusively. Early signs, as in many other vitamin deficiencies, are nonspecific and include anorexia, failure to thrive, and irritability. With time, a scaly dermatitis develops and is accompanied by tenderness of the extremities and hemorrhage into the skin, mucous membranes, gingiva, and under the periosteum of the long bones. A "scorbutic rosary," comprising swollen osteochondral junctions along the anterior rib cage has been described, mimicking that seen in rickets. Laboratory findings may show a normochromic, normocytic anemia due to blood loss into the tissues, as well as radiographic evidence of arrested bone growth.

Recommended Intake

Oral. Enteral feeding with either human milk or proprietary bovine milk formula supplies approximately 8 mg/100 kcal. Preterm infant formulas typically contain 8.5 to 40 mg/100 kcal. The current recommended dietary allowance (RDA) for vitamin C is 30 mg/day for the neonate (see Table 9.3). No studies have been published evaluating blood concentrations of VLBW infants receiving enteral vitamin C. Assuming that an infant consumes 120 kcal of breast milk, about 10 mg/100 kcal should meet normal needs. Because of the likelihood of increased renal losses and increased protein catabolism/anabolism in preterm infants, a higher intake of 20 mg/100 kcal is suggested.

Parenteral. Parenteral administration of ascorbic acid (80 mg/day) to term infants sufficiently maintained "normal" plasma concentrations. In VLBW infants, doses of 52 mg/day for 28 days caused a threefold increase of plasma ascorbic acid concentrations compared with concentrations in cord blood.[12] Based on body weight, an expert panel of the American Society for Clinical Nutrition (ASCN) suggests a dose of 25 to 31 mg/kg/day for preterm infants up to 3 kg.[13] This dose has not been tested in VLBW infants, but it seems appropriate pending further study.

Toxicity

In term gestation infants and adults, renal clearance of ascorbic acid far exceeds doses in general use, making toxicity extremely uncommon. The compromised (immature) renal function in VLBW infants may result in an accumulation of circulating ascorbic acid and there is a theoretical risk of increased urinary oxalate and uric acid, although the significance of and actual clinical risk from urinary oxalate stone formation is uncertain.

Vitamin B$_1$ (Thiamine)

Biochemistry and Metabolism

The primary functional form of thiamine is thiamine pyrophosphate (TPP), which serves as a cofactor for three enzyme complexes involved in carbohydrate metabolism: (1) pyruvate dehydrogenase, which catalyzes the conversion of pyruvate to acetyl coenzyme A (CoA); (2) α-ketoglutarate dehydrogenase, which catalyzes the conversion of α-ketoglutarate to succinate; and (3) transketolase, which is involved in the production of ribose for the synthesis of RNA and also provides nicotinamide adenine dinucleotide phosphate, a requirement for fatty acid synthesis. Other roles for this vitamin include the decarboxylation of branched-chain amino acids and facilitation of nerve conduction through its influence on membrane sodium ion conductance.

At low concentrations (~2 μmol/L), thiamine is absorbed in the small intestine in its free form by a carrier-mediated process, while at higher concentrations passive diffusion assumes greater importance.[14] Following absorption, thiamine is converted to the primary active cofactor TPP chiefly in the liver, a process that consumes adenosine triphosphate. Further phosphorylation to thiamine triphosphate (TTP) occurs in the central nervous system. The specific role of TTP in neuronal tissues is not entirely clear; some patients with depressed content of TTP in cerebrospinal fluid have reportedly improved with pharmacologic doses of the vitamin.[15,16] Both thiamine and TPP circulate in the serum, although thiamine predominates. Total adult body stores are thought to be around 30 mg, composed of 80% TPP, 10% TTP, with free thiamine and the monophosphorylated form comprising the remainder. Since amounts present in human milk are directly proportional to intake, alcoholic and malnourished mothers frequently have low milk thiamine.[17] Free thiamine and several metabolites are excreted in the urine. Thiamine requirements vary with the intake of carbohydrate, and symptoms of vitamin B$_1$ deficiency can occur much sooner with a diet consisting predominantly of carbohydrate.

Measurement

The most reliable index of thiamine status is whole blood thiamine concentrations. Erythrocyte transketolase activity, determined both with and without added TPP, is a useful screening method; an increase in transketolase activity of >26% upon introduction of TPP indicates deficiency. This method does not detect marginal or elevated concentrations of the vitamin, however. An alternative is to measure the 24-hour excretion of thiamine or the thiamine:creatinine ratio.[18] A more accurate indicator of thiamine status, though, is the direct measurement of plasma and erythrocyte thiamine and TPP coupled with urinary excretion. This approach is particularly relevant in the evaluation of parenteral vitamin B_1 since the dose provided is relatively high[19] (Table 9.2).

Deficiency

Thiamine deficiency, or beriberi, occurs most commonly in Asia, where polished rice serves as the dietary staple. Codeficiencies of riboflavin and niacin are not unusual. The Wernicke-Korsakoff syndrome occurs in adult alcoholics. In infants, deficiency is more prone to occur in breast-fed infants of malnourished mothers. Onset is typically between the second day and the fifth month of life, although it may be delayed for as long as 10 months, or triggered earlier by an intercurrent infection. Initial signs may include edema, restlessness, insomnia, and anorexia. Later, cardiac signs predominate. A weak cry or aphonia may be present because of paralysis of the recurrent laryngeal nerve. Inadvertent omission of vitamins from children receiving TPN with glucose as the source of energy has resulted in lactic acidosis and congestive heart failure in as little as 2.5 weeks. Death may ultimately ensue with cardiomegaly and extensive central nervous system degeneration. Laboratory evaluation in cases of beriberi shows decreased urinary excretion of thiamine and low blood concentrations of thiamine with simultaneous elevation of pyruvate, lactate, and α-ketoglutarate.

Recommended Intake

Oral. The current neonatal RDA for thiamine is 300 µg/day. The thiamine content of human milk and infant formula is 29 and 78 to 100 µg/100 kcal, respectively (Table 9.1). No studies have been reported on VLBW infants consuming the amounts currently present in preterm formulas (100 to 250 µg/100 kcal) or in infants consuming human milk. Because of the higher metabolic rate of VLBW infants, it seems reasonable to provide an enteral dose greater than that in human milk. Since there is no documentation of deficiency or toxicity at levels typically used in preterm infant formulas, the suggested dose for future study is 200 µg/100 kcal.

Parenteral. A parenteral dose of 1.2 mg/day in term infants is sufficient to prevent deficiency. Preterm infants reportedly showed a normal erythrocyte transketolase activity while receiving about 0.78 mg/kg/day; however, this dose appears excessive since subsequent analysis of plasma thiamine showed values about 10-fold higher than cord blood concentrations. The ASCN committee suggests a lower dose of 0.35 mg/kg body weight for VLBW infants.[13] No blood levels have been performed in infants receiving this dose.

Toxicity

Thiamine is safe even in large doses, although there have been rare reports of respiratory depression with excessive administration. A rare anaphylactic reaction associated with intravenous administration of doses <100 mg has resulted in death or severe morbidity. While high blood concentrations of thiamine in VLBW infants have not been specifically tied to signs of toxicity, there does not appear to be any advantage in maintaining blood concentrations in excess of those present in fetal circulation.

Riboflavin

Biochemistry and Metabolism

Riboflavin serves as an essential component of flavoproteins, which function as hydrogen carriers in a number of crucial oxidation-reduction reactions such as energy metabolism, glycogen synthesis, erythrocyte production, and the conversion of folate to its active coenzyme. Furthermore, because of its photooxidative activity, riboflavin has been shown to facilitate bilirubin photocatabolism.[20] It is present in human milk at about 60 µg/100 kcal; however, if milk is exposed to ultraviolet and visible sunlight, rapid reduction of vitamin content occurs within a few hours.

Under normal conditions, intestinal riboflavin absorption and renal elimination are tightly controlled by balanced mechanisms. Uptake occurs predominantly in the proximal small intestine by means of a high-affinity, low-capacity carrier. This allows for efficient absorption even at low gut concentrations, while excessive absorption is reduced because the carrier is easily saturated. Operating in parallel is a high-capacity renal tubular secretory pathway to enhance riboflavin elimination when blood concentrations are elevated.

In the intestinal mucosa, riboflavin is phosphorylated to riboflavin 5'-phosphate, also known as flavin mononucleotide (FMN). Further phosphorylation produces flavin adenine dinucleotide (FAD), the other main coenzyme. Riboflavin is carried bound largely to albumin, although in fetal serum a specific high-affinity riboflavin-binding protein has been identified that may play a role in transplacental transport during gestation.[21] Riboflavin is stored primarily in the liver and kidney, but stores are small and depleted in as little as 2 weeks. The vitamin circulates in a labile tissue pool that can be turned over in times of increased need, as well as a highly protein-bound pool that serves to maintain local tissue stores. Excess intake is eliminated, unchanged, chiefly in the urine, with lesser amounts eliminated in the bile.

Measurement

A useful screen for riboflavin sufficiency can be obtained by measuring erythrocyte–glutathione reductase activity both in the presence and in the absence of excess added active cofactor FAD. An increase of >20% in the enzyme's activity indicates riboflavin deficiency, although glucose 6-phosphate dehydrogenase deficiency is a common cause for falsely normal results. A more accurate measure of riboflavin status is measurement of riboflavin and its phosphorylated cofactors FMN and FAD in plasma and erythrocytes.[22] Urinary riboflavin concentrations, coupled with blood concentrations, provide the best measure of riboflavin status.[23]

Deficiency

Deficiency of riboflavin usually occurs in the setting of more generalized malnutrition associated with multiple vitamin deficiencies. A particularly high-risk setting is the pregnant teenager, because as many as one half of all teenagers have been estimated to be riboflavin-deficient.[24] Oral contraceptives, other corticosteroids, and imipramine may impair riboflavin metabolism,[25] and boric acid increases renal loss of riboflavin.[26] Negative nitrogen balance, a common condition in the severely stressed infant, increases urinary excretion of the vitamin. Since riboflavin is utilized in the reduction of bilirubin during phototherapy, breast-fed infants receiving phototherapy are often riboflavin depleted. This has been documented repeatedly by measurement of erythrocyte–glutathione reductase activity coefficient, although no clearly defined clinical signs of deficiency have been documented.

The principal manifestations of riboflavin deficiency are dermatologic and ophthalmologic, including angular stomatitis, cheilosis, glossitis, seborrhea, photophobia, and increased corneal vascularity. Severe deficiency has been reported to cause electrocardiographic abnormalities and developmental delay.

Recommended Intake

Oral. The minimum oral intake of riboflavin for infants is 60 μg/100 kcal, while the current RDA for neonates is 400 μg/day. Human milk and standard formula riboflavin content is 60 and 400 μg/100 kcal, respectively (Table 9.1). Preterm infant formulas typically contain 160 to 620 μg/100 kcal. Increased utilization rate of riboflavin is related to increased nitrogen intake. The higher nitrogen needs of VLBW infants coupled with the increased photooxidation present during treatment for hyperbilirubinemia suggest that the content in human milk may be insufficient to meet the needs of VLBW infants. A dose of 300 μg/100 kcal is therefore suggested.

Parenteral. The current parenteral recommendation of 1.4 mg/day for full-term infants is probably more than required; however, this dose appears to be safe. Preterm infants show reduced renal clearance of riboflavin relative to term infants, so that previously administered doses of 0.66 mg/kg/day resulted in serum concentrations exceeding cord blood levels by as much as 100-fold.[22] Using dose response data from three dosages (0.23, 0.41, and 0.66 mg/kg/day) of riboflavin, an intake of 0.15 mg/kg/day was recommended by the ASCN Committee for VLBW infants.[13]

Toxicity

There are no clearly defined toxic effects from high blood concentrations of this vitamin. However, Baeckert et al. have described plasma riboflavin concentrations approximately 100 times the cord blood levels in preterm infants receiving parenteral multiple vitamins (0.66 mg/kg/day for 7 days).[22] It is notable that sustained elevations of this magnitude have not been studied in either humans or animals, since renal tubular excretion is extremely high in the mature kidney. In animals, the LD_{50} is determined by renal failure stemming from riboflavin precipitation in renal tubules.[27] The urinary concentration in one infant was reported by Baeckert to be only slightly below that which causes precipitation of riboflavin and obstructive tubular damage.[27] In addition, riboflavin reduction by photoexcitation generates free radicals.[28] The elevated blood concentrations of riboflavin may provide a mechanism for increased free-radical generation and therefore pose some risk for free-radical damage. Future work should be aimed at identifying this potential complication from excessive intake in VLBW infants in an effort to fully justify reduced intake during the first 3 weeks of extrauterine life.

Vitamin B₆

Biochemistry and Metabolism

Vitamin B_6 serves as a cofactor for a large number of reactions involved in the synthesis, interconversion, and catabolism of amino acids.[29] The vitamin exists in three forms which are readily interconverted in vivo: pyridoxal is the chief metabolite, which is phosphorylated to the cofactor form of vitamin B_6, pyridoxal phosphate (PLP); pyridoxamine, like pyridoxal, is widely available in meat, fish, and poultry, and its phosphorylated form serves as a cofactor in transaminase reactions; pyridoxine is widely present in plants, and it can be converted to pyridoxal or pyridoxamine. The vitamin is absorbed in the dephosphorylated forms by passive diffusion in the jejunum[30] and transported to the liver where it is efficiently converted to the active forms, PLP or pyridoxamine phosphate, in reactions that require the presence of flavin. From there, it is carried on albumin to tissues. Body stores of this vitamin are small, with nearly 50% of its activity present in muscle phosphorylase.[31] However, because of its ubiquitous supply, deficiency is uncommon even in infancy. In addition to its role in amino acid metabolism, pyridoxine is required for the synthesis of niacin, neurotransmitters (histamine, serotonin, dopamine, norepinephrine, and γ-aminobutyric acid), heme, and prostaglandins. Ultimately the vitamin is dephosphorylated by alkaline phosphatase in the liver and degraded predominantly to 4-pyridoxic acid, which is excreted in the urine. Blood specimens high in alkaline phosphatase may degrade the phosphorylated vitamin in vitro and thus give falsely low concentrations of PLP. Theophylline may also reduce the blood PLP concentrations through inactivation of pyridoxal kinase.[32]

Measurement

Several measures of pyridoxine status are available. Plasma PLP concentrations may be measured directly by radioimmunoassay, although determination of erythrocyte–aspartate aminotransferase activity, both with and without added PLP, is the most widely used screen for vitamin sufficiency.[33,34] Most recently, high-performance liquid chromatography methods to quantitate all the B_6 vitamins in plasma and erythrocytes promise to provide the most accurate and reliable measure of vitamin B_6 status.[35]

Because of the requirement for B_6 in the normal metabolism of tryptophan, the measurement of certain urinary metabolites following a tryptophan load in the infant has been proposed as a functional in vivo test for vitamin deficiency. Greater than 50 mg xanthurenic acid per 24 hours following a 2 to 5 g tryptophan load is interpreted as evidence of deficiency. No comparative studies using this test have been performed in VLBW infants.

Deficiency

Due to widespread availability, true deficiency of this vitamin is quite uncommon. Malabsorption syndromes such as celiac disease or cystic fibrosis may result in deficiency. Inadequate intake during pregnancy has been linked to adverse gestational outcomes.[24] Deficiency in infants results in a syndrome including a hypochromic, microcytic anemia, vomiting, diarrhea, failure to thrive, irritability, and seizures. Very low levels of blood PLP concentrations have been reported in patients with chronic renal disease and high concentrations of alkaline phosphatase.[36]

Recommended Intake

Considering the central role of pyridoxine in amino acid metabolism, it is not surprising that requirements are directly proportional to protein intake. In the early days of bovine milk feeding of infants, pyridoxine deficiency was occasionally observed because milk is a poor source of this otherwise abundant vitamin. Furthermore, it is extremely heat labile, so that even the small amounts present were easily inactivated in the processing of formulas or other foods. Today, commercial formulas are made with pyridoxine hydrochloride, a relatively heat-stable form of the vitamin, so deficiency is rarely seen. Formula-fed infants overall tend to have higher blood concentrations of this vitamin than breast-fed infants. Vitamin B_6 deficiency is most commonly diagnosed in the breast-fed infant of the malnourished, typically adolescent, mother.

Oral. Human milk contains 28 μg/100 kcal of vitamin B_6, mostly in the form of pyridoxal. Milk-based routine formulas contain about 60 μg/100 kcal, while preterm formulas contain 60 to 250 μg/100 kcal. Plasma B_6 (pyridoxine, pyridoxal, pyridoxic acid) concentrations in three infants receiving B_6 250 μg/100 kcal for 14 days had plasma concentrations approximately six times cord blood levels. Based on the content of human milk and this sparse information, the recommended oral intake is 150 μg/100 kcal.

Parenteral. In term infants, 1.0 mg/day vitamin B_6 as pyridoxine given parenterally in TPN is sufficient to prevent deficiency. A lower dose of 0.3 mg/kg/day in preterm infants is adequate to prevent deficiency[37]; however, serum concentrations measured after this dose for 7 to 14 days gave a 10- to 20-fold increase in circulating B_6 levels (mostly as pyridoxic acid relative to cord blood). This dose appears excessive and the marked elevation in plasma may be secondary to the relative immaturity of the preterm liver and kidneys to excrete the higher dose of 0.3 mg/kg/day of the vitamin. The current intravenous recommendation of the ASCN is 0.18 mg/kg/day for infants requiring TPN.

Toxicity

Toxicity is rare and not observed at the doses given in infant formulas or standard parenteral preparations. Megadoses in adults have been reported to produce a sensory neuropathy.[38] It is postulated that the persistently elevated blood concentrations of pyridoxic acid represent the likely toxin from this vitamin. In this case, the persistent elevation in pyridoxic acid indicates toxicity, and the high dose of pyridoxin should be avoided.

Niacin

Biochemistry and Metabolism

Niacin is the term used to describe two equivalent compounds, nicotinic acid and nicotinamide, which are widely available in meats and grains. Niacin is converted in the liver to the active cofactors nicotinamide adenine dinucleotide (NAD) and nicotinamide adenine dinucleotide phosphate (NADP). These cofactors play central roles in body metabolism in a wide variety of oxidation-reduction reactions including glycolysis, electron transport, and fat synthesis; as a result, a deficiency in this vitamin has diffuse manifestations. Transport to tissue sites occurs largely in erythrocytes.[24] There is no storage form of the vitamin. Further metabolism of NAD to N^1-methyl nicotinamide and NAD to N^1-methyl-2-pyridone-5-carboxylamide allows urinary excretion of these compounds.[39]

In strict terms, niacin is not a vitamin because the active cofactors NAD and NADP can be synthesized in vivo from the amino acid tryptophan by reactions that require vitamin B_6. Niacin requirements depend on the amount of dietary tryptophan available and on vitamin B_6 status.

Measurement

The most commonly employed method of determining niacin status is the measurement of the urinary metabolite N^1-methyl nicotinamide, which declines late in niacin deficiency simultaneously with or just before the development of overt clinical signs.[40] The other major urinary metabolite, N^1-methyl-2-pyridone-5-carboxylamide, declines much earlier in the course of niacin deficiency, making the ratio of these compounds a much more sensitive index of niacin status. However, difficulties in the laboratory measurement of the latter compound make this approach impractical. Blood niacin concentrations have also been used as a measure of niacin status.

Deficiency

Niacin deficiency today is limited to developing areas of Central and South America, which rely heavily on corn as a dietary staple. Corn is poor in tryptophan and rich in the amino acid lysine, which interferes with niacin metabolism. Additionally, the niacin present is in a poorly absorbable form.[24] Other settings of high risk include alcoholic subjects,[41] who often have multiple vitamin deficiencies because of malnutrition, and, occasionally, isoniazid-treated patients, due to vitamin B_6 depletion with its secondary effects on NAD synthesis. Infants born in these contexts are at increased risk for niacin deficiency.

Pellagra is the classic syndrome of niacin deficiency, with the four D's of dermatitis, diarrhea, dementia, and death. The dermatologic manifestation—an erythematous, sunburned appearance predominantly in areas exposed to sunlight and trauma—is generally the first to appear. Gastrointestinal symptoms include glossitis, angular stomatitis, anorexia, diarrhea, malabsorption, and weight loss due to villous atrophy. Neurologic manifestations are not as easily recog-

nized in infancy but may appear as lassitude, irritability, and eventually coma.

Recommended Intake

Oral. Human milk contains about 210 μg/100 kcal of niacin and routine infant formulas contain about 1,000 μg/100 kcal. Formulas for preterm infants typically contain 750 to 5,000 μg/100 kcal. Enteral requirements are generally met by intakes of 0.25 mg/100 kcal for both term and preterm infants, although the current RDA for term neonates is more generous at 5 mg/day. No data on blood or urine concentrations are available for VLBW infants receiving oral niacin. Based on the above considerations plus the data on VLBW infants receiving TPN, an intake of 4 mg/100 kcal should be adequate to prevent deficiency, although this dose may be higher than necessary and further studies should be encouraged.

Parenteral. Parenteral administration of 17 mg/day in term infants and 11 mg/day in preterm infants receiving TPN is sufficient to prevent deficiency while simultaneously avoiding excessive plasma concentrations.[12] When calculated based on approximate body weight, these doses lead to the current recommendations of the ASCN Committee of 6.8 mg/kg/day for preterm infants.[13] The quantities of tryptophan present in standard neonatal TPN are not sufficient to decrease niacin requirements.

Toxicity

Toxicity is not described at the doses administered in TPN or standard infant formulas. Megadoses have been widely used in the treatment of certain hyperlipidemic conditions, for which niacin is effective in reducing serum concentrations of low-density lipoprotein cholesterol and very low-density lipoprotein triglyceride.[42] At these megadoses (on the order of 2 to 4 g/day in adults), side effects have included flushing, nausea and vomiting, dry skin, and, less commonly, elevated liver-function tests and hyperuricemia. A substantial number of patients may also develop insulin-resistant hyperglycemia.

Biotin

Biochemistry and Metabolism

Biotin is important as a cofactor for four known mammalian enzymes involved in carboxylation and carbon dioxide transfer reactions. These include: (1) propionyl CoA carboxylase, which is involved in the degradation of valine, leucine, and methionine; (2) 3-methylcrotonyl-CoA carboxylase, also required for leucine degradation; (3) pyruvate carboxylase, which catalyzes the rate-limiting step of gluconeogenesis from alanine and pyruvate; and (4) acetyl CoA carboxylase, the cytosolic enzyme catalyzing the formation of methyl malonyl CoA, which is the first step in fatty acid synthesis. Biotin is also active in folate metabolism.[2,43]

Intestinal absorption of biotin in humans has not been well studied; however, absorption in lower mammals occurs in the first half of the small intestine through mechanisms that include a saturable carrier.[44,45] In addition, intestinal flora synthesize biotin, although the importance of this source in biotin nutriture is uncertain. Biotin is widely available in a variety of foods. Once absorbed, it circulates bound to plasma proteins and is taken up by hepatocytes by way of a sodium-dependent carrier. It is then converted to 5-adenylate biotin, which is used for the synthesis of carboxylase enzymes.

Biotin-containing enzymes are degraded to biocytin, from which biotin can be recovered by liver and plasma biotinidase. This mechanism of biotin conservation makes biotin deficiency extremely uncommon even with marginal intakes of the vitamin. However, a number of children showing the clinical signs of biotin deficiency have been identified with inborn errors of biotin metabolism. These children are effectively treated with physiologic amounts of the vitamin.[46]

Measurement

Recent studies using newer technology provide evidence that the concentration of biotin bound to plasma protein is about half of the concentration of free biotin.[47] This contrasts with earlier reports that the concentration of protein-bound biotin exceeds that of free biotin by 6- to 30-fold in human plasma. Using this new technique, measurement of biotin in human milk indicates a mean concentration of 6 μg/100 kcal with a range of 1 to 10 μg/100 kcal.[48,49] Furthermore, observations based on a rat model of biotin deficiency indicate that urinary excretion of 3-HIA will be a useful indicator of biotin status at the tissue level.[50] These new methods for analysis of biotin and its metabolites will lead to a reevaluation of reports on biotin requirements in health and disease over the next decade.

Deficiency

Due to widespread availability of biotin in food and through intestinal bacterial production, deficiency is uncommon. Low plasma concentrations are reported in pregnant women. Chronic diarrhea or antibiotic use may increase requirements due to decreased availability from intestinal sources. Chronic ingestion of large amounts of raw egg whites may result in biotin deficiency because of the presence of avidin, a glycoprotein of egg albumin, which is a high-affinity binder of the vitamin. Because of the mechanism of biotin conservation, isolated biotin deficiency was not noted in humans until Mock et al.[51] described the syndrome in parenterally fed infants receiving biotin-deficient solutions for several weeks. Clinical signs of deficiency include alopecia, an exfoliative dermatitis, and conjunctivitis. If prolonged, progression to nausea, anorexia, and mental and neurologic signs occur. Laboratory data may include anemia and elevated plasma cholesterol concentrations. At present, the intravenous pediatric multiple vitamin formulation includes biotin, and infants receiving this formulation of TPN have shown no evidence of deficiency.

Recommended Intake

Oral. Human milk contains biotin at about 0.56 μg/100 kcal, as compared with approximately 3 μg/100 kcal in milk-based formulas. The RDA has not been determined, although 10 μg/day is considered to be a safe and adequate dietary intake. Enteral requirements for term neonates are probably about 10 μg/day. No data are available concerning blood concentrations in enterally fed VLBW infants. Based on human milk content and the data from VLBW infants fed TPN, a suggested dose is 5 μg/100 kcal.

Parenteral. Parenteral administration of 20 μg/day to term infants maintains normal plasma concentrations for 21 days. Parenteral doses of 12 μg/kg/day in preterm infants produced excessive plasma concentrations 10-fold greater than cord blood concentrations over 28 days. A smaller dose of 6 μg/kg/day has been recommended by the ASCN Committee.[13]

Toxicity

Biotin toxicity has not been reported.

Pantothenic Acid

Biochemistry and Metabolism

As signified by its name, pantothenic acid is widely distributed in plant and animal sources, including milk. The vitamin forms an important part of the ubiquitous acyl transfer group CoA and, as such, is essential for the metabolism of fat, carbohydrate, and protein in reactions involved in fatty acid elongation, energy release, and gluconeogenesis. Approximately half of the ingested vitamin is biologically available for absorption. Intestinal flora produce pantothenate, but the importance of this source in humans is unknown. Following absorption, pantothenic acid is converted to 4′-phosphopantetheine and then either covalently linked to form CoA or bound to acyl-carrier protein, the two functional forms of the vitamin. Pantothenic acid has been identified in the liver, adrenals, brain, heart, and kidneys, and circulates in the plasma as the free vitamin. Excretion is in the urine, predominantly as the unchanged vitamin.

Measurement

Plasma concentrations of pantothenic acid can be measured by means of a two-stage assay that involves, first, the enzymatic cleavage of the bound vitamin to its carrier protein, and second, bioassay or radioimmunoassay of the liberated pantothenic acid. Measurement of urine pantothenic acid contents is also useful in assessing deficiency states.

Deficiency

Widespread availability of biotin makes isolated deficiency of pantothenic acid rare, but deficiency may occur as a part of more generalized malnutrition, or under experimentally induced conditions employing a specific pantothenic acid antagonist. Such experimental deficiency is characterized in adults by apathy, headache, depression, paresthesias, muscle weakness, vomiting, and intermittent diarrhea. Inborn errors involving defects in pantothenic acid metabolism have not been described.

Recommended Intake

Oral. Human milk pantothenic acid contents are about 250 μg/100 kcal and milk-based formulas about 400 μg/100 kcal. Preterm infant formulas typically contain 450 to 1,900 μg/100 kcal. The RDA is not determined but the estimated safe and adequate dietary intake is 1.4 μg/day. To date, there are no published studies on VLBW infants receiving oral intakes of pantothenate. Based on human milk content and data from parenterally fed infants, a dose of 1.4 μg/100 kcal is suggested. Future studies are recommended.

Parenteral. Term infants given 5 μg/day parenterally maintained stable plasma concentrations over 21 days. Preterm infants given 2.9 μg/kg/day parenterally have elevated plasma levels, such that a dose of 2.0 μg/kg/day was recommended by the ASCN Committee.[13]

Toxicity

Pantothenic acid toxicity has not been reported.

CASE STUDY _____

A 4-month-old infant with short bowel syndrome who required TPN is seen in the emergency room. He appears severely acidotic and exhibits generalized cyanosis, which improves with 100% oxygen. The following laboratory tests are obtained:

	Sodium (mmol)	Potas- sium (mmol)	Chlo- ride (mmol)	HCO$_3$ (mmol)	Lactate (mmol)	Glu- cose (mmol)
Patient	137	3.5	90	10	21	18.2
Normal	126– 145	4.1– 5.4	95– 110	20–26	< 3.0	3.9–5

Because of poor perfusion, a chest radiograph is obtained which shows a cardiac silhouette three times

normal and evidence of pulmonary edema. Despite infusions with bicarbonate, insulin, digoxin, diuretics, and glucose over the next 18 hours, the acidosis and congestive heart failure worsen. He sustains cardiac arrest which does not respond to resuscitative measures.

The infant was previously well-known to the neonatology service as a 1,000-g preterm infant who required extensive bowel resection because of necrotizing enterocolitis. The parents had omitted vitamins from the TPN solution for the past 12 days.

This unfortunate patient illustrates the following points: (1) Regular intakes of water-soluble vitamins are required for growing infants. (2) Adequate energy intake in the absence of vitamin B$_1$ promotes vitamin depletion more rapidly than one would expect judging from studies on the half-life of the vitamins. (3) Metabolic acidosis appears to be the first clinical manifestation of vitamin B$_1$ deficiency.

References

1. Food and Drug Administration Rules and Regulations. Nutrient requirements for infant formulas. *Fed Reg* 1985; 50:45106–45108.
2. Food and Nutrition Board. *Recommended dietary allowances.* 10th Edition. National Academy Press, 1989.
3. American Medical Association, Department of Foods and Nutrition. Multivitamin preparations for parenteral use: a statement by the Nutrition Advisory Group, 1975. *JPEN* 1979; 3:258–265.
4. Moran JR, Greene HL. Nutritional biochemistry of water-soluble vitamins. In: Grand RJ, Sutphen JL, Dietz WH Jr, eds. *Pediatric nutrition: theory and practice.* Boston: Butterworths, 1987:51–71.
5. Tajima S, Pinell SR. Regulation of collagen synthesis by ascorbic acid: ascorbic acid increases type I procollagen mRNA. *Biochem Biophys Res Commun* 1982;106:632–637.
6. Wallerstein RO, Wallerstein RO Jr. Scurvy. *Semin Hematol* 1976; 13:211–218.
7. Finn FM, Johns PA. Ascorbic acid transport by isolated bovine adrenal cortical cells. *Endocrinology* 1980; 106: 811–817.
8. Streeter M, Rosso P. Transport mechanisms for ascorbic acid in the human placenta. *Am J Clin Nutr* 1981; 34:1706–1711.
9. Norkus EP, Bassi JA, Rosso P. Maternal hyperglycemia and its effect on the placental transport of ascorbic acid. *Pediatr Res* 1982; 16:746–750.
10. Heller RM, Howard L, Greene HL. Skeletal changes of copper deficiency in infants receiving prolonged total parenteral nutrition. *J Pediatr* 1978; 92:942–949.
11. Prockop DJ, Guzman NA. Collagen diseases and the biosynthesis of collagen. *Hosp Pract* 1977; 12:61–68.
12. Moore MC, Greene HL, Phillips B, et al. Evaluation of a pediatric multiple vitamin preparation for total parenteral nutrition in infants and children. I. Blood levels of water-soluble vitamins. *Pediatrics* 1986; 77:530–538.
13. Greene HL, Hambidge KM, Schanler R, et al. Guidelines for the use of vitamins, trace elements, calcium, magnesium and phosphorus in infants and children receiving total parenteral nutrition: report of the Subcommittee on Pediatric Parenteral Nutrient Requirements from the Committee on Clinical Practice Issues of the American Society for Clinical Nutrition. *Am J Clin Nutr* 1988; 48:1324–1342.
14. Rindi G, Ventura U. Thiamine intestinal transport. *Physiol Rev* 1972; 52:817–821.

15. Pincus JH, Copper JR, Murphy JV, et al. Thiamine derivatives in subacute necrotizing encephalomyelopathy: a preliminary report. *Pediatrics* 1973; 51:716–721.

16. Shah N, Wolff JA. Thiamine deficiency: probable Wernicke's encephalopathy successfully treated in a child with acute lymphocytic leukemia. *Pediatrics* 1973;51:750–751.

17. Davis ED, Icke GC. Clinical chemistry of thiamine. *Adv Clin Chem* 1983; 23:93–140.

18. Ariaey-Nejad MR, Balaghi M, Baker EM, et al. Thiamine metabolism in man. *Am J Clin Nutr* 1970; 23:764–778.

19. Sauberlich HE. Biochemical alterations in thiamine deficiency: their interpretation. *Am J Clin Nutr* 1967;20: 528–546.

20. Kostenbauder HB, Sanvordecker DR. Riboflavin enhancement of bilirubin photocatabolism in vivo. *Experientia* 1973; 29:282–283.

21. Bartlett K. Vitamin-responsive inborn errors of metabolism. *Adv Clin Chem* 1986; 23:141–198.

22. Baeckert PA, Greene HL, Fritz I, et al. Vitamin concentrations in very low birth weight infants given vitamins intravenously in a lipid emulsion: measurement of vitamins A, D, and E and riboflavin. *J Pediatr* 1988;113: 1057–1065.

23. Horwitt MK. Interpretations of requirements for thiamin, riboflavin, niacin-tryptophan and vitamin E, plus comments on balance studies and vitamin B_6. *Am J Clin Nutr* 1986; 44:973–985.

24. Brewster MA. Vitamins. In: Kaplan L, Pesce A, eds. *Clinical chemistry*. St. Louis: CV Mosby, 1984: 656–685.

25. Pinto J, Huang YP, Rivlin RS. Inhibition of riboflavin metabolism by chlorpromazine, imipramine and amitriptyline. *J Clin Invest* 1981; 67:1500–1506.

26. Pinto J, Huang YP, McConnell R, et al. Increased urinary riboflavin excretion resulting from boric acid ingestion. *J Lab Clin Med* 1978; 92:126–134.

27. Christensen S. Renal excretion of riboflavin in the rat. *Acta Pharmacol et Toxicol* 1971; 29:428–440.

28. Brown MC, Roe DA. Role of riboflavin in drug-induced photohemolysis. *Clin Res* 1988; 36:755A.

29. Barker BM, Bender DA. Vitamin B_6. In: Barker BM, Bender DA eds. *Vitamins in medicine*. 4th ed. London: Heinemann Medical Books, 1980:348.

30. Wilson RG, Davis RE. Clinical chemistry of vitamin B_6. *Adv Clin Chem* 1983; 23:1–68.

31. Sebrell WM, Jr, Harris RS. *The vitamins*. New York: Academic Press, 1968.

32. Ubbink, JB, Delport R, Becker PJ, et al. Evidence of a theophylline-induced vitamin B_6 deficiency caused by noncompetitive inhibition of pyridoxal kinase. *J Lab Clin Med* 1989; 113:15–22.

33. Sauberlich HE, Canham JE. The vitamins. In: Goodhart RS, Shils ME, eds. *Modern nutrition in health and disease*. Philadelphia: Lea & Febiger, 1980:216.

34. Leklem JE, Reynolds RD. *Methods in vitamin B_6 nutrition*. New York: Plenum Publishing, 1979.

35. Ubbink JB, Schnell AM. Assay of erythrocyte enzyme activity levels involved in vitamin B_6 metabolism by high-performance liquid chromatography. *J Chromatogr* 1988; 431:406–412.

36. Spannuth CL, Jr, Laken GW, Wagner C, et al. Increased plasma clearance of pyridoxal 5'-phosphate in vitamin B_6-deficient uremic man. *J Lab Clin Med* 1977; 90:632–637.

37. Greene HL, Baeckert PA, Murrell J, Oelburg DG, Adcock EW. III. Blood pyridoxine levels in preterm infants receiving TPN. *JPEN* 1989; 24:113A.

38. Schaumburg H, Kaplan J, Windebank A, et al. Sensory neuropathy from pyridoxine abuse: a new megavitamin syndrome. *N Engl J Med* 1983; 309:445–448.

39. Moran JR, Greene HL. The B vitamins and vitamin C in human nutrition. II. "Conditional" B vitamins and vitamin C. *Am J Dis Child* 1979; 133:308–314.

40. Sauberlich HE, Skala JH, Dowdy RP. *Laboratory tests for the assessment of nutritional status*. Cleveland, OH: CRC Press, 1974.

41. Spivak JL, Jackson DL. Pellagra: an analysis of 18 patients and a review of the literature. *Johns Hopkins Med J* 1977; 140:295–309.

42. Carlson LA. Nicotinic acid and inhibition of fat-mobilizing lipolysis: present status of effects on lipid metabolism. *Adv Exp Med Biol* 1978; 109:225–238.

43. National Academy of Sciences. *Recommended dietary allowances*. 8th ed. Washington, DC: GPO, 1974.

44. Spencer RP, Brody KR. Biotin transport by the small intestine of rat, hamster and other species. *Am J Physiol* 1964; 206:653–657.

45. Rose RC, McCormick DB, Li TK, et al. Transport and metabolism of vitamins. *Fed Proc* 1986; 45:30–39.

46. Wolf B, Heard GS. Disorders of biotin metabolism. In: Seriver CR, Beaudet AL, Sly WS, eds. *The metabolic basis of inherited disease*. New York: McGraw Hill, 1989: 2083–2099.

47. Mock DM, Malik M. Distribution of biotin in human plasma: most of the biotin is not bound to protein. *Am J Clin Nutr* 1992; 56:427–432.

48. Mock DM, Mock NI, Langbehn SE. Biotin in human milk: methods, location and chemical form. *J Nutr* 1992; 122:535–545.

49. Mock DM, Mock NI, Dankle JA. Secretory patterns of biotin in human milk. *J Nutr* 1992; 122:546–552.

50. Mock DM, Jackson H, Lankford GL, Mock NI, Weintraub ST. Quantitation of urinary 3-hydroxyisovaleric acid using deuterated 3-hydroxyisovaleric acid as internal standard. *Biomed Env Mass Spectrom* 1989; 18:652–656.

51. Mock DM, DeLorimer AA, Liebman WM, et al. Biotin deficiency: an unusual complication of parenteral alimentation. *N Engl J Med* 1981; 304:820–823.

10. Calcium, Magnesium, Phosphorus, and Vitamin D

Winston W.K. Koo

Reginald C. Tsang

Reviewers: Stephanie Atkinson, Frank R. Greer, Jacques Senterre

Calcium (Ca), magnesium (Mg), and phosphorus (P) are essential for tissue structure and function. The physiology and metabolism of these minerals are interrelated and modulated by other nutrients and hormones, including vitamin D metabolites. Nutrient requirements for these minerals and vitamin D should aim to maintain biochemical homeostasis and normal growth in physical stature, with minimal stress to the functions of regulatory organs. They should also prevent the complications of chronically inadequate intake of these nutrients, specifically bone demineralization, fractures, and rickets. For infants born prematurely, the interruption of the period of most rapid in utero mineral accretion, along with the presence of respiratory insufficiency and other illnesses, can influence the route of delivery and requirements for these nutrients.

Physiology

Calcium, Magnesium, and Phosphorus

Calcium is the most abundant mineral in the body and, together with P, forms the major inorganic constituent of bone. Magnesium is the fourth most abundant mineral and is the second most common intracellular electrolyte in the body. At all ages, 99% of total body Ca is in bone. The tissue distribution of P and Mg varies somewhat according to the extent of bone mineralization and the rate of soft tissue growth. However, near the end of the third trimester, approximately 80% of total body P is in bone, 9% is in skeletal muscle, and the remainder is in viscera and extracellular fluid. Approximately 60% of the body's Mg is in bone, 20% is in muscle, and most of the remainder is found in intracellular space of other tissues. Although the major portions of Ca, P, and Mg are found in the skeleton, all three elements are essential to the function of soft tissues.

There are discrepancies in the published data on in utero accretion of Ca, Mg, and P.[1-4] However, it is generally agreed that approximately 80% of Ca, P, and Mg accrue in the fetus from 25 weeks to term gestation. During this period, the estimated daily accretion per kg fetal bodyweight is 2.30 to 2.98 mmol (92 to 119 mg) Ca, 0.10 to 0.14 mmol (2.51 to 3.44 mg) Mg, and 1.90 to 2.39 mmol (59 to 74 mg) P. The peak accretion rates occur at 36 to 38 weeks gestation. In newborn term infants, the total body Ca, P, and Mg content averages approximately 28 g, 16 g, and 0.8 g, respectively.[3,4]

Serum or plasma is readily available for measurement of Ca, Mg, and P, but the fraction of Ca, Mg, and P in the circulation is <1% of their respective total body contents. Acute and transient fluctuations of serum concentrations of Ca, Mg, and P may occur in response to acute changes in intake of each mineral, or to compartmental shifts of these elements, and may not reflect actual tissue changes. However, chronic and severely lowered serum concentrations of these minerals may reflect the presence of a deficiency state.

The major determinant of mineral retention for enterally fed infants, particularly for Ca and Mg, is the amount of mineral intake and mineral absorption. However, differences in the distribution and concentration of minerals (and vitamin D) between human milk and infant formulas theoretically may affect mineral absorption and retention. Approximately half of the Ca and Mg is found in the protein fraction of milk. The majority of Ca and Mg is present in the whey protein of human milk, in contrast to the casein fraction of bovine milk. Another one third of Ca content and one half of Mg content are bound to low molecular-weight compounds. The final 20% of the Ca is found in the fat fraction of human milk.[5,6] There are no major differences in the contents of Ca, Mg, and P in milk between mothers delivering term and preterm infants.[7,8] The reported range of mean content of minerals in human milk is 6.7 to 7.9 mmol (270 to 320 mg) Ca per liter, 1.2 to 1.6 mmol (30 to 40 mg) Mg per liter, and 4.2 to 4.9 mmol (130 to 150 mg) P per liter, with Ca:P ratios by weight ranging from 1.8:1 to 2.2:1. Variations in individuals and differences in study design and assay methodologies account for some of the differences in the reported human milk content of Ca, Mg, and P.[9,10] In longitudinal studies, human milk Ca content decreases by an average of approximately 10% and P content probably also decreases to a similar extent, but Mg content remains stable during the first 6 months of lactation.[11,12] Preterm infant formulas have Ca contents varying from 18.8 to 36.5 mmol (750 to 1,460 mg)/L, P contents from 12.9 to 23.5 mmol (400 to 730 mg)/L, and Mg contents from 1.7 to 4.2 mmol (40 to 100 mg)/L.[13]

Intestinal absorption of Ca occurs by active transport and by facilitated diffusion. Active Ca absorption occurs primarily in the proximal small intestine and is under adaptive hormonal control by 1,25-dihydroxyvitamin D.[14-16] Adaptive changes in Ca absorption occur in the colon only in patients with extensive small bowel resection. Standard Ca balance studies represent a ''net'' balance of intake minus stool and urinary losses. Endogenous (intestinal secretory) losses of Ca are included in fecal losses and markedly affect measures of true percent Ca absorption. Thus, based on recent stable isotope studies,[17-20] true Ca absorption is approximately 10% higher than the net Ca absorption reported by standard balance studies in infants. However, significant individual variabilities in intestinal Ca absorption (21% to 90%) and retention (14% to 78%) rates were also noted.[17-22] The average net Ca absorption in preterm infants fed high mineral-containing bovine milk–based ''preterm'' formulas ranges from 36% to 75% and is comparable to the range of 35% to 75% reported for those fed human milk fortified with Ca.[23-31]

Magnesium absorption occurs mainly in the distal small intestine, with colonic absorption occurring at low Mg intake. Over the usual intake range, intestinal absorption of Mg is linear in adults and infants, consistent with a diffusion process. However, decreased fractional absorption with larger intakes is more consistent with a facilitated diffusion or saturable component as well. Quantitatively, vitamin D metabolites have little effect on intestinal Mg absorption, although Mg is a necessary cofactor in vitamin D metabolism.[32,33] It is not known to what extent the endogenous fecal excretion of Mg influences net intestinal Mg absorption in infants. The endogenous fecal excretion of Mg for adults appears small and is approximately 0.015 mmol (0.36 mg)/kg/day. The net Mg absorption in preterm infants is reported to range from 33% to 63% and is similar between those fed human milk or preterm infant formula.[26,30,34] In one report, true fractional Mg absorption of human milk averaged 88% (range, 75% to 93%) using intrinsic and extrinsic stable isotope labeling techniques.[19]

Phosphorus absorption occurs throughout the small intestine but is greatest in the jejunum and least in the ileum. It is absorbed by simple and facilitated diffusion and by an active sodium-phosphate co-transport system. The active transport is subject to adaptive hormonal control in which 1,25-dihydroxyvitamin D and thyroid hormone play major roles,[35] although vitamin D supplementation does not appear to significantly affect P absorption or retention in preterm infants.[36] Phosphorus retention approaches ≥90% in preterm infants fed low P-containing milks, including human milk.[23,28,34,36-39] Intestinal P absorption and urinary P excretion both increase with high P milks, but percent P retention usually remains >50%.[25,27,29-31] The extent of endogenous intestinal P secretion is not known.

Specific nutrients affect mineral absorption and retention.[40-43] In preterm infants fed low-mineral milk, Ca absorption and retention may be increased by vitamin D[36] and P[23,37] supplementation, but the effect of dietary lactose remains controversial.[30,44,45] Extreme reduction in dietary P may impair Ca absorption, whereas large excesses of P and fat intake also may impair Ca absorption.[32,33,35,40] With Ca supplementation, fractional phosphate absorption is slightly decreased at a total Ca intake of >3.75 mmol (150 mg)/kg/day,[38] fecal Ca excretion is correlated with fecal fat excretion,[23] and there is also a 5% to 10% increase in fecal fat loss noted in preterm[46] and term[47] infants. The absorption of major fatty acids in human milk and bovine milk–based infant formulas is decreased with supplementation of 2 mmol (80 mg) elemental Ca per day as Ca lactate to preterm infants.[48] Conflicting data exist on the possible interaction of Ca and Mg during absorption and retention of these minerals.[26,30,49,50] Magnesium retention may be lowered by high Ca and P supplementation to standard infant formula unless Mg supplementation is also provided.[50] In soy formula, phytate is thought to be responsible for binding P and reducing its absorption.[47,51]

In contrast, preterm infants fed high mineral bovine milk–based ''preterm'' formulas showed no significant alteration in net absorption of fat compared to infants fed human milk with commercial mineral fortifier,[25,27] although Ca retention is negatively correlated with fecal fat excretion.[27] Balance studies showed consistently positive retention of Mg,[30,50] zinc, copper,[25,30,52] and manganese[30] retention at amounts similar to in utero retention when the high-mineral formulas were fortified with these nutrients. Mass balance and stable isotope studies demonstrated that high-mineral premature infant formula does not affect iron absorption, and that net iron balance varies directly with daily iron intake.[53]

Normally, there are large amounts of minerals filtered through the nephron each day. For example, in an infant with a glomerular filtration rate of 20 mL/min (28.8 L/day) and 60% of serum Ca (2.5 mmol/L) being ultrafiltrable, the daily amount of filtered Ca would be 43.2 mmol (1,728 mg). Similarly, the daily amount of filtered Mg and P would be 18.4

mmol (442 mg) and 46.6 mmol (1,445 mg), respectively. However, only 1% to 2% of Ca, 3% to 4% of Mg, and 10% to 15% of P are excreted. Thus, a small percent increase in renal loss of any of the minerals may significantly affect mineral balance, particularly at low ranges of intake.

Some common factors of clinical importance that may increase urinary excretion of Ca, Mg, and P include: increased intake of the respective minerals; increased sodium intake with resultant positive sodium balance and extracellular fluid expansion; and intravenous and oral glucose loading.[40,42,43,54-56] Magnesium infusion inhibits Ca reabsorption in the loop of Henle, while hypercalcemia inhibits Mg reabsorption in the loop of Henle. Phosphorus deficiency is typically associated with hypercalciuria, whereas P intake, either orally or intravenously, decreases urinary Ca and Mg excretion. The kidney in the human infant adapts well to retaining P, particularly under conditions of low P intake (e.g., human milk feeding) and increased need (e.g., for bone growth and mineralization).

Vitamin D

Vitamin D is produced endogenously as vitamin D_3 (cholecalciferol) in the skin upon exposure to ultraviolet irradiation or derived exogenously as vitamin D_2 (ergocalciferol) or vitamin D_3 from enteral or parenteral delivery. Vitamin D is transported in plasma primarily by vitamin-D-binding protein. In the liver, vitamin D is hydroxylated to 25-hydroxyvitamin D (25-OHD), and its serum concentration is often used as an indicator of vitamin D status. The 25 OHD is further hydroxylated to 1,25-dihydroxyvitamin D $(1,25[OH]_2D)$ in the kidney, a process stimulated by parathyroid hormone and deficiencies in Ca and P. Both vitamin D_2 and D_3 undergo the same metabolic transformation, and there is little functional difference between their metabolites.

There are >30 metabolites of vitamin D, but $1,25(OH)_2D$ is biologically the most active and most important. A major physiologic action of $1,25(OH)_2D$ is to increase bone mineralization. This action is thought to be primarily related to the capacity of $1,25(OH)_2D$ to increase intestinal Ca and P absorption, although $1,25(OH)_2D$ is known to affect the function of cells from many tissues besides the enterocytes of the small intestine. The other major action (together with parathyroid hormone) is the maintenance of normal circulating Ca concentrations. The direct action of $1,25(OH)_2D$ on bone is the mobilization of bone Ca and P to the extracellular fluid.[14-16]

Human and bovine milk contain very little vitamin D or its metabolites. The total biologic antirachitic steroid activity of human milk is probably in the range of 3 to 7 IU/dL (0.08 to 0.18 µg/dL), depending on the maternal vitamin D status, race, and the season of the year.[57-62] Quantitatively, vitamin D (parent compound) accounts for the largest contribution to human milk vitamin D content. However, 25-OHD in milk accounts for the major component of biologic activity when tested by rat skeletal growth and maintenance of Ca homeostasis.[60] Preterm infant formulas currently are fortified with vitamin D in varying amounts from 480 to 2,675 IU/L.[13]

The ability of preterm infants to absorb and metabolize vitamin D is present even in the most immature infants within days after birth, as shown by changes in serum 25-OHD and $1,25(OH)_2D$ concentrations following different amounts of vitamin D supplementation.[31,63-67]

Determination of Mineral and Vitamin D Requirements

There are no data to demonstrate significant differences among preterm infants in the absorption and excretion of Ca, Mg, and P, and vitamin D metabolism appears adequate (in the presence of adequate substrate availability) even in the smallest preterm infants. Thus, if one of the major goals of high mineral intake is to achieve tissue accretion comparable to in utero accretion, the major difference in the requirement of Ca, Mg, and P among preterm infants, for practical purposes, is primarily that of the duration of high mineral intake. This difference is due to the fact that small preterm infants at risk for ''mineral and vitamin D deficiency'' are born before the peak in utero accretion which occurs primarily at >34 weeks gestation.

Parenteral Nutrition

Parenteral nutrition (PN) usually is the major source of nutrient intake during the transition period, since few preterm infants, particularly extremely low-birthweight (ELBW) (<1 kg) infants, can tolerate complete enteral feeding from birth. The requirement for minerals during the transition period is primarily to maintain biochemical homeostasis until clinical stabilization from acute illnesses.[55,68] For practical purposes, calcium homeostasis is the most disturbed and is usually manifested as hypocalcemia in the early neonatal period. Hypocalcemia can be prevented or treated with calcium infusions of 1.25 to 1.88 mmol (50 to 75 mg) elemental Ca per kg per day in the first 2 to 3 days of life. Alternately, PN solutions with high mineral content intended for use during the stable period (see following discussion) can be utilized (with additional Ca if necessary) and appear to be clinically well tolerated.[69-74] Parenteral vitamin D requirements during this period also are not well defined but are likely to be minimal, since vitamin D metabolites act primarily at the intestinal level and there is little enteral mineral intake.

During the stable period when acute illnesses have stabilized and postnatal adjustments in the fluid compartments have been completed, the maintenance of biochemical homeostasis as well as the resumption of rapid tissue accretion of minerals are the major determinants of nutritional needs. Requirements of Ca, Mg, P, and vitamin D for infants who need PN can now be estimated from recent biochemical and hormonal data of mineral homeostasis, metabolic balance studies, and radiographic studies of bone mineralization.[69-75]

The use of PN solution with Ca, P, and Mg contents of 15 mmol (60 mg)/dL, 15 mmol (46.5 mg)/dL, and 3 mmol (7.2 mg)/dL, respectively, can maintain desirable biochemical and calciotropic hormone indices of mineral homeostasis in the management of preterm infants. These goals include normal and stable serum concentrations of Ca, P, parathyroid hormone, calcitonin, 25 OHD, and $1,25(OH)_2D$, as well as renal tubular reabsorption of phosphate.[69,72] However, transient hypocalcemia, hypermagnesemia, and relatively low serum P concentrations may occur occasionally in ELBW infants at these levels of intake.[72]

Studies have shown that fluctuations in serum concentration of Mg can occur secondary to changes in the amount of Mg delivered in PN solution, losses from gastrointestinal fluid, and the presence of underlying renal dysfunction. Parenteral nutrition solutions containing 1 mmol (24 mg) Mg per L resulted in hypomagnesemia in 11 of 42 infants.[76] In contrast, PN solutions with 4 mmol (96 mg) Mg per L delivering an average of 0.5 mmol (12 mg) Mg per kg per day resulted in transient episodes of hypermagnesemia in 5 of 18 infants.[69] None of these reports used Mg replacement for gastrointestinal fluid losses, which can have Mg contents as high as 7 mmol/L (16.8 mg/dL). Parenteral nutrition solutions with an Mg content of 3 mmol/L that deliver approximately 0.3 to 0.4 mmol (7.2 to 9.6 mg) Mg per kg per day appear to maintain stable serum Mg concentrations. Transient hypermagnesemia may occur in ELBW infants at this level of intake,[72] however, presumably in part due to a delay in adaptive renal excretory response to the intravenous Mg load. Furthermore, the additional protection from the gut barrier to Mg absorption in enterally fed infants is not a factor in infants receiving PN.

Balance studies in clinically stable infants on PN receiving 1.45 to 1.9 mmol (58 to 76 mg) Ca per kg per day and 1.23 to 1.74 mmol (38 to 54 mg) P per kg per day have demonstrated that average retention was 88% to 94% for Ca and 83% to 97% for P[71,73,74] (Tables 10.1 and 10.2). Thus, 60% to 70% of in utero accretion of Ca and P could be achieved with current PN solutions. Average Mg retention of 61% was reported in preterm infants receiving an average total daily Mg intake of 0.51 mmol (122 mg) from PN solutions containing 0.34 mmol (8 mg)/dL.[75] This amount is approximately twice the in utero accretion rate for Mg. Negative balances for Mg and other nutrients (e.g., sodium, potassium, and zinc) may result from loss of large volumes of gastrointestinal fluid without appropriate replacement.[77-79]

Standard biochemical and radiographic findings showed that metabolic bone disease was less severe when the Ca and P delivered in PN solutions were doubled to 1.36 mmol (54.4 mg) Ca and 1.22 mmol (37.8 mg) P per kg per day.[70] However, there has been no systematic study of bone mineralization in such infants using newer and more sensitive absorptiometric techniques.

The kidneys normally represent the main mineral excretory route in infants receiving total PN, and as previously reviewed,[40,42,54,56] urinary losses may have a significant impact on mineral balance. Increased urinary Ca excretion may result from an increased filtered load (with or without extracellular fluid expansion), decreased reabsorption of Ca (e.g., from parathyroid hormone resistance associated with P deficiency), and increased inorganic sulfate, oxalate, or acid loads. In clinical practice, P deficiency, along with excessive intakes of intravenous fluid, sodium, Ca, Mg, vitamin D, or amino acids, are reported to increase urinary Ca losses.[40,80] Calciuria of >40% of Ca intake can occur with low P intake in PN in spite of associated low Ca intake.[81,82] The calciuria with P deficiency may be reduced by as much as 75% when P delivery is increased to correct hypophosphatemia and result in phosphaturia; >1 mmol (31 mg) of P per kg per day may be necessary to achieve this effect.[56,81-83] Cyclic PN with delivery of PN over shorter periods (10 to 18 h/day) results in greater urine Ca loss compared to a continuous 24-hour infusion of PN or periods without PN infusion. Nonnutritional factors, including diuretics (furosemide, spironolactone, and occasionally thiazide) and theophylline, also increase urine Ca loss and theoretically may be associated with disturbed bone mineralization.

Urinary loss of Mg and P also may be increased by similar factors affecting urinary loss of Ca and may significantly affect Mg and P balances. However, renal handling of Mg appears to be unaffected by the quantity or type of amino acids infused, as well as independent of the Ca and P content of currently used PN solutions or the urinary excretion of Ca, P, and sodium. In infants receiving low P intake, the renal tubular reabsorption of phosphate may approach 100%.

Factors such as Ca and P ratios may be important to achieve optimal mineral retention in infants receiving PN therapy. Parenteral nutrition solutions with

Table 10.1. Calcium Balance in Preterm Infants Receiving Parenteral Nutrition

Reference	n	Vitamin D (IU/day)	Content (mmol/L)	Intake (mmol/kg/day)	Urinary Excretion (mmol/kg/day)	Retention (mmol/kg/day)	%
Pelegano et al.[71]	5	100–200	14.5 (580)	1.79 (72)	0.10 (4)	1.39 (56)	91
Chessex et al.[73]	16	200	12.8 (510)	1.80 (72)	0.23 (9)	1.58 (63)	88
Pelegano et al.[74]	16	100–200	15.0 (600)	1.90 (76)	0.13 (5)	1.79 (72)	93
Pelegano et al.[74]	12	100–200	15.0 (600)	1.90 (76)	0.10 (4)	1.80 (72)	94
Pelegano et al.[74]	13	100–200	10.1 (400)	1.45 (58)	0.10 (4)	1.35 (54)	93
Hanning et al.[75]	9	150	8.8 (352)	1.32 (53)	0.11 (4)	1.21 (48)	92

Conversion: Ca 1 mmol = 40 mg; number in parentheses is in mg.

Table 10.2. Phosphorus Balance in Preterm Infants Receiving Parenteral Nutrition

Reference	n	Vitamin D (IU/day)	Content (mmol/L)	Intake (mmol/kg/day)	Urinary Excretion (mmol/kg/day)	Retention (mmol/kg/day)	%
Pelegano et al.[71]	5	100–200	11.0 (341)	1.32 (41)	0.13 (4)	1.17 (36)	89
Chessex et al.[73]	16	200	12.7 (394)	1.74 (54)	0.06 (2)	1.67 (52)	97
Pelegano et al.[74]	16	100–200	9.7 (282)	1.23 (38)	0.10 (3)	1.13 (35)	92
Pelegano et al.[74]	12	100–200	11.3 (350)	1.45 (45)	0.13 (4)	1.32 (41)	90
Pelegano et al.[74]	13	100–200	11.0 (341)	1.45 (45)	0.23 (7)	1.23 (38)	83
Hanning et al.[75]	9	150	10.4 (322)	1.56 (48)	0.39 (12)	1.10 (34)	71

Conversion: P 1 mmol = 31 mg; number in parentheses is in mg.

extremes of Ca:P ratios by weight from 4:1 to 1:8 have been used in infants and previously reviewed.[40,54] However, a Ca:P ratio of 1:1 to 1.3:1 by molar ratio or 1.3:1 to 1.7:1 by weight minimizes the disturbance to the Ca:P homeostatic mechanism and results in the highest Ca:P retention. A Ca:P ratio of <0.78:1 by molar ratio or <1:1 by weight should not be used because of potential risk for disturbance of Ca and P homeostasis, specifically hyperphosphatemia and hypocalcemia.[83–85]

There are no documented major complications associated with the Ca (12.5 to 15 mmol [500–600 mg]/L), P (12.9 to 14.5 mmol [400–450 mg]/L), and Mg (2 to 3 mmol [50–70 mg]/L) contents of PN solutions recommended here for preterm infants.[69–74] Serial abdominal ultrasound examination has shown that "biliary sludge" did not occur with greater frequency in infants receiving this higher Ca-P solution compared to those with lower mineral intake. Biliary sludge appeared to resolve upon enteral feeding. In the absence of chronic diuretic therapy, abnormal renal ultrasound findings have not been reported at this Ca and P intake.[69,72]

There are extensive clinical and research data on the use of current preparations of inorganic salts, primarily Ca gluconate and mixed mono- and dibasic phosphate salts of sodium and potassium. The inorganic Ca and P salts will remain in solution with thorough mixing and addition of the P salt in PN solution prior to the addition of Ca salt, and with careful attention to technical details in the preparation of PN solution.[86,87] The solubility of Ca and P salts is enhanced by higher amino acid concentrations recommended for use in preterm infants (see Chapter 3). Limited information exists on the use of alternate sources of inorganic[73,88] and organic salts[75,89,90] of Ca and P in PN solutions.

If the nutritional goal in preterm infants is to match the estimated rate of in utero mineral accretion,[3] the current PN solutions achieve only 60% to 70% of the maximum requirements for Ca and P but contain sufficient amounts of Mg. The use of alternate infusions of Ca and P to increase the delivery of these minerals and to avoid Ca-P precipitation in PN solutions has been shown to result in lower Ca and P retention (42% to 63%)[84,85] compared to the Ca and P retention rates when Ca and P are infused simultaneously (83% to 97%).[71,73,74] In addition, hypercalcemia and hypophosphatemia may occur during high Ca infusion, whereas hyperphosphatemia and hypocalcemia may occur during high P infusion.[84] Furthermore, infusion of P alone results in elevated urinary cyclic adenosine monophosphate, presumably reflecting the presence of increased circulating parathyroid hormone.[83,84] A consistent, moderate PN mineral intake appears to be best suited for most preterm infants,

since it is impractical and probably impossible to mimic the exact in utero changes during postnatal life. In addition, higher Ca and P intakes may be associated with a greater risk of side effects as described earlier.

Recent studies have demonstrated that about 30 IU/kg/day up to a maximum of 400 IU/day of vitamin D delivered in amino acid dextrose solution[69,71–75,91,92] or 160 IU/kg/day up to a maximum of 400 IU/day in lipid emulsion[93] is adequate to maintain normal vitamin D status for infants requiring PN.

At present, few preterm infants continue to receive PN therapy postdischarge (i.e., home PN therapy). There are no systematic data to determine the mineral and vitamin D requirements for these patients. However, PN solution with a vitamin D content of 250 IU/L can maintain normal vitamin D status in preterm infants for >3 months as indicated by normal serum 25-OHD concentrations.[92] Based on systematic studies of preterm infants receiving PN solutions with high Ca and P content of 12.5 to 15 mmol/L each during hospitalization[69,71–74] and clinical experience since its recommendation for general use,[94] these amounts of Ca and P (and the currently recommended Mg content) appear suitable for use in preterm infants for at least the first 6 months after birth.

Enteral Nutrition

Most ELBW infants require several weeks to achieve total enteral feeding. During the transitional period, multiple physiologic adaptations occur in the preterm infant, including gastrointestinal adaptation to postnatal feeding. Enteral mineral requirement during this period is relatively low compared to subsequent rapid growth during the stable period. Human milk, if available, has multiple potential benefits and can be used without mineral supplementation during the first 2 to 3 weeks after birth (i.e., during transition from parenteral to enteral feeding). Nevertheless, preterm infant formulas with high mineral content appear to be well tolerated during this period. Vitamin D requirement is also likely to be minimal during this period when the major nutrients are delivered parenterally and there is little growth.

Some units with aggressive enteral feeding policy have preterm infants achieving full enteral feeding by 7 days postnatally. In these situations, unfortified human-milk feeding may not be justified at any time. (S. Atkinson)

During the *stable period* of rapid growth, human milk contains insufficient Ca and P but probably sufficient Mg to meet the estimated intrauterine accretion rates[3] or the estimated requirement by factorial approach. This latter approach takes into account the estimated intestinal absorption, and urine and skin losses, in addition to tissue increment.[95] Based on these data, the advisable intake per kg bodyweight per day may be as high as 5.25 mmol (210 mg) Ca, 4.52 mmol (140 mg) P, and 0.42 mmol (10 mg) Mg for a 1 kg preterm infant.[95]

Evidence supporting inadequacy of mineral intake from human milk and standard infant formulas includes biochemical (low serum and urine P, elevated serum and urine Ca, elevated serum alkaline phosphatase activity)[2,28,34,38,39,43,54,80,96-102] and hormonal (elevated serum 1,25[OH]$_2$D) disturbances,[103,104] lower bone mineral content (BMC),[103,105-108] and abnormal x-rays showing fractures and rickets.[109,110] These abnormalities are improved or normalized with increases in Ca and P intake.[24,28,34,38,39,97-99,101-103,105,108,111,112]

The data from preterm infants fed pooled human milk, own mother's milk, standard-term infant formulas, or human milk supplemented with individual components or a combination of components (vitamin D, Ca, or P) have been previously reviewed.[2,41,43,54,80,113-115] Recent standard balance studies in infants fed mother's milk fortified with lyophilized human milk powder (and Ca and P),[24] bovine milk–based powder,[25] or liquid[27] formulation, as well as in infants fed formulas with high mineral content,[25,27,29,30] have demonstrated that within a few weeks after birth preterm infants can absorb and retain Ca and P (Tables 10.3 and 10.4) in sufficient amounts to approximate estimated in utero accretion rates and requirements based on factorial approach.

Preterm infants fed human milk at 200 mL/kg/day would receive an intake of 0.29 to 0.33 mmol (7 to 8 mg) Mg per kg per day and consistently showed Mg retention rates comparable to in utero accretion values.[24,34] Preterm infants fed standard bovine milk–based formulas with Mg content similar to human milk[26,34,38,49] can achieve rates of Mg retention comparable to in utero retention rates as early as the first 3 days after birth.[49] Preterm infants fed high Ca and P formulas can consistently achieve similar Mg retention rates if there is Mg fortification to a level of approximately 4.2 mmol (100 mg)/L[30,50] (Table 10.5).

The unequal distribution of a stable isotopic Ca tracer between casein and whey fractions of infant formulas, human milk, and bovine milk[116] may in part explain the reported differences in bioavailability of minerals in infant formulas.[26] However, studies using either standard balance techniques[25,27,29,30] or stable isotope techniques[17,19] indicate that the mineral preparations in bovine milk–based preterm infant formulas are usually well absorbed. It is possible that, as shown in adults, the difference in bioavailability between well-formulated supplements is small relative to differences in absorptive performance between individuals.[117,118] In small preterm infants, the variance in mineral retention rate appears to depend more on individual patient variability than the effect of bodyweight and postnatal age,[119] but the effect of gestational age in the small preterm infant has not been clearly demonstrated.

Urinary loss of minerals also may affect mineral retention in enterally fed infants. Preterm infants fed human milk or "humanized" infant formula with low mineral content and a Ca:P ratio of about 2:1 by weight can develop hypercalciuria to an extent similar to those receiving PN solutions with relatively low Ca and P content.[39,97-100] In these situations, P supplementation increases Ca and P retention but also increases urine P excretion.[37,39] In adults, high intakes of some nutrients (e.g., protein) are reported to increase urine Ca loss, but there is no specific evidence that increased protein intake to the range of 3.0 to 3.6 g/kg/day in currently available preterm infant formulas will increase urine Ca loss. Chronic diuretic therapy is the major cause of increased urinary loss of minerals and increased risk of nephrocalcinosis.[120,121] Other drugs such as theophylline also may increase urine loss of minerals.[122]

Currently, there is a low rate of sustained human-milk feeding for preterm infants in the United States, and many of these infants are fed bovine milk–based preterm infant formulas with a Ca and P content several times greater than that found in human milk. Mineral content of bovine milk–based infant formulas varies over a wide range. Since Ca and P are partly linked to casein,[5,6] their content is generally related to the protein content and whey:casein ratio in the formula. Preterm infant formulas contain additional sources of Ca, P, and Mg, including Ca carbonate, Ca phosphate tribasic, Ca chloride, and Mg chloride. A loss of 30% to 40% of Ca and P may occur from sedimentation in these formulas, especially during constant infusion over a period of 3 to 6 hours.[123-125] The mineral loss is less with newer formulations and with vigorous shaking of the containers prior to the bolus delivery of feeds.[25,29,126]

The effect of Ca:P ratio on mineral retention rates varies, depending on the type of infant feeding and the Ca and P content. In one report[127] of preterm infants fed standard bovine milk formulas plus varying amounts of mineral mixture to achieve a final Ca:P ratio of 1.4:1 to 3.8:1 by weight (1:1 to 2.9:1 molar ratio), the Ca and P combination that resulted in retention rates closest to in utero values occurred in infants fed formulas with a Ca:P ratio of 3.8:1 by weight (2.9:1 molar ratio) at a Ca intake of 6.25 mmol (250 mg)/kg/day.

Table 10.3. Calcium Balance in Preterm Infants Receiving Enteral Nutrition

Reference		n	Vitamin D* (IU/day)	Intake† (mmol/kg/day)	Urine† (mmol/kg/day)	Absorption† (mmol/kg/day)	%	Retention† (mmol/kg/day)	%
Mother's milk									
Salle et al.[23]	+ Ca, P	8	1,200	2.25 (90)	0.08 (3)	1.65 (66)	73	1.58 (63)	73
Schanler et al[24]	+ lyophilized human milk, Ca, P	16	800	3.28 (131)	0.15 (6)	2.33 (93)	71	2.15 (86)	66
Ehrenkranz et al.[25]	+ bovine milk-based powder fortifier	6	200	3.07 (123)	0.25 (10)	2.31 (92)	75	2.06 (82)	67
Schanler et al.[26]	+ bovine milk-based liquid formula	12	800 (150)	3.43 (137)	0.13 (5)	1.20 (48)	35	1.08 (43)	31
Raschko et al.[27]	+ bovine milk-based liquid formula	10	400 (150)	4.18 (167)	0.34 (14)	2.45 (98)	59	2.13 (85)	51
Bovine milk–based preterm infant formula									
Intermediate Ca content (23[26] and 19[28] mmol/L, respectively)									
Schanler et al.[26]		10	800 (100)	3.68 (147)	0.13 (5)	1.98 (79)	54	1.85 (74)	50
Lyon et al.[28]		5	2,000 (100)	3.20 (128)	0.03 (1)	1.35 (54)	42	1.32 (53)	41
High Ca content (>23 mmol/L)									
Ehrenkranz et al.[25]		6	200 (700)	3.69 (148)	0.19 (8)	2.58 (103)	70	2.38 (95)	65
Raschko et al.[27]		10	400 (270)	5.75 (230)	0.13 (5)	2.73 (109)	48	2.60 (104)	45
Rowe et al.[29]		13	400 (300)	5.48 (219)	—	4.15 (166)	74	3.98 (159)	70
Wirth et al.[30]		8	240 (250)	5.83 (233)	0.04 (2)	4.35 (174)	75	4.30 (172)	74
Cooke et al.[31]		11	200 (250)	5.40 (216)	0.11 (4)	2.03 (81)	36	1.90 (76)	34

*Number in parentheses indicates estimated daily vitamin D intake from infant formula.

†Number in parentheses is in mg.

Conversion: Ca 1 mmol = 40 mg

Table 10.4. Phosphorus Balance in Preterm Infants Receiving Enteral Nutrition

Reference		n	Vitamin D* (IU/day)	Intake† (mmol/kg/day)	Urine† (mmol/kg/day)	Absorption† (mmol/kg/day)	%	Retention† (mmol/kg/day)	%
Mother's milk									
Salle et al.[23]	+ Ca, P	8	1,200	2.0 (62)	0.16 (5)	1.87 (58)	94	1.71 (53)	93
Schanler et al.[24]	+ lyophilized human milk	160	800	2.35 (73)	0.42 (13)	2.23 (69)	95	1.81 (56)	77
Ehrenkranz et al.[25]	+ bovine milk–based powder fortifier	6	200	2.31 (72)	0.08 (2)	1.97 (61)	86	1.89 (58)	82
Schanler et al.[26]	+ bovine milk–based liquid formula	12	800 (150)	2.29 (71)	0.16 (5)	1.42 (44)	63	1.26 (39)	55
Raschko et al.[27]	+ bovine milk–based liquid formula	10	400 (150)	2.71 (84)	0.03 (1)	1.84 (57)	68	1.81 (56)	67
Bovine milk–based preterm infant formula									
Intermediate P content (13.9[26] and 12.9[28] mmol/L, respectively)									
Schanler et al.[26]		10	800 (100)	2.23 (69)	0.23 (7)	1.97 (61)	89	1.61 (50)	72
Lyon et al.[28]		5	2,000 (100)	2.18 (68)	0.30 (9)	1.84 (57)	84	1.51 (47)	69
High P content (>16 mmol/L)									
Ehrenkranz et al.[25]		6	200 (700)	2.46 (76)	0.27 (8)	2.10 (65)	85	1.83 (56)	75
Raschko et al.[27]		10	400 (270)	4.13 (128)	0.15 (5)	2.65 (82)	64	2.48 (77)	61
Rowe et al.[29]		13	400 (300)	3.74 (116)	—	2.87 (89)	76	2.81 (87)	74
Wirth et al.[30]		8	240 (250)	3.97 (123)	0.23 (7)	2.35 (73)	59	2.13 (66)	54
Cooke et al.[31]		11	200 (250)	3.87 (120)	0.39 (12)	2.45 (76)	64	2.06 (64)	53

*Number in parentheses indicates estimated additional daily vitamin D intake from infant formula.
†Number in parentheses is in mg.
Conversion: P 1 mmol = 31 mg

143

Table 10.5. Magnesium Balance in Preterm Infants Receiving Enteral Nutrition

Reference	n	Vitamin D* (IU/day)	Intake† (mmol/kg/day)	Urine† (mmol/kg/day)	Absorption† (mmol/kg/day)	%	Retention† (mmol/kg/day)	%
Mother's milk								
Schanler et al.[34]	14	800	0.34 (8)	0.06 (1)	0.22 (5)	63	0.15 (4)	45
Atkinson et al.[38]	7	500	0.20 (5)	—	—	—	0.08 (2)	40
Schanler et al.[24] + lyophilized human milk	16	800	0.30 (7)	—	—	—	0.18 (4)	58
Schanler et al.[26] + bovine milk–based liquid formula	12	800 (150)	0.46 (11)	0.04 (1)	0.25 (6)	55	0.17 (4)	57
Bovine milk–based infant formula								
Low Ca, P								
Atkinson et al.[38]	7	500 (100)	0.60 (14)	—	—	—	0.15 (4)	25
Schanler et al.[34]	14	800 (100)	0.50 (12)	0.04 (1)	0.17 (4)	33	0.13 (3)	25
Moya et al.[49]	8	0	0.30 (7)	—	—	—	0.18 (4)	58
Moya et al.[49] + Ca lactate	8	0	0.42 (10)	—	—	—	0.24 (6)	57
Giles et al.[50] +Ca gluconate/Cl & K phosphate/Cl	8	550	0.42 (10)	0.04 (1)	0.08 (2)	20	<0.02 (0.5)	<5
Giles et al.[50] +Ca gluconate/Cl & K phosphate/Cl & Mg supplement	10	550	0.84 (20)	0.10 (2.4)	0.42 (10)	50	0.29 (7)	35
Schanler et al.[26] **Intermediate Ca, P**	10	800 (100)	0.50 (12)	0.08 (2)	0.25 (6)	50	0.25 (6)	42
Wirth et al.[30] **High Ca, P**	8	240 (250)	0.71 (17)	0.09 (2)	0.38 (9)	53	0.29 (7)	42

*Number in parentheses indicates estimated additional daily vitamin D intake from infant formula.
†Number in parentheses is in mg.
Conversion: Mg 1 mmol = 24 mg

Caution is needed in the use of high Ca:P ratio of >2.2:1 by weight because, in the presence of good Ca absorption (or absence of Ca sedimentation), this ratio could theoretically lead to a relative P deficiency syndrome. (J. Senterre)

In contrast, Ca:P ratios of high-mineral formula and human-milk mineral fortifier designed for preterm infants are 1.4:1 to 1.6:1 molar ratio (approximately 1.8:1 to 2:1 by weight). When delivered at about 3.70 to 5.80 mmol (148 to 232 mg) of Ca and 2.45 to 4.13 mmol (76 to 128 mg) of P per kg per day, the Ca and P retention rates in these infants have been consistently at or above the values for in utero accretion.[25,27,29,30]

Metabolic bone disease, as indicated by standard biochemical and radiographic findings, has been successfully treated with small doses of P alone (0.81 to 1.29 mmol [25 to 40 mg]/kg/day)[98,99] or Ca at 0.75 to 1.50 mmol (30 to 60 mg)/kg/day and P at 0.67 to 1.0 mmol (20 to 30 mg)/kg/day.[97,101] The severity and frequency of standard radiographic changes of bone disease were less in preterm infants fed mineral-fortified, bovine milk–based formulas with an average intake of about 5.5 mmol (220 mg) Ca, 2.8 mmol (87 mg) P per kg per day, and 460 IU vitamin D per day when compared with those fed standard bovine-milk formula[112]; they were also less in very low-birthweight infants fed human milk supplemented from the third day after birth with mixed mono- and dibasic phosphate solution given as 25 to 50 mg of elemental P in two divided doses daily compared with an unsupplemented group.[128] However, treatment or prevention of metabolic bone disease based on interpretation of standard radiographs may not equate with normal bone mineralization, since significant radiographic changes of bone demineralization are not evident until approximately 40% of mineral has been lost from the skeleton.

Conflicting reports on the success in matching postnatal changes in bone mineral content (BMC) (as determined by single photon absorptiometry) to the in utero rate of increase in BMC[105,111,129,130] may be due in part to individual variations in mineral absorption and differences in bioavailability of mineral fortifiers. Studies reporting the achievement of fetal rates of increase in BMC used a total Ca intake of 5.25 to 6.25 mmol (210 to 250 mg)/kg/day and total P intake of 3.61 to 4.03 mmol (112 to 125 mg)/kg/day.[105,111] Thus, in selected infants, higher amounts of mineral intake may be needed. However, if this approach is taken, complete delivery of intended amounts of Ca and P should be confirmed, and infants should be evaluated for clinical tolerance as well as monitored by laboratory tests (see Recommendations section).

Duration of Ca and P supplementation is inversely related to the gestational age or birthweight of the infant. Six to 8 weeks of increased mineral supplementation may be insufficient to prevent rickets and fractures in ELBW infants with birthweights <800 g.[110,131] In small preterm infants who received 6 to 8 weeks of high mineral formula, BMC as determined by single photon absorptiometry continues to remain significantly lower than the "intrauterine" BMC curve.[108,129] The occurrence of rickets and fractures is greatest at 2 to 4 months and is rare beyond 6 months after birth.[109,110,132] Several studies have documented that by 6 to 9 months after birth, the distal forearm BMC of small preterm infants is within the normal range of BMC for infants born at term. Bone mineral content continues to increase throughout infancy and childhood in association with increasing skeletal size; i.e., height and weight are significant covariates of BMC.[106,133–136] In one report, the mid-forearm BMC of 15 preterm infants 25 to 34 weeks gestational age had reached the BMC values for term infants after 60 weeks postmenstrual age.[137] According to anecdotal reports,[97,99,101,102] only preterm infants who never received adequate amounts of mineral supplementation from birth (e.g., infants who received low or no Ca and P in PN solution followed by intermittent periods of low-mineral milk feedings) required prolonged mineral supplementation beyond term-postmenstrual age. Some infants' mineral status may be further compromised by the use of diuretics and steroids. There is no proven advantage if Ca and P intake matches the maximum in utero accretion rate beyond a bodyweight of 3 to 3.5 kg.

Theoretically, the requirement for vitamin D may be affected by the availability of substrates, including vitamin D, Ca, and P,[138–141] and the effect of $1,25(OH)_2D$, which increases the metabolic clearance of 25-OHD.[142–144] Early studies reported that preterm infants had poor vitamin D status[145–149] as indicated by low serum 25-OHD concentrations in some preterm infants with early onset hypocalcemia[145] and a decrease in serum 25-OHD concentration in preterm infants at 1 week after birth compared to cord values, in spite of oral (about 500 to 600 IU/day) and intravenous (171 to 464 IU/day) vitamin D supplementation.[146] With enteral vitamin D supplementation of 400 IU[147,148] or 750 IU/day,[149] low serum 25-OHD concentrations were reported in small preterm infants fed human milk[147,149] or standard (low Ca and P) infant formulas.[147,148] Prolonged feeding of low Ca/low P milk and low vitamin D intake in small preterm infants may result in low serum 25-OHD concentration and suggests a diagnosis of vitamin D deficiency, as has been reported in term infants who received prolonged, exclusive human-milk feeding.[139,142] However, it is likely that elevation of serum $1,25(OH)_2D$ concentrations related to mineral deficiency could enhance the metabolism of 25-OHD and further lower serum 25-OHD concentrations. Thus, a higher vitamin D intake theoretically may be needed with low mineral intake and a lower vitamin D intake with high mineral intake.

In contrast, in infants at >30 weeks gestation serum 25-OHD and $1,25(OH)_2D$ concentrations can be increased to normal or even supranormal ranges for older infants and children within the first 5 days of supplementation with 1,200 to 2,100 IU of vitamin D per day.[63-65] Serum 25-OHD concentrations also were normalized and serum $1,25(OH)_2D$ concentrations were elevated within 9 days from a daily supplementation with 500 IU of vitamin D.[66,67] Preterm infants of birthweight <1,250 g and gestational age <32 weeks who received high mineral–containing bovine milk–based formulas and a daily intake of approximately 400 IU vitamin D maintained normal serum 25-OHD and elevated $1,25(OH)_2D$ concentrations from as early as 2 weeks after birth.[31] One longitudinal study of 71 preterm infants with mean birthweight of 1 kg demonstrated that normal serum 25-OHD and appropriately elevated $1,25(OH)_2D$ concentrations can be maintained between 3 and 12 months with a daily vitamin D supplement of 400 IU.[104] In preterm very low-birthweight infants fed human milk or standard infant formula, longitudinal measurements over 2 to 3 months showed that serum 25-OHD concentrations were within normal ranges with a daily vitamin D supplementation of 400 IU or 800 IU.[150-153] However, with a daily vitamin D supplementation of 2,000 IU, serum 25-OHD concentrations were consistently at the high normal level or slightly above the upper limit of normal.[153] Furthermore, an increase of vitamin D supplementation of 2,000 IU/day in preterm infants did not prevent development of radiographic osteopenia and rickets[153,154] and was not more effective than a daily vitamin D supplement of 400 IU.[154]

The use of soy formula, in spite of its relatively high Ca and P content, is associated with high frequency of fractures and rickets in small preterm infants.[132] The phytate in soy formula is thought to be responsible for binding the P and reducing absorption.[47,51] Use of soy formula in term infants is reported to result in lower BMC as measured by photon absorptiometry when compared to infants fed bovine milk–based formula or human milk.[155,156] However, newer formulations of soy formula with lower protein content and improved mineral suspension appear to result in appropriate mineral retention[47] and normal BMC,[157,158] at least in infants born at term. Nevertheless, until more data are available, there is no specific indication for the use of soy formula in preterm infants.

Deficiency

In many infants, there is no easily recognizable syndrome allowing early diagnosis of specific nutritional deficiency of Ca, Mg, or P, since many of the clinical signs are nonspecific and can occur in the sick infant for other reasons.

Nutritional deficiency of Ca alone is rarely diagnosed. It may, in part, contribute to the cause of early neonatal hypocalcemia that occurs within the first 2 to 3 days after delivery.[55,68] Late-onset neonatal hypocalcemia that usually occurs about 1 to 2 weeks after delivery is probably associated with a relative excess of P intake from infant formulas with Ca:P ratio <1.5:1 by weight and possibly coupled with a relatively inadequate parathyroid response.[159] Prolonged, limited Ca intake coupled with increased urinary loss of Ca from chronic diuretic usage in sick infants also may contribute to bone demineralization and rickets in small preterm infants.[42,54,55,160]

Nutritional deficiency of P has typical biochemical features, including hypophosphatemia, hypercalcemia, hypophosphaturia, and hypercalciuria. Phosphorus deficiency contributes to bone demineralization and rickets in small preterm infants with low mineral intake.[39,97-99] In preterm infants who receive unsupplemented human-milk feedings, hypophosphatemia (serum P<1.30 mmol/L; <4 mg/dL) and sometimes hypercalcemia (serum Ca>2.75 mmol/L; >11 mg/dL) are noted.[161] In infants receiving intravenous fluid or PN, extreme hypophosphatemia (serum P<0.49 mmol/L or <1.5 mg/dL) may occur with inadequate or no P administration, and be further aggravated by injudicious use of fluid and electrolyte therapy which increases urinary P loss and intercompartmental shifts of P.[40,69,72] In growing preterm infants, addition of Ca salts or protein without phosphate supplementation in human milk should be avoided since it may theoretically aggravate the P depletion syndrome by further increasing urinary Ca excretion and risk of nephrocalcinosis. Rapid increase in nutrient delivery after a prolonged period of inadequate nutrition is responsible for a relative deficiency in P and resultant hypophosphatemia as a part of the "refeeding" syndrome.[162] Phosphorus deficiency is often only one facet of the typical "hypophosphatemic syndrome,"[163,164] since the condition usually occurs in the sick infant with complex disorders and multiple nutrient deficiencies.

Biochemical evidence of mineral deficiency, specifically hypophosphatemia, raised serum-alkaline phosphatase activity,[165] and lower BMC,[106,107] persists for longer periods in preterm infants fed human milk compared to formula-fed infants. In small preterm infants with nutritional rickets and fractures, longitudinal study showed that their growth and

BMC as determined by photon absorptiometry remained less than in those who did not develop rickets and fractures throughout the first year after birth.[135] In one series of preterm infants with birthweights <1,850 g, the number of infants with extremely elevated serum–alkaline phosphatase activity, presumably a reflection of Ca and P deficiency, was twice as high in those fed human milk compared to those who received an average of 4 weeks of a preterm infant formula with Ca and P content of 18.8 mmol (750 mg)/L and 11.3 mmol (350 mg)/L, respectively. Follow-up at 9 and 18 months showed significantly shorter body length in those infants with the highest serum–alkaline phosphatase activities.[166] Other reports showed that by 1 year after birth, preterm infants fed unsupplemented human milk after hospital discharge reached within one[165] or two[106] standard deviations of the growth recorded for term infants.

Unreplaced Mg losses from chronic gastrointestinal or biliary fistula, combined with injudicious use of fluid and electrolyte therapy, probably are the major causes of Mg deficiency in infants.[40,76] Specific Mg malabsorption syndromes as a cause of Mg deficiency occur rarely.

Vitamin D deficiency as indicated by low serum 25-OHD concentrations have been reported in preterm infants fed low-mineral milks despite the provision of 500 to 750 IU of vitamin D daily.[147–149] The potential for development of vitamin D deficiency increases if there is poor vitamin D status in the mother, since the vitamin D store of most infants is depleted in <8 weeks, even in those born to mothers with normal vitamin D status.[62,139]

Toxicity

Under usual circumstances, toxicity associated with Ca, Mg, and P is usually iatrogenic. Fortunately, most of the potential toxicity associated with disturbed serum concentrations and tissue content of these elements is preventable by meticulous attention to details of fluid and electrolyte management, mechanical ventilatory efforts to minimize acid-base disturbances, and judicious use of diuretic therapy.

The major source of potential toxicity occurs with parenteral administration of these minerals. Excessive or unbalanced administration of Ca, Mg, or P results in abnormally elevated circulating concentrations of these minerals, with their clinical sequelae.[40,55,68] Metastatic calcification may occur from excess Ca and P.[167,168] Hypermagnesemia is a well-known complication of PN (see earlier comments). In contrast, the intestinal tract and the physicochemical dietary interactions described earlier are to some extent effective barriers against excessive absorption of orally administered Ca, Mg, and P.

Calcium, Mg, and P toxicity can also result from therapeutic maneuvers not directly related to the administration of these minerals. For example, fluid restriction in association with Ca and P supplementation apparently can cause intestinal milk curds and intestinal obstruction. Calcium- and P- containing bezoars have been reported in relation to Ca and P supplementation of human milk to a total high intake of about 6.3 mmol (250 mg) Ca and 6.5 mmol (200 mg) P per kg per day[169] or Ca and P supplementation of infant formula to a total intake of about 5.9 mmol (235 mg) Ca and 3.6 mmol (112 mg) P per kg per day.[125] Chronic furosemide administration may be associated with nephrocalcinosis[120,170] and cholelithiasis[171] when coupled with high Ca intake. Thiazide diuretics are effective in reducing the calciuric effect of furosemide.[170] However, use of a thiazide diuretic may be associated with hypokalemia, hypercalcemia, and other metabolic disturbances,[172] and its efficacy and safety in the neonate require further study.

Vitamin D toxicity is usually iatrogenic, and it is characterized by nausea, vomiting, failure to thrive, hypercalcemia, hypercalciuria, polyuria, and ectopic calcification. These signs are usually associated with very large vitamin D intakes of >10,000 IU/kg/day, but cases have been described with prolonged intake of 4,000 IU/kg/day over many weeks.[139,173]

Toxins also may be given to infants incidental to the delivery of Ca, Mg, and P. Aluminum contamination of parenteral[174] and enteral[175] nutrients has not been documented to result in toxicity.[176] However, aluminum may persist in the bone for long periods[177] and tissue aluminum can be mobilized to the rest of the body; aluminum contamination of infant nutrients should remain a cause of some concern.

Recommendations

The following recommended intakes should be considered a guideline, and serial biochemical monitoring—in particular, of serum concentrations of Ca, Mg, and P and alkaline phosphatase activity—are necessary throughout the period of high mineral intake. The frequency of monitoring initially may be once daily during initial adjustments in mineral content of PN solution or oral Ca and P supplements until the measured variables become stabilized; thereafter, measurements can be made once every 1 to 2 weeks until ''catch-up'' growth is completed (i.e., until 40 weeks postmenstrual age and >3 kg in bodyweight). Other biochemical measurements (serum osteocalcin, procollagen, urinary excretion of Ca and P), serum vitamin D metabolites, radiograph of wrists, bone densitometry, and renal ultrasound studies may be performed as needed.[40,43,54,80,178–180]

In addition, many very small preterm infants have complex illnesses, and prudence in the use of therapeutic measures is critical to optimize delivery and retention of Ca, Mg, and P, and minimize potential side effects of high mineral intake.

Parenteral Intake (Table 10.6)

The mineral needs of preterm infants are relatively low during the *transition period,* although current PN solutions with high Ca and P contents appear well tolerated and no persistent adverse biochemical changes have been reported. We suggest that these solutions can be used throughout the first 6 months after birth.

Attention to details during the preparation of PN solutions should ensure the solubility of the recommended amounts of Ca and P under normal nursery conditions,[86,87] although each institution should establish Ca and P solubility curves for their PN solutions. The recommended amounts of Ca and P should be increased stepwise over the first 3 days from approximately 70% of the intended maximum content. This buildup allows for physiologic adaptation to the increased mineral loading. Daily monitoring of serum Ca, Mg, and P concentrations for the first 3 to 4 days and thereafter at weekly intervals are the minimum necessary to monitor disturbances in the Ca, Mg, and P homeostasis.

The Mg needs are probably comparable in all preterm infants, but a Mg content of 3 mmol (72 mg)/L may be needed if there is gastrointestinal fluid loss.

Vitamin D needs for infants receiving total PN are minimal. However, the upper range of advisable intake (i.e., 160 IU/kg/day) may be useful for the majority of preterm infants who are also given some enteral feeding. In any case, a maximum total intake of 400 IU/day appears sufficient to maintain normal vitamin D status.

Enteral Intake (Table 10.7)

During the transition period, human milk has many potential benefits and can be used without mineral supplementation provided that PN solution is the major source of Ca and P intake. Alternately, human milk fortified with minerals or high-mineral preterm infant formula also appears to be well tolerated clinically and can be used during this period.

During the stable period of rapid growth, the best means to increase retention of Ca and P appears to be early introduction of high Ca- and P-containing enteral feeding. This early introduction should be possible in all but the most ill infants, particularly infants who have reached 30 weeks gestation (i.e., prior to the period of maximal mineral needs).

For breast-fed infants, powder[25,115] or liquid[27] fortifier can be mixed with expressed breast milk as per manufacturer's recommendations; use of liquid fortifier without mixing with human milk is inappropriate. Alternately, in thriving infants being fed human milk ad libitum (i.e., who are probably at low risk for deficiency of other nutrients), direct supplementation with Ca and P may be adequate. There are a number of Ca and P salts used successfully for this purpose.[23,97–99,101,114,115,128,181] Suitable preparations include Ca as calcium glubionate (2.88 mmol [115 mg] elemental Ca per 5 mL) or calcium gluceptate (2.25 mmol [90 mg] elemental Ca per 5 mL), and P as sodium or potassium mixed mono- and dibasic (less soluble) phosphate (3 mmol [93 mg] elemental P per mL) which may be given directly to the infant at time of feeding[97–99,101] or by mixing P with expressed milk followed by addition of Ca.[23] Based on the above reports, the

Table 10.6. Advisable Parenteral Intake for Calcium (Ca), Magnesium (Mg), Phosphorus (P), and Vitamin D

	Ca	Mg	P	Vitamin D
mmol/L	12.5–15.0	1.5–2.0	12.5–15.0	
(mg/L)	(500–600)	(36–48)	(390–470)	250–1,000 IU/L[†]
mmol/kg/day*	1.5–2.25	0.18–0.30	1.5–2.25	
(mg/kg/day)	(60–90)	(4.3–7.2)	(47–70)	40–160 IU/kg/day[†]

*Based on an intake of 120–150 mL/kg/day. **Note:** For Ca, Mg, and P, concentration-based (mmol/L or mg/L), NOT per kg per day, recommendations should be used since alterations of fluid volumes by clinical circumstances (such as fluid restriction) could inadvertently result in high mineral concentrations and *precipitation* of minerals. Ca and P content may be adjusted according to biochemical measurements (see text) within the range of 1:1 to 1.3:1 molar ratio or 1.3:1 to 1.7:1 by weight.

[†]Maximum daily total 400 IU.

Conversion: Ca 1 mmol = 40 mg; Mg 1 mmol = 24 mg; P 1 mmol = 31 mg

Table 10.7. Advisable Enteral Intake for Calcium (Ca), Magnesium (Mg), Phosphorus (P), and Vitamin D

	Ca	Mg	P	Vitamin D
mmol/L	20–38.3	2.2–4.2	12.9–30.1	
(mg/L)	(800–1,533)	(55–100)	(400–933)	1,000–2,700 IU/L[†]
mmol/kg/day*	3.0–5.63	0.33–0.63	1.94–4.52	
(mg/kg/day)	(120–230)	(7.9–15)	(60–140)	150–400 IU/kg/day[†]

*Based on an average intake of 150 mL/kg/day at 504 kJ (120 kcal)/kg/day.

[†]Aim to deliver 400 IU daily. Alternately, 400 IU daily supplement can be given directly to infants fed formulas with low vitamin D content.

Conversion: Ca 1 mmol = 40 mg, Mg 1 mmol = 24 mg, P 1 mmol = 31 mg, 1 kJ = 4.2 kcal

amount of elemental Ca and P should be started at 1.25 and 1.0 mmol (50 and 30 mg)/kg/day, respectively, in 4 to 6 equally divided doses. Dose adjustments can be made according to biochemical monitoring. Hypercalcemia with marked hypercalciuria may occur with the use of Ca alone, whereas hypocalcemia with hyperphosphatemia may occur with the use of P alone[97,99]; hypokalemia has been observed in some infants receiving Ca and P supplementation.[181] Serum potassium also should be monitored and potassium phosphate solution used as necessary.

There is currently no evidence that Mg should be supplemented for preterm infants receiving mother's milk. An intake of 0.34 mmol (8 mg)/kg/day should be sufficient to meet the needs of preterm infants, assuming a retention rate of 50%. Magnesium deficiency or overload has not been reported in formula-fed preterm infants, and there is no evidence that the Mg content should exceed 4.2 mmol (100 mg)/L in preterm infant formulas.

During the postdischarge phase, after the body-weight reaches 3 to 3.5 kg (i.e., becomes comparable to the bodyweight of infants born at term), a daily intake equal to the currently recommended daily allowance for term infants[182] (i.e., up to approximately 2.5 mmol [100 mg] Ca, 2.68 mmol [83 mg] P, and 0.42 mmol [10 mg] Mg per kg per day, with a maximum total daily intake of 15 mmol [600 mg] Ca, 16.13 mmol [500 mg] P, and 2.5 mmol [60 mg] Mg) appears to be appropriate.

Vitamin D intake of 400 IU/day should be sufficient and need not exceed 800 IU/day in the presence of adequate mineral intake during the first 6 months after birth.

The higher vitamin D dose may be necessary for 1 to 2 weeks in preterm infants who have poor vitamin D status at birth and relative fat malabsorption during the transition to full enteral feeding. (J. Senterre)

Many nurseries provide multivitamin preparations including vitamin D directly as supplements to preterm infants. Thus it is important to know whether the infant formula is already fortified with vitamin D in order not to provide overdosage. The use of vitamin D metabolites, 25-OHD, 1α-OHD, and 1,25(OH)$_2$D has no proven role except in the presence of cholestasis, when 25-OHD is relatively better absorbed compared to vitamin D.[151,152,183]

Future Research

The enteral intake of nutrients remains the safest and most efficient route to meet the mineral requirements of preterm infants. The multiple factors that influence enteral feeding should be studied in order to maximize the clinical tolerance, absorption, and retention of enterally administered minerals. The need for further increase in parenteral mineral intake as well as the safety and efficacy of alternate sources of Ca and P in PN solutions remain to be defined.

With the increasing survival of ELBW infants and widespread use of mineral-containing infant formulas, the extent of metabolic bone disease in these infants needs to be redefined. There is also a need for more sensitive techniques to determine the rate of change of bone mineralization in preterm infants after birth. The effects of subclinical or marginal mineral deficiency, nonnutritional factors such as aluminum toxicity,[176,177] and physical therapy[184] on skeletal growth, bone mineralization, and the development of rickets and fractures remain to be determined.

CASE STUDY

A female infant with a birthweight of 680 g is born at 26 weeks gestation with a complicated postnatal course. She requires prolonged ventilatory support, one course of dexamethasone, and multiple intermittent doses of furosemide. She is weaned from supplemental oxygen by 8 months of age. Chest percussion (using a rubber conductive face mask) and chest vibration (using a battery-operated vibrator) are prescribed as therapeutic and preventive measures for pulmonary atelectasis. Passive exercises are also prescribed "to minimize increased muscle tone" of the infant. The infant receives repeated courses of PN (containing 1,000 IU of vitamin D_2 [ergocalciferol], 4.5 mmol [180 mg] of elemental calcium, and 6 mmol [186 mg] of phosphorus per liter of infusate) via the peripheral and central venous route. Consistently adequate enteral feeding with preterm infant formula (100 kcal/kg/day) is not achieved until 15 weeks postnatally. Incidental skeletal abnormalities, including severe demineralization and fracture of ribs, are noted on a chest roentgenogram at 15 weeks postnatally. Roentgenograms of forearms and hands obtained immediately afterwards show rickets and fractures of radius and ulna.

Questions and Answers

Q. What are the important risk factors in this infant for osteopenia, fractures, and rickets?
A. Extremely low birthweight; low Ca and P content of PN solution and inadequate intake of enteral feeding during the first 3 months after birth; steroid and diuretic therapy; and physical therapy.

Q. Should $1,25(OH)_2D$ be added to the therapeutic regimen?
A. With adequate mineral intake, 400 IU/day of vitamin D is sufficient to maintain normal vitamin D status. There is no documented advantage to using $1,25(OH)_2D$ or other vitamin D metabolites.

Q. What is the treatment for this infant if she has been fed human milk?
A. Powder or liquid fortifier for human milk and, in certain circumstances, direct Ca and P supplementation.

Q. What could have been done differently in this infant to prevent the osteopenia and fractures?
A. We suspect that a much more aggressive approach to maximize both parenteral and enteral mineral intake early in the course might have helped to prevent this condition. However, at times, even with fairly "aggressive" mineral supplementation, osteopenia and fractures may not be prevented. We need also to be careful to handle such "fragile" infants with gentleness, since "trauma" even in the form of chest percussion and physical therapy can precipitate fractures in a vulnerable infant.

References

1. Sparks JW: Human intrauterine growth and nutrient accretion. *Semin Perinatol* 1984;8:74–93.
2. Greer FR, Tsang RC. Calcium, phosphorus, magnesium, and vitamin D requirements for the preterm infant. In: Tsang RC, ed. *Vitamin and mineral requirements in preterm infants*. New York: Marcel Dekker, 1985:99–136.
3. Ziegler EE, O'Donnell AM, Nelson SE, Fomon SJ. Body composition of the reference fetus. *Growth* 1976; 40:329–341.
4. Widdowson, EM Southgate DAT, Hey E. Fetal growth and body composition. In: Lindblad BS, ed. *Perinatal nutrition*. New York: Academic Press, 1988;4–14.
5. Fransson GB, Lonnerdal B. Zinc, copper, calcium, magnesium in human milk. *J Pediatr* 1982;101:504–508.
6. Fransson GB, Lonnerdal B. Distribution of trace elements and minerals in human and cow's milk. *Pediatr Res* 1983; 17:412–415.
7. Sann L, Bienvenu J, Bienvenu F, Lahet C, Bethenod M. Comparison of the composition of breast milk from mothers of term and preterm infants. *Acta Paediatr Scand* 1981;70:115–160.
8. Lemons JA, Moye L, Hall D, Simmons M. Differences in the composition of preterm and term human milk during early lactation. *Pediatr Res.* 1982;16:113–117.
9. Picciano MF. What constitutes a representative human milk sample? *J Pediatr Gastroenterol Nutr* 1984;3:280–283.
10. Lonnerdal B, Smith C, Keen CL. Analysis of breast milk: current methodologies and future needs. *J Pediatr Gastroenterol Nutr* 1984;3:290–295.
11. Greer FR, Tsang RC, Levin RS, Searcy JE, Wu R, Steichen JJ. Increasing serum calcium and magnesium concentrations in breast-fed infants: longitudinal studies of minerals in human milk and in sera of nursing mothers and their infants. *J Pediatr* 1982;100:59–64.
12. Allen JC, Keller RP, Archer P, Neville MC. Studies in human lactation: milk composition and daily secretion rates of macronutrients in the first year of lactation. *Am J Clin Nutr* 1991;54:69–80.
13. Tsang RC, Nichols BL, eds. *Nutrition in infancy*. Philadelphia: Hanley & Belfus, 1988:420.
14. Reichel H, Koeffler HP, Norman AW. The role of the vitamin D endocrine system in health and disease. *N Engl J Med* 1989;320:980–990.
15. Mundy GR. *Calcium homeostasis: hypercalcemia and hypocalcemia*. 2nd ed. London: Martin Dunitz, 1990:17–28.
16. Fraser DR. Physiology of vitamin D and calcium homeostasis. In: Glorieux FH, ed. *Rickets*. New York: Raven Press, 1991:23–24.
17. Ehrenkranz RA, Ackerman BA, Nelli CM, Janghorbani M. Absorption of calcium in premature infants as measured with a stable isotope ^{46}Ca extrinsic tag. *Pediatr Res* 1985;19:178–184.
18. Moore LJ, Machlan LA, Lim MO, Yergey AL, Hansen JW. Dynamics of calcium metabolism in infancy and childhood. I. Methodology and quantification in the infant. *Pediatr Res* 1985;19:329–334.
19. Liu Y-M, Neal P, Ernst J, et al. Absorption of calcium and magnesium from fortified human milk by very low birth weight infants. *Pediatr Res* 1989;25:496–502.
20. Abrams SA, Esteban NV, Viera NE, Yergey AL. Dual tracer stable isotopic assessment of calcium absorption and endogenous fecal excretion in low birth weight infants. *Pediatr Res* 1991;29:615–618.
21. Barltrop D, Mole RH, Sutton A. Absorption and endogenous faecal excretion of calcium by low birthweight infants on feeds with varying contents of calcium and phosphate. *Arch Dis Child* 1977;52:41–49.
22. Hillman LS, Tack E, Covell DG, Vieira NE, Yergey AL. Measurement of true calcium absorption in premature infants using intravenous ^{46}Ca and oral ^{44}Ca. *Pediatr Res* 1988;23:589–594.
23. Salle B, Senterre J, Putet G, Rigo J. Effects of calcium and phosphorus supplementation on calcium retention and fat absorption in preterm infants fed pooled human milk. *J Pediatr Gastroenterol Nutr* 1986;5:638–642.

24. Schanler RJ, Garza C. Improved mineral balance in very low birth weight infants fed fortified human milk. *J Pediatr* 1988;112:452–456.
25. Ehrenkranz RA, Gettner PA, Nelli CM. Nutrient balance studies in premature infants fed premature formula or fortified human milk. *J Pediatr Gastroenterol Nutr* 1989;8:58–67.
26. Schanler RJ, Abrams SA, Garza C. Bioavailability of calcium and phosphorus in human milk fortifiers and formula for very low birth weight infants. *J Pediatr* 1988;113:95–100.
27. Raschko PK, Hiller JL, Benda GI, NRM Buist, Wilcox K, Reynolds JW. Nutritional balance studies of VLBW infants fed their mothers' milk fortified with a liquid human milk fortifier. *J Pediatr Gastroenterol Nutr* 1990; 9:212–218.
28. Lyon AJ, McIntosh N. Calcium and phosphorus balance in extremely low birthweight infants in the first six weeks of life. *Arch Dis Child* 1984;59:1145–1150.
29. Rowe JC, Goetz CA, Carey DE, Horak E. Achievement of in utero retention of calcium and phosphorus accompanied by high calcium excretion in very low birth weight infants fed a fortified formula. *J Pediatr* 1987;110:581–585.
30. Wirth FH Jr, Numerof B, Pleban P, Neylan MJ. Effects of lactose on mineral absorption in preterm infants. *J Pediatr* 1990;117:283–287.
31. Cooke R, Hollis B, Conner C, Watson D, Werkman S, Chesney R. Vitamin D and mineral metabolism in the very low birth weight infant receiving 400 IU of vitamin D. *J Pediatr* 1990;116:423–428.
32. Fine KD, Santa Ana CA, Porter JL, Fordtran JS. Intestinal absorption of magnesium from food and supplements. *J Clin Invest* 1991;88:396–402.
33. Hardwick LL, Jones MR, Brautbar N, Lee DBN. Magnesium absorption: mechanisms and the influence of vitamin D, calcium and phosphate. *J Nutr* 1991;121:13–23.
34. Schanler RJ, Garza C, Smith EO. Fortified mothers' milk for very low birth weight infants: results of macromineral balance studies. *J Pediatr* 1985;107:767–774.
35. Cross HS, Debiec H, Peterlik M: Mechanism and regulation of intestinal phosphate absorption. *Miner Electrolyte Metab* 1990;16:115–124.
36. Senterre J, Salle B. Calcium and phosphorus economy of the preterm infant and its interaction with vitamin D and its metabolites. *Acta Paediatr Scand* 1982;296(suppl):85–92.
37. Senterre J, Putet G, Salle B, Rigo J. Effects of vitamin D and phosphorus supplementation on calcium retention in preterm infants fed banked human milk. *J Pediatr* 1983; 103:305–307.
38. Atkinson SA, Radde IC, Anderson GH. Macromineral balances in premature infants fed their own mothers' milk or formula. *J Pediatr* 1983;102:99–106.
39. Carey DE, Goetz CA, Horak E, Rowe JC. Phosphorus wasting during phosphorus supplementation of human milk feedings in preterm infants. *J Pediatr* 1985;107:790–794.
40. Koo WWK, Tsang RC. Calcium, magnesium and phosphorus. In: Tsang RC, Nichols BL, eds. *Nutrition in infancy*. Philadelphia: Hanley and Belfus, 1988:175–189.
41. Schanler RJ. Calcium and phosphorus absorption and retention in preterm infants. In: *Wyeth ayerst: nutrition seminar series*. New York: Exerpta Medica, 1991;4: 24–36.
42. Atkinson SA, Shah JK. Calcium and phosphorus fortification of preterm formulas: drug-mineral and mineral-mineral interactions. In: *Wyeth Ayerst: nutrition seminar series*. New York: Exerpta Medica, 1991;4:58–74.
43. Senterre J. Osteopenia versus rickets in premature infants. In: Glorieux F, eds. *Rickets*. New York: Raven Press, 1991:145–152.
44. Ziegler EE, Fomon SJ. Lactose enhances mineral absorption in infancy. *J Pediatr Gastroenterol Nutr* 1983;2: 288–294.
45. Moya M, Cortes E, Ballester MI, Vento M, Juste M. Short-term polycose substitution for lactose reduces calcium absorption in healthy term babies. *J Pediatr Gastroenterol Nutr* 1992;14:57–61.
46. Katz L, Hamilton JR. Fat absorption in infants with birth weight less than 1,300 g. *J Pediatr* 1974;85:608–614.
47. De Vizia B, Fomon SJ, Nelson SE, Edwards BE, Ziegler EE. Effect of dietary calcium on metabolic balance of normal infants. *Pediatr Res* 1985;19:800–806.
48. Chappell JE, Clandinin MT, Kearney-Volpe C, Reichman B, Swyer PW. Fatty acid balance studies in premature infants fed human milk or formula: effect of calcium supplementation. *J Pediatr* 1986;108:439–447.
49. Moya M, Domenech E. Role of calcium-phosphate ratio of milk formulae on calcium balance in low birth weight infants during the first three days of life. *Pediatr Res* 1982;16:675–681.
50. Giles MM, Laing IA, Elton RA, Robins JB, Sanderson M, Hume R. Magnesium metabolism in preterm infants: effects of calcium, magnesium, and phosphorus, and of postnatal and gestational age. *J Pediatr* 1990;117: 147–154.
51. Shenai JP, Jhaveri BM, Reynolds JW, Huston RK, Babson SG. Nutritional balance studies in very low birth weight infants: role of soy formula. *Pediatrics* 1981; 67:631–637.
52. Ehrenkranz RA, Gettner PA, Nelli CM, Sherwonit EA, Williams JE, Ting BT. Zinc and copper nutritional studies in very low birth weight infants: comparison of stable isotopic extrinsic tag and chemical balance methods. *Pediatr Res* 1989;26:298–307.
53. Ehrenkranz RA, Gettner PA, Nelli CM, et al. Iron absorption and incorporation into red blood cells by very low birthweight infants: studies with the stable isotope [58]Fe. *J Pediatr Gastroenterol Nutr* 1993. In press.
54. Koo WWK, Tsang RC. Bone mineralization in infants. *Prog Food Nutr Sci* 1984;8:229–302.
55. Koo WWK, Tsang RC. Calcium and magnesium metabolism. In: Werner M, ed. *CRC handbook of clinical chemistry*. Boca Raton, FL: CRC Press, 1989;2: 51–91.
56. Senterre J, Salle B. Renal aspects of calcium and phosphorus metabolism in preterm infants. *Biol Neonate* 1988;53:220–229.
57. Hollis BW, Roos BA, Draper HH, Lambert PW. Vitamin D and its metabolites in human and bovine milk. *J Nutr* 1981;111:1240–1248.
58. Reeve LE, Chesney RW, DeLuca HF. Vitamin D of human milk: identification of biologically active forms. *Am J Clin Nutr* 1982;36:122–126.
59. Lammi-Keefe CJ, Jensen RG. Fat soluble vitamins in human milk. *Nutr Rev* 1984;42:365–370.
60. Hollis BW, Pittard WB III, Reinhardt TA. Relationship among vitamin D, 25-hydroxyvitamin D, and vitamin D-binding protein concentrations in the plasma and milk of human subjects. *J Clin Endocrinol Metab* 1986; 62:41–44.
61. Specker BL, Tsang RC, Hollis BW. Effect of race and diet on human-milk vitamin D and 25-hydroxyvitamin D. *Am J Dis Child* 1985;139:1134–1137.
62. Hoogenboezem T, Degenhart HJ, De Muinck SMPF, et al. Vitamin D metabolism in breast-fed infants and their mothers. *Pediatr Res* 1989;25:623–628.
63. Glorieux F, Salle B, Delvin E, David L. Vitamin D metabolism in premature infants: serum calcitriol values during the first five days of life. *J Pediatr* 1981;99:640–643.

64. Salle B, David L, Glorieux F, Delvin E, Senterre J, Renaud H. Early oral administration of vitamin D and its metabolites in premature neonates on mineral homeostasis. *Pediatr Res* 1982;16:75–78.

65. Salle BL, Glorieux FH, Delvin EE, David LS, Meunier G. Vitamin D metabolism in preterm infants. Serial serum calcitriol values during the first four days of life. *Acta Paediatr Scand* 1983;72:203–206.

66. Markestad T, Asknes L, Finne P, Aarskog D. Vitamin D nutritional status of premature infants supplemented with 500 IU vitamin D_2 per day. *Acta Paediatr Scand* 1983;72:517–520.

67. Markestad T, Asknes L, Finne P, Aarskog D. Plasma concentrations of vitamin D metabolites in premature infants. *Pediatr Res* 1984;18:269–272.

68. Koo WWK, Tsang RC. Neonatal calcium and phosphorus disorders. In: Lifshitz F, ed. *Pediatric endocrinology: a clinical guide.* 2nd ed. New York: Marcel Dekker, 1990:569–611.

69. Koo WWK, Tsang RC, Steichen JJ, et al. Parenteral nutrition for infants: effect of high versus low calcium and phosphorus content. *J Pediatr Gastroenterol Nutr* 1987;6:96–104.

70. MacMahon P, Blair ME, Treweeke P, Kovar IZ. Association of mineral composition of neonatal intravenous feeding solutions and metabolic bone disease of prematurity. *Arch Dis Child* 1989;64:489–493.

71. Pelegano JF, Rowe JC, Carey DE, et al. Simultaneous infusion of calcium and phosphorus in parenteral nutrition for premature infants: use of physiologic calcium/phosphorus ratio. *J Pediatr* 1989;114:115–119.

72. Koo WWK, Tsang RC, Succop P, Krug-Wispe SK, Babcock D, Oestreich AE. Minimal vitamin D and high calcium and phosphorus needs of preterm infants receiving parenteral nutrition. *J Pediatr Gastroenterol Nutr* 1989;8:225–233.

73. Chessex P, Pineault M, Brisson G, Delvin EE, Glorieux FH. Role of the source of phosphate salt in improving the mineral balance of parenterally fed low birth weight infants. *J Pediatr* 1990;116:765–772.

74. Pelegano JF, Rowe JC, Carey DE, et al. Effect of calcium/phosphorus ratio on mineral retention in parenterally fed premature infants. *J Pediatr Gastroenterol Nutr* 1991;12:351–355.

75. Hanning RM, Atkinson SA, Whyte RK. Efficacy of calcium glycerophosphate vs conventional mineral salts for total parenteral nutrition in low-birth-weight infants: a randomized clinical trial. *Am J Clin Nutr* 1991;54:903–908.

76. Koo WWK, Fong T, Gupta JM. Parenteral nutrition in infants. *Aust Paediatr J* 1980;16:169–174.

77. Randall HT. Water and Electrolyte balance in surgery. *Surg Clin North Am* 1952;32:445–469.

78. Thoren L. Magnesium deficiency in gastrointestinal fluid loss. *Acta Chir Scand* 1963;306(suppl):1–65.

79. Wolman SL, Anderson GH, Marliss EB, Jeejeebhoy KN. Zinc in total parenteral nutrition. requirement and metabolic effects. *Gastroenterology* 1980;76:458–467.

80. Koo WWK, Tsang RC. Mineral requirements of low-birth-weight infants. *J Am Coll Nutr* 1991;10:474–486.

81. Ricour C, Millot M, Balsan S. Phosphorus depletion in children on long term total parenteral nutrition. *Acta Paediatr Scand* 1975;64:385–392.

82. Chessex P, Pineault M, Zebiche H, Ayotte RA. Calciuria in parenterally fed preterm infants: role of phosphorus intake. *J Pediatr* 1985;107:794–796.

83. Vileisis RA. Effect of phosphorus intake in total parenteral nutrition infusates in premature neonates. *J Pediatr* 1987;110:586–590.

84. Kimura S, Nose O, Seino Y, et al. Effect of alternate and simultaneous administrations of calcium and phosphorus on calcium metabolism in children receiving total parenteral nutrition. *J Parenter Enteral Nutr* 1986;10:513–516.

85. Hoehn GJ, Carey DE, Rowe JC, Horak E, Raye JR. Alternate day infusion of calcium and phosphate in very low birth weight infants: wasting of the infused mineral. *J Pediatr Gastroenterol Nutr* 1987;6:752–757.

86. Koo WWK. Calcium, phosphorus and vitamin D requirements of infants receiving parenteral nutrition. *J Perinatol* 1988;8:263–268.

87. Dunham B, Marcuard S, Khazanie PG, Meade G, Craft T, Nichols K. The solubility of calcium and phosphorus in neonatal total parenteral nutrition solutions. *J Parenter Enteral Nutr* 1991;15:608–611.

88. MacMahon P, Mayne PD, Blair M, Pope C, Kovar IZ. Calcium and phosphorus solubility in neonatal intravenous feeding solutions. *Arch Dis Child* 1990;65:352–353.

89. Draper HH, Yuen DE, Whyte RK. Calcium glycerophosphate as a source of calcium and phosphorus in total parenteral nutrition solutions. *J Parenter Enteral Nutr* 1991;15:176–180.

90. Raupp R, von Kries R, Pfahl H-G, Manz F: Glycero- vs glucose-phosphate in parenteral nutrition of premature infants: a comparative in vitro evaluation of calcium phosphorus compatibility. *J Parenter Enteral Nutr* 1991;15:469–473.

91. Greene HL, Moore CME, Phillips B, et al. Evaluation of a pediatric multivitamin preparation for total parenteral nutrition. II. Blood levels of vitamins A, D, and E. *Pediatrics* 1986;77:539–547.

92. Koo WWK, Tsang RC, Steichen JJ, et al. Vitamin D requirement in infants receiving parenteral nutrition. *J Parenter Enteral Nutr* 1987;11:172–176.

93. Baeckert PA, Greene HL, Fritz I, Oelberg DG, Adcock EW. Vitamin concentrations in very low birth weight infants given vitamins intravenously in a lipid emulsion: measurement of vitamins A, D, and E and riboflavin. *J Pediatr* 1988;113:1057–1065.

94. Greene HL, Hambidge KM, Schanler R, Tsang RC. Guidelines for the use of vitamins, trace elements, calcium, magnesium, and phosphorus in infants and children receiving total parenteral nutrition: report of the Subcommittee on Pediatric Parenteral Nutrient Requirements from the Committee on Clinical Practice Issues of the American Society for Clinical Nutrition. *Am J Clin Nutr* 1988;48:1324–1342.

95. Committee on Nutrition, American Academy of Pediatrics. Nutritional needs of low birth weight infants. *Pediatrics* 1985;75:976–986.

96. Committee on Nutrition of the Preterm Infant, European Society of Paediatric Gastroenterology and Nutrition. Nutrition and feeding of preterm infants. *Acta Paediatr Scand* 1987;336(suppl):1–14.

97. Rowe JC, Wood DH, Rowe DW, Raisz LG. Nutritional hypophosphatemic rickets in a premature infant fed breast milk. *N Engl J Med* 1979;300:293–296.

98. Sagy M, Birenbaum E, Balin A, Orda S, Barzilay Z, Brish M. Phosphate-depletion syndrome in a premature infant fed human milk. *J Pediatr* 1980;96:683–685.

99. Koo WWK, Antony G, Stevens LHS. Continuous nasogastric phosphorus infusion in hypophosphatemic rickets of prematurity. *Am J Dis Child* 1984;138:172–175.

100. Rowe JC, Carey DE. Phosphorus deficiency syndrome in very low birth weight infants. *Pediatr Clin North Am* 1987;34:997–1017.

101. Greer RF, Steichen JJ, Tsang RC. Calcium and phosphate supplements in breast milk-related rickets. *Am J Dis Child* 1982;136:581–583.

102. Raupp P, von Kries R, Schmiedlau D, Manz F. Biochemical evidence for the need of long-term mineral supplementation in an extremely low birth weight infant fed own mother's milk exclusively during the first six months of life. *Eur J Pediatr* 1990;149:806–808.

103. Steichen JJ, Tsang RC, Greer FR, Ho M, Hug G. Elevated serum 1,25 dihydroxyvitamin D concentration in rickets of very low birth weight infants. *J Pediatr* 1981;99:293–298.

104. Koo WWK, Sherman R, Succop P, Ho M, Buckley D, Tsang RC. Serum vitamin D metabolites in very low birth weight infants with and without rickets and fractures. *J Pediatr* 1989;114:1017–1022.

105. Steichen JJ, Gratton TL, Tsang RC. Osteopenia of prematurity: the cause and possible treatment. *J Pediatr* 1980;96:528–534.

106. Abrams SA, Schanler RJ, Tsang RC, Garza C. Bone mineralization in former very low birth weight infants fed either human milk or commercial formula: one year followup observation. *J Pediatr* 1989;114:1041–1043.

107. Chan GM, Mileur LJ. Post-hospitalization growth and bone mineral status of preterm infants: feeding with mother's milk or standard formula. *Am J Dis Child* 1985;139:896–898.

108. Horsman A, Ryan SW, Congdon PJ, Truscott JG, Simpson M. Bone mineral accretion rate and calcium intake in preterm infants. *Arch Dis Child* 1989;64:910–918.

109. Lyon AJ, McIntosh N, Wheeler K, Williams JE. Radiological rickets in extremely low birth weight infants. *Pediatr Radiol* 1987;17:56–58.

110. Koo WWK, Sherman R, Succop P, et al. Fractures and rickets in very low birth weight infants: conservative management and outcome. *J Pediatr Orthop* 1989;9:326–330.

111. Greer FR, Steichen JJ, Tsang RC. Effects of increased calcium, phosphorus, and vitamin D intake on bone mineralization in very low birth weight infants fed formula with polycose and medium chain triglycerides. *J Pediatr* 1982;100:951–955.

112. Laing, IA, Glass EJ, Hendry GMA, et al. Rickets of prematurity: calcium and phosphorus supplementation. *J Pediatr* 1985;106:265–268.

113. Bremer HJ, Brooke EG, Orzalesi M, et al. Calcium, phosphorus and magnesium. In: *Nutrition and feeding of preterm infants*. Oxford, UK: Blackwell Scientific Publications, 1987:117–132.

114. Atkinson SA. Calcium, phosphorus and vitamin D needs of low birthweight infants on various feedings. *Acta Paediatr Scand* 1989;351(suppl):104–108.

115. Raupp P, von Kries R, Schmidt E, Manz F, Tonz O. Human milk fortification. *Lancet* 1988;1:1160–1161.

116. Abrams SA, Vieira NE, Yergey AL. Unequal distribution of a stable isotopic calcium tracer between casein and whey fractions of infant formulas, human milk and cow's milk. *J Nutr* 1990;120:1672–1676.

117. Allen LH. Calcium bioavailability and absorption. *Am J Clin Nutr* 1982;35:783–808.

118. Heaney RP, Recker RR, Stegman MR, Moy AJ. Calcium absorption in women: relationships to calcium intake, estrogen status, and age. *J Bone Mineral Res* 1989;4:469–475.

119. Cooke RJ, Perrin F, Moore J, Paule C, Ruckman K. Nutrient balance studies in the preterm infant: crossover and parallel studies as methods of experimental design. *J Pediatr Gastroenterol Nutr* 1988;7:718–722.

120. Ezzedeen F, Adelman RD, Ahlfors CE. Renal calcification in preterm infants: pathophysiology and long-term sequelae. *J Pediatr* 1988;113:532–539.

121. Jacinto JS, Modanlou HD, Crade M, Strauss AA, Bosu SK. Renal calcification incidence in very low birth weight infants. *Pediatrics* 1988;81:31–35.

122. Joad JP, Ahrens RL, Lindgren SD, Weinberger MM. Extra-pulmonary effects of maintenance therapy with theophylline and inhaled albuterol in patients with chronic asthma. *J Allergy Clin Immunol* 1988;78:1147–1153.

123. Bhatia J, Fomon SJ. Formulas for preterm infants: fate of the calcium and phosphorus. *Pediatrics*. 1983;72:37–40.

124. Bhatia J, Rassin DK. Human milk supplementation. Delivery of energy, calcium, phosphorus, magnesium, copper and zinc. *Am J Dis Child* 1988;142:445–447.

125. Koletzko B, Tangermann R, von Kries R, et al. Intestinal milk-bolus obstruction in formula fed premature infants given high doses of calcium. *J Pediatr Gastroenterol Nutr* 1988;7:548–553.

126. Bhatia J. Formula fixed. *Pediatrics* 1985;75:800–801.

127. Giles MM, Fenton MH, Shaw B, et al. Sequential calcium and phosphorus balance studies in preterm infants. *J Pediatr* 1987;110:591–598.

128. Holland PC, Wilkinson AR, Diez J, Lindsell DRM. Prenatal deficiency of phosphate, phosphate supplementation, and rickets in very-low-birthweight infants. *Lancet* 1990;335:697–701.

129. Greer FR, McCormick A. Improved bone mineralization and growth in premature infants fed fortified own mother's milk. *J Pediatr* 1988;112:961–969.

130. Modanlou H, Lim MO, Hansen JW. Growth, biochemical status and mineral metabolism in very low birth weight infants receiving fortified preterm human milk. *J Pediatr Gastroenterol Nutr* 1986;5:762–767.

131. Cooke RJ. Rickets in a very low birth weight infant. *J Pediatr Gastroenterol Nutr* 1989;9:397–399.

132. Callenbach JC, Sheehan MB, Abramson J, Hall RT. Etiologic factors in rickets of very low birth weight infants. *J Pediatr* 1981;98:800–805.

133. Helin I, Landin LA, Nilsson BE. Bone mineral content in preterm infants at age 4 to 16. *Acta Paediatr Scand* 1985;74:264–267.

134. Greer FR, McCormick A. Bone mineral content and growth in very low birth weight infants. *Am J Dis Child* 1987;141:179–183.

135. Koo WWK, Sherman R, Succop P, et al. Sequential bone mineral content in very low birth weight infants with and without fractures and rickets. *J Bone Miner Res* 1988;3:193–197.

136. Steichen J, Koo W, Mimouni F, Tsang RC. Bone mineralization of very low birth weight preterm, average for gestational age and small for gestational age infants: followup at age 18 to 36 months. *J Bone Miner Res* 1988;3(suppl 1):S184.

137. Congdon PJ, Horsman A, Ryan SW, Truscott JG, Durward H. Spontaneous resolution of bone mineral depletion in preterm infants. *Arch Dis Child* 1990;65:1038–1042.

138. Fox J, Ross R. The effects of low phosphorus and low calcium diets on the production and metabolic clearance rates of 1,25 dihydroxycholecalciferol in pigs. *J Endocrinol* 1985;105:169–173.

139. Specker BL, Greer F, Tsang RC. Vitamin D. In: Tsang RC, Nichols BL, eds. *Nutrition during infancy*. Philadelphia: Hanley & Belfus, 1988:264–276.

140. Bhowmick SK, Johnson KR, Rettig KR. Rickets caused by vitamin D deficiency in breast-fed infants in the southern United States. *Am J Dis Child* 1991;145:127–130.

141. Bell NH, Shaw S, Turner RT. Evidence that calcium modulates circulating 25-hydroxyvitamin D in man. *J Bone Miner Res* 1987;2:211–214.

142. Clements MR, Johnson L, Fraser DR. A new mechanism for induced vitamin D deficiency in calcium deprivation. *Nature* 1987;325:62–65.

143. Halloran BP, Bikle DD, Levens MJ, Castro ME, Globus RK, Holton E. Chronic 1,25-dihydroxyvitamin D_3 administration in the rat reduces the serum concentration of 25-hydroxyvitamin D by increasing metabolic clearance rate. *J Clin Invest* 1986;78:622–628.

144. Clements MR, Davies M, Fraser DR, Lumb GA, Mawer FB, Adams PH. Metabolic inactivations of vitamin D is enhanced in primary hyperparathyroidism. *Clin Sci* 1987;73:659–664.

145. Rosen J, Roginsky M, Nathenson G, Finberg L. 25-hydroxyvitamin D. Plasma levels in mothers and their premature infants with neonatal hypocalcemia. *Am J Dis Child* 1974;127:220–223.

146. Hillman L, Haddad J. Perinatal vitamin D metabolism. II. Serial 25-hydroxyvitamin D concentrations in sera of term and premature infants. *J Pediatr* 1975;86:928–935.

147. Hillman LS, Salmons SJ, Slatopolsky E, McAlister WH. Serial serum 25-hydroxyvitamin D and mineral homeostasis in very premature infants fed preterm human milk. *J Pediatr Gastroenterol Nutr* 1985;4:762–770.

148. Hillman LS, Hoff N, Salmons S, Martin L, McAlister W, Haddad J. Mineral homeostasis in very premature infants: serial evaluation of serum 25 hydroxyvitamin D, serum minerals, and bone mineralization. *J Pediatr* 1985;106:970–980.

149. Pettifor JM, Stein H, Herman A, Ross FP, Blumenfeld T, Moodley GP. Mineral homeostasis in very low birth weight infants fed either own mother's milk or pooled pasteurized preterm milk. *J Pediatr Gastroenterol Nutr* 1986;5:248–253.

150. Koo WWK, Gupta JM, Nayanar VV, Wilkinson M, Posen S. Skeletal changes in premature infants. *Arch Dis Child* 1982;57:447–452.

151. Hillman LS, Hollis B, Salmons S, et al. Absorption, dosage, and effect on mineral homeostasis of 25-hydroxycholecalciferol in premature infants: comparison with 400 and 800 IU vitamin D_2 supplementation. *J Pediatr* 1985;106:981–989.

152. Pittard WB III, Geddes KM, Hulsey TC, Hollis BW. How much vitamin D for neonates? *Am J Dis Child* 1991;145:1147–1149.

153. McIntosh N, Livesey A, Brooke OG. Plasma 25-hydroxyvitamin D and rickets in infants of extremely low birthweight. *Arch Dis Child* 1982;57:848–850.

154. Evans JR, Allen AC, Stinson DA, et al. Effect of high-dose vitamin D supplementation on radiographically detectable bone disease of very low birth weight infants. *J Pediatr* 1989;115:779–786.

155. Steichen JJ, Tsang RC. Bone mineralization and growth in term infants fed soy based or cow milk based formula. *J Pediatr* 1987;110:687–692.

156. Chan GM, Leeper L, Book LS. Effects of soy formulas on mineral metabolism in term infants. *Am J Dis Child* 1987;141:527–550.

157. Hillman LS, Chow W, Salmons SS, Weaver E, Erickson M, Hansen J. Vitamin D metabolism, mineral homeostasis, and bone mineralization in term infants fed human milk, cow milk based formula or soy based formula. *J Pediatr* 1988;112:864–874.

158. Mimouni F, Donovan D, Harris L, Landi T, Tsang RC. Bone mineralization in infants fed milk-based or soy-based infant formulae. *J Am Coll Nutr* 1990;9:528.

159. Venkataraman PS, Tsang RC, Greer FR, Noguchi A, Laskarzewski P, Steichen JJ. Late infantile tetany and secondary hyperparathyroidism in infants fed humanized cow milk formula. *Am J Dis Child* 1985;139:664–668.

160. Venkataraman PS, Han BK, Tsang RC, Daugherty CC. Secondary hyperparathroidism and bone disease in infants receiving long term furosemide therapy. *Am J Dis Child* 1983;137:1157–1161.

161. Lyon AJ, McIntosh N, Wheeler K, Brooke OG. Hypercalcemia in extremely low birthweight infants. *Arch Dis Child* 1984;59:1141–1144.

162. Weinsler RL, Krumdieck CL. Death from overzealous total parenteral nutrition: the refeeding syndrome revisited. *Am J Clin Nutr* 1980;34:393–399.

163. Stoff JS. Phosphate homeostasis and hypophosphatemia. *Am J Med* 1982;72:489–495.

164. Knochel JP. The clinical status of hypophosphatemia. *N Engl J Med* 1985;313:447–449.

165. Hall RT, Wheeler RE, Montalto MB, Benson JD. Hypophosphatemia in breast-fed low-birth-weight infants following initial hospital discharge. *Am J Dis Child* 1989;143:1191–1195.

166. Lucas A, Brooke OG, Baker BA, Bishop N, Morley R. High Alkaline phosphatase activity and growth in preterm neonates. *Arch Dis Child* 1989;64:902–909.

167. Laflamme GH, Jowsey J. Bone and soft tissue changes with oral phosphate supplements. *J Clin Invest* 1972;51:2834–2840.

168. Robbins SL, Cotran RS, Kumar V. *Pathologic basis of disease*. 3rd ed. Philadelphia: WB Saunders, 1984:35–36.

169. Cleghorn GJ, Tudehope DI. Neonatal intestinal obstruction associated with oral calcium supplementation. *Aust Paediatr J* 1981;17:298–299.

170. Hufnagle KG, Khan SN, Penn D, Cacciarelli A, Williams P. Renal calcifications: a complication of long term furosemide therapy in preterm infants. *Pediatrics* 1982;70:360–363.

171. Barth RA, Brasch RC, Filly RA. Abdominal pseudotumor in childhood: distended gallbladder with parenteral hyperalimentation. *Am J Roentgenol* 1981;136:341–343.

172. Reynolds JEF, Prasad AB, eds. *Martindale: the extra pharmacopoeia*. 28th ed. London: The Pharmaceutical Press, 1982:600–602.

173. American Academy of Pediatrics. The prophylactic requirement and the toxicity of vitamin D. *Pediatrics* 1963;31:512–525.

174. Koo WWK, Kaplan LA, Horn J, Tsang RC, Steichen JJ. Aluminum in parenteral nutrition solution—sources and possible alternatives. *J Parenter Enteral Nutr* 1986;10:591–595.

175. Koo WWK, Kaplan LA, Krug-Wispe SK. Aluminum contamination of infant formulas. *J Parenter Enteral Nutr* 1988;12:170–173.

176. Koo WWK, Kaplan LA. Aluminum and bone disorders: with specific reference to aluminum contamination of infant nutrients. *J Am Coll Nutr* 1988;7:199–214.

177. Koo WWK, Krug-Wispe SK, Succop P, Bendon R, Kaplan LA. Sequential serum aluminum and urine aluminum: creatinine ratio and tissue aluminum loading in infants with fractures and rickets. *Pediatrics* 1992;89:877–881.

178. Hauschka PV, Lian JB, Cole DEC, Gundberg CM. Osteocalcin and matrix gla protein: vitamin K-dependent proteins in bone. *Physiol Rev* 1989;69:990–1047.

179. Lyon AJ, Hawkes DJ, Doran M, McIntosh N, Chan F. Bone mineralization in preterm infants measured by dual energy radiographic densitometry. *Arch Dis Child* 1989;64:919–923.

180. Trivedi P, Risteli J, Risteli L, Hindmarsh PC, Brook CGD, Mowat AP. Serum concentrations of the type I and III procollagen propeptides as biochemical markers of growth and velocity in healthy infants and children and in children with growth disorders. *Pediatr Res* 1991;30:276–280.

181. Koo WWK, Tsang RC. Rickets in infants. In: Nelson NM, ed. *Current therapy in neonatal perinatal medicine*. 2nd ed. Philadelphia: B.C. Decker, 1990:353–357.

182. Subcommittee on the Tenth Edition of the RDAs, National Research Council. *Recommended Dietary Allowances*. 10th ed. Washington, DC: National Academy Press, 1989:174–194.

183. Heubi JE, Hollis BW, Tsang RC. Bone disease in chronic childhood cholestasis. II. Better Absorption of 25-OH vitamin D than vitamin D in extrahepatic biliary atresia. *Pediatr Res* 1989;27:26–31.

184. Helfer RE, Scheurer SL, Alexander R, Reed J, Solvis TL. Trauma to the bones of small infants from passive exercise: a factor in the etiology of child abuse. *J Pediatr* 1984;104:47–50.

11. Sodium, Chloride, and Potassium

Billy S. Arant, Jr.

Reviewers: Stephen Baumgart, Jonathan Shaw, Jayant P. Shenai

Few topics in neonatal medicine are more controversial than fluid and electrolyte therapy for preterm infants, especially the amount of sodium chloride (NaCl) that should be provided at various stages of postnatal life.

The requirement for water is considered more completely in Chapter 1, but it is futile to discuss Na or Cl apart from the concomitant volume of fluid the infant receives. Not only do these principal electrolytes determine the distribution of body water between the intracellular and extracellular compartments, but changes in their concentrations in body fluids also prompt physicians to alter clinical management.

Much of the failure to understand electrolyte requirements of neonates at any gestational or postnatal age can be attributed in large measure to the potpourri of uncontrolled observations made in human neonates. The conclusions of such studies are based on incomplete information and apparently made to fit the clinical problem being investigated. How else could one explain two phenomena reported under similar conditions: (1) the kidney of the preterm infant has an unlimited ability to reabsorb Na along the nephron, probably because of unusually high aldosterone secretion[1]; yet (2) frequent hyponatremia in the premature infant is secondary to renal Na wasting due, perhaps, to tubular insensitivity to aldosterone.[2,3]

The notion that kidney function in neonates is immature was based initially on the finding that glomerular filtration rate (GFR) remained low relative to the adult, even when corrected for body size.[4] Later, the neonatal kidney was observed to have a limited capacity to excrete an exogenous salt load.[5] However, that study was conducted under conditions that were not physiologic: 10% NaCl solution was infused intravenously into full-term infants, which raised their plasma osmolarities acutely by 100 mOsm/L. The conclusion of the study, however, was readily accepted at the time as an explanation for the frequent occurrence of hypernatremia in the nursery.

When preterm infants were first admitted to neonatal intensive care units, parenteral fluids (dextrose and water) were prescribed routinely. Although hypernatremia became less common, hyponatremia was observed more frequently—so frequently, in fact, that the definition of hyponatremia was reduced in some neonatal units from 135 mmol/L to 130 mmol/L or even as low as 125 mmol/L. Such low values are associated with central nervous system complications, including apnea in neonates[6] and central pontine myelinolysis in adults.[7] The marked urinary Na wasting in preterm infants given parenteral fluids from birth seemed a logical explanation for the frequent hyponatremia observed.[8] Similar observations of negative Na balance had been reported many years earlier in neonates given no fluid intake for several days after birth, with one important difference: hyponatremia was rare.[9] Nevertheless, the conclusion drawn from these and additional studies was that kidneys of preterm infants could not conserve Na even in the presence of hyponatremia, so Na was added to parenteral fluids or formula.

If one point is to be made clear in this chapter, it is that any two infants born prematurely will have similar, but not necessarily the same, daily requirements for Na, Cl, and potassium (K), particularly in the immediate postnatal period. Moreover, electrolyte balance is inexorably linked to fluid therapy. Differences among sick neonates are more variable. Finally, plasma concentrations of electrolytes alone cannot be relied upon to reflect balance and should not be used as the only criterion for changing therapy.

Physiology

Developmental Changes in Body Composition

Total Body Water   Chemical development of the human from conception is characterized by gradual accretion of water and electrolytes, which are incorporated into an ever enlarging volume of both intracellular fluid (ICF) and extracellular fluid (ECF) as the infant grows. The fraction of body weight attributable to water decreases during gestation from 96% at 8 weeks to 78% at 40 weeks, then decreases further to 70% immediately after birth at term. The percentage of body weight as water continues to decrease more gradually thereafter, until the adult proportion of 60% is attained when body weight is 10 to 15 kg.[10-12]

The ratio of ECF to ICF decreases from 2:1 in the second trimester to 1:1 when birth occurs at term. The ratio gradually decreases further during infancy to 1:2, which is like the adult ratio.[11-13] The change in the ratio results mainly from a relative decrease in ECF, rather than an increase in ICF relative to body weight.

157

Total Body Sodium, Chloride, and Potassium
Like body water, total body Na relative to body weight also decreases, from 110 to 120 mmol/kg at 8 weeks gestation to 85 mmol/kg at 40 weeks. During the first days of life, the relative Na content of the full-term infant is reduced further by continued urinary losses. Then it continues to be reduced by growth, until an adult-like relative Na content is reached when body weight is 10 to 15 kg.[12,14] The change in the fractional content of Cl follows a similar developmental pattern; the fetus contains 85 to 90 mmol/kg at 8 weeks and 60 mmol/kg at 40 weeks, but the Cl content of the adult is only 35 mmol/kg. Unlike water and NaCl, however, the relative body content of K increases, from 40 mmol/kg body weight at 8 weeks to 50 mmol/kg at 40 weeks; an adult proportion of 69 mmol/kg is attained when body weight is 10 to 15 kg.[12,14] Except for the period of fetal adaptation to postnatal life (transitional period), the daily balances of Na, Cl, K, and water should be positive, with intakes exceeding losses (mainly in the urine and, to a lesser degree, in the stool, sweat, and respiratory tract).

Active transport mechanisms in cell membranes exclude most Na and Cl from the cell and favor K entry, maintaining the Na:K gradient across the membrane. In muscle and nerve, this gradient propagates the action potential. Therefore, the majority of K in the body is located within cells, where its concentration is about 160 mmol/L; outside the cell, the K concentration is only 5 mmol/L. By comparison, the concentration of Na or Cl in cell water is about 4 mmol/L; but outside the cell, in plasma or interstitial fluid, the concentration of Na is 135 to 145 mmol/L and that of Cl is 97 to 106 mmol/L. The osmotic activity (270 to 290 mmol/L) is the same across the cell membrane. Any change in either the ICF or ECF osmolarity will result in the movement of water into the compartment with the higher osmotic activity or with relatively less water.

Extracellular Fluid The relative volume of the ECF is gradually reduced during gestation, from 60% of body weight during the first trimester to 35% at 40 weeks.[11–13,15–17] This is accomplished by incorporation of NaCl and water into growing tissues and by continuous natriuresis and diuresis in utero.[18,19] The osmotic activity and thus the integrity of the ECF volume are maintained primarily by the concentrations of Na and Cl. Following birth, ECF is reduced further as the relative body contents of NaCl and water decrease, until the adult proportion of 20% of body weight is attained.

The ECF is distributed between the vascular and interstitial spaces in a ratio of 1:4 or 1:5. The vascular volume is maintained by the colloid oncotic pressure (COP) contributed by plasma proteins, primarily albumin. When COP is reduced, capillary hydrostatic forces favor the movement of plasma into the interstitial space, where much of it remains. Continued intake of water or NaCl will increase the ECF volume, but the blood volume does not expand proportionally, because plasma water is lost into the interstitium when COP is low.

The COP of a preterm infant is about 11 mm Hg, compared with 16 mm Hg in the full-term infant[20,21] and 25 mm Hg in the adult. The serum albumin concentration increases with gestational age, from 2.52 to 3.31 g/dL in infants whose birthweights are between 690 g and 4,020 g.[22] The only explanation offered to date for the lower serum albumin concentrations and, thus, lower COP in preterm infants, is reduced synthesis of protein by the immature liver. However, this theory has never been proved. In fact, COP in normal preterm infants was shown to increase to 19 mm Hg within the first 3 hours of life—too rapidly to be explained by liver maturation or increased protein intake.[21] Alternatively, it could be that factors favoring accumulation of excess interstitial fluid that may be important to the fetus normally include an increase in capillary permeability to protein, or the "leaky capillary syndrome" more familiar in a discussion of septic shock.

Brace[23] infused enough isotonic saline into fetal lambs over 5 minutes to, hypothetically, raise blood volume immediately by 20% if all the saline remained in the circulation. However, only 7% of the infused volume actually remained in the vascular space for more than 5 minutes. After a second infusion, 94% of the total infusate left the vascular space within 5 minutes. This physiologic finding is relevant to understanding the neonatal kidney's alleged inability to excrete NaCl and water. If the infused saline does not reach the renal circulation because 80% or more is distributed into the interstitium, then the neonatal kidney cannot be expected to excrete the NaCl load like the adult kidney.

When intravenous saline loading was used to examine the renal handling of Na during development, both human[5] and canine[24,25] neonates excreted less than 10% of the administered load within 2 hours; adults excreted, on average, about 50%. In one such study,[24] the saline did increase the ECF volume as expected, but it also diluted plasma protein concentration and, presumably, COP, which permitted plasma water to enter the interstitium. As a result of intravenous saline loading, therefore, plasma volume and blood pressure (BP) actually decreased slightly. When the saline infusion caused an increase in plasma volume or BP, more than 50% of the saline was excreted in the urine, regardless of the age of the animal. The functional response of the neonatal kidney to saline loading has given some investigators an impression of its immaturity, but the identical qualitative responses to volume expansion can be demonstrated in the adult kidney.

Blood Volume The relative blood volume of the preterm neonate is 90 to 120 mL/kg, which is 1.5 to 2 times greater than that of the adult.[26] Placental transfusion of up to 30 mL/kg in very preterm infants can increase this volume further, without causing cardiovascular overload or hypertension.[27,28] The neonatal cardiovascular system, therefore, appears to adapt rapidly to a sudden increase in circulating blood volume and high hematocrit. This may well be the same physiologic mechanism that prevented any increase in BP of preterm infants given either 5%[26] or 20%[29] albumin solution intravenously. Moreover, mean arterial BP in normal dogs at every age[30] and diastolic BP in normal human adults[31] varied inversely with simultaneously measured blood volume—i.e., BP decreases as blood volume increases. In patients with hypertension, however, BP varied directly with blood volume.[31] Hypotensive patients whose circulating blood volumes are reduced respond to volume loading with an increase in BP.

Transitional Adaptation
In the fetus, the peripheral vasculature is maximally dilated, and BP is maintained by the high blood volume and nearly maximal cardiac output.[32] Following birth, ECF is reduced during the first 3 days of life, as excess NaCl and water are excreted in the urine.[15,33] Simultaneously, a decrease in synthesis of vasodilator prostaglandins, primarily prostacyclin but also PGE_2,[34,35] is associated with a decrease in capillary permeability to protein, an increase in COP,[21] and closure of the ductus arteriosus. Blood pressure increases as COP rises,[21] peripheral resistance increases, and the vasculature becomes more responsive to endogenous vasoconstrictor substances.[36-38] However, high-volume fluid therapy, saline loading, or acute blood volume expansion can reverse this pattern of normal physiologic transition. In that case, BP decreases or does not increase after birth, renal excretion of NaCl and water remains high, and the ductus arteriosus either fails to close spontaneously or reopens.[17,30,39-41] Except in cases of fetal blood loss, therefore, a neonate always has adequate circulating volumes of blood and ECF at birth. Confirmation of this statement comes from the survival of neonates, but not adults, for up to a week in the debris of a collapsed maternity hospital after a major earthquake in Mexico.

A major role of the kidney at every stage of development is to regulate the ECF volume. When needed, every renal hemodynamic and reabsorptive mechanism is activated to conserve NaCl and water and preserve or restore the ECF. In general, NaCl and water are reabsorbed isotonically along the nephron, except in the ascending thick limb (which is water impermeable) and in the collecting duct (where a large volume of water can be returned to the circulation without much NaCl when arginine vasopressin [AVP] is present).

When the effective arterial blood volume (EABV)—the combined effect of blood volume and BP on baroreceptors—is increased, the kidney, in both the neonate and the adult, will decrease the fraction of glomerular filtrate reabsorbed along the tubule, regardless of plasma osmolarity or plasma Na concentration. Consequently, renal NaCl wasting in the presence of severe hyponatremia should be anticipated when EABV is increased above normal, as it is in the syndrome of inappropriate antidiuretic hormone secretion (SIADH). Moreover, when EABV is decreased below normal, as occurs with hypernatremic dehydration, the kidney will conserve NaCl maximally, even with worsening hypernatremia. This physiologic response is not an indicator of immature renal function, because it is present in normal individuals at every stage of postnatal development.

The relative ECF volume is reduced gradually in the fetus during development, primarily by growth but also by marked urinary excretion of both NaCl and water. The fractional excretion of Na (FE_{Na}) by the human fetal kidney is 12% to 21%,[19] compared with less than 1% in the 2-day-old normal infant born at term.[42] Moreover, urine volume is about 10 mL/kg/h between 30 and 40 weeks gestation[18] but decreases rapidly immediately after birth to 1 mL/kg/h or less in full-term infants. Meanwhile, the urine osmolarity increases to 350 to 400 mOsm/L as more water is reabsorbed along the collecting duct by AVP-mediated mechanisms.[33] The urine volume of the extremely low-birthweight (ELBW) infant ($<1,000$ g) or preterm infant, however, remains high for many days after birth, and during this "diuretic phase" the urine osmolarity usually remains at 200 mOsm/L or more because of the quantity of NaCl in the urine and the minimal influence of AVP to conserve water.[43,44] Once the excess NaCl has been excreted, the osmolarity of the urine decreases, depending upon water balance. Thereafter, the urine volume and osmolarity assume a normal reverse relationship: when urine volume decreases, osmolarity increases.

If an adult were subjected to enough isotonic saline loading to double or triple the volume of ECF, similar to that measured in the fetus or preterm infant at birth,[15-17,26,45] there would be a marked decrease in proximal tubule reabsorption of NaCl and water.[46]

Arginine vasopressin release would be inhibited, and urine volume would increase. But instead of producing very dilute urine with little or no AVP, the adult would have urine osmolarity that is isotonic or only slightly hypotonic to plasma, because of all the osmotically active substances not reabsorbed along the nephron. An evaluation of overall renal function in this adult would identify glucosuria,[47] calciuria,[48] phosphaturia,[49] bicarbonaturia,[50] uricosuria,[51] and beta$_2$-microglobulinuria,[52] representing a state of glomerulotubular imbalance with limited functional capacity of proximal tubules. These findings are the very same criteria used to characterize the fetal or neonatal kidney as immature.[53] Once the ECF excess was reduced, proximal tubule reabsorption would increase, glomerulotubular balance would be reestablished, and the kidney would return to its "mature" state.[54]

In animal studies, an acute reduction in the EABV of the fetus or neonate by hemorrhage, fluid restriction, peritoneal dialysis, or diuretic therapy "matures" kidney function.[55,56] Negative NaCl and water balances in the neonate can be changed to positive balances with renal conservation of NaCl and water in a matter of hours — too brief a time for the kidney to have actually matured. When EABV in these studies was restored to that considered normal for the fetus, kidney function reverted to an "immature" state, with NaCl and water wasting.

Clinical anecdotes confirm similar renal responses when the management of an ELBW infant does not proceed as planned. The usual story is that parenteral fluid therapy, through some oversight in management, has not replaced urinary and insensible water losses adequately for a limited period. The rapid loss of body weight, which may have exceeded 10% to 15% in less than 24 hours, is associated not only with a predictable reduction in urine volume (<1 mL/kg/h) but also with an unexpected decrease in urinary Na excretion (FE$_{Na}$ <1%) and an increase in urine specific gravity (>1.018) or osmolarity (>500 mOsm/L). Even more surprising is the fact that, despite the rapid reduction in total body water, BP remains normal or may actually increase slightly. Most importantly, this rather abrupt loss of weight does not have any untoward effect on the infant. The clinical notion that such an event is undesirable or dangerous may prompt intervention, on misguided principle, to restore the acute ECF "deficit" in what by all measures is a stable neonate. Quite predictably, however, aggressive fluid replacement would not only "rehydrate" an otherwise stable infant but would also cause kidney function to revert to the fetal or "immature" state, as manifested by diuresis (urine volume > 3 mL/kg/h), NaCl wasting (FE$_{Na}$ >3%), and less concentrated urine (specific gravity <1.010).

Glomerular Filtration Rate

It is well known that GFR is lower in infants than in children or adults, even when corrected for body weight or surface area.[4] A few reports, mainly from a single center, have suggested that GFR increases from birth even in very preterm infants.[57] However, it was first reported[42] and later confirmed at several centers and by different investigators[58–60] that the developmental pattern of GFR in preterm infants correlates best with postconceptional age (gestational plus postnatal ages), not postnatal age alone. Infants born after 34 weeks gestation exhibit a postnatal increase in absolute GFR like full-term infants do,[61] but those born more prematurely have little or no increase in GFR until a postconceptional age of 34 weeks. For instance, the neonate born at 28 weeks gestation would not be expected to have a significant increase in GFR until 5 or 6 weeks after birth. During these 6 weeks, urinary creatinine excretion equals or barely exceeds the ELBW infant's creatinine production of 8 to 10 mg/kg/day,[62] so the plasma creatinine concentration may remain relatively unchanged or decrease slowly when GFR is not changing much. Thereafter, GFR increases rapidly, as it does in the first week of life in infants born at term, while urinary creatinine excretion increases and plasma creatinine concentration decreases by 50% within a week, as happens in infants born after 34 weeks gestation.[63] The abrupt change in the developmental pattern of GFR occurs around 34 weeks after conception, which is the same stage in renal development at which nephrogenesis is completed.[64] This developmental pattern of change in GFR about the time that nephrogenesis is completed has been identified as well in other mammals.[65,66] Throughout the first year of life, the rate of increase in GFR parallels the change in body surface area; GFR factored for body surface area changes very little.[67]

Renal Handling of Electrolytes and Water

Failure of GFR to increase in the immediate postnatal period in very preterm infants should not be interpreted to mean that the kidney has a limited ability to excrete or reabsorb electrolytes and water. The relatively low GFR limits only the absolute amount of electrolytes and water filtered and handled by the renal tubule. Glomerular filtrate has the same concentration of Na, Cl, and K as plasma. About 40% of NaCl and water filtered is reabsorbed isotonically along the proximal tubule of the fetus and neonate,[68,69] compared with 60% to 70% in the adult. The amount is influenced by COP and hematocrit in the peritubular capillary and by other physical factors, including the various renal responses for volume regulation.[46]

Half of the NaCl remaining in the tubular lumen beyond the proximal tubule that reaches the distal nephron is reabsorbed in the ascending thick limb—the site of action for loop diuretics. Nearly all the K in the glomerular filtrate is reabsorbed in the proximal nephron. Additional Na is reabsorbed in the distal tubule in exchange for either K or hydrogen ion; this aldosterone-sensitive, Na-K-ATPase–dependent mechanism is the means by which extracellular K is regulated. Some electrolyte may be reabsorbed beyond the distal tubule, but the collecting duct is mainly the site of additional water conservation. Water reabsorption is dependent not only on the presence of AVP but also on the effect of locally produced substances that interfere with the action of AVP, like prostaglandins, as well as the osmotic gradient established by Na and urea in the renal medulla through the countercurrent multiplier mechanism.[70]

Even when GFR is only 0.5 mL/min in a preterm infant weighing 1.0 kg, the kidneys will filter about 100 mmol of Na or Cl each day. If just 1 mmol/day of NA is excreted in the urine (0.067 mmol/min), the FE_{Na} will be 1%. An increase in the FE_{Na} by an additional 1% will double the urinary loss of Na. The amount of Na rejected by the fetal kidney (or by the ELBW infant whose FE_{Na} is 7% to 12%) is remarkable indeed. This is not the consequence of functional immaturity. Rather, it is mostly an exaggerated normal renal response to a combination of stimuli, such as atrial natriuretic peptide, prostaglandins, aldosterone, angiotensin II, catecholamines, low COP, and low EABV—all of which participate in regulating ECF volume.

Urine Volume

There is a widely held clinical notion that urine volume in preterm infants must be maintained above 1 mL/kg/h to protect the kidneys and prevent acute renal failure. The rationale for this practice is not well founded; it is based, most likely, on two clinical principles. First, acute renal failure should be considered in the differential diagnosis for neonates whose urine volumes fall below 1 mL/kg/h. What seems to be forgotten often, however, is that for a diagnosis of acute renal failure to be made, the renal indices—namely, the tubular handling of Na—must be abnormal (i.e., $FE_{Na} >1\%$) and the urinary osmolarity lower than plasma osmolarity.[71] Moreover, weight gain is usually observed with acute renal failure and with SIADH; both conditions can be associated with hyponatremia, but blood urea nitrogen (BUN) is increased in renal failure and decreased in SIADH. If the oliguria is accompanied by weight loss, an increase in BUN, and an increase in urine osmolarity, but FE_{Na} is less than 1%, then a decrease in EABV (as with dehydration, nephrotic syndrome, or heart failure) should be suspected.

The other well-established fact is that the neonatal kidney cannot concentrate urine as well as the normal adult kidney. The volume of urine produced must be sufficient to excrete the "obligatory solute load," which represents the nonwater excess or waste that the kidney must remove from the body under usual circumstances plus any additional solute filtered by the glomerulus or secreted by the tubule that is not reabsorbed. The majority of that solute load comprises electrolytes and nitrogenous waste. The minimum volume of urine required to excrete the obligatory solute load was calculated primarily on the basis of studies of infants fed bovine milk.[72] When infants were fed modified bovine milk formula, the solute load was only about half that produced by bovine milk.[73] The urinary excretion of nitrogenous waste depends on the infant's protein intake and degree of catabolic activity. The rapidly growing infant has less nitrogenous waste to excrete because the protein in human milk and, to a lesser extent, modified bovine milk formula has relatively high biologic value, and a greater fraction is incorporated into tissue growth. When the kidney conserves Na or has little nitrogenous waste to excrete, the solute load is reduced, and less water is required to maintain a minimum urine volume. Therefore, all infants do not have the same "minimally safe" urine volume—the less solute to be excreted, the lower is the urine volume required.

Although solute excretion is relatively high in preterm infants during the diuretic phase in the days following birth, the volume of water to be excreted is also high. The limited concentrating capacity of the neonate is rarely challenged in clinical practice and should cause little or no concern in most situations. Moreover, there is no difference in the maximum ability of preterm and term infants to concentrate the urine. Preterm neonates (28 to 34 weeks gestational age) deprived of fluid intake for 72 hours after birth were found to concentrate urine above 600 mOsm/L (specific gravity >1.018), which was actually higher than the concentration in full-term infants studied simultaneously.[33] Rees et al.[74] observed that in response to a reduction in blood volume, AVP release was sufficient to produce a urine concentrated in excess of 500 mOsm/L (specific gravity >1.015) in an 800-g infant born at 26 weeks gestation.

It is important to understand that maintaining urine volume above 1 mL/kg/h, as is usually recommended in the literature, may have unwanted clinical consequences. As outlined in Table 11.1, for an adult to have a urine volume of 1 mL/kg/h, the fractional volume of glomerular filtrate excreted as urine (V/GFR) is 0.9%. For an infant born at term, 1.7% of glomerular filtrate must be excreted. For a preterm infant born at 28 weeks, 3.0% of glomerular filtrate must be excreted, and the ELBW infant must excrete 5.0% if

Table 11.1. Comparison of Fractional Urine Flow Rate (V/GFR) and Sodium Excretion (FE$_{Na}$) in the Adult and Neonates

Age	Weight (kg)	Urine Volume (mL/kg/h)	GFR (mL/kg/h)	V/GFR (%)	FE$_{Na}$ (%)
Adult	70	1.0/3.0	110	0.9/2.7	0.3/0.9
Neonates					
40 wks	3.5	1.0/3.0	60	1.7/5.0	0.8/2.4
32 wks	1.4	1.0/3.0	50	2.0/6.0	1.1/3.3
28 wks	0.9	1.0/3.0	33	3.0/9.0	2.5/7.5
25 wks	0.6	1.0/3.0	20	5.0/15.0	3.2/9.6

the urine volume is maintained at 1 mL/kg/h. If the preterm infant has a urine volume of 3 mL/kg/h, which is not uncommon, it means that 10% of glomerular filtrate was not reabsorbed along the nephron.

Expecting the preterm infant's kidney to satisfy an arbitrary notion of a "minimally safe" urine volume is not only unphysiologic but wasteful. The volume of urine excreted is not only water. When V/GFR is increased abnormally, the proximal tubule also rejects solute that is ordinarily reabsorbed, like Na, Cl, K, calcium, phosphorus, glucose, β_2-microglobulin, and nitrogen. This higher urine volume and fractional electrolyte excretion are normal for the fetus and the neonate who is still excreting excess ECF during transitional adaptation. Then V/GFR decreases gradually as spontaneous diuresis ends, and the stable period begins with evidence of NaCl and water conservation.[15,33,37]

Tubular Reabsorption of Sodium, Chloride, and Potassium

When it was considered that the neonatal human kidney could not excrete Na efficiently, clearance studies were interpreted to mean that the distal tubule had an unlimited capacity to reabsorb Na.[1] This observation was supported further when plasma concentrations and urinary excretion of aldosterone were reported to be much higher and urinary ratios of Na to K (an indication of the aldosterone effect to excrete K and reabsorb Na) much lower in neonates than in children or adults.[2,3] Subsequently, hyponatremia was recognized in neonatal intensive care units as a major clinical problem. The negative Na balance that was observed transiently during the first week of life when preterm infants were thirsted for 2 to 3 days after birth[33,75] and that was noted to persist for weeks when infants were given large volumes of parenteral fluids and NaCl from birth[76,77] was reinterpreted to

mean that distal tubular reabsorption of Na and secretion of K were in fact limited, despite the presence of very large amounts of aldosterone.[2,3,43] This has been the explanation as well for elevated plasma K concentrations in preterm infants.[78]

What determines how much Na is reabsorbed along the proximal tubule? Other than "physical factors,"[46] intrarenal synthesis of angiotensin II has been shown to affect proximal tubule Na reabsorption.[79,80] The concentration of angiotensin II in proximal tubule fluid and efferent arterioles of the rat is 1,000 times greater than the concentration in circulating blood.[81] When the concentration of angiotensin II in proximal tubule fluid was increased experimentally above 10^{-8} mol/L, Na reabsorption was reduced; when it was lowered below 10^{-8} mol/L, Na reabsorption was increased.[79] An increase in angiotensin II also stimulates aldosterone secretion, which in turn increases Na reabsorption in the distal tubule. If angiotensin II is high enough to inhibit proximal tubule Na reabsorption, which it may well be in the neonate, then distal delivery of Na will increase, and the level may exceed the limit of distal sites to recover Na even when aldosterone is high. The concentration of angiotensin II in tubular fluid of neonatal kidneys has not been measured, but the urinary excretion of angiotensin II by newborn dogs[82] and by ELBW infants (Arant, unpublished observation), whose FE$_{Na}$ is normally above 3%, is higher than in adults.

In the first clearance studies ever done in neonates according to strict experimental criteria, Rodriguez-Soriano et al.[83] observed that the fraction of filtered Na and Cl reaching distal tubule sites decreased as gestational age of the neonates increased. Whereas 60% of Na filtered by the glomerulus was reabsorbed in the proximal tubule of the adult kidney, only 40% was reabsorbed there in the preterm infant, just as Schoeneman and Spitzer[69] had found in the guinea pig. The limit to the reabsorptive capacity for Na in the distal tubule in the neonatal dog is about 50% of filtered load[84]—higher than previously thought but not unlimited, as implied from earlier human studies.[1] Regardless of the amount of aldosterone present, this limit is exceeded in preterm infants, and the Na that cannot be reabsorbed in the distal tubule is "wasted" in the urine.

A similar observation in adults is referred to as the deoxycorticosterone acetate (DOCA) escape phenomenon. An individual given a high NaCl intake and treated with mineralocorticoid will retain much of the ingested NaCl and an equivalent amount of water, and the ECF will expand. Once a critical ECF volume is reached, however, the volume-regulating mechanisms cause less tubular fluid to be reabsorbed proximally, and distal delivery of NaCl increases. When the capacity of the distal tubule to reabsorb Na is exceeded, the remaining Na is excreted in the urine. The mechanism for volume regulation, therefore, appears to override the mineralocorticoid effect on Na reabsorption in the distal tubule.

When Leake et al.[85] gave preterm infants an intravenous infusion of 10% dextrose in water at a rate of either 3.6 mL/kg/h (86 mL/kg/day) or 10.3 mL/kg/h (247 mL/kg/d), FE_{Na} was 1.6% and 2.8% respectively. The amount of urinary Na excreted would have represented 2.8 mmol/kg/day and 7.5 mmol/kg/day respectively if the results are extrapolated to 24 hours. Fractional urine flow rate was 6.6% in the low-volume group, compared with 14.2% in the high-volume group. Absolute urine volume expressed in more familiar terms was 3.5 mL/kg/h with the low-volume infusion and 11.8 mL/kg/h at the higher infusion rate. The same response was observed in term infants when Aperia et al.[86] increased fluid intake from 135 to 219 mL/kg/day; both FE_{Na} and V/GFR doubled.

When spontaneous V/GFR in preterm infants was 5% or higher Arant[38,87] observed that distal tubule Na reabsorption increased until a limit was reached, and beyond that the remaining Na was excreted in the urine. Failure to reabsorb the additional Na was reflected by an increase in FE_{Na}. Although preterm infants usually exceeded the limit more often than more mature infants, it was related not to gestational or postconceptional age, as Rodriguez-Soriano et al.[83] had concluded, but to V/GFR, regardless of age.[87] It was V/GFR that varied with gestational age.[38]

When 40 preterm infants of 34 weeks gestation or less were grouped in another study (Arant, unpublished observations) according to their spontaneous diuretic states, the FE_{Na} was less than 1% in all infants whose Na intake was less than 2.0 mmol/kg/day (Fig. 11.1). When the Na intake exceeded 2 mmol/kg/day, however, urinary Na excretion increased. Moreover, the FE_{Na} varied directly with Na intake in every diuretic state except in infants with hydropenia, whose V/GFR was 2% or less and whose urine osmolarity exceeded 250 mOsm/L. This latter condition indicated a slight reduction in EABV below normal, because the kidney was conserving NaCl and water to maintain or restore ECF volume.

Neonatal Requirements

Sodium Chloride

More than 40 years ago, weight gain was always greater in infants given bovine milk than in those fed human milk. One important difference between these milks is that bovine milk contains three times more NaCl than mature human milk. Kagan et al.[88] compared isocaloric feedings in five groups of preterm infants in which the Na intake varied from 1.16 mmol/kg/day with human milk to 3.53 mmol/kg/day with formula. The infants were studied at the 6th and 28th days of life. Those on higher NaCl intake had the most weight gain, but they failed to show the characteristic pattern of decreasing total body water and ECF relative to body weight. The dry weights of the infants were not different among the groups; those given the higher Na intake, therefore, had an expanded ECF volume.

Based on careful metabolic balance studies, Ziegler and Foman[89] determined that term infants need a total of 2.4 mmol/day of NaCl for growth during the first 4 months of life. Factored for body weight, this represents only about 0.35 to 0.7 mmol/kg/day. In case the NaCl requirement had been underestimated, the authors recommended tripling that amount or giving 1.0 to 2.0 mmol/kg/day, which should be adequate to cover incidental losses from skin or gastrointestinal tract.

Because NaCl balance seems to vary greatly with fluid intake, the following discussion divides representative studies arbitrarily into three groups: daily fluid intake >170 mL/kg/day, between 140 and 170 mL/kg/day, and <140 mL/kg/day.

Daily Fluid Intake >170 mL/kg Where did the notion arise that preterm infants, especially ELBW infants, need more NaCl than more mature infants? The reports referred to most often, perhaps, are those of Day et al.,[90] Roy et al.,[76] and Chance et al.,[91] all of whom observed that preterm infants given more NaCl than would be provided in human milk or formula exhibited less hyponatremia and greater growth. A major criticism of those studies is that no information was provided on the management of the infants during the first 2 weeks of life, before the observations began. If fluid intake had been relatively high or if negative Na balance had been prolonged, the infants could have

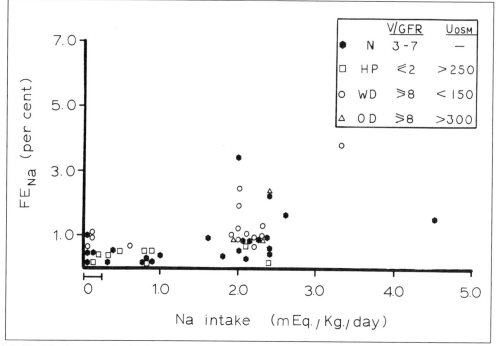

Fig. 11.1. The FE_{Na} is compared to Na intake in 40 preterm infants, 26 to 34 weeks gestation, with birthweights between 780 and 1,630 g. The symbols represent four different diuretic states: N = euvolemia; HP = hydropenia, or renal Na and water conservation; WD = water diuresis, or a large volume of dilute urine; and OD = osmotic diuresis.

begun the study with a deficit in total body Na. This is certainly true of these studies by Day et al.[90] and Roy et al.[76] because infants were given a fluid intake of 150 to 200 mL/kg/day, and although none were hyponatremic when selected for study just after birth, all infants exhibited hyponatremia (plasma Na concentration <135 mmol/L) by the time the study began. Infants given an Na intake of 2.8 mmol/kg/day excreted an average of 0.92 mmol/kg/day in the urine, while those given only 1.6 mmol/kg/day excreted only 0.45 mmol/kg/day. Infants given a fluid intake of 150 mL/kg/day appeared to excrete less Na in their urine compared to those given 200 mL/kg/day, regardless of whether the Na intake was high or low. Assuming no difference in NaCl losses in stool and sweat between groups, NaCl balance was positive in both groups, and growth, as measured by length and head circumference, was not different. The only difference between the infants was greater weight gain in those given more NaCl. The recommendation that preterm infants be given NaCl at a rate of 3 mmol/kg/day to prevent late hyponatremia between 3 to 5 weeks, therefore, really was *treatment* for the Na deficit that had developed during the first 2 weeks of life. Sodium supplementation for 2 weeks was beneficial in restoring the Na deficit in one group of infants, while

hyponatremia became more pronounced in the unsupplemented infants.

Kashyap et al.[92] fed preterm infants one of three formulas, which did not differ in electrolyte content but were different in protein content and total calories. The infants were introduced to a formula by the fourth day of life and were ingesting, on average, 178 mL/kg/day by the third week. Each formula provided Na 2.6 mmol/kg/day, Cl 3.6 mmol/kg/day, and K 4.2 mmol/kg/day. Positive balance of each electrolyte was achieved, but those infants given a higher protein intake had significantly more Na retention, while those given more calories retained more Cl and K. Overall growth, measured by weight gain, was greater in those infants given more calories and was attributed to more fat deposition. The important point of this study was that the differences observed were unrelated to Na, Cl, or K intake.

When Saigal and Sinclair[73] fed preterm infants Na at a rate of 1.4 or 2.7 mmol/kg/day in the same volume of formula (~200 mL/kg/day), infants given more Na excreted a greater fraction of it in the urine. However, Na balance was positive with either intake. No occurrence of hyponatremia was mentioned in the report.

When Engelke et al.[93] gave very low-birthweight infants who were appropriate for gestational age

(AGA) a fluid intake in excess of 200 mL/kg/day for 8 days, urinary Na excretion was 17.6 mmol/kg on the third day and Na balance was -9.3 mmol/kg/day, despite an intake of 7.5 mmol/kg/day. This is more urinary NaCl wasting than was reported for fasting infants given no NaCl at all during the first days of life. When the Na intake was increased to 10 mmol/kg/day, more than 90% was excreted in the urine. The FE_{Na} exceeded 15% on the third day and had decreased only to 5% by the eighth day. Half the infants developed hyponatremia (<130 mmol/L) despite the large Na intake provided. The infants lost an average of 12.7% of birthweight by the fifth postnatal day; however, only one of these 12 infants appears to have received other nutritional support during this period. The conclusion of these authors that preterm infants require very high Na supplementation, therefore, does not seem warranted, and the paucity of physiologic data provided in this unusual report does not support such a recommendation.

Preterm infants studied by Sulyok et al.[94] were given no NaCl supplementation, only human milk, for the first 6 weeks of life. The total volume of fluid given to the infants was approximately 220 mL/kg/day. The average plasma Na concentration decreased from 137 to 131 mmol/L. Although Na intake was not measured, the average urinary Na excretion was between 1 and 3 mmol/kg/day in the final 2 weeks of the study, when the infants exhibited hyponatremia. It should be noted, however, that V/GFR in these infants, on average, remained greater than 5% during the entire 6 weeks after birth; it should have decreased to <1.0% after the first week of life, as it does in neonates given less fluid intake.

In a subsequent report, Sulyok et al.[95] compared the renal handling of Na on the sixth day of life in preterm and term infants fed human milk to which 5% dextrose in water was added, providing a total fluid intake of about 180 mL/kg/day. On a similar Na intake, the preterm infants had higher FE_{Na} (1.44% versus 0.36%), which was attributed to less Na being reabsorbed in the proximal tubule. When this additional amount of Na was presented to the distal tubule, only 70% was recovered, compared to 86% in term infants. Although the fraction of Na reabsorbed distally was less in preterm infants, they actually transported more Na than the full-term infants (0.465 versus 0.32 mL/min/1.73 m^2). An aldosterone effect was definitely manifested in those preterm infants. A more plausible explanation of the finding might be the difference in V/GFR between the infant groups: 6.1% in preterm and 3.3% in term infants. The influence of excess ECF volume was less in the more mature infants.

Al-Dahhan et al.[58] recommended that preterm infants be given Na at a rate of 4 to 5 mmol/kg/day during the first 2 weeks of life. The basis for this recommendation was that the ELBW neonates (27 to 29 weeks gestational age) that they studied exhibited negative Na balance during the first week of life, and 43% of them developed hyponatremia. The gastrointestinal losses of Na were minimal, <0.1 mmol/kg/day.[96] The fluid intake of these infants was 170 to 180 mL/kg/day. When this recommendation was tested in other infants given supplemental NaCl during the first 2 weeks of life to provide 4.5 mmol/kg/day, a positive Na balance was achieved.[97] A comparison group of infants received a total of only 1.5 mmol/kg/day, and their Na balance remained slightly negative. The Na-supplemented infants gained more weight on the same calorie and protein intake as the unsupplemented infants. The greater weight gain was, as demonstrated acutely and chronically in earlier studies, more likely a difference in ECF volume; water retention was facilitated by excess NaCl. When compared 3 days after the supplement was discontinued at age 14 days, however, there was no difference in Na balance between the supplemented and unsupplemented infants. The supplemented infants certainly seemed to fare much better. A fact that cannot be ignored is that the unsupplemented infants received more daily fluid intake than similar infants in other studies who exhibited a positive Na balance with little or no hyponatremia on the same or even lower Na intake.

Daily Fluid Intake of 140 to 170 mL/kg Babson and Bramhall[98] provided preterm infants with a Na intake of either 1.1 or 3.0 mmol/kg/day during the first month of life and varied the protein intake. The infants given more protein exhibited greater linear growth, but the high-salt diet resulted in only about a 3 g/kg difference in daily weight gain, which could be attributable to Na and water retention.

Räihä et al.[99] studied preterm infants given pooled human milk (170 mL/kg/day) or one of four formulas (150 mL/kg/day), which differed primarily in protein or carbohydrate content. The Na, Cl, and K intakes of the infants were identical, 1.2, 1.95, and 2.55 mmol/kg/day respectively. No differences in growth were observed among the groups. Weight gain in the smallest preterm infants was about 20 g/day.

Polberger et al.[100] fed preterm infants human milk that provided an average Na intake of 1.9 to 2.0 mmol/kg/day in a volume of 170 mL/kg/day; only the protein intake varied. Like the study of Day et al.[90] this study began during the third week of life, and observations continued until the infants weighed 2.2 kg, or about 4 weeks. The growth rate was considered satisfactory and was unrelated to Na intake. In fact, some infants given less than 2 mmol/kg/day gained more than 40 g/day. Plasma Na concentration fell below 130 mmol/L in only one infant, and the mean value for all infants was 138 mmol/L.

Schanler and Oh[101] compared the growth of preterm infants given Na intakes of 1.6 to 1.9 mmol/kg/day for the first 5 weeks of life in about 170 mL/kg/day of fluid, either preterm or mature human milk or formula. Regardless of the feeding, Na retention by the infants was similar, and no differences in growth rate were observed.

Daily Fluid Intake <140 mL/kg Lorenz et al.[102] compared Na balance in two groups of preterm infants—one given enough fluid to permit an 8% to 10% decrease in body weight during the first 5 days of life, the other given enough fluid to permit a 13% to 15% decrease. The average Na intake was 2.2 mmol/kg/day in those infants losing less weight (i.e., those given more fluid) compared with 0.9 mmol/kg/day in those losing more weight (given less fluid). The Na intake for these groups among ELBW infants on average, was either 3.1 or 1.6 mmol/kg/day, which was more than the Na received by preterm infants weighing 1,000 to 1,750 g. Although hyponatremia was encountered in only 1 of 44 infants given the lower Na intake, the infants given more Na actually had significantly lower plasma Na concentrations overall, and 5 of 44 developed hyponatremia. There was no increase in morbidity among infants given less Na and less fluid. Even the ELBW infants did well on a daily Na intake <2 mmol/kg.

Engle et al.[44] permitted preterm infants to gradually lose an average of 12% of their birthweight during the first week of life. The average Na intake of the infants during the first 3 weeks of life was 2.3 mmol/kg/day. Sodium balance was positive by the third day of life, and no infant developed hyponatremia. By the end of the third week, not only had birthweights been exceeded by 12%, but body weight actually increased by 25% over the lowest weight recorded 8 days after birth—an average daily weight gain of 20.9 g/day during the last 14 days of the study.

Asano et al.[103] fed preterm infants, born at 25 to 36 weeks gestation, human milk in a volume that increased from 50 to 110 mL/kg/day and provided Na at a rate of 2.0 mmol/kg/day during the first week of life. The infants lost between 10% and 20% of birthweight, and plasma Na concentrations remained between 130 and 150 mmol/L.

Ekblad et al.[104] fed preterm infants human milk, with Na intake of either 2 or 4 mmol/kg/day. They concluded that the higher Na intake was "better" for the infants, although there was no difference in plasma Na or K concentrations, COP, or in BP between the groups. Plasma Na concentrations tended to be lower in infants given less Na, but hyponatremia was not reported.

Kojima et al.[105] fed sick preterm infants only human milk. The infants received no Na on the first day of life and an average daily Na intake of 2.2 mmol/kg for the remainder of the 2-week study. The volume of fluid given increased from 65 to 120 mL/kg/day during the first week of life. All infants were in positive Na balance at the end of the second week of life, when the FE_{Na} was 0.7%. Plasma aldosterone concentrations decreased with postnatal age and were inversely related to FE_{Na}. Hyponatremia was not a problem in these infants, and weight gain was 24 g/day, compared with 21 g/day in healthy full-term infants treated similarly.

In similar preterm infants, Shaffer and Meade[15] gave an average fluid intake of 125 mL/kg/day and Na intake of either 1 or 3 mmol/kg/day for the first 10 days of life. Both groups of infants lost weight, and ECF volume, measured as corrected bromide space, decreased. In both groups Na balance was positive on the 10th day, after which the NA intake was 2 to 2.5 mmol/kg/day for all infants. Sodium balance remained positive, and plasma Na concentrations remained between 130 and 135 mmol/L in those infants originally given only 1 mmol/kg/day. It is likely that the lower Na intake for the first 10 days could explain the lower plasma Na concentrations, both before and after the period of study. This study confirmed this group's earlier observation[106] that the Na requirement in ELBW infants may be more than 1 but less than 3 mmol/kg/day.

Most recently, Costarino et al.[107] provided ELBW infants with Na intake of either 4.3 or 0.85 mmol/kg/day in parenteral fluids during the first 5 days of life. The volume of fluid administered was varied to maintain hemodynamic stability and plasma Na concentration between 130 and 150 mmol/L. Those infants given the higher Na intake received an average fluid intake of 134 mL/kg/day, and the Na-restricted infants received 85 mL/kg/day. The urinary Na excretion was similar in the two groups, 4.5 to 5.0 mmol/kg/day. Infants given more Na nearly maintained Na balance, while those given very little Na had a negative Na balance of −3.9 mmol/kg/day or, on average, a 19.4 mmol Na deficit by the end of the first 5 days of life; this is similar to the finding in infants studied more than 30 years earlier by Butterfield et al.[75] Only two of the Na restricted infants developed hyponatremia, whereas two infants given the higher Na intake developed hypernatremia. Although not statistically significant in this small group of infants, the incidences of patent ductus arteriosus and bronchopulmonary dysplasia were higher in infants given more Na and a higher fluid intake, similar to reports by others.[39,108]

It should be obvious from these various studies that it is the infant, not the clinician, who determines

NaCl balance, provided that a minimum NaCl intake of about 1 mmol/kg/day is given in a moderate volume of fluid, 140 mL/kg/day or less. If more fluid is administered, even to replace higher insensible water loss, additional NaCl must be prescribed. When fluid therapy exceeds 200 mL/kg/day, most ELBW infants will not be able to maintain NaCl balance, regardless of the amount of NaCl provided. In my opinion, it would seem more reasonable, therefore, to minimize insensible water loss so that the volume of fluids administered can maintain the infant's optimal hydration without causing urinary NaCl wasting.

Potassium

The actual requirement for K in preterm infants has not been studied definitively. Controversy about providing K to preterm infants is usually based on clinicians' anxiety. There has been a general concern for complications attributed to K, namely cardiac arrhythmias.[109] Leslie et al.[110] found that among 43 ELBW infants, 60% had at least one plasma K concentration above 5.5 mmol/L, and 30% had a value in excess of 7 mmol/L. The highest value was observed, on average, 25 hours after birth. Five of the infants developed cardiac arrhythmias, and four of them died. The plasma K concentration varied inversely with urinary volume but not with K intake, arterial blood pH, asphyxia, respiratory distress, gestational age, or birthweight.

Most episodes of hyperkalemia in the neonate have no observable consequences. In fact, the range of normal values for plasma K concentration given in standard references exceed the upper limit for every other age. Whether this is due to the frequent occurrence of hemolyzed blood specimens, blood sampling in a hypoperfused extremity, or a greater tolerance to extracellular K is uncertain. What is certain is that hyperkalemia and cardiac arrhythmia can account for many deaths of preterm infants, and this problem occurs in the absence of K administration, either parenterally or with feeding. Prevention of hyperkalemia should be directed more at keeping K within cells than at providing the daily requirement recommended for stable and growing infants.

Compared with the pronounced negative Na and Cl balance of normal and sick preterm infants, K balance is only minimally negative during the first days of life. Al-Dahhan et al.[97] observed that preterm infants retained more K when given NaCl supplements to prevent hyponatremia. Sulyok et al.[111] reported that the plasma K concentration was 6.5 ± 0.5 mmol/L in preterm infants born at 30 to 32 weeks gestation, compared with 5.1 ± 0.2 mmol/L in infants born at 40 weeks gestation. Moreover, urinary K excretion and K balance did not change with increasing gestational age of preterm infants.

In a balance study of preterm infants with respiratory distress syndrome, Engle and Arant[112] observed plasma K concentrations of 4.9 ± 0.2 mmol/L on the first day of life, which decreased to 3.8 mmol/L by the fourth day; plasma K concentration in preterm infants without respiratory distress decreased from 6.5 ± 0.4 to 5.9 ± 0.1 mmol/L during the same period. Urinary K excretion in these infants varied directly with urinary PGE_2 excretion. In at least one infant studied, a single dose of furosemide, which stimulates PGE_2 synthesis, increased urinary K excretion tenfold. In a subsequent metabolic balance study of preterm infants, Engle et al.[44] found plasma K concentrations of 5.6 ± 0.3 mmol/L on the first day of life, 4.8 ± 0.2 at 3 days of age, and unchanged values by the end of the third week. No infant developed hyperkalemia. Furthermore, urinary K excretion varied directly with urinary aldosterone excretion. It could be that a rise in plasma K concentration following birth stimulated the renin-angiotensin-aldosterone axis in these neonates, just as K loading does in rats.[113]

Most foods and milks contain K in quantities similar to or exceeding their Na contents. Moreover, when neonates are deprived of K following birth or are treated by measures such as diuretic therapy that increase renal K excretion, hypokalemia will develop quite predictably. It is appropriate, therefore, for K to be prescribed when a preterm infant has become stabilized and the plasma K concentration has either remained or returned to within the range of normal values (4.0 to 5.5 mmol/L). In balance studies by various investigators,[75,82,85,96,97] regardless of K intake, thriving preterm infants retained K at about 1.0 to 1.5 mmol/kg/day, which is about the same as fetal accretion. The amount of K usually recommended is similar to the amount provided in human milk, about 2 to 3 mmol/kg/day.[114] Certain milk formulas provide even more K without any untoward effects on the infant, unless renal function is impaired or mineralocorticoid deficiency is present.

Recommendations

Although the daily requirement for nutrients such as protein may vary according to the gestational age or body weight of the neonate, there is no discernible difference in the minimum requirement for NaCl to achieve optimal growth among infants of various maturities. The variable that confounds clinical practice is the need to maintain adequate NaCl balance so that NaCl is always available but never in either excess or deficiency.

In some nurseries preterm infants rarely exhibit wide fluctuations in plasma Na concentrations, while other nurseries combat this problem in many infants almost daily. Certainly, the difference is not the infants themselves. Could it be the amount of NaCl provided to the infants? Perhaps, except that when treated prospectively in controlled studies, preterm infants given less NaCl (0.9 mmol/kg/day) maintained plasma Na concentrations and NaCl balance better than those given more salt (2.2 to 4.3 mmol/kg/day).[102,107] The differences in clinical management have usually been the total volume of fluid given each day and reduction of the excess ECF after birth before maintenance fluid therapy was initiated. Extremely low-birthweight and preterm infants given high-volume fluid therapy,[77] fresh frozen plasma,[17] and higher NaCl intakes[88] had no postnatal decrease in ECF volume during the first week of life. Failure to achieve this normal reduction in ECF following birth has been associated with a higher morbidity rate among preterm infants.[39,77,107]

Transitional Period
It is easy to understand the urgency some clinicians feel to replace urinary losses of Na and thus implicate kidney function as the cause of hyponatremia in preterm infants. For the fetus, the Na lost in the urine can be replaced by ingestion of amniotic fluid and from the maternal circulation across the placenta. What is the risk in failing to maintain Na balance following birth and replacing only insensible weight loss (IWL), not urine volume, precisely with water to which nutrients, not electrolytes, may be added? If we are to learn from nature, there should be no risk to normal preterm neonates, even ELBW infants, if they are permitted to excrete the excess of ECF—NaCl and water—in the urine until body composition, particularly ECF, is more like that of the term neonate. The effectiveness of this approach has been proven in numerous studies.[15,102,107] Sick neonates or those considered high risk because of prematurity could be managed similarly by replacing insensible water loss precisely with water to which nutrients, but not electrolytes, may be added. Urinary excretion of Na and urine volume tend to be less in ventilated infants with and without respiratory distress syndrome.[38,115,116]

If 0.25% NaCl solution is given as a parenteral fluid to replace all of the anticipated insensible water losses and to provide some NaCl to offset urinary excretion, the ELBW or preterm infant under a radiant warmer would receive approximately 200 mL/kg/day. This amount, combined with intravenous saline "flushes" and drugs, would come to a Na intake of at least 7.5 mmol/kg/day. Whereas the infused water is lost from the skin, the 0.25% NaCl is effectively concentrated in the infant, and it may become more like isotonic, even hypertonic, NaCl solution, which maintains a higher ECF volume. When there is continued urinary NaCl wasting, the transitional period is prolonged and, more than likely, optimal nutritional support will be delayed.

Immediately after birth, there may be little or no urine production for several hours or perhaps longer. Plasma AVP concentrations have been shown to be increased during this time.[117] Subsequently, spontaneous diuresis, noted as increases in both urine volume and NaCl excretion, is sustained for 1 to 5 days when only insensible water loss is replaced with water, carbohydrate, lipid, amino acids, and minerals other than NaCl or K. When the ECF has been reduced, further loss of body weight will be minimal if insensible water loss is 20 to 30 mL/kg/day, and a period of oliguria (urine volume <1 mL/kg/h), increased urinary osmolarity (>300 mOsm/L) or increased specific gravity (>1.012), and conservation of NaCl (FE_{Na} <1%) are observed. The fractional weight loss will be between 10% and 15% in preterm infants but may exceed 20% in ELBW infants. Because frequent weighing is considered hazardous to these infants, an electronic scale with a digital readout, made to fit under the sleeping pad in an incubator, is an ideal way of following the infant's change in body weight as often as desired. At this point, the infant can, in my opinion, be given enough enteral or parenteral fluid volume to deliver appropriate nourishment, which would be at least the volume of fluid to replace an idealized urine volume (about 1 to 2 mL/kg/h) and the estimated insensible water loss. This volume can be increased daily to provide additional calories so long as the infant exhibits no complication, such as unexpected weight loss, and neither urinary volume nor insensible water loss decreases.

During the transitional phase, very little NaCl is required to maintain plasma Na concentration between 135 and 145 mmol/L if the volume of fluid administered replaces insensible water losses and is enough to keep the plasma Na concentration within that range, as described by Costarino et al.[107] These investigators gave ELBW infants less than 1.0 mmol/kg/day of Na during the first 5 days of life, mainly with medications, and plasma Na concentrations were easily maintained within the normal range. In fact, management seemed easier than in other infants given more Na, 4 mmol/kg/day, who required a larger volume of water to prevent hypernatremia. The addition of K to parenteral fluids should be postponed until the plasma K concentration is stable within the range of normal values, 4 to 5.5 mmol/L. The same recommendation applies to both ELBW and preterm infants.

Stable and Growing Period
Once the ECF volume has been reduced, loss of body weight has slowed, urinary NaCl excretion has diminished, and an inverse relationship between urine volume and specific gravity is observed, the infant can be

Table 11.2. Recommended Total Allowances of Sodium, Chloride, and Potassium for Preterm Infants*

	Transitional Period† (0–7 days)	Stable and Growing Period (1–8 weeks)	Postdischarge Period (2–6 months)
Sodium (mmol/kg/day)	0–1	2–3	2–3
Chloride (mmol/kg/day)	0–1	2–3	2–3
Potassium (mmol/kg/day)	0–1	2–3	2–3

*Includes that given with medication and blood products.

†The period of transition may be of variable duration and last only 2 or 3 days in individual infants; however, the transitional period tends to be longer in extremely low-birthweight infants.

given a daily intake of 2 to 3 mmol/kg each of Na, Cl, and K (Table 11.2). The amounts of Na, Cl, and K should not exceed that recommended for normal growing term infants. Despite suggestions that the preterm infant must maintain a generous ECF volume for satisfactory growth and therefore needs more NaCl than more mature infants, such a requirement has not been documented. This is certainly not the case during other periods of rapid growth in infancy and adolescence.

If parenteral nutrition must be continued beyond the transitional period, the same daily amount of electrolytes should be provided. Such amounts are provided in preterm human milk during the first 4 weeks[114,118] and in modified bovine milk formulas for preterm infants (Table 11.3). However, preterm infants fed pooled mature human milk may require some Na supplementation, at least until full volume is achieved; Cl and K contents are adequate, and no supplements are needed. Occasionally, healthy infants will require more or less electrolyte intake. Most sick infants require frequent adjustments in intake, depending upon renal function, fluid therapy, drug therapy, and ventilator settings, all of which can alter renal electrolyte excretion.[38]

Electrolyte Derangements

The ranges of normal values for plasma concentrations of Na, Cl, and K in humans have been based on assays performed on plasma samples drawn from thousands, even millions, of normal individuals. Studies of normal humans involving a variety of intakes have shown how well homeostatic mechanisms can maintain electrolyte concentrations within a relatively narrow range. Moreover, the electrical poten-

Table 11.3. Approximate Electrolyte Contents of Human Milk* and Preterm Formulas

	Na	Cl (mmol/100mL/day)	K
Preterm human milk			
1st week	1.7	1.9	1.7
2–3 weeks	1.3	1.3	1.5
4–8 weeks	0.8	1.2	1.4
Mature human milk			
0–14 days	0.9	1.4	1.6
>14 days	0.7	1.1	1.4
Preterm formula			
24 cal/oz	1.4	1.9	2.1

*Average mean values.[114,118]

tials across cellular membranes are optimal within these ranges.

Deficiencies

Hyponatremia and Hypochloremia Relative or absolute hyponatremia occurs when the plasma Na concentration decreases, either within the range of normal values between 135 and 145 mmol/L (e.g., from 140 to 136 mmol/L) or to an abnormal value below 135 mmol/L. In preterm infants the most common cause is relative hyponatremia, or excess body water relative to a normal body Na content. This clinical situation is attributable most often to inappropriate AVP secretion, which is usually triggered and sustained by a change in intrathoracic pressure that alters cardiac output.[38,74] The clue to this disorder is a decrease in urine volume that is associated either with an increase in body weight or a failure to lose weight normally during the transitional period, which precedes the fall in plasma Na concentration. Other changes in blood chemistries include a parallel decrease in BUN and serum Cl concentration and, perhaps, blood hematocrit, which are indications of hemodilution; however, in the neonate, the hematocrit may change for other reasons. The FE_{Na} will be above 1.0%, which misleads the clinician into thinking that the hyponatremia is due to renal Na wasting. Administering Na rarely raises the plasma Na concentration, which remains nearly unchanged as the additional Na acts osmotically to pull water from the intracellular compartment. Appropriate treatment is restriction of water intake until the plasma Na concentration increases to within the range of normal values.

With an absolute Na deficiency state, there is difficulty in maintaining ECF volume. Extracellular fluid volume depletion alters cardiovascular hemodynamics and organ perfusion unless total body water has been maintained. However, as plasma Na concentration decreases, the ECF osmolarity falls in parallel, and cells, particularly brain cells, begin to swell. In addition, hyponatremia can slow nerve conduction, reduce neuroexcitation of muscle, and, as most clinicians recognize, cause seizures.[105] Even the occurrence of neonatal apnea has been associated with hyponatremia.[6] If hyponatremia is permitted to persist, as it is in many infants whose plasma Na concentrations are considered "satisfactory" at 125 to 134 mmol/L or higher, there is potential risk for central pontine demyelinolysis. Just how often this occurs in neonates has not been considered thoroughly, but its incidence in older children and adults is remarkable.[7]

The decision to administer Na to an infant whose plasma Na concentration is low, therefore, can be no more than guesswork when prior Na or water balance is unknown or ignored. When the exact etiology of the hyponatremia cannot be determined, supplemental Na should be administered. If possible, the Na should be given orally or with feedings to correct the deficit over 24 hours. If Na must be given parenterally, care must be given not to raise the plasma osmolarity acutely more than 5 to 6 mmol/L, to prevent a reduction in brain water.[119] This would mean that the maximum safe increment in plasma Na concentration is 2.5 mmol/L or a total increase in plasma osmolarity of 5 mOsm/L. The osmotic load of the anion, given either as NaCl or $NaHCO_3$, contributes an additional 2.5 mOsm/L. In the case of a seizure associated with hyponatremia, Na administration may need to exceed this guideline, because the relative risk of seizures, which cannot be controlled with the usual drugs but only with Na, is greater than the potential brain injury from the sudden increase in plasma osmolarity.

If the infant is clinically dehydrated and has hyponatremia, the FE_{Na} will be less than 1%, oliguria will be accompanied by urine that is more concentrated than plasma, and BUN will be increased. Treatment of an infant under these circumstances is the same as for any other patient with hyponatremia and dehydration.

For the infant with bronchopulmonary dysplasia, electrolyte deficiency is manifested both as water excess and urinary electrolyte losses from chronic diuretic therapy. The treatment of this condition is to concentrate feedings and provide less water, thereby avoiding further diuretic therapy and the need to replace electrolytes. Such correction is easier said than done; however, when these infants are treated prospectively, much of the electrolyte deficiency can be prevented. The goal in these patients is to promote adequate growth, which is slowed when infants suffer from chronic electrolyte deficiency.

The previously unrecognized importance of Cl on growth was identified in infants who were selectively deprived of Cl when the formula[120,121] or human milk[122] they ingested was deficient. Inadequate Cl in growing infants is associated with plasma Cl concentrations below 97 mmol/L and is manifested by failure to gain weight, followed by reduction in the rate of linear growth and, finally, reduction in growth of the head. Moreover, hyponatremia and hypokalemia accompany the hypochloremia, and a metabolic alkalosis develops. Little or no Cl is lost in the urine of these infants. Restitution of the Cl deficiency (plasma Cl concentration ≥97 mmol/L) permits prompt correction of the other biochemical abnormalities. Growth resumes, first with a prompt increase in body weight, followed by an increase in length and, finally, by an accelerated rate of head growth. Chloride deficiency also can develop from excessive loss of Cl in the urine (due to Bartter's syndrome or diuretic therapy), from the gut (due to chronic vomiting, chronic diarrhea, or, more rarely, Cl-losing diarrhea), and from the skin (as in cystic fibrosis).

Hypokalemia Hypokalemia results most often from diuretic therapy and from failure to provide adequate K to preterm infants. Because concern is more for the development of hyperkalemia and its consequences, many clinicians are reluctant to add K to parenteral fluids. Moreover, only glucose and, in some nurseries, amino acids and lipids are provided in parenteral fluids given sick infants soon after birth. Such treatment not only keeps most of the K within cells but also moves additional K out of the ECF into cells. In the absence of exogenous K, the preterm infant can develop hypokalemia rather quickly, especially if urine volume is maintained high, diuretics are given, or insulin is administered to combat hyperglycemia.[112]

The signs of K deficiency include lethargy, muscle weakness (even paralysis), and cardiac arrhythmia (first manifested as bradycardia with subsequent electrocardiographic abnormalities). There may also be ileus and a decrease in urinary concentrating ability. Chronic K deficiency can be associated with histopathologic changes in the renal tubules; AVP resistance, so that there is a loss of urinary concentrating ability and polyuria; increased renal production of PGE_2, with resulting renin release; and increased angiotensin formation and aldosterone secretion, which worsens the K deficiency and increases renal vascular resistance and GFR.[123] Polydipsia develops, and an infant who depends on caregivers for water intake will become dehydrated, develop hypernatremia, and seem to have developed nephrogenic diabetes insipidus.

The management of K deficiency calls for anticipation in infants at risk and prevention when possible. In an emergency, K can be administered intravenously as KCl or K phosphate, with close electrocardiographic monitoring. Otherwise, chronic K deficiency is best treated by selectively increasing the K intake.

Excesses

Hypernatremia The usual cause of hypernatremia in preterm infants is inadequate replacement of insensible water losses—with enough water alone or through provision of excess Na, either in parenteral fluids to replace water losses, as a supplement in routine practice, or as $NaHCO_3$ treatment for systemic acidosis. Absolute Na excess may not be suspected in any infant until the plasma Na concentration increases above 145 mmol/L. Further, correction of hyponatremia requires that the deficit be calculated on the basis of total body water. The excess Na in the ECF osmotically draws water from cells; otherwise, the rate of rise in plasma Na concentration would proceed at a higher rate. Treatment for hypernatremia includes reduction in Na intake, slow correction of any water deficit, and administration of a loop diuretic such as furosemide to increase urinary NaCl losses. Again, one must recognize the risk of excessive Na administration to preterm infants: the consequences are just as serious, maybe more so, than those of hyponatremia.[124]

Hyperkalemia As stated before, hyperkalemia has serious consequences. Moreover, if the clinician waits until the plasma K concentration has exceeded 7 mmol/L or electrocardiographic changes associated with a lower concentration occur, the likelihood of treatment being successful is reduced. Therefore, every preterm infant should be monitored at regular intervals during the first 48 hours after birth for an increasing plasma K concentration. No K should be administered until the plasma K concentration has remained between 4 and 5.5 mmol/L for 24 hours. Cellular injury from asphyxia or hypoxia should prompt even closer monitoring for hyperkalemia. Maintaining blood glucose concentrations slightly above the range of normal will stimulate endogenous insulin production and drive K into the cells. In the event of symptomatic hyperkalemia or a plasma K concentration that is potentially dangerous, additional glucose and insulin should be administered to drive K out of the ECF and into cells, while the volume of fluid therapy is increased and furosemide is given intravenously to increase urinary K excretion.[112] Calcium gluconate can be given intravenously in an emergency to treat an arrhythmia while other treatments are prepared. A cation exchange resin may be given by enema or by nasogastric tube, but this is a secondary maneuver to reduce plasma K concentration.

CASE STUDY

An 870-g infant was born to a healthy mother at 27 weeks gestation. The pregnancy had been uncomplicated. There was some respiratory distress on the first day of life, which was treated eventually by assisted ventilation. Parenteral fluid therapy was initiated with 5% dextrose in 0.25N NaCl solution, 150 to 180 mL/kg/day. Due to the anticipated high insensible water loss in a very preterm infant, the volume was increased to an average of 240 mL/kg/day during the first week of life. Urine volume was usually 3 to 4 mL/kg/h, and urine specific gravity was 1.012.

Plasma Na concentration was 138 mmol/L on admission to the nursery. By the second day, plasma Na concentration had decreased to 128 mmol/L, and the infant was given additional Na, 4 mmol/kg as NaCl over 4 hours. By the third day, plasma Na concentration had decreased further to 124 mmol/L, and the urine volume had increased to 5 mL/kg/h. The FE_{Na} was calculated to be 6.1%, which meant that despite a total Na intake of 9 mmol/kg/day, 12.4 mmol/kg/day was excreted into the urine. Concluding that the infant exhibited renal Na wasting due to immature kidney function, the clinicians changed parenteral fluid therapy to 5% dextrose in 0.5N NaCl, which would provide Na at a rate of 18.5 mmol/kg/day. Yet on the fourth day, the plasma Na concentration had decreased further to 118 mmol/L, the urine volume had increased to 10.4 mL/kg/h, and the FE_{Na} was 8.8%. Although the NaCl intake was raised to nearly four times the amount that should be sufficient to prevent hyponatremia in preterm infants, Na balance was not restored and in fact worsened as the Na intake was systematically increased. Moreover, hyponatremia had become more pronounced. Additional Na as 3% NaCl was given in an amount calculated to raise the plasma Na concentration to 124 mmol/L over 6 hours.

The infant's body weight remained unchanged from birth until the third day of life, when it was 820 g, and it decreased to 805 g by the fourth day; this was 7.5% lower than birthweight. Blood sugar remained between 240 and 300 mg/dL. No nutrition other than the glucose in the parenteral fluids had been given since birth. Enteral feeding was begun on the fourth day, and the intravenous fluid rate was reduced so that the infant received a total fluid intake of only 240 mL/kg/day. The total Na intake was reduced to 9 mmol/kg/day.

By the end of the first week of life, when the infant was gradually weaned from the ventilator, body weight had not decreased further on 60 kcal/kg/day. The plasma Na concentration remained between 120 and 123 mmol/L. Urinary Na wasting was again confirmed by a FE_{Na} of 5.4%, which meant that Na was excreted at a rate of 11.8 mmol/kg/day in a urine volume of 7 to 8 mL/kg/h. During the second week of life, total caloric intake was increased to 105 kcal/kg/day, and gradual weight gain was observed. The hyponatremia persisted but did not worsen, because an intravenous infusion of 3% NaCl was given almost daily in an amount that maintained the plasma Na concentration between 123 and 125 mEq/L.

When consultation with a nephrologist was requested during the third week of life, the infant still exhibited renal Na wasting and persistent hyponatremia. The infant's weight, however, had increased to 920 g. Urine volume was 6.9 mL/kg/h, urine osmolarity was 240 mOsm/L, and the FE_{Na} was 5.3%. The GFR was estimated to be 1 mL/min or 65 mL/kg/h. The V/GFR would have been approximately 10.6%, indicating an increased effective arterial blood volume. The recommendation was to reduce the Na intake to 5 mmol/kg and the total fluid intake to 100 mL/kg for 24 hours. Body weight was recorded every 8 hours, and if a decrease of more than 50 g was noted, the infant was to be examined for evidence of circulatory compromise or dehydration and plasma Na concentration measured. At the end of 24 hours, the infant had lost 80 g, BP was 70/55 mm Hg, heart rate was 140 beats per minute, urine volume had

decreased to 4.4 mL/kg/h, estimated V/GFR would be 7.3%, and urine osmolarity was 188 mOsm/L. Plasma Na concentration had increased slightly to 127 mmol/L, and the FE_{Na} had decreased to 2.8%. Sodium balance was negative, -1.1 mmol/kg.

For the next 24 hours, fluid intake was maintained at 100 mL/kg but the Na intake was reduced to 2.5 mmol/kg. The infant was still monitored closely for any sign of circulatory compromise or change in plasma Na concentration. By the next day, body weight had decreased further to 780 g, urine volume was 2.3 mL/kg/h, V/GFR would now be about 3.8%, and the urinary osmolarity was 70 mOsm/L. Plasma Na concentration increased to 132 mmol/L, and FE_{Na} was 1.4%. Na balance was slightly negative, -0.1 mmol/kg/day. From that point on, the volume of formula and caloric intake were increased daily as the infant tolerated, but the total amount of Na given was kept at 2.5 mmol/kg/day. Plasma Na concentration increased further, and a positive Na balance was achieved without any further change in Na intake. Urine volume was between 1 and 3 mL/kg/h, V/GFR was 1.6% to 3.0%, and urine osmolarity was 110 to 235 mOsm/L.

The explanation for the change from a markedly negative to a positive Na balance with an increase in plasma Na concentration when the amount of NaCl provided was reduced is that the normally expanded ECF of the preterm infant at birth had been maintained with parenteral fluids to which increasing amounts of NaCl were added in an effort to treat or prevent hyponatremia. When a neonate is given 0.25N NaCl solution, the Na intake is 3.75 mmol/kg/day for each 100 mL/kg of fluid administered. The normal renal response to the expanded ECF is to increase the volume and NaCl content of the urine until euvolemia is achieved. This clinical scenario is repeated hundreds of times each day in nurseries by clinicians who prescribe treatment more from the way they were trained than from the clinical knowledge available in the literature, some of it for more than 30 years. Such treatment not only places the infant at jeopardy but prolongs the stay in the neonatal intensive care unit.

References

1. Aperia A, Broberger O, Thodenius K, Zetterstrom R. Developmental study of the renal response to an oral salt load in preterm infants. *Acta Paediatr Scand* 1974; 63: 517–524.
2. Sulyok E, Nemeth M, Tenyi I, et al. Postnatal development of renin-angiotensin-aldosterone system, RAAS, in relation to electrolyte balance in premature infants. *Pediatr Res* 1979; 13:817–820.
3. Aperia A, Broberger O, Herin P, Zetterström R. Sodium excretion in relation to sodium intake and aldosterone excretion in newborn preterm and full-term infants. *Acta Paediatr Scand* 1979; 68:813–817.
4. Barnett HL, Hare K, McNamara H, Hare R. Measurement of glomerular filtration rate in premature infants. *J Clin Invest* 1948; 27:691–699.
5. Dean RFA, McCance RA. The renal responses of infants and adults to the administration of hypertonic solutions of sodium chloride and urea. *J Physiol* 1949; 109: 81–97.

6. Daily WJR, Laus M, Myer HBP. Apnea in premature infants: monitoring, incidence, heart rate changes and an effect of environmental temperatures. *Pediatrics* 1969; 43:510–518.

7. Burcar PJ, Norenberg MD, Yarnell PR. Hyponatremia and central pontine myelinolysis. *Neurology* 1977; 27: 223–226.

8. Siegel SR, Oh W. Renal function as a marker of human fetal maturation. *Acta Paediatr Scand* 1976; 65:481–485.

9. Smith CA, Yudkin S, Young W, Minkowski A, Cushman M. Adjustment of electrolytes and water following premature birth (with special reference to edema). *Pediatrics* 1949; 3:34–47.

10. Givens MH, Macy IG. The chemical composition of the human fetus. *J Biol Chem* 1933; 102:7–17.

11. Friis-Hansen B. Body water compartments in children: changes during growth and related changes in body composition. *Pediatrics* 1961; 28:169–181.

12. Widdowson E, Dickerson JWT. Chemical composition of the body. In: Assali NS, ed. *Biology of gestation.* New York: Academic Press, 1968:2–247.

13. Cheek DB, Wishart J, MacLennan AH, Haslam R. Cell hydration in the normally grown, the premature and the low weight for gestational age infant. *Early Hum Dev* 1984; 10:75–84.

14. Forbes GB, Reid AF, Bondurant J, Etheridge J. Changes in total body chloride during growth. *Pediatrics* 1956; 17: 334–340.

15. Shaffer SG, Meade VM. Sodium balance and extracellular volume regulation in very low birth weight infants. *J Pediatr* 1989; 115:285–290.

16. Shaffer SG, Ekblad H, Brans YW. Estimation of extracellular fluid volume by bromide dilution in infants less than 1000 grams birth weight. *Early Hum Dev* 1991; 27: 19–24.

17. Ekblad H, Kero P, Shaffer SG, Korvenranta H. Extracellular volume in preterm infants: influence of gestational age and colloids. *Early Hum Dev* 1991; 27:1–7.

18. Wladimiroff JW, Campbell S. Fetal urine-production rates in normal and complicated pregnancy. *Lancet* 1974; 1:151–154.

19. Houston IB, Zeis PM. Intrauterine renal function and the amniotic fluid. *J Physiol* 1976; 257:20P–21P.

20. Wu PYK, Rockwell G, Chan L, Wang S-M, Udani V. Colloid osmotic pressure in newborn infants: variations with birth weight, gestational age, total serum solids, and mean arterial pressure. *Pediatrics* 1981; 68:814–819.

21. Ekblad H. Postnatal changes in colloid osmotic pressure in premature infants: in healthy infants, in infants with respiratory distress syndrome, and in infants born to mothers with premature rupture of membranes. *Gynecol Obstet Invest* 1987; 24:95–100.

22. Saito M, Gittleman IF, Pincus JB, Sobel AE. Plasma protein patterns in premature infants of varying weights on the first day of life. *Pediatrics* 1956; 17:657–661.

23. Brace RA. Fetal blood volume responses to intravenous saline solution and dextran. *Am J Obstet Gynecol* 1983; 147:777–781.

24. Arant BS, Jr. Effects of changing plasma volume on sodium excretion by the neonatal kidney. *Pediatr Res* 1978; 12:538.

25. Goldsmith DI, Drukker A, Blaufox MD, Edelmann CM, Jr, Spitzer A. Hemodynamic and excretory response of the neonatal canine kidney to acute volume expansion. *Am J Physiol* 1979; 237:F392–F397.

26. Barr PA, Bailey PE, Sumners J, Cassady G. Relation between arterial blood pressure and blood volume and effect of infused albumin in sick preterm infants. *Pediatrics* 1977; 60:282–289.

27. Arcilla RA, Oh W, Lind J, Blankenship W. Portal and atrial pressures in the newborn period. *Acta Paediatr Scand* 1966; 55:305–315.

28. Taylor PM, Egan TJ, Birchard EL, Bright NH, Wolfson JH. Venous hypertension in the newborn infant associated with delayed clamping of the umbilical cord. *Acta Paediatr* 1961; 50:149–159.

29. Greenough A, Greenall F, Gamsu HR. Immediate effects of albumin infusion in ill premature neonates. *Arch Dis Child* 1988; 63:307–317.

30. Arant BS, Jr. The relationship between blood volume, prostaglandin synthesis and arterial blood pressure in neonatal puppies. In: Spitzer A, ed. *The kidney during development: morphology and function.* New York: Masson, 1981:167–172.

31. London GM, Safar ME, Weiss YA, et al. Volume-dependent parameters in essential hypertension. *Kidney Int* 1977; 11:204–208.

32. Klopfenstein HS, Rudolph AM. Postnatal changes in the circulation and responses to volume loading in sheep. *Circ Res* 1978; 42:839–845.

33. Hansen JDL, Smith CA. Effects of withholding fluid in the immediate postnatal period. *Pediatrics* 1953;12: 99–113.

34. Arant BS, Jr, Stapleton FB, Engle WD, Stephenson WH. Urinary prostaglandin excretion rates and renal function in human infants at birth. *Pediatr Res* 1982; 16:317A.

35. Kaapa P, Viinikka L, Ylikoohala O. Plasma prostacyclin from birth to adolescence. *Arch Dis Child* 1982; 57: 459–461.

36. Arant BS, Jr. Prostaglandin-angiotensin interactions for blood pressure regulation in the newborn. In: Strauss J, ed. *Homeostasis, nephrotoxicity, and renal anomalies in the newborn.* Boston: Martinus Nijhoff, 1986:11–15.

37. Arant BS, Jr. Adaptation of the infant to an external milieu. In: Gruskin A, Norman M, eds. *Pediatric nephrology.* The Hague: Martinus Nijhoff, 1981:265–272.

38. Arant BS, Jr. Neonatal adjustments to extrauterine life. In: Edelmann CM Jr, Bernstein J, Meadow R, Spitzer A, Travis LB, eds. *Pediatric kidney disease.* 2nd ed. Boston: Little Brown, 1992:1015–1042.

39. Bell EF, Warburton D, Stonestreet BS, Oh W. Effects of fluid administration on the development of symptomatic patent ductus arteriosus and congestive heart failure in premature infants. *N Engl J Med* 1980; 302:598–604.

40. Arant BS, Jr. Nonrenal factors influencing renal function during the perinatal period. *Clin Perinatol* 1981; 8: 225–240.

41. Stevenson JG. Fluid administration in the association of patent ductus arteriosus complicating respiratory distress syndrome. *J Pediatr* 1977; 90:257–261.

42. Arant BS, Jr. Developmental patterns of renal functional maturation compared in the human neonate. *J Pediatr* 1978; 92:705–712.

43. Sulyok E, Kovacs L, Lichardus B, et al. Late hyponatremia in premature infants: role of aldosterone and arginine vasopressin. *J Pediatr* 1985; 106:990–994.

44. Engle WD, Magness RR, Faucher DJ, Arant BS, Jr, Rosenfeld CR. Sodium balance in the growing preterm infant. *Pediatr Res* 1985; 19:376A.

45. Morris JA, Hustead RF, Robinson RG, Haswell GL. Measurement of fetoplacental blood volume in the human previable fetus. *Am J Obstet Gynecol* 1974; 118: 927–934.

46. Daugharty TM, Belleau LJ, Martino JA, Earley LE. Interrelationship of physical factors affecting sodium reabsorption in the dog. *Am J Physiol* 1968; 215:1442–1447.

47. Kurtzman NA, White, MG, Rogers PW, Flynn JJ III. Relationship of sodium reabsorption and glomerular fil-

tration rate to glucose reabsorption. *J Clin Invest* 1972; 51:127–133.

48. Blythe WB, Getelman HJ, Welt LG. Effect of expansion of the extracellular space on the rate of urinary excretion of calcium. *Am J Physiol* 1968; 214:52–61.

49. Massry SG, Coburn JW, Kleeman CR. The influence of extracellular volume expansion on renal phosphate reabsorption in the dog. *J Clin Invest* 1969; 48:1237–1245.

50. Kurtzman NA. Regulation of renal bicarbonate reabsorption by extracellular volume. *J Clin Invest* 1970; 49: 586–595.

51. Weinman EJ, Eknoyan G, Suki WN. The influence of the extracellular fluid volume on the tubular absorption of uric acid. *J Clin Invest* 1975;55:283–291.

52. Hall PW, Chung-Park M, Vacca CV, London M, Crowley AQ. The renal handling of beta$_2$-microglobulin in the dog. *Kidney Int* 1982; 22:156–161.

53. Edelmann CM Jr, Spitzer A. The maturing kidney: a modern view of well-balanced infants with imbalanced nephrons. *J Pediatr* 1969; 75:509–519.

54. Arant BS Jr. Glomerulo-tubular balance following saline loading in the developing canine kidney. *Am J Physiol* 1978; 235:F417–F424.

55. Robillard JE, Sessions C, Burmeister L, Smith FG Jr. Influence of fetal extracellular volume contraction on renal reabsorption of bicarbonate in fetal lambs. *Pediatr Res* 1977; 11:649–655.

56. Stapleton FB, Nash D, Arant BS Jr. The role of extracellular fluid volume upon renal clearance of uric acid in puppies. *Pediatr Res* 1982; 16:378A.

57. Fawer C-L, Torrado A, Guignard J-P. Maturation of renal function in full-term and premature neonates. *Helv Paediat Acta* 1979; 34:11–21.

58. Al-Dahhan J, Haycock GB, Chantler C, Stimmler L. Sodium homeostasis in term and preterm neonates. I. Renal aspects. *Arch Dis Child* 1983; 58:335–342.

59. Engle WD, Arant BS Jr. Renal handling of beta-2-microglobulin in the human neonate. *Kidney Int* 1983; 24:358–363.

60. Vanpee M, Herin P, Zetterstrom R, Aperia A. Postnatal development of renal function in very low birthweight infants. *Acta Paediatr Scand* 1988; 77:191–197.

61. Sertel H, Scopes J. Rates of creatinine clearance in babies less than 1 week of age. *Arch Dis Child* 1973; 48: 717–720.

62. Sutphen JL. Anthropometric determinants of creatinine excretion in preterm infants. *Pediatrics* 1982; 69:719–723.

63. Arant BS, Jr. The newborn kidney. In: Rudolph AJ, ed. *Pediatrics.* 19th ed. Norwalk, CT: Appleton and Lange, 1991:1233–1236.

64. Potter EL, Thierstein ST. Glomerular development in the kidney as an index of fetal maturity. *J Pediatr* 1943; 22:695–706.

65. Horster M, Kemler BJ, Valtin H. Intracortical distribution of number and volume of glomeruli during postnatal maturation in the dog. *J Clin Invest* 1971; 50:796–800.

66. Arant BS, Jr., Edelmann CM Jr, Nash MA. The renal reabsorption of glucose in the developing canine kidney: a study of glomerulo-tubular balance. *Pediatr Res* 1974; 8:638–645.

67. Aperia A, Broberger O, Elinder G, Herin P, Zetterstrom R. Postnatal development of renal function in preterm and full-term infants. *Acta Paediatr Scand* 1981; 70:183–187.

68. Merlet-Benichou C, de Rouffignac C. Renal clearance studies in fetal and young guinea pigs: effect of salt loading. *Am J Physiol* 1977; 232:F178–F185.

69. Schoeneman MJ, Spitzer A. The effect of intravascular volume expansion on proximal tubular reabsorption. *Proc Soc Exp Biol Med* 1980; 165:319–322.

70. Scherer B, Weber PC. Urinary prostaglandins in the newborn: relationship to urinary osmolality, urinary potassium, and blood pressure. *Adv Prost Thromb Res* 1980; 7:1033–1038.

71. Norman ME, Asadi FK. A prospective study of acute renal failure in the newborn infant. *Pediatrics* 1979; 63: 475–479.

72. Ziegler EE, Foman SJ. Fluid intake, renal solute load, and water balance in infancy. *J Pediatr* 1971; 78:561–568.

73. Saigal S, Sinclair JC. Urine solute excretion in growing low-birth-weight infants. *J Pediatr* 1977; 90:934–938.

74. Rees L, Brook CGD, Shaw JCL, Forsling ML. Hyponatraemia in the first week of life in preterm infants. II. Arginine vasopressin secretion. *Arch Dis Child* 1984; 59:414–422.

75. Butterfield J, Lubchenco LO, Bergstedt J, O'Brien D. Patterns in electrolyte and nitrogen balance in the newborn premature infant. *Pediatrics* 1960; 26:777–791.

76. Roy RN, Chance GW, Radde IC, Hill MDE, Willis DM, Sheepers J. Late hyponatremia in very low birthweight infants (<1.3 kilograms). *Pediatr Res* 1976; 10:526–531.

77. Stonestreet BR, Bell EF, Warburton D, Oh W. Renal response in low-birth-weight neonates. *Am J Dis Child* 1983; 137: 215–219.

78. Gruskay J, Costarino AT, Polin RA, Baumgart S. Nonoliguric hyperkalemia in the premature infant weighing less than 1000 grams. *J Pediatr* 1988; 113: 381–386.

79. Schuster VL, Kokko JP, Jacobson HR. Angiotensin II directly stimulates sodium transport in rabbit proximal convoluted tubules. *J Clin Invest* 1984; 73:507–515.

80. Liu F-Y, Cogan MG. Role of angiotensin II in glomerulotubular balance. *Am J Physiol* 1990; 259:F72–F79.

81. Seikaly MG, Arant BS Jr, Seney F. Endogenous angiotensin concentrations in specific intrarenal fluid compartment of the rat. *J Clin Invest* 1990; 86:1352–1357.

82. Arant BS, Jr, Seikaly MG. Intrarenal angiotensin II may regulate developmental changes in renal blood flow. *Pediatr Nephrol* 1989; 3:C142.

83. Rodriguez-Soriano J, Vallo A, Oliveros R, Castillo G. Renal handling of sodium in premature and full-term neonates: a study using clearance methods during water diuresis. *Pediatr Res* 1983; 17:1013–1016.

84. Kleinman LI. Renal sodium reabsorption during saline loading and distal blockade in newborn dogs. *Am J Physiol* 1975; 228:1403–1408.

85. Leake RD, Zakauddin S, Trygstad CW, Fu P, Oh W. The effects of large volume intravenous fluid infusion on neonatal renal function. *J Pediatr.* 1976; 89:968–972.

86. Aperia A, Herin P, Lundin S, Melin P, Zetterstrom R. Regulation of renal water excretion in newborn full-term infants. *Acta Paediatr Scand* 1984; 73:717–721.

87. Arant BS, Jr. Distal tubular sodium handling in human neonates. *Contrib Nephrol* 1988; 24:101–107.

88. Kagan BM, Stanincova V, Felix NS, Hodgman J, Kalman D. Body composition of premature infants: relation to nutrition. *Am J Clin Nutr* 1972; 25:1153–1164.

89. Ziegler EE, Foman SJ. Major minerals. In: Foman SJ, ed. *Infant nutrition.* 2nd ed. Philadelphia: WB Saunders, 1974:267–297.

90. Day GM, Radde IC, Balfe JW, Chance GW. Electrolyte abnormalities in very low birth weight infants. *Pediatr Res* 1976; 10:522–526.

91. Chance GW, Ingeborg CR, Willis DM, Park E, Ackerman I. Postnatal growth of infants of <1.3 kg birth weight: effects of metabolic acidosis, of caloric intake, and of calcium, sodium, and phosphate supplementation. *J Pediatr* 1977; 91:787–793.

92. Kashyap S, Forsyth M, Zucker C, Ramakrishnan R, Dell RB, Heird WC. Effects of varying protein and energy

intakes on growth and metabolic response in low birth weight infants. *J Pediatr* 1986; 108:955–963.

93. Engelke SC, Shah BL, Vasan U, Raye JR. Sodium balance in low-birth-weight infants. *J Pediatr* 1978; 93: 837–841.

94. Sulyok E, Varga F, Györy E, Jobst K, Csaba IF. Postnatal development of renal sodium handling in premature infants. *J Pediatr* 1979; 95:787–792.

95. Sulyok E, Varga F, Gyory E, Jobst K, Csaba IF. On the mechanism of renal sodium handling in newborn infants. *Biol Neonate* 1980; 37:75–79.

96. Al-Dahhan J, Haycock GB, Chantler C, Stimmler L. Sodium homeostasis in term and preterm neonates. II. Gastrointestinal aspects. *Arch Dis Child* 1983; 58:343.

97. Al-Dahhan J, Haycock GB, Nichol B, Chantler C, Stimmler L. Sodium homeostasis in term and preterm neonates. III. Effect of salt supplementation. *Arch Dis Child* 1984; 59:945–950.

98. Babson SG, Bramhall JL. Diet and growth in the premature infant. *J Pediatr* 1969; 74:890–900.

99. Räihä NCR, Heinonen K, Rassin DK, Gaull GE. Milk protein quantity and quality in low-birthweight infants. I. Metabolic responses and effects on growth. *Pediatrics* 1976; 57:659–674.

100. Polberger SKT, Axelsson IA, Räihä NCE. Growth of very low birth weight infants on varying amounts of human milk protein. *Pediatr Res* 1989; 25:415–419.

101. Schanler RJ, Oh W. Nitrogen and mineral balance in preterm infants fed human milks or formula. *J Pediatr Gastroenterol Nutr* 1985; 4:214–219.

102. Lorenz JM, Kleinman LI, Kotagal UR, Reller MD. Water balance in very low-birth-weight-infants: relationship to water and sodium intake and effect on outcome. *J Pediatr* 1982;101:423–432.

103. Asano H, Taki M, Igarashi I. Sodium homeostasis in premature infants during the early postnatal period: results of relative low volume of fluid and sodium intake. *Pediatr Nephrol* 1987; 1:C38.

104. Ekblad H, Kero P, Takala J, Korvenranta H, Välimäki I. Water, sodium and acid-base balance in premature infants: therapeutical aspects. *Acta Paediatr Scand* 1987; 76: 47–53.

105. Kojima T, Fukuda Y, Hirata Y, Matsuzaki S, Kobayashi Y. Effects of aldosterone and atrial natriuretic peptide on water and electrolyte homeostasis of sick neonates. *Pediatr Res* 1989; 25:591–594.

106. Shaffer SG, Bradt SK, Meade VM, Hall RT. Extracellular fluid volume changes in very low birth weight infants during first 2 postnatal months. *J Pediatr* 1987; 111: 124–128.

107. Costarino AT Jr, Gruskay JA, Corcoran L, Polin RA, Baumgart S. Sodium restriction versus daily maintenance replacement in very low birth weight premature neonates: a randomized, blind therapeutic trial. *J Pediatr* 1992; 120: 99–106.

108. Brown ER, Stark A, Sosenko I, Lawson EE, Avery ME. Bronchopulmonary dysplasia: possible relationship to pulmonary edema. *J Pediatr* 1978; 92:982–984.

109. Usher R. The respiratory distress syndrome of prematurity, I: changes in potassium in the serum and the electrocardiogram and effects of therapy. *Pediatrics* 1959; 24:562–576.

110. Leslie GI, Carman G, Arnold JD. Early neonatal hyperkalaemia in the extremely premature newborn infant. *J Paediatr Child Health* 1990; 26:58–61.

111. Sulyok E, Németh M, Tényi I, et al. Relationship between maturity, electrolyte balance and the function of the renin-angiotensin-aldosterone system in newborn infants. *Biol Neonate* 1979; 35:60–65.

112. Engle WD, Arant BS, Jr. Urinary potassium excretion in the critically ill neonate. *Pediatrics* 1984; 74:259–264.

113. Nakamaru M, Misono KS, Naruse M, Workman RJ, Inagami T. A role for the adrenal renin-angiotensin system in the regulation of potassium-stimulated aldosterone production. *Endocrinology* 1985; 117:1772–1778.

114. Gross SJ. Growth and biochemical response of preterm infants fed human milk or modified infant formula. *N Engl J Med.* 1983; 308:237–241.

115. Engle WD, Arant BS Jr, Wiriyathian S, Rosenfeld CR. Diuresis and respiratory distress syndrome: physiologic mechanisms and therapeutic implications. *J Pediatr* 1983; 102:917–921.

116. Tulassay T, Machay T, Kiszel J, Varga J. Effects of continuous positive airway pressure on renal function in prematures. *Biol Neonate* 1983; 43:152–157.

117. Pohjavuori M, Fyhrquist F. Hemodynamic significance of vasopressin in the newborn infant. *J Pediatr* 1980; 97: 462–465.

118. Lemons JA, Moye L, Hall D, Simmons M. Differences in the composition of preterm and term human milk during early lactation. *Pediatr Res* 1982; 16:113–117.

119. Finberg L. The relationship of intravenous infusions and intracranial hemorrhage: a commentary. *J Pediatr* 1977; 91:777–778.

120. Roy S III, Arant BS Jr. Hypokalemic metabolic alkalosis in normotensive infants with elevated plasma renin activity and hyperealdosteronism: the role of dietary chloride deficiency. *Pediatrics* 1981; 67:423–429.

121. Rodriguez-Soriano J, Vallo A, Castillo G, Oliveros R, Cea JM, Balzategui MJ. Biochemical features of dietary chloride deficiency syndrome: a comparative study of 30 cases. *J Pediatr* 1983; 103:209–214.

122. Asnes RS, Wisotsky DH, Migel PF, Seigle RI, Levy J. The dietary chloride deficiency syndrome occurring in a breast-fed infant. *J Pediatr* 1982; 100:923–924.

123. Bevan M, Arant B, Hogg R, Kokko J. Effect of chronic prostaglandin inhibition on the renal concentrating defect in potassium deficiency. *Clin Res* 1982; 30:881A.

124. Arieff AI, Guisado R. Effects on the central nervous system of hypernatremic and hyponatremic states. *Kidney Int* 1976; 10:104–116.

12. Iron, Folic Acid, and Vitamin B₁₂

Richard A. Ehrenkranz

Reviewers: C. Lawrence Kien, Winston W.K. Koo

Iron

The goal of nutritional management of preterm infants is often stated to be the provision of nutrient intakes that will permit prompt postnatal resumption of growth and nutrient accretion at a rate approximating that of the third trimester of intrauterine life.[1] Controversy exists over the amount of dietary iron that should be provided to growing premature infants during the early postnatal period and the optimal time to begin providing supplemental iron.[1-11] Initiation of iron supplementation shortly after birth does not prevent the development of the "physiologic anemia" that occurs at about 1 month of age in "healthy" growing premature infants.[3-11] However, such supplementation has been shown to prevent the development of iron deficiency after the age of 2 months.[3-11] Therefore, the objective of nutritional management in preterm infants with respect to iron should be the provision of sufficient iron supplementation to enhance iron stores and to prevent the development of iron deficiency.

In this chapter, recommendations aimed at achieving this objective will be presented after discussion of the following: (1) the iron endowment of infants at birth, (2) iron and postnatal erythropoiesis, (3) iron absorption and retention, (4) the use of supplemental iron to prevent iron deficiency, (5) iron availability from human milk and infant formulas, (6) the effect of red blood cell (RBC) transfusions on iron absorption and iron needs, (7) the potential impact of erythropoietin therapy on iron needs, (8) the need for iron supplementation with parenteral nutrition, (9) the interaction between supplemental iron and vitamin E, and (10) the interactions between iron and zinc and copper.

Intrauterine Iron Accumulation
During the third trimester, the growing fetus accumulates iron at a relatively steady rate, between 1.6 and 2.0 mg/kg/day. Total body iron content remains approximately 75 mg/kg.[5,10,12-14] Iron is present as hemoglobin iron, tissue iron, and storage iron within the fetus. Hemoglobin iron accounts for almost 80% of total body iron content, about 60 mg/kg body weight.[5,10,14] Tissue iron is estimated to be about 7 mg/kg body weight, or about 9% of total body iron

content, whereas iron stored within the liver and spleen accounts for the remaining portion, about 10% of total body iron.[10,14] Tissue iron includes myoglobin and iron-containing enzymes such as those involved in the mitochondrial respiratory chain and in redox reactions within the cell involving oxygen. Storage iron exists as ferritin and hemosiderin.[15]

The iron endowment of an infant at birth is not influenced by maternal iron status, except under conditions of severe maternal iron deficiency.[16-18] However, the neonate's iron status is affected by factors that influence RBC mass.[18] For example, iron endowment is decreased by early clamping of the umbilical cord, by fetal blood loss from abruptio placentae or placenta previa, and by fetal-to-maternal or a twin-to-twin transfusion. It is increased by delivery procedures that result in enhanced placental transfusion, such as late clamping of the umbilical cord, and in the recipient of a twin-to-twin transfusion. Although premature birth disrupts the steady intrauterine accumulation of iron that is associated with fetal weight gain, prenatal expansion of blood volume, and increase in the hemoglobin concentration, the total body iron content per kilogram body weight at birth is similar for preterm and term infants.

Iron and Postnatal Erythropoiesis
Postnatal erythropoiesis has been divided into three stages (Fig. 12.1).[5,8,10,11] In the first stage, which begins immediately after birth and lasts during the first 6 to 8 weeks of life in a term infant, there is an abrupt decrease in erythropoiesis. This decrease reflects the increased postnatal delivery of oxygen to tissues and is manifested by a decrease in marrow erythroid precursors, a fall in the reticulocyte count, and a fall in the hemoglobin concentration. The rate of decline in hemoglobin concentration is largely related to the shorter lifespan of fetal RBCs, about two thirds that of the normal adult RBC. Because erythropoiesis is depressed, reticuloendothelial iron stores become augmented, and serum ferritin concentrations increase. This "physiologic anemia" cannot be prevented by provision of iron and/or other nutritional supplements.

During the second stage, which occurs between the second and fourth postnatal month in term infants, erythropoiesis becomes more active because of de-

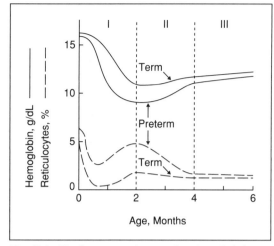

Fig. 12.1. The three postnatal stages of erythropoiesis in premature and term infants. Mean values for hemoglobin concentration and reticulocyte count are shown. The duration of the stages (dotted vertical lines) is shown for term infants. Stage I: Immediately after birth, the rate of erythropoiesis (reticulocyte count) and hemoglobin concentration decrease; storage iron is augmented. Stage II: At about 2 months of age, the hemoglobin concentration has fallen to its lowest point, and the rate of erythropoiesis is increased; storage iron gradually decreases. Stage III: After the third month of life in preterm infants and the fourth month of life in term infants, erythropoiesis is dependent upon iron stores and dietary iron intake. Iron deficiency anemia develops if an adequate exogenous supply of iron is not provided. (Reprinted, with permission, from Dallman PR, Siimes MA.[5])

creased oxygen delivery to the tissues associated with physiologic anemia.[5,8,10,11] Blood erythropoietin concentration, erythroid precursors in the marrow, and reticulocyte count all increase. Although total body hemoglobin increases, the concentration of circulating hemoglobin may not rise substantially because of dilution of the red cell mass by the expanded blood volume that results from increased body weight. Storage iron declines during this stage, as reflected by decreased serum ferritin concentrations.

The third stage of postnatal erythropoiesis begins after the fourth month of life in term infants and is characterized by its dependence upon dietary iron.[5,8,10,11] Infants who receive sufficient dietary iron to maintain body iron stores are able to support the increased erythropoiesis started in the second stage and will maintain a relatively constant hemoglobin concentration during the remainder of the first year of life. However, if the decreased iron stores are not replenished by provision and absorption of sufficient dietary iron, that increased erythropoiesis will not be maintained, and iron deficiency anemia will develop.

Although postnatal erythropoiesis in premature infants has been shown to have the same three stages (Fig. 12.1), there are some differences.[5,8,10,11] The hemoglobin concentration in preterm infants reaches values that are 2 to 3 g/dL lower than those observed in term infants during the first stage. Furthermore, the more premature the infant at birth, the lower will be the eventual nadir of the hemoglobin concentration, and it may be reached earlier. In healthy preterm infants, the second stage of erythropoiesis may begin earlier than in term infants; by 1 month of age, rising reticulocyte counts may already suggest evidence of active RBC production. Furthermore, because the absolute total body iron content at birth is less in preterm than in term infants, and because preterm infants have a more rapid rate of postnatal weight gain, they may deplete their iron stores earlier and thus reach the stage of iron-dependent erythropoiesis earlier. Blood sampling, such as for diagnostic purposes, especially if the blood is not replaced with transfused RBCs, results in an even more rapid depletion of iron stores. However, if the supply of dietary iron is adequate, the hemoglobin concentration in most preterm infants will be equivalent to that of term infants by about 9 months of age.[3,7] This physiologic anemia of prematurity cannot be prevented by initiating dietary iron supplementation or by providing other nutritional supplements shortly after birth.

Determining Postnatal Iron Requirements

During the first year of life, the iron requirements of preterm infants are determined by birthweight, the initial hemoglobin concentration, the rate of growth, and the extent of any blood losses.[8,10,11] Oski[10] has estimated that, in the absence of iron supplementation and blood losses, a very low-birthweight (VLBW) preterm infant will remain iron replete until the birthweight has doubled, usually at about 2 months of age.

Because an infant's iron endowment at birth is directly related to birthweight and initial hemoglobin concentration, and because blood volume expands in direct proportion to weight gain, iron needs during the first year of life can be approximated. For example, an infant that has a birthweight of 1 kg and an initial hemoglobin concentration of 17 g/dL will require about 280 mg of additional iron to become a 10-kg 1-year-old with a hemoglobin concentration of 11 g/dL (assuming a blood volume of 75 mL/kg, 3.47 mg of iron per g of hemoglobin, and iron tissue needs of about 7 mg/kg).[10] This would require a daily iron accumulation of about 0.8 mg once birthweight has doubled in an infant who has had minimal blood losses. Blood sampling in excess of blood replacement would increase iron needs.

Absorption and Retention of Iron

Dietary iron is absorbed mainly from the duodenum in the ferrous form.[19–22] The regulation of intestinal iron absorption and transfer to the plasma is an area of active research.[21-24] Some investigators[21-24] have proposed that transferrin is an important mediator of intestinal iron absorption; others[25] have proposed a role for free fatty acids in the transfer of ionic iron across brush border cell membranes. Iron absorption is influenced by an individual's age, iron status, and state of health; the form of iron ingested; and various dietary components.[5,17,19,20,26-28] Ascorbic acid enhances iron absorption; food fiber, cereals, and high intakes of phosphate, oxalate, zinc, copper, calcium, and manganese decrease iron absorption by forming insoluble iron salts or competing for iron-binding sites in the intestinal mucosa. Heme iron is absorbed within the heme moiety directly by intestinal mucosal cells.

Although the preterm infant can absorb iron, the percentage of iron absorbed appears to be related to the age of the infant, the growth rate, the infant's hemoglobin concentration, and the type of feeding.[3,5,8,10,11,26-28] Oettinger et al.[29] administered a test dose of radioactive iron (^{59}Fe) as ferrous chloride to 10 preterm infants (birthweight <2,500 g). The radiolabelled iron was given without formula in the first 7 days of life. From 0.29% to 6.8% (mean 2.8%) of the test dose was present in the infants' circulating RBC 2 to 6 weeks later, leading the investigators to conclude that from birth, preterm infants can absorb iron from the gastrointestinal tract and incorporate it into hemoglobin.

Gorten et al.[30] studied gastrointestinal absorption of iron and utilization of iron for hemoglobin formation. They gave formulas extrinsically labelled with ^{59}Fe to 14 preterm infants (birthweight 928 to 2,112 g) between 1 and 10 weeks of age. Intestinal absorption of iron ranged from 6.8% to 74.0% (mean ± SD, 31.5 ± 19.2%). Further, intestinal iron absorption appeared to be inversely related to the amount of dietary iron and directly related to postnatal age and incremental weight gain. Utilization of the absorbed ^{59}Fe for hemoglobin formation, determined at a mean of 8.4 days after administration of the test dose of radiolabelled iron, ranged from 7.1% to 102.5% (mean, 52.3% ± 28.1%). Incorporation of the total ^{59}Fe dose in hemoglobin ranged from 2.8% to 47.8% (mean, 15.3% ± 12.4%). Grouping the infants by severity of anemia and degree of erythropoietic activity, as determined by reticulocyte counts, revealed that infants with higher reticulocyte counts incorporated a significantly greater percentage of the test dose of radioactive iron into hemoglobin, even though the mean percentage of intestinal iron absorbed and the mean percentage of absorbed iron utilized were similar in the two groups.

Data from these studies[29,30] are frequently compared. It is important to note differences in addition to study design (i.e., age of subjects and administration of the test dose of ^{59}Fe with or without formula).

Oettinger et al.[29] assumed that all gastrointestinally absorbed iron would be found in circulating red cells. Gorten et al.[30] reported incorporation of ^{59}Fe into hemoglobin as a function of the amount absorbed and administered and found wide variability in utilization of absorbed ^{59}Fe.

More recently, Ehrenkranz et al.[31] measured iron absorption and incorporation into RBCs after administration of a reference dose of the stable isotope ^{58}Fe in 11 VLBW infants (birthweight 780 to 1,520 g; gestational age 24 to 33 weeks; postnatal age 9 to 54 days). Their findings were consistent with the ^{59}Fe studies in preterm infants.[29,30] The percentage of ^{58}Fe absorption was 41.6% ± 17.6% (mean ± SD), with 12.0% ± 9.6% of the ^{58}Fe dose and 28.7% ± 22.3% of the absorbed ^{58}Fe dose incorporated into RBCs 2 weeks after administration. Absorption of ^{58}Fe was significantly correlated with postnatal age, but not with postconceptional age. The percentages of ^{58}Fe absorption and of ^{58}Fe incorporation into RBCs 2 weeks after administration were significantly correlated with the hemoglobin concentration and reticulocyte count obtained prior to administration of ^{58}Fe. Transfusion history did not affect ^{58}Fe absorption or incorporation into RBCs, but study infants had not been transfused during the 2 weeks before or 1 week after ^{58}Fe administration.

In addition to the observations by Gorten et al.[30] and Ehrenkranz et al.[31] that iron absorption increases with postnatal age, other investigators[5,10] have demonstrated, with whole-body counting following administration of a dose of ^{59}Fe, that iron retention increases with postnatal age in preterm infants. However, the concurrent measurement of isotopic iron absorption with fecal monitoring and of isotopic iron incorporation into RBCs permits a better understanding of the fate of iron ingested by preterm infants than does either measurement alone. As shown in Table 12.1, such studies[30,31] indicate that although a significant percentage of the absorbed iron is incorporated into circulating RBCs, a substantial amount of absorbed iron is presumably stored for later utilization or is incorporated into tissue iron. By contrast, studies with radiolabelled iron in adults with normal iron stores demonstrate that approximately 10% of a test dose of iron is absorbed and about 90% of the absorbed iron is incorporated in hemoglobin.[32,33]

Dauncey et al.[34] used serial nutritional balance studies to measure iron absorption in six preterm infants (birthweight 1,050 to 1,400 g) from 10 to 72 days of age. Chemical methods were used to determine the amount of iron intake and fecal and urinary iron excretion. The infants were initially fed pooled pasteurized human milk (iron content 0.043 ± 0.002 mg/dL). These infants were found to be in negative iron balance during the first 30 days of life, presumably secondary to an endogenous fecal iron loss of

Table 12.1. Iron Absorption by Preterm Infants in Studies with Extrinsic Isotopic Iron

Reference	Subject Characteristics* (n)	Method	% Intestinal Absorption of Extrinsic Label[†]	% Incorporation of Extrinsic Label into RBCs[†]	% Incorporation of Absorbed Extrinsic Label into RBCs[†]
Oettinger et al.[29]	BW <2,500 g Age <7 days (10)	Single dose ^{59}Fe given between feedings; blood samples obtained 2–6 weeks later		2.8 (0.29–6.8)	
Gorten et al.[30]	BW 928–2,112 g Age 1–10 weeks (14)	Single feeding of iron-fortified formula extrinsically labelled with ^{59}Fe; 5-day stool collection; blood samples obtained 7–14 days later	31.5 ± 19.2 (6.8–74.0)	15.3 ± 12.4 (2.8–47.8)	52.3 ± 28.1 (7.1–102.5)
Ehrenkranz et al.[31]	BW 780–1,520 g GA 24–33 weeks Age 9–54 days (11)	Single dose ^{58}Fe given with ascorbic acid; 7-day stool collection; blood samples obtained 2 weeks later	41.6 ± 17.6 (14.1–72.5)	12.0 ± 9.6 (1.6–31.4)	28.7 ± 22.3 (6.2–68.2)

*BW = birthweight; GA = gestational age.
[†]Mean ± SD (range).

0.21 mg/kg/day.[35] However, after the introduction of iron-fortified pooled pasteurized human milk on day 30 (iron content 3.82 ± 1.4 mg/dL), iron absorption increased and iron balance became positive. In infants who were not given transfusions, absorption of dietary iron was found to be a function of iron intake; absorption averaged about 34%. Interestingly, blood transfusion was followed by a marked decrease in iron absorption, which appeared to remain depressed until the hemoglobin concentration fell below about 12.0 g/dL.

Supplemental Iron and Prevention of Iron Deficiency

Supplemental iron is usually provided to preterm infants by an iron-fortified formula or by a daily oral iron supplement. A parenteral iron supplement, iron dextran (Imferon,® Fisons Pharmaceuticals, Rochester, NY), is available, but it is infrequently used today.[36]

A meta-analysis performed by Doyle and Zipursky[37] demonstrated no difference in the incidence of iron deficiency anemia or of biochemical iron deficiency at 6 months of age in term infants fed iron-fortified formulas (iron content, 12 to 15 mg/L) or non-iron-fortified formulas (iron, 0.5 to 1.5 mg/L). However, non-iron-supplemented preterm infants have a high incidence of iron deficiency anemia after age 4 months,[3-11,37-39] and the incidence of iron deficiency has been consistently demonstrated to decrease with iron supplementation regimens. Randomized controlled trials with this outcome have compared nonsupplemented preterm infants and infants receiving intramuscular iron dextran (250 mg over 5 days upon reaching a body weight of 2,000 g[38];

100 mg over 2 to 4 days upon reaching a body weight of 1,500 g[39]), iron-fortified formula (12.7 mg/L) from birth,[3] or daily oral iron supplements (2 mg/kg/day) from 2 weeks of age.[4]

Iron supplementation does not affect the development of early or "physiologic" anemia. But, as shown in Tables 12.2 and 12.3, the meta-analyses[37] demonstrate that iron supplementation results in significant benefits: a 72.5% reduction in the incidence of iron deficiency anemia and a mean increase in hemoglobin concentration of 2.34 g/dL.

Lundström et al.[4] reported findings from 117 infants with birthweights between 1,000 and 2,000 g who were divided into two groups; infants received banked human milk and either elemental iron 2 mg/kg/day as ferrous sulfate or no iron supplementation from 2 weeks of age. In addition to the blood hemoglobin concentrations, the mean corpuscular volume, transferrin saturation, and serum ferritin concentration were all significantly lower in the unsupplemented infants after 2 months of age (Fig. 12.2).

Similar findings were recently reported by Melnick and co-workers,[40] who compared iron status in 38 VLBW infants fed an iron-fortified preterm formula (15 mg/L) with that of a group fed a low-iron preterm formula (3.5 mg/L). Study formulas were started at about 2 weeks of age. Although hemoglobin and serum transferrin concentrations remained similar after 29 days of formula feeding, serum ferritin concentration was significantly higher in the infants receiving the iron-fortified formula, suggesting an improved iron status.

Several studies have compared two levels of iron supplementation in preterm infants.[6,41] Studying 28

Table 12.2. Meta-Analysis of Effect of Iron Supplement, Compared with No Supplement, on Anemia in Preterm Newborns*

Reference	Anemia Measure	Treatment		Control		ERD† (%)	95% CI
		n	%	n	%		
James and Combes[38]	at 11 months Hb <9.5 g/dL	0/32	0	43/48	89.6	−88.2	−97.7,−78.6
Gorten and Cross[3]	at 6 months Hb <9.0 g/dL	1/49	2.0	17/49	34.7	−32.7	−46.6,−18.7
Lundström et al.[4]	at 6 months Hb <10.4 g/dL	0/60	0	44/57	77.2	−76.6	−87.6,−65.5
Typical estimates						−72.5	−78.9,−66.0

*Adapted from Doyle and Zipuvsky.[37]

†Event Rate Difference (ERD) measures the difference in the proportion of outcome events (anemia) between treated and untreated patients. A negative ERD indicates the percentage reduction in the incidence of outcome events in the treated group. If the 95% confidence intervals (CI) of the ERD excludes zero, the effect of the intervention is significant at $p < 0.05$. It was significant in all three studies.

Table 12.3. Meta-Analysis of Effects of Iron Supplement, Compared with No Supplement, on Hemoglobin Concentration (g/dL) at 6 Months in Preterm Newborns*

Reference	Treatment			Control			MD[†]	95% CI
	n	x$_t$	SD	n	x$_c$	SD		
James and Combes[38]	42	12.2	1.07	44	8.8	1.17	3.4	2.93, 3.87
Hammond and Murphy[39]	8	12.1	1.10	13	11.3	0.80	0.8	−0.08, 1.68
Gorten and Cross[3]	37	11.3	1.00	32	9.8	1.30	1.5	0.95, 2.05
Weighted mean difference[‡]							2.34	2.00, 2.67

*Adapted from Doyle and Zipursky.[37]

[†]Mean difference (x$_t$ − x$_c$).

[‡]If the 95% confidence intervals (CI) of the weighted mean difference exclude 0.0, the difference is significant at $p < 0.05$.

premature infants with birthweights about 1,800 g, Jansson et al.[6] reported that serum ferritin values, hemoglobin concentrations, and reticulocyte counts were not different at 2 months of age in infants who received an iron-fortified formula (10 mg ferrous sulfate per L) with or without an iron supplement (2 to 3 mg/kg/day as ferrous succinate) from 3 weeks of age. Data from a recent study[41] also demonstrated similar hematologic measures of iron status at 4 months of age in 36 VLBW infants who were fed non-iron-fortified formulas initially and were randomized after reaching a body weight of 2,000 g to receive an iron supplement of either 2 mg/kg/day or 4 mg/kg/day. Previously, Siimes and Järvenpää[7] had suggested that 4 mg/kg/day provided by a combination of a daily iron supplement (2 mg/kg/day) and an iron-fortified formula (2 mg/kg/day) from about 2 months of age might be necessary to prevent iron deficiency in preterm infants with birthweights of 1,000 g or less. Furthermore, Sitarz et al.[42] reported that intramuscular iron dextran was as effective as daily oral iron supplementation for prevention of late iron deficiency anemia in preterm infants.

In summary, physiologic anemia of prematurity cannot be prevented by providing increased dietary iron, either as iron-fortified formula or as supplemental oral iron, to growing preterm infants during the early postnatal period. However, a dietary iron intake of about 2 mg/kg/day started during the early postnatal period is clearly beneficial.[3,4,6,37,40] Such supplementary iron is not only absorbed, but is utilized to improve iron status and reduce the risk of later iron deficiency.

Iron Availability in Human Milk and Infant Formulas

The iron content of human milk falls from about 1 mg/L to less than 0.5 mg/L during the first 6 months of lactation, decreasing further if lactation continues.[27,43,44] Iron levels in preterm human milk do not differ from iron levels in milk from women delivering at term.[43,44] In addition, maternal iron status does not appear to affect the iron concentration of milk.[27]

Few studies have directly compared iron absorption or availability from human milk with that from infant formula in preterm infants. Siimes[9] reported that Järvenpää and her colleagues compared a group of VLBW infants exclusively fed human milk who received iron supplementation (2 mg/kg/day) from 2 months of age with a group of formula-fed VLBW infants who received an iron-fortified formula (12 mg/L) from birth. The concentration of hemoglobin and serum ferritin was higher at 4 months of age in the human milk–fed infants, suggesting that supplementary iron was better absorbed from human milk than from formula.

Studies in older infants and in adults given feedings of human milk, bovine milk, bovine milk formula, or soy-based formula have usually demonstrated that iron absorption and utilization is significantly better with human milk than with infant formula or bovine milk.[9,27,45–50] The factor or factors responsible for the enhanced iron availability from human milk are unclear.[26–28] Therefore, despite the low iron content of human milk, iron supplementation for exclusively breast-fed full-term infants does not appear necessary until about 6 months of age.[51] Formula-fed term infants often require supplemental iron earlier and are commonly started on an iron-fortified formula from birth.[9,45–50] In comparison, iron supplementation appears necessary by about 2 months of age for preterm infants, especially VLBW infants, regardless of whether they are fed human milk or formula.[5,8,10,11]

Iwai et al.[52] compared the iron status in 15 preterm infants who received only preterm human milk during

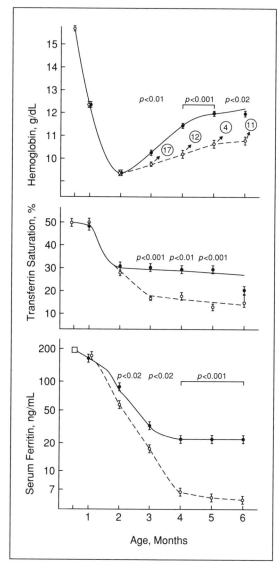

Fig. 12.2. Hemoglobin concentration, transferrin saturation, and serum ferritin concentration in low-birthweight infants. All infants received banked breast milk during their hospital stay and were randomly assigned to receive either no iron supplementation (open circles, broken lines) or iron supplementation 2 mg/kg/day from 2 weeks of age (solid circles and lines). Means ± SEM are indicated. The circled numbers indicate unsupplemented infants who were started on iron supplementation on the basis of anemia. Serum ferritin concentration became significantly lower in the unsupplemented infants at 2 months of age. Hemoglobin concentration and transferrin saturation were significantly decreased from 3 months of age. (Reprinted, with permission, from Lundstöm U, Siimes MA, Dallman PR.[4])

the first 6 months of life and the status of 30 infants who had been fed preterm human milk until about 3 months of age and then were given an iron-fortified formula (8 mg/L). Serum ferritin and hemoglobin concentrations were significantly lower in the infants

who received only preterm human milk between 4 and 6 months of age, and the incidence of iron deficiency anemia was significantly greater in those infants (86% versus 33%).

Table 12.4 displays the iron content of the currently available preterm formulas and human milk fortifiers.

Red Blood Cell Transfusions and Iron Needs

Because the total blood volume of preterm infants, especially VLBW infants, is small, approximately 75 mL/kg, blood sampling for diagnostic purposes frequently leads to a need for packed RBC transfusion. A common practice in the care of acutely ill neonates is to administer a packed RBC transfusion whenever blood sampling exceeds 10 mL/kg. An infant with moderate to severe respiratory disease who requires assisted ventilation or greater than 35% to 40% inspiratory oxygen often receives a packed RBC transfusion whenever the packed red cell volume (hematocrit) falls below 35% or 40%. Transfusion guidelines for preterm infants with anemia of prematurity vary, but often accepted indications for packed RBC transfusion in a 1- to 2-month-old VLBW infant with a hematocrit of 30% or less include the following: persistent tachycardia, persistent tachypnea, increased lethargy, increased severity of apneic or bradycardic episodes, pallor, and cessation of previously steady weight gain.[8,53]

As noted above, Dauncey et al.[34] performed serial iron absorption studies in six VLBW infants and reported that iron absorption was markedly decreased after transfusion and remained depressed until the hemoglobin concentration fell below 12.0 mg/dL. Because the serum ferritin concentration in multiply transfused VLBW infants remains elevated without supplemental iron until after 12 postnatal weeks and then gradually declines, Shaw[35] and Austria et al.[54] have suggested that such infants do not require supplemental iron as early as other preterm infants. Serum ferritin concentrations fall significantly as iron-dependent erythropoiesis begins and iron absorption increases.[5,8,10,11] This observation is consistent with findings that serum ferritin concentration is inversely related to iron absorption.[55] However, Ehrenkranz et al.[31] observed that [58]Fe absorption was not influenced by transfusion history and was not related to serum ferritin concentrations in VLBW infants, concurring with the suggestion of other investigators[35] that iron absorption is poorly regulated in these infants. Furthermore, mobilization of storage iron might be inhibited by elevated serum ferritin concentration.[9] A higher than normal transferrin saturation might be required to support the production of hemoglobin by infants[56]; a serum transferrin saturation of 16% is considered the lower limit of normal.

Table 12.4. Iron, Folic Acid, and Vitamin B$_{12}$ Content of Bovine Milk Formulas, Mature Human Milk, and Human Milk Fortifiers

	Iron*		Folic acid		Vitamin B$_{12}$	
	mg/dL	mg/100 kcal	µg/dL	µg/100 kcal	µg/dL	µg/100 kcal
Enfamil Premature[†]	0.20(1.52)	0.25(1.88)	29.0	35.0	0.24	0.30
Similac Special Care[†]	0.30(1.5)	0.37(1.80)	30.0	37.0	0.45	0.55
SMA "Preemie"[†]	0.30	0.38	10.0	12.5	0.20	0.30
Enfamil[‡]	0.11(1.27)	0.16(1.88)	10.5	15.6	0.15	0.23
Similac[‡]	0.15(1.2)	0.22(1.8)	10.0	15.0	0.17	0.25
SMA[‡]	0.15(1.2)	0.20(1.8)	5.0	7.5	0.16	0.20
Mature Human Milk[‡]	0.05	0.40	5.0	7.4	0.05	0.07
Enfamil Human Milk Fortifier	none added	none added	23.2[§]	28.6[§]	0.20[§]	0.25[§]
Similac Natural Care Human Milk Fortifier[†]	0.30	0.37	30.0	37.0	0.45	0.55

*Non-iron-fortified (iron-fortified formula values in parentheses).

[†]81 kcal/dL.

[‡]67 kcal/dL.

[§]In four 0.96-g packets.

Thus, supplementary iron would be necessary to provide a readily available source of iron that would maintain the serum iron concentration and sustain hemoglobin production by being preferentially incorporated into hemoglobin.[56,57]

Erythropoietin Therapy and Iron Needs

Inadequate erythropoietin production has been suggested as a major cause of physiologic anemia of prematurity, based on two lines of reasoning. First, Brown et al.[58] demonstrated that despite a marked fall in hemoglobin values during the second postnatal month, plasma erythropoietin concentrations in untransfused premature infants did not rise above values characteristic of healthy nonanemic adults. Although plasma erythropoietin levels in VLBW infants have been shown to vary inversely with hemoglobin concentration, central venous oxygen tension, and "available oxygen," the response is much smaller than that observed in older children and adults at any given hemoglobin level or degree of hypoxia.[58-60]

"Available oxygen" is an expression of the capacity of the blood to release oxygen to the tissues; it takes into account both oxygen-carrying capacity, which is proportional to the concentration of hemoglobin, and oxygen affinity of blood. The erythropoietin response to low available oxygen improves with maturity and increasing age; with similar levels of available oxygen, erythropoietin levels rose signifi-

cantly with either increasing postconceptional age (studied at three intervals: from 27 to 31 weeks, from 32 to 36 weeks, and from 37 to 41 weeks) or increasing postnatal age (studied at three ages: from 1 to 5 weeks, from 6 to 10 weeks, and from 11 to 15 weeks).[60] This maturational change in the responsiveness of erythropoietin to low levels of hemoglobin, central venous oxygen tension, and available oxygen may be related to a shift in the site of erythropoietin production: from an extrarenal site during fetal life to the kidney postnatally.[61,62]

The second line of reasoning in support of inadequate erythropoietin production is that erythroid progenitors obtained from the blood and bone marrow of VLBW infants with anemia of prematurity are normally responsive to erythropoietin.[63,64] Three clinical trials have evaluated the response to recombinant human erythropoietin (r-HuEPO) by preterm infants with anemia of prematurity.[65-67] Ohls and Christensen[65] recently reported the results of a preliminary study in which 19 preterm infants with hematocrits <30% were randomized to receive a packed RBC transfusion or r-HuEPO (200 units/kg every other day for 20 days, for a total of 10 doses). Each r-HuEPO-treated infant also received iron, 2 mg/kg/day. Treatment with r-HuEPO stimulated erythropoiesis; reticulocyte counts increased from 2.2% ± 0.4% to 7.1% ± 0.3%, and hematocrits rose from 27% ± 2% to 30% ± 4%, and no infant required a transfusion. Five of the nine infants randomized to the transfusion therapy group required a second transfusion. The investigators concluded that r-HuEPO therapy could reduce the need for packed RBC transfusions in preterm infants with anemia of prematurity.

However, the other two studies[66,67] reported more variable results, leading investigators to suggest that the effectiveness of r-HuEPO therapy in VLBW infants might be limited by their low iron stores and that r-HuEPO therapy would increase iron requirements. Halpérin et al.[66] described the results of a pilot study in which seven infants were treated with doses of 75 to 300 units/kg/week. Treatment was administered subcutaneously three times per week, starting between 21 and 33 days of age, and was maintained for 4 weeks. At least a twofold increase in the absolute number of reticulocytes was observed in all infants, with the peak reticulocyte count noted between 10 and 21 days of therapy. However, only a slight change in hematocrit was observed in six of the seven infants; in these infants the mean baseline hematocrit increased from 26.3% to 29.6% on day 21 of treatment. Serum iron and ferritin concentrations significantly decreased after the initiation of r-HuEPO therapy; mean ($\pm$SD) serum iron fell from 14.2 ± 4.4 μmol/L to 7.0 ± 2.3 μmol/L and mean ferritin from 222 ± 127 ng/mL to 60 ± 34 ng/mL between the start of therapy and day 28. Although each infant received an oral supplement of elemental iron (2 mg/kg/day), two infants treated with the highest dose of r-HuEPO developed iron deficiency; one of these infants had only a transient increase in hematocrit, and the other was the infant who did not respond to r-HuEPO.

Shannon et al.[67] reported the results of a double-blind pilot study of r-HuEPO treatment in VLBW infants at risk of requiring transfusions for anemia of prematurity. Twenty infants were randomly assigned to receive r-HuEPO doses of 100 units/kg or placebo intravenously twice weekly for 6 weeks; treatment was started at a mean age of 22 days. Absolute reticulocyte counts tended to rise earlier in infants treated with r-HuEPO, but after 2 weeks of therapy no differences in the absolute reticulocyte counts were observed between treated and control infants. In addition, there were no differences between treated and control infants with respect to hematocrit values or transfusion requirements. The administration of supplemental oral iron was variable during the study period.

Serum iron and ferritin levels and the percent transferrin saturation have been observed to fall in children and adults with chronic renal failure who are treated with r-HuEPO.[68-72] Because a transferrin saturation less than 16% implies iron deficiency, Eschbach et al.[69,70] have suggested that the transferrin saturation be maintained above 20% in r-HuEPO-treated

adults to ensure an adequate iron supply for erythropoiesis. Stockman[73] has commented on the possibility that r-HuEPO-induced erythropoiesis could produce iron deficiency in VLBW infants. If r-HuEPO therapy is shown to be effective in the prevention or treatment of anemia of prematurity and becomes part of standard care, attention will have to be paid to the sufficiency of dietary iron intake.

Iron Supplementation with Parenteral Nutrition

Because a VLBW preterm infant will remain iron replete until birthweight has doubled, usually at about 2 months of age, iron supplementation of parenteral nutrition is typically omitted.[36] Enteral nutrition has usually been initiated by the time iron stores are depleted, and supplementary iron can be provided with an iron-fortified formula or with daily oral iron supplements. However, an infant who develops iron deficiency while receiving prolonged total parenteral nutrition for problems such as severe short-gut syndrome can have iron dextran added to parenteral alimentation (0.1 to 0.2 mg/kg/day) or can be administered iron intramuscularly.[36,42]

Iron and Vitamin E

An association between vitamin E deficiency and hemolytic anemia in preterm infants was first reported by Oski and Barness in 1967.[74] Additional reports[75,76] demonstrated that preterm infants were predisposed to develop vitamin E-deficiency anemia; the causes were limited vitamin E stores at birth and consumption of infant formulas with high polyunsaturated fatty acid (PUFA) and low vitamin E content. Intake of such formulas not only increased the PUFA content of erythrocyte membranes but also increased erythrocyte susceptibility to peroxidation because of insufficient antioxidant protection of membrane PUFAs.

Studies by Melhorn and Gross[77] demonstrated that daily administration of therapeutic doses of iron (about 8 mg/kg/day) between 2 and 6 weeks of age exaggerated hemolysis in preterm infants not receiving supplemental vitamin E; administration of vitamin E (25 IU/day) decreased the iron-induced hemolysis. Subsequently, Williams et al.[78] demonstrated in VLBW infants that iron fortification (12 mg/L) of formulas with inadequate vitamin E:PUFA ratios increased the likelihood that vitamin E deficiency anemia would occur. Iron fortification of formulas with adequate vitamin E:PUFA ratios, however, was well tolerated and did not promote hemolysis.

These findings were supported by a randomized, controlled, blinded trial of the effectiveness of supplemental vitamin E in the prevention of anemia in VLBW.[79] In that study of 178 infants, Zipursky et al.[79] administered 25 IU vitamin E daily to infants fed formulas containing, per liter, 10 to 12 IU vitamin

E, and 12.7 to 15.2 mg iron sulfate; the vitamin E:P-UFA ratio was 1.3:1. The supplemental vitamin E offered no additional benefit with respect to hemoglobin concentration, erythrocyte peroxide fragility, erythrocyte morphology, and reticulocyte and platelet counts.

Most proprietary formulas now available, including the iron-fortified premature formulas, have satisfactory vitamin E:PUFA ratios and should not predispose a VLBW infant to develop vitamin E-deficiency hemolytic anemia (see Chapter 7).[1,8,10,75,76,80] In addition, Gross and Gabriel[80] have shown that infants fed preterm human milk may safely receive an iron supplement (2 mg/kg/day) if a small vitamin E supplement (4.1 mg/day) is provided; routine daily multivitamin supplementation fulfills that recommendation.

Iron-Zinc and Iron-Copper Interactions

Interactions within the gastrointestinal tract among dietary minerals and between dietary minerals and other nutrients may affect the bioavailability of a mineral by interfering with its absorption.[81,82] Dietary excess of one mineral may decrease the bioavailability of other minerals, while deficiency of a mineral may inhibit the absorption of another mineral. An excess of iron has been shown to decrease zinc and copper absorption. An excess of zinc decreases iron and copper absorption, whereas an excess of copper decreases iron and zinc absorption. Also, copper deficiency lowers iron absorption.

Solomons and Jacob[83] demonstrated that zinc absorption is impaired by iron when the iron:zinc ratio increases from 1:1 to 3:1. They suggested that the improved growth and apparent zinc nutriture observed by Walravens and Hambidge[84] in infants fed a zinc-fortified (5.8 mg/L), iron-fortified (12 mg/L) formula compared with the growth in infants fed a non-zinc-fortified (1.8 mg/L), iron-fortified formula was related to the increased bioavailability of zinc due to the change in the iron:zinc ratio from 6.7:1 to 2.1:1.

However, more recent clinical data have not demonstrated significant iron-zinc or iron-copper interactions with the currently recommended levels of iron supplementation or iron fortification of formulas.[85,86] Yip et al.[85] showed that iron supplementation (30 mg of ferrous sulfate daily) of 1-year-old infants for 3 months did not alter serum zinc or copper concentrations and did not produce any signs of zinc deficiency. Haschke et al.[86] determined mineral balance in infants who were fed each of two nearly identical formulas whose composition differed in iron content, 10.2 mg/L and 2.5 mg/L. The iron:zinc ratios were 5.4 and 1.4 and the iron:copper ratios were 34 and 8.7 in the iron-fortified and low-iron formulas, respectively. Zinc absorption and retention were similar from these formulas, but copper absorption and retention were lower from the iron-fortified formula.

Although the effect on copper was statistically significant, the investigators considered its clinical significance questionable.[86]

The American Academy of Pediatrics Committee on Nutrition (AAPCON)[87] has stated that, given the levels of zinc and copper presently in infant formulas, iron fortification of the formulas does not impair the absorption of those minerals to a nutritionally important degree. The zinc and copper contents of the preterm formulas have been increased to support intrauterine accretion rates (zinc, 8.0 to 12.7 mg/L; copper, 0.7 to 2 mg/L).[1] Fortifying those formulas with iron (about 15 mg/L) would not be expected to alter absorption of zinc and copper.

Conclusions and Recommendations

The AAPCON has recommended that some form of iron supplementation be started no later than 2 months of age in VLBW preterm infants and that it be continued at least through the remainder of the first year of life.[1,2] This recommendation is based upon two facts: (1) the lack of response to supplemental iron by infants with physiologic anemia of prematurity and (2) the need for multiple transfusions of packed RBCs in many of these infants. Iron supplements are necessary for preterm infants fed either human milk or formula. The recommended dose is 2 mg/kg/day, up to a maximum of 15 mg/day. However, as discussed above, controversy exists as to the optimal time to begin supplemental iron.[1–11] Some authors[3,4,40] suggested that supplemental iron be started by 2 weeks of age and others[10] by the time birthweight has doubled. The objective of iron supplementation is the enhancement of iron stores and the prevention of iron deficiency.

Preterm infants, including VLBW preterm infants, absorb dietary iron well.[5,10,29–31] The percentage of iron absorbed appears to be directly related to postnatal age, growth rate, hemoglobin concentration, and the type of feeding.[5,8,10,11] Although packed RBC transfusion decreases dietary iron absorption acutely,[34] multiple transfusions increase serum ferritin but do not appear to impair iron absorption,[31] suggesting that the regulation of iron absorption in preterm infants is not tightly controlled.[35] In addition, mobilization of storage iron might be inhibited by elevated serum ferritin concentrations,[9] and normal blood transferrin saturations might be a limiting factor in the production of hemoglobin by infants.[56] Thus, supplemental iron would be necessary to provide newly absorbed iron that would be preferentially incorporated into hemoglobin.[56,57]

Therefore, existing data[3,4,40] suggest that preterm infants, especially VLBW preterm infants, should receive iron supplementation of 2 mg/kg/day. Such supplementation should be initiated by 2 months of age but may be offered throughout the initial hospitalization. Formula-fed infants may receive either an iron-fortified preterm formula (providing iron at 1.33 mg/dL or 1.67 mg/100 kcal, assuming an intake of 150 mL/kg/day of an 81 kcal/dL formula) or a daily oral iron supplement after full enteral nutrition is achieved with a non-iron-fortified preterm formula. Infants fed human milk may receive a daily oral iron supplement after full enteral nutrition with fortified human milk is achieved; current human milk fortifiers are not iron fortified. Multiply transfused infants may receive the same regimen of iron supplementation. Supplemental iron is not usually required during total parenteral nutrition. However, if it is provided exclusively for more than the first 2 months of life or if iron deficiency develops, parenteral iron, 0.1 to 0.2 mg/kg/day, can be delivered with parenteral alimentation.[36] If r-HuEPO therapy is shown to effectively prevent and/or treat anemia of prematurity and becomes part of standard clinical care, iron in excess of 2 mg/kg/day may be necessary to support erythropoiesis.[66-72] Finally, supplemental iron (2 mg/kg/day up to a maximum of 15 mg/day) should be continued throughout the first year of life.

Folic Acid

Folate refers to a group of compounds having the nutritional and chemical properties of folic acid (pteroylglutamic acid).[36,88-90] The parent compound consists of a double-ringed structure (pteridine), p-aminobenzoic acid, and glutamic acid. Tetrahydrofolic acid is the metabolically active form of folic acid and functions as a coenzyme, serving as an acceptor and donor of one-carbon units in amino acid and nucleotide metabolism.

Folic acid is a water-soluble vitamin. It is not stored to any great extent and therefore daily provision, often in excess, is desirable.[36,89] Although there is active transport of folate from mother to fetus and although the folate content of serum, RBCs, and liver increases during gestation,[90-92] folate stores in preterm infants are sufficient to cover needs only for several weeks.[36,89-91]

Folic acid is absorbed rapidly from the proximal small intestine following hydrolysis by mucosal polyglutamate hydrolases.[88-90] Folate passes into the portal circulation as a free monoglutamate derivative and is stored in the liver. In adults, total body folate turnover is slow, averaging 1% per day.[36,88] High doses of folic acid are generally viewed as nontoxic in humans.[91]

Deficiency of Folic Acid
Nutritional folate deficiency is one of the most common vitamin deficiencies in humans.[11,36,88-90] Preterm infants are predisposed to folate deficiency because of limited intrauterine hepatic stores and be-

cause of their rapid postnatal growth.[11,88-93] The risk of folate deficiency is increased if the dietary intake of folic acid is inadequate, if the infant has any malabsorption syndrome, or if the infant is receiving medications that interfere with folate absorption (such as diphenylhydantoin) or antibiotics that interfere with colonic bacterial production of folate.[11,88-93] The main metabolic consequence of folic acid deficiency is a disturbance in DNA synthesis that may alter cell division in a variety of tissues, especially those with high rates of cell multiplication, such as bone marrow and intestine.[89]

The folic acid status of preterm infants is best evaluated by measurement of serum and RBC folate concentrations and by assessment of blood smears.[11,88,91] The serum folate concentration reflects recent dietary intake of folic acid, whereas the RBC folate concentration is more stable and more accurately reflects folate status.[11,88] A serum folate level of 3 ng/mL and an RBC folate level of 140 ng/mL are considered the lower limits of normal.[11] Hematologic and clinical manifestations of folate deficiency occur after low plasma folate concentrations develop; they include hypersegmentation of neutrophils, megaloblastic changes on blood smears, and poor growth.[11,36,88-91,93,94] Macrocytic anemia and neurologic manifestations, such as hypotonia, are evident only in severe cases. Urinary excretion of formiminoglutamate, an intermediate in the metabolism of histidine to glutamic acid, is also an indicator of folate deficiency.

Folic Acid Availability in Human Milk and Infant Formulas
The folate concentration of human milk increases as lactation advances, with mature human milk containing about 50 µg/L[95-100]; however, due to differences in assay technique, reported mean values range from 26 to 141 µg/L.[100] Lower levels have been reported in milk from poorly nourished mothers.[98] Although the folate content of milk increases when these women receive folic acid supplementation,[88,97,98] milk from women with adequate folate status is unaffected by supplementation.[96,98,100] The presence of a folate-binding protein in human milk may facilitate folate absorption; heat treatment (such as pasteurization) decreases folate availability of human milk.[11,91,93,95,96,98]

The folate content of human milk fortifiers is shown in Table 12.4. The need for such fortification in preterm infants has not been demonstrated.

The folate content of preterm formulas and full-term bovine milk infant formulas also is shown in Table 12.4. These levels exceed the content of human milk and the minimum level recommended by the AAPCON,[1] 4 µg/100 kcal. Preterm and term infants appear able to absorb folic acid well from these formulas, but folate absorption is greater from human milk.[91,101–103]

Folic Acid Supplementation and Prevention of Folate Deficiency

Although no randomized controlled trials of folic acid supplementation in full-term infants have been performed,[94] there is little evidence to support the need for supplementation beyond the amount present in human milk. Low serum folate levels or clinical signs of folate deficiency have not been described in breast-fed full-term infants.[11,88,89] Formula-fed full-term infants usually have elevated folate levels, most likely reflecting the high level of folic acid fortification in the currently available term formulas (Table 12.4).[11,88,89]

Three trials[104–106] on prevention of megaloblastic anemia have investigated the effect of folic acid supplementation on RBC folate and hemoglobin concentrations in preterm infants. Burland et al.[104] studied 30 preterm infants with birthweight under 1,800 g; 10 infants received 100 μg folic acid intramuscularly every other day for 14 doses, beginning by 5 days of age, and 20 infants received no additional folic acid. All infants had similar diets, without additional vitamins or iron, during the treatment period. Kendall and coworkers[105] performed a controlled trial in which 130 preterm infants (birthweight <2,500 g) were randomized to receive 50 μg folic acid daily or placebo. All infants were fed reconstituted bovine milk formula; semi-solid foods were started after 2 months of age. Stevens et al.[106] assigned 246 preterm infants (birthweight <2,500 g) to receive either 100 μg folic acid daily with an iron supplement (10 mg/day) or the iron supplement alone from 3 weeks to 12 months of age; the clinical team on duty when the infant was born made the group assignment. All infants received a formula containing 3.5 μg folic acid per dL. These three studies found that folate supplementation resulted in a significant increase in RBC folate concentration. However, no study infant developed anemia. Specker et al.[94] performed a meta-analysis of these studies and demonstrated a mean weighted difference in hemoglobin concentration at 6 months of age of 1.0 g/dL (95% confidence intervals, 0.7 and 1.3 g/dL). Although this increase was statistically significant, it was of questionable clinical significance. Nonetheless, these authors[94] suggest that a folate intake of about 50 μg/day is probably sufficient for most preterm infants and speculate that the needs of the smallest infants might be greater.

Similar findings were reported by Ek and coworkers[91,103] in a study in which 41 preterm infants (mean gestational age, 31.6 weeks) were randomized at 2 weeks of age to receive a supplement of 50 μg folic acid daily or no additional folic acid throughout the first year of life. All infants were fed pasteurized human milk from birth and began at 1 month of age to receive a formula containing 2.1 μg folate per dL. At 3 months of age, folate intakes were about 65 μg/day (14 μg/kg/day) in the supplemented group and 15 μg/day (3.5 μg/kg/day) in the nonsupplemented group. Although plasma and RBC folate concentrations were significantly different between 2 months and 6 months, no infant manifested folate deficiency, and no differences between groups were observed in growth and hematologic indices. Because the infants supplemented with 50 μg folic acid daily had plasma and RBC folate concentrations similar to those observed in breast-fed term infants,[91,101] Ek et al.[91,103] recommended an intake of about 65 μg/day (15 μg/kg/day) during the first several months of life. Thus, the recommended folic acid intake for enterally fed preterm infants is similar to that for full-term infants.[88]

Folic Acid Supplementation and Parenteral Nutrition

Water-soluble vitamins are often administered in excess of enteral recommendations in parenteral feedings.[36] It is unclear whether excess administration is necessary to compensate for renal losses of vitamins associated with the continuous infusion of parenteral nutrition.[36]

Moore et al.[107] described folic acid status during total parenteral nutrition of 18 preterm infants and 26 full-term infants and children. The folate supplement was provided by an intravenous multivitamin preparation, M.V.I. Pediatric (distributed by Astra Pharmaceutical Products, Inc., Westborough, Mass.), in accordance with suggested dosage guidelines.[108] In the full-term infants and children, who received 140 μg/day (15 μg/100 kcal), whole blood folate was slightly elevated, but RBC folate was maintained near the upper limit of the reference values throughout the treatment period (reference values were derived from measurements in unfasted children 2 months to 11 years of age). The preterm infants received 65% of the full dose, 91 μg/day (120 μg/100 kcal or about 75 μg/kg/day). Their RBC folate concentrations were slightly greater than the reference values, but were essentially stable during the treatment period (reference values for the preterm infants were based upon cord blood samples from 55 healthy term infants).

Due to concern about the amount of polysorbate 80 administered with intravenous vitamin preparations, the manufacturer (Armour Pharmaceutical Company, Kankakee, Ill.) has suggested the following dosage guidelines for M.V.I. Pediatric[109]: infants weighing less than 1,000 g should receive 30% of a full dose (52 μg/day); infants weighing between 1,000 and 3,000 g should receive 65% of a full dose

(91 μg/day); infants weighing more than 3,000 g (and children up to 11 years of age) should receive 140 μg/day, the full dose. Serum and RBC folate levels have not been reported in preterm infants treated in accordance with these recommendations.

An intravenous multivitamin preparation for VLBW infants is supposedly being considered.[110]

Conclusions and Recommendations

The minimal enteral intake of folic acid recommended by the AAPCON[1] for preterm infants is the same as that recommended for full-term infants, 4 μg/100 kcal. However, the AAPCON has suggested that preterm infants weighing less than 2,000 g receive 50 μg folic acid daily, because an intake of about 20 μg/day did not prevent low plasma and RBC folate levels.[1,9,103] The Recommended Dietary Allowance (RDA) for folic acid is 25 μg/day for infants from birth to 6 months.[111] Therefore, based upon existing data and recommendations, an enteral folic acid intake of 25 to 50 μg/kg/day is recommended for VLBW preterm infants until 40 weeks postconceptional age. Thereafter, the minimal recommended intake for full-term infants, 4 μg/100 kcal, should be sufficient.

For formula-fed preterm infants, the suggested folate requirement for infants less than 40 weeks postconceptional age is readily satisfied by an adequate intake (150 to 200 mL/kg/day) of two of the current preterm formulas (Table 12.4). The folate contents of the currently available term infant formulas (Table 12.4) satisfy the folate requirements of full-term infants. Although low serum and RBC folate levels and folate deficiency have not been described in breast-fed full-term infants,[11,88,89] a folic acid supplement of 50 μg/day appeared sufficient for preterm infants fed human milk.[91,94,103] The use of human milk fortifiers should facilitate meeting that recommendation in human milk–fed VLBW infants during the early postnatal period. Liquid multivitamin preparations do not contain folate, because it is labile under the pH conditions used in such formulations.[11,89]

The recommended parenteral folic acid intake is 140 μg/day for full-term infants and 56 μg/kg/day for preterm infants.[36,88,89] The dose for preterm infants is provided by 40% of a full dose of M.V.I. Pediatric. A dose of this size should decrease the likelihood that preterm infants would experience elevated RBC concentrations similar to those observed in preterm infants who received a parenteral dose of 75 μg/kg/day.[107]

Vitamin B$_{12}$

Vitamin B$_{12}$, or cobalamin, is an organometallic complex consisting of two major moieties, a corrin nucleus containing a covalently bonded cobalt atom and a nucleotide base lying at right angles to it. Vitamin B$_{12}$ participates in reactions involving the synthesis of DNA nucleotides and the transfer of methyl groups.[36,88–90]

Vitamin B$_{12}$ is a water-soluble vitamin that is actively transported across the placenta. Neonates have twice the serum concentrations of their mothers.[90,91] Hepatic stores are large at birth, averaging 25 μg in full-term infants,[92] and are rarely depleted before 1 year of age.[11,88–91] Toxicity from vitamin B$_{12}$ has not been described.[91]

The absorption of vitamin B$_{12}$ requires the formation of a complex between the vitamin and a glycoprotein, intrinsic factor, which is produced by the parietal cells of the stomach.[11,88–90] Prior to formation of the intrinsic factor-vitamin B$_{12}$ complex, the vitamin is freed from its attachment to food protein by gastric juice and then is transiently complexed with R-binders, proteins that are normally present in saliva, gastric juice, bile, and milk. R-binders have a greater affinity for vitamin B$_{12}$ than does intrinsic factor. However, in the alkaline pH of the duodenum, pancreatic proteases degrade R-binders, permitting vitamin B$_{12}$ to bind with intrinsic factor. The intrinsic factor-vitamin B$_{12}$ complex appears to be absorbed intact in the distal ileum. Within the ileal mucosal cells, vitamin B$_{12}$ is released from intrinsic factor and binds to transcobalamin II, a specific serum transport protein, as it is released into the circulation.

The vitamin is stored within the liver. Bile is a primary route of vitamin B$_{12}$ excretion, but an effective enterohepatic circulation salvages it.

Deficiency of Vitamin B$_{12}$

Vitamin B$_{12}$ deficiency is rarely seen in infancy and early childhood.[11,36,88–91, 94] Nutritional deficiency can develop in infants who are exclusively fed human milk from strict vegetarian mothers or vitamin B$_{12}$-deficient women. Other potential causes of vitamin B$_{12}$ deficiency in young children are a congenital defect in the absorption or metabolism of the vitamin (such as lack of intrinsic factor or an inherited deficiency or abnormality of transcobalamin II), surgical resection of the terminal ileum (due to necrotizing enterocolitis or intestinal malformations, for example), and bacterial overgrowth in the ileum.

Clinical manifestations of vitamin B$_{12}$ deficiency usually do not become apparent until late infancy because of the normally abundant neonatal liver stores in full-term infants.[11,88–92,94] Depression of serum vitamin B$_{12}$ concentrations below 100 pg/mL and the appearance of hypersegmented neutrophils are the earliest findings. Megaloblastic anemia and neurologic changes occur later; the neurologic changes may become irreversible. High folic acid intake may mask a vitamin B$_{12}$ deficiency. Therefore, serum and RBC folate levels should also be determined if vitamin B$_{12}$ deficiency is considered as a clinical diagnosis.[11,91]

Vitamin B$_{12}$ Availability in Human Milk and Infant Formulas

The vitamin B$_{12}$ content of human milk falls from about 2.4 μg/L in colostrum to about 0.3 μg/L in mature milk.[88,94,98,112] Human milk has a high vitamin B$_{12}$-binding capacity; however, the role played by these binding proteins is not well defined.[94,98,112] Mature human milk and maternal serum have similar vitamin B$_{12}$ concentrations.[112] Supplementation of nursing mothers with vitamin B$_{12}$ will increase the vitamin B$_{12}$ content of their milk, but it is unnecessary unless the maternal diet is deficient or conditions exist that interfere with maternal vitamin B$_{12}$ absorption.[88,98] Human milk provides sufficient vitamin B$_{12}$ to term infants, and serum vitamin B$_{12}$ concentrations are maintained within normal limits.[88,89] Preterm infants also appear to absorb vitamin B$_{12}$ well from human milk.[91] The vitamin B$_{12}$ contents of human milk fortifiers are shown in Table 12.4; the need for such fortification in preterm infants has not been demonstrated.

The vitamin B$_{12}$ contents of the preterm and common term infant formulas (Table 12.4) exceed the content of human milk and the minimal level recommended by the AAPCON, 0.15 μg/100 kcal.[1] Preterm infants appear able to absorb vitamin B$_{12}$ well from these formulas. There are no data suggesting that vitamin B$_{12}$ is absorbed better from human milk than from bovine milk formula.[91]

Vitamin B$_{12}$ Supplementation and Deficiency Prevention

There are no data from controlled clinical trials supporting vitamin B$_{12}$ supplementation in full-term infants in the neonatal period.[94] Vitamin B$_{12}$ deficiency has not been described in infants born to healthy, well-nourished mothers.[11,88–91,94] The amount of vitamin B$_{12}$ contained in human milk and in the current infant formulas is well absorbed,[88–91] and additional vitamin B$_{12}$ supplementation is unnecessary for full-term infants.

No clinical trials have evaluated the effect of vitamin B$_{12}$ supplementation in preterm infants.[94] Since the hepatic stores of vitamin B$_{12}$ correlate with the duration of pregnancy,[92] preterm infants, especially VLBW infants, would be expected to have lower stores of vitamin B$_{12}$ and possibly could be predisposed to vitamin B$_{12}$ deficiency. In addition, VLBW infants might experience a delay in achieving full enteral nutrition, a limitation of fluid intake, or a condition that interferes with vitamin B$_{12}$ absorption. Nonetheless, preterm infants appear to absorb a sufficient amount of vitamin B$_{12}$ from human milk and

the current infant formulas to prevent vitamin B$_{12}$ deficiency.[89,91]

Vitamin B$_{12}$ Supplementation and Parenteral Nutrition

Moore et al.[107] described vitamin B$_{12}$ status during total parenteral nutrition in 18 preterm infants and 26 full-term infants and children. The vitamin B$_{12}$ supplement was provided by the recommended amount of M.V.I. Pediatric.[108] The full-term infants and children received about 1 μg/day (0.1 μg/100 kcal) and maintained serum vitamin B$_{12}$ concentrations above reference values. The premature infants received 0.65 μg/day (0.85 μg/100 kcal; 0.6 μg/kg/day), and their serum vitamin B$_{12}$ levels remained markedly higher than reference values throughout the 28-day study. Revised dosage guidelines for M.V.I. Pediatric suggested by the manufacturer[109] would provide a daily vitamin B$_{12}$ supplement of 0.3 μg to infants weighing less than 1,000 g, 0.65 μg to infants weighing between 1,000 and 3,000 g, and 1 μg to infants weighing more than 3,000 g. Serum vitamin B$_{12}$ concentrations have not been reported in preterm infants treated in accordance with these recommendations.

Conclusions and Recommendations

The minimal enteral intake of vitamin B$_{12}$ recommended by the AAPCON[1] for preterm infants is the same as that recommended for full-term infants, 0.15 μg/100 kcal. The RDA for vitamin B$_{12}$ is 0.3 μg/day for infants from birth to 6 months.[111] An enteral vitamin B$_{12}$ intake of 0.3 μg/kg/day is recommended for VLBW preterm infants until 40 weeks postconceptional age. Thereafter, the minimal recommended intake for full-term infants, 0.15 μg/100 kcal, should be sufficient. Because the vitamin B$_{12}$ content is 0.20 to 0.45 μg/dL in the preterm formulas and 0.15 to 0.17 μg/dL in the term formulas (Table 12.4), vitamin B$_{12}$ requirements should be readily satisfied by adequate formula intake. Although low serum vitamin B$_{12}$ concentrations and vitamin B$_{12}$ deficiency have not been described in preterm infants fed human milk,[89,91] the use of human milk fortifiers should insure that the minimal recommended intake of vitamin B$_{12}$ is achieved in VLBW infants during the early postnatal period (Table 12.4).

The recommended parenteral intake of vitamin B$_{12}$ is 1 μg/day in full-term infants and 0.3 μg/kg/day in preterm infants.[36,88,89] The dose for preterm infants is provided by 30% of a full dose of M.V.I. Pediatric. Such a dose should prevent the elevation in serum vitamin B$_{12}$ concentrations that was observed in preterm infants who received a parenteral intake of 0.6 μg/kg/day.[107]

CASE STUDY

A 1,130-g baby girl was born at 28 weeks gestation to a 35-year-old gravida 1 woman with O+ blood type. The pregnancy was complicated by premature rupture of the fetal membranes followed by development of amniotitis. After delivery, the infant developed moderate respiratory distress syndrome, which was treated with surfactant replacement therapy, positive-pressure mechanical ventilation for 3 days, and then supplemental inspiratory oxygen for 3 days. Her initial hemoglobin was 10.0 g/dL.

Enteral feedings with a non-iron-fortified (0.2 g/dL) preterm formula were initiated on the fourth day of life and were slowly advanced to full enteral nutrition (150 mL/kg/day) on day 10. Birthweight was regained on the 14th day of life.

At age 25 days, the infant weighed 1,320 g and had a hemoglobin concentration of 8.1 g/dL, hematocrit of 24.2%, mean corpuscular volume of 81 fL, reticulocyte count of 1.4%, and serum ferritin concentration of 160 ng/mL. She had received two packed RBC transfusions, totaling 22 mL, on days 1 and 9, and approximately 25 mL of blood had been withdrawn for laboratory studies. Aside from occasional episodes of apnea and bradycardia, which were well controlled with caffeine therapy, the baby's course was unremarkable, and she gained weight steadily. At 40 days of age, she weighed 1,750 g and had a hemoglobin concentration of 6.8 g/dL, hematocrit of 20.7%, mean corpuscular volume of 78 fL, reticulocyte count of 10.6%, and serum ferritin of 90 ng/mL. An iron-fortified (1.2 mg/dL) term formula was initiated at that time. She was discharged 3 weeks later weighing 2,255 g. Laboratory studies at discharge revealed a hemoglobin concentration of 7.6 g/dL, hematocrit of 23.9%, mean corpuscular volume of 74 fL, reticulocyte count of 6.2%, and serum ferritin concentration of 38 ng/dL.

Questions. Should iron supplementation or an iron-fortified formula have been started earlier? If so, when?

If iron supplementation had been started at about 2 weeks of age, would the laboratory values be different at discharge?

Assume that an iron-fortified (1.2 mg/dL) formula is continued throughout the first year of life and that the baby has no extraordinary blood loss. What is the likelihood that she will develop iron deficiency anemia?

Commentary. By 25 days of age, this baby had anemia of prematurity. Although she had been transfused with a total of 22 mL of packed RBCs, she had had a low hemoglobin concentration at birth, and a significant amount of blood had been withdrawn for laboratory studies. She had gained weight steadily from 14 days of age, and her blood volume had increased about 16% in association with weight gain. An iron-fortified formula was started at 40 days of age, meeting the recommendation of the AAPCON that some form of iron supplementation be started no later than 2 months of age in VLBW preterm infants. At that time, the baby appeared to be in the second stage of erythropoiesis. Although her hemoglobin concentration had fallen from 8.1 g/dL to 6.8 g/dL, her total body hemoglobin had increased from 8.6 g to 9.5 g, her reticulocyte count was elevated, and her serum ferritin concentration had decreased. Three weeks later she appeared to be reaching the stage of iron-dependent erythropoiesis; her hemoglobin concentration had increased to 7.6 g/dL, but her mean corpuscular volume had fallen to 74 and her serum ferritin concentration to 38 ng/dL.

Iron supplementation could have been started once full enteral nutrition with a non-iron-fortified preterm formula was reached at 10 days of age, or an iron-fortified preterm formula could have been initiated when enteral feedings were begun at 4 days of age. However, earlier initiation of iron supplementation or introduction of an iron-fortified formula would not have prevented development of anemia of prematurity. Initiation of some form of iron supplementation by 2 weeks of age might have resulted in a higher serum ferritin concentration at discharge, but the hemoglobin concentration and the hematocrit would not be different.

The risk of later iron deficiency is reduced by early initiation of some form of iron supplementation. Continuation of an iron-fortified formula or some form of iron supplementation throughout the first year of life should prevent the development of iron deficiency anemia.

Acknowledgments

The author thanks Debra Camputaro and Marcel Nabors for secretarial assistance in the preparation of this manuscript.

References

1. American Academy of Pediatrics Committee on Nutrition. Nutritional needs of low-birth-weight infants. *Pediatrics* 1985; 75:976–986.
2. American Academy of Pediatrics Committee on Nutrition. Iron supplementation for infants. *Pediatrics* 1976; 58:765–768.
3. Gorten MK, Cross ER. Iron metabolism in premature infants, II: prevention of iron deficiency. *J Pediatr* 1964; 64:509–520.
4. Lundström U, Siimes MA, Dallman PR. At what age does iron supplementation become necessary in low-birthweight infants? *J Pediatr* 1977; 91:878–883.
5. Dallman PR, Siimes MA. Iron deficiency in infancy and childhood: a report for the international nutritional anemia consultative group. Washington, DC: The Nutrition Foundation, 1979.
6. Jansson L, Holmberg L, Ekman R. Medicinal iron to low birth weight infants. *Acta Paediatr Scand* 1979; 68:705–708.
7. Siimes MA, Järvenpää A-L. Prevention of anemia and iron deficiency in very low-birth-weight infants. *J Pediatr* 1982; 101:277–280.
8. Oski FA, Naiman JL. Anemia in the neonatal period. In: Oski FA, Naiman JL, eds. *Hematologic problems in the newborn*. 3rd ed. Philadelphia: WB Saunders, 1982: 56–86.
9. Siimes MA. Iron nutrition in low-birth-weight infants. In: Stekel A, ed. *Iron nutrition in infancy and childhood*. New York: Raven Press, 1984:75–94.
10. Oski FA. Iron requirements of the premature infant. In: Tsang RC, ed. *Vitamin and mineral requirements in preterm infants*. New York: Marcel Dekker, 1985:9–21.

11. Dallman PR. Nutritional anemia of infancy: iron, folic acid, and vitamin B$_{12}$. In: Tsang RD, Nichols BL, eds. *Nutrition during infancy*. Philadelphia: Hanley and Belfus, 1988:216–235.

12. Widdowson EM, Spray CM. Chemical development in utero. *Arch Dis Child* 1951; 26:205–214.

13. Shaw JCL. Parenteral nutrition in the management of sick low birthweight infants. *Pediatr Clin N Am* 1973; 20:333–358.

14. Oski FA, Naiman JL. The hematologic aspects of the maternal-fetal relationship. In: Oski FA, Naiman JL, eds. *Hematologic Problems in the Newborn*. 3rd ed. Philadelphia: WB Saunders, 1982:32–55.

15. Chang LL. Storage iron in foetal livers. *Acta Paediatr Scand* 1972; 62:173–175.

16. Stekel A. Iron requirements in infancy and childhood. In: *Iron nutrition in infancy and childhood*. New York: Raven Press, 1984:1–10.

17. Dallman PR. Review of iron metabolism. In: Filer LJ, ed. *Dietary iron: birth to two years*. New York: Raven Press, 1989:1–18.

18. Oski FA, Naiman JL. Normal blood values in the newborn period. In: *Hematologic problems in the newborn*. 3rd ed. Philadelphia: WB Saunders, 1982:1–31.

19. Moore CV, Dubach R. Iron. In: Comar CL, Bronner F, eds. *Mineral metabolism*. New York: Academic Press, 1962;2(pt B):287–348.

20. Fomon SJ. Iron. In: *Infant nutrition*. 2nd ed. Philadelphia: WB Saunders, 1974:298–319.

21. Seligman PA, Klausner RD, Huebers HA. Molecular mechanisms of iron metabolism. In: Stamatoyannopoulos G, Nienhuis AW, Leder P, Majerus PW, eds. *The molecular basis of blood diseases*. Philadelphia: WB Saunders, 1987:219–244.

22. Flanagan PR. Mechanisms and regulation of intestinal uptake and iron transfer. *Acta Paediatr Scand* 1989; 361 (supp):21–30.

23. Huebers HA, Finch CA. The physiology of transferrin and transferrin receptors. *Physiol Rev* 1987; 67:520–582.

24. Klausner RD. From receptors to genes: insights from molecular iron metabolism. *Clin Res* 1988; 36:494–500.

25. Peters JH, Raja KB, Simpson RJ, Snape S. Mechanisms and regulation of intestinal iron absorption. *Ann NY Acad Sci* 1988; 526:141–147.

26. Cook JD, Bothwell TH. Availability of iron from infant foods. In: Stekel A, ed. *Iron nutrition in infancy and childhood*. New York: Raven Press, 1984:119–145.

27. Lönnerdal B. Iron in human milk and cow's milk: effects of binding ligands on bioavailability. In: Lönnerdal B, ed. *Iron metabolism in infants*. Boca Raton, FL: CRC Press, 1990:87–107.

28. Lynch SR, Hurrell RF. Iron in formulas and baby foods. In: Lönnerdal B, ed. *Iron metabolism in infants*. Boca Raton, FL: CRC Press, 1990:109–126.

29. Oettinger L, Jr, Mills WB, Hahn PF. Iron absorption in premature and full-term infants. *J Pediatr* 1954; 45:302–306.

30. Gorten MK, Hepner R, Workman J. Iron metabolism in premature infants, I: absorption and utilization of iron as measured by isotope studies. *J Pediatr* 1963; 63:1063–1071.

31. Ehrenkranz RA, Gettner PA, Nelli C, et al. Iron absorption and incorporation into red blood cells by very low birthweight infants: studies with the stable isotope ^{58}Fe. *J Pediatr Gastroenterol Nutr* 1992; 15:270–278.

32. Larsen L, Milman N. Normal iron absorption determined by means of whole body counting and red cell incorporation of ^{59}Fe. *Acta Med Scand* 1975; 198:271–274.

33. Bothwell TH, Charlton RW, Cook JD, Finch CA. *Iron metabolism in man*. Oxford, UK: Blackwell Scientific, 1979:401–438.

34. Dauncey MJ, Davies CG, Shaw JCL, Urman J. The effect of iron supplements and blood transfusion on iron absorption by low birthweight infants fed pasteurized human breast milk. *Pediatr Res* 1978; 12:899–904.

35. Shaw JCL. Iron absorption by the premature infant: the effect of transfusion and iron supplements on the serum ferritin levels. *Acta Paediatr Scand* 1982;299 (suppl):83–89.

36. Greene HL, Hambidge KM, Schanler R, Tsang RC. Guidelines for the use of vitamins, trace elements, calcium, magnesium, and phosphorus in infants and children receiving total parenteral nutrition: report of the Subcommittee on Pediatric Parenteral Nutrient Requirements from the Committee on Clinical Practice Issues of The American Society for Clinical Nutrition. *Am J Clin Nutr* 1988; 48:1324–1342.

37. Doyle JJ, Zipursky A. Neonatal blood disorders. In: Sinclair JL, Bracken MB, eds. *Effective care of the newborn infant*. Oxford, UK: Oxford University Press, 1992:426–453.

38. James JA, Combes M. Iron deficiency in the premature infant. Significance, and prevention by the intramuscular administration of iron-dextran. *Pediatrics* 1960; 26:368–374.

39. Hammond D, Murphy A. The influence of exogenous iron on formation of hemoglobin in the premature infant. *Pediatrics* 1960; 25:362–374.

40. Melnick G, Grouch JB, Caksackkas HL, Churella HR. Iron status of low-birth-weight infants fed formulas containing high or low iron content. *Pediatr Res* 1988; 23:488A.

41. Groh-Wargo SL, Danish EH, Super DM. Iron therapy in the premature infant. *Pediatr Res* 1990; 27:284A.

42. Sitarz AL, Wolff JA, Van Hofe FH. Comparison of oral and intramuscular administration of iron for prevention of the late anemia of premature infants. *Pediatrics* 1960; 26:375–386.

43. Lemons JA, Moye L, Hall D, Simmons M. Differences in the composition of preterm and term human milk during early lactation. *Pediatr Res* 1982; 16:113–117.

44. Mendelson RA, Anderson GH, Bryan MH. Zinc, copper and iron content of milk from mothers of preterm and full-term infants. *Early Hum Dev* 1982; 6:145–151.

45. McMillan JA, Landaw SA, Oski FA. Iron sufficiency in breast-fed infants and the availability of iron from human milk. *Pediatrics* 1976; 58:686–691.

46. Saarinen UM, Siimes MA, Dallman PR. Iron absorption in infants: high bioavailability of breast milk iron as indicated by the extrinsic tag method of iron absorption and by the concentration of serum ferritin. *J Pediatr* 1977; 91:36–39.

47. Saarinen UM, Siimes MA. Iron absorption from breast milk, cow's milk, and iron-supplemented formula: an opportunistic use of changes in total body iron determined by hemoglobin, ferritin, and body weight in 132 infants. *Pediatr Res* 1979; 13:143–147.

48. Picciano MF, Deering RH. The influence of feeding regimens on iron status during infancy. *Am J Clin Nutr* 1980; 33:746–753.

49. Garry PJ, Owen GM, Hopper EM, Gilbert BA. Iron absorption from human milk and formula with and without iron supplementation. *Pediatr Res* 1981; 15:822–828.

50. Hertrampf E, Cayazzo M, Pizarro F, Stekel A. Bioavailability of iron in soy-based formula and its effect on iron nutriture in infancy. *Pediatrics* 1986; 78:640–645.

51. Saarinen UM. Need for iron supplementation in infants on prolonged breast feeding. *J Pediatr* 1978; 93:177–180.

52. Iwai Y, Takanashi T, Nakao Y, Mikawa H. Iron status in low birth weight infants on breast and formula feeding. *Eur J Pediatr* 1986; 145:63–65.

53. Stockman JA III. Anemia of prematurity: current concepts in the issue of when to transfuse. *Pediatr Clin North Am* 1986; 333:111–128.

54. Austria JR, Brodsky NL, Hurt H. Multiply-transfused (M-Tx) preterm infants may not require iron-supplementation (Iron-S) at recommended times. *Pediatr Res* 1987; 21:391A.

55. Bezwoda WR, Bothwell TH, Torrance JD, et al. The relationship between marrow iron stores, plasma ferritin concentrations and iron absorption. *Scand J Haematol* 1979; 22:113–120.

56. Siimes MA, Saarinen UM, Dallman PR. Relationship between hemoglobin concentration and transferrin saturation in iron-sufficient infants. *Am J Clin Nutr* 1979; 32:2295–2300.

57. Siimes MA, Heikinheimo M. Regulation of erythropoiesis during early infancy. *Pediatr Hematol Oncol* 1991; 8:9–12.

58. Brown MS, Phibbs RH, Garcia JF, Dallman PR. Postnatal changes in erythropoietin levels in untransfused premature infants. *J Pediatr* 1983; 103:612–617.

59. Stockman JA, Graeber JE, Clark DA, McClellan K, Garcia JF, Kavey REW. Anemia of prematurity: determinants of the erythropoietin response. *J Pediatr* 1984; 105: 786–792.

60. Brown MS, Garcia JF, Phibbs RH, Dallman PR. Decreased response of plasma immunoreactive erythropoietin to "available oxygen" in anemia of prematurity. *J Pediatr* 1984; 105:793–798.

61. Zanjani ED, Poster J, Burlington H, Mann LI, Wasserman LR. Liver as the primary site of erythropoietin formation in the fetus. *J Lab Clin Med* 1977; 89:640–644.

62. Dallman PR. Erythropoietin and the anemia of prematurity. *J Pediatr* 1984; 105:756–757.

63. Shannon KM, Naylor GS, Torkildson JC, et al. Circulating erythroid progenitors in the anemia of prematurity. *N Engl J Med* 1987; 317:728–733.

64. Rhondeau SM, Christensen RD, Ross MP, Rothstein G, Simmons MA. Responsiveness to recombinant human erythropoietin of marrow erythroid progenitors from infants with the "anemia of prematurity," *J Pediatr* 1988; 112:935–940.

65. Ohls RK, Christensen RD. Recombinant erythropoietin compared with erythrocyte transfusion in the treatment of anemia of prematurity. *J Pediatr* 1991; 119:781–788.

66. Halpérin DS, Wacker P, Lacourt G, et al. Effects of recombinant human erythropoietin in infants with the anemia of prematurity: a pilot study. *J Pediatr* 1990; 116: 779–786.

67. Shannon KM, Mentzer WC, Abels RI, et al. Recombinant human erythropoietin in the anemia of prematurity: results of a placebo controlled pilot study. *J Pediatr* 1991; 118:949–955.

68. Winearls CG, Oliver DO, Pippard MJ, Reid C, Downing MR, Cotes PM. Effect of human erythropoietin derived from recombinant DNA on the anaemia of patients maintained by chronic haemodialysis. *Lancet* 1986; 2: 1176–1178.

69. Eschbach JW, Egrie JC, Downing MR, Browne JK, Adamson JW. Correction of the anemia of end-stage renal disease with recombinant human erythropoietin: results of a combined phase I and II clinical trial. *N Engl J Med* 1987; 316:73–78.

70. Eschbach JW, Kelly MR, Haley NR, Abels RI, Adamson JW. Treatment of the anemia of progressive renal failure with recombinant human erythropoietin. *N Engl J Med* 1989; 321:158–163.

71. Lim VS, DeGowin RL, Zavala D, et al. Recombinant human erythropoietin treatment in pre-dialysis patients: a double-blind placebo-controlled trial. *Ann Intern Med* 1989; 110:108–114.

72. Sinai-Trieman L, Salusky IB, Fine RN. Use of subcutaneous recombinant human erythropoietin in children undergoing continuous cycling peritoneal dialysis. *J Pediatr* 1989; 114:550–554.

73. Stockman JA III. Erythropoietin: off again, on again. *J Pediatr* 1988; 112:906–908.

74. Oski FA, Barness LA. Vitamin E deficiency: a previously unrecognized cause of hemolytic anemia in the premature infant. *J Pediatr* 1967; 70:211–220.

75. Ehrenkranz RA. Vitamin E and the neonate. *Am J Dis Child* 1980; 134:1157–1166.

76. Bell EF, Filer LJ Jr. The role of vitamin E in the nutrition of premature infants. *Am J Clin Nutr* 1981; 34:414–422.

77. Melhorn DK, Gross S. Vitamin E-dependent anemia in the premature infant, I: effects of large doses of medicinal iron. *J Pediatr* 1971; 79:569–580.

78. Williams ML, Shott RJ, O'Neal P, Oski FA. Role of dietary iron and fat on vitamin E deficiency anemia of infancy. *N Engl J Med* 1975; 292:887–890.

79. Zipursky A, Brown EJ, Watts J, et al. Oral vitamin E supplementation for the prevention of anemia in premature infants: a controlled trial. *Pediatrics* 1987; 79:61–68.

80. Gross SJ, Gabriel E. Vitamin E status in preterm infants fed human milk or infant formula. *J Pediatr* 1985; 106:635–639.

81. O'Dell BL. Bioavailability of and interactions among trace elements. In, Chandra RK, ed. *Trace elements in nutrition of children*. New York: Raven Press, 1985:41–62.

82. Mills CF. Dietary interactions involving the trace elements. *Annu Rev Nutr* 1985; 5:173–193.

83. Solomons NW, Jacob RA. Studies on the bioavailability of zinc in humans: effects of heme and nonheme iron on the absorption of zinc. *Am J Clin Nutr* 1981; 34:475–482.

84. Walravens PA, Hambidge KM. Growth of infants fed a zinc supplemented formula. *Am J Clin Nutr* 1976; 29: 114–121.

85. Yip R, Reeves JD, Lönnerdal B, Keen CL, Dallman PR. Does iron supplementation compromise zinc nutrition in healthy infants? *Am J Clin Nutr* 1985; 42:683–687.

86. Haschke F, Ziegler EE, Edwards BB, Fomon SJ. Effect of iron fortification of infant formula on trace mineral absorption. *J Pediatr Gastroenterol Nutr* 1986; 5:768–773.

87. American Academy of Pediatrics Committee on Nutrition. Iron-fortified infant formulas. *Pediatrics* 1989; 84: 114–115.

88. Schanler RJ. Water-soluble vitamins. In, Lebenthal E, ed. *Textbook of gastroenterology and nutrition in infancy* New York: Raven Press, 1989:377–391.

89. Moran RJ, Greene HL. Vitamin requirements. In: Polin RA, Fox WW, eds. *Fetal and neonatal physiology*. Philadelphia: WB Saunders Company, 1992:248–257.

90. Shojania AM. Folic acid and vitamin B_{12} deficiency in pregnancy and in the neonatal period. *Clin Perinatol* 1984; 11:433–459.

91. Ek J. Folic and vitamin B_{12} requirements in premature infants. In: Tsang RC, ed. *Vitamin and mineral requirements in preterm infants* New York: Marcel Dekker, 1985:23–38.

92. Loria A, Vaz-Pinto A, Arroyo P, Ramirez-Mateos C, Sánchez-Medal L. Nutritional anemia, VI: fetal hepatic

storage of metabolites in the second half of pregnancy. *J Pediatr* 1977; 91:569–573.

93. Hoffbrand AV. Folate deficiency in premature infants. *Arch Dis Child* 1970; 45:441–444.

94. Specker BL, DeMarini S, Tsang RC. Vitamin and mineral supplementation. In: Sinclair JC, Bracken MB, eds. *Effective care of the newborn infant.* Oxford, UK: Oxford University Press, 1992:162–177.

95. Matoth Y, Pinkas A, Sroka CH. Studies on folic acid in infancy, III: folates in breast fed infants and their mothers. *Am J Clin Nutr* 1965; 16:356–359.

96. Tamura T, Yoshimura Y, Arakawa T. Human milk folate and folate status in lactating mothers and their infants. *Am J Clin Nutr* 1980; 33:193–197.

97. Cooperman JW, Dweck HS, Newman LJ, Garbarino C, Lopez R. The folate in human milk. *Am J Clin Nutr* 1982; 36:576–580.

98. Gaull GE, Jensen RG, Rassin DK, Malloy MH. Human milk as food. *Adv Perinat Med* 1982; 2:47–120.

99. Ek J. Plasma, red cell, and breast milk folacin concentrations in lactating women. *Am J Clin Nutr* 1983; 38:929–935.

100. Picciano MF. Analysis of water-soluble vitamins in human milk: folacin and vitamin B$_{12}$. In: Jensen RG, Neville MC, eds. *Human lactation, milk components and methodologies.* New York: Plenum Press, 1985:143–151.

101. Ek J, Magnus EM. Plasma and red blood cell folate in breastfed infants. *Acta Paediatr Scand* 1979; 68:239–243.

102. Ek J, Magnus E. Plasma and red cell folate values and folate requirements in formula-fed term infants. *J Pediatr* 1982; 100:738–744.

103. Ek J, Behncke L, Halvorsen KS, Magnus E. Plasma and red cell folate values and folate requirements in formula-fed premature infants. *Eur J Pediatr* 1984; 142:78–82.

104. Burland WL, Simpson K, Lord J. Response of low birth-weight infants to treatment with folic acid. *Arch Dis Child* 1971; 46:189–194.

105. Kendall AC, Jones EE, Wilson CID, Shinton NK, Elwood PC. Folic acid in low birthweight infants. *Arch Dis Child* 1974; 49:736–738.

106. Stevens D, Burman D, Strelling MK, Morris A. Folic acid supplementation in low birth weight infants. *Pediatrics* 1979; 64:333–335.

107. Moore MC, Greene HL, Phillips B, et al. Evaluation of a pediatric multiple vitamin preparation for total parenteral nutrition in infants and children, I: blood levels of water-soluble vitamins. *Pediatrics* 1986; 77:530–538.

108. American Medical Association, Department of Foods and Nutrition. Multivitamin preparations for parenteral use: a statement by the Nutrition Advisory Group. *JPEN* 1979; 3:258–262.

109. Phillips B, Franck LS, Greene HL. Vitamin E levels in premature infants during and after intravenous multivitamin supplementation. *Pediatrics* 1987; 80:680–683.

110. Greene HL. Vitamins A, E, B$_2$, and B$_6$ in very-low-birth weight infants receiving total parenteral nutrition. *J Am Coll Nutr* 1990; 9:543.

111. Committee on Dietary Allowances, Food and Nutrition Board. *Recommended dietary allowances.* 10th ed. Washington, DC: National Academy of Sciences, 1989.

112. Samson RR, McClelland DBL. Vitamin B$_{12}$ in human colostrum and milk. *Acta Paediatr Scand* 1980; 69:93–99.

13. Microminerals

R.M. Reifen

Stanley Zlotkin

Reviewers: *Billy S. Arant, Jr., Winston W.K. Koo, Kenneth Hambidge, Bo Lonnerdal*

Eight trace elements (or trace minerals) are nutritionally essential for the human: zinc, copper, selenium, chromium, molybdenum, manganese, iodine, and iron. Iron is considered separately in Chapter 12. This chapter reviews the major metabolic functions of the other seven trace minerals, comments on the currently recommended intakes of these minerals, and gives specific recommendations, where appropriate, on the need for supplementation in the very low-birthweight preterm infant and other survivors of preterm birth.

Although quantitatively the trace elements make up a small fraction of the total mineral content of the human body, they play an important role in numerous metabolic pathways. Clinical deficiencies have been described for six of the elements. The infant born prematurely is at increased risk of developing trace mineral deficiencies. Premature birth is associated with low stores at birth, because accretion of trace minerals takes place during the last trimester of pregnancy. Rapid postnatal growth, unknown requirements, and variable intake of trace minerals also put the preterm infant at risk for deficiencies.

The content of trace minerals in human milk is the accepted "gold standard" for the full-term infant, provided that an adequate volume of milk is ingested. For the infant born prematurely, there is no gold standard for trace mineral intakes. There are, however, three acceptable objectives for trace mineral intakes: (1) intake of an amount that will prevent trace mineral deficiencies; (2) intake of an amount that will allow for accretion of stores that would have been deposited in the developing fetus had the infant stayed in the womb until term; and (3) avoidance of toxicity from excess intakes.

During the *transitional period* (between birth and 2 weeks of age), when the infant is likely to be clinically unstable, intake of trace minerals may not be necessary, because deficiencies are unlikely to develop over this short period of time. If trace minerals are included in the diet, the intake should be adequate simply to prevent deficiency. If parenteral nutrition is used during the transitional period, trace minerals need not be included, with the possible exception of zinc. During the *stable period,* which directly follows the transitional period, rapid growth resumes, and trace minerals should be included in the diet, either at concentrations that will prevent deficiency or at the

higher concentrations that will also meet the needs for replacing body stores. These higher intakes should generally continue during the *postdischarge period,* when growth is rapid and the risk of trace mineral deficiencies is increased. The recommended intakes for the parenterally fed infant are in keeping with the recent recommendations by the Committee on Clinical Practice Issues of the American Society of Clinical Nutrition.[1]

Zinc

Despite the paucity of research on the other trace elements, zinc has been relatively well studied. Zinc is nutritionally essential for the human and is especially important for the maintenance of cell growth and development. A major function of zinc is as a metalloenzyme. Over 200 zinc metalloenzymes have been associated with carbohydrate and energy metabolism, protein catabolism and synthesis, nucleic acid synthesis, heme biosynthesis, and many other vital reactions.[2] Zinc is required in all stages of the cell cycle.[3] A few of the more common zinc-dependent enzymes include erythrocyte carbonic anhydrase, alkaline phosphatase, and DNA and RNA polymerases. Through its role in the superoxide dismutase enzyme systems, zinc acts in stabilizing cell membranes and protecting them from lipid peroxidation. Zinc is involved in protein and collagen synthesis and degradation (collagenase is a zinc enzyme). The role of zinc in protein metabolism is not simply in DNA synthesis, but also in the structuring of chromatin and in the regulatory action of some proteins in gene transcription via "zinc finger" elements in their structure.

Under normal circumstances, zinc homeostasis appears to be maintained primarily by changes in the fecal excretion of endogenous zinc and by alterations in fractional zinc absorption. The primary route of excretion of endogenous zinc is in the feces, with smaller quantities being excreted in the urine.[4] The only exception is in the parenterally fed infant, where the primary route of excretion is via the kidneys.

Intrauterine Accretion

Zinc is essential for embryogenesis and fetal growth. Most of the zinc present in the infant born at full term is accumulated during the final trimester of preg-

Table 13.1. Hepatic Metallothionein and Zinc Concentration*

	Metallothionein	Zinc
	(μg/g wet weight)	
Premature	234.5 ± 214.6[†]	226.0 ± 85.6[‡]
Full-term	217.6 ± 218.0[†]	142.2 ± 60.8[‡]
Infants	52.2 ± 47.0	49.8 ± 14.6[‡]
Controls[§]	34.9 ± 37.6	64.2 ± 14.8

*Mean ± SD. (Adapted, with permission, from Zlotkin SH, Cherian G.[6])
[†]$p < 0.01$ (premature and full-term vs. infants and controls).
[‡]$p < 0.05$ (premature vs. full-term vs. infants vs. controls).
[§]All control subjects (n = 9) died from accidents and were older than 1 year of age (mean age was 7.9 ± 4.4 years).

nancy.[5] A recent study examined hepatic metallothionein as a source of zinc storage in the preterm and full-term infant to test the hypothesis that zinc bound to metallothionein, the major zinc-binding protein in the liver, may protect the infant from zinc deficiency during the first weeks of life when dietary intake of zinc is limited.[6] During the first week of life, there was no difference in the concentration of metallothionein between premature and full-term infants (Table 13.1). The concentration of metallothionein, however, was significantly lower in older infants than in newborns. The hepatic zinc concentrations were significantly higher in preterm than in full-term infants. Due to the smaller size (and therefore smaller liver) of the preterm infants, however, total zinc stores at birth in the premature compared to the full-term infants were significantly lower.

When Widdowson and colleagues[7] updated the original estimates of zinc accretion for fetuses between 24 and 34 weeks gestation, only one value was provided for the entire last trimester of gestation.

Zinc accretion was given as 0.85 mg/day. Using this updated value, we have calculated new estimates of zinc accretion (Table 13.2). These new estimates of intrauterine zinc accretion are significantly higher than the older estimates. Further information on the changing rate of zinc accretion throughout the last trimester is necessary before definitive recommendations based on intrauterine accretion can be made.

Zinc Absorption
Data on the principle sites of zinc absorption are conflicting. Dietary zinc is absorbed in the proximal small intestine and, possibly, over the entire length of the small bowel. Following cellular uptake, zinc is actively secreted into the portal circulation. Two thirds of the zinc in plasma is bound to albumin, one third is bound to α_2-macroglobulin, and a small portion is bound to amino acids.

Absorption of zinc is decreased in the presence of phytate and fiber. At alkaline pH, phytate, zinc, and

Table 13.2. Estimates of Intrauterine Zinc Accretion Based on Old and New Data of Widdowson and Colleagues

Gestational Age (weeks)	Weight (kg)	Zinc Accretion	
		Old Values*	New Values[†]
		(μg/kg/day)	
24	0.6	600	1,416
28	1.0	360	850
32	1.8	200	472
34	2.4	150	354

*Data from Widdowson et al.[5]
[†]Data from Widdowson et al.[7]

Table 13.3. Estimate of Zinc Intake (the Dietary Requirement) from Breast Milk at 4, 12, and 24 Weeks after Birth[*]

Age (weeks)	Zinc[†] content (mg/L)	Milk[‡] Intake (mL/day)	Zinc[§] Intake (mg/day)
4	2.5	700	1.75
12	1.1	750	0.83
24	0.5	790	0.40

[*]Reproduced, with permission, from Zlotkin SH. Assessment of trace element requirements (zinc) in newborns and young infants, including the infant born prematurely. In: Chandra RK, ed. *Trace elements in nutrition of children—II*. New York: Raven Press, 1991;23:51.
[†]The mean zinc content of milk.[16]
[‡]The mean volume of intake of human milk.[71]
[§]Zinc intake calculated as zinc content of milk (mg/L) × milk intake (mL/day), expressed as mg/day.

calcium form an insoluble complex, which retards zinc absorption. Zinc absorption is facilitated by certain amino acids, such as histidine and cysteine.[8] Zinc is better absorbed from human milk than from formula or bovine milk.[9] The difference in availability is likely due to the tight binding of zinc to casein, which is the predominant protein in bovine milk.[10] Citrate has a positive effect on zinc absorption from human milk.[11] The estimated absorption of zinc in the adult is in the range of 20% to 40%.[12]

Ehrenkranz et al.[13] demonstrated that 60% of zinc was absorbed from preterm human milk, compared with 36% from fortified preterm human milk, 24% from "term formula," and 14% from "premature formula." Despite the significant differences in absorption, net retention of zinc from these four different feeding types was not significantly different. The two factors that most significantly affected absorption of zinc were the type of formula used and the concentration of zinc in the feed (the higher the concentration, the lower the percent absorption).

Another important finding from that study[13] was that infants were in positive zinc balance from the first week or two of life. Previous balance studies[14,15] examining zinc retention in preterm infants demonstrated large negative zinc balances during the first weeks of life, regardless of the types of feedings provided to the infants. The study of Ehrenkranz et al.[13] was the only one to use a combination of stable isotope (^{70}Zn) and traditional balance techniques to measure zinc status. Thus, different study methodologies may explain the differences in outcomes.

Sources of Zinc in the Diet

The concentration of zinc in colostrum is high, but the zinc concentration of human milk decreases rapidly. One month after birth, the zinc concentration of human milk is 2.5 mg/L.[16] The zinc concentration decreases as postpartum time increases, while the volume of milk ingested slowly rises. Thus, for the full-term infant at age 3 months who has an average daily intake of 750 mL of human milk with a zinc concentration of 1.1 mg/L, the zinc intake would be 0.83 mg/day (Table 13.3). The content of zinc in formula is variable, but it is usually higher than the amount in human milk.

Unlike the situation for the full-term infant, the content of zinc (or of any nutrient) in human milk cannot be used a priori as a gold standard to establish dietary zinc requirements for the preterm infant. In fact, a sizeable number of preterm infants who have been breast fed have developed frank zinc deficiency. As an example, five such infants are shown in Table 13.4. Although frank zinc deficiency is quite rare, many premature infants fed human milk may be zinc depleted, but without frank zinc deficiency. The clinical effects of acute zinc deficiency include growth failure, diminished food intake, skin lesions, poor wound healing, hair loss, decreased protein synthesis, and depressed immune function. Cases of severe zinc deficiency are relatively easy to diagnose because of the severity of the clinical and biochemical presentation. Patients have distinctive skin lesions, diarrhea, growth, and behavioral changes. Plasma zinc levels and alkaline phosphatase activity are usually below normal. Although such cases are relatively rare, subclinical zinc deficiency in premature infants fed human milk may be more common. Unfortunately, biochemical confirmation of subclinical zinc deficiency is not universally obtainable. The only definitive method of diagnosing zinc deficiency is to note the clinical and biochemical responses to zinc supplementation.

Friel et al.[17] examined longitudinally the trace element status of low-birthweight premature infants during the first year of life. Zinc content in hair of

Table 13.4. Characteristics of Premature Infants with "Zinc Deficiency" Due to Inadequate Human Milk Zinc Content*

Birthweight (kg)	Gestational Age (weeks)	Sex	Age at Onset (months)	Zinc Content of Milk (mg/L)	Reference Values[†16] (mg/L)
1.05[72]	27	Male	3	0.26	0.75 ± 0.3
1.98[73]	32	Male	2	0.58	0.78 ± 0.3
1.62[74]	32	Male	2	0.30	0.95 ± 0.3
1.58[74]	32	Female	2.5	0.50	0.78 ± 0.3
0.71[75]	26	Female	6.0	0.09	0.49 ± 0.4

*Reproduced, with permission, from Zlotkin SH. Assessment of trace element requirements (zinc) in newborns and young infants, including the infant born prematurely. In: Chandra RK, ed. *Trace elements in nutrition of children—II.* New York: Raven Press, 1991;23:59.

[†]This value corresponds to the postnatal date at which the milk sample was taken.

premature infants was significantly lower than that of full-term infants at 6 months of age (81 μg/g versus 144 μg/g, $p. < 0.05$). At that age, 37% of the preterm infants and 7% of full-term infants had hair zinc concentrations below 70 μg/g, the level that reportedly indicates zinc deficiency (in older children).[18] Median hair zinc concentrations of the male infants (preterm and full-term) were significantly lower than corresponding values for females at the same age. Of interest was the finding that length at 3 months of age could be best predicted, using multiple regression equations, by length at birth and dietary zinc intake. These data, although limited, support the suggestion that zinc, which plays an important role in early growth in the preterm infant, may be limiting to growth.

Recommended Enteral Zinc Intake (Table 13.5)
Transitional period: 500 to 800 μg/kg/day
Stable and postdischarge periods: 1 mg/kg/day

The American Academy of Pediatrics (AAP)[19] recommended a zinc intake for the preterm infant of 600 μg/kg/day. The European Society of Paediatric Gastroenterology and Nutrition (ESPGAN)[20] recommended a zinc intake of 720 to 1,400 μg/kg/day.

There is no information on the zinc needs of the infant whose birthweight is < 1,000 g. Although such small infants receive formulas with varying amounts

Table 13.5. Recommended Micromineral Intakes for Preterm Infants

	Transitional Period (0–14 days)		Stable/Postdischarge Periods	
	Enteral (μg/kg/day)	Parenteral (μg/kg/day)	Enteral (μg/kg/day)	Parenteral (μg/kg/day)
Zn	500–800	150	1,000*	400
Cu	120	0, ≤ 20[†]	120–150	20[†]
Se	1.3	0, ≤ 1.3	1.3–3.0	1.5–2.0
Cr	0.05	0, ≤ 0.05	0.1–0.5	0.05–0.2
Mo	0.3	0	0.3	0.25[‡]
Mn	0.75	0, ≤ 0.75[†]	0.75–7.5	1.0[†]
I	11–27	0, ≤ 1.0	30–60	1.0

*Postdischarge supplement of 0.5 mg/kg/day for infants fed human milk.
[†]Should be withheld when hepatic cholestatis is present.
[‡]For long-term TPN only.

of zinc, there are no reliable markers of safety or efficacy. No cases of acute zinc deficiency have been described in this population during the first weeks after birth. Therefore, during the transitional period, the amount of zinc found in human milk is likely adequate.

Recommendations of zinc intake during the stable period must consider efficacy, clinical experience, and safety. Based on the recalculated nutrient accretion data of Widdowson et al.[7] and the absorption estimates of Ehrenkranz et al.[13] the zinc intakes necessary to duplicate intrauterine accretion would be higher than any currently in clinical use. Although zinc is relatively nontoxic, high zinc intakes may be associated with adverse nutrient interactions (protein-mineral or mineral-mineral). For example, supplementation of zinc at a level of 30 mg/day in one infant resulted in copper deficiency.[21] Until data are available on the safety of these high intakes, they should not be recommended.

As previously discussed, during the first weeks of life infants may be protected from zinc deficiency through the release of zinc bound to metallothionein. Although there is controversy regarding the ability of the premature infant to absorb zinc from the diet, the recent work of Ehrenkranz et al.[13] indicates that infants in the 700 g to 1,500 g birthweight range likely can absorb zinc even in the first weeks of life. Intakes of zinc from preterm human milk when fed in adequate amounts will be in the range of 500 to 800 μg/kg/day. Since intake of this size has not been associated with zinc deficiency in the first 4 to 6 weeks of life and is likely safe, recommendations for zinc intake during the first weeks of life for infants <1,750 g birthweight are set at 500 to 800 μg/kg/day.

During the stable and postdischarge periods the zinc content of human milk may not be adequate to meet the needs of the rapidly growing preterm infant. Based on the recalculated data of Widdowson et al.[7] and the absorption estimates of Ehrenkranz et al.,[13] the recommended safe and adequate zinc intake is 1,000 μg/kg/day (1 mg/kg/day) until 6 months of age. This intake can be achieved through the use of "full-term" or "preterm" formula. Infants fed human milk may not be able to achieve this intake and will need a zinc supplement of 0.5 mg/kg/day, as zinc gluconate or sulfate.

Recommended Parental Zinc Intake (Table 13.5)

Transitional period: 150 μg/kg/day

Stable and postdischarge periods: 400 μg/kg/day

NOTE: The intake suggested for stable and postdischarge periods is likely adequate to maintain serum zinc levels within the normal range and to support growth, but it may be inadequate to parallel rates of intrauterine accretion.

With the intravenous infusion of nutrients, all nutrients are absorbed, compared with the 15% to 60% absorption estimates for the enterally fed infant. Infants receiving total parenteral nutrition (TPN) may become zinc deficient when not enough zinc is included in the parenteral formulation, when growth and zinc utilization are rapid, and when urinary losses are excessive.

Under normal conditions, fecal loss of zinc is the major excretory route. However, infants who receive no oral nutrients and who are parenterally fed pass little stool. Losses in the urine, therefore, are the main route of zinc excretion for the parenterally fed infant. About 60% of parenterally infused zinc is retained.[22] Of the zinc that is not retained, 87% is excreted in the urine, compared with 8% urinary excretion in healthy breast-fed full-term infants.

Although observed relatively frequently in the early 1970s, zinc deficiency has not been seen in preterm infants receiving TPN. We examined zinc retention in preterm infants receiving TPN and determined that positive zinc retention could be obtained with intakes >150 μg/kg/day.[22] Intakes of 440 μg/kg/day were adequate to duplicate Widdowson's original estimates of intrauterine zinc accretion.[5] Lockitch et al.[23] observed that intakes of about 400 μg/kg/day were adequate to maintain serum zinc levels in the normal range. The Committee on Clinical Practice Issues of the American Society of Clinical Nutrition[1] recommends a zinc intake of 400 μg/kg/day for the preterm infant.

In some infants the needs for zinc will be considerably higher due to abnormal losses from the gastrointestinal tract (e.g., with persistent diarrhea or excessive ileostomy drainage) or via urine (e.g., with high-output renal failure). In these cases, zinc intakes may have to be doubled or even tripled, depending on the volume and concentration of the losses.

Copper

Copper, like zinc, is an essential constituent of many enzymes. Of special importance are the copper-dependent oxidative enzymes, including cytochrome oxidase, the terminal oxidase in the electron transport chain. The most abundant copper-containing enzymes are the superoxide dismutase enzymes, which help protect cell membranes against oxidative damage. Ceruloplasmin, a weak oxidase, represents about 60% of the copper in plasma and interstitial fluids. Its main function is copper transport, but ceruloplasmin may also play a role in iron transport from hepatic storage sites to transferrin and may be necessary for the conversion of ferric to ferrous iron prior to attachment of iron to transferrin.

Metabolism

Copper is primarily absorbed in the upper small intestine. Its absorption seems to be enhanced by the presence of proteins, amino acids, and other chelating agents in the gut, which likely enhance its solubility.[3] Using stable isotope techniques, Ehrenkranz et al.[13] demonstrated significant net absorption in preterm infants fed various types of milk. The range was from 27% absorption with term bovine milk formula to 57% with fortified preterm human milk. High levels of dietary zinc can induce intestinal metallothionein synthesis and thus inhibit copper absorption.

After absorption from the gut, copper is bound to albumin and a copper-protein, transcuprein. It is transported to the liver, where it is incorporated into ceruloplasmin and metalloenzymes, or excreted via the biliary tract. Only small amounts of copper are lost in the urine. The liver plays the central role in copper metabolism through the synthesis of ceruloplasmin. Ceruloplasmin is synthesized in the liver and secreted into the plasma to carry copper to various sites in the body. Plasma copper and ceruloplasmin concentrations are low at birth in the preterm infant and remain low until ceruloplasmin synthesis is initiated, 6 to 12 weeks after birth. Synthesis begins earlier in more gestationally mature infants.

Metallothionein-bound copper accumulates in the fetal liver during the last 3 months of gestation. Fetal accretion of copper is approximately 0.9 μmol (56 μg)/kg/day. The fetal liver concentration is reported to be 16 times greater than the concentration in the adult.[5] This store of copper is thought to provide a reserve that is available to the term infant in early postnatal life. Except for the fetal period, there is little storage of copper in body tissues. After birth, concentrations of copper in the liver remain constant throughout life, except in states of disease or deficiency.

Copper Deficiency

Copper deficiency has been reported in infants who were fed primarily bovine milk[24] and in infants fed copper-free parenteral formulations.[25] The infusion of amino acids, as with TPN, may enhance urinary excretion. Copper deficiency has been reported in an infant receiving high-dose zinc therapy.[26]

The principal features of copper deficiency are hypochromic anemia unresponsive to iron therapy, neutropenia, and osteoporosis. Early radiologic features are osteoporosis of the metaphysis and retarded bone age. Other clinical findings associated with copper deficiency in premature infants may include pallor, decreased pigmentation of skin and hair, prominence of superficial veins, skin lesions similar to those of seborrheic dermatitis, failure to thrive, diarrhea, and hepatosplenomegaly. Features suggestive of central nervous system involvement are hypotonia, psychomotor retardation, lack of visual responses, and apneic episodes.[27]

Copper deficiency, although very rare, should be suspected in the presence of a combination of physical signs, abnormal laboratory measurements, and radiologic changes. An X-linked, recessively inherited disease, the Menkes kinky hair syndrome, is associated with a defect in copper absorption. The syndrome is characterized by subnormal copper levels in the blood, liver, and hair; hypothermia; defective keratinization of hair; metaphysical lesions; degenerative changes in aortic elastin; and progressive mental deterioration.[28]

Copper Toxicity

Although acute copper toxicity is rare, chronic excessive intake or reduced hepatic excretion can result in liver cirrhosis.

Copper Concentration of Feedings

The concentration of copper in early preterm mother's milk is high, 0.8 mg/L, but it decreases gradually. At 4 weeks after birth, preterm human milk contains about 0.6 mg/L.[29] In full-term milk, the copper concentration decreases as postpartum time increases. The content of copper in formula is variable, ranging from 0.01 to 1.4 mg/L.[30]

Recommended Enteral Copper Intake (Table 13.5)

Transitional period: Equivalent to content of human milk: 120 μg/kg/day

Stable and postdischarge periods: 120 to 150 μg/kg/day

Data on copper requirements in the preterm infant are limited. On intakes currently in use, copper deficiency is rarely, if ever, seen. Infants fed their own mother's milk do not become copper deficient. In addition, there is no documentation of copper deficiency in long-term survivors of premature birth. The current AAP recommendation for copper intake in the preterm infant is 108 μg/kg/day.[31] ESPGAN recommends a range between 117 and 156 μg/kg/day.[20]

Recommended Parenteral Copper Intake (Table 13.5)

Transitional period: May be omitted; if given, $\leq$20 μg/kg/day

Stable and postdischarge periods: 20 μg/kg/day

NOTE: Copper should be withheld when hepatic cholestasis is present.

Zlotkin and Buchanan[22] provided varying intakes of copper to parenterally fed preterm infants. They demonstrated that intakes in excess of 16 μg/kg/day were adequate to replace ongoing losses and prevent acute deficiencies. With this intake, plasma copper concentrations remained within the normal range. Intake of copper at a rate of 63 μg/kg/day resulted in duplication of intrauterine accretion rates. Lockitch et al.[23] demonstrated normal plasma copper levels with parenteral intakes varying from 19 to 38 μg/kg/day.

The Committee on Clinical Practice Issues of the American Society of Clinical Nutrition[1] recently recommended parenteral intakes of 20 μg/kg/day for the preterm infant. They also suggested that copper supplementation of short-term TPN may not be necessary.

Infants with cholestasis should not receive parenteral copper, because biliary excretion is the major excretory route for copper.

Selenium

Although selenium deficiency has been described infrequently in the infant, selenium is recognized as a nutritionally essential trace element.[32] The role of selenium in pediatric nutrition has recently been thoroughly reviewed.[33] Its only established physiologic function is as an integral part of the selenium-dependent enzyme glutathione peroxidase. Selenium and vitamin E have overlapping functions. Selenium, through glutathione peroxidase, is involved in protecting cell membranes from peroxidase damage through detoxification of peroxides and free radicals.

Selenium deficiency is one of the etiologic factors responsible for Keshan disease, an often fatal cardiomyopathy primarily affecting children and young women in more than a dozen provinces within the belt of endemic selenium deficiency in China.[34,35] Cases of cardiac and skeletal myopathy resembling Keshan disease have been reported in patients with depressed selenium status in the United States. Two of these patients were on long-term TPN and had little or no selenium in their parenteral formulations.[36] Loss of hair pigment and macrocytosis apparently attributable to mild selenium deficiency have also been reported in intravenously fed children.[37] Clinical selenium deficiency has not been described in preterm infants, although biochemical evidence of selenium deficiency (low serum concentrations and decreased glutathione peroxidase activity) has been cited. The preterm infant is at risk because of low stores at birth[38] and the use of selenium-free TPN.

All soluble selenium compounds, including selenite, selenomethionine, and Se-cysteine, are absorbed in the duodenum. Ehrenkranz et al.,[39] using stable isotopes of selenium in a study of 20 premature infants, recently demonstrated absorption of 60% to 80% of dietary selenium in formula. Selenium absorption and retention were not found to correlate with gestational age, postconceptional age, or weight gain. Although selenium is generally thought to be lost from the body via urine following metabolism, about twice as much selenium was excreted in stool as in urine.[39]

Human milk, bovine milk, and infant formulas all provide biologically available sources of dietary selenium. Colostrum contains twice as much selenium as mature human milk. The selenium content of mature human milk falls from 20 μg/L at 1 month postpartum to 15 μg/L at 3 and 6 months postpartum. The selenium content of infant formulas varies according to the amounts of intrinsic selenium in the ingredients. Dietary selenium is normally associated with proteins. The content of selenium in formula, therefore, depends mainly on the amount, source, and type of protein in the formulation. A usual range is 7 to 14 μg/L.

Infants born prematurely have decreased hepatic selenium stores compared to full-term infants at birth.[38] Intrauterine accretion of selenium during the third trimester of gestation is estimated to be 1 μg/kg/day. This estimate is likely an underestimate of gestational accretion, since it was based on tissues obtained from fetuses in New Zealand, where tissue selenium contents are known to be low. Ehrenkranz and colleagues,[39] using a stable isotope methodology, showed that preterm infants who were fed selenium at a rate of 3 μg/kg/day were able to absorb and retain dietary selenium at a rate that exceeded this rate of intrauterine selenium accretion. In another study, infants receiving formula that provided about 1 μg/kg/day had normal serum selenium levels after 6 weeks but declining plasma glutathione peroxidase activity.[40] Smith et al.[41] demonstrated that premature infants fed either preterm human milk (selenium content 24 μg/L), standard premature formula (7.8 μg/L), or premature formula supplemented with selenium in the amount of 30 μg/L had similar plasma and red blood cell selenium and glutathione peroxidase levels. There are no accounts in the literature of older preterm infants developing selenium deficiency independent of their dietary selenium intake.

Previous recommendations for selenium intake for the very low-birthweight infant were 1.5 to 2.5 μg/kg/day, with 1.0 μg/kg/day the minimum requirement.[42]

Recommended Enteral Selenium Intake (Table 13.5)

Transitional period: Equivalent to human milk, 1.3 μg/kg/day

Stable and postdischarge periods: 1.3 to 3 μg/kg/day

Plasma glutathione peroxidase levels have been noted to fall with selenium intakes <1 μg/kg/day, yet they remain in the normal range with intakes of about 1.3 μg/kg/day. Infants receiving their own mother's milk would receive about 3 μg/kg/day.

Recommended Parenteral Selenium Intake (Table 13.5)

Early transitional period: May be omitted; if given, ≤1.3 μg/kg/day

Stable and postdischarge periods: 1.5 to 2.0 μg/kg/day
NOTE: Because selenium is excreted primarily via the kidneys, the dosage should be lowered in the presence of decreased renal output.

Huston and colleagues[43] have examined selenium metabolism in the parenterally fed infant over the past decade. Their earlier studies in infants <1,250 g birthweight demonstrated that the use of selenium-free TPN resulted in low serum selenium concentrations and glutathione peroxidase activity.[43] More recently, they studied infants weighing <1,000 g at birth who received either selenium-free TPN or formulations containing selenium to achieve an intake of 1.34 μg/kg/day.[44] Supplemented infants receiving TPN maintained normal serum selenium levels and higher white blood cell glutathione peroxidase activity than infants receiving selenium-free TPN.

The Committee on Clinical Practice Issues of the American Society of Clinical Nutrition has recommended parenteral intakes of selenium at 2 μg/kg/day for the preterm infant.

Chromium

Chromium is somehow involved in the prevention of glucose intolerance. Early work suggested that chromium is part of, or necessary for, a glucose tolerance factor, described as being a water-soluble component of liver, blood, plasma, and other biologic cells.[45] More recently, Yamamoto et al.[46] reported the isolation from liver and milk of an amino acid component containing chromium that had biologic activity, stimulated adipocytes to take up glucose, and potentiated insulin action. The role of chromium in glucose homeostasis is the only biologic role postulated for this micromineral.

There have been no studies on chromium absorption by infants and only a few studies in adults. Adults absorb less than 2% of a chromium load. Chromium is excreted primarily via the urine, with excretion rates reflecting dietary intake.[47]

Although chromium deficiency has been described in three adult patients on long-term chromium-free TPN, it has not been documented in the pediatric population. The adult patients with chromium deficiency all had received chromium-free TPN for periods ranging from 5 months to 3 years.[48,49] The chromium deficiency was associated with weight loss, peripheral neuropathy, hyperglycemia, and abnormally high insulin requirements. The symptoms disappeared with parenteral chromium supplementation.

There are no satisfactory laboratory methods to assess chromium status, because samples are readily contaminated. Current estimates for normal blood chromium values (mean, 0.2 ng/mL) are at least eight times lower than values reported 10 years ago. The current normal values are so low that they are just at the detection limits of modern-day atomic absorption spectrophotometers.

Trivalent chromium has a very low order of toxicity.[27] Up to 6 mg/kg/day can be provided intravenously without ill effect.

The concentration of chromium in bovine milk and formula based on bovine milk (15 μg/L) is considerably higher than the concentration in human milk. The chromium content of human milk is 0.3 to 0.5 μg/L.[50,51] There is no information on the chromium content of preterm human milk.

There are insufficient data to recommend a specific chromium intake for the infant born prematurely. Because infants fed their own mother's milk have not become obviously chromium deficient, this intake is likely adequate for the preterm infant. Furthermore, because infants fed formula with significantly higher amounts of chromium have not developed overt toxicity, there is likely a wide safe range of intake.

Recommended Enteral Chromium Intake (Table 13.5)

Transitional period: Equivalent to human milk (0.05 μg/kg/day)
Stable and postdischarge periods: 0.1 to 0.5 μg/kg/day

Recommended Parenteral Chromium Intake (Table 13.5)

Early transitional period: May be omitted; if given, ≤0.05 μg/kg/day

Stable and postdischarge periods: 0.05 to 0.2 μg/kg/day
NOTE: Because chromium is excreted primarily via the kidneys, the dosage should be lowered in the presence of decreased renal output.

The Committee on Clinical Practice Issues of the American Society of Clinical Nutrition[1] recommended parenteral intakes of chromium at 0.2 μg/kg/day for the preterm infant. This recommendation was based on the dose known to prevent chromium deficiency in adults on long-term TPN (0.3 μg/kg/day) and the realization that infants fed human milk receive intakes of only about 0.05 μg/kg/day. No adverse effects have been reported in infants receiving this amount of chromium. There are no data to justify an intake higher than that received by the breast-fed infant.

Molybdenum

Molybdenum is necessary in very small amounts for the function of three mammalian enzymes: xanthine, aldehyde, and sulfite oxidases. Xanthine oxidase is necessary for the terminal oxidation of purines, to allow their excretion as uric acid. Sulfite oxidase is necessary for the disposal and excretion of sulfur.

Only one case of molybdenum deficiency has been reported in the literature.[52] An adult on long-term TPN had tachycardia and tachypnea, followed by vomiting, and central scotomas, and eventually became comatose. Urinary excretion of the end products of methionine metabolism was decreased, while serum uric acid levels were increased. This patient responded clinically and biochemically to the addition of molybdenum, 2.5 μg/kg/day, to the parenteral formulation. Molybdenum deficiency has not been described in the premature infant.

In adults, molybdenum is readily absorbed from the diet. Excretion is primarily via the urine, although small amounts may also be lost in bile. No information is available on the metabolism of molybdenum in the infant or child.

In the only study that examined fetal accretion of molybdenum, intrauterine molybdenum accretion was estimated at 1 μg/kg/day. The authors caution that this is probably a significant overestimation of the accretion rate.[53]

The molybdenum content of mature human milk is about 2 μg/L. No data are available on the molybdenum content of preterm milk. Based on an average intake of 150 mL/kg/day, a premature infant ingesting human milk would receive 0.3 μg/kg/day.

Recommended Enteral Molybdenum Intake (Table 13.5)

Transitional period: Equivalent to human milk (0.3 μg/kg/day)

Stable and postdischarge periods: 0.3 μg/kg/day

Recommended Parenteral Molybdenum Intake (Table 13.5)

Early transitional period: 0

Stable and postdischarge periods: 0.25 μg/kg/day (for long-term TPN only)

The Committee on Clinical Practice Issues of the American Society of Clinical Nutrition[1] recommended parenteral intakes of molybdenum at 0.25 μg/kg/day for the preterm infant. This intake is probably in the appropriate range. However, because molybdenum deficiency has not been described in the pediatric population, intravenous molybdenum is recommended only for those infants needing long-term TPN.

Manganese

Manganese is known to function in three main areas of metabolism: (1) it acts as an activator of the gluconeogenic enzymes pyruvate carboxylase and isocitrate dehydrogenase; (2) it is involved in protecting mitochondrial membranes through superoxide dismutase, a manganese-containing enzyme; and (3) per-

haps most important, manganese activates glycosyl transferase, which is involved in mucopolysaccharide synthesis.

Manganese deficiency has not been conclusively demonstrated in humans. Manganese deficiency in animals, however, has a significant effect on the production of hyaluronic acid, chondroitin sulfate, heparin, and other mucopolysaccharides that are important for growth and maintenance of connective tissue, cartilage, and bone. Although manganese is involved as a cofactor in numerous enzyme systems, manganese deficiency does not appear to have broad effects other than on mucopolysaccharide and lipopolysaccharide formation. This is probably because magnesium can be substituted for manganese in many of its enzyme-related functions.

Whereas manganese deficiency has not been reported in humans, manganese toxicity has been well described. Miners of manganese in India and Peru, for example, develop a toxicity syndrome that consists of extrapyramidal signs similar to those seen in Parkinson's disease.[54] Apparently, manganese crosses the blood-brain barrier and displaces catecholamines from storage sites in the central nervous system, resulting in a central catecholamine depletion state.[55] The signs of manganese toxicity respond quickly to treatment with levodopa, thus confirming the depletion of brain catecholamines.

Adult populations are protected from manganese toxicity by three barriers: the intestinal barrier, the blood-brain barrier, and the liver. Newborn premature infants, especially those receiving manganese-supplemented TPN, may be at increased risk of toxicity because manganese homeostasis is poorly developed in the premature infant. In addition, absorptive control (in the intestine) is bypassed by TPN, and because little or no stool is passed, excretion is minimal.[56] Intravenous infusions likely result in altered tissue distribution.[57] Finally, the blood-brain barrier of the preterm infant is immature and, therefore, more permeable. Zlotkin and Buchanan[58] looked for manganese toxicity in parenterally fed preterm infants by measuring the urinary excretion of catecholamine metabolites. Despite high manganese intakes in the infants studied (48 μg/kg/day), no evidence of manganese toxicity was detected. Unfortunately, there are no readily usable laboratory assays to assess manganese status adequately.

Manganese absorption in humans is low. In adults, 2% of the manganese from bovine milk was absorbed, 8% from human milk, and <1% from soy formula.[59] Studies in animals show that absorption varies inversely with the level of manganese.[60] In the plasma, manganese is bound to transferrin. More than 90% of manganese is excreted through the bile, with only a small portion excreted through the kidneys.[61] Manganese is rapidly cleared from the blood, with only 1.5% of an ingested adult dose being retained 10 days later.[62]

The manganese content of human milk is about 5 μg/L. With a milk intake of 150 mL/kg/day, intake of manganese would be 0.75 μg/kg/day. Formulas contain variable amounts of manganese, ranging from undetectable amounts to 340 μg/L. It has been estimated that formula-fed infants may receive between 5 and 90 μg/kg/day, depending on the formula provided.[30] There is no evidence that the low intake of manganese in breast-fed infants, even premature infants, is associated with manganese deficiency, nor is there any indication that higher intakes with the use of formulas is associated with toxicity. We therefore conclude that the safe and adequate range for manganese intake is 0.75 to 7.5 μg/kg/day. Based on data reported by Casey and Robinson,[63] a 1-kg infant would accumulate manganese at a rate of 9 μg/kg/day during the last trimester of pregnancy. Although the above recommendation would not duplicate intrauterine accretion rates, the absence of deficiency signs in infants receiving these lower intakes, combined with the potential for toxicity in the small preterm infant, leads to recommendation of the lower amounts.

Recommended Enteral Manganese Intake (Table 13.5)

Transitional period: Equivalent to human milk (0.75 μg/kg/day)

Stable and postdischarge periods: 0.75 to 7.5 μg/kg/day

Recommended Parenteral Manganese Intake (Table 13.5)

Transitional period: May be omitted; if given, ≤0.75 μg/kg/day

Stable and postdischarge periods: 1.0 μg/kg/day

NOTE: Manganese supplements should be withheld when hepatic cholestasis is present.

Parenteral solutions contain variable quantities of manganese contaminants.[64] For example, Zlotkin and Buchanan[58] found levels of 7 ± 1 μg/L in apparently manganese-free TPN formulations. Little manganese is secreted into the gut during TPN; thus, retention of intravenously infused manganese is close to 100%.[58] The majority of premature infants on TPN will be in positive manganese balance with intakes of 1.0 μg/kg/day. Quantities ten times that high have been used without evidence of toxicity, although serum manganese levels are elevated above normal. The addition of 5 μg/L has been associated with normal concentrations of serum manganese except in cholestatic liver disease.[65]

The Committee on Clinical Practice Issues of the American Society of Clinical Nutrition[1] deemed parenteral intakes of manganese at 1.0 μg/kg/day to be in the appropriate range for the preterm infant.

Iodine

The only known role of iodine is in thyroid function, where it is part of triiodothyronine (T_3) and tetraiodothyronine (T_4) (60% iodine by weight). The physiologic response to iodine deficiency in humans is increased secretion of thyroid-stimulating hormone, thyroid hyperplasia and hypertrophy, increased thyroid iodine uptake, and increased ratio of secretion of T_3 relative to T_4. Iodine deficiency depresses the production of thyroid hormones, especially T_4. Endemic goiter occurs in specific geographic areas throughout the world when dietary iodine intake is <15 μg/day.

In the intestinal tract, iodine is converted to I^- prior to absorption. Iodine is stored in the thyroid gland, and after peroxidation it becomes attached to the tyrosine residues of thyroglobulin.

The major concern regarding iodine nutrition in infants is endemic cretinism due to maternal iodide deficiency. Overt cretinism is said to occur in 5% to 15% of cases of endemic neonatal goiter. Milder degrees of iodine deficiency, both in utero and after birth, may have detrimental effects on growth and intellectual performance, even in the absence of more severe manifestations.[66]

Excess iodine intake can also cause hypothyroidism, especially in the 4% of the population who are sensitive to excess iodine. Even in a patient who receives no iodine by mouth or parenterally, iodine intake may be excessive from skin absorption of iodine in topical disinfectants, detergents, and other sources. Despite this theoretical risk of toxicity, iodine intakes of up to 1,000 μg/day in children have not resulted in deleterious outcomes.

In infants born prematurely, mechanisms to deal with iodine excess and deficiency are immature. When the diet is deficient in iodine, the premature infant is not able to compensate by retaining more iodine, and thus a higher iodine intake is needed to maintain a euthyroid state. Premature infants may develop transient hypothyroidism on iodine intakes of 10 to 30 μg/kg/day.[67] Iodine excess can also be deleterious to young infants. If premature infants (<34 weeks gestation) are exposed to high iodine intakes (>100 μg/day) via cutaneous administration of povidone-iodine and alcohol-iodine solutions, decreased T_4 and increased serum thyroid-stimulating hormone may result.[68]

The content of iodine in human milk is variable, depending on the dietary intake of the mother. The average iodine content of mature human milk in European mothers is 70 to 90 μg/L; in the United States, the iodine content is higher, 140 to 180 μg/L. An American infant ingesting 150 mL/kg/day will receive iodine at about 24 μg/kg/day. The average iodine content of bovine milk, also quite variable, is about three times higher than that of human milk (average 415 μg/L). Formulas based on bovine milk contain about 50 μg/L iodine, while special premature formulas contain between 50 and 146 μg/L. The concentrations of iodine in formula are well below the advised upper safety limit of 50 μg/100 kcal recommended at a symposium on upper limits in infant formulas.[69]

Delange has suggested a daily iodine requirement for the preterm infant of >30 μg/kg/day (personal communication). Some premature infants may be in negative iodine balance on intakes <30 μg/kg/day.[70] Based on the average iodine content of human milk, in Europe human milk would definitely not be an adequate iodine source for the preterm infant, while in the United States human milk would be slightly below this recommended intake.

Recommended Enteral Iodine Intake
(Table 13.5)

Transitional period: Equivalent to human milk (11 to 27 μg/kg/day)

Stable and postdischarge periods: 30 to 60 μg/kg/day.

If a preterm infant is exclusively fed human milk after discharge, an iodine supplement will be necessary to achieve the recommended intake.

Recommended Parenteral Iodine Intake
(Table 13.5)

Transitional period: May be omitted; if given, ≤1.0 μg/kg/day

Stable and postdischarge periods: 1.0 μg/kg/day

Most infants receiving TPN will have iodine-containing disinfectants or detergents used on their skin. Thus, one may assume a significant amount of iodine absorption through the skin. Based on this assumption, The Committee on Clinical Practice Issues of the American Society of Clinical Nutrition recently recommended parenteral intakes of iodine at 1.0 μg/kg/day for the preterm infant. In patients on long-term TPN, 1 μg/kg/day will avoid any risk of iodine deficiency, yet is not sufficient to add significantly to the risk of toxicity from topical iodine absorption.

This intake is deemed by the authors to be in the appropriate range.

Future Research

The recent use of stable isotopes of zinc and selenium has increased our knowledge about the absorption of these two elements. Further research with the stable isotope methodology is necessary to learn more about the absorption of the other trace minerals, especially in very low-birthweight preterm infants. In addition, the effect on mineral absorption of increasing or decreasing the amounts of trace minerals in enteral formulas should be determined. For example, will the high zinc content in enteral formulas for the preterm

infant affect iron absorption? Will a higher iron content in formulas designed for the preterm infant affect zinc absorption?

Further research is needed to document the changing concentration of trace minerals in human milk with increasing lactation time.

Our ability to assess the trace mineral status of infants is very limited. Currently, plasma levels of the minerals or mineral-dependent enzymes (as with selenium) are the primary means of assessment. Functional measures of deficiency need to be developed. Measurement of pentane/ethane concentrations in expired air as a measure of fatty acid oxidation secondary to vitamin E deficiency is a good example of a functional (although complex) measure of a nutrient deficiency.

Although the clinical signs and laboratory measurements of acute trace mineral deficiencies are relatively easy to recognize, there is most likely a stage between normal trace mineral status and profound deficiency. We currently have no means, either clinical or laboratory, to recognize marginal trace mineral deficiencies. This should be a focus for future research.

References

1. Greene HL, Hambidge KM, Schandler R, Tsang RC. Guidelines for the use of vitamins, trace elements, calcium, magnesium, and phosphorus in infants and children receiving total parenteral nutrition: report of the Subcommittee on Pediatric Parenteral Nutrient Requirements from the Committee on Clinical Practice Issues of the American Society of Clinical Nutrition. *Am J Clin Nutr* 1988; 48: 1324–1342.
2. Vallee BL, Galdes A. The metallobiochemistry of zinc enzymes. *Adv Enzymol* 1984; 56:283–430.
3. Linder M, ed. *Nutritional biochemistry and metabolism (with clinical applications).* 2nd ed. New York: Elsevier, 1991:215–276.
4. Zlotkin SH, Casselman C. Urinary zinc excretion in normal subjects. *J Trace Elem Exp Med* 1990; 3:13–21.
5. Widdowson EM, Dauncey J, Shaw JCL. Trace elements in fetal and early postnatal development. *Proc Nutr Soc* 1974; 33:275.
6. Zlotkin SH, Cherian G. Hepatic metallothionein as a source of zinc and cysteine during the first year of life. *Pediatr Res* 1988; 24:326–329.
7. Widdowson EM, Southgate DAT, Hey E. Fetal growth and body composition. In: Lindblad B, ed: *Perinatal nutrition.* New York: Academic Press, 1988:3–14.
8. Prasad AS, Oberleas D. Binding of zinc to amino acids and serum proteins in vitro. *J Lab Clin Med* 1970; 76:416–425.
9. Hambidge KM, Walravens PA, Casey CE, Brown RM, Bender C. Plasma zinc concentration of breast-fed infants. *J Pediatr* 1979; 94:607–608.
10. Lonnerdal B, Keen CL, Bell JG, Hurley LA. Zinc uptake and retention from chelates and milk fractions. In: Mills CF, Bremner I, Chesters JK, eds. *Trace elements in man and animals.* Farnham Royal, UK: Commonwealth Agricultural Bureaux, 1985; 5:427–430.
11. Sandstrom B, Davidson L, Lederblad A, Lonnerdal B. Zinc absorption from human milk, cow's milk and infant formulas. *Am J Dis Child* 1983; 137:726–729.

12. Prasad AS, Halsted JA, Nadhimi M. Syndrome of iron deficiency anemia, hepatosplenomegaly, dwarfism, hypogonadism and geophagia. *Am J Med* 1961; 31:532–546.
13. Ehrenkranz RA, Gettener PA, Nelli CMO, et al. Zinc and copper nutritional studies in very low birth weight infants: comparison of stable isotopic extrinsic tag and chemical balance methods *Pediatr Res* 1989; 26:298–307.
14. Dauncey MJ, Show JCL, Urman J. The absorption and retention of magnesium, zinc and copper by low birth weight infants fed pasteurized human breast milk. *Pediatr Res* 1977; 11:991–997.
15. Higashi A, Ikeda T, Iribe K, Matsuda I. Zinc balance in premature infants given the minimal dietary zinc requirements. *J Pediatr* 1988; 112:262–266.
16. Vuori E, Kuitunen J. The concentration of copper and zinc in human milk. *Acta Pediatr Scand* 1979; 68:33–37.
17. Friel JK, Gibson RS, Kwash G, Watts JL. Dietary zinc intake and growth during infancy. *J Pediatr Gastroenterol Nutr* 1985; 4:746–751.
18. Strain WH, Steadman LT, Lankau CA Jr, et al. Analysis of zinc levels in hair for the diagnosis of zinc deficiency in man. *J Lab Clin Med* 1966; 68:244–255.
19. American Academy of Pediatrics Committee on Nutrition. Nutritional needs of low birth weight infants. *Pediatrics* 1977; 60:519–530.
20. Committee on Nutrition of the Preterm Infant, European Society of Paediatric Gastroenterology and Nutrition. *Nutrition and feeding of preterm infants.* Oxford, UK: Blackwell Scientific, 1987.
21. Hambidge KM, Walravens PA, Neldner KH, Daugherty NA. Zinc, copper and fatty acids in acrodermatitis enterohepatica. In: Kirchgessner M, ed: *Trace elements: metabolism in man and animals.* Munich: Freisig-Weihenstephan, 1978:413–417.
22. Zlotkin SH, Buchanan BE. Meeting zinc and copper intake requirements in the parenterally fed preterm and full term infant. *J Pediatr* 1983; 103:441–446.
23. Lockitch G, Godolphin W, Pendray MR, et al. Serum zinc, copper retinol-binding protein, prealbumin, and ceruloplasmin concentrations in infants receiving intravenous zinc and copper supplementation. *J Pediatr* 1983; 102:304–307.
24. Graham GG, Cordano A. Copper depletion and deficiency in the malnourished infant. *John Hopkins Med J* 1966; 124:139.
25. Karpel JT, Peden VH. Copper deficiency in long-term parenteral nutrition. *J Pediatr* 1972; 80:83.
26. Yadrick MK, Kenney MA, Winterfeldt EA. Iron, copper and zinc status: response to supplementation with zinc and iron in adult females. *Am J Clin Nutr* 1989; 49:145–150.
27. Langard S, Norseth T. Chromium. In: Friberg L, Nordberg GF, Vouk VB, eds. *Handbook on the toxicology of metals.* Vol II. Amsterdam: Elsevier, 1986:185–210.
28. Danks DM, Campbell PE, Stevens BJ, et al. Menkes' kinky hair syndrome: an inherited defect in copper absorption with widespread effects. *Pediatrics* 1972; 50:188–201.
29. Mendelson RA, Anderson GH, Bryan MH. Zinc, copper, and iron content of milk from mothers of preterm infants. *Early Hum Dev* 1982; 6:145–151.
30. Lonnerdal B, Keen CL, Ohtake M, Tamura T. Iron, zinc, copper, and manganese in infant formulas. *Am J Dis Child* 1983; 137:433–437.
31. American Academy of Pediatrics Committee on Nutrition. Nutritional needs of low birth weight infants. *Pediatrics* 1985; 75:976–986.
32. Combs GF Jr, Combs SB. The role of selenium in nutrition. In: Walker WA, Watkins JB, eds. *Nutrition in pediatrics: science and clinical application.* Boston: Little Brown, 1985:17–45.
33. Litov RE, Combs GF. Selenium in pediatric nutrition, *Pediatrics* 1991; 87:339–352.
34. Chen X, Yang G, Chen J, et al. Studies on the relations of selenium and Keshan disease. *Biol Trace Elem Res* 1980; 2:91–107.
35. Sokoloff L. Kashin-Bech disease: current status. *Nutr Rev* 1988; 46:113–119.
36. Levander OA, Burk RF. Report on the 1986 ASPEN Research Workshop on Selenium in Clinical Nutrition. *JPEN* 1986; 10:545–549.
37. Vinton NE, Dahlstrom KA, Strobel CT, Ament ME. Macrocytosis and pseudoalbinism: manifestations of selenium deficiency. *J Pediatr* 1987; 111:711–717.
38. Bayliss PA, Buchanan BE, Hancock RGV, Zlotkin SH. Tissue selenium accretion in premature and full-term human infants and children. *Biol Trace Elem Res* 1985; 7:755–761.
39. Ehrenkranz RA, Gettner PA, Newlli CM, et al. Selenium absorption and retention by very-low-birth-weight infants: studies with the extrinsic stable isotope tag 74 Se. *J Pediatr Gastroenterol Nutr* 1991; 13:125–133.
40. Rudolph N, Preis O, Bitzos EL, Reale MM, Wong SL. Hematologic and selenium status of low-birth-weight-infants fed formulas with and without iron. *J Pediatr* 1981; 9:57–62.
41. Smith AM, Picciano MF, Milner JA, et al. Influence of feeding regimens on selenium concentrations and gluthathione peroxidase activities in plasma on erythrocytes of infants. *J Trace Elem Exp Med* 1988; 1:209–216.
42. Casey CE, Hambidge KM. Trace minerals. In: Tsang RC, ed. *Vitamin and mineral requirements in preterm infants.* New York: Marcel Dekker, 1985:152–184.
43. Huston RK, Benda GI, Carlson CV, et al. Selenium and vitamin E sufficiency in premature infants requiring total parenteral nutrition. *JPEN* 1982; 6:507–510.
44. Huston RK, Jelen BJ, Vidgoff J. Selenium supplementation in low-birthweight premature infants: relationship to trace metals and antioxidant enzymes. *JPEN* 1991;15:556–559.
45. Mertz W. Chromium occurrence and function in biological systems. *Physiol Rev* 1969; 49:163–239.
46. Yamamoto A, Wado O, Suzuki H. Purification and properties of biologically active chromium complex from bovine colostrum. *J Nutr* 1988; 118:39–45.
47. Anderson RA, Kozlovsky AS. Chromium intake, absorption and excretion of subjects consuming self-selected diets. *Am J Clin Nutr* 1985; 41:1177–1183.
48. Jeejeebhoy DN, Chu RC, Marliss EB, Greenberg GR, Bruce-Robertson A. Chromium deficiency, glucose intolerance, and neuropathy reversed by chromium supplementation, in a patient receiving long-term total parenteral nutrition. *Am J Clin Nutr* 1977; 30:531–538.
49. Freund H, Atamian S, Fischer JE. Chromium deficiency during total parenteral nutrition. *JAMA* 1979; 241:496–499.
50. Kumpulaninen J, Vuori E. Longitudinal study of chromium in human milk. *Am J Clin Nutr* 1980; 33:2299–2302.
51. Casey CE, Hambidge KM. Chromium in human milk from American mothers. *Br J Nutr* 1984; 52:73–77.
52. Johnson J, Wadman SK. Molybdenum cofactor deficiency. In: Scriver CR, Beaudet AL, Sly WS, Valle D, eds. *Metabolic basis of inherited diseases.* 6th ed. New York: McGraw Hill, 1989:1463–1475.
53. Abumrad NN. Molybdenum—is it an essential trace metal? *Bull NY Acad Med* 1984; 60:163–171.
54. Cotzias GC, Papavasiliou MI, Tang LC, Miller ST. Manganese and catecholamines. *Adv Neurol* 1974; 5:235–243.

55. Mena I, Count J, Fuenzalida S, Papavasiliou PS, Cotzias GC. Modification of chronic manganese poisoning. *N Engl J Med* 1970; 282:5–10.

56. Papavasiliou PS, Miller ST, Cotzias GC. Role of liver in regulating distribution and excretion of manganese. *Am J Physiol* 1966; 211:211–216.

57. Cotzias GC, Horiuchi K, Fuenzalida S, et al. Chronic manganese poisoning. *Neurology* 1968; 18:376–382.

58. Davidson L, Cederblad A, Lonnerdal B, Sandstorm B. Manganese retention in man: a method for estimating manganese absorption in man. *Am J Clin Nutr* 1989; 49:170–179.

59. Zlotkin SH, Buchanan BE. Manganese intake in intravenously fed infants. *Biol Trace Elem Res* 1986; 9:271–279.

60. Weigand E, Kirchgessner M. Radioisotope studies on true absorption of manganese. In: Mills CF, Bremner I, Chesters JK, eds. *Trace elements in man and animals.* Slough, UK: Commonwealth Agricultural Bureaux, 1985; 5:506–509.

61. Gan LS, Tan KT, Kwok SF. Biological threshold limit values for manganese dust exposure. *Sing Med J* 1988; 29:105–109.

62. Mena I, Horiuchi K, Burke K, Cotzian GC. Chronic manganese poisoning: individual susceptibility and absorption of iron. *Neurology* 1964; 19:1000.

63. Casey CE, Robinson MF. Copper, manganese, zinc, nickel, cadmium and lead in human foetal tissue. *Br J Nutr* 1978; 39:639–646.

64. Kurkus J, Alcock NW, Shiles ME. Manganese content of large volume parenteral solutions and of nutrient additives. *JPEN* 1984; 8:254–257.

65. Hambidge KM, Sokol RJ, Fidanza SJ, Goodall MA. Plasma manganese concentrations in infants and children receiving parenteral nutrition. *JPEN* 1989; 13:168–171.

66. Infant Formula Act, USA. 1980. Public Law 96–359.

67. Delange F, Dalhem A, Bourdoux P, et al. Increased risk of primary hypothyroidism in preterm infant. *J Pediatr* 1984; 105:462–469.

68. Castaing H, Fournet JP, Lager FA, Kiesgen FC, Dupard MC, Savoie JC. Thyroide du ne et surcharge en iode apres la naissance. *Arch Rf Perinatal* 1979; 36(4):365–368.

69. Fisher DA. Upper limit of iodine in infant formulas. *J Nutr* 1989; 119:1865–1868.

70. Delange F, Bourdoux P, Senterre J. Evidence of a high requirement of iodine in preterm infants. *Pediatr Res* 1984; 18:106.

71. Neville MC, Keller R, Seacat J, et al. Studies in human lactation: milk volumes in lactating women during the onset of lactation and full lactation. *Am J Clin Nutr* 1988; 48:1375–1386.

72. Weymouth RD, Kelly R, Lansdell BJ. Symptomatic zinc deficiency in a premature infant. *Aust Pediatr J* 1982; 18:208–210.

73. Aggett PJ, Atherton DJ, More J, et al. Symptomatic zinc deficiency in a breast-fed, preterm infant. *Arch Dis Child* 1980; 55:547–550.

74. Zimmerman AW, Hambidge KM, Lepow ML, et al. Acrodermatitis in breast-fed, preterm infants: evidence for a defect of mammary zinc secretion. *Pediatrics* 1982; 69:176–183.

75. Parker P, Helinek GL, Meneely RL, et al. Zinc deficiency in a premature infant fed exclusively human milk. *Am J Dis Child* 1982; 136:77–78.

14. Enteral Nutrition

Alan Lucas

Reviewers: Stephen Baumgart, Edward Bell, Guy Putet, Brian A. Wharton

When a preterm infant is born, its continuous intravenous nutrition via the placenta and maternal controls over fetal metabolism cease. This cessation occurs up to 4 months too soon in biological terms, at a time when rapid fetal growth and nutrient accretion are quite different from those at term. The complex postnatal adaptive events in the gut and intermediary metabolism that equip the infant for extrauterine nutrition must be initiated at an "unphysiological" time in development. The enterally fed preterm infant may successfully switch on some adaptive events months ahead of time (e.g., the ability to digest lactose,[1] which is normally poor until term). Other events, however, appear to be more rigidly controlled by an endogenous biological clock (e.g., the ability to suck and swallow effectively[2]). Thus, not only is it unphysiological for a preterm infant to be fully enterally fed, but the concomitant adaptive changes are not synchronized in the "normal" way.

In view of this, the normal principles of enteral feeding for healthy full-term infants cannot be applied directly to the preterm infant. The critical questions of what and how a preterm infant should be enterally fed have needed scientific exploration de novo as in other new areas of therapeutics. It is an objective of this chapter to provide, as far as possible, support for proposed feeding policy options with published data from clinical trials.

Indeed, there have been more published clinical trials on enteral nutrition than in any other area of neonatal care.[3] Yet this large body of work has focused principally on short-term physiological studies of nutrient handling and growth. Many of these investigations have unknown significance for outcome. However, as the focus of attention in neonatal intensive care has progressively switched from neonatal survival to quality of survival, it has become apparent that dietary management of preterm infants can have a major impact not only on their morbidity in the short term, but also on the quality of their long-term outcome and development. Such data, reviewed briefly here, have important implications for those concerned with formulating nutrition policy in neonatal units.

Available diets, summarized in Table 14.1, are discussed individually in the following section before their relative merits in comparative clinical trials are considered.

Table 14.1. Diets Available for the Preterm Infant

Human milk
Mother's own
  Donor breast milk
    Drip milk
    Expressed milk
Standard formulas
Preterm formulas (see Appendix, Table A.3)
Fortified diets
  Human milk plus multinutrient fortifier
  "Human milk formula"

Mother's Own Milk

The perceived value of human milk in neonatal intensive care has waxed and waned throughout this century, though more recent outcome data (see discussion that follows) are beginning to establish its role. Human milk is not an inert multinutrient medium like a formula, but may be seen as a living tissue like blood. It contains live cells (macrophages, polymorphonuclear leukocytes, T and B lymphocytes) and a wide variety of biologically active factors[4] that include: (1) a range of antimicrobial factors (including IgA, lactoferrin, lysozyme, B_{12} and folate-binding proteins, complement and antiviral factors); (2) a large number of hormones, hormone-releasing hormones, and growth factors (see Table 14.2[5,6]); and (3) at least 60 enzymes,[7] (e.g., milk lipase).

Since it would not normally be physiological for such factors to be received preterm, their role in infants undergoing neonatal intensive care needs consideration. Some evidence supports an anti-infective action of human milk in preterm infants (see data that follow). A role for the many milk hormones and trophic agents has not been clearly established in term or preterm infants. These hormones are often secreted actively into human milk in high concentrations,[5,8,9] and animal data indicate potential roles in the suckled infant in vivo.[10] Recent evidence shows that epidermal growth factor is absorbed from the gut in human preterm infants,[11]

Table 14.2. Examples of Hormones in Breast Milk

Steroids	Prolactin
Thyroxine	Erythropoietin
Gonadotrophins	Melatonin
LH-RH	Prostaglandins
TRH	Calcitonin
TSH	Epidermal growth factor
ACTH	

raising the possibility that it could be involved in tissue growth and maturation (e.g., of the lung[12]). Breast milk lipase may assist fat digestion in preterm infants,[13] a potential advantage in view of the reduced pancreatic and lingual lipase activities, and reduced bile acid pool size and excretion that impair fat lipolysis at early gestation.[14]

The nutrient composition of human milk normally varies considerably between individual mothers and during the course of lactation.[15] Nevertheless, the term infant has the potential to protect its nutrient needs by regulating intake. Moreover, the changing content of milk during lactation (with the exception of lactose, most factors decline with time) might be geared to the term infant's changing needs. For example, there is a marked fall in milk protein from 2 to 3 g/100 mL in early lactation to around 1 g/100 mL in mature milk. Since immunoprotein (which largely accounts for the high protein content in early milk) is probably nutritionally available,[16] it could be argued that this falling protein content is linked to the falling growth rate in early infancy.

In the preterm infant, however, the inherent variability of milk poses two problems: (1) intake is not regulated by the baby but by the clinician, who usually does not know the composition of the milk, and (2) the time-course of nutrient needs for preterm infants is different from that for term infants in view of the more rapid growth and nutrient retention. It has been suggested that mothers who deliver preterm have milk that is more adapted to the preterm infant's needs, with a higher content of protein, non-protein nitrogen, sodium, chloride, magnesium, iron, copper, zinc and IgA.[17-20] It seems unlikely that this adaptation would have evolved, since very small preterm babies would not normally have survived. Indeed, data on protein content[21] suggest that the high protein content of early milk is a fortuitous consequence of the relatively small milk volume often produced by mothers when they must express their milk; when mothers of preterm infants produce large milk volumes, protein content is similar to that in term breast milk. In any case, unfortified preterm milk

frequently fails to meet estimated nutrient needs for protein, energy, sodium, calcium, phosphorus, magnesium, iron, copper, zinc, and vitamins B_2, B_6, C, D, E, and K, and folic acid (see other chapters). In one study—taking the European Society of Paediatric Gastroenterology and Nutrition (ESPGAN) recommendation for protein intake of 2.9 to 4.0 g/kg/day—200 mL/kg/day of mother's milk did not achieve even the modest, minimum recommended protein intake in 28% of babies during the second week (even if full intake had been achieved), 36% by the third week, and 83% by the fourth.[21] Nutrient monitoring of milk from individual mothers could be undertaken, but this is expensive and impractical for many units, given that day-to-day variation increases the need for repeated measurement.

Since breast-feeding is not usually possible <34 weeks gestation, expressed milk must be fed to these infants. Expressed milk may not have the same composition as milk obtained by an infant during normal suckling.[22,23] For example, if mothers express small milk volumes principally of foremilk, this will have a low fat and therefore energy content, often <60 kcal/100 mL. Expressed milk is unphysiologically exposed to light, resulting in photodegradation of riboflavin and vitamin A.[24] Bacteriological contamination may occur during expression and subsequent storage, and milk fat may be lost by its adherence to collection vessels.

Naturally, many mothers do not find long-term manual or mechanical expression of breast milk as effective at stimulating milk release as breast-feeding (see following discussion for practical aspects), and milk supply may not meet the infant's needs, necessitating the use of another enteral diet as well. In a large multicenter study,[25] mothers who choose to provide milk for preterm infants met a median of only 46% of their infants' needs, and only 17% of infants were successfully breast-feeding when discharged. These figures vary greatly according to the enthusiasm of the unit staff. In one U.K. investigation,[26] however, the proportion of mothers choosing initially to provide milk was little influenced by medical staff but was low in association with low maternal education, single-parent status, multiparity, low maternal age and, interestingly, a female child. Mothers with all of these features were nearly 1,000 times less likely to provide their milk than when the opposite applied.

Donor Breast Milk

Human milk banking is a significant undertaking for a neonatal unit, and in recent years doubts about its value and theoretical concerns about HIV (human immunodeficiency virus) transmission have resulted in the closing of most milk banks in the West.

Human Milk Banking

Detailed instructions for human milk banking[27] are beyond the scope of this chapter. Briefly, the problems that need to be considered are as follows:

1. Funding and organizing milk collection and transportation.
2. Creation of a milk kitchen and its staffing.
3. Canvassing donors.
4. Screening donors for HIV, with counseling if needed.
5. Selecting the type of donor milk to be used: drip or expressed.
6. Monitoring and giving advice on milk storage facilities in the home.
7. Issuing donors with apparatus for milk collection (pumps/collecting shells, sterilizing tanks, hypochlorite agents, collecting bottles and labels).
8. Providing adequate advice and care for donors.
9. Installing, checking, and running accurate pasteurization equipment in the milk kitchen.
10. Organizing milk storage and retrieval facilities (4°C refrigerator(s) and -20°C freezer(s) are required).
11. Arranging bacteriological monitoring and developing criteria for milk rejection.
12. Establishing nutrient quality control of donor milk, either in collaboration with the biochemistry department or using simple analytical methods on the unit.
13. Planning the preparation of individual feeds over a 24-hour period.

It is important to appreciate that once milk has been collected, bacterially decontaminated, stored, frozen and thawed, pasteurized, exposed to light, aliquotted, and instilled into feeding apparatus, it may have undergone qualitative alterations that render it significantly different from milk obtained by an infant during normal suckling. Freezing, thawing, and heat treatment damage antimicrobial factors in milk and denature milk lipase; milk cells seldom survive the banking process. Evans et al.[28] showed that accurate pasteurization for 30 minutes at 62.5°C destroyed 24% of the lysozyme, 57% of the lactoferrin, 34% of the IgG but little IgA (though loss of biological activity of IgA was not assessed), whereas after treatment at 73°C (as might occur with inaccurate pasteurization) only minimal quantities of these constituents remained intact. Heating milk may reduce vitamin C content. In addition, pasteurization may reduce fat absorption, perhaps by damaging milk lipase.[13] Short-time, low-temperature pasteurization (56°C for 15 minutes) may be effective at removing bacteria and preserves 90% of lactoferrin and IgA intact.[29] Exposing breast milk to light results, within 3 hours, in a 50% reduction in riboflavin content and 70% loss of vitamin A.[24] Nevertheless, as discussed in the next paragraph, donor milk can have a valuable role in neonatal care.

Most donor milk collected is manually or mechanically expressed from the breast. Expressed donor milk can be foremilk or hindmilk, obtained either before or after the donor's own infant has fed from the breast. These two types of milk will have, respectively, lower or higher fat and energy contents than the milk received by the breast-fed infant.[23,30] Mature donor milk will have a lower protein, sodium, zinc, and copper content than that of milk produced in early lactation. Often donor milk has a low fat content, partly because it is often foremilk[31] and perhaps also because of fat losses during collection. Breast milk fat is often <3 g/100 mL (as opposed to 4 g/100 mL usually reported in most studies on expressed milk), with the result that milk energy is often <60 kcal/100 mL.

Some centers in the U.K. have collected so-called drip breast milk (DBM), which drips spontaneously from the contralateral breast during feeding in a proportion of lactating mothers.[31] About 20% of mothers who lactate in this manner produce significant quantities. This milk can be collected during feeding into a presterilized glass or plastic shell worn over the contralateral nipple and areola. Drip breast milk has a similar composition to foremilk, with a low fat and energy values that correlate positively with the volume of DBM obtained and negatively with postpartum duration.[32] Pools of DBM may have energy contents as low as 45 to 50 kcal/100 mL.[25]

While most units would favor use of mother's own milk in the raw state, donor milk is usually pasteurized to destroy vegetative organisms and, of recent concern, HIV. Raw donor milk may contain a variety of pathogens, including group B streptococci,[33] and few units are prepared to undertake the rigorous testing and repeated donor screening required to use untreated milk.

Standard Term Formulas

Formulas designed for full-term infants have been used for many years to feed preterm infants. Since formula composition is modeled on mature breast milk, limitations of human milk in meeting calculated needs of preterm infants will often apply to standard formulas. These formulas, however, lack the nonnutrient properties of human milk. If, for example, the ESPGAN recommendation[34,35] for protein intake of 2.9 to 4.0 g/kg/day is taken, term formulas typically containing 1.45 to 1.50 g protein per 100 mL will meet only the lower end of this range when fed at 200 mL/kg/day; this is an unacceptably high intake for some small babies, especially those with ductal patency.

Soy formulas have lower amounts of essential amino acids; they contain phytate, which may reduce trace mineral availability and, more recently, concern has been expressed over their high aluminum content.[36] These formulas have no established place in the nutritional management of preterm infants.

Preterm Infant Formulas

Since the 1970s, special formulas designed to meet the calculated increased requirement of preterm infants for nutrient accretion at the in utero rate have been available. These formulas, based on current nutrient recommendations, contain increased amounts of protein, energy, sodium, calcium, phosphorus, copper, zinc, and selected micronutrients compared with standard formulas or human milk (see Appendix, Table A.3). Preterm formula design continues to evolve. Not all manufacturers have solved the technical problems of getting sufficient calcium and phosphorus into solution or microsuspension in order to approach the increased needs of preterm infants for bone mineralization at the rate seen in the third trimester. Fat blends are currently under consideration; some preterm formulas contain unphysiologically large contents of medium-chain triglyceride (up to 40% of fats) of uncertain benefit, and recently recommendations have been made for adding long-chain fatty acids (e.g., arachidonic and docosahexaenoic acid), ostensibly to ensure adequate brain and retinal deposition.

Fortification of Human Milk

If mothers want to provide their milk or if neonatologists wish to use donor milk, calculated nutrient requirement may be met by human milk fortification. Two strategies have been used. The most practical is to add a commercially available human milk fortifier, either as a powder or as a liquid mixed with equal volumes of breast milk. The compositions of commercially available fortifiers are shown in the Appendix, Table A.4. While these products have an important place, breast milk fortifiers, like preterm formulas, continue to evolve. The ideal fortifier should not result in precipitation or reduced availability of nutrients in human milk, and this aspect needs continued exploration. Furthermore, since the human milk–based diet has a very variable composition, addition of a fixed nutrient supplement (e.g., protein) could still fail to produce a diet that meets estimated requirement in some infants, while in others the intake would exceed recommended upper limits.

Using complex modeling based on our own (unpublished) analytic data on 6,000 samples of breast milk, our nutrition unit calculated that a protein supplement of approximately 0.7 g/100 mL was an optimal compromise, though a proportion of infants will still fall outside the recommended range. For instance, if a fortifier supplying 0.7 g/100 mL was used when a mother produced milk with a protein content >1.8 g/100 mL (which may occur in preterm milk in the early weeks[21]), protein intake at 180 mL/kg would exceed 4.5 g/kg/day. However, the effects, if any, of exceeding recommended protein intakes in this circumstance remain unexplored.

Another strategy has been to use "lactoengineering" to prepare human milk components that can fortify human milk. Over a decade ago, the first "human milk formula" was produced by adding dialysed human milk protein and milk fat, obtained by centrifugation, to whole milk.[37] The theoretical argument for this procedure is that any inherent biological properties of human milk protein (e.g., immunoproteins) or fat (e.g., long-chain lipids) would be given while nutrient needs were met at the same time. This procedure has been used in some units,[38–40] but is quite impractical for most, since it requires a large supply of donor milk.

Clinical Trial Comparisons of Available Diets

In the large number of clinical trials of preterm nutrition, choice of diet has been shown to have significant effects on many short-term outcomes, including growth, nutrient retention, intermediary metabolism, mineral and vitamin status, hormone secretion, enzyme activities, immunological response, gastrointestinal function, infection, and necrotizing enterocolitis. It would not be possible to review all these outcomes here and, in any case, many short-term responses to diet (e.g., effects on hormone secretion) are of unknown significance. In this section, therefore, only selected outcomes that may be influential in making practical dietary choices are considered.

Short-Term Outcomes

Growth

Growth is the traditional measure of nutritional status in early life. Weight gain has been given most attention, yet some caution is required in interpreting results of dietary trials. For weight gain to be a valid measure of growth, it must reflect nutrient deposition. It has been shown, however, that preterm infants may protect weight gain to some extent at the expense of body composition.[41] For instance, an infant fed on unfortified donor breast milk, rather than preterm formula, may lay down a lower concentration of energy and protein in each gram of new tissue, so that the observed difference in weight gain between feed groups could be a substantial underestimation of the real difference in nutrient (especially protein). Steady-state weight gain is often compared with the expected intrauterine rate of weight increment of around 15 g/kg/day for the third trimester. However, this comparison fails to take account of the considerable growth faltering seen after birth in small, sick preterm infants, who may often not regain birthweight for 3 to 4 weeks. These infants must exhibit catch-up growth to regain in utero growth status, which often demands weight gains of nearer 20 g/kg/day.

Linear growth has been argued to be a better measure of growth, though in preterm infants bone mineral deficiency might impair linear bone growth selectively without necessarily affecting muscle and fat deposition. Thus linear growth and tissue deposition are both important. It should be appreciated that while weight gain falters after birth, linear growth is protected and proceeds from birth at term.[42] Our data (unpublished) show that preterm infants in a large study gained an average of 1.5 cm in length before regaining birthweight, at a median of 15 days, which represents a faster linear growth rate than at any other time after birth. These data emphasize that growth processes need "fueling" from birth, even when weight gain is not occurring.

Head circumference is a good reflection of brain weight in the perinatal period[43] and can be used as a measure of brain growth. Around 15% of a preterm infant is brain (as opposed to 2% in an adult) and a 28-week gestation baby should be expected to double the weight of its brain in the succeeding 8 weeks. Brain growth failure is commonly observed in preterm infants and is a legitimate cause for concern at this critical period of brain development.[44]

In a number of trials, growth performance in infants fed unfortified donor or mother's own milk has been shown to be reduced compared with infants on a nutrient-enriched formula. This finding was first shown by Gordon in 1947.[45] More recent studies comparing term donor breast milk with preterm formula have shown a 40% to 95% increase in rate of weight gain on preterm formula along with significant increases in linear and head growth.[25,46–48] Infants grow faster when fed their own mother's early preterm milk rather than mature donor milk[48] but, nevertheless, still significantly slower in all respects than when fed a preterm formula.[49–51] These studies indicate collectively that preterm infants fed preterm formula are more likely to show in utero growth performance and to have "caught up" to their original birth centile by discharge from hospital.[25] Typically, infants fed breast milk gain weight at approximately 13 to 15 g/kg/day (according to milk type and quality), while those fed preterm formula gain closer to 20 g/kg/day. Estimates based on head circumference data suggest that, in the first postnatal months, infants fed preterm formula could have up to twice the rate of brain weight increase compared with infants fed unfortified mature donor milk.[52]

As expected, infants fed on standard term formula also grow more slowly, notably in weight and head circumference, than those fed a preterm formula.[53] Infants fed unfortified human milk or standard formula, rather than preterm formula, also regain birthweight more slowly; they may be already on a low weight centile before steady-state weight gain is achieved, thus increasing their chances of being discharged from the hospital with growth retardation (see following discussion).[25]

Fortification of human milk to address the problem of reduced growth rate has been undertaken in at least six randomized trials.[38–40,50,54–56] Some of these trials have employed human milk protein, others bovine milk protein. Other fortifier constituents have included human milk fat, medium-chain triglyceride, calcium, phosphorus, and other minerals, and protein intake has usually been increased from an average of 1.9 to 2.5 g/kg/day (below current recommendations) to an average of 3.2 to 3.6 g/kg/day. Increased rates of weight, length, and head circumference gain were found, with weight gains in most studies comparable to those seen with preterm formula.

Other Measures of Nutrition The use of growth-promoting, nutrient-enriched diets in preterm infants has been shown to improve a number of aspects of nutritional status in addition to growth rate. These improvements are largely reviewed in other sections of this book and include favorable effects on body composition[41,57] and nutrient retention, vitamin status, trace mineral status, bone mineralization, and biochemical measures of bone status.[58]

Overview Extensive evidence shows improvement in growth and nutritional status resulting from diets designed to supply the calculated increase in nutritional needs of third-trimester rates of nutrient accretion. These increased needs may be met by using preterm formula or multinutrient-fortified human milk, or a combination of the two. One important aspect is that infants fed on these diets may have a reduced hospital stay, which has psychosocial and economic implications.

Necrotizing Enterocolitis and Infection
The importance of enteral feeding as a risk factor in necrotizing enterocolitis (NEC) has been emphasized by some investigators,[59–62] though 5% to 10% of cases occur in babies who have never been enterally fed.[59,63] Further risk factors relating to feeding include early initiation of enteral feeds,[62] rapid escalation of feed volumes,[61] and hyperosmolar feeding,[64,65] although some have doubted the importance of these factors.[66,67] While several older studies suggest that human milk is protective,[68–70] NEC may occur in infants fed exclusively fresh, frozen, or pas-

teurized milk.[62,66] The notion that breast milk is protective was supported by the finding in a rat model that live milk leukocytes are prophylactic,[71,72] but this may not be an appropriate model for humans. Necrotizing enterocolitis is not explained by any single known etiological factor, but the possible contributory importance of diet and dietary practice has again emerged in a recent study on 926 preterm infants, 51 of whom developed NEC.[73] In stringently confirmed cases, infants fed formula exclusively had a rate of NEC that was six times as common as in infants fed human milk alone, and three times as common in infants fed human milk plus formula compared with breast milk alone. This study showed that in babies >30 weeks gestation, NEC was a rarity in those who received human milk, and was 20 times as common in those receiving formula alone. Interestingly, in formula-fed, but not breast-fed infants, delayed enteral feeding was associated with a reduced incidence of NEC; for example, if enteral formula feeding was started on day 9 rather than day 2, the risk of NEC was reduced threefold.

The possibility that human milk might be protective against infection has not been established in Western neonatal units, although Naraynan[74] demonstrated a major protective effect in a neonatal unit in India where infection rates were high. Further studies are needed in the West.

Diet and Feed Tolerance
In a randomized comparison, babies fed preterm formula took significantly longer to become established on full enteral feeds than those fed donor human milk.[75] The proportion of babies receiving preterm formula who required more than 2 and 3 weeks to tolerate full enteral feeds was 33% and 17%, respectively, compared with the significantly lower values of 11% and 5% in the group fed human milk. The formula-fed group also showed more gastric stasis and vomiting. These findings are not specific to special preterm formulas; delay in establishing enteral feeding has been found to be equally prolonged using term formulas.[52]

Long-Term Outcomes

Growth
Some evidence suggests that reduced growth rates seen in infants fed human milk in the neonatal period may have an impact on later growth status; infants fed human milk have been found to be shorter at 18 months than those previously fed formula.[58] Moreover, biochemical evidence of bone disease of prematurity (high alkaline phosphatase activity) in one study was the strongest independent predictor of body length identified at 18 months.[58] In this study, most of the infants who developed evidence of bone disease had been fed human milk.

Allergic Disease
A major problem in the interpretation of many reports on early dietary associations with childhood allergy is the lack of random assignment of babies to breast or formula feeding. In preterm infants, however, random comparison is feasible and ethical. There has been only one published randomized trial of the role of human milk versus bovine milk formula in later incidence of allergic disease.[76] While no overall effect of early diet on later allergy was shown in this trial, in the subgroup of infants with a positive family history of allergy (in first-degree relatives) brief exposure to bovine milk formula in the early weeks resulted in a significant increase in a wide range of allergic reactions at 18 months, including eczema (41% incidence, versus 16% of infants fed human milk); reactions to bovine milk, other foods, and drugs; and wheezing or asthma.

Early Diet and Later Neurodevelopment
The possibility that early diet, at a potentially vulnerable period of brain development, could have an impact on long-term developmental outcome is a key question with important implications for practice. In a large randomized outcome study,[53] babies fed a standard term formula rather than a preterm formula for just, on average, the first postnatal month, had a major disadvantage in developmental scores using the Bayley psychomotor index (PDI) and mental development index (MDI) at 18 months post-term. This disadvantage was especially marked in infants born small for gestation. In this subgroup, who were already malnourished in utero, feeding a standard term formula was associated with a 16-point reduction in later cognitive development (MDI) and a 23-point reduction in the PDI (see Fig. 14.1). In a further randomized comparison,[77] infants fed donor human milk also had a small disadvantage in developmental quotient at 9 months post-term compared with infants fed preterm formula, although unpublished data show this disadvantage was no longer seen at 18 months. It was speculated that non-nutrient factors in human milk promoted neurodevelopment and compensated for its low nutrient density. Indeed, in a nonrandomized study, use of the mother's own milk, which has a higher nutrient content than donor milk, was associated with a positive advantage in cognitive performance at 18 months[78] and 7½ to 8 years[79] even after adjusting for social and educational differences between the groups. At 7½ to 8 years, the advantage in IQ associated with mother's milk feeding, independent of the mother's education and social class, was approximately eight points (half a standard deviation). This advantage was related to being fed milk by tube in the neonatal period and not with subsequent breast-feeding, and was dose-related to the proportion of breast milk consumed. While genetic and

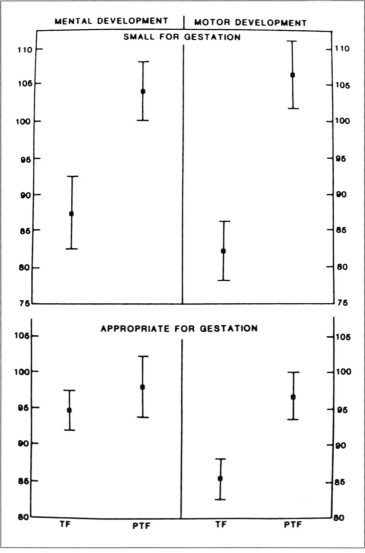

Fig. 14.1. Mental and motor development indices (Bayley Scales) at 18 months in infants randomly assigned to a standard "term" formula (TF) or a special nutrient-enriched "preterm" formula (PTF) during the early weeks postpartum, in babies born small (above) and appropriately sized for gestation (below). Bars represent mean (SE) neurodevelopmental scores. (Adapted, with permission, from Lucas et al.[53] © The Lancet Ltd. 1990.)

parenting factors might still explain these findings, the possibility that human milk contains substances that influence neurodevelopment (e.g., long-chain lipids, hormones, or growth factors) requires further exploration.

Choice of Diet: Practical Implications

In summary, extensive data from many studies show that diets suitable for full-term infants, including standard formula, unfortified donor milk, or the mother's own milk, do not meet the nutritional needs of small preterm infants. Infants fed on these diets are likely to develop growth failure, have a prolonged hospital stay, and develop biochemical or clinical evidence of deficiency of specific nutrients including protein, minerals, microminerals, and vitamins. In the longer term, such infants may have reduced growth in early childhood, and infants fed standard formulas (but not human milk) may have major deficits in subsequent neurocognitive and motor development.

These data argue in favor of using preterm formulas, multinutrient-fortified human milk, or a combination. Such diets may (with the exception of iron) provide complete nutrition for preterm infants, provided that adequate enteral volume intakes are achieved. If infants are not on full enteral feeds, or are receiving human milk with limited fortification, micronutrient supplementation is required (see other sections).

An important question is whether preterm formulas are equivalent to fortified human milk, or whether there is some benefit for the infant if human milk forms part of the diet. From the evidence discussed, the merits of human milk include: (1) greater enteral feed tolerance (even when given in conjunction with formula) and more rapid weaning from intravenous nutrition, which has numerous well-described hazards (see Chapter 15); (2) probable (though not proven in a strictly randomized trial) reduction in NEC risk; (3) reduced risk of later allergy if there is a positive family history of allergy (but only if human milk is used exclusively, which is often impractical); and (4) possible, though not proven, favorable effects on neurocognitive development.

It would seem good practice to encourage mothers to provide their own milk and to fortify it using a researched and tested multinutrient fortifier. However, many mothers do not choose to provide milk or do not produce enough, in which case a preterm formula should be used alone or in conjunction with the mother's milk. There have been no published outcome studies on fortified milk, but if adequate nutrition (supplied by preterm formula or fortified milk) and breast milk itself both have independent and additive effects in promoting neurodevelopment, theoretically the best outcome would be for infants to be fed at least some maternal milk. Clearly, further exploration of the long-term consequences of breast-milk feeding is a priority for the future.

If mothers are to provide milk successfully, however, they need good care and advice. The most common reason for failure of milk supply in a motivated mother is an inadequate number of milk expression sessions per day. We advise at least six and preferably more, bearing in mind that very young infants are frequently suckled, on demand, 8 to 12 times per day, which constitutes a sustained stimulus to prolactin output. Naturally, many mothers find a breast pump does not induce such an effective ''let-down'' reaction as breast feeding. We have found that this situation may be improved if the mother looks at a photograph of her baby during expression or, if practical, expresses milk in her baby's presence. Non-nutritive suckling at the breast by the baby may also improve efficacy of milk production, perhaps by increasing maternal prolactin secretion.

If mothers do not provide breast milk, an important question is whether milk banking is worthwhile. Some data show that even pasteurized donor milk is as effective as mother's milk in promoting enteral feed tolerance and reducing the risk of NEC.[73] If donor milk is in limited supply, one approach, used in our own unit, is to give it to babies whose mothers have elected not to provide their own milk, just until enteral feed tolerance has been established (intake of 150 mL/kg/day) and then change, over a 48-hour period, to a preterm formula.

There is increasing evidence that the choice of diet influences the quality of survival in preterm infants. Recent clinical trials have looked at unselected populations of infants, but high-risk subgroups, e.g., small-for-gestation-age infants (see Fig. 14.1) and infants of extremely low gestation, need special consideration. The next generation of clinical trials will need to focus on how nutrition can be optimized for individual infants.

Feeding Techniques and Feed Scheduling

How much, how often, and by what route infants should be fed are questions that have received much less scientific attention than the aspects discussed above. In this section, an appraisal of current trial data is made before formulating suggested practical feeding policies in the neonatal unit.

Feeding Tube Routes

Since most infants <34 weeks cannot suck effectively or coordinate sucking, swallowing, and breathing, they must be tube fed. Most units use nasogastric tube placement because a nasally inserted tube is easy to fix. However, indwelling nasogastric tubes cause increased airway resistance and the alternative of repeated tube placement is unpleasant for the infant, time-consuming, and may provoke apnea. The alternative of orogastric versus nasogastric tube placement was researched in a small randomized trial by Van Someren et al.[80] An orogastric tube was fitted to an orthodontic palatal appliance with grooves to hold the tube. The orogastric-fed group showed less central apnea and periodic breathing, but no difference in obstructive apnea. More research is needed.

Transpyloric rather than intragastric feeding has been in vogue in the past. At least seven randomized trials have compared either nasojejunal or nasoduodenal feeding with intragastric feeding.[81-87] While none of the trials were large or conclusive, collectively they provided disappointing data for this approach to tube feeding. There is no convincing evidence that transpyloric feeding improves enteral feed tolerance and growth, or reduces aspiration pneumonia. Among the five trials that report death as an outcome,[82,83,85-87] the overall death rate was 15% higher (95% CI 5.4, 23.8%)[3] in infants fed via the transpyloric rather than intragastric route. While this finding could have been confounded by the unsatisfactory randomization in the trials, current data do not support the use of transpyloric feeding for preterm infants.

Gastrostomy rather than conventional feeding has been examined in a randomized trial.[88] As with transpyloric feeding, no benefit was identified for enteral volume intake or growth. There also was a significantly higher death rate in the gastrostomy group.

Continuous versus Bolus Feeding

It is "physiological" for a fetus to be fed continuously and for a normal newborn infant (usually) to be fed intermittently with phasic changes in organ function and metabolism. Intermittent feeding is known to induce dynamic changes in regional and cerebral blood flow, blood pressure, respiratory pattern, lung volume, and chemical control of breathing,[89–91] raising questions as to whether these events would be desirable in sick and clinically unstable preterm infants. Nutrient handling in the gut and metabolic response to feeding theoretically could be affected by intermittent versus continuous feeding, but in randomized comparison Toce et al.[92] found no difference between groups in any aspect of growth when nutrient intakes were constrained to be the same.

Feed Scheduling

Two trials of immediate (2 to 4 hours after birth) versus delayed (12 to 36 hours after birth) introduction of enteral feeds in babies unsupported by parenteral nutrition showed a higher death rate in the immediate groups, largely from aspiration, but a higher incidence of symptomatic hypoglycemia in the delayed group.[93,94] These studies date from the 1960s, however, when enteral and parenteral management was quite different. There is also little recent trial information on the merits of different feed advancement schedules. In a recent randomized study, Currao et al.[95] compared infants fed a 67 kcal/100mL formula with those fed the same formula at "half strength" but twice the volume. Interestingly, those fed the diluted formula attained an intake of 100 kcal/kg/day faster, had lower gastric residual volumes, and no increase in apnea, vomiting, or abdominal distension.

Non-nutritive Sucking

Tube feeding bypasses the "cephalic phase" of the digestive process. Normal oral feeding may result in preparatory events in gut function, hormone secretion, and intermediary metabolism that might be altered in infants fed intragastrically. The hypothesis that beneficial physiological events might result from non-nutritive sucking on a pacifier during gavage feeding has triggered at least seven randomized trials.[96–102] Those that looked at nutritional outcomes, despite encouraging early results,[98] have not

collectively provided convincing data that this technique promotes growth or favorable changes in gastrointestinal function. It may, however, reduce hospital stay (by about 6 days[3]), perhaps by reducing the subsequent learning time for effectively taking sucking feeds. This approach needs further testing.

Demand Feeding

Some studies in full-term babies have shown that after a period infants may regulate volume intake when offered milks of different energy content.[103,104] A number of published studies imply that preterm babies may regulate their volume intake, but not sufficiently to offset differences in nutrient intakes when given milks of different composition.[46] In our own (unpublished) studies, preterm infants fed ad libitum after discharge consumed substantially larger milk volumes than they would receive in the hospital, and frequently have intakes for protein and energy that exceed recommended maximum intakes for preterm infants (>4.0 g/kg/day and 165 kcal/kg/day, respectively).

Practical Feeding Policies

The following practical guidelines are based as much as possible on the available evidence discussed in the previous section. Otherwise, they are based on personal practice and consensus views.

Tube Feeding

Intragastric feeding is the route of choice. Transpyloric and gastrostomy feeding may increase mortality rate and have no proven benefit (see previous section). Nasogastric feeding is likely to remain the most commonly used technique, although the orogastric route should be considered in infants whose nasal passages are partially blocked by secretions.

A No. 4 French-gauge gavage tube is usually adequate for infants <1.3 kg: for heavier infants, a 6-gauge tube may be used. The distance between the nares and left hypochondrium should be measured, and the tube passed this distance and taped in place. Correct placing should be checked by testing the aspirate for acidity with litmus paper. As an additional check, a few mL of air may be pushed from a syringe into the tube, while listening with a stethoscope placed over the stomach. It is suggested that nasogastric tubes be replaced at 48- to 72-hour intervals.

An important pitfall to remember when giving human milk by tube is the adherence of fat to the feeding vessels. This process may be accentuated by the change in physical characteristics of the fat induced by freezing for long periods.

When a syringe pump is used to infuse human milk continuously via a feeding tube, the syringe should be below the infant; otherwise the fat rises up the connecting tubing back towards the syringe and may never be received by the infant before the tube is discarded. My own (unpublished) in vitro studies using perfuser pumps in various positions show that 33% of human milk energy can be lost over a 40-hour infusion if the syringe is placed above the baby.

It is neither possible nor desirable to adhere to rigid feeding policies for low-birthweight infants. Gastrointestinal "tolerance" of enteral feeding is very variable. Concomitant illness may impose additional constraints, and therefore feeding needs to be managed on an individual basis.

The following guidelines are suggested for large, well infants >1,500 g birthweight. Feeding, by nasogastric tube if necessary, should start early to prevent hypoglycemia, at approximately 2 hours of age or before. A commonly employed schedule for increasing feed volumes is, successively, 60, 90, 120, and 150 mL/kg/day during the first 4 days. Infants on diets requiring feed volumes greater than these amounts should receive further daily increments up to 180 mL/kg/day on day 10 and 200 mL/kg/day by day 14. There are few data on the rate at which bolus feeds should be instilled down a tube; most units favor gravity feeding over 10 to 20 minutes rather than injection from a syringe.

Most infants weighing 1,500 g will tolerate feeding every 3 hours; smaller infants will need to be fed every 1 to 2 hours. Initially, the nasogastric tube should be aspirated at least 4 to 6 times hourly, just before a feed. If the volume of aspirate is small (e.g., up to 10% of the accumulated feed intake since the previous aspirate), the aspirate may be replaced without altering the feed schedule. If the aspirate is significantly larger, feed intake should be reduced accordingly. This reduction is critical in infants who develop significant abdominal distension and/or blood in the stools, for whom enteral feeds should be stopped temporarily and NEC considered.

If feed volumes need to be reduced below the total fluid requirement for more than a few hours, an intravenous infusion must be considered.

Sick and Immature Infants

In sick or very small preterm infants, it is undesirable and often impossible to commence enteral nutrition after birth; an intravenous infusion is required.

If, after 48 hours, an infant has only mild respiratory disease and there is no ileus, enteral feeds may be introduced gradually and increased at the rate of 10 to 20 mL/kg/day, proceeding to full volumes after several days. This feeding should be accompanied by intravenous nutrition (see Chapter 15). As enteral feeds are increasingly tolerated, the intravenous infusion may be reduced correspondingly. If, however, enteral feeds are not tolerated, as indicated by vomiting, large gastric aspirates, or abdominal distension, total parenteral nutrition should be instituted.

When enteral feeding is commenced in very immature (see following discussion) or sick infants, it is advisable to use either a continuous infusion pump suitable for accurately administering volumes to the nearest 0.5 mL/h or less, or slowly infused hourly boluses. Subsequent increments in feed frequency are a matter for clinical judgment and require careful monitoring of enteral tolerance.

Routine Nutritional Monitoring

In very sick and immature infants, plasma urea, sodium, potassium, calcium, albumin, and acid-base status need to be measured daily (or more often) at least for the first few days. Even in well and growing preterm infants, it is advisable to make these measurements weekly. Recording daily intakes of each diet used, stool frequency, and volumes of gastric aspirate is an essential part of monitoring.

In healthy neonates, it is suggested that blood glucose be monitored at 2 hours of age and subsequently 4 to 6 times hourly for the first 48 hours, and for a longer period if glucose concentrations are low.

Accurate daily weights are important and, if at all possible, should be obtained in sick patients in order to calculate fluid needs. An electronic balance with a digital display, which rapidly averages a sequence of weights to reduce infant movement artifact, is ideal for use in neonatal intensive care units. Head circumferences should be measured weekly using a disposable paper tape measure. Although informative, length measurements are more difficult to perform accurately and require an appropriate stadiometer, preferably one that will fit into an incubator.

Feeding Problems

Vomiting, large gastric aspirates, and abdominal distension are common in very immature infants; it often takes several weeks to establish full enteral feeding. Occasionally a switch from formula to human milk results in a dramatic improvement in feed tolerance. However, in intractable cases, the possibility of an underlying structural anomaly of the gut or NEC should be considered. While enteral feeds are being increased or decreased repeatedly, several days may pass during which the nutrient intake is grossly deficient. If such a situation is identified, parenteral nutrition should be commenced.

Lacto-bezoars have been described in the American literature, especially in infants receiving high caloric density preterm formulas. These bezoars may increase in size progressively, causing obstruction and even gut perforation.[105] Fortunately, this increase is rare on diets currently available, but as new preterm formulas are introduced their incidence might rise. Increasing abdominal distension, vomiting, and gastric residual volumes raise the possibility of this diagnosis. Lacto-bezoars can be seen on plain abdominal x-ray, especially after air insufflation of the stomach. They resolve on intravenous feeding and gastric lavage.

A further potential danger with preterm formulas is milk curd obstruction in the small intestine, which may require surgical disimpaction at laparotomy.[75] The high-risk group comprises very immature infants in whom preterm formula feeds are introduced as the initial diet and feed volumes escalated rapidly (e.g., >20 mL/kg/day). A clue to the development of this problem is a sudden reduction in stool frequency (e.g., from four to six stools per day to one to two per day); at this early stage, formula feeds should be stopped and replaced with intravenous nutrition or cautious use of human milk. The problem is avoidable, however, with careful early use of preterm formulas and, preferably in small, sick infants, the establishment of full enteral feeds using human milk.

Milk curd obstruction might relate to calcium palmitate soap formation in the gut (unpublished data) and, if so, would not be expected with current U.S. formulas that are low in palmitate and high in medium-chain triglycerides (although the high medium-chain triglyceride content poses other potential problems).

Psychosocial Aspects

A major problem for parents with preterm infants is that the care of their child is delegated to others. Practical involvement of parents in infant feeding during the period when suckling is not possible has social and psychological benefits. For well infants, parents (under supervision) may be encouraged to measure out and give nasogastric tube feeds.

Mothers who wish ultimately to breast-feed may start to put their infant to the breast from an early stage, even at 1,000 g, provided the infant is well. Aspiration and choking do not occur in our experience and, as described above, such non-nutritive sucking may have additional benefits.

The difficulties for a mother who has delivered a 28-week infant and wishes to eventually take her baby home fully breast-fed should not be underestimated. Her chances of success are influenced greatly by the sympathetic attitude of the nursing staff, by skilled assistance, and by frequent milk expression (at least six times a day). If a mother manages to maintain lactation for several weeks by mechanical expression, she may then face problems in getting her infant to feed from the breast. One specific difficulty arises when the infant's mouth is too small to encompass a large nipple. It is important for attendant staff to explain that it requires patience and time to establish breast-feeding in this special situation.

Postdischarge Nutrition

Few studies have addressed postdischarge nutrition, yet the preterm infant frequently leaves the hospital severely growth retarded and with poor nutrient stores. Since many of these infants remain growth retarded throughout infancy, specific nutritional management policies may be required for this population. In a small randomized study of 32 infants (to be published), those fed a specially designed nutrient-enriched postdischarge formula grew significantly faster in weight and length (with a trend towards increased head size) throughout the first 9 months. The new formula contained 1.8 g protein and 72 kcal/100 mL (as opposed to 1.45 g protein and 68 kcal/100 mL in the standard formula), and was enriched with calcium, phosphorus, and selected micronutrients. More studies are needed.

The Micropreemie <1,000 g

Preterm infants surviving at 23 to 26 weeks gestation pose a considerable challenge. These babies have very low nutrient and energy stores, and establishing effective intravenous nutrition is the immediate priority. It is of course entirely possible to avoid enteral feeding until the infant is >1,000 g, but the key question for the micropreemie is whether this is desirable. Given the paucity of specific trials, this question can be addressed only on the basis of physiological research.

Enteral feeding is not a new experience for the newborn infant. Amniotic fluid is swallowed throughout most of gestation and may have a trophic effect on the gut.[106] In infants born with complete congenital blocks in the upper intestine (e.g., duodenal atresia), hypotrophy below the block has been noted. By the end of the third trimester, the fetus is swallowing approximately 500 mL of amniotic fluid per day, providing around 3 g protein per day, which contributes to nutrition.[107,108] Thus the fetus eventually consumes nearly the same fluid volume and 25% of the protein intake of a fully breast-fed infant. After birth, enteral feeding continues, although it changes in its quality and has been shown in numerous animal studies to induce a wide variety of adaptive events in the gut and in intermediary metabolism that equip the infant for extrauterine nutrition.[106,109] This postnatal adaptation may be, in part, controlled by gastrointestinal hormones secreted in response to the first postnatal enteral feeds.[70]

It is therefore fundamentally unphysiological to deprive an infant of any gestation of enteral feeding, since this deprivation would never normally occur at any stage. Animal studies show that after only a few days of deprivation of enteral feeds, atrophic changes occur in the gut (e.g., decreased weight of small intestine, pancreas, and stomach, and dramatic reduction in small intestinal DNA.[110-113] Human studies show that infants who have never been enterally fed do not have the normal gut peptide surges,[114] including those of the trophic hormones, enteroglucagon and gastrin, and gastric inhibitory polypeptide, which may be a key effector in the enteroinsular axis.[115]

One concern is whether the preterm infant's gut, deprived of enteral nutrition, will atrophy to the point that it becomes vulnerable (e.g., in terms of excluding pathogenic organisms in the gut lumen or resisting NEC when enteral feeding commences). A more theoretical concern is whether the gut would be deprived of critical signals during its development, with long-term consequences for its handling of nutrients.

For these reasons it makes biological sense to give small, subnutritional, enteral feeds, since these feeds should stimulate gut development. Indeed, "minimal enteral feeding"[116] has been shown to stimulate normal postnatal gut hormone surges within days, even with feed volumes (e.g., 0.5 mL) that would have no nutritional significance. In one study, such feeding was shown to have potentially beneficial effects on gut function and nutritional status.[117] The increase in gastric inhibitory polypeptide following minimal enteral feeding may stimulate insulin release (via the enteroinsular axis[115]). If so, this type of feeding would be expected to decrease glucose intolerance, which is a significant problem in the intravenously fed micropremie.

There has been some concern that when papers on minimal enteral feeding are viewed collectively (see Chapter 15), a trend towards a high incidence of NEC is found compared with infants fed intravenously. Nevertheless, LaGamma and coworkers[67] tested the hypothesis that delayed oral feeding would lessen the risk of NEC, yet they found a significantly higher rate of NEC in those fed parentally during the first 2 weeks than in those fed diluted formula or breast milk. Clearly, this area is unresolved, but in view of the data on NEC just discussed, it would seem prudent to use human milk for minimal enteral feeding whenever possible.

In extremely immature infants, even minimal enteral feeds may not be tolerated initially, but in my view it is worth establishing small enteral feeds as soon as possible, cautiously. These feeds are best given by continuous nasogastric infusion using a perfuser pump. Especially vigilant monitoring for excessive gastric aspirates and abdominal distension is required.

CASE STUDY

A white female infant was born at 27 weeks gestation weighing 860 g to a primiparous mother aged 18. The Apgar score was 6 at 5 minutes. The infant required intubation and ventilation for increasing respiratory dis-

tress. Within 4 days the baby was weaned from ventilation and put on oxygen. Intravenous nutrition was then decreased and enteral feeding with full-strength preterm formula was introduced, starting at 20 mL/kg/day and working up to 70 mL/kg/day by day 7.

At this stage the infant deteriorated, became hypoxemic, and required ventilation again. A right upper lobe pneumonia was diagnosed from the x-ray. In view of the presumptive diagnosis of aspiration pneumonia and requirement for ventilation, intravenous feeding was restarted and enteral feeds stopped completely. It proved difficult to wean the infant from the ventilator, largely due to recurrent apnea.

After 7 days, on day 14, the infant was extubated again and transpyloric feeds, via a nasojejunal tube, were initiated because of previous concern over aspiration pneumonia. Enteral feeds of full-strength preterm formula were increased by 20 mL/kg/day over the next 3 days to 60 mL/kg/day, at which time (day 17) the infant became acutely ill with a tense swollen abdomen, bloody diarrhea, and thrombocytopenia. Abdominal x-ray confirmed a diagnosis of NEC with free gas in the abdomen. The infant became hypotensive and required ventilation again. After stabilization the infant was transferred to our hospital for abdominal surgery. Following gut resection, the infant became increasingly sick and died on day 23.

Commentary. This abbreviated history of a complex case poses three important questions: (1) Was enteral nutrition management contributory to this infant's demise? (2) Was transpyloric feeding a logical decision in this circumstance? (3) Could transpyloric feeding have played a role in the infant's morbidity?

The evidence that rapid escalation of early feed volume is deleterious is poor. However, increments of 20 mL/kg/day or above with full-strength formula, as employed on both occasions here, theoretically may be more risky in the micropreemie than in the sick but larger infant. Hard evidence, however, that the aspiration pneumonia on the first occasion and NEC on the second could be attributed to this policy is lacking. Nevertheless, our own policy for the micropreemie would be to escalate feed volumes more cautiously, especially on day 4.

There is evidence, however, discussed in this chapter, that formula-fed infants are more prone to NEC than those fed human milk. We use human milk (mother's own or donor) to establish full enteral feeds (150 mL/kg), especially in a micropreemie, before resorting to preterm formula. Furthermore, on the basis of the data just discussed, we would be especially concerned about introduction of exclusive undiluted formula feeding in the first week in a vulnerable infant, since "early" formula-fed infants <28 weeks are the highest risk group for NEC.

It is theoretically possible that after 1 week of complete intravenous feeding (from days 7 to 14) the gut had become atrophic and more vulnerable to NEC. However, the decision to withhold enteral feeds in an apneic, ventilated baby with aspiration pneumonia was sound.

The choice to use transpyloric feeding here was not unconventional, since many believe that aspiration pneumonia is an indication. However, the studies cited in this chapter do *not* provide support for this application. Transpyloric feeding has been associated with NEC, especially in the past, when older tubes used to leach plastics that may have been toxic to the gut. Although modern clinical trial data, from six studies, collectively do not show that modern transpyloric feeding is a cause of NEC, they do show an associated increase in death rate that is relevant today.

Establishment of enteral feeding in small babies is desirable and, if achievable, is the preferred mode of nutrition. It is likely that a more cautious introduction of enteral feeds either with human milk or diluted formula would have been entirely successful in this case. We are left with the uncomfortable thought that dietary management decisions could have played an important part in the death of this baby.

References

1. Auricchio S, Rubino A, Murset G. Intestinal glycosidase activities in the human embryo, fetus, and newborn. *Pediatrics* 1965;35:944–954.
2. Herbst JJ. Development of suck and swallow. *J Pediatr Gastroenterol Nutr* 1983;2:S131–135.
3. Steer P, Lucas A, Sinclair JC. Feeding the low birthweight infant. In: Sinclair JC, Bracken MB, eds. *Effective care of the newborn infant*. New York: Oxford University Press, 1992:94–160.
4. Lucas A. Human milk and infant feeding. In: Battaglia F, Boyd R, eds. *Perinatal medicine*. London: Butterworths, 1983:172–200.
5. Read LC. Milk growth factors. In: Cockburn F, ed. *Fetal and neonatal growth*. Chichester, England: John Wiley & Sons, 1988:131:152.
6. Koldovsky O. Hormones in milk. *Life Sci* 1980;26:1833–1836.
7. Shahani KM, Kwan AJ, Friend BA. Role and significance of enzymes in human milk. *Am J Clin Nutr* 1980;33:1861–1869.
8. Werner S, Widstro A-M, Wahlberg V, Eneroth P, Winberg J. Immunoreactive calcitonin in maternal milk and serum in relation to prolactin and neurotensin. *Early Hum Dev* 1982;6:77–82.
9. Lucas A, Mitchell MD. Plasma prostaglandins in preterm neonates before and after treatment for patent ductus arteriosus. *Lancet* 1978;2:130–132.
10. Koldovsky O, Vaucher Y, Gasparo M, et al. TSH and ACTH are present in rat's milk: they retain physiological activity when given perorally to sucking rats. *Pediatr Res* 1980;14(4, II):502.
11. Gale SM, Read LC, George-Nascimento C, Wallace JC, Ballard FJ. Is dietary epidermal growth factor absorbed by premature human infants? *Biol Neonate* 1989;55:104–110.
12. Adamson ED, Dellar MJ, Warshaw JB. Functional EGF receptors are present on mouse embryo tissues. *Nature* 1981;291:656–659.
13. Williamson S, Finucane E, Ellis HJ, Gamsu HR. Effect of heat treatment of human milk on absorption of nitrogen, fat, sodium, calcium and phosphorus by preterm infants. *Arch Dis Child* 1978;53:555–563.
14. Rey J, Schuri ZJ, Amedee-Manesme O. Fat absorption in low birthweight infants. *Acta Paediatr Scand* 1982;296 (suppl):81–84.
15. Lonnerdal B, Forsum E, Hambraeus L. A longitudinal study of the protein, nitrogen and lactose contents of human milk from Swedish well-nourished mothers. *Am J Clin Nutr* 1976;29:1127–1233.
16. Prentice A, Ewing G, Roberts SB, et al. The nutritional role of breast-milk IgA and lactoferrin. *Acta Paediatr Scand* 1987;76:592–598.
17. Atkinson SA, Bryan MH, Anderson GH. Human milk: difference in nitrogen concentration in milk from mothers of term and premature infants. *J Pediatr* 1978;93:67–69.
18. Lemons JA, Moyle L, Hall D, Simmons M. Differences in the composition of preterm and term human milk during early lactation. *Pediatr Res* 1982;16:113–117.
19. Atinmo T, Omololu A. Trace element content of breast milk of mothers of preterm infants in Nigeria. *Early Hum Dev* 1982;6:309–313.
20. Gross SJ, Buckley RH, Wakil SS, et al. Elevated IgA concentration in milk produced by mothers delivered of preterm infants. *J Pediatr* 1981;99:289–293.
21. Lucas A, Hudson G. Preterm milk as a source of protein for low birthweight infants. *Arch Dis Child* 1984;59:831–836.
22. Lucas A, Gibbs JH, Baum JD. What's in breast milk? *Lancet* 1977;2:1011.
23. Lucas A, Lucas PJ, Baum JD. The Nipple Shield Sampling System: a device for measuring the dietary intake of breast fed infants. *Early Human Dev* 1980;4(pt 4):365–372.
24. Bates CJ, Liu D-S, Fuller NJ, Lucas A. Susceptibility of riboflavin and vitamin A in breast milk to photodegradation and its implications for the use of banked breast milk in infant feeding. *Acta Paediatr Scand* 1985;74:40–44.
25. Lucas A, Gore SM, Cole TJ, et al. A multicentre trial on the feeding of low birthweight infants: effects of diet on early growth. *Arch Dis Child* 1984;59:722–730.
26. Lucas A, Cole TJ, Morley R, et al. Factors associated with maternal choice to provide breast milk for low birthweight infants. *Arch Dis Child* 1988;63:48–52.
27. Department of Health and Social Security. Report on health and social subjects: the collection and storage of human milk. London: HMSO, 1981.
28. Evans TJ, Ryley JC, Neale LM. Effect of storage and heat on antimicrobial proteins in human milk. *Arch Dis Child* 1978;53:239–241.
29. Wills ME, Han VEM, Harris DA, Baum JD. Short time low temperature pasteurisation of human milk. *Early Hum Dev* 1982;7:71–80.
30. Hytten FE. Clinical and chemical studies in human lactation. II. Variation in major constituents during a feeding. *Br Med J* 1954;1:176–179.
31. Lucas A, Gibbs JD, Baum JD. Human milk banking with drip breast milk. In: Stern L, ed. *Intensive care of the newborn II*. New York: Masson; 1978:369–379.
32. Lucas A, Gibbs JH, Baum JD. The biology of drip breast milk. *Early Hum Dev* 1978;2(pt 4):351–361.
33. Lucas A, Roberts CD. Bacteriological quality control in human milk banking. *Br Med J* 1979;1:80–82.
34. Committee on Nutrition of the Preterm Infant, European Society of Paediatric Gastroenterology and Nutrition. Nutrition and feeding of preterm infants. *Acta Paediatr Scand* 1987;336(suppl):1–14.
35. Wharton BA. *Use of formulas in nutrition and feeding of preterm infants*. Oxford, UK: Blackwell Scientific, 1987:208–223.
36. Bishop N, McGraw M, Ward N. Aluminium in infant formulas. *Lancet* 1989;1:490, 565.
37. Lucas A, Lucas PJ, Chavin S, Lyster RLJ, Baum JD. A human milk formula. *Early Hum Dev* 1980;4:15–21.
38. Ronnholm KAR, Simell O, Siimes MA. Human milk protein and medium-chain triglyceride oil supplementation of human milk: plasma amino acids in very low-birth-weight infants. *Pediatrics* 1984;74:792–799.
39. Ronnholm KAR, Perheentupa J, Siimes MA. Supplementation with human milk protein improves growth of

small premature infants fed human milk. *Pediatrics* 1986;77:649–653.

40. Polberger SKT, Axelsson IA, Raiha NCE. Growth of very low birth weight infants on varying amounts of human milk protein. *Pediatr Res* 1989;25:414–419.

41. Roberts SB, Lucas A. Energetic efficiency and nutrient-accretion in preterm infants fed extremes of dietary intake. *Hum Nutr Clin Nutr* 1987;41C:105–113.

42. Bishop NJ, King FJ, Lucas A. Linear growth in the early neonatal period. *Arch Dis Child* 1990;65:707–708.

43. Cooke RWI, Lucas A, Yudkin PLN, Pryse-Davies J. Head circumference as an index of brain weight in the fetus and newborn. *Early Hum Dev* 1977;1(pt 2):145–149.

44. Dobbing J. The later development of the brain and its vulnerability. In: Davis JA, Dobbing J, eds. *Scientific foundations of paediatrics*. 2nd ed. London: Heinemann; 1981:744–759.

45. Gordon HH, Levine SZ, McNamara H. Feeding of premature infants. A comparison of human and cow's milk. *Am J Dis Child* 1947;73:442–452.

46. Tyson JE, Lasky RE, Mize CE, et al. Growth, metabolic response, and development in very low-birthweight infants fed banked human milk or enriched formula. I. Neonatal findings. *J Pediatr* 1983;103:94–104.

47. Davies DP. Adequacy of expressed breast milk for early growth of preterm infants. *Arch Dis Child* 1977;52:296–301.

48. Gross SJ. Growth and biochemical response of preterm infants fed human milk or modified infant formula. *N Engl J Med* 1983;308:237–241.

49. Bell A, Halliday H, McClure G, Reid M. Controlled trial of new formulae for feeding low birth weight infants. *Early Hum Dev* 1986;13:97–105.

50. Modanlou HD, Lim MO, Hansen JW, Sickles V. Growth, biochemical status, and mineral metabolism in very low-birthweight infants receiving fortified preterm human milk. *J Pediatr Gastroenterol* 1986;5:762–767.

51. Chan GM, Mileur L, Hansen JW. Calcium and phosphorus requirements in bone mineralization of preterm infants. *J Pediatr* 1988;113:225–229.

52. Lucas A. AIDS and human milk banking. In: Hudson CN, Sharp F, eds. *Proceedings of 19th Royal College of Obstetricians and Gynecologists study group: AIDS and obstetrics and gynaecology*. London: RCOG, 1988:271–281.

53. Lucas A, Morley R, Cole TJ, et al. Early diet in preterm babies and developmental status at 18 months. *Lancet* 1990;335:1477–1481.

54. Carey DE, Rowe JC, Goetz CA, Horak E, Clark RM, Goldbert B. Growth and phosphorus metabolism in premature infants fed human milk, fortified human milk, or special premature formula. *Am J Dis Child* 1987;141:511–515.

55. Greer FR, McCormick A. Improved bone mineralization and growth in premature infants fed fortified own mother's milk. *J Pediatr* 1988; 112:961–969.

56. Kashyap S, Schulze KF, Forsyth M, Dell RB, Ramakrishnan R, Heird WC. Growth, nutrient retention, and metabolic response of low-birth-weight infants fed supplemented and unsupplemented preterm human milk. *Am J Clin Nutr* 1990;52:254–262.

57. Roberts SB, Lucas A. The effects of two extremes of dietary intake on body composition in preterm infants. *Early Hum Dev* 1985;12:301–307.

58. Lucas A, Brooke OG, Baker BA, Bishop N, Morley R. High alkaline phosphatase activity and growth in preterm neonates. *Arch Dis Child* 1989;64:902–909.

59. Kliegman RM, Fanaroff AA. Neonatal necrotizing enterocolitis: a nine-year experience. I. Epidemiology and uncommon observations. *Am J Dis Child* 1981;135:603–607.

60. Santulli TV, Schullinger JN, Heird WC, et al. Acute necrotizing enterocolitis in infancy: a review of 64 cases. *Pediatrics* 1975;55:376–387.

61. Goldman HI. Feeding and necrotizing enterocolits. *Am J Dis Child* 1980;134:553–555.

62. Eyal F, Sagi E, Arad I, Avital A. Necrotizing enterocolitis in the very low birthweight infant: expressed breast milk feeding compared with parenteral feeding. *Arch Dis Child* 1982;57:274–276.

63. Stoll BJ, Kano WP, Glass RI, Nahmias AJ, Brannon AW. Epidemiology of necrotizing enterocolitis: a case-control study. *J Pediatr* 1980; 96:447–451.

64. Book LS, Herbert JJ, Atherton SO, Jung AL. Necrotizing enterocolitis in low-birthweight infants fed an elemental formula. *J Pediatr* 1975;87:602–605.

65. Willis DM, Chabot J, Radde IC, Chance GW. Unsuspected hyperosmolality of oral solutions contributing to necrotizing enterocolitis in very low-birthweight infants. *Pediatrics* 1977;60:535–538.

66. Bunton GL, Durbin GM, McIntosh N, et al. Necrotizing enterocolitis: controlled study of 3 years' experience in a neonatal intensive care unit. *Arch Dis Child* 1977;52:772–777.

67. LaGamma EF, Ostertag SG, Birenbaum H. Failure of delayed oral feedings to prevent necrotizing enterocolitis. Results of studying very low-birthweight neonates. *Am J Dis Child* 1985;139:385–389.

68. DeCurtis M, Paone C, Vetrano G, Romano G, Paludetto R, Ciccimarra F. A case control study of necrotizing enterocolitis occurring over 8 years in a neonatal intensive care unit. *Eur J Pediatr.* 1987; 146:398–400.

69. Kliegman RM, Pittard WB, Fanaroff AA. Necrotizing enterocolitis in neonates fed human milk. *J Paediatr* 1979;95:450–453.

70. Kosloske AM. Pathogenesis and prevention of necrotizing enterocolitis: a hypothesis based on personal observation. *Pediatrics* 1984;74:1086–1092.

71. Barlow B, Santulli TV, Heird WC, Pitt J, Blanc WC, Schullinger JN. An experimental study of acute neonatal enterocolitis—the importance of breast milk. *J Pediatr Surg* 1974;9:587–595.

72. Pitt J, Barlow B. Heird WC. Protection against experimental necrotizing enterocolitis by maternal milk. I. Role of milk leukocytes. *Pediatr Res* 1977;11:906–909.

73. Lucas A, Cole TJ. Breast milk and neonatal necrotising enterocolitis. *Lancet* 1990;336:1519–1523.

74. Narayanan I, Prakash K, Gujral VV. The value of human milk in the prevention of infection in the high-risk low-birthweight infant. *J Pediatr* 1982;99:496–498.

75. Lucas A. AIDS and milk bank closures. *Lancet* 1987;1:1092–1093.

76. Lucas A, Brooke OG, Morley R, Cole TJ, Bamford MF. Early diet of preterm infants and development of allergic or atopic disease: randomised prospective study. *Br Med J* 1990;300:837–840.

77. Lucas A, Morley R, Cole TJ, et al. Early diet in preterm babies and developmental status in infancy. *Arch Dis Child* 1989;11:1570–1578.

78. Morley R. Cole TJ, Lucas PJ, et al. Mother's choice to provide breast milk and developmental outcome. *Arch Dis Child* 1988;63:1382–1385.

79. Lucas A, Morley RM, Cole TJ, Lister G, Leeson-Payne C. Breast milk and subsequent intelligence quotient in children born preterm. *Lancet* 1992;339:261–264.

80. Van Someren V, Linnett SJ, Stothers JK, Sullivan PG. An investigation into the benefits of resisting nasoenteric feeding tubes. *Pediatrics* 1984;74:379–383.

81. Van Caillie M, Powell GK. Nasoduodenal versus nasogastric feeding in the very low birthweight infant. *Pediatrics* 1975;56:1065–1072.

82. Wells, DH, Zachman RD. Nasojejunal feedings in low-birthweight infants. *J Pediatr* 1975;87:276–279.

83. Roy RN, Pollnitz RP, Hamilton JR, Chance GW. Impaired assimilation of nasojejunal feeds in healthy low-birth-weight newborn infants. *J Pediatr* 1977;90:431–434.

84. Drew JH, Johnston R, Finocchiaro C, Taylor PS, Goldberg HJ. A comparison of nasojejunal with nasogastric feedings in low-birthweight infants. *Aust Paediatr J* 1979;15:98–100.

85. Pereira GR, Lemons JA. Controlled study of transpyloric and intermittent gavage feeding in the small preterm infant. *Pediatrics* 1981;67:68–72.

86. Whitfield MF. Poor weight gain of the low birthweight infant fed nasojejunally. *Arch Dis Child* 1982;57:597–601.

87. Laing IA, Lang MA, Callaghan O, Hume R. Nasogastric compared with nasoduodenal feeding in low birthweight infants. *Arch Dis Child* 1986;61:138–141.

88. Vengusamy S, Pildes RS, Raffensperger JF, Levine HD, Cornblath M. A controlled study of feeding gastronomy in low birth weight infants. *Pediatrics* 1969;43:815–820.

89. Yao AC, Wallgren CG, Sinha SN, Lind J. Peripheral circulatory response to feeding in the newborn. *Pediatrics* 1971;47:378–383.

90. Pitcher-Wilmott R, Shutack JG, Fox WW. Decreased lung volume after nasogastric feeding of neonates recovering from respiratory disease. *J Pediatr* 1979;95:119–121.

91. Dear PRF. Effect of feeding on jugular venous blood flow in the newborn infant. *Arch Dis Child* 1980;55:365–370.

92. Toce SS, Keenan WJ, Horman SM. Enteral feeding in very-low-birth-weight infants. *Am J Dis Child* 1987;141:439–444.

93. Wharton BA, Bower BD. Immediate or later feeding for premature babies? A controlled trial. *Lancet* 1965;2:996–972.

94. Wu PYK, Teilmann P, Gabler M, Vaughan M, Metcoff J. "Early" vs "late" feeding of low birth weight neonates: effect on serum bilirubin, blood sugar and responses to glucagon and epinephrine tolerance tests. *Pediatrics* 1967;39:733–739.

95. Currao WJ, Cox C, Shapiro DL. Diluted formula for beginning the feeding of premature infants. *Am J Dis Child* 1988;142:730–731.

96. Measel CP, Anderson GC. Nonnutritive sucking during tube feedings: effect on clinical course in premature infants. *J Obstet Gynecol Nurs* 1979;8:265–272.

97. Field T, Ignatoff E, Stringer S, et al. Nonnutritive sucking during tube feelings: effects on preterm neonates in an intensive care unit. *Pediatrics* 1982;70:381–384.

98. Bernbaum JC, Pereira GR, Watkins JB, Peckham GJ. Nonnutritive sucking during gavage feeding enhances growth and maturation in premature infants. *Pediatrics* 1983;71:41–45.

99. Szabo JC, Hillemeier C, Oh W. Effect of non-nutritive and nutritive suck on gastric emptying in premature infants. *J Pediatr Gastroenterol Nutr* 1985;4:348–351.

100. Decurtis M. McIntosh N. Ventura V, Brooke O. Effect of nonnutritive sucking on nutrient retention in preterm infants. *J Pediatr* 1986;109:888–890.

101. Widstrom AM, Marchini G, Matthiesen AS, Werner S, Winberg J, Uvnas-Mobert K. Nonnutritive sucking in tube-fed preterm infants: effects on gastric motility and gastric contents of somatostatin. *J Pediat Gastroenterol Nutr* 1988;7:517–523.

102. Ernst JA, Rickard KA, Neal PR, Yu PL, Oei TO, Lemons JA. Lack of improved growth outcome related to nonnutritive sucking in very low birthweight premature infants fed a controlled nutrient intake: a randomized prospective study. *Pediatrics* 1989;83:706–716.

103. Fomon SJ, Filer LJ, Thomas LN, Rogers RR, Proksch AM. Relationship between formula concentration and rate of growth of normal infants. *J Nutr* 1969;98:241–254.

104. Fomon SJ, Filer LJ, Thomas LN, Anderson TA, Nelson SE. Influence of formula concentration on caloric intake and growth or normal infants. *Acta Paediatr Scand* 1975;64:172–181.

105. Schreiner RL, Lemons JAS, Gresham EL. A new complication of nutritional management of the low-birthweight infants. *Pediatrics* 1979;63:683–685.

106. Lucas A. Gut hormones and the adaptation to extrauterine nutrition. In: Milla PJ, Muller DPR, eds. *Essentials of paediatric gastroenterology*. Edinburgh: Churchill Livingstone, 1987:302–317.

107. Abbas TM, Tovey JE. Proteins of the liquor amnii. *Br Med J* 1960; 1:476–479.

108. Friis-Hansen B. Body water metabolism in early infancy. *Acta Paediatr Scand* 1982;296(suppl):44–48.

109. Lucas A, Bloom SR, Aynsley-Green A. Gastrointestinal peptides and the adaptation to extrauterine nutrition. *Can J Physiol Pharmacol* 1985;63:527–537.

110. Johnson LR, Copeland EM, Dudrick SJ, Lichtenberger LM, Castro GA. Structural and hormonal alterations in the gastrointestinal tract of parenterally fed rats. *Gastroenterology* 1975;68:1177–1183.

111. Heird WC. Effects of total parenteral alimentation on intestinal function. In: Sunshine P, ed. *Gastrointestinal function and neonatal nutrition*. Columbus, OH: Ross Laboratories, 1977:16.

112. Hughes CA, Dowling RH. Speed of onset of adaptive mucosal hypoplasia and hypofunction in the intestine of parenterally fed rats. *Clin Sci* 1980;59:317–327.

113. Hughes CA. Intestinal adaptation. In: Tanner MS, Stocks RJ, eds. *Neonatal gastroenterology*. Newcastle-upon-Tyne, England: Intercept 1984:69–91.

114. Lucas A, Bloom SR, Aynsley-Green A. Metabolic and endocrine consequences of depriving preterm infants of enteral nutrition. *Acta Paediatr Scand* 1983;72:245–249.

115. Lucas A, Sarson D, Adrian TE, Bloom SR, Aynsley-Green A. Developmental aspects of gastric inhibitory polypeptide (GIP) and its possible role in the enteroinsular axis in preterm neonates. *Acta Paediatr Scand* 1980;69:321–325.

116. Lucas A, Bloom SR, Aynsley-Green A. Gut hormones and "minimal enteral feeding." *Acta Paediatr Scand* 1986;75:719–723.

117. Dunn L, Hulman S, Weiner J, Lkiegman R. Beneficial effects of early hypocaloric enteral feeding on neonatal gastrointestinal function: preliminary report of a randomized trial. *J Pediatr* 1988;112:622–629.

15. Parenteral Nutrition

William C. Heird

Michael R. Gomez

Reviewers: Harry L. Greene, Brian A. Wharton, Victor Yu, Stanley Zlotkin

The first report of successful use of parenteral nutrition in the clinical management of a pediatric patient appeared in 1944.[1] The patient, a 5-month-old male with severe marasmus, received alternate peripheral vein infusions of a mixture of 50% glucose and 10% casein hydrolysate and a noncommercial homogenate of olive oil and lecithin providing 130 kcal/kg/day and a total volume of 150 mL/kg/day. The ultimate fate of the child is unknown but, after 5 days of the regimen, "the fat pads of the cheek had returned, the ribs were less prominent, and the general nutritional status was much improved."

Most attempts to administer nutrients parenterally were not as successful. Among many other problems, lack of an acceptable parenteral oil emulsion made delivery of adequate energy difficult. Thus, for a brief period, there was some enthusiasm for the use of ethanol and various polyalcohols (e.g., sorbitol, xylitol) as alternative parenteral sources of energy. Although peripheral vein infusions of a mixture of protein hydrolysate, glucose, and ethanol along with electrolytes, minerals, and vitamins permits achievement of weight gain and general improvement in nutritional and clinical status,[2] maintenance of the infusions requires considerable effort. In addition, the amount of ethanol tolerated by individual patients is both variable and unpredictable. Infusion of large volumes of less concentrated mixtures of glucose and protein hydrolysate, even with administration of diuretics to prevent fluid overload, also enjoyed a brief period of popularity but was soon abandoned because of the severe plasma electrolyte and acid base disturbances that frequently ensued.

The technique of total parenteral nutrition as practiced today was introduced to clinical medicine in the late 1960s with a case report describing normal growth and development of an infant who had virtually no remaining small intestine and was, therefore, totally dependent upon parenterally delivered nutrients.[3] By the early 1970s, this technique was being used extensively in infants and children with congenital or acquired surgically correctable lesions of the gastrointestinal tract,[4,5] as well as in infants with intractable diarrhea.[5,6] Use of the technique in nutritional management of low-birthweight (LBW) infants soon followed.[7,8] Currently, most infants who weigh <1,500 g at birth, more than 1% of all births in the United States, receive parenterally delivered nutrients as their major source of nutrition for the first several days to weeks of life. For example, 81% of infants with birthweights between 500 g and 1,500 g who were discharged from the seven participating NICHD Neonatal Intensive Care Network Centers between November of 1987 and October of 1988 received parenteral nutrients for a mean duration of 19 days (range, 12 to 26 days).[9]

Since the endogenous nutrient stores of LBW infants are limited and their rate of ongoing energy expenditure is relatively high, these infants theoretically are at great risk for development of malnutrition or actual starvation within the first few days of life.[2] The total endogenous nutrient stores of the infant weighing 1,000 g, for example, are sufficient to support survival without exogenous nutrients for only about 5 days. Nonetheless, it is not clear that the increasing use of parenteral nutrition in LBW infants over the past 2 decades has contributed to the concurrent dramatic improvement in survival of LBW infants. During this time, there have been improvements in other aspects of neonatal care and, in the absence of controlled studies, it is impossible to distinguish between the contributions to improved survival of advances in other aspects of care versus the ability to provide nutrients exogenously.

Despite uncertainty concerning the contribution of parenteral nutrition to the markedly better survival of LBW infants today versus 10 to 15 years ago, this therapy obviously is a firmly established part of the care of many LBW infants. Yet, the lack of understanding of a number of aspects of the technique probably limits its use in many more infants who might benefit from better nutritional management. The purpose of this chapter is to enhance understanding of all aspects of parenteral nutrition. Practical aspects of the therapy that may enhance its efficacy as well as a variety of unsolved problems will be discussed.

Techniques of Parenteral Nutrition Therapy

The basic concept of parenteral nutrition therapy as described by Wilmore and Dudrick in 1968[3] is quite simple. A hypertonic nutrient solution is infused at a constant rate through an indwelling catheter, the tip of which is in the superior vena cava just above the right atrium. In infants, the catheter usually is placed through a surgical cutdown into either the internal or external jugular vein and tunneled subcutaneously to exit some distance from the site of insertion, usually the scalp or anterior chest, thereby protecting the catheter from both inadvertent dislodgment and contamination by microorganisms.

Despite its apparent simplicity, this technique resulted in a number of predictable as well as unpredictable complications (see following section). Although many of these complications can be reduced to an acceptable level, doing so requires considerable effort, as well as expense. Thus infusion of parenteral nutrition regimens by peripheral vein became and remains very popular. By necessity, the glucose concentration of such regimens cannot be much >10%; as a result, the nutrient intake that can be delivered by this route without excessive fluid intake is limited. Use of parenteral lipid emulsions helps compensate for this drawback but, if fluid intake is limited to a total volume of 150 mL/kg/day and intravenous lipid intake is limited to 3 g/kg/day, the maximum energy intake that can be delivered is approximately 80 kcal/kg/day.[2] While the growth achievable with such an intake is less than that achievable with conventional central vein parenteral nutrition regimens, which deliver up to 50% more energy, few LBW infants are able to tolerate the maximal energy intakes that can be delivered by central vein. Moreover, many infants require parenteral nutrition for only a few days or weeks. Thus, if the infant can tolerate a fluid intake of at least 120 to 150 mL/kg/day, the nutrient intakes achievable with peripheral vein infusions are adequate.

The concept that delivery of nutrients by peripheral vein is easier and less time-consuming than successful delivery by central vein is not necessarily valid. The supervision required for successful peripheral vein delivery is at least equal to that required for successful central vein delivery. In addition, since a single infusion site rarely lasts for more than 24 hours, considerable time and effort are required to maintain peripheral vein infusions. Further, the complications per day of therapy associated with the two routes of delivery, although different in nature and severity, are similar.[10] Thus it seems reasonable to base the choice of delivery route for parenteral nutrients on an individual patient's clinical condition and nutritional needs rather than on the perceived ease or difficulty of a particular technique. For example, infants who are likely to require parenterally delivered nutrients for a prolonged period as well as infants with fluid intolerance are likely to benefit from central vein delivery.

Currently, use of small Silastic or polyurethane catheters inserted into the superior vena cava through a needle placed percutaneously into a peripheral vein, a technique described initially some 20 years ago,[11,12] is quite popular. To date, the advantages and disadvantages of this technique versus those of conventional central and/or peripheral vein techniques of nutrient delivery have not been evaluated extensively. Available data suggest that these catheters may not remain functional as long as central catheters placed in the conventional manner,[13] but that they can be used for a much longer period than can a single peripheral vein site.[14] Moreover, they appear to be as safe as conventional central vein catheters.[13,15] Since they allow infusion of a more concentrated nutrient infusate, they permit delivery of more nutrients without excessive fluid intake.

Infusate Composition and Delivery

The parenteral nutrition infusate, whether delivered by central or peripheral vein, should include a nitrogen source as well as adequate energy, electrolytes, minerals, and vitamins. The amount of each nutrient it should include, however, varies considerably as a function of the infant's age, maturity, and clinical condition, as well as the results to be achieved with the parenteral nutrition regimen. Suitable central vein and peripheral vein infusates for LBW infants are shown in Table 15.1. In general, the infusate intended for peripheral vein delivery is appropriate for the transitional period and the infusate intended for central vein delivery is more appropriate for the stable, growing infant who is dependent on parenterally delivered nutrients. Modifications of these that may be indicated for specific categories of infants are discussed subsequently.

One of several crystalline amino acid mixtures (Table 15.2) is usually used as the nitrogen source. The amount of amino acids provided ranges from 2 to 4 g/kg/day; an intake of 2 to 2.5 g/kg/day results in nitrogen retention comparable to that observed in enterally fed, normal term infants, but a higher intake is required to achieve a rate of nitrogen retention equal to the intrauterine rate.

Glucose is the major energy source of most parenteral nutrition regimens. An intake >15 g/kg/day rarely is tolerated by any infant on the first day of therapy and the amount tolerated by LBW infants frequently is less. However, intake usually can be increased by 2 to 5 g/kg/day until the desired intake is achieved.

Since any patient who receives a fat-free parenteral nutrition regimen will develop essential fatty acid deficiency within a relatively short period (preterm and nutritionally depleted infants do so within days, particularly if growth is rapid),[16] a sufficient amount of a parenteral lipid emulsion to prevent this deficiency (i.e., 0.5 to 1.0 g/kg/day) is indicated. It is usually

Table 15.1. Composition of Nutrient Infusates Suitable for Central Vein and Peripheral Vein Infusion*

Component	Central Vein (Amount/kg/day)[†]	Peripheral Vein (Amount/kg/day)[†]
Amino acids	3–4 g	2.5–3.0 g
Glucose	15–25 g (83–139 mmol)	10–15 g (56–83 mmol)
Lipid emulsion	0.5–3.0 g	0.5–3.0 g
Sodium	2–3 mEq (46–69 mg)	2–3 mEq (46–69 mg)
Potassium[‡]	2–4 mEq (78–156 mg)	2–4 mEq (78–106 mg)
Calcium	80–100 mg (4–5 mEq)	40–80 mg (2–4 mEq)
Magnesium	3–6 mg (0.125–0.25 mmol)	3–6 mg (0.125–0.25 mmol)
Chloride	2–3 mEq (71–107 mg)	2–3 mEq (71–107 mg)
Phosphorus[‡]	43–62 mg (1.4–2.0 mmol)	43–62 mg (1.4–2.0 mmol)
Zinc[§]	200–400 μg (3–6 μmol)	200–400 μg (3–6 μmol)
Copper[§]	20 μg (0.3 μmol)	20 μg (0.3 μmol)
Other trace minerals[§]		
Iron[§]		
Vitamins (M.V.I. Pediatric)[‖]		
Total volume	120–130 mL	150 mL

*In general, the peripheral vein regimen is appropriate for the transitional period and as a supplement to tolerated enteral feedings; the central vein regimen is appropriate for the stable growing infant dependent upon parenteral nutrition.

[†]For all nutrients, the amount/kg/day is expressed in the most commonly used unit; these amounts expressed in alternative units are shown in parentheses.

[‡]With a lower calcium intake (40 to 60 mg/kg/day or 1 to 1.5 mmol/kg/day), a phosphorus intake in excess of 1.4 mmol/kg/day or 43 mg/kg/day, the amount given with a daily potassium intake of 2 mEq/kg/day or 78 mg/kg/day as a mixture of KH_2PO_4 and K_2HPO_4, frequently results in hyperphosphatemia. Although this may not be true with the calcium intakes suggested here, a potassium intake of more than 2 mEq/kg/day should be given initially as KCl and the infant should be monitored carefully to assess the adequacy of phosphorus intake.

[§]See text and Table 15.5. Iron Dextran (Imferon, Fisons Corp., Bedford, Mass) can be added to the infusate of patients requiring parenteral nutrition but the dose should be limited to 0.1 mg/kg/day. Alternatively, the indicated intramuscular dose can be used intermittently, either as the sole source of iron or as an additional dose.

[‖]M.V.I. Pediatric (distributed by Astra Pharmaceutical Products, Inc., Westborough, Mass; manufactured by Armour Pharmaceutical Co., Kankakee, Ill) is a lypholized product. When reconstituted as directed, 2 mL added to the daily infusate provides 280 μg vitamin A, 2.8 mg vitamin E, 80 μg vitamin K, 4 μg (64 IU) vitamin D, 32 mg ascorbic acid, 520 μg thiamine, 560 μg riboflavin, 400 μg pyridoxine, 6.8 mg niacin, 2 mg pantothenic acid, 8 μg biotin, 56 μg folic acid, and 0.4 μg vitamin B_{12}. See Table 15.3.

recommended that parenteral lipid intake not exceed 3 g/kg/day,[17] and many advocate 2 g/kg/day as the maximum intake for LBW infants.

Convenient additive preparations of electrolytes and minerals are available. Multivitamin preparations also are available but the amounts of the various vitamins in these preparations are not necessarily optimal (see following section). Inclusion of sufficient amounts of calcium and phosphorus in parenteral nutrition infusates is particularly problematic because of the relative incompatibility of these elements in aqueous solution. The amounts of calcium and phosphorus suggested in Table 15.1 usually are compatible, but whether they support optimal skeletal mineralization remains to be demonstrated. Zinc deficiency develops relatively rapidly if zinc is not provided; thus any infant likely to require parenteral nutrients for more than a few days should receive zinc. If exclusive parenteral nutrition is required for more than 2 weeks, the infusate also should include other trace minerals (e.g., copper, chromium,[18] selenium,[19] molybdenum[20]).

The nutrient infusate, whether delivered by peripheral or central vein, should be infused at a constant rate using a constant infusion pump. Although some consider placement of a 0.22 μ-membrane filter between the catheter and the administration tubing optional, the author feels that use of the filter is desirable. Otherwise, any microscopic particulate matter and bacteria that may be present in the infusate will be infused into the infant.

Many infants tolerate the same infusate for the total duration of parenteral nutrition; others, particularly

Table 15.2. Amino Acid Content (mg/g) of Commercially Available Amino Acid Mixtures

	Aminosyn*	Aminosyn PF*	Travasol B†	FreAmine III‡	Trophamine‡	Novamine§
Isoleucine	72	76	48	70	82	50
Leucine	94	119	62	91	140	70
Lysine	72	68	58	73	82	79
Methionine	40	18	58	53	33	50
Phenylalanine	44	43	62	56	48	70
Threonine	52	52	42	40	42	50
Tryptophan	16	18	18	15	20	16
Valine	80	64	46	66	78	65
Histidine	30	32	44	28	48	59
Cystine	0	0	0	<3	<3	<5
Tyrosine	4.4	6	4	0	23‖	4
Taurine	0	7	0	0	2	0
Alanine	128	70	207		53	141
Aspartate	0	53	0	0	32	30
Glutamate	0	82	0	0	50	50
Glycine	128	38	207	71	37	70
Proline	86	82	42	112	68	59
Serine	42	50	0	59	38	40
Arginine	98	123	103	95	122	99

*Abbott Laboratories, N. Chicago, Ill.
†Clintec, Morton Grove, Ill.
‡McGaw Laboratories, Irvine, Calif.
§Kabi-Vitrum, Inc, Franklin, Ohio.
‖Mixture of L-tyrosine and N-acetyl-L-tyrosine.

more immature and clinically unstable infants, require frequent adjustment of the intake of one or more nutrients. For this reason, ability to change the composition of the infusate in response to clinical and chemical monitoring or to increase or decrease the volume in response to greater or lesser fluid losses than anticipated is important.

Rationale for Recommended Parenteral Nutrient Intakes

The parenteral requirements for various nutrients depend upon the end points to be achieved and any peculiarities of metabolism of specific nutrients incident to the route of administration. The requirements for normal growth, for example, are considerably greater than the requirements for merely preserving existing body composition. Although the requirements for achieving either goal have not been studied extensively, considerable information is available concerning the amounts of some nutrients needed, particularly protein and energy. Virtually no information is available concerning special requirements imposed by parenteral versus enteral delivery of nutrients.

Amino Acid Intake. According to Zlotkin et al.,[21] stable growing LBW infants require a parenteral amino acid intake of approximately 3 g/kg/day to assure accretion of nitrogen at the intrauterine rate (i.e., approximately 300 mg/kg/day). This amino acid intake with an energy intake of 80 kcal/kg/day also results in a rate of weight gain approximating the intrauterine rate (i.e., approximately 15 g/kg/day). Whether these intakes also are appropriate for smaller infants has not been established. Greater amino acid intakes result in somewhat greater rates of nitrogen retention and may be desirable for most LBW infants, who generally require considerable catch-up growth.

Anderson et al.[22] found that LBW infants who received a regimen providing an energy intake of 60 kcal/kg/day with an amino acid intake of 2.5 g/kg/day during the first week of life were in positive nitrogen balance (178 mg/kg/day versus −132 mg/kg/day in infants who received the same energy intake) but did not gain weight. These general findings have recently been confirmed in smaller, sicker, more immature infants.[23-25] These more recent studies suggest that infants who receive no amino acid intake lose from 130 to 180 mg/kg/day of nitrogen, which also is in agreement with earlier estimates of "endogenous nitrogen losses."[26] Assuming that these nitrogen losses reflect tissue breakdown, as is likely, infants who receive no nitrogen intake for the first few days of life lose from 0.8 to 1.1 g/kg/day of protein, equivalent to a daily loss of at least 1% of endogenous protein stores. This loss can be prevented by provision of an amino acid intake at least equal to endogenous losses, but a higher intake is necessary for achievement of positive nitrogen balance or protein accretion. Recent studies in small, sick LBW infants suggest that a parenteral amino acid intake of 2 g/kg/day with an energy intake as low as 35 to 50 kcal/kg/day consistently results in positive nitrogen retention without significant metabolic abnormalities.[25]

The quality of the parenteral amino acid intake also is important. Both Duffy et al.[27] and Helms et al.[28] observed differences in nitrogen utilization between groups of infants receiving isonitrogenous and isocaloric parenteral nutrition regimens in which the quality of the nitrogen source differed. Duffy et al.[27] found that infants who received a regimen containing a crystalline amino acid mixture retained more of the nitrogen intake than those who received a regimen containing casein hydrolysate; protein synthesis also accounted for a greater percentage of total nitrogen flux in those who received the crystalline amino acid regimen. Helms et al.[28] observed that infants who received a regimen containing a parenteral amino acid mixture designed for infants retained 78% of the amino acid intake, whereas infants who received an isocaloric regimen containing a parenteral amino acid mixture designed for adults retained only 66% of intake.

Neither of these studies provides insight into the reason one regimen was utilized better than the other. The more efficiently utilized regimen studied by Helms et al.[28] contained more cyst(e)ine (see Chapter 17) and tyrosine, both considered indispensable amino acids for the infant[29]; thus, the investigators suggested that provision of more optimal intakes of these two amino acids improved nitrogen retention. This is a logical suggestion, although perhaps not a valid explanation.

Cystine and tyrosine are insoluble, and cysteine is unstable in aqueous solution; hence, no currently available parenteral amino acid mixture contains appreciable amounts of either amino acid. Consequently, plasma cyst(e)ine and tyrosine concentrations of infants receiving cyst(e)ine- and tyrosine-free amino acid mixtures are quite low.[30] Moreover, greater intakes of methionine and phenylalanine do not result in greater plasma concentrations, respectively, of cyst(e)ine and tyrosine.[30] Hepatic activity of cystathionase, which is required for endogenous conversion of methionine to cysteine, is absent or low throughout gestation and for some time postnatally.[31,32] This developmental deficit, although not apparent in other tissues,[33] is an acceptable explanation for the low plasma cyst(e)ine concentration of infants receiving cyst(e)ine-free parenteral nutrition regimens. Since there appears to be no developmental delay in the hepatic activity of phenylalanine hydroxylase (which converts phenylalanine to tyrosine),[34] the low plasma tyrosine concentration of infants receiving tyrosine-free parenteral nutrition regimens is not explicable on this basis.

Chawla et al.[35] found lower plasma concentrations of cyst(e)ine and tyrosine in adult patients receiving cyst(e)ine- and tyrosine-free parenteral nutrition regimens than in patients receiving a cyst(e)ine- and tyrosine-free elemental enteral diet. Those who received the parenteral regimen also had lower plasma concentrations of carnitine, creatine, and choline, all of which, when synthesized endogenously, require a methyl group from S-adenosyl-methionine, the first intermediate in the usual pathway of conversion of methionine to cysteine. These differences between patients receiving similar enterally versus parenterally administered regimens led the investigators to suggest that parenterally delivered methionine is metabolized by an alternative pathway, perhaps immediate transamination. The specific reason for the apparent requirement for tyrosine is less clear, but a similar mechanism seems reasonable.

In both adults and infants, therefore, it appears that parenterally administered methionine and phenylalanine may not be metabolized by the expected pathways and, hence, are not effectively converted, respectively, to cyst(e)ine and tyrosine. Although evidence that other amino acids are metabolized differently when delivered parenterally versus enterally is less convincing, there are some indications that the same may also be true for other amino acids. If so, it is clear that the amino acid needs of infants who require parenteral nutrition cannot be extrapolated from intakes of normally growing, enterally fed infants.

Cysteine hydrochloride is soluble and also is reasonably stable for short periods in aqueous solutions; thus it is possible to supplement parenteral nutrition infusates with cysteine, as was done in the study of Helms et al.[28] However, trials of cysteine supplementation[36,37] have not shown a beneficial effect of parenteral cysteine intake on nitrogen retention, perhaps because the tyrosine content of the control regimens of these studies also was low and any beneficial effect of cysteine intake on nitrogen retention was masked by concurrent tyrosine deficiency. Some of the newer parenteral amino acid mixtures contain N-acetyl-L-tyrosine (Table 15.2), which is soluble. Although the absolute efficacy of this tyrosine derivative has not been determined, infants receiving one of the parenteral amino acid mixtures that contains it have higher plasma tyrosine concentrations than infants receiving mixtures without it.[30,38] If N-acetyl-L-tyrosine proves to be an efficacious source of tyrosine, it should be possible to define the need for both tyrosine and cyst(e)ine in infants requiring parenteral nutrition.

Parenteral Energy Intake. Theoretically, if amino acid intake is adequate, an energy intake approximating the resting energy expenditure (i.e., 50 to 60 kcal/kg/day) is sufficient for maintenance (i.e., prevention of weight loss), whereas an energy intake in excess of resting energy expenditure is necessary to achieve weight gain. This theoretical consideration is confirmed by the findings of a number of investigators. However, because of genetic differences as well as differences in other factors affecting energy expenditure, the resting energy requirement varies considerably from infant to infant. Thus, the total energy intake necessary to produce a specific rate of weight gain will be greater in infants with higher resting energy expenditures. For example, the resting energy expenditure of infants with bronchopulmonary dysplasia is 10% to 30% greater than that of infants without bronchopulmonary dysplasia.[39] Hence, for the same rate of weight gain, infants with bronchopulmonary dysplasia require a greater energy intake than infants without this condition. The same is likely to be true for infants with other chronic or acute clinical conditions, but definitive data are not available.

As discussed above, LBW infants who receive an energy intake of 80 kcal/kg/day with a concomitant amino acid intake of 3 g/kg/day gain weight at a rate approximating the intrauterine rate. Theoretically, those who receive a greater energy intake will experience an even greater rate of weight gain. However, this greater rate most likely will represent only deposition of additional adipose tissue. Hence, if the rate of weight gain of a LBW infant receiving 80 kcal/kg/day is at or near the intrauterine rate, it is unlikely that a greater energy intake will be particularly desirable unless it is accompanied by a greater amino acid intake that supports greater rates of deposition of both protein and adipose tissue. Unfortunately, there are no data concerning this theoretical consideration.

In addition to the absolute energy requirements for maintenance and growth, the relationship between energy intake and nitrogen utilization must be considered. The accepted concept, developed primarily in animals and adults, is that increases in energy intake increase utilization of any single adequate protein intake.[40] One of the few such studies in LBW infants is that of Zlotkin et al.[21] documenting greater retention of amino acid intakes of both 3 g and 4 g/kg/day with a concomitant energy intake of 80 versus 50 kcal/kg/day. In another such study, Pineault et al.[41] observed a minimal additional effect of an energy intake of 80 versus 60 kcal/kg/day on nitrogen retention of LBW infants receiving an amino acid intake of 2.7 g/kg/day. These two sets of data suggest that an energy intake >60 kcal/kg/day will not appreciably enhance retention of an amino acid intake of 2.7 g/kg/day, but that an energy intake >50 kcal/kg/day will enhance retention of the slightly greater amino acid intake of 3 g/kg/day.

The distribution of energy intake between glucose and lipid also may be important with respect to amino acid utilization. In general, the nitrogen-sparing effect of carbohydrate in the absence of nitrogen intake is not shared by fat, but the effect of parenterally administered glucose versus lipid on utilization of concomitantly administered amino acids is less well understood. Studies in adults suggest both that the two energy substrates are equal in this regard[42] and that lipid does not exert this effect unless at least 85% of the resting energy requirement is provided as glucose.[43] This apparent discrepancy may reflect differences in the patient populations of the two studies (i.e., depleted adults in the former and stressed patients in the latter) or differences in duration of observation. In studying the effects of parenteral lipid intakes of 3 versus 1 g/kg/day in infants at total energy intakes of both 60 and 80 kcal/kg/day, Pineault et al.[41] found that the higher carbohydrate regimens, regardless of total energy intake, resulted in somewhat lower plasma concentrations of most amino acids. Although this finding suggests that the amino acid intake was used more efficiently by infants who received the greater carbohydrate intakes, rates of nitrogen retention with the two regimens at each energy intake did not differ significantly. A more recent study in infants also shows no effect of the quality of energy intake on nitrogen utilization and suggests that inclusion of lipid, in fact, may be preferable.[44]

The foregoing interpretation of the available data, coupled with the observed relationship between urinary nitrogen excretion and the amino acid:energy (g/kcal) intake ratio,[45] suggest that utilization of the amino acid content of a parenteral nutrition infusate with an amino acid:energy ratio similar to the lower energy infusates studied by Pineault et al.[41] (i.e., 4.5 g amino acid per 100 kcal) will be acceptable, although perhaps not maximal. Although this suggestion has not been tested extensively in clinical studies, it is not refuted by the available data.

In practical terms, this suggestion implies that an infant who can tolerate an energy intake of only 30 kcal/kg/day should easily tolerate an amino acid intake of 1.35 g/kg/day. Since the nitrogen content of this intake is somewhat greater than expected urinary nitrogen losses, it should result in nitrogen equilibrium or a minimally positive nitrogen balance. This does not mean necessarily that an infant who is receiving only 30 kcal/kg/day will not tolerate a somewhat greater amino acid intake; however, the amount of additional amino acid intake that will be tolerated is not known. This also does not mean that an amino acid intake as low as 1.35 g/kg/day will not be utilized more efficiently at an energy intake above 30 kcal/kg/day; but, at this low amino acid intake, an increase in energy intake is not likely to be nearly as effective in terms of nitrogen retention as an increase in the intakes of both amino acids and energy.

Parenteral Lipid Intakes. Parenteral lipid emulsions containing soybean oil and a mixture of safflower and soybean oils are currently available (Table 15.3). In both types, the emulsifying agent is egg yolk phospholipid and the emulsion particles are roughly the size of chylomicrons or very low-density lipoproteins (VLDL). After infusion, the triglyceride portion of these particles is hydrolyzed by endothelial lipoprotein lipase, and the free fatty acids and glycerol released are metabolized by the usual pathways.[46] The ability to hydrolyze the infused emulsion particles increases with increasing gestational age and, at any gestational age, the capacity for hydroly-

sis is greater in the infant whose size is appropriate for gestational age versus the infant who is small for gestational age.[47] A number of clinical conditions (e.g., infection, surgical stress, malnutrition) adversely affect the hydrolysis step,[46] but less information is available concerning the factors that affect metabolism of free fatty acids and glycerol.

If the lipid emulsion is infused at a rate that is equal to or less than the rate of hydrolysis, a dramatic change in plasma triglyceride concentration reflecting accumulation of the infused triglyceride emulsion is unlikely. However, if the rate of infusion exceeds the rate of hydrolysis, plasma triglyceride concentration will rise and the adverse effects of elevated triglyceride concentrations on pulmonary diffusion[48,49] and polymorphonuclear leukocyte function[50,51] may be seen. Moreover, if the rate of hydrolysis exceeds the rate at which the released free fatty acids are oxidized, the plasma concentration of free fatty acids will increase. Since free fatty acids displace bound bilirubin from albumin,[52] this possibility is of some concern in infants with hyperbilirubinemia. Unfortunately, the concentration of free fatty acids likely to result in displacement of albumin-bound bilirubin in vivo is not known.[46]

It has been suggested that low plasma carnitine concentrations, commonly observed in infants and adults (see preceding discussion) receiving carnitine-free parenteral nutrition regimens,[35,53] may inhibit fatty acid oxidation. However, most trials of the effect of carnitine supplementation show no effect on

Table 15.3. Composition (Amount/Liter) of Representative Parenteral Lipid Emulsions

Component	Soybean Oil Emulsion*	Soybean/Safflower Oil Emulsion†
Soybean oil (g)	100‡	50‡
Safflower oil (g)	—	50‡
Egg yolk phospholipid (g)	12	up to 12
Glycerol (g)	22.5	25
Fatty acids (% of total):		
16:0	10	8.8
18:0	3.5	3.4
18:1	26	17.7
18:2	50	65.8
18:3	9	4.2
Particle size (microns)	0.5	0.4

*Intralipid (Kabi-Vitrum, Sweden).

†Liposyn II (Abbott Laboratories, N. Chicago, Ill).

‡20% emulsions also are available; these contain twice as much of the oils but roughly the same amounts of all other ingredients (see text).

fatty acid oxidation.[54,55] One exception is the study of Helms et al.,[56] which shows that carnitine supplementation following a prolonged period of carnitine-free parenteral nutrition improves fatty acid oxidation.

Based on the linoleic acid content of soybean oil (i.e., approximately 50%), the amount of the soybean oil emulsion necessary to prevent linoleic acid deficiency (i.e., 2% to 4% of total energy intake) is approximately 0.5 g/kg/day, a dose that is likely to be tolerated by almost all infants. Since the linoleic acid content of safflower oil is approximately 50% higher than that of soybean oil, an even smaller dose of the safflower plus soybean oil emulsion should provide the linoleic acid requirement. A previously available emulsion of safflower oil, which contains little or no linolenic acid, was associated with linolenic acid deficiency[57] but, so far as is known, both types of emulsions currently available in the United States contain an adequate, although perhaps not optimal, amount of linolenic acid (see subsequent discussion).

A prudent approach for use of the currently available lipid emulsions in LBW infants is to limit intake initially to 0.5 g/kg/day, particularly in infants who are likely to experience difficulties hydrolyzing the emulsions and in those with hyperbilirubinemia. Subsequently, as tolerance of the emulsion is demonstrated and/or hyperbilirubinemia resolves, the amount can be increased. This approach is common in clinical practice but it appears to be based on the assumption that slow introduction of the lipid emulsion increases the recipient infant's ability to utilize the infused lipid. The data of Brans et al.[58] suggest that this assumption is not valid. They show, instead, that plasma triglyceride and free fatty acid concentrations of LBW infants receiving parenteral lipid emulsions, regardless of the method or duration of lipid infusion, are a function of the amount of emulsion administered over a given time. In this study, plasma triglyceride and free fatty acid concentrations were acceptable if the dose of emulsion did not exceed 0.08 to 0.12 g/kg/h, or 2 to 3 g/kg/day.

Although there appears to be little physiological reason to gradually increase the dose of lipid emulsion over several days, gradual introduction, nonetheless, is more prudent in the smaller infant, the small-for-gestational-age infant, or the infant who is infected or experiencing other complications associated with delayed triglyceride hydrolysis. In such infants, the graded introduction permits assessment of lipid tolerance before the next increase in dose.

Parenteral Intakes of Other Nutrients. The electrolyte content of parenteral nutrition regimens has always been the same as that of maintenance parenteral fluid regimens (i.e., approximately 3 mmol/kg/day of sodium and chloride, and 2 mmol/kg/day of potassium) and, indeed, these intakes seem to be appropriate for most stable, growing infants.[59] Very small LBW infants, however, may require lesser or greater intakes of sodium to maintain a normal plasma sodium concentration (see Chapter 11), and nutritionally depleted infants may require greater potassium intakes to maintain a normal plasma potassium concentration. In all infants, frequent monitoring of plasma electrolyte concentrations and appropriate reformulation of the nutrient infusate in order to maintain normal plasma electrolyte concentrations is recommended, particularly during the first few days of parenteral nutrition.

The recommended parenteral intakes of phosphorus (i.e., 1.4 to 2.0 mmol/kg/day) and magnesium (i.e., 3 to 6 mg/kg/day) were established in the same manner as the recommended electrolyte intakes. These intakes, too, appear to maintain "normal" plasma phosphorus and magnesium concentrations in most infants. However, frequent monitoring of the plasma concentration of both and, if indicated, appropriate reformulation of the infusate are recommended.

Because of the insolubility of calcium phosphate, most commonly used parenteral nutrition regimens, although they maintain "normal" calcium concentration, do not provide an adequate calcium intake. Hence, osteopenia, rickets, and collapsed vertebrae have been reported in both LBW and term infants who require parenteral nutrition as their sole source of nutrient intake for prolonged periods.[60,61] The fetus deposits ~ 100 mg (2.5 mmol/kg/day) of calcium[62] during the last trimester of gestation but, until recently, it was impossible to provide more than half this amount (i.e., 40 to 60 mg [1 to 1.5 mmol/kg/day]) parenterally unless the phosphorus intake was lowered sufficiently to result in hypophosphatemia.

The lower pH of some of the newer amino acid mixtures permits administration of more calcium without sacrificing phosphorus intake. Koo et al.[63] studied the effects of regimens containing 25 IU/dL of vitamin D and either 0.5 or 1.5 to 2.0 mmol/dL of calcium and phosphorus. Serum 1,25-dihydroxy-D concentrations of the high calcium/phosphorus group were stable and within the normal range; tubular reabsorption of phosphorus also was stable and consistently <90%. Serum 1,25-dihydroxy-D concentrations of the low calcium/phosphorus group, on the other hand, were high, and tubular reabsorption of phosphorus was consistently >90%. Thus it appears that delivery of calcium and phosphorus intakes approaching those required to achieve intrauterine accretion rates exerts less stress on calcium and phosphorus homeostatic mechanisms than delivery of smaller intakes. A recent study[64] suggests that higher parenteral calcium and phosphorus intakes also result in more optimal skeletal mineralization although, interestingly, serum alkaline phosphatase activity of the two groups studied by Koo et al.[63] did not differ.

A peculiarity of calcium phosphate is its greater solubility at cooler temperatures. This peculiarity raises serious concerns about the overall safety of recently advocated three-in-one or ''complete'' parenteral nutrition infusates that contain glucose, amino acids, and the lipid emulsion along with required electrolytes, minerals, and vitamins in the same bottle. These infusates must be administered without an in-line filter, and presence of lipid in the infusate obscures any precipitate of calcium phosphate that may occur upon removal from refrigeration and warming prior to administration or during infusion; therefore, use of these infusates in LBW infants, particularly those for whom efforts are being made to maximize calcium and phosphate intakes, seems unwise.

Vitamin mixtures for parenteral use have been available since the early days of parenteral nutrition and have been used to formulate parenteral nutrition infusates. Hence, the amounts provided were (and are) determined to a large extent by the preparations available. During the early years of parenteral nutrition, it was thought that frequent plasma and/or blood transfusions provided needed trace minerals. Reports of zinc and copper deficiencies, even in infants who had received these transfusions, demonstrated the inadequacy of this approach and led to the availability of zinc and copper additives. Today, additives of all trace minerals for which a deficiency has been demonstrated are available. However, little definitive information is available concerning the parenteral requirements of either trace minerals or vitamins. Research concerning the parenteral requirements of these nutrients by infants, of course, is hindered by the difficulties both of measuring plasma concentrations of the nutrients using small volumes of plasma and of interpreting the physiological significance of plasma concentrations. Accurate studies of the retention of these nutrients also are notoriously difficult. The current recommendations for parenteral vitamin and trace mineral intakes[65] (Tables 15.4 and 15.5) are based on the most reliable information available, much of it theoretical, rather than data from randomized trials of various intakes.

Strategies for Improving Tolerance of Parenterally Delivered Nutrients

Many LBW infants, particularly smaller infants and infants with a variety of medical problems, are unable to tolerate appreciable amounts of many nutrients. However, even during the first several days of life, most will tolerate an amino acid intake of 1.2 to

---

Table 15.4. Suggested Parenteral Intakes of Vitamins*

Vitamin	(Amount/kg/day)[†]
Vitamin A (μg)[‡]	280–500
Vitamin E (mg)	2.8
Vitamin K (μg)	100
Vitamin D (μg)	4
(IU)	160
Ascorbic acid (mg)	25
Thiamine (μg)	350
Riboflavin (μg)	150
Pyridoxine (μg)	180
Niacin (mg)	6.8
Pantothenate (mg)	2
Biotin (μg)	6
Folate (μg)	56
Vitamin B$_{12}$ (μg)	0.3

*Data from Greene et al.[65]

†Total daily dose should not exceed amounts provided by 5 mL of reconstituted M.V.I. Pediatric (see notes to Table 15.1) 700 μg vitamin A, 7 μg vitamin E, 200 μg vitamin K, 10 μg vitamin D, 80 mg ascorbic acid, 1.2 mg thiamine, 1.4 mg riboflavin, 1.0 mg pyridoxine, 17 mg niacin, 5 mg pantothenic acid, 20 μg biotin, 140 μg folic acid, 1 μg vitamin B$_{12}$.

‡Infants with lung disease may benefit from higher doses (see Chapter 6).

Table 15.5. Recommended Parenteral Intakes of Trace Minerals*

Trace Mineral	Preterm Infants (μg/kg/day)(μmol/kg/day)[†]
Zinc	400 (6.1)
Iron	200 (3.6)
Copper	15–20 (0.24–0.31)
Selenium	1.5–2 (0.020–0.025)
Manganese	1.0 (0.018)
Iodide	1.0 (0.008)
Molybdenum	0.25 (0.003)
Chromium	0.20 (0.004)

*If parenteral nutrients are used as a supplement to tolerated enteral feedings or as the sole source of nutrients for <2 weeks, only zinc is needed. (Data from Greene et al.[65])

[†]For all nutrients, the amount/kg/day expressed in the most commonly used units is followed by the amount expressed in alternative units.

1.5 g/kg/day, a glucose intake of 5 g/kg/day, and a lipid intake of 1 g/kg/day. This combination provides about 40 kcal/kg/day, at least 90% of which is retained. While this intake is somewhat less than required for positive energy balance, it almost certainly will result in nitrogen equilibrium, if not a positive nitrogen balance. A 5% to 10% glucose and electrolyte infusion, on the other hand, will definitely result in negative nitrogen balance equivalent to a daily loss of about 1% of endogenous protein stores.[22,25] Equally important, neither marked hyperaminoacidemia nor azotemia is likely with the suggested regimen containing amino acids.

According to Collins et al.,[66] the glucose intolerance of most LBW infants can be alleviated by careful administration of insulin that permits delivery of considerably greater intakes of glucose. Moreover, in these investigators' hands, insulin administration did not result in hypoglycemia or other problems. Even though use of insulin may be safe, some question the advisability of using it routinely to circumvent what can best be described as physiological insulin resistance rather than insulin deficiency (see Chapter 16).

Infusion of 20% versus 10% lipid emulsions appears to lessen the likelihood of hyperlipidemia.[67] The mechanism, most likely, is related to the lower phospholipid:triglyceride ratio of the 20% versus the 10% emulsion and, hence, less inhibition of lipoprotein lipase activity secondary to infused phospholipid.[68] Although not available in the United States, emulsions containing medium-chain triglycerides are being used with increasing frequency in other parts of the world. Since the triglycerides of these emulsions are hydrolyzed more rapidly by lipoprotein lipase[69]

and the medium-chain fatty acids released are oxidized more rapidly,[70] they may permit safe administration of larger parenteral doses of lipid than is possible with conventional emulsions.

For most LBW infants, some combination of the strategies just discussed makes it relatively easy to achieve reasonable intakes of most nutrients within the first 24 to 48 hours of life. While definitive data are lacking, this approach appears preferable to the common practice of ignoring nutritional needs for the first several days after birth.

Complications of Parenteral Nutrition

The complications of total parenteral nutrition can be classified into two general categories: (1) those related to the technique, particularly the presence of an indwelling catheter (infusion-related complications), and (2) those related to composition of the infusate (metabolic complications).

The major infusion-related complication is infection. Although many of the infusate components support growth of various microorganisms,[71,72] a contaminated infusate rarely is the underlying cause of infection. Most infections appear to result either from improper care of the catheter, particularly failure to follow meticulously the requirement for frequent changes of the catheter exit site dressing, or frequent use of the catheter for purposes other than delivery of the nutrient infusate. Other complications related to the technique of infusion include malposition, dislodgment, and thrombosis, including superior (or inferior) vena cava thrombosis. Malposition can be avoided by radiographic confirmation of the location of the catheter tip prior to infusion of the hypertonic nutrient infusate and reconfirmation as indicated thereafter. The other complications in this category cannot be completely avoided; however, it is widely believed that careful attention to all procedures involving the catheter will reduce their incidence to an acceptable level.

Infusion-related complications associated with peripheral vein delivery of nutrients include thrombophlebitis as well as skin and subcutaneous sloughs secondary to infiltration of the hypertonic infusate. Infection appears to be much less common with peripheral than with central vein delivery, probably because infusion sites must be changed so frequently.

The metabolic complications of parenteral nutrition can be subdivided into three categories: (1) those related to the patient's limited metabolic capacity for the various components of the infusate; (2) those related to the infusate per se; and (3) those related to the fact that nutrients are administered by vein rather than by the gastrointestinal tract. (These complications are summarized in Table 15.6.) Metabolic complications related to the patient's metabolic tolerance of the infusate are likely to be less with the less concentrated

peripheral vein regimens. Certainly, glucose intolerance is less frequent with peripheral vein delivery, which limits glucose intake to about 15 g/kg/day. Electrolyte and mineral disorders usually result from provision of either too much or too little of the particular nutrient, although electrolyte disorders also can result from hyperglycemia and attendant osmotic diuresis.

Since infusates delivered by central vein and peripheral vein are qualitatively similar, metabolic complications related to the infusate are similar with the two routes of delivery. One of the major concerns in this category is related to the fact that none of the currently available amino acid mixtures results in a completely normal plasma amino acid pattern.[30] In part, this concern is based on the long-recognized coexistence of mental retardation and elevated plasma concentrations of specific amino acids in patients with inborn errors of metabolism (e.g., hyperphenylalaninemia in patients with phenylketonuria). However, in patients receiving parenteral nutrition the plasma concentration of many amino acids is low rather than high, suggesting that the intake of these amino acids may be inadequate. As discussed,

Table 15.6. Metabolic Complications of Parenteral Nutrition and Their Most Common Cause(s)

Disorder	Most Common Cause(s)
1. Disorders Related to Metabolic Capacity of Patient:	
Hyperglycemia	Excessive intake relative to infant's metabolic capacity: either excessive concentration or excessive infusion rate (e.g., pump dysfunction); change in metabolic state (e.g., infection)
Hypoglycemia	Sudden cessation of infusion; inappropriate use of insulin
Azotemia	Excessive nitrogen intake
Electrolyte, mineral, and vitamin disorders	Excessive or inadequate intake
Hypertriglyceridemia; elevated free fatty acid concentration	Excessive lipid emulsion relative to patient's metabolic capacity (see text)
2. Disorders Related to Infusate Composition:	
Abnormal plasma	
Aminograms	Amino acid pattern of nitrogen source
Hypercholesterolemia/phospholipidemia	Characteristics of lipid emulsion
Abnormal fatty acid pattern	Characteristics of lipid emulsion or its route of metabolism
3. Disorders Related to Parenteral Delivery:	
GI tract development	See text
Hepatic disorders	See text

plasma concentrations of the possibly indispensable amino acids cysteine and tyrosine are quite low, presumably because these amino acids are either unstable or insoluble in aqueous solution and, therefore, are not present in appreciable amounts in available parenteral amino acid mixtures.

In animals, the abnormal plasma amino acid pattern associated with administration of parenteral nutrition regimens is accompanied by an abnormal tissue amino acid pattern.[73] Although this relationship is not necessarily a direct one, the abnormal plasma and tissue amino acid patterns are of concern with respect to possible adverse effects on ongoing protein synthesis. They also raise theoretical concerns regarding the relationship between plasma concentrations of specific amino acids and concentration of various neurotransmitters within the central nervous system (CNS), (e.g., plasma tryptophan concentration and CNS serotonin, plasma tyrosine concentration and CNS catecholamines, and plasma concentrations of amino acids that may function as neurotransmitters as well as CNS concentration of that amino acid). Unfortunately, this relationship has not been studied sufficiently to warrant major concern or to allay fears.

Many of the metabolic problems related to use of available parenteral lipid emulsions are better understood than those related to available parenteral amino acid mixtures (see preceding discussion).[46] Perhaps the most pressing concern is related to the fatty acid pattern of these emulsions. These emulsions contain adequate amounts of linoleic and linolenic acids, which are the parent fatty acids, respectively, of the n-6 and n-3 fatty acid series, but none of the longer chain, more unsaturated fatty acids of either series (Table 15.7). Although adults can convert the parent fatty acids to the longer chain, polyunsaturated fatty acids,[74] the activity of the various desaturases and elongases required for this conversion may not be fully developed in infants. In addition, in both adults

and infants, fatty acids of the two series compete for the same desaturases and elongases which appear to prefer the n-3 fatty acids. Thus both the absence of long-chain, polyunsaturated fatty acids and the ratio of linoleic to linolenic acid in available parenteral lipid emulsions raise at least theoretical concerns. Furthermore, the validity of some of these concerns has been confirmed in enterally fed infants.[75,76]

Since appreciable amounts of the longer chain, more unsaturated members of both the ω-3 and ω-6 fatty acid families accumulate during development,[77,78] particularly in the developing CNS (Table 15.7), the possibility that the infant cannot convert the parent fatty acids of either family to the longer chain, more unsaturated derivatives gives rise to concern regarding the fatty acid pattern of tissue lipids. Indeed, the long-chain, polyunsaturated fatty acid content of both the liver and brain of infants who succumb after receiving only parenteral nutrition reportedly is low compared to that of normal infants.[79] Whether such an abnormal pattern is associated with functional abnormalities remains unknown. However, recent studies in enterally fed infants[80,81] show that development of retinal function and visual acuity is slower in infants fed formulas containing only vegetable oils than in infants fed the same formula supplemented with long-chain, polyunsaturated ω-3 fatty acids.

Some of the elongated, desaturated derivatives of linoleic and linolenic acids are precursors of the various prostaglandin series. Thus, if the precursors cannot be formed or are formed in inappropriate ratios to each other, infants receiving available lipid emulsions, theoretically, may develop derangements in prostaglandin metabolism secondary to specific long-chain, polyunsaturated fatty acid deficiencies. Indeed, the arachidonic acid content of serum lipids decreases in infants who receive the available soybean oil emulsion. Urinary excretion of a stable metabolite of prostaglandin E, which is synthesized

Table 15.7. Accretion of n-6 and n-3 Fatty Acids in the Developing Human Brain*

Fatty Acid	Prenatal (mg/week)	Postnatal (mg/week)
Total n-6	31	78
18:2	<1	2
20:4	19	45
Total n-3	15	4
18:3	181	149

*Data from Clandinin et al.[77,78]

from arachidonic acid, is also very low in these infants.[82] Although these abnormalities have not been associated with clinical abnormalities, they are disturbing. To date, however, they have received very little attention.

The final subcategory of metabolic problems resulting from parenteral nutrition probably is related to bypassing of the gastrointestinal tract. Since the one unquestioned clinical indication for use of parenteral nutrition is to maintain or restore the nutritional status of patients with deranged gastrointestinal function, there has been considerable interest in the consequences of this therapy with respect to gastrointestinal function. In normal animals, parenteral nutrition, like starvation, results in an appreciable decrease in enteric mucosal mass.[83–85] However, parenteral nutrition following a period of starvation prevents a further decrease in mucosal mass, although it does not support regrowth of the enteric mucosa as occurs in animals that are refed (Mones RL, Heird WC, Rosensweig SN. Unpublished data). The effect of parenteral nutrition on mucosal enzyme activities is unclear. Some studies suggest that the specific activity of some disaccharidases decreases relative to that of control animals[83]; others suggest that the specific activity of these enzymes does not differ between control animals and animals receiving parenteral nutrition.[84] These discrepancies may be related to the nature of the diet consumed by the control animals in the different studies. Interestingly, none of the available clinical studies of the effects of parenteral nutrition on intestinal tract structure and function demonstrate morphological involution.[86,87] However, disaccharidase activities, which usually are low when parenteral nutrition begins, are not fully restored until enteral intake is reinstituted.[87]

Many infants maintained solely on parenteral nutrition develop a typical clinical and histological picture of cholestasis.[88] Whether this results from a toxic effect of some component of the parenteral nutrition infusate or simply from bypassing the gastrointestinal tract is not clear. Various studies, none rigorously controlled, suggest a number of etiologies. Two randomized trials suggest that the cholestasis is related to parenteral amino acid intake.[89,90] In an uncontrolled study, infants receiving one of the newer parenteral amino acid mixtures had an incidence of cholestasis that was lower than expected.[91] A randomized trial of the effects of the same amount of amino acids with taurine versus no taurine revealed no effects of taurine on liver function during the first 10 days of life[92]; however, none of the infants in either group developed hepatic dysfunction. The results of another trial[93] suggest that cholestasis can be reduced by minimal enteral feeding. Since the release of a number of gastrointestinal hormones appears to be delayed by exclusive parenteral nutrition,[94] it might be particularly informative to determine if parenteral nutrition affects the release of cholecystokinin, which stimulates contraction of the gall bladder, and if development of cholestasis is related to the pattern of cholecystokinin release.

Minimizing the Complications of Parenteral Nutrition

The complications of parenteral nutrition can be minimized by a monitoring system that permits detection of both infusion-related and metabolic complications. It also is important to monitor the actual intake of specific nutrients rather than simply the volume of a standard infusate delivered. In addition, the clinical results of the intake delivered must be monitored carefully to realize the full potential of the technique. Adequate clinical monitoring to prevent infiltration of infusates delivered by peripheral vein and assure long-term function of the central vein catheters usually requires considerable time as well as personnel who are familiar with the intricacies of the intravenous infusion apparatus, including the many varieties of constant infusion pumps that are an absolute necessity both for central vein and peripheral vein delivery.

A suggested schedule for chemical monitoring is shown in Table 15.8. This schedule allows detection of metabolic complications in sufficient time to permit correction by altering the infusate. It differs somewhat from other suggested schedules; instead of routinely monitoring blood glucose concentration, as often suggested, checking urine regularly for glucose (at least three times daily, perhaps more frequently during the first few days of the technique) and determining blood glucose concentrations only when glucosuria is present appear to be adequate. This monitoring schedule also omits determinations of plasma osmolality which, in the absence of hyperglycemia, can be estimated with sufficient accuracy as twice the plasma sodium concentration. In addition, routine monitoring of the plasma amino acid pattern, which is predictable from the pattern of the mixture of amino acids used,[30] is omitted, as is routine monitoring of the leukocyte count and routine cultures.

The monitoring required to ensure safe and efficacious use of intravenous fat emulsions is somewhat problematic. The most common clinical practice (i.e., periodic visual or nephelometric inspection of the plasma for presence of lipemia) is not reliable for detecting elevated plasma concentrations of both triglyceride and free fatty acids[95]; accurate detection requires actual chemical determinations of both of these types of fatty acids. Since microtechniques for these assays are not routinely available or, if avail-

Table 15.8. Suggested Monitoring Schedule during Parenteral Nutrition

Variables to Be Monitored	Suggested Frequency (per week)*	
	Initial Period	Later Period
Growth Variables:		
Weight	7	7
Length	1	1
Head circumference	1	1
Metabolic Variables:		
Blood or plasma		
Electrolytes	2–4	1
Ca, Mg, P	2	1
Acid base status	2	1
Urea nitrogen	2	1
Albumin	1	1
Liver function studies	1	1
Lipids†		
Hemoglobin	2	1
Urine glucose	2–6/day	2/day
Prevention and Detection of Infection:		
Clinical observations (activity, temperature)	Daily	Daily
White blood count and differential	As indicated	As indicated
Cultures	As indicated	As indicated

*"Initial Period" refers to the time before full intake is achieved as well as any period during which metabolic instability is present or suspected (e.g., postoperative period, presence of infection). "Later Period" refers to the time during which the patient is in a metabolic steady state and desired nutrient intakes have been achieved. In general, the schedule suggested for the "initial period" is appropriate for the transitional period and that suggested for the "later period" is appropriate for the stable, growing infant.

†See text.

able, are performed only two or three times per week, such monitoring is not practical. A reasonable compromise is to inspect the plasma frequently, either visually or by nephelometry, and to determine actual triglyceride and free fatty acid concentrations once or twice weekly. Careful monitoring is particularly important during the first few days of parenteral nutrition and when the patient develops a clinical condition likely to interfere with triglyceride hydrolysis. Other serum lipid abnormalities associated with use of parenteral lipid emulsions (e.g., hypercholesterolemia, hyperphospholipidemia, and deranged free fatty acid patterns of serum and tissue lipids) are predictable and/or of uncertain clinical relevance; thus monitoring to detect these is not necessary.

Other Considerations

Some of the questions most commonly asked concerning parenteral nutrition include: (1) When should

the therapy be started? (2) How long should therapy be continued? (3) When should enterally delivered nutrients be introduced? Unfortunately, there are few definitive data on which to base answers to these questions. Thus it is not surprising that some nurseries routinely start parenteral nutrition soon after birth and continue this form of nutritional management exclusively for several days to weeks, while others start parenteral nutrition much later, with or without enterally delivered nutrients, and discontinue it as soon as possible.

In the authors' opinion, the question of when to start parenteral nutrients can be addressed, although not answered definitively. As discussed elsewhere, infants who receive only glucose lose at least 1% of endogenous nitrogen stores daily, whereas those who receive an isocaloric infusate containing amino acids are in positive nitrogen balance without marked hyperaminoacidemia or azotemia. Thus it is difficult to argue against a policy of starting a parenteral nutrition regimen containing amino acids as soon after birth as feasible, preferably within the first 24 to 48 hours.

Whether a policy of exclusive parenteral nutrition for some arbitrary period is advantageous is not clear. The issue has been addressed by two controlled trials.[96,97] In one,[96] 34 VLBW infants (birthweight <1,200 g) who survived the first 24 hours of life were assigned randomly to receive either total parenteral nutrition (glucose, amino acids, lipid, electrolytes, vitamins, and trace minerals infused through an umbilical artery or peripheral vein) or intermittent gavage feedings (fresh expressed milk from the baby's mother or a commercial formula) for a 2-week period. The enterally fed (control) group also received intravenous dextrose, water, and electrolytes as needed to maintain fluid and electrolyte homeostasis. Parenteral feeding, available as backup for infants who were assigned to the enterally fed group but did not tolerate enteral feedings, was required by 3 of the 14 surviving infants assigned to the control group. In the other trial,[97] 59 infants (birthweight, 750 to 1,500 g) were assigned alternately within the first 24 hours of life to receive either total parenteral nutrition or continuous transpyloric feeding (fresh expressed milk from the baby's mother or a commercial formula). In the parenteral feeding group, supplementary transpyloric milk feeds were introduced at a mean age of 7 days (range, 1 to 26 days). In the transpyloric feeding group, supplementary intravenous infusions of dextrose, water, and electrolytes were used, as needed, to maintain fluid and electrolyte homeostasis. Partial or full parenteral feeding was available as backup for the transpyloric group if full enteral nutrition could not be established by the seventh day of life, and was necessary in 10 of the 25 infants who were assigned to this group and survived the first week.

The results of these two trials show that exclusive parenteral nutrition for the first 1 to 2 weeks of life versus enteral feeding with parenteral feeding backup has no advantages with respect to acute survival. While such a policy may reduce the incidence of necrotizing enterocolitis, it appears to result in a greater incidence of conjugated hyperbilirubinemia, the usual biochemical marker of cholestasis.

Because of the concern that lack of enteral nutrients decreases secretion of gastrointestinal hormones and might impair intestinal tract development (see preceding discussion), the practice of minimal enteral feeding (i.e., infusion of 1 to 2 mL/kg/h of human milk or a standard formula) during the early days to weeks of life, when the bulk of nutrient intake is supplied by parenteral nutrients, currently is quite popular. The effects of this strategy have been tested in two randomized trials.[93,98] In each trial, the provision of 1 to 2 mL/kg/h of a standard infant formula or human milk led to earlier tolerance of full enteral intakes. However, this observation as well as other apparent benefits may be biased by the exclusion of infants who developed complications (including necrotizing enterocolitis which, in both trials, was more frequent in infants randomized to the minimal enteral feeding group).

Based on the information available, it is impossible to recommend a single strategy for use of parenteral nutrition in LBW neonates because: (1) early enteral feeding, even minimal enteral feeding, may contribute to development of necrotizing enterocolitis, and (2) prolonged use of exclusive parenteral feeding may contribute to development of cholestasis. Perhaps the most appropriate strategy is to individualize the early nutritional management of each infant. For example, those with a number of predisposing factors for development of necrotizing enterocolitis might receive only parenteral nutrients until some of these factors resolve, while those deemed less likely to develop necrotizing enterocolitis might be started on enteral feedings much earlier. Although many nurseries have standard policies for increasing the enteral intake of all infants, this aspect of feeding also is one that might best be determined on an individual basis.

Regardless of the method chosen for nutritional management, there inevitably is a period during which infants receive a combination of parenterally and enterally delivered nutrients. During this period, careful monitoring of the intake of each major nutrient received by each route is crucial if nutrient imbalances are to be avoided. Differences in likely retention of nutrients delivered parenterally versus enterally also must be considered.

When to stop parenteral nutrition is frequently debated. Usually, the time selected to do so is when sufficient enteral intake to supply minimal fluid requirements can be tolerated. Although this practice may result in nutrient intake being less than optimal for a few days, it seems reasonable, particularly if nutrient intake prior to this time has been adequate.

There is a major void in knowledge concerning the advantages, disadvantages, and costs of the various ways parenteral nutrition is managed at individual institutions. Current methods of management range from those that are very tightly controlled (i.e., only a few individuals supervise the parenteral nutrition program for all patients) to those in which any physician is allowed to order any regimen desired for any patient, with or without an assessment of the patient's need for parenteral nutrition and with or without requirements for monitoring either the efficacy or the safety of the particular regimen ordered. A system in which one of a few standard parenteral nutrition infusates can be ordered by any physician represents a common intermediate system for management of parenteral feeding.

This issue has been addressed by only one randomized, controlled study. Dice et al.[99] alternately assigned neonates requiring parenteral feeding to receive either a standardized formulation or an individualized formulation monitored by a pharmacist. The group assigned to the individualized formulation with pharmacist monitoring received higher intakes of amino acids (2.2 versus 1.9 g/kg/day), lipid (2 versus 1.5 g/kg/day), and total energy (63 versus 53 kcal/kg/day); this group also exhibited a greater rate of weight gain (11.8 versus 4.9 g/day). Although the total cost of the individualized system was approximately 40% greater, the cost per gram of weight gain was approximately 40% less. It also is important to note that this cost analysis included neither the cost of wasted solutions, which was greater in the standardized versus the individualized group, nor the cost of nursing time, which also was greater in the standardized group. The results of this study confirm earlier impressions that a centralized system of managing parenteral nutrition is most likely to both maximize benefits and minimize risks of the technique.[59] Nonetheless, more such studies are needed.

In fact, randomized, controlled studies assessing every aspect of parenteral nutrition are needed. Without the information that such studies can provide, decisions concerning many aspects of the therapy (e.g., catheter A versus catheter B, pump A versus pump B, amino acid mixture A versus amino acid B, policy A versus policy B) will continue to be made, frequently by administrators rather than professionals, on the basis of cost rather than efficacy. Obviously, this situation must change before the technique of parenteral nutrition can be improved beyond its current status. It no longer is sufficient to view the technique simply as one that permits provision of nutrients to infants who cannot be fed; rather, it must be viewed as a method of feeding that may permit better nutritional management but undoubtedly can be improved further. Additional data from carefully conducted, randomized trials are crucial for further improvements.

References

1. Helfrick FW, Abelson NM. Intravenous feeding of a complete diet in a child: a report of a case. *J Pediatr* 1944; 25:400–403.
2. Heird WC. Parenteral nutrition. In: Grand RJ, Sutphen JL, Dietz WH, Jr, eds. *Pediatric nutrition: theory and practice*. Boston: Butterworths, 1987:747–761.
3. Wilmore DM, Dudrick SJ. Growth and development of an infant receiving all nutrients by vein. *JAMA* 1968;203: 860–864.
4. Filler RM, Eraklis AJ, Rubin VG, Das JB. Long-term parenteral nutrition in infants. *N Engl J Med* 1969;281:589–594.
5. Heird WC, Driscoll JM Jr, Schullinger JN, et al. Intravenous alimentation in pediatric patients. *J Pediatr* 1972;80: 351–372.
6. Keating JP, Ternberg JL. Amino acid-hypertonic glucose treatment for intractable diarrhea in infants. *Am J Dis Child* 1971;122:226–228.
7. Driscoll JM Jr, Heird WC, Schullinger JN, et al. Total intravenous alimentation in low birth weight infants: a preliminary report. *J Pediatr* 1972;81:145–153.
8. Peden VH, Karpel JT. Total parenteral nutrition in premature infants. *J Pediatr* 1972;81:137–144.
9. Hack M, Horbar JD, Malloy MH, et al. Very low birth weight outcomes of the National Institutes of Child Health and Human Development Neonatal Network. *Pediatrics* 1991;87:587–597.
10. Jacobowski D, Ziegler MD, Perreira G. Complications of pediatric parental nutrition: central versus peripheral administration [Abstract]. *J Parent Ent Nutr* 1979;3:29.
11. Shaw JCL. Parenteral nutrition in the management of sick low birth weight infants. *Pediatr Clin of North Am.* 1973;20:333–358.
12. Morgan WW, Harkins GW. Percutaneous introduction of long term indwelling vascular catheters in infants. *J Pediatr Surg* 1972;7:583.
13. Shulman RJ, Pokorny WJ, Martin CG, et al. Comparison of percutaneous and surgical placement of central venous catheters in neonates. *J Pediatr Surg* 1986;21:348–350.
14. Nakamura KT, Sato Y, Erenberg A. Evaluation of a percutaneously placed 27-gauge central venous catheter in neonates weight <1200 grams. *JPEN* 1990;14:295–299.
15. Chathas MK, Paton JB, Fisher DE. Percutaneous central venous catheterization. *Am J Dis Child* 1990;144: 1246–1250.
16. Friedman Z, Danon A, Stahlman MT, et al. Rapid onset of essential acid deficiency in the newborn. *Pediatrics* 1976; 58:640–649.
17. Committee on Nutrition, American Academy of Pediatrics. Use of intravenous fat emulsions in pediatric patients. *Pediatrics* 1981;68:738–743.
18. Jeejeebhoy KN, Chu RC, Marliss EB, et al. Chromium deficiency, glucose intolerance, and neuropathy reversed by chromium supplementation, in a patient receiving long-term total parenteral nutrition. *Am J Clin Nutr* 1977;30: 531–538.
19. Kien CL, Ganther HE. Manifestations of chronic selenium deficiency in a child receiving total parenteral nutrition. *Am J Clin Nutr* 1983;37:319–328.
20. Abumrad NN, Schneider AJ, Steel D, et al. Amino acid intolerance during prolonged total parenteral nutrition reversed by molybdate therapy. *Am J Clin Nutr* 1981;34: 2551–2559.
21. Zlotkin SH, Bryan MH, Anderson GH. Intravenous nitrogen and energy intakes required to duplicate in utero nitrogen accretion in prematurely born human infants. *J Pediatr* 1981;99:115–120.
22. Anderson TL, Muttart C, Bieber MA, et al. A controlled trial of glucose vs glucose and amino acids in premature infants. *J Pediatr* 1979;94:947–951.
23. Rivera A, Jr, Bell EF, Stegink LD, Ziegler EE. Plasma amino acid profiles during the first three days of life in infants with respiratory distress syndrome: effect of parenteral amino acid supplementation. *J Pediatr* 1989;115: 465–468.
24. Saini J, MacMahon P, Morgan JB, Kovar IZ. Early parenteral feeding of amino acids. *Arch Dis Child* 1989;64: 1362–1366.
25. Kashyap S. Nutritional management of the extremely low-birth-weight infant. In: Cowett RM, Hay WW, eds. *The micropremie: the next frontier.* Report of the 99th Ross Conference on Pediatric Research. Columbus, OH: Ross Laboratories, 1990:115–122.

26. Pencharz PB, Stefee WP, Cochran W, et al. Protein metabolism in human neonates: nitrogen-balance studies, estimated obligatory losses of nitrogen and whole-body turnover of nitrogen. *Clin Sci Mol Med* 1977;52:485–498.

27. Duffy B, Gunn T, Collinge J, et al. The effect of varying protein quality and energy intake on the nitrogen metabolism of parenterally fed very low birth weight (1600 g) infants. *Pediatr Res* 1981;15:1040–1044.

28. Helms RA, Christensen ML, Mauer EC, et al. Comparison of a pediatric versus standard amino acid formulation in preterm neonates requiring parenteral nutrition. *J Pediatr* 1987;110:466–472.

29. Snyderman SE. The protein requirements of the premature infant. In: Jonxis JHP, Visser HKA, Troelsta JA, eds. *Metabolic processes in the fetus and newborn infant*. Leiden, The Netherlands: Stenfert Kruesse, 1971:128–141.

30. Winters RW, Heird WC, Dell RB, et al. Plasma amino acids in infants receiving parenteral nutrition. In: Greene HL, Holliday MA, Munro HN, eds. *Clinical nutrition update: amino acids*. Chicago: American Medical Association, 1977:147–154.

31. Sturman JA, Gaull GA, Räihä, NCR. Absence of cystathionase in human liver: is cystine essential? *Science* 1970;169:74–76.

32. Gaull GE, Sturman JA, Räihä NCR. Development of mammalian sulfur metabolism: absence of cystathionase in human fetal tissues. *Pediatr Res* 1972;6:538–547.

33. Zlotkin SH, Anderson GH. The development of cystathionase activity during the first year of life. *Pediatr Res* 1982;16:65–68.

34. Räihä NCR. Phenylalanine hydroxylase in human liver during development. *Pediatr Res* 1973;7:1–4.

35. Chawla RK, Berry CJ, Kutner MH, et al. Plasma concentrations of transsulfuration pathway products during nasoenteral and intravenous hyperalimentation of malnourished patients. *Am J Clin Nutr* 1985;42:577–584.

36. Zlotkin SH, Bryan MH, Anderson GH. Cysteine supplementation to cysteine-free intravenous feeding regimens in newborn infants. *Am J Clin Nutr* 1981;34:914–923.

37. Malloy MH, Rassin DK, Richardson CJ. Total parenteral nutrition in sick preterm infants: effects of cysteine supplementation with nitrogen intakes of 240 & 400 mg/kg/d. *J Pediatr Gastroenterol Nutr* 1984;3:239–244.

38. Heird WC, Hay W, Helms RA, et al. Pediatric parenteral amino acid mixture in low birth weight infants. *Pediatrics* 1988;81:41–50.

39. Weinstein MR, Oh W. Oxygen consumption in infants with bronchopulmonary dysplasia. *J Pediatr* 1981;99:958–961.

40. Munro HN. General aspects of the regulation of protein metabolism by diet and hormone. In: Munro HN, ed. *Mammalian protein metabolism. Vol. 1: Biochemical aspects of protein metabolism*. New York: Academic Press, 1964:381–481.

41. Pineault M, Chessex P, Bisaillon S, et al. Total parenteral nutrition in the newborn: impact of the quality of infused energy on nitrogen metabolism. *Am J Clin Nutr* 1988;47:298–304.

42. Jeejeebhoy KN, Anderson GK, Nakhooda AF, et al. Metabolic studies in total parenteral nutrition with lipid in man: comparison with glucose. *J Clin Invest* 1976;57:125–136.

43. Long JM III, Wilmore DW, Mason AD, Jr, et al. Effect of carbohydrate and fat intake on nitrogen excretion during total intravenous feeding. *Ann Surg* 1977;185:417–422.

44. Bresson JL, Bader B, Rocchiccioli F, et al. Protein-metabolism kinetics and energy-substrate utilization in infants fed parenteral solutions with different glucose-fat ratios. *Am J Clin Nutr* 1991;54:370–376.

45. Kashyap S, Ramikrishnan R, Heird WC. Effect of concomitant energy (E) intake on nitrogen (N) retention of low birth weight (LBW) infants. *Pediatr Res* 1991;29:298A.

46. Heird WC. Lipid metabolism in parenteral nutrition. In: Fomon SJ, Heird WC, eds. *Energy and protein needs during infancy*. New York: Academic Press, 1986:215–229.

47. Andrew G, Chan G, Schiff D. Lipid metabolism in the neonate. I. The effect of intralipid infusion on plasma triglyceride and free fatty acid concentrations in the neonate. *J Pediatr* 1976;88:273–278.

48. Greene HL, Hazlett D, Demaree R. Relationship between intralipid-induced hyperlipidemia and pulmonary function. *Am J Clin Nutr* 1976;29:127–135.

49. Pereira GR, Fox WW, Stanley CA, et al. Decreased oxygenation and hyperlipidemia during intravenous fat infusions in premature infants. *Pediatrics* 1980;66:26–30.

50. Loo LS, Tang JP, Kohl S. The inhibition of leukocyte cellular cytotoxicity to herpes simplex virus in vitro and in vivo by intralipid. *J Infect Dis* 1982;146:64–70.

51. Cleary TC, Pickering LK. Mechanisms of intralipid effect on polymorphonuclear leukocytes. *J Clin Lab Immunol* 1983;11:21–26.

52. Odell GB, Cukier JO, Ostrea EM, Jr, et al. The influence of fatty acids on the binding of bilirubin to albumin. *J Clin Med* 1977;89:295–307.

53. Penn D, Schmidt-Sommerfeld E, Pascu F. Decreased carnitine concentration in newborn infants receiving total parenteral nutrition. *Early Hum Dev* 1979;4:23–28.

54. Schmidt-Sommerfeld E, Penn D, Wolf H. Carnitine deficiency in premature infants receiving total parenteral nutrition: effect of L-carnitine supplementation. *J Pediatr* 1983;102:931–935.

55. Orzali A, Donzelli F, Enzi G, et al. Effect of carnitine on lipid metabolism in the newborn. I. Carnitine supplementation during total parenteral nutrition in the first 48 hours of life. *Biol Neonate* 1983;43:186–190.

56. Helms RA, Whitington PF, Mauer EC, et al. Enhanced lipid utilization in infants receiving oral L-carnitine during long-term parenteral nutrition. *J Pediatr* 1986;109:984–988.

57. Holman RT, Johnson SB, Hatch TF. A case of human linolenic acid deficiency involving neurological abnormalities. *Am J Clin Nutr* 1982;35:617–623.

58. Brans YW, Andrew DS, Carrillo DW, et al. Tolerance of fat emulsions in very-low-birth-weight neonates. *Am J Dis Child* 1988;142:145–152.

59. Heird WC, Winters RW. Total parenteral nutrition: the state of the art. *J Pediatr* 1975;86:2–16.

60. Koo WWK, Tsang RC. Bone mineralization in infants. *Prog Food Nutr Sci* 1984;8:229–302.

61. Koo WWK, Tsang RC. Rickets in infants. In: Nelson NM, ed. *Current therapy in neonatal perinatal medicine*. Philadelphia: BC Decker, 1985:299–304.

62. Ziegler EE, O'Donnell AM, Nelson SE, et al. Body composition of the reference fetus. *Growth* 1986;40:329–341.

63. Koo WWK, Tsang RC, Steichen JJ, et al. Parenteral nutrition for infants: effect of high versus low calcium and phosphorus content. *J Pediatr Gastroenterol Nutr* 1987;6:96–104.

64. Prestridge LL, Schanler RJ, Shulman RJ, et al. Parenteral calcium and phosphorus intake early after birth affects long-term mineral retention and bone mineral content (BMC) in very low birth weight (VLBW) infants. *Pediatr Res* 1992;31:293A.

65. Greene HL, Hambidge KM, Schanler R, et al. Guidelines for the use of vitamins, trace elements, calcium, magnesium, and phosphorus in infants and children receiving total parenteral nutrition: report of the subcommittee on

pediatric parenteral nutrient requirements from the committee on clinical practice issues of the American Society for Clinical Nutrition. *Am J Clin Nutr* 1988;48: 1324–1342.

66. Collins JN, Hoope M, Brown K, et al. A controlled trial of insulin infusion in parenteral nutrition in extremely low birth weight infants with glucose intolerance. *J Pediatr* 1991;118:921–927.

67. Haumont D, Deckelbaum RJ, Richelle M, et al. Plasma lipid and plasma lipoprotein concentrations in low birth weight infants given parenteral nutrition with 20% compared to 10% Intralipid. *J Pediatr* 1989;115:787–793.

68. Fielding CJ. Human lipoprotein lipase inhibition of activity by cholesterol. *Biochim Biophys Acta* 1970;218:221–226.

69. Deckelbaum RJ, Hamilton J, Moser A, et al. Medium chain versus long chain triacylglycerol emulsion hydrolysis by lipoprotein lipase and hepatic lipase: implications for the mechanisms of lipase action. *Biochemistry* 1990; 29:1136–1142.

70. Paust H, Park W, Knoblach G, Keles T. Studies of fatty acid metabolism by ^{13}C-triglyceride infusion technique in children. In: Ahnefeld FW, Hartig W, Holm E, Kleinberger G, eds. *Klin Ern.* München, Germany: W Zuckschwerdt Verlag, 1988;34:127–140.

71. Goldman DA, Martin WT, Worthington JW. Growth of bacteria and fungi in total parenteral nutrition solutions. *Am J Surg* 1973;126:314–318.

72. McKee KT, Melly MA, Greene HL, et al. Gram-negative bacillary sepsis associated with use of lipid emulsion in parenteral nutrition. *Am J Dis Child* 1979;133:649–650.

73. Heird WC, Malloy MH. Brain composition of beagle puppies receiving total parenteral nutrition. In: Visser HKA, ed. *Nutrition and growth of the fetus and infant.* The Hague: Martinus Nijhoff, 1979:365–375.

74. Emken EA, Adlof RO, Rakoff H, Rohwedder WK. Metabolism of deuterium-labeled linolenic, linoleic, oleic, stearic and palmitic acid in human subjects. In: Baillie TA, Jones JR, eds. *Synthesis and applications of isotopically labeled compounds 1988.* Amsterdam: Elsevier Science Publishers, 1989:713–716.

75. Carlson SE, Rhodes PG, Ferguson MG. Docosahexaenoic acid status of preterm infants at birth and following feeding with human milk or formulas. *Am J Clin Nutr* 1986; 45:798–804.

76. Innis SM, Foote KD, Mackinnon MJ, King DJ. Plasma and red blood cell fatty acids of low birthweight infants fed their mother's expressed breast milk or preterm infant formula. *Am J Clin Nutr* 1990;51:994–1000.

77. Clandinin MT, Chappell JE, Leong S, et al. Intrauterine fatty acid accretion rates in human brain: implications for fatty acid requirements. *Early Hum Dev* 1980;4:121–129.

78. Clandinin MT, Chappell JE, Leong S, et al. Extrauterine fatty acid accretion in infant brain: implications for fatty acid requirements. *Early Hum Dev* 1980;4:131–138.

79. Martinez M, Ballabriga A. Effect of parenteral nutrition with high doses of linoleate on the developing human liver and brain. *Lipids* 1987;22:133–138.

80. Uauy RD, Birch DG, Birch EE, et al. Effect of dietary omega-3 fatty acids on retinal function of very-low-birthweight neonates. *Pediatr Res* 1990;28:485–492.

81. Carlson S, Cooke R, Werkman S, Peeples J. Docosahexaenoate (DHA) and eicosapentaenoate (EPA) supplementation of preterm infants: effects on phospholipid DHA and visual acuity [Abstract]. *FASEB J* 1989;3:A1056.

82. Friedman Z, Frolich JC. Essential fatty acids and the major urinary metabolites of the E prostaglandins in thriving ne-

onates and in infants receiving parenteral fat emulsions. *Pediatr Res* 1979;13:926–932.

83. Levine GM, Deren JJ, Steiger E, et al. Role of oral intake in maintenance of gut mass and disaccharidase activity. *Gastroenterology* 1974;67:975–982.

84. Johnson LR, Copeland EM, Dudrick SJ, et al. Structural and hormonal alterations in the gastrointestinal tract of parenterally fed rats. *Gastroenterology* 1975;68: 1177–1183.

85. Feldman EJ, Dowling RH, McNaughton J, et al. Effects of oral versus intravenous nutrition on intestinal adaptation after small bowel resection in the dog. *Gastroenterology* 1976;70:712–719.

86. Shwachman H, Lloyd-Still JD, Khaw KT, et al. Protracted diarrhea of infancy treated with intravenous alimentation. II. Studies of small intestinal biopsy results. *Am J Dis Child* 1973;125:365–368.

87. Greene HL, McCabe DR, Merenstein GB. Intractable diarrhea and malnutrition in infancy: changes in intestinal morphology and disaccharidase activities during treatment with total intravenous nutrition or oral elemental diets. *J Pediatr* 1975;87:695–704.

88. Merritt RJ. Cholestasis associated with total parenteral nutrition. *J Pediatr Gastroenterol Nutr* 1980;5:9–22.

89. Black DD, Suttle EA, Whitington PF, et al. The effect of short-term total parenteral nutrition on hepatic function in the human neonate: a prospective randomized study demonstrating alteration of hepatic canalicular function. *J Pediatr* 1981;99:445–449.

90. Brown MR, Thunberg BJ, Golub L, et al. Decreased cholestasis with enteral instead of intravenous protein in the very low-birth-weight infant. *J Pediatr Gastroenterol Nutr* 1989;9:21–27.

91. Heird WC, Dell RB, Helms RA, et al. Amino acid mixture designed to maintain normal plasma amino acid patterns in infants and children requiring parenteral nutrition. *Pediatrics* 1987;80:401–408.

92. Cooke RJ, Whitington PF, Kelts D. Effect of taurine supplementation on hepatic function during short-term parenteral nutrition in the premature infant. *J Pediatr Gastroenterol Nutr* 1984;3:234–238.

93. Dunn L, Hulman S, Weiner J, Kliegman R. Beneficial effects of early hypocaloric enteral feeding on neonatal gastrointestinal function: preliminary report of a randomized trial. *J Pediatr* 1988;112:622–629.

94. Lucas A, Bloom SR, Aynsley-Green A. Metabolic and endocrine effects of depriving preterm infants of enteral nutrition. *Acta Paediatr Scand* 1983;72:245–249.

95. Schreiner RL, Glick MR, Nordschow CD, et al. An evaluation of methods to monitor infants receiving intravenous lipids. *J Pediatr* 1979;94:197–200.

96. Yu VYH, James B, Hendry P, MacMahon RA. Total parenteral nutrition in very low birthweight infants: a controlled trial. *Arch Dis Child* 1979;54:653–661.

97. Glass EJ, Hume R, Lang MA, Forfar JO. Parenteral nutrition compared with transpyloric feeding. *Arch Dis Child* 1984;59:131–135.

98. Slagle TA, Gross SJ. Effect of early enteral substrate on subsequent feeding tolerance. *J Pediatr* 1988;113: 526–531.

99. Dice JE, Burckart GJ, Woo JT, Helms RA. Standardized versus pharmacist-monitored individualized parenteral nutrition in low-birth-weight infants. *Am J Hosp Pharm* 1981;8:1487–1489.

16. Conditions Requiring Special Nutritional Management

Patti J. Thureen

William W. Hay, Jr.

Reviewers: Edward Bell, Richard A. Ehrenkranz, Alan Lucas, Brian A. Wharton

In practice, nutritional management of preterm infants has been adapted to meet observed or anticipated unique requirements in certain special conditions. Little has been studied or written about such management; thus it is not surprising that practices vary considerably among newborn intensive care centers. In this chapter we shall focus arbitrarily on infants with seven conditions that appear to require special nutritional management:

1. *Extremely low-birthweight (ELBW)* infants with extreme immaturity (<1,000 g birthweight, <27 to 28 weeks gestation) and unique biology who require nutritional management that is adjusted or scaled to their needs on more than a weight-specific basis compared with older, more mature infants;
2. Infants with *necrotizing enterocolitis (NEC)*;
3. Infants with *short bowel syndrome (SBS)*, which is usually the result of surgical resection for NEC or anatomical anomalies;
4. Infants with *bronchopulmonary dysplasia (BPD)*;
5. Infants with *patent ductus arteriosus (PDA)*;
6. *Small-for-gestational-age (SGA)* infants who may have altered growth potential as well as nutritional deficits;
7. *Infants of diabetic mothers (IDMs)*.

There are, of course, many other infants who develop certain medical complications or diseases that require changes in the type and amount of nutrition (at least alterations in requirements are presumed). Such conditions include abnormal neuromuscular status following hypoxic-ischemic encephalopathy, congestive heart failure, sepsis, and drug intoxications or withdrawal, to name a few. Too little is known about the metabolism and thus requirements of nutrients in such conditions to profitably discuss, or even speculate about, recommended changes in nutritional management.

The Extremely Low-Birthweight Infant

As presented in Table 16.1, ELBW infants are unique creatures; they are not simply smaller infants. As a result, adjusting nutrient requirements simply on a body weight basis may be highly inaccurate. Compared with older, more mature infants, ELBW infants are markedly different in those biological and developmental factors that determine nutritional requirements: body composition, expected growth rate, metabolic rate, and the capacity for metabolic regulation. Unfortunately, there have been few attempts to quantify nutrient intakes in such infants or to measure the rates of metabolism and growth that the nutrients serve. Thus a rational (i.e., experimentally determined) basis for nutritional management of ELBW infants is not available, except by rather tenuous extrapolation from management practices used for larger, more mature infants. Nevertheless, much of the recent improvement in survival and health of ELBW infants has been accomplished with the adaptation (albeit extrapolated, arbitrary, and variable) of nutrient mixtures and feeding regimens used for larger and more mature infants.

Nutritional Goals

The optimal nutrition for ELBW infants is commonly debated but poorly defined. Traditionally, nutritional management has been used to mimic postnatally the rates of in utero fetal growth and nutrient accretion. Whether this method is optimal or even desirable is not clear. Postnatally, the infant quickly achieves an entirely different metabolic milieu from that of the fetus (distribution of water, hormonal influences, enzyme activity, etc.) and is exposed to many more stresses than the fetus. Comparable growth rates can be attained using a variety of different nutrient solutions, but whether these solutions will produce similar proportions of nutrient accretion has not been adequately determined. Actual nutrient content studies of human fetuses at different gestational ages are few in number, have analyzed small numbers of fetuses, and have used differing analytical techniques.[1,2] Also, they are commonly hampered by assumptions that fetuses of similar weights are of similar gestational age (and therefore comparable) or that gestational age dating is reliable.

243

Table 16.1. Conditions in ELBW Infants That May Require Special Nutritional Management

Low energy reserves (both carbohydrate and fat)

Higher metabolic rate (intrinsic due to a higher ratio of more metabolically active organs [brain, heart, liver] to bone and skeletal muscle)

Higher protein turnover rate (if matching the very high in utero growth rate)

Higher glucose needs for energy and brain requirements

Higher lipid requirements (if matching the in utero fat deposition rates)

Excessive evaporative rates from the immature skin

Excessive urinary water and solute losses (depending on intake)

Low rates of gastrointestinal peristalsis

Limited production of gut digestive enzymes and growth factors

Higher incidence of stressful events and unique responses to these stresses

Abnormal neurological outcome if not fed adequately

There are other goals for providing proper nutrition for ELBW infants. One is to meet fetal nutrient accretion rates as determined by direct measurement of net nutrient transfer rates from the placenta to the fetus in utero via the umbilical circulation. To date, however, these studies have been limited to nonhuman species. Another goal is to provide nutrition that prevents clinical nutritional deficiency states (i.e., rickets of prematurity, zinc enteropathy) and/or avoids complications that might be attributable to a suboptimal (though not necessarily subphysiological) nutrient level (i.e., vitamin E and prevention of intraventricular hemorrhage [IVH] or retinopathy of prematurity [ROP]).

It also can be argued that the best nutritional strategy for the ELBW infant is one which produces an infant with a favorable developmental outcome. Lucas et al.[3,4] have undertaken the most comprehensive studies to date aimed at measuring the effect of dietary intake on developmental outcome in preterm infants. The first report from these trials indicated that among 501 low-birthweight infants fed differing diets for a median of 30 days, the developmental quotient at 9 months of age was significantly lower in those infants fed unfortified donor breast milk than those fed preterm infant formula.[3] In a second study of 424 preterm infants fed either term infant formula or a nutrient-enriched preterm infant formula for a median of 4 weeks, follow-up at 18 months of age demonstrated moderate developmental impairment (particularly motor deficits) considerably more often in the infants fed term formula.[4] Unfortunately, this type of study will be very difficult to confirm, because the ELBW infant's course is a mine field of complications that can affect development; factoring

out these complications will require progressive studies of large numbers of very similar infants in many centers that practice common medical care for this unique group of infants.

Fetal Growth Rates and Growth Potential

In 1977 the American Academy of Pediatrics stated that the major goal of nutrition in premature infants should be "the optimal diet that supports a rate of growth approximating that of the third trimester of intrauterine life, without imposing stress on the developing metabolic and excretory system." Lacking sufficient data to contraindicate mimicking of in utero growth, attempting to achieve ex utero growth rates that parallel published fetal growth curves has become in many nurseries, by default, the method of tracking adequate nutrition. The first step in using this system to assess adequacy of growth is to assign a baseline gestational age using a combination of maternal pregnancy history, ultrasound dating,[5] and clinical gestational age assessment. The commonly used Ballard Score has recently been expanded to become the first system for assessing gestation in the extremely premature infant.[6] Use of this system allows infant growth to be tracked on one of several growth charts,[7–12] each of which is based on different populations.

On a weight-specific basis, growth rate actually declines over the second half of gestation (Fig. 16.1). Thus nutritional requirements for growth, when estimated from the weight of the fetus or newborn ELBW infant, are actually higher in the 24- to 28-week gestational age range. For this period, growth of total body weight can be approximated at 1.5% per day.[2] However, this figure does not take into account the

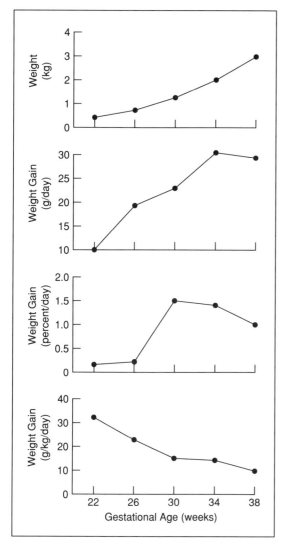

Fig. 16.1. Mean changes in weight and weight gain over the second half of gestation in human infants based on cross-sectional data at birth. (Reproduced, with permission, from Hay.[17] Adapted from data of Widdowson.[188])

change in composition of the fetus. Total water content of the fetus decreases from 90% at 20 weeks to 75% at term.[13] Cell number and size increase, with the ratio of intracellular to extracellular fluid volume increase changing from approximately 1:2 at 20 weeks to approximately 1:1 at term.[13] Fetal nitrogen content increases exponentially over time (Fig. 16.2). Studies in animal models (particularly in fetal sheep) indicate that both fractional protein synthetic and accretion rates decrease over gestation (Fig. 16.3). A similar situation is presumed to occur in the human fetus; in both sheep and humans, fetal skeletal muscle mass with relatively low protein synthetic rates increases significantly during gestation, while fetal or-

gans with higher protein synthetic rates (liver, brain, heart) grow more slowly.[14] Furthermore, unlike the placentas of most other species, the human placenta readily transports lipids to the fetus and allows for the progressive and unique accumulation of white fat (Fig. 16.2), resulting in a term fetus that is nearly 20% fat by body weight.[15]

As for mineral balance and mineral accretion, Tsang et al. have estimated the fetal accretion rate of calcium to be approximately 150 mg/kg/day, with a constant calcium:phosphorus ratio throughout pregnancy of 1.8:1.[16] It has been difficult, in fact nearly impossible, to provide this calcium accretion rate postnatally in ELBW infants, either enterally or intravenously.

The appropriateness of applying fetal nutrient accretion rates to the ELBW infant remains to be determined, but indirectly this process has been confirmed by noting empirically that higher weight-specific nutrient intakes are necessary to produce growth in such infants compared with older, more mature infants. For example, 3 to 4 g/kg/day of protein appear necessary to support the estimated in utero growth rate in healthy, growing, ELBW infants, compared with 1.5 to 2.5 g/kg/day for infants 34 to 40 weeks gestation.[17,18] This difference has led to the enrichment of preterm formulas to ≥2 g protein per 100 mL, while term infants grow normally using milk and formulas with only 1.2 to 1.5 g protein per 100 mL.

Fluid and Electrolyte Requirements

Fluid requirements are primarily determined by a combination of evaporative plus renal water losses, with fecal loss and water for growth making minimal contributions, particularly in the ELBW infant. Evaporative water loss is the major determinant of fluid needs in the ELBW infant and is highly variable among infants, depending on weight, maturity of the infant (Fig. 16.4), and the environment in which the infant is nursed. Respiratory evaporative losses can be minimized by providing warm, 100% humidified air or air/oxygen (O_2) mixed gas to the respiratory tract. Significant evaporation from the skin occurs in the ELBW infant because of a relatively large body surface area relative to body mass, a thin and permeable epidermis that lacks a protective keratin layer, and a large interstitial water pool that is exposed to evaporation.[19] Baumgart et al. determined evaporative water loss on an open radiant warmer to be 6 to 8 mL/kg/h for a typical infant weighing 750 g.[20] This loss can be reduced by providing humidity under a clear plastic blanket.[21] Evaporative losses are also lower in a humidified incubator, although access to a critically ill infant and maintenance of adequate temperature may preclude this form of nursing, at least in

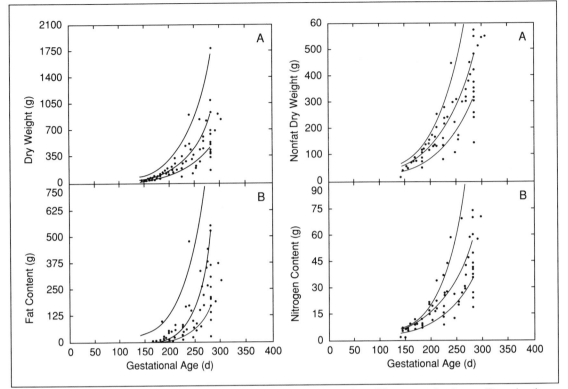

Fig. 16.2. Cross-sectional data of body composition of "normal" infants at birth at different gestational ages. (Reproduced, with permission, from Sparks.[2])

the first few days of life when evaporative losses are highest.[22] Minimizing water loss also decreases energy requirements for heat loss, because 0.58 kcal are utilized for each gram of water evaporated.

For the ELBW infant, the first 1 to several days of life often are marked by a low glomerular filtration rate (GFR), with oliguria and difficulty preventing the hypernatremic, hyperosmolar state that may accompany the evaporative losses.[23] Overhydration must be guarded against during this period. After 2 to 4 days of life there usually is a several-day period of massive urine output (6 to 9 mL/kg/h) associated with high urine sodium (and other electrolyte and mineral) losses of up to 4 to 8 mEq/kg/day. Over this period, a significant weight loss secondary to urinary excretion of the relatively large extracellular fluid volume and its contents is anticipated. Although some nurseries consider up to a 20% weight loss to be within acceptable limits,[19] most tend to take a more conservative approach and titrate fluid intake to keep weight loss during this period between 5% and 10% of birthweight. The authors of Chapters 1 and 11 make cogent arguments that until the "excess" extracellular fluid and its contents are removed from the body, renal function will remain responsive to the relative hypervolemia and produce a high urine flow

rate with large electrolyte losses. Thereafter, the infant seems to have a more normal regulation of both urine volume and electrolyte output.

Clearly, uniform fluid recommendations cannot be made for the ELBW infant, particularly over the first week of life. Each child should have individualized fluid and electrolyte management based on frequent weights, close monitoring of fluid intake and output, estimates of insensible losses, and frequent determinations of serum and urine electrolyte status. Very accurate scales (± 1 g) built into isolettes and radiant warmers are making measurements of weight change easier, safer, and more accurate, allowing much tighter control of water balance.

Energy Requirements

Most of the newborn infant's fat and carbohydrate stores are established during the third trimester. As a result, the ELBW infant has an endogenous energy reserve of ≤ 200 kcal.[24] Most infants are started on glucose and electrolyte infusions; seldom are the quantities of glucose given sufficient to meet basal caloric requirements. Thus even in the first few days of life and without supplemental amino acid intake, these infants undergo protein catabolism. Kashyap et al. have shown that ELBW infants receiving only

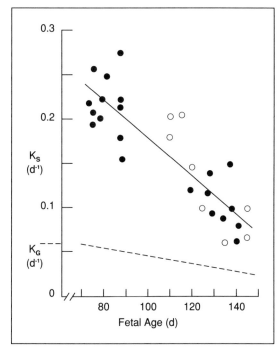

Fig. 16.3. Fractional protein synthetic rate (K_S) in fetal sheep decreases with gestational age at a greater rate than does fractional growth rate (K_G). Closed circles represent data derived from leucine tracer studies; open circles represent data from lysine tracer studies. (Reproduced, with permission, from Hay.[17] Adapted from data of Meier et al.[189] and Kennaugh et al.[190])

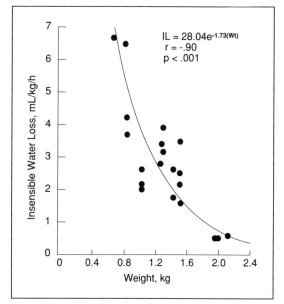

Fig. 16.4. Exponential increase in insensible (evaporative) water loss (IL) with decreasing body size in preterm infants. (Reproduced, with permission, from Costarino and Baumgart.[191])

glucose (approximately 40 kcal/kg/day) lose >1% of protein stores per day.[18,25]

Even when the ELBW infant is more stable and receiving a combination of substrate intakes, the best proportions of nutrients to achieve optimal growth must be estimated by extrapolating from data on more mature infants and then individualized for each infant's specific condition—e.g., an infant with significant lung disease may develop excessive carbon dioxide (CO_2) production with relatively high glucose loads.[26] For most infants, the goal in the stabilization period should be the establishment of enteral feeding to provide enough energy to gain 10 to 15 g/day. More aggressive energy intakes should be balanced also by the observations of Kashyap et al.[25] (Fig. 16.5) who showed that at adequate protein intakes (i.e., weight gain was >10 g/kg/day, with length and head circumference also growing) excess energy only produced fatter babies. The value (beneficial or detrimental) of such adiposity is not known.

In conjunction with the gradual introduction of nutrients in the ELBW infant, detailed attention should be paid to minimizing energy losses. This can be achieved by minimal handling, maintaining a neutral thermal environment, and avoiding undue heat and fluid losses.

Carbohydrate Requirements

Glucose alone is insufficient to prolong survival for more than a few days in ELBW infants, and does not prevent protein catabolism. Nevertheless, glucose is often the sole nutrient supplied to ELBW infants in the first days of life. Human ELBW infants also have uniquely increased glucose requirements because of their excessively large brain:body weight ratio, obligatory glucose requirements for brain energy metabolism, and limited capacity for glucose production.[17] In fact, it has been suggested reasonably, if never proven definitively, that ELBW infants may be more susceptible than more mature infants to neurological injury from hypoglycemia, even of modest degree. Furthermore, in a recent retrospective study, recurrent, moderate hypoglycemia in preterm infants correlated positively with significant developmental and intellectual handicaps.[27] In this study, deviation below normal in terms of neurological function occurred at approximately 45 mg/dL, suggesting this concentration as a reasonable choice for a lower limit at which to maintain plasma glucose concentration in ELBW infants. Although no study has shown definitive neurological damage from some measured degree or duration of hypoglycemia, and several studies have shown preservation of neuronal function and viability in spite of severe and prolonged hypoglycemia, it seems prudent to maintain normal glucose concentrations and glucose supply rates as much of the time as possible to ELBW infants.

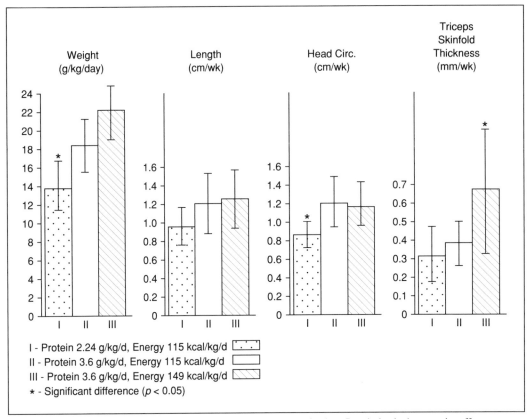

Fig. 16.5. The graphs show growth rates with varying protein and energy intakes. Protein intake has a major effect on promoting growth in preterm human infants. Additional calories add slightly to weight gain and significantly to triceps skinfold thickness. Dotted bars = protein 2.24 g/kg/day, energy 115 kcal/kg/day; open bars = protein 3.6 g/kg/day, energy 115 kcal/kg/day; hatched bars = protein 3.6 g/kg/day, energy 149 kcal/kg/day. (Adapted from Kashyap et al.[25] Reproduced, with permission, from Kennaugh J, Hay WW Jr. Nutrition of the fetus and newborn. *West J Med* 1987;147:435–448.)

One must be careful, however, of giving too much glucose. Hyperglycemia is a common problem in ELBW infants, with reported incidences as high as 20% to 86%,[28,29] particularly during the first few days of life. High serum glucose concentrations are attributed to both increased secretion of hypoglycemia counter-regulatory hormones and diminished end-organ sensitivity to insulin. The addition of intravenous amino acids and lipids to parenteral glucose infusions tends to further increase the serum glucose concentration.[30] Several studies have reported increased glucose tolerance and enhanced weight gain with simultaneous insulin infusions,[31–33] but further studies are needed to determine the possible deleterious effects of this practice on respiratory status, metabolic rate, and body composition.

From a different perspective concerning the dangers of too much glucose administration, particularly intravenously, Van Aerde et al. have shown that in full-term newborns administered intravenous nutrition, CO_2 production and O_2 consumption increased when glucose intake exceeded 40 kcal/kg/day (the point at which lipogenesis from glucose occurs), and

above this level each kcal of energy supplied by glucose increases basal expenditure by 0.31 kcal.[26] Therefore the percentage of calories from glucose above approximately 40 kcal/kg must be carefully considered in newborns in whom increased CO_2 production might further compromise an already tenuous respiratory status. A significant increase in basal metabolic rate has been noted in infants administered hyperalimentation fluid composed of only glucose and amino acids compared to infants who also received some lipid supplementation.[34]

Protein Requirements

In ELBW infants, positive nitrogen balance occurs when at least 2 to 2.5 g/kg/day of amino acids are administered intravenously with at least 60 kcal/day of energy,[35] supplied either as glucose, lipid, or a combination of the two.[36] In utero nitrogen accretion rates can be achieved with 70 kcal/kg/day and 2.7 to 3.5 g/kg/day protein.[37]

Animal studies demonstrate high protein synthetic and turnover rates earlier in fetal life (Fig. 16.3), and suggest the need for high protein intakes in the

ELBW infant. This need is due to: (1) an intrinsically higher rate of protein synthesis during the rapid growth phase, and (2) the greater body proportion of rapidly growing organs earlier in gestation. In a preceding study, amino acid intakes of >5 g/kg/day often were associated with increased concentrations of blood urea nitrogen (BUN) and metabolic acidosis.[38] However, Kashyap showed more recently that introduction of protein (approximately 2 g/kg/day) in infants <1,000 g as early as the second day of life resulted in positive nitrogen balance, did not elevate markedly the BUN, and produced a plasma amino acid profile similar to that seen in cord blood of healthy infants at term.[39]

Fat Requirements

As noted in the preceding discussion, intravenous nutrient mixtures that contain exclusively glucose and amino acids produce an increased basal metabolic rate[34] and an increased CO_2-production:O_2-consumption ratio (RQ).[39] However, when calories are supplied solely as lipid, there may also be an increase in O_2 consumption.[40] Caloric-based glucose:lipid ratios of 3:1 or 2:1 minimize CO_2 stress.[41-43] Early use or rapid advancement of lipid emulsions in the preterm infant has been cautious because of a variety of potential complications including lipid intolerance, impaired pulmonary function, increased free bilirubin concentrations,[44,45] and potential interference with immune function.[46,47] The nature of the lipid-related pulmonary dysfunction includes pulmonary microemboli that have been noted at autopsy,[48,49] a diffusion block secondary to lipid overload,[50] and, most convincingly, increases in pulmonary vascular tone secondary to infusion of precursors of the vasoactive prostanoid system.[51-53] An echocardiographic study by Lloyd and Boucek demonstrated increasing pulmonary vascular resistance with increasing lipid infusion rate; the range of the lipid infusion rates, however, was the equivalent of 2.4 to 10.8 g/kg/day, and the greatest effect of the lipids was seen at the highest of these infusion rates (which are unlikely to be used in the newborn).[54] A recent study of lipid infusions early in the postnatal course of sick, ventilator-dependent infants <1,500 g showed no deleterious effects of increasing intravenous lipid from 1 to 3 g/kg/day over days 1 to 4 of life compared to isocaloric, isonitrogenous intravenous feedings with lipid added only after day 8.[55]

If tolerated, early introduction of lipid is desirable, and only 0.5 to 1.0 g/kg/day is needed to prevent essential fatty acid deficiency.[56] Because of impaired tolerance to intravenous lipids,[57] current recommendations for ELBW infants are a maximum of 2 g/kg/day.[58] Clearly, some ELBW infants tolerate higher infusion rates than this amount. Careful monitoring of serum triglyceride concentrations, changes in blood gas tensions, and bilirubin levels can determine which infants may tolerate higher lipid infusion rates.

Twenty percent rather than 10% lipid emulsions are recommended because of the greater phospholipid intake and increased triglyceride concentrations seen with the 10% emulsion.[59]

Feeding Routes

A survey of feeding practices in neonatal intensive care units reported in 1985 by Churella et al. showed that 80% of all units used parenteral nutrition exclusively for at least the first week of life in infants <1,000 g birthweight.[60] Nevertheless, Lucas et al.[61] have shown that even minimal enteral feeding produces a surge in serum concentrations of enteral hormone similar to that seen in term newborns. Two recent studies have shown the safety of early enteral feedings in ELBW infants.[62,63] Beneficial effects in these studies included earlier attainment of full enteral feeds, greater decline in serum bilirubin concentrations with less time under phototherapy, less cholestasis, and significantly lower serum alkaline phosphatase concentrations. Although both continuous and intermittent nasogastric feedings have been shown to produce postprandial increases in serum concentrations of enteral hormones, significantly more pronounced cyclical surges are seen with bolus feedings.[64] At the present time, the clinical significance of this difference is not clear. Continuous feedings have been shown to be more energy efficient than intermittent feedings in preterm infants.[65]

If enteral feedings are contraindicated, early use of central venous access should be considered to allow for higher nutrient density in feedings at relatively lower fluid infusion rates.

Guidelines for Feeding

Stabilization (Days 0 to 3) Unless the baby is edematous, fluid and nutrient administration calculations should be based on birthweight until birthweight is regained; then the daily weight should be used.

1. Start intravenous fluids at 100 to 150 mL/kg/day (estimate based on gestational age, use of radiant warmer, and need for phototherapy); reduce this rate if acute renal failure develops.
2. Determine weight two to three times per day depending on patient stability; use this weight to adjust fluid requirements up or down to maintain weight loss within 5% to 10% of birthweight.
3. Monitor serum electrolyte concentrations every 6 to 8 hours. Expect concentration hypernatremia and do not add sodium supplements until serum sodium concentration starts to fall and is <140 mEq/dL. If serum sodium concentration is >145 mEq/dL, increase free water intake. Do not begin potassium supplementation until urine

output is established (>1 mL/kg/h) and/or serum potassium concentration is <3.5 mEq/L.

4. Start intravenous glucose infusion at 4 to 6 mg/kg/min and alter to keep plasma glucose concentration >45 mg/dL and <120 mg/dL. Begin intravenous amino acid infusion at 0.5 to 1.0 g/kg/day and intravenous 20% lipid emulsion at 0.5 g/kg/day (infused over a period of 20 to 24 hours) within the first day of life or as soon after birth as possible (i.e., after gross physiological and metabolic disturbances have been properly treated). Monitor blood or serum acid-base balance, BUN, bilirubin and triglyceride concentrations, and advance as tolerated.

5. If the baby is stable, begin continuous enteral feedings at 1 to 2 mL/kg/h within the first 2 to 3 days of life. While initial feedings are customarily diluted (e.g., 10 kcal/oz or 50% of normal formula strength), there are no convincing data to prove that dilute feedings are truly better than those with normal concentrations found in human milk or routine formulas. However, concentrated formulas designed for the growing, normally feeding preterm infant should be avoided as initial feedings at full strength.

Transition (Days 3 to 5)

1. Move the baby to an incubator to decrease evaporative losses.

2. Continue twice-daily weight measurements and closely monitor intake and output. There may be marked diuresis. Magnitude of urine volume can be used to anticipate weight and serum electrolyte changes. Adjust fluid intake to parallel urine output.

3. Measure serum electrolyte concentrations two to three times daily, and urine electrolyte concentrations at least once per day. Adjust potassium and sodium intake to correct for urine losses (for potassium, often 2 to 4 mEq/kg/day; for sodium often 4 to 8 mEq/kg/day).

4. Advance intravenous glucose and lipid infusions to achieve intakes of 6 to 10 mg/kg/min and 1.5 to 2 g/kg/day, respectively. Intravenous amino acids should be increased to 2 to 3.5 g/kg/day, provided that 50 to 60 kcal/kg/day of nonprotein energy are also administered.

5. Enteral feedings may remain at small volumes. If the infant is stable, increase enteral volumes by no more than 5 to 10 mL/kg/day initially and later by 10 to 20 mL/kg/day.

Nutritional Advancement (After Days 5 to 7)

Fluid and nutrient intakes will vary depending on clinical stability and underlying disease processes (e.g., fluid restriction for respiratory distress or

PDA; fluid liberalization if a radiant warmer is required to achieve optimal thermoregulation and/or phototherapy is required to treat hyperbilirubinemia). The goal during this period is to progressively increase nutrient intake so that the infant is able to achieve weight gain of 10 to 20 g/day by the third week of life.

1. During the first week of this period, fluids should be administered to keep the baby near birthweight. By the end of 3 weeks, most infants will tolerate 130 to 160 mL/kg/day.

2. Advance to 24 kcal/oz preterm infant formula, or use human breast milk supplemented with nutrient mixtures to provide an appropriate balance of nutrients to meet the unique needs of preterm infants.

Necrotizing Enterocolitis

Epidemiology

Necrotizing enterocolitis is a significant neonatal complication, with an incidence of up to 5% of all newborn intensive care unit admissions.[66] In a large British collaborative study, the incidence increased as birthweight decreased.[67] In an American multicenter study, NEC was seen in 6.3% of infants with birthweights 1,000 to 1,249 g, 9.2% of those 750 to 999 g, and 13.5% of those 500 to 749 g.[68]

Etiology (Effect of Feeding)

The etiology of NEC has not been clearly delineated. This disease state probably represents a common pathological response that is triggered by a variety of risk factors acting singly or in combination. Implicated etiologic factors include hypoxia, ischemia, infection, hypertonic feedings, rapid advancement of feedings, severe polycythemia, milk-protein allergy, exchange transfusions, and both the presence and prolonged use of umbilical catheters.[69] Nearly all infants with NEC have received enteral feedings.[69]

Volume and Rate of Feeding. Retrospective analyses suggest that both early and aggressive enteral feeding regimens put an infant at increased risk for NEC, while later and more slowly advanced feedings appear to reduce the risk.[70,71] Several difficulties have been encountered in trying to compare results of NEC studies, including the different definitions of "early" (day 1 versus within the first week of life after birth), the rate of volume advancement considered "rapid," the density of feeding (hypo- versus hyperosmotic), and the type of feeding (continuous versus bolus). Although the numbers of infants are small, most of the prospective, controlled trials on enteral feeding and the occurrence of NEC in preterm infants have not demonstrated that either early enteral feedings or rapid advancement of enteral feedings increase the risk of this disease.[62,72,73]

For example, a recent case-control study implicated large increments in enteral feedings as a cause of NEC.[74] In this study, however, the average "rapid" feeding rate was nearly 28 mL/kg/day (with the NEC group receiving an average increment of 56.7 mL/kg on day 3); this is a relatively large volume advance compared with most other studies. Also in this study, the "slow"-feeding, low NEC-incidence control group had a daily feeding increment of 16.8 mL/kg/day. This so-called slow advancement of feeding volume was comparable to the "rapid" feeding increase of 20 mL/kg/day seen in the only randomized, prospective study on the connection between feeding volume increases and the development of NEC that did not show that either early enteral feedings or rapid advancement of enteral feedings increased the risk for NEC.[73] On the basis of these studies, maintaining feeding increments at ≤20 mL/kg/day seems prudent.

To test the hypothesis that delayed oral feedings would decrease the incidence of NEC in a population of infants <1,500 g at birth who were specifically selected for study because they were at very high risk for developing NEC, LaGamma et al. prospectively randomized neonates over the first 2 weeks of life to receive exclusively parenteral nutrition versus parenteral nutrition plus incremental (both volume and density) enteral feedings.[72] Although the details for the enteral feeding regimen were not described, the incidence of NEC in the parenterally fed group of 20 infants was 60% (12) versus 22% (4) (significantly different, $p<0.02$) in the 18 infants who received a mixture of parenteral and enteral feedings. Thus there appears to be little evidence to justify restricting early enteral feedings simply to avoid the development of NEC.

To help determine the optimal time for initiating enteral feedings in sick infants <1,500 g, Ostertag et al. prospectively randomized neonates to receive enteral feedings beginning on day 1 versus 7 of life.[62] The early feeding group received 1 mL/h continuous enteral infusion; density was increased gradually from sterile water to full-strength Portagen (Mead Johnson, Inc., Evansville, Ind.) over the first 7 days, with volume advances thereafter. Necrotizing enterocolitis was seen in 29% (5 of 17) of the early versus 35% (6 of 17) of the late-fed group (not significantly different). In a similar study of infants <1,500 g who received early hypocaloric enteral feedings starting at 48 hours of age versus intravenous nutrition only for 9 days, the incidence of NEC was only 5% in the early feeding group, considerably less (although not significantly) than the 16% incidence in the intravenous nutrition group.[63] On balance, therefore, it appears that early, minimal enteral feeding may reduce the risk of NEC; at least there appears to be no contraindication to early, minimal enteral feeding for fear of increasing the risk of NEC.

Type of Feeding. Hyperosmolar feedings have been implicated in producing NEC,[69,74,75] and current feeding practices tend to use iso- or hypo-osmolar feeds. Attention should be given also to diluting hyperosmolar enteral medications commonly used in preterm infants (particularly the multivitamin preparations).

It has been suggested that immunoprotective factors in human milk may help prevent NEC. However, there are numerous observations and case reports of NEC occurring in infants who were fed only human milk.[66] In the only prospective study of the association of type of diet and the development of NEC by Lucas and Cole (among 926 preterm infants with birthweights <1,850 g), NEC was 6 to 10 times more common among exclusively formula-fed infants than among infants fed human milk exclusively.[76] Among infants fed a combination of human milk and formula, NEC was reported three times more often than in those infants fed only human milk. This study also indicated that there might be a decreased incidence of NEC with delayed enteral feedings in those infants fed formula but not in those infants fed human milk. In studies demonstrating no increased risk of NEC with early, minimal enteral feeding, the culprit, therefore, appears to be formula and not early enteral feeding that increases the risk of NEC.

With respect to immune protection from NEC, the results of one study have indicated that oral administration of an IgA-IgG preparation in infants <2,000 g for whom human milk was not available might prevent the development of NEC.[77]

Enteral Feeding in the Presence of Other Risk Factors. Bowel hypoxia or ischemia are the presumed common denominators for many of the risk factors (e.g., hypotension, respiratory distress, asphyxia, infection) associated with NEC in preterm infants. Although these risk factors are frequently just as common in studies which compare NEC patients with age-matched controls,[66] from a pathophysiological standpoint it seems prudent to avoid enteral feedings for at least a brief period after such events have occurred. Then one can commence feedings if there is evidence of relatively normal gut function (absence of gastric contents or abdominal distension, presence of bowel sounds, passage of meconium or stool).

Data from studies that have compared the use of umbilical catheters with the risk of developing NEC are contradictory; some have reported an increased incidence of NEC,[78] while others have not.[72,74] There are no prospective data to help one decide whether or not enteral feedings should be given while umbilical catheters are in place. This may be a situation where use of "minimal enteral feeding" regimens have a role, given the apparent reduction in the incidence of NEC with this mode of feeding.

Similarly, because of the reduced blood flow to the gut in the presence of a PDA and/or indomethacin therapy, it probably is advisable to withhold enteral feedings until the ductus is closed or indomethacin therapy is concluded (see later section on PDA). Data to support this position, however, are not available.

Guidelines for Feeding

Prevention   Available data do not contraindicate starting small, dilute (5 to 10 kcal/oz [0.15 to 0.35 kcal/mL]) feedings in the first 48 to 72 hours in infants <1,500 g, as long as these infants are closely monitored for evidence of feeding intolerance and/or NEC. As with the ELBW infant, not enough solid data are available to prove that "dilute" feedings are necessary, although their use is customary. (The effects of small feedings on prevention or modulation of cholestasis and stimulation of gut growth, motility, and digestive enzyme development will be discussed in the section on short bowel syndrome to follow.)

Therapy   With any degree of NEC, nutrient delivery should not be interrupted but switched from an enteral to a parenteral route. The duration of withholding of enteral feedings following the diagnosis of NEC is variable and depends on the severity of the disease, with ranges from 2 to 3 days in cases of mild, "medical" NEC to 7 to 14 days with NEC that requires surgical intervention for gut resection or diverting procedures.

Once it is deemed safe to begin feeding, small (2 to 3 mL/kg), dilute (5 to 10 kcal/oz) feedings should be given, with advances dependent on tolerance and severity of prior NEC. Human milk may be better tolerated initially in milder cases of NEC, although this type of feeding has not been studied. In more severe cases, theoretically a more easily digested formula such as

Pregestamil (Mead Johnson, Inc., Evansville, Ind.) or Alimentum (Ross Laboratories, Columbus, Ohio) is recommended. Those infants with the most severe sequelae may require elemental formulas (see Short Bowel Syndrome section that follows).

Feeding intolerance may indicate residual NEC, poor gut motility, or possible sequelae such as stricture formation. With the latter, feeding difficulties may arise late (up to 6 to 8 weeks post-NEC) or only at very large feeding volumes.

Short Bowel Syndrome

Short bowel syndrome refers to a state of malabsorption and accompanying malnutrition that occurs when significant portions of the small bowel are lost. There are many etiologies for the loss of intestinal surface area in SBS, but most commonly SBS is seen following surgical resection of the intestine for NEC, gastroschisis, omphalocoele, and intestinal atresias. In most cases, significant fluid and nutrient losses do not occur until >50% of the small intestine is lost.[79, 80] The nature of these losses, however, depends on the portion of the intestine that is missing, since the functional capacities of each area are different (Table 16.2).

In general, the more proximal and extensive the small bowel loss, the more severe the morbidity.[81] Fortunately, the small bowel has many adaptive processes that develop after resection (Table 16.3), allowing for new growth in the length of the intestine or in the luminal surface area.

Until the advent of neonatal parenteral alimentation approximately 12 years ago, the prognosis for infants undergoing resection of large portions of the small bowel was dismal.[82–84] Very early administration of normal amounts of protein and energy with intravenous feeding helps with reparative processes and

Table 16.2.   Principal Sites (X) of Intestinal Absorption in Normal Small Bowel*

Nutrient	Proximal	Distal
Carbohydrate	X	
Protein	X	
Fat	X	
Vitamins (not B_{12})	X	
Minerals (iron, calcium, copper)	X	
Vitamin B_{12}		X
Bile salts		X
Fluids	X	X

*Reproduced, with permission, from Taylor SF, Sokol RJ.[81]

Table 16.3. Adaptive Small Bowel Changes Following Resection*

Anatomical

Increased epithelial cell number per villus
Increased rate of enterocyte proliferation
Increased depth of crypts
Increased villus height
Increased bowel diameter, wall thickness, and length

Functional

Increased glucose absorption per segment of bowel
Increased disaccharidase activity segmentally
Increased enterokinase and peptide hydrolase activity
Increased water, electrolyte, and mineral absorption per length of remnant small bowel
Increased colonic absorption of short-chain fatty acids

*Reproduced, with permission, from Taylor SF, Sokol RJ.[81]

growth. Initially, relatively high energy intravenous feedings (up to 130 kcal/kg/day) may be required. Electrolyte and trace element losses must be monitored carefully because of their frequently high rates of loss from ostomy drainage and the limited absorptive surface area of the intestine. Infants with SBS are prone to deficiencies of sodium, zinc, copper, manganese, magnesium, iron, selenium, and chromium, and these elements need careful monitoring and replacement. Most infants with SBS require prolonged intravenous nutrition. There is some evidence also that consolidated, intermittent intravenous feeding (i.e., only part of the day) to supplement partial enteral feedings may reduce the risk of hepatobiliary complications from hyperalimentation fluids.[81]

Early initiation of small enteral feedings increases the rate of intestinal adaptation after gut resection. In general, continuous feedings are better tolerated than bolus feedings, although this issue remains somewhat controversial.[85] Infants with SBS may also show intolerance to a variety of specific nutrients. Carbohydrate malabsorption is a significant problem and primary cause of diarrhea. Glucose polymers may be better hydrolyzed, digested, and absorbed (glucose is more slowly released near the luminal villi) than either starches or lactose because of a much higher residual maltase activity compared to lactase or sucrase.[86] Fat malabsorption secondary to bile acid depletion, decreased pancreatic exocrine secretion (often seen in preterm, especially ELBW, infants), and decreased intestinal absorptive surface area also contribute to intolerance of enteral nutrients.[87] Medium-chain triglycerides (MCTs) are the lipids that are absorbed best, since they do not require the presence of bile acids to form micelles necessary for the absorption of longer chain triglycerides. Protein intolerance

does not appear to play a significant role in enteral feeding intolerance in SBS infants, although protein malabsorption does occur because of decreased pancreatic exocrine secretions and reduced absorptive surface area. Amino acids and protein hydrolysates appear to be well absorbed.

The choice of formula for an infant with SBS depends on the length and type of residual bowel. A formula that contains glucose polymers, MCTs, and either amino acids or protein hydrolysates seems a reasonable choice. Enteral feeding should begin with slow, preferably continuous feedings of a dilute mixture; it should be advanced first on volume to determine tolerance, then on concentration when approximately half of the total fluid intake is enteral. If intolerance is encountered after several attempts at advancement, a more elemental formula (primarily amino acids and glucose, plus vitamins, minerals, and trace elements) can be initiated in small volumes and in dilute mixture. Such elemental formulas appear to be well tolerated and absorbed but provide incomplete nutrition because they contain low levels of fat, particularly essential fatty acids,[81] and certain minerals, particularly calcium and phosphorous. Thus, with these formulas, supplemental intravenous feeding must be provided, particularly with lipids. Once full enteral feedings are established, serum electrolyte and mineral (macro and trace) concentrations should still be monitored. Both fat- and water-soluble vitamin supplements are usually required.

Both surgical techniques and parenteral hyperalimentation have significantly increased the survival of infants with SBS. Goulet et al.[82] reported in 1991 that in infants with resection >50% of the length of the small bowel (but, obviously, <100%), survival was >90%. The length of time required for intestinal adaptation depended on the length of the residual small intestine (27 months with <40 cm of small bowel remaining, and 14 months if >40 cm were left in place), and the presence (shorter adaptation time) or absence (longer adaptation time) of the ileocecal valve.

Guidelines for Feeding

1. Advance early to "full" amounts of protein and energy to aid in gut repair.
2. Pay close attention to additional fluid, electrolyte, and micronutrient losses above basal requirements from orogastric and stoma output.
3. Monitor serum concentrations of sodium, potassium, zinc, copper, manganese, iron, selenium, magnesium, and chromium.
4. Consider "consolidated" (i.e., intravenous feeding only part of the day) parenteral feedings if hepatobiliary complications are present (e.g., 12 hours "on," 12 hours "off").
5. Continuous feedings generally appear to be better tolerated than bolus feedings. When ready to start bolus enteral feedings, gradually consolidate continuous feedings (i.e., provide 2 hours of continuous feeding in only 1 hour, then in 30 minutes, and so on).
6. Although choice of feeding depends on the site and severity of the injury, generally commence with human milk or a formula that contains glucose polymers, medium-chain triglycerides, and either amino acid mixtures or protein hydrolysates. Start with a dilute concentration of about 5 kcal/oz. Generally advance volume of feedings first, then concentration.

Bronchopulmonary Dysplasia

Nutritional Factors

The preterm infant is at increased risk for development of hyaline membrane disease and subsequent BPD. Both disease processes may increase energy expenditure and thus energy requirements by as much as 25% above basal needs in preterm, especially ELBW, infants who, by virtue of their immaturity and size, already are severely compromised in their ability to achieve adequate nutrition.[88,89] Infants with BPD recover more quickly if they have sufficient caloric intake; the metabolism of this energy, however, results in increased CO_2 production and O_2 consumption in infants whose respiratory function already is limited.

There are many mechanisms that contribute to development and persistence of BPD. Nutritional deficiencies in the premature infant that may exacerbate these mechanisms are summarized in Table 16.4 and have been reviewed by Van Aerde.[41]

Energy and Nutrient Requirements

Failure to thrive is a major complication of BPD. Theoretical possibilities for growth impairment include increased energy expenditure, suboptimal energy intake (often secondary to fluid restriction), chronic hypoxia, metabolic disturbances related to drug therapy, decreased gastrointestinal absorption of nutrients, and congestive heart failure.

Energy studies have concluded that energy expenditure is increased in infants with BPD.[89,115-117] As pointed out in a recent review by Kalhan and Denne,[118] however, there are difficulties with interpreting studies of infants who required supplemental oxygen.[88,115-117] Such studies are prone to error because current calorimetry systems are inaccurate under conditions of increased oxygen. Studies in room air,[89,119] however, were performed on infants who were clinically well, producing an inadequate control group. Hypotheses for increased energy expenditure in infants with BPD include increased work of breathing, higher basal metabolic rate (perhaps secondary to medications such as theophylline), and increased energy expenditure and CO_2 production accompanying the metabolism of concentrated (particularly high carbohydrate) formula.[120]

Energy requirements in the infant with BPD, therefore, include not only increased total energy because of the disease process itself, but also additional energy to try to prevent the slower rate of growth observed in these infants. The magnitude of growth delay in these infants is directly related to the severity and duration of the disease.[41] What portion of intake is distributed to each of these demands is not clear, and undoubtedly varies depending on such factors as severity of disease and infant maturity.

In general, infants with BPD are treated with relative fluid restriction, because pulmonary edema appears to complicate the pathology of BPD.[121] The presence of a PDA also is associated with large fluid intakes and with increased risk of developing BPD.[122] More recently, Van Marter et al. suggested that excessive fluid therapy, even in the first days of life, may increase the risk of BPD in low-birthweight infants.[123] Based on this information, it is advisable to refrain from excessive water administration during all stages of BPD.

It has been demonstrated that infants with BPD have improved growth if oxygenation is maintained in a higher range.[124] The mechanisms responsible for the effect of oxygen on growth are not known.

As noted earlier in this chapter, the dietary distribution of energy clearly has been shown to influence metabolic rate, CO_2 production, and O_2 consumption in studies of intravenous feedings in infants[26,34, 40-43] and enteral alimentation in adults.[125,126] Glucose: lipid calorie ratios of 3:1 or 2:1 minimize CO_2

Table 16.4. Potential Pulmonary Effects of Undernutrition in the VLBW Infant Susceptible to BPD

Energy reserves
Early onset of catabolic state[39,90]

Effects on respiratory distress syndrome
Altered surfactant production[91-96]
Decreased respiratory muscle function[92,97-99]

Protection from hyperoxia and barotrauma
Decreased epithelial integrity (insufficient vitamin A)[92,100-102]
Decreased antioxidant defense systems (antioxidant enzymes, glutathione, vitamin E, vitamin C, polyunsaturated fatty acids [PUFAs])[91,92,103-107]
Decreased lung biosynthesis/cell replication for lung repair[92,97,108,109]

Lung repair and development of BPD
Decreased replacement of damaged cells[92,97,108,109]
Decreased replacement of damaged extracellular components (elastin, collagen)[92,110,111]

Lung growth and replication
Decreased lung biosynthesis[92,97,108,109]
Decreased lung structural maturation[92,97,108,109]

Susceptibility to infection
Decreased cellular/humoral defenses[112-114]
Decreased epithelial cell integrity[92,97,100,102]
Decreased foreign material clearance mechanisms[92,97]

stress.[41] The upper limit of desirable energy intake in these infants remains to be determined. Further research also is needed to determine optimal enteral feeding methods and types of formula supplements.

Guidelines for Feeding

1. Restrict fluid relative to normal infants of comparable gestational age.
2. Increase caloric density formula or calorie-enriched milk for adequate growth (i.e., 24 to 27 kcal/oz) due to increased caloric requirements for lung repair and growth.
3. Establish glucose:lipid ratios of 3:1 or 2:1 to avoid excessive CO_2 production.
4. Maintain oxygenation in higher range in the chronic disease phase.

Patent Ductus Arteriosus

The ductus arteriosus of many preterm infants remains open for days or weeks,[127] and its persistent patency is associated with significant neonatal morbidity that can be significantly reduced with its closure.[128] Studies in the preterm lamb have shown that with PDA shunts greater than 50% of left ventricular output, effective systemic blood flow falls and organ perfusion decreases, with blood flow to the gas-trointestinal tract showing some of the earliest compromise.[129] Very low-birthweight (VLBW) infants with a PDA have decreased blood flow in the descending aorta[130,131] that has been implicated as a cause of the increased incidence of NEC seen with PDA.[128] Indomethacin is the primary nonsurgical therapy for PDA in low-birthweight infants. Use of indomethacin in preterm infants is associated with decreased gastrointestinal blood supply by Doppler ultrasound measurements,[133] and its administration has been implicated in neonatal NEC.[132,134]

No studies have determined optimal feeding practices in infants with PDA. Fluid restriction is practiced in most centers because of the association of increased intravenous fluid infusion rates with PDA.[135] With the reduction of gastrointestinal blood flow induced independently by a PDA or indomethacin therapy, it seems prudent to withhold or at least limit enteral feedings when an infant with a PDA exhibits symptoms or is undergoing indomethacin treatment.

Small-for-Gestational-Age Infants

The definition of SGA infants or those with "intrauterine growth retardation (or restriction)" (IUGR) varies but usually refers to growth parameters more than 2 standard deviations below the mean or less than the 10th percentile for gestational age for normally growing infants. This definition will miss some SGA infants depending on which infants and which populations are used for the reference growth chart, whether or not the study infants are from a similar population as that in the reference chart, and whether or not infants are assigned appropriate gestational ages.

Intrauterine growth retardation is estimated to affect 3% to 7% of all deliveries,[136] and accounts for significant perinatal morbidity and mortality.[137–139] In an analysis of published fetal carcass studies, Sparks has demonstrated that the proportion of SGA infants is probably much higher (as much as 20% to 30% of deliveries) than these estimates when one considers only the deliveries of preterm (and especially ELBW) infants.[2] In general, SGA infants have been classified into two groups: (1) symmetrical or early-onset growth retardation, and (2) asymmetrical or late-onset growth retardation, in which head size and (less frequently) linear growth are relatively normal (Table 16.5).[140,141] This division is artificial and there is considerable overlap between the two groups. Nevertheless, these categories have been considered useful to determine nutritional strategies and predict growth outcome.

As a group, SGA infants do not demonstrate as much catch-up growth in the first year of life as appropriate-for-gestational-age (AGA) infants of a similar gestational age.[142–145] However, SGA infants with asymmetrical growth retardation tend to have more catch-up growth than those with symmetrical growth.[145,146] Hack et al.[147] reported on other features associated with poor compensatory growth, including poor intrauterine head growth, severe and early IUGR, multiple births, and lower socioeconomic status. Most SGA infants who exhibit catch-up growth do so within the first year of life.[146,148]

The reported incidence of significant neurological handicap in preterm SGA infants varies widely, from 3% to 35%, but the risk for neurological problems or developmental delay has not been conclusively established for the term SGA infant.[149] The majority of full-term SGA infants are of normal intelligence.[150] The most significant predictor of neurological outcome is head circumference.[151,152] Fetuses who have poor in utero head growth and newborns who have head circumferences <10% have a high incidence of developmental and neurological abnormalities.[153,154] Several studies have shown that nutrition affects neurological outcome more significantly in SGA infants than AGA infants.[149,155]

In the immediate newborn period, SGA infants are prone to problems that include asphyxia, meconium aspiration, hypoglycemia, hypocalcemia, polycythemia, hyperviscosity, and poor temperature regulation. Neonatal hypoglycemia is a common problem in SGA infants, particularly during the first 2 to 3 days of life, and may be secondary to a number of factors, including decreased hepatic glycogen stores,[156,157] impaired hepatic gluconeogenesis and glycogenolysis,[158,159] decreased counter-regulatory hormones, and hyperinsulinism.[140] Infants with these problems should be monitored closely for several days after birth. If clinically stable, they may be started on enteral feedings with short, 1- to 2-hour feeding intervals. Low reagent strip or other screening serum or blood glucose concentration tests should be confirmed by serum glucose determinations; if the serum (or plasma) glucose concentration is <45 mg/dL, an intravenous glucose infusion of 4 to 8 mg/kg/min should be started. Enteral feedings

Table 16.5. Growth Variables and Fetal Development*

First Trimester/Altered Growth Potential	Third Trimester/Impaired Nutrient Supply

Dependence on fetal genome
  Expression of growth factors
  Expression of growth factor receptors
	Dependence on placental transfer of oxygen and nutrients

Less dependent on maternal nutrition	Partial dependence on fetal genome
Symmetrical body growth	Asymmetrical body growth
Low-profile growth pattern	Late-flattening growth pattern
Reduced cell number	Reduced cell size
Catch-up growth improbable	Catch-up growth probable
Examples: Teratogens (drugs, infectious agents), chromosomal abnormalities, metabolic disorders, malformation syndromes	**Examples:** maternal vascular disease, maternal malnutrition

*Adapted and reproduced, with permission, from Kliegman RM, Johnston VL.[140]

should be continued if the serum glucose concentration quickly returns to the normal range. In many infants, however, the serum glucose concentrations fluctuate widely; therefore, enteral feedings should be limited and given continuously while the intravenous glucose administration is titrated to achieve a stable serum glucose. This method allows enteral feedings to be advanced cautiously. Intravenous bolus glucose therapy should be avoided to prevent insulin fluctuations and rebound hypoglycemia. However, if the serum glucose concentration is <20 mg/dL, 200 mg/kg (2 mL of 10% dextrose in water) of glucose can be infused slowly over 3 to 5 minutes, before starting the continuous glucose infusion.

The most appropriate way to feed SGA babies on a long-term basis has not been determined. Although there is significant overlap between groups, infants whose growth delay began early in gestation show a significant probability for altered growth potential and therefore less chance of responding to any feeding regimen with catch-up growth. For infants who exhibit late-gestation onset (more characteristic of asymmetrical growth retardation), probability is greater that the relative decrease in weight is due to "nutrient starvation" in utero and that optimal feeding will enhance postnatal catch-up growth. Reports of specific nutrient deficiencies in SGA infants are limited.[160] Frequently it is noted that SGA infants need a higher caloric intake to gain weight at a rate comparable to their AGA counterparts, but there are no prospective studies on the effectiveness of feedings with different protein:energy ratios and compositions.

Nutrient abnormalities have been studied in several IUGR models in different species.[161] In general, these studies show decreased plasma or blood concentrations of fetal glucose and many amino acids, and decreased rates of oxygen consumption and umbilical blood flow. Interpretation of these results is difficult, since most of these studies only addressed fetal plasma (or blood) nutrient concentrations and not mechanisms of growth retardation. The question thus becomes: Are the nutrient deficiencies causing growth retardation, or is nutrient intake merely scaled down to provide the same intake on a body weight basis in a fetus that is growth retarded from other causes? Several groups have tried to augment fetal growth in IUGR animal models by administering nutrients in utero via the amniotic,[162,163] intragastric,[164] intraintestinal, and intravenous routes.[165,166] In general, fetuses do show plasma elevations of nutrients administered by these routes, but long-term effects on safety and enhanced growth rates have not been demonstrated.

Similar studies of fetal plasma or blood nutrient concentrations have not been performed as readily in pregnant women because of the difficulty in obtaining in vivo fetal blood samples. In a study of amino acid levels obtained by cordocentesis at both mid- and late-gestation in normal and SGA fetuses, there was a significant reduction in alpha-amino nitrogen and in most essential amino acids at both stages of gestation in the IUGR group.[167]

Guidelines for Feeding

1. Institute early feeding and intravenous glucose infusion to prevent or treat hypoglycemia.
2. Avoid too much intravenous glucose to prevent hyperglycemia.
3. Increase energy intake if needed to promote growth. SGA infants may have higher rates of energy expenditure.

NOTE: There is no evidence that forced feeding of SGA infants promotes catch-up growth.

Infants of Diabetic Mothers

Frequently born or intentionally delivered preterm, IDMs have many unique metabolic conditions that may require special nutritional management.[168,169] Such conditions include: (1) an excessive first phase and perhaps sustained insulin response to acute and sustained hyperglycemia; (2) suppressed concentrations of free fatty acids, ketoacids, and glycerol; and (3) impaired counter-regulatory hormonal response (e.g., with glucagon and epinephrine) to hypoglycemia.[170,171] Because of the excessive insulin secretion, they also may have impaired glucose production,[172,173] as well as the potential for very high rates of glucose utilization, especially if glucose infusions are allowed to produce hyperglycemia and secondary hyperinsulinemia.[174] As a result, hypoglycemia is a frequent and often severe complication. Also, under similar conditions of excessive insulin secretion and glucose utilization in animal models, hypoxemia has been observed, along with elevated blood concentrations of lactic acid and hydrogen ion.[175]

Many nutritional regimens have been tried with IDMs to prevent progressive stimulation of insulin secretion, increased glucose requirements, dangers of hypoglycemia, and persistence or aggravation of obesity. Early feeding, small and frequent feedings, or even continuous enteral feedings have been used, all with the intent of decreasing postprandial hyperglycemia and secondary insulin release. In this regard, enteral feedings are preferred, if possible, to intravenous feedings alone because less insulin appears to be secreted following gastric feeding compared with intravenous glucose infusions.[176] Probably this is due largely to the relatively smaller increase in serum glucose concentration after gastric feedings (even if feedings consist of enteral glucose, such as 5% or 10% dextrose) compared with intravenous boluses of glucose.[177] Furthermore, milk feedings appear more successful than glucose (dextrose in water) feedings. This occurs because half of milk sugar or lactose is galactose, which is cleared almost completely by the liver after portal venous absorption and contributes more to glycogen formation than to direct hepatic glucose release and subsequent hyperglycemia.[178] Galactose also stimulates insulin secretion less effectively than glucose.[179] Galactose has been used also by the intravenous route (in research trials only) and appears to allow an increase in total carbohydrate intake above what would have been possible with glucose alone, probably because it does not cause as marked a degree of hyperglycemia as does glucose alone.[180]

Infants of diabetic mothers also have difficulty with hypocalcemia, which is related partly to prematurity, delayed feedings, hyperphosphatemia, and maternal magnesium balance disturbances that suppress fetal parathyroid function.[181,182] Such hypocalcemia occurs early in the neonatal course of these infants, particularly those who are born prematurely, and can present with signs of jitteriness that confuse the ability to diagnose clinically important hypoglycemia.

Guidelines for Feeding
1. Use early small frequent feedings, preferably of milk or formula.
2. Establish low rates of intravenous glucose infusion if significant hypoglycemia occurs and persists in spite of the enteral feedings.
3. Try to maintain plasma glucose concentrations in the low normal range (45 to 80 mg/dL) to prevent excessive insulin secretion.
4. Advance feedings and reduce intravenous glucose infusion slowly and in tandem.
5. If intravenous glucose infusions are >50% of total fluids, add intravenous calcium to prevent hypocalcemia.

NOTE: In very polycythemic IDMs (blood hematocrit >70% and especially if symptomatic), correction of hypoglycemia may be easier after partial exchange transfusion with 5% albumin solution to lower the blood hematocrit.

CASE STUDIES _____

Average-for-gestational-age ELBW Infant. J.O. was a male infant born at 25 weeks gestation, birthweight 950 g, to a 29-year-old gravida 2 white woman whose first pregnancy ended with a late first-trimester spontaneous abortion. Apgar scores were 5 and 7 at 1 and 5 minutes, respectively. The baby was treated with artificial surfactant and mechanical ventilation for severe respiratory distress syndrome. Intravenous glucose was started at birth; intravenous amino acids were started on day 2 of life and gradually increased to 3 g/kg/day; in-

travenous lipids were started on day 7 of life and gradually increased to 2.5 g/kg/day. Continuous enteral feedings with mother's breast milk were started per gavage on day 8 of life and gradually increased to total nutrition by 3 weeks of life. The milk was supplemented at that time with Human Milk Fortifier (Mead Johnson, Inc., Evansville, Ind.) to approximately 24 kcal/oz. At approximately the same time, corticosteroid treatment (Decadron) was started to treat BPD; this therapy lasted 6 weeks. From about 4 weeks until discharge, the baby received 24 kcal/oz "preterm" formula as an increasing fraction of total nutrition, which ultimately replaced mother's breast milk by 12 weeks postnatally. Neurodevelopmental exams were always within normal limits. No other medical complications were observed. In Figure 16.6, J.O.'s weight gain is plotted with closed circles and a solid line in the upper panel; his caloric intake per day is plotted as the entire shaded area under the closed line in the lower panel.

Small-for-gestational-age ELBW Infant. N.D. was a female infant with severe intrauterine growth retardation who was born at 29 weeks gestation, birthweight only 420 g, to a 28-year-old primigravida white woman. Growth retardation was suspected at the first ultrasound at 16 weeks and oligohydramnios was noted at 26 weeks. Delivery was by emergency cesarean section for fetal distress evidenced by late decelerations on the fetal tococardiogram. Two separate courses, each of two doses of corticosteriod (betamethasone) were given to the mother over the 2 weeks prior to delivery. At birth the baby had no respiratory effort and required vigorous resuscitation. Apgar scores were 1 at 1 minute and 5 at 5 minutes. She was placed on the ventilator at moderate settings. The initial blood glucose reagent strip reading was "0" and she was immediately given an intravenous dextrose infusion of 8 mg/kg/min after a bolus dose of 200 mg/kg. On the second day of life, she developed glucose intolerance and required only 4 mg/kg/min of intravenous dextrose. Intravenous amino acids were started at 24 hours of age. Small, dilute, continuously infused feedings of routine 20 kcal/oz formula were started on the fourth day of life and slowly advanced. By day 13, she was receiving 112 kcal/kg/day of nonprotein energy, 2.5 g/kg/day of amino acid and 2 g/kg/day of intravenous lipids. She was receiving only enteral feedings by day 20 and advanced then to 24 kcal/oz preterm formula or her mother's breast milk supplemented with Human Milk Fortifier to approximately 24 kcal/oz. Over the next 3 months she had slow weight gain in spite of receiving 113 to 130 kcal/kg/day. She was extubated on day 45 of life but was not discharged until 6 months of life because of slow weight gain and a persistent, marked oxygen requirement. In Figure 16.6, her weight gain is shown by solid circles and a dotted line in the upper panel; her daily caloric intake is shown as the area under the closed circles connected by the dotted line in the lower panel.

Commentary. It has been over 40 years since Dancis et al. observed that the smaller, more immature newborn infant took much longer to start postnatal growth, regain birthweight, achieve a normal rate of postnatal growth,

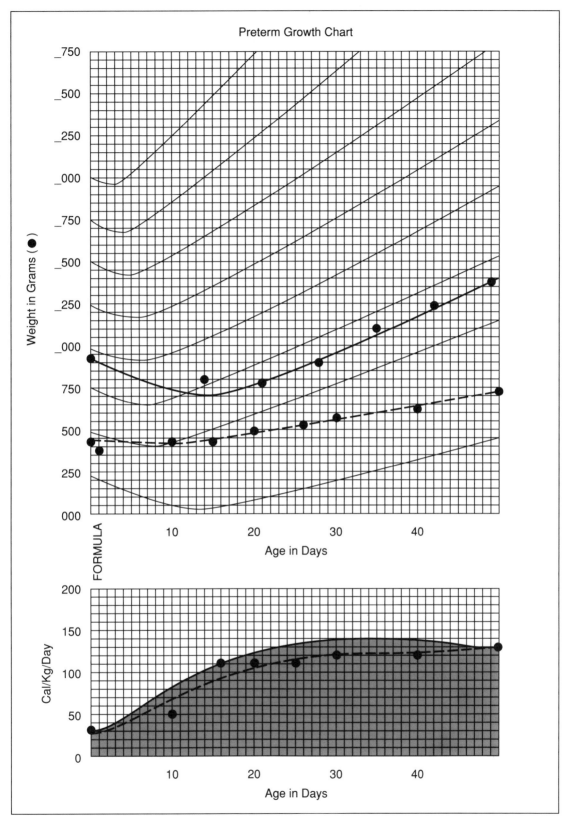

Fig. 16.6. Growth (as weight in grams, top panel) and nonprotein calorie intake (as cal/kg/day, lower panel) of a 25-week extremely low-birthweight (*ELBW*), appropriate-for-gestational-age male infant (heavy solid lines) and a 29-week *ELBW*, severely small-for-gestational-age female infant (heavy dotted lines), both born at University Hospital, Denver, Colo, in 1991, compared with growth curves presented by Dancis et al.[183]

and catch up in growth rate and size when compared with larger, more mature infants.[183,184] This lag was particularly true for those ELBW infants who weighed <1,000 g at birth. As shown in Figure 16.6, which compares caloric intake and growth of two representative ELBW infants today (one AGA and one SGA) with the "Dancis curves" of 1948, there has been little or no improvement in the onset and early growth rates of this group of infants. Why, in spite of vastly improved medical care for these infants and provision of superior intravenous and enteral formulas and supplemented human milk, does this abnormal postnatal growth pattern persist?[185]

There are several possible explanations. First, it may be that modern obstetrical and neonatal care allows survival of ELBW infants who are sicker and less physiologically stable. Certainly, it would be difficult to imagine that either of the two infants described above would have survived in 1948, or even 20 years ago; surely, their requirements for ventilation, artificial surfactant, and intravenous nutrition could not have been provided. Second, we continue to be quite ignorant of how these infants grow in utero at this early gestational age, and what we do know of in utero nutrition, metabolism, and growth indicates that we still have very inadequate means of providing appropriate amounts and kinds of nutrients in the postnatal period. Third, the vast array of growth factors, hormones, and metabolic cofactors, for example, that are part of normal fetal nutrition, metabolism, and growth are not well known or well understood, and they are not necessarily present in the postnatal period at normal fetal blood concentrations or provided at appropriate rates (whatever such rates may be). Finally, the physiological instability of these infants, stresses of the postnatal environment that affect these infants so uniquely, and necessity to feed these infants by peripheral or central venous routes or the immature gastrointestinal tract rather than by umbilical vein, make it extremely difficult to extrapolate nutritional needs from in utero conditions or from older, more mature infants.[185,186]

Perhaps it is time to learn more about these infants and their unique nutritional, metabolic, and growth requirements. It also may be time to simply feed them more aggressively. Certainly, these are two major themes of this book. The authors of the chapters on water (Chapter 1) and sodium, chloride, and potassium (Chapter 11) present cogent arguments for aggressively restricting these infants in water and electrolytes in the first day or so of postnatal life in order to reduce the "excessive" extracellular volume, thereby allowing the kidney to function in response to euvolemia rather than hypervolemia. Furthermore, the authors of the chapters on energy (Chapter 2), protein (Chapter 3), carbohydrates (Chapter 4), fat (Chapter 5), and parenteral nutrition (Chapter 15) all are suggesting strongly a very aggressive approach to postnatal nutrition that involves nearly "normal" rates of nutrients to be provided very soon after birth (first day or "as soon as possible"). Recent data presented in these chapters indicate that this more aggressive approach is probably a lot safer than previously suspected (obstetrical and neonatal care probably

are providing healthier infants). Whether or not improved growth will result remains to be proven. Nevertheless, as Lucas and his colleagues have pointed out, more than growth may be at stake; this group of infants also may be suffering from under- and malnutrition that have impaired neurological development significantly,[3,4] with impairment appearing to last into the school years.[187] Considering such neurological-developmental impairment and the potential for learning impairment in school, what can be left but to project limited function as adults? A great deal remains to be learned, but the outcome certainly seems worth the effort.

References

1. Ziegler EE, O'Donnell AM, Nelson SE, Fomon SJ. Body composition of the reference fetus. *Growth* 1976;40:329–341.
2. Sparks JW. Human intrauterine growth and nutrient accretion. *Semin Perinatol* 1984;8:74–93.
3. Lucas A, Morley R, Cole TJ, Gore SM, Davis JA, Bamford MF, et al. Early diet in preterm babies and developmental status in infancy. *Arch Dis Child* 1989;64:1570–1578.
4. Lucas A, Morely R, Cole TJ, Gore SM, Lucas PJ, Crowle P, et al. Early diet in preterm babies and developmental status at 18 months. *Lancet*. 1990;335:1477–1481.
5. Creasy RK, Resnik R. Intrauterine growth retardation. In: Creasy RK, Resnik R, eds. *Maternal-fetal medicine: principles and practice*. 2nd ed. Philadelphia: WB Saunders, 1989:557.
6. Ballard JL, Khoury JC, Wedig K, Wang L, Eilers-Waisman BL, Lipp R. New Ballard score, expanded to include extremely premature infants. *J Pediatr* 1991;119:417–423.
7. Lubchenco LO, Hansman C, Dressler M, Boyd E. Intrauterine growth as estimated from liveborn birth-weight data at 24 to 42 weeks of gestation. *Pediatrics* 1963;32:793–800.
8. Gruenwald P. Growth of the human fetus. 1. Normal growth and its variation. *Am J Obstet Gynecol* 1966;94:1112–1119.
9. Usher R, McLean F. Intrauterine growth of live-born Caucasian infants at sea level: standards obtained from measurements in 7 dimensions of infants born between 25 and 44 weeks of gestation. *J Pediatr* 1969;74:901–910.
10. Babson SG, Behrman RE, Lessel R. Fetal growth. Liveborn birth weights for gestational age of white middle class infants. *Pediatrics* 1970;45:937–944.
11. Wong KS, Scott KE. Fetal growth at sea level. *Biol Neonate* 1972;20:175–188.
12. Tanner JM, Thomson AM. Standards for birth weight at gestation periods from 32 to 42 weeks, allowing for maternal height and weight. *Arch Dis Child* 1970;45:566–569.
13. Friis-Hansen B. Body water compartments in children: changes during growth and related changes in body composition. *Pediatrics* 1961;28:169–181.
14. Waterlow JC, Garlick PJ, Millward DJ. Protein turnover and growth. In: Waterlow JC, Garlick PJ, Millward DJ, eds. *Protein turnover in mammalian tissues and in the whole body*. Amsterdam: Elsevier/North-Holland Biomedical Press, 1978:541.
15. Sparks JW, Girard JR, Battaglia FC. An estimate of the caloric requirements of the human fetus. *Biol Neonate* 1980;38:113–119.

16. Tsang RC, Steichen JJ, Brown DR. Perinatal calcium homeostasis: neonatal hypocalcemia and bone demineralization. *Clin Perinatol* 1977;4:385–409.

17. Hay WW Jr. Nutritional requirements of the extremely low-birth-weight infant. In: Hay WW Jr, ed. *Neonatal nutrition and metabolism*. St. Louis: Mosby Year Book, 1991;361–391.

18. Kasyhap S, Schulze KF, Forsyth M, Zucker C, Dell RB, Ramakrishnan R, et al. Growth, nutrient retention, and metabolic response in low birth weight infants fed varying intakes of protein and energy. *J Pediatr* 1988; 113:713–721.

19. Baumgart S. Water metabolism in the extremely low-birthweight infant. In: Cowett RM, Hay WW Jr, eds. *The micropremie: The next frontier*. Report of the 99th Ross Conference on Pediatric Research. Columbus, OH: Ross Laboratories, 1990:83–93.

20. Baumgart S, Langman CB, Sosulski R, Fox WW, Polin RA. Fluid, electrolyte, and glucose maintenance in the very low birth weight infant. *Clin Pediatr (Phila)* 1982;21:199–206.

21. Baumgart S. Reduction of oxygen consumption, insensible water loss, and radiant heat demand with use of a plastic blanket for low-birth-weight infants under radiant warmers. *Pediatrics* 1984;74:1022–1028.

22. Fanaroff AA, Wald M, Gruber HS, Klaus MH. Insensible water loss in low birth weight infants. *Pediatrics* 1972; 49:236–245.

23. Aperia A, Broberger O, Elinder G, et al. Postnatal development of renal function in pre-term and full-term infants. *Acta Paediatr Scand* 1981;70:183–187.

24. Widdowson EM. Changes in body proportions and composition during growth. In: Davis JA, Dobbing J, eds. *Scientific foundations of paediatrics*. Philadelphia: WB Saunders, 1974:153–163.

25. Kashyap S, Forsyth M, Zucker C, Ramakrishnan R, Dell RB, Heird WC. Effects of varying protein and energy intakes on growth and metabolic response in low birth weight infants. *J Pediatr* 1986;108:955–963.

26. Van Aerde JE, Sauer PJ, Heim T, Smith J, Pencharz P, Swyer P, et al. Effect of increasing glucose loads on respiratory exchange in the newborn infant. *Pediatr Res* 1986;20:420A.

27. Lucas A, Morley R, Cole TJ. Adverse neurodevelopmental outcome of moderate neonatal hypoglycaemia. *Med J* 1988;297:1304–1308.

28. Louik C, Mitchell AA, Epstein MF, Shapiro S. Risk factors for neonatal hyperglycemia associated with 10% dextrose infusion. *Am J Dis Child* 1985;139:783–786.

29. Dweck HS, Cassady G. Glucose intolerance in infants of very low birth weight. I. Incidence of hyperglycemia in infants of birth weight 1,100 grams or less. *Pediatrics* 1974;53:189–195.

30. Savich RD, Finley SL, Ogata ES. Intravenous lipid and amino acids briskly increase plasma glucose concentrations in small premature infants. *Am J Perinatol* 1988; 5:201–205.

31. Collins JW Jr, Hoppe M, Brown K, et al. A controlled trial of insulin infusion and parenteral nutrition in extremely low birth weight infants with glucose intolerance. *J Pediatr* 1991;118:921–927.

32. Binder N, Raschko P, Benda G, Reynolds JW. Insulin infusion with parenteral nutrition in extremely low birth weight infants with hyperglycemia. *J Pediatr* 1989; 114:273–280.

33. Ostertag SG, Jovanovic L, Lewis B, Auld PAM. Insulin pump therapy in the very low birth weight infant. *Pediatrics* 1986;78:625–630.

34. Nose O, Tipton JR, Ament ME, Yabuuchi H. Effect of the energy source on changes in energy expenditure, respiratory quotient and nitrogen balance during total parenteral nutrition in children. *Pediatr Res* 1987;21:538–541.

35. Anderson T, Muttart C, Bieber M, Nicholson JF, Heird WC. A controlled trial of glucose versus glucose and amino acids in preterm infants. *J Pediatr* 1979;94: 947–951.

36. Rubecz I, Mestyan J, Varga P, Klujber L. Energy metabolism, substrate utilization, and nitrogen balance in parenterally fed postoperative neonates and infants. *J Pediatr* 1981;98:42–46.

37. Zlotkin S, Bryan M, Anderson G. Intravenous nitrogen and energy intakes required to duplicate in utero nitrogen accretion in prematurely born human infants. *J Pediatr* 1981;99:115–120.

38. Goldman HI, Freudentha R, Holland B, Karelitz S. Clinical effects of two different levels of protein intake on low birth weight infants. *J Pediatr* 1969;74:881–889.

39. Kashyap S. Nutritional management of the extremely low-birthweight infant. In: Cowett RM, Hay WW Jr, eds. *The micropremie: The next frontier*. Report of the 99th Ross Conference on Pediatric Research. Columbus, OH: Ross Laboratories, 1990:115–119.

40. Heim T, Putet G, Verellen G, et al. Energy cost of intravenous alimentation in the newborn infant. In: Stern L, Salle B, Friis-Hansen B, eds. *Intensive care in the newborn III*. New York: Masson Publishing, 1981:219–238.

41. Van Aerde JE. Acute respiratory failure and bronchopulmonary dysplasia. In: Hay WW Jr, ed. *Neonatal nutrition and metabolism*, St. Louis: Mosby Year Book, 1991: 476–506.

42. Van Aerde JE, Sauer PJ, Pencharz PB, Smith JM, Swyer PR. The effect of replacing glucose with lipid on the energy metabolism of newborn infants. *Clin Sci* 1989;76:581–588.

43. Sauer PJ, Van Aerde JE, Pencharz PB, et al. Beneficial effect of the lipid system on energy metabolism in the intravenously alimented newborn. *Pediatr Res* 1986; 20:248A.

44. Spear ML, Stahl GE, Paul MH, Egler JM, Pereira GR, Polin RA. The effect of fifteen hour fat infusion of varying dosage on bilirubin binding to albumin. *JPEN* 1985; 9:144–147.

45. Andrew G, Chan G, Schiff D. Lipid metabolism in the neonate. II. The effect of Intralipid on bilirubin binding in vitro and in vivo. *J Pediatr* 1976;88:279–284.

46. Helms RA, Herrod HG, Burckart GJ, Christensen ML. E-rosette formation, total T cells and lymphocyte transformation in infants receiving intravenous safflower oil emulsion. *JPEN* 1983;7:541–545.

47. English D, Roloff JS, Lukens JN, Parker P, Greene HL, Ghishan FK. Intravenous fat emulsions and human neutrophil function. *J Pediatr* 1981;99:913–916.

48. Puntis JWL, Rushton DI. Pulmonary intravascular lipid in neonatal necropsy specimens. *Arch Dis Child* 1991; 66:26–28.

49. Levene MI, Batisti O, Wigglesworth JS, et al. A prospective study of intrapulmonary fat accumulation in the newborn lung following Intralipid infusion. *Acta Paediatr Scand* 1984;73:454–460.

50. Greene J, Hazlett D, Demaree R. Relationship between Intralipid-induced hyperlipemia and pulmonary function. *Am J Clin Nutr* 1976;29:127–135.

51. Hageman JR, McCulloch K, Gora P, Olsen EK, Pachman L, Hunt CE. Intralipid alterations in pulmonary prostaglandin metabolism and gas exchange. *Crit Care Med* 1983;10:794–798.

52. Inwood R, Gora P, Hunt C. Indomethacin inhibition of intralipid-induced lung dysfunction. *Prostaglandins Med* 1981;6:503–513.

53. Skeie B, Askanazi J, Rothkopf J, Rosenbaum SH, Kvetan V, Thomashaw B. Intravenous fat emulsions and lung emulsions: a review. *Crit Care Med* 1988;16:183–194.
54. Lloyd T, Boucek M. Effect of Intralipid on the neonatal pulmonary bed. An echographic study. *J Pediatr* 1986; 108:130–133.
55. Gilbertson N, Kovar IZ, Cox DJ, Crowe L, Palmer NT. Introduction of intravenous lipid administration on the first day of life in the very low birth weight neonate. *J Pediatr* 1991;119:615–623.
56. Adamkin D. Nutrition in very low birth weight infants. *Clin Perinatol* 1986;13:419–443.
57. Stahl GE, Spear ML, Hamosh M. Intravenous administration of lipid emulsions to premature infants. *Clin Perinatol* 1986;13:133–162.
58. American Academy of Pediatrics Committee on Nutrition. Use of intravenous fat emulsions in pediatric patients. *Pediatrics* 1981;68:738–743.
59. Haumont D, Deckelbaum RJ, Richelle M, Dahlan W, Coussaert E, Bihain BE, et al. Plasma lipid and plasma lipoprotein concentrations in low birth weight infants given parenteral nutrition with twenty or ten percent lipid emulsion. *J Pediatr* 1989;115:787–793.
60. Churella JR, Bachhuber WL, MacLean WC Jr. Survey: methods of feeding low-birth-weight infants. *Pediatrics* 1985;76:243–249.
61. Lucas A, Bloom S, Aynsley-Green A. Gut hormones and minimal enteral feeding. *Acta Paediatr Scand* 1986; 75:719–723.
62. Ostertag SG, LaGamma EF, Reisen CE, Ferrintino FL. Early enteral feeding does not affect the incidence of necrotizing enterocolitis. *Pediatrics* 1986;77:275–280.
63. Dunn L, Weiner J, Kliegman R. Beneficial effects of early hypocaloric enteral feeding on neonatal gastrointestinal function: preliminary report of a randomized trial. *J Pediatr* 1988;112:622–629.
64. Aynsley-Green A, Adrian T, Bloom S. Feeding and the development of enteroinsular hormone secretion in the preterm infant: effects of continuous gastric infusions of human milk compared with intermittent boluses. *Acta Paediatr Scand* 1982;71:379–383.
65. Grant J, Denne SC. Effect of intermittent versus continuous enteral feeding on energy expenditure in premature infants. *J Pediatr* 1991;118:928–932.
66. Kliegman RM, Fanaroff AA. Necrotizing enterocolitis: a nine-year experience. I. Epidemiology and uncommon observations. *Am J Dis Child* 1981;135:603–606.
67. Palmer SR, Biffin A, Gamsu HR. Outcome of neonatal necrotizing enterocolitis: results of the BAPM/CDSC surveillance study, 1982–1984. *Arch Dis Child* 1989;64: 388–394.
68. Kanto WP Jr, Wilson R, Breart GL, et al. Perinatal events and necrotizing enterocolitis in premature infants. *Am J Dis Child* 1987;141:167–169.
69. Kliegman RM, Fanaroff AA. Necrotizing enterocolitis. *N Engl J Med* 1984;310:1093–1103.
70. Brown E, Sweet A. Preventing necrotizing enterocolitis in neonates. *JAMA* 1978;240:2452–2454.
71. Goldman H. Feeding and necrotizing enterocolitis. *Am J Dis Child* 1980;134:553–555.
72. La Gamma E, Ostertag S, Birenbaum H. Failure of delayed oral feedings to prevent necrotizing enterocolitis. *Am J Dis Child* 1985;139:385–389.
73. Book LS, Herbst J, Jung AL. Comparison of fast- and slow-feeding rate schedules to the development of necrotizing enterocolitis. *J Pediatr* 1976;89:463–466.
74. Anderson DM, Kliegman R. The relationship of neonatal alimentation practices to the occurrence of endemic necrotizing enterocolitis. *Am J Perinatol* 1991;8:62–67.
75. Book LS, Herbert JJ, Atherton SO, Jung AL. Necrotizing enterocolitis in low-birth-weight infants fed an elemental formula. *J Pediatr* 1975;87:602–605.
76. Lucas A, Cole TJ. Breast milk and neonatal necrotising enterocolitis. *Lancet* 1990;336:1519–1523.
77. Eibl MM, Wolf HM, Furnkranz H, Rosenkranz A. Prevention of necrotizing enterocolitis in low-birth-weight infants by IgA-IgG feeding. *N Engl J Med* 1988;319:1–7.
78. Santuli TV, Schullinger JN, Heird WC, et al. Acute necrotizing enterocolitis in infancy: a review of 64 cases. *Pediatrics* 1975;55:376–387.
79. Clark JH. Management of short bowel syndrome in the high-risk infant. *Clin Perinatol* 1984;11:189–197.
80. Klish WJ, Putnam TC. The short gut. *Am J Dis Child* 1982;125:1056–1061.
81. Taylor SF, Sokol RJ. Infants with short bowel syndrome. In: Hay WW Jr, ed. *Neonatal nutrition and metabolism*. St. Louis: Mosby Year Book, 1991:432–450.
82. Goulet OJ, Revillon Y, Jan D, et al. Neonatal short bowel syndrome. *J Pediatr* 1991;119:18–23.
83. Young WF, Swain VA, Pringle EM. Long-term prognosis after major resection of small bowel in early infancy. *Arch Dis Child* 1969;44:465–470.
84. Wilmore DW. Factors correlating with a successful, outcome following extensive intestinal resection in newborn infants. *J Pediatr* 1972;80:88–95.
85. Parker P, Stroop S, Greene J. A controlled comparison of continuous versus intermittent feeding in the treatment of infants with intestinal disease. *J Pediatr* 1981;99: 360–364.
86. Ameen V, Powell GK, Jones LA. Quantitation of fecal carbohydrate excretion in patients with short bowel syndrome. *Gastroenterology* 1987;92:493–500.
87. Weser E. Nutritional aspects of malabsorption: short gut adaptation. *Am J Med* 1979;67:1014–1021.
88. Weinstein MR, Oh W. Oxygen consumption in infants with bronchopulmonary dysplasia. *J Pediatr* 1981;99:958–961.
89. Kurzner SI, Garg M, Bautitsa DB, Sargent CW, Bowman CM, Keens TG. Growth failure in bronchopulmonary dysplasia: elevated metabolic rates and pulmonary mechanics. *J Pediatr* 1988;112:73–80.
90. American Academy of Pediatrics, Committee on Nutrition. Nutritional needs of low-birth-weight infants. *Pediatrics* 1985;75:976–986.
91. Farrell P. Nutrition and infant lung functions. *Pediatr Pulmonol* 1986;2:44–59.
92. Edelman NH, Rucker RB, Peavy HH. NIH workshop summary. Nutrition and the respiratory system. *Am Rev Respir Dis* 1986;134:347–352.
93. Brown LAS, Bliss AS, Longmore WJ. Effect of nutritional status on the long surfactant system: food deprivation and caloric restriction. *Exper Lung Res* 1984;6: 133–147.
94. Gail DB, Massaro GD, Massaro D. Influence of fasting on the lung. *J Appl Physiol* 1977;42:88–92.
95. Gross I, Ilie I, Wilson CM, Rooney SA. The influence of postnatal nutritional deprivation on the phospholipid content of developing rat lung. *Biochim Biophys Acta* 1976; 441:412–422.
96. Gross I, Rooney SA, Warshaw JB. The inhibition of enzymes related to pulmonary fatty acid and phospholipid synthesis by dietary deprivation in the rat. *Biochem Biophys Res Commun* 1975;64:59–63.
97. O'Brodovich HM, Mellins RB. Bronchopulmonary dysplasia: unresolved neonatal acute lung injury. *Am Rev Respir Dis* 1985;132:694–709.
98. Arora N, Rochester D. Respiratory muscle strength and maximal voluntary ventilation in undernourished patients. *Am Rev Respir Dis* 1982;126:6–8.

99. Kelsen S, Ference M, Kapoor S. Effects of prolonged undernutrition on structure and function of the diaphragm. *J Appl Physiol* 1985;58:1354–1359.

100. Zachman RD. Vitamin A. In: Farrell PM, Taussig LM, eds. *Bronchopulmonary dysplasia and related chronic respiratory disorders*. Report of the 90th Ross Conference on Pediatric Research. Columbus, OH: Ross Laboratories, 1986:86–96.

101. Hustead V, Gutcher G, Anderson S. Relationship of vitamin A status to lung disease in the preterm infant. *J Pediatr* 1984;105:610–615.

102. Anzano MA, Olson JA, Lamb AJ. Morphologic alterations in the trachea and the salivary gland following the induction of rapid synchronous vitamin A deficiency in rats. *Am J Pathol* 1980;98:7171–7180.

103. Sullivan J. Iron, plasma antioxidants, and the oxygen radical disease of prematurity. *Am J Dis Child* 1988; 132:1341–1344.

104. Deneke S, Gershoff S, Fanburg B. Potentiation of oxygen toxicity in rats by dietary protein or amino acid deficiency. *J Appl Physiol* 1983;54:147–151.

105. Cross C, Haegawa G, Reddy K, Omaye ST. Enhanced lung toxicity of oxygen in selenium-deficient rats. *Res Commun Chem Pathol Pharmacol* 1977;16:695–706.

106. Ehrenkranz RA, Ablow RC. Effect of vitamin E on the development of oxygen-induced lung injury in neonates. *Ann NY Acad Sci* 1982;93:452–466.

107. Sosenko IRS, Innis SM, Frank L. Polyunsaturated fatty acids and protection of newborn rats from oxygen toxicity. *J Pediatr* 1988;112:630–637.

108. Roberts RJ. Implications of nutrition in oxygen-related pulmonary diseases in the human premature infant. *Adv Pharmacol Ther* 1978;8:53–64.

109. Frank L, Groseclose EE. Oxygen toxicity in newborns: the adverse effect of undernutrition. *J Appl Physiol* 1982; 53:1248–1255.

110. Myers BA, Dubick MA, Gerreits J, Rucker RB, Jackson AC, Reiser KM, et al. Protein deficiency. Effects on lung mechanics and the accumulation of collagen and elastin in rat lung. *J Nutr* 1983;113:2308–2315.

111. Sahebjami H, Vassalo C. Effects of starvation and refeeding on lung mechanics and morphometry. *Am Rev Respir Dis* 1979;119:443–451.

112. Martin T, Altman Z, Alvares L. The effects of severe protein-calorie malnutrition on antibacterial defense mechanisms in the rat lung. *Am Rev Respir Dis* 1983; 128:1013–1019.

113. Chandra RK. Nutrition, immunity and infection. Present knowledge and future directions. *Lancet* 1983;1:688–691.

114. Mata L. The malnutrition-infection complex and its environmental factors. *Proc Nutr Soc* 1979;38:29–40.

115. Yunis KA, Oh W. Effects of intravenous glucose loading on oxygen consumption, carbon dioxide production, and resting energy expenditure in infants with bronchopulmonary dysplasia. *J Pediatr* 1989;115:127–132.

116. Yeh TF, McClenan DA, Ayahi OA, Pildes RS. Metabolic rate and energy balance in infants with bronchopulmonary dysplasia. *J Pediatr* 1989;114:448–451.

117. Kao LC, Durand DJ, Nickerson BG. Improving pulmonary function does not decrease oxygen consumption in infants with bronchopulmonary dysplasia. *J Pediatr* 1988; 112:616–621.

118. Kalhan SC, Denne SC. Energy consumption in infants with bronchopulmonary dysplasia. *J Pediatr* 1990; 116:662–664.

119. Kurzner SI, Garg M, Bautista DB, et al. Growth failure in infants with bronchopulmonary dysplasia: nutrition and elevated resting metabolic expenditure. *Pediatrics* 1988; 81:379–384.

120. Van Aerde JE, Sauer R, Heim T, Smith J, Swyer P. Is bountiful nutrient intake beneficial for the orally fed very low birth weight infant? *Pediatr Res* 1988;23:427A.

121. Brown E, Stark A, Sosenko I, Lawson EE, Avery ME. Bronchopulmonary dysplasia: possible relationship to pulmonary edema. *J Pediatr* 1978;92:982–984.

122. Brown E. Increased risk of bronchopulmonary dysplasia in infants with patent ductus arteriosus. *J Pediatr* 1979; 95:865–866.

123. Van Marter LJ, Leviton A, Allred EN, Pagano M, Kuban KCK. Hydration during the first days of life and the risk of bronchopulmonary dysplasia in low birth weight infants. *J Pediatr* 1990;116:942–949.

124. Groothuis J, Rosenberg A. Home oxygen promotes weight gain in infants with bronchopulmonary dysplasia. *Am J Dis Child* 1987;141:992–995.

125. Heymsfield SB, Erbland M, Casper K, et al. Enteral nutritional support: metabolic, cardiovascular, and pulmonary interrelations. *Clin Chest Med* 1986;7:41–67.

126. Heymsfield SB, Head CA, McManus CB, Seitz S, Staton GW, Grossman GD. Respiratory, cardiovascular and metabolic effects of enteral hyperalimentation: influence of formula dose and composition. *Am J Clin Nutr* 1984; 40:116–160.

127. Dudell GG, Gersony WM. Patent ductus arteriosus in neonates with severe respiratory disease. *J Pediatr* 1984; 104:915–920.

128. Cotton RB, Stahlman MR, Berder HW, Graham TP, Catterton WZ, Kovar I. Randomized trial of early closure of symptomatic patent ductus arteriosus in small preterm infants. *J Pediatr* 1978;93:647–651.

129. Clyman RI, Heymann MA, Mauray F. Cardiopulmonary effects of a patent ductus arteriosus. *Pediatr Res* 1985; 19:126A.

130. Johnson DS, Rogers JH, Null DM, de Lemos RA. The physiologic consequences of the ductus arteriosus in the extremely immature newborn. *Clin Res* 1978;26:826A.

131. Murphy DJ, Vick GW, Ramsay JM, Danford DA, Huhta JC. Continuous wave Doppler echocardiography in patent ductus arteriosus. *J Cardiovasc Ultrason* 1987;6: 273–278.

132. Kitterman JA. Effects of intestinal ischemia in necrotizing enterocolitis in the newborn infant. In: Moore TD, ed. *Necrotizing enterocolitis in the newborn infant*. Report of the 68th Ross Conference on Pediatric Research. Columbus, OH: Ross Laboratories, 1975:38–41.

133. Van Bel F, Van Zoeren D, Schipper J, Gult GL, Boan J. Effect of indomethacin on superior mesenteric artery blood flow velocity in preterm infants. *J Pediatr* 1990; 116:965–970.

134. Walters M. Tolerance in intravenous indomethacin treatment for premature infants with patent ductus arteriosus. *Br Med J* 1988;297:773–774.

135. Bell EF, Warburton D, Stonestreet B, Oh W. Effect of fluid administration on the development of symptomatic patent ductus arteriosus and congestive heart failure in premature infants. *N Engl J Med* 1980;302:598–604.

136. Galbraith RS, Karchmar EJ, Pievey WN, Low JA. The clinical prediction of intrauterine growth retardation. *Am J Obstet Gynecol* 1979;133:281–286.

137. Teberg AJ, Hotrakitya S, Wu PYK, Yeh S-Y, Hoppenbrowers T. Factors affecting nursery survival of very low birth weight infants. *J Perinatol Med* 1987;15:297–306.

138. Cefalo RC. The hazards of labor and delivery for the intrauterine growth retarded fetus. *J Reprod Med* 1978;21:300–304.

139. Gruenwald P. Growth and maturation of the foetus and its relation to perinatal mortality. In: Butler NR, Alberman ED, eds. *Perinatal problems*. Second Report of British

Perinatal Mortality Survey. Edinburgh, Scotland: Livingstone, 1969:141–162.

140. Kliegman RM, Johnston VL. The metabolism and endocrinology of intrauterine growth retardation. In: Hay WW Jr, ed. *Neonatal nutrition and metabolism.* St. Louis: Mosby Year Book; 1991:392–418.

141. Brar JS, Rutherford SE. Classification of intrauterine growth retardation. *Semin Perinatol* 1988;12:2–10.

142. Kimble KJ, Ariagno RL, Stevenson DK, Sunshine P. Growth to age 3 years among very low-birth-weight sequelae-free survivors of modern neonatal intensive care. *J Pediatr* 1982;100:622–624.

143. Davies DP. Growth of "small for dates" babies. *Early Hum Dev* 1981;5:95–105.

144. Kumer SP, Anday EK, Sacks LM, Ting RY, Delivoria-Papadopoulos M. Follow-up studies of very low birth weight infants (1,250 grams or less) born and treated within a perinatal center. *Pediatrics* 1980;66:438–444.

145. Villar J, Smeriglio V, Martorell R, Brown CH, Klein RE. Heterogeneous growth and mental development of intrauterine growth-retarded infants during the first 3 years of life. *Pediatrics* 1984;74:783–791.

146. Davies DP, Platts P, Pritchard JM, Wilkinson PW. Nutritional status of light-for-date infants at birth and its influence on early postnatal growth. *Arch Dis Child* 1979;54:703–706.

147. Hack M, Merkatz IR, McGrath SK, Jones PK, Fanaroff AA. Catch-up growth in very-low-birthweight infants. *Am J Dis Child* 1984;138:370–375.

148. Hack M, Merkatz IR, Gordon D, Jones PK, Fanaroff AA. The prognostic significance of postnatal growth in very low birth weight infants. *Am J Obstet Gynecol* 1982;143:693–699.

149. Teberg AJ, Walther FJ, Pena IC. Mortality, morbidity, and outcome of the small-for-gestational age infant. *Semin Perinatol* 1988;12:84–94.

150. Allen MC. Developmental outcome and follow-up of the small for gestational age infant. *Semin Perinatol* 1984;8:123–156.

151. Parkinson CE, Wallis S, Harvey D. School achievement and behavior of children who were small-for-dates at birth. *Dev Med Child Neurol* 1981;23:41–50.

152. Harvey DR, Prince J, Bunton WJ, Campbell S. Abilities of children who were small for dates at birth and whose growth in utero was measured by ultrasonic cephalometry. *Pediatr Res* 1976;10:891.

153. Gross SJ, Kosmetatos N, Grimes CT, Williams ML. Newborn head size and neurological status. *Am J Dis Child* 1978;132:753–756.

154. Lipper E, Lee KS, Gartner LM, Grellong B. Determinant of neurobehavioral outcome in low-birth-weight infants. *Pediatrics* 1981;67:502–505.

155. Lucas A, Morley R, Cole TJ, Gore SM, Davis JA, Bamford MFM, et al. Early diet in preterm babies and developmental status in infancy. *Arch Dis Child* 1989;64:1570–1578.

156. Naeye RL, Kelly JA. Judgment of fetal age. III: The pathologist's evaluation. *Pediatr Clin North Am* 1966;13:849–862.

157. Shelly J, Neligan G. Neonatal hypoglycemia. *Br Med Bull* 1966;22:34–39.

158. Hay WW. Fetal and neonatal glucose homeostasis and their relation to the small-for-gestational-age infant. *Semin Perinatol* 1984;8:101–116.

159. Haymond MW, Karl IE, Pagliara AS. Increased gluconeogenic substrates in the small-for-gestational-age infant. *N Engl J Med* 1974;291:322–328.

160. Cassady G, Strange M. The small-for-gestational-age (SGA) infant. In: Avery GB, ed. *Pathophysiology and management of the newborn,* 3rd ed. Philadelphia: Lippincott, 1987:299–331.

161. Charlton V. Nutritional supplementation of the growth-retarded fetus. *Advances Perinatol Med* 1986;5:1–42.

162. Charlton V, Johengen M. Intraamniotic administration of nutrients. *Pediatr Res* 1984;118:136A.

163. Mulvihill S, Albert A, Synn A, Fonkalsrud EW. In utero supplemental fetal feeding in an animal model: effects on fetal growth and development. *Surgery* 1985;98:500–505.

164. Charlton V, Reis B. Effects of gastric nutritional supplementation on fetal umbilical uptake of nutrients. *Am J Physiol* 1981;241:E178–E185.

165. Young M, Soltesz G, Noakes D, Joyce J, McFadyen IR, Lewis BV. The influence of intrauterine surgery and of fetal intravenous nutritional supplements (in utero) on plasma free amino acid homeostasis in the pregnant ewe. *J Perinatol Med* 1975;3:180–197.

166. Charlton V, Johengen, M. Fetal intravenous nutritional supplementation ameliorates the development of embolization-induced growth retardation in sheep. *Pediatr Res* 1987;22:55–61.

167. Cetin I, Corbetta C, Sereni LP. Umbilical amino acid concentrations in normal and growth-retarded fetuses sampled in utero by cordocentesis. *Am J Obstet Gynecol* 1990;162:253–261.

168. Cowett RM. The metabolic sequelae in the infant of the diabetic mother. In: Cohen MR, Foa PP, eds. *Endocrinology and metabolism.* Vol: Jovanovic L, ed. *Controversies in diabetes and pregnancy.* New York: Springer-Verlag; 1988:149–171.

169. Cowett RM, Schwartz R. The infant of the diabetic mother. *Pediatr Clin North Am* 1982;29:1212–1231.

170. Bloom SR, Johnston DT. Failure of glucagon release in infants of diabetic mothers. *Br Med J Clin Res* 1972;4:169–173.

171. Light IJ, Sutherland JM, Loggie JM, Gaffney TE. Impaired epinephrine release in hypoglycemic infants of diabetic mothers. *N Engl J Med* 1967;277:394–398.

172. Kalhan SC, Savin SM, Adam PAJ. Attenuated glucose production rate in newborn infants of insulin-dependent diabetic mothers. *N Engl J Med* 1977;296:375–376.

173. Cowett RM, Susa JB, Giletti B, Oh W, Schwartz R. Variability of endogenous glucose production in infants of insulin dependent diabetic mothers. *Pediatr Res* 1980;14:570A.

174. Cowett RM, Susa JB, Giletti B, Oh W, Schwartz R. Glucose kinetics in infants of diabetic mothers. *Am J Obstet Gynecol* 1983;146:781–786.

175. Hay WW Jr. Fetal metabolic consequences of maternal diabetes. In: Jovanic L, Peterson CM, Fuhrmann K, eds. *Diabetes and pregnancy: teratology, toxicity, and treatment.* New York: Praeger Publishers, 1986:185–221.

176. Pildes RS, Hart RJ, Warrner R, Cornblath M. Plasma insulin response during oral glucose tolerance tests in newborns of normal and gestational diabetic mothers. *Pediatrics* 1969;44:76–82.

177. Siegel CD, Sparks JW, Battaglia FC. Patterns of serum glucose and galactose concentrations in term newborn infants after milk feedings. *Biol Neonate* 1988;54:301–306.

178. Kliegman RM, Sparks JW. Perinatal galactose metabolism *J Pediatr* 1985;107:831–841.

179. Grodsky CM, Balts AA, Bennett LL. Effect of carbohydrate on secretion of insulin from isolated rat pancreas. *Am J Physiol* 1983;205:638–644.

180. Pribylova J, Kozlova J. Glucose and galactose infusions in newborns of diabetic and healthy mothers. *Biol Neonate* 1979;36:193–197.

181. Cruikshank DP, Pitkin RM, Reynolds WA, Williams GA, Hargis GK. Altered maternal calcium homeostasis in di-

abetic pregnancy. *J Clin Endocrinol Metab* 1980;50: 264–267.

182. Demarini S, Tsang RC. What causes neonatal hypocalcemia? *Contemp Obstet Gynecol* 1990;35;107–121.

183. Dancis J, O'Connell JR, Holt LE Jr. Grid for recording weight of premature infants. *J Pediatr* 1948;33:570–572.

184. Hay WW Jr. Nutritional needs of the extremely low-birth-weight infant. *Sem Perinatol* 1991;15:482–492.

185. Hay WW Jr. A biologic perspective on the nutritional requirements of the extremely LBW infant. In: Cowett RM, Hay WW Jr, eds. *The micropremie: The next frontier*. Report of the 99th Ross Conference on Pediatric Research. Columbus, OH: Ross Laboratories, 1990: 103–110.

186. MacLean WC. What matters in feeding the extremely low-birthweight infant? In: Cowett RM, Hay WW Jr, eds. *The micropremie: The next frontier*. Report of the 99th Ross Conference on Pediatric Research. Columbus, OH: Ross Laboratories, 1990:111–115.

187. Ross G, Lipper EG, Auld PAM. Educational status and school-related abilities of very low birth weight premature children. *Pediatrics* 1991;88:1125–1134.

188. Widdowson EM. Changes in body composition during growth. In: Davis JA, Dobbing J, eds. *Scientific foundations of paediatrics*. Philadelphia: WB Saunders, 1974:44–45.

189. Meier PR, Peterson RG, Bonds DR, Meschia G, Battaglia FC. Rates of protein synthesis and turnover in fetal life. *Am J Physiol* 1981;240:E320–E324.

190. Kennaugh JM, Bell AW, Meschia G, Battaglia FC. Ontogenetic changes in protein synthesis rate and leucine oxidation rate during fetal life. *Pediatr Res* 1987;22: 688–692.

191. Costarino AT, Baumgart S. Modern fluid and electrolyte management of the critically ill premature infant. *Pediatr Clin North Am* 1986;33:153.

17. Conditionally Essential Nutrients: Cysteine, Taurine, Tyrosine, Arginine, Glutamine, Choline, Inositol, and Nucleotides

Ricardo Uauy

Harry L. Greene

William C. Heird

Dietary recommendations usually focus on the nutrients that cannot be synthesized by humans. Insufficient dietary supplies of these nutrients induce deficiency diseases.[1] Less attention has been given to nutrients that are traditionally considered nonessential. That is, the biochemical pathways to synthesize the nonessential compounds are present, and their endogenous synthesis is sufficient for normal function. However, certain disease conditions or developmental states may reduce the synthetic capacity below functional metabolic demands.[1,2] During the past few decades, several nutrients have been identified that may be required dietary constituents, but only in unusual situations. These have been referred to as "conditionally essential" nutrients.

Evidence accumulated suggests that taurine, cysteine, tyrosine, carnitine, and choline may be conditionally essential for immature newborn infants.[3-6] More recent findings suggest that inositol, arginine, glycine, and dietary nucleotides (purine and pyrimidine bases) may also be conditionally essential.[7-11] For example, dietary inositol (at intakes similar to that provided by human milk) reduced the severity of respiratory distress, improved survival after hyaline membrane disease, and ameliorated the sequelae from oxygen-induced injury in preterm neonates[8]; also, nucleotides in amounts present in human milk appear to promote intestinal epithelial healing following infection.[7]

The purpose of this chapter is to summarize information concerning several "conditionally essential" nutrients which may be important dietary or intravenous constituents for preterm infants. A summary of the suggested additions of the nutrients to preterm infant formulas and total parenteral nutrition (TPN) solutions is provided in Table 17.1.

Amino Acids

Individual amino acids are often described as essential as determined by optimal growth rate and maintenance of positive nitrogen balance.[9,10] More recently there is increasing evidence indicating that several amino acids dispensable for normal infants may be required for preterm infants. Examples are arginine, glutamine, and glycine—which may be necessary for optimal function during development or recovery from injury.[10,11] The demarcation of amino acids into essential (i.e., cannot be synthesized) and nonessential (i.e., can be made de novo) is becoming less sharp. The use of the terms "indispensable" and "dispensable" to represent extremes in a spectrum of requirements better typifies the metabolic fates of and the interconversions that occur with dietary amino acids. The only absolutely essential amino acids are lysine and threonine, because they cannot be made from transamination of carbon skeletons. Conversely, alanine and aspartate can be considered absolutely nonessential, because they can be readily formed by transamination from available carbon skeletons, pyruvate, and oxaloacetate.[10,11] The first section of this chapter summarizes information on several amino acids that may be rate limiting for optimal cellular function in the absence of an exogenous source.

Cyst(e)ine

Note: "Cyst(e)ine" is used throughout to designate any undefined combination of cysteine and cystine; the terms "cysteine" and "cystine" are used to designate the specific amino acids.

Cyst(e)ine, in addition to being an important amino acid component of most proteins, is a precursor for taurine and is one of the amino acid components of the peptide glutathione. In the normal adult and older child, cyst(e)ine is formed endogenously via the transsulfuration pathway (Fig. 17.1) from the essential amino acid methionine. Thus, in these populations, cyst(e)ine is not an essential amino acid. However, the hepatic activity of cystathionase, the enzyme catalyzing the final step of the transsulfuration pathway, is absent or low during development and remains low for the first few months of postnatal life.[4,12] Although cystathionase activity of nonhepatic tissues (e.g., the kidney and the adrenal) reaches adult values early in development,[13] extrahepatic cystathionase activity appears to be inadequate to supply the growing infant's total needs for

Table 17.1. Intakes of Cyst(e)ine, Taurine, Inositol, and Choline in Preterm Infant Formulations

| | Human Milk Content | | Advisable Intake | | |
| | | | Formula Content* | | TPN Content[†] |
	μmol/dL	μmol/100 kcal	μmol/dL	μmol/100 kcal	μmol/dL
Cyst(e)ine[‡]	150–200	225–300	150–265	225–395	400–800
Taurine	20–40	30–60	20–40	30–60	40–120
Tyrosine	290–360	430–540	430–540	640–800	200
Inositol	100–250	148–375	100–250	150–375	300[§]
Choline	75–150[¶]	115–225[¶]	75–150	115–225	—[∥]

*Contents of 20 kcal/30 mL preterm infant formula; amounts of cyst(e)ine and tyrosine reflect the range of these amino acids in either 18:82 or 60:40 bovine milk protein, assuming protein intakes of 3 to 3.5 g/kg/day.

[†]Amounts of each nutrient are based on assumption that infant will receive 125 mL/kg/day.

[‡]As cysteine equivalents; if expressed as cystine, contents will be one half of amounts shown.

[§]Refers to only one publication using intravenous inositol.[8] This suggested intravenous intake is based on the positive results of that study and is the basis for the single intravenous recommendation.

[∥]No data on intravenous intakes.

[¶]Recent analyses indicate early human milk contains approximately 145 μmol/dL (S. Zeisel, personal communication).

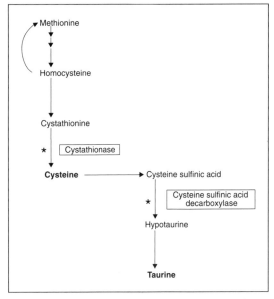

Fig. 17.1. Metabolic conversion of methionine to cysteine and taurine.

cyst(e)ine. For example, Snyderman found that removal of cysteine from an otherwise adequate synthetic diet of 2- to 4-month-old infants who had been born prematurely resulted in lower rates of weight gain and nitrogen retention as well as lower plasma cyst(e)ine concentrations.[14] The cyst(e)ine intake required to restore the rates of weight gain and nitrogen retention and the concentration of plasma cyst(e)ine to control values was 85 mg/kg/day; intakes of either

44 or 66 mg/kg/day restored neither the rates of weight gain and nitrogen retention nor the plasma cyst(e)ine concentration to control values.

The proteins commonly used in infant feeding contain cyst(e)ine as well as methionine, but their cyst(e)ine content differs considerably. The cyst(e)ine content of human milk protein, for example, is 17 mg/g whereas that of bovine milk protein is only 8 mg/g; the whey fraction of bovine milk protein contains 22 mg/g but the casein fraction contains only 3 mg/g.[15] Today, most formula-fed low-birthweight (LBW) infants receive formulas containing modified bovine milk protein (60% whey proteins and 40% caseins) with a cyst(e)ine content (calculated from the above values) of about 15 mg/g. Thus, at a total protein intake of 3 to 3.6 g/kg/day, these infants receive a cyst(e)ine intake of 45 to 55 mg/kg/day, or only one half to two thirds of the apparent requirement as estimated by Snyderman.[14] Infants fed the same amount of human milk protein would receive a cyst(e)ine intake of only 51 to 61 mg/kg/day; in reality, infants fed their own mother's milk without protein supplementation receive a total protein intake of only about 2.5 g/kg/day, providing a cyst(e)ine intake of about 42 to 43 mg/kg/day. Infants fed a casein-predominant bovine milk formula providing 3 to 3.6 g/kg/day of protein receive only 24 to 29 mg/kg/day of cyst(e)ine.

Despite the twofold difference in cyst(e)ine content between whey-predominant and casein-predominant bovine milk formulas, both provide adequate growth and neither provides as much cyst(e)ine as Snyderman found to be necessary.[14,16-22] However, plasma cyst(e)ine concentration generally is higher in infants fed whey-predominant formulas.[21-23] Thus, on balance, the cyst(e)ine intake of infants fed whey-predominant formulas (50 mg/kg/day) seems preferable to that of infants fed casein-predominant formulas (25 mg/kg/day). The desirability of an even greater cyst(e)ine intake—e.g., 85 mg/kg, as found necessary by Snyderman[14]—is not clear.

Unfortunately, Snyderman[14] did not state the methionine intake of the infants studied. If the methionine intake was less than the roughly 75 to 90 mg/kg/day of infants fed casein- or whey-predominant formulas at a protein intake of 3.0 to 3.6 g/kg/day, the apparent higher cyst(e)ine requirement of the infants studied by Snyderman possibly could be related to their low methionine intake. This explanation, of course, implies that there is sufficient nonhepatic cystathionase activity to provide at least a portion of the infant's cyst(e)ine requirement if methionine intake is generous.[13]

Since cysteine is unstable and cystine is only sparingly soluble in aqueous solution, no parenteral amino acid mixture contains appreciable amounts of cyst(e)ine, and infants who receive parenteral nutrition infusates containing these mixtures have quite low plasma cyst(e)ine concentrations.[24] Cysteine hydrochloride can be added to the parenteral infusate when it is prepared, and doing so results in higher plasma cyst(e)ine concentrations but not in the improvement in either nitrogen retention or weight gain[25-27] that would be expected if cyst(e)ine were a required nutrient. A possible explanation is the fact that tyrosine intake and resulting plasma tyrosine concentrations also were quite low.[24] Thus, concurrent tyrosine deficiency obscured any positive effect of cysteine supplementation on growth and nitrogen retention.

There is no definitive proof of this argument for tyrosine deficiency, but the results of two subsequent studies are at least supportive of this concept. First, Helms et al.[28] reported greater rates of both weight gain and nitrogen retention in LBW infants who received a parenteral nutrition regimen containing both tyrosine (as N-acetyl-L-tyrosine) and cysteine hydrochloride than in a control population who received an isocaloric, isonitrogenous regimen without either supplement. The authors suggested that the observed differences were attributable to provision of both tyrosine and cyst(e)ine. However, although the supplemented group retained 78% of the nitrogen intake and the control group only 66%, the amino acid intakes of the two groups differed in other respects, and the overall plasma amino acid pattern of the supplemented group was more ''normal'' (closer to that of normal-term infants) than was that of the control group.[29] Thus, in this study, provision of more optimal amounts of all amino acids, not only cyst(e)ine

and tyrosine, is an equally tenable explanation of the findings. In a more recent study, Kashyap et al.[30] found that cyst(e)ine supplementation of the amino acid mixture containing N-acetyl-L-tyrosine resulted in somewhat greater utilization of the total amino acid intake than was the case in the control group that received no cyst(e)ine supplementation. Thus, on balance, it appears that cyst(e)ine is a conditionally essential amino acid for infants requiring parenteral nutrition.

Interestingly, adults and older children receiving parenteral nutrition regimens without cyst(e)ine also develop quite low plasma cyst(e)ine concentrations. Whereas this finding in infants can be explained on the basis of low to absent hepatic cystathionase activity, this is an unlikely explanation for the finding in adults. To help explain this discrepancy, Stegink and Denbesten[31] reported that intravenous administration of a cyst(e)ine-free parenteral nutrition infusate resulted in low plasma cyst(e)ine concentrations but that intragastric administration of the same infusate did not. Similar findings were reported more recently by Chawla et al.[32]; plasma concentrations of taurine, creatine, choline, and carnitine also were lower in adults receiving a cysteine-free parenteral nutrition regimen than in adults receiving a cysteine-free enteral nutrition regimen. Chawla et al. also suggested that parenterally administered methionine may be metabolized by a pathway other than the transsulfuration pathway.[32] Suggested alternatives include direct transamination or accelerated remethylation of homocysteine to methionine (Fig. 17.1). Whatever the mechanism, it appears that cyst(e)ine is a conditionally essential nutrient for the adult as well as for the infant who requires parenteral nutrition.

Low-birthweight infants have markedly lower plasma glutathione concentrations than older children or adults.[33] Since cysteine is required for glutathione synthesis, it is intriguing to postulate that inadequate cyst(e)ine intake at least contributes to the low plasma, and presumably tissue, glutathione concentrations. However, insufficient data are available to warrant this postulate. For example, in infants receiving parenteral nutrition exclusively, Kashyap et al.[30] found no difference in plasma glutathione concentration between infants who did and those who did not receive cysteine hydrochloride supplementation of an otherwise isonitrogenous and isocaloric parenteral nutrition regimen.

Toxicity. Toxicity related to cyst(e)ine has not been linked to clinical abnormalities in term infants. However, it is quite clear that many preterm infants who receive parenteral nutrition regimens supplemented with cysteine hydrochloride develop metabolic acidosis, particularly those weighing less than approximately 1,250 g at birth. With appropriate monitoring, the acidosis can be detected and treated in a timely manner. Alternatively, appropriate base therapy (e.g., acetate or lactate) for the prevention of acidosis can be incorporated into the parenteral nutrition infusate. Theoretically, an equimolar amount of base should prevent the acidosis associated with cysteine hydrochloride; however, from experience and available data[30,34] we suggest that base intake must be roughly double the intake of cysteine hydrochloride to prevent acidosis.

Before we discuss the effect of cyst(e)ine intake on plasma cyst(e)ine concentration, some discussion of the plasma cyst(e)ine concentration is in order. There are two major plasma fractions of cyst(e)ine—bound and free.[35] In general, the bound fraction, which is roughly equal to the free fraction, is not measured by conventional methods. However, if plasma is not deproteinized immediately, the bound fraction may increase at the expense of the free, resulting in a perhaps falsely low free fraction.[36] The free plasma cyst(e)ine fraction includes primarily cystine, but some cysteine; the relative proportions are roughly 3 or 4 cystine to 1 cysteine.[37] Plasma cyst(e)ine concentration as usually measured by amino acid analyzer includes the free cystine plus some but not all of the bound cysteine. Thus, plasma cyst(e)ine concentration as measured by amino acid analyzer usually is somewhat lower than free cyst(e)ine as measured calorimetrically,[35] because the calorimetric measurement includes all of the free cystine and cysteine. Both free cystine and cysteine can be quantitated separately by amino acid analyzer, but additional steps (and plasma) are required and this usually is not done. Another peculiarity is that plasma cyst(e)ine concentration is reported sometimes as cystine, which is measured directly by the analyzer, and sometimes as $\frac{1}{2}$-cystine, which is twice the cystine concentration (i.e., the cystine concentration expressed as molecular cysteine equivalents); frequently, it is impossible to tell which is reported.

The major effect of parenteral cyst(e)ine supplementation on plasma cyst(e)ine concentration is to increase the free cysteine fraction. Little effect on either free cystine or the bound cyst(e)ine fraction is seen. In part, this effect reflects accumulation in plasma of D-glucose-L-cysteine that forms in the parenteral infusate; within 24 hours of adding cysteine hydrochloride to the complete infusate, approximately 50% is present as D-glucose-L-cysteine rather than as cyst(e)ine.[38] There is some concern as to whether D-glucose-L-cysteine is a bioavailable form of cysteine. However, Kashyap et al.[30] found no difference in plasma cyst(e)ine concentration or nitrogen retention between infants who received an infusate containing half of its cyst(e)ine content in the form of D-glucose-L-cysteine and another group who received only cysteine.

Suggested Intakes. Suggested intakes of dietary cyst(e)ine for both LBW and term infants fed human milk or conventional formulas could approximate 0.2 to 0.5 mmol of cysteine equivalents per kg per day, or 0.13 to 0.33 mmol cysteine equivalents per dL of 24 kcal/oz formula. Although the higher intakes characteristic of human milk and whey-predominant formulas may be preferable, there is no clinical data to support this preference. Whether cyst(e)ine supplementation of parenteral nutrition regimens does more than increase the plasma concentration of free cyst(e)ine, a questionably favorable effect, is not entirely clear. There is some evidence that cyst(e)ine supplementation in the absence of a limiting intake of another essential or conditionally essential amino acid improves nitrogen retention. Thus, supplementation of parenteral nutrition regimens with cysteine hydrochloride (as is commonly done to increase calcium phosphate solubility) can be recommended.[38] The amount of supplementation, however, is somewhat more problematical. The requirement as defined by Snyderman in infants fed a synthetic diet is 85 mg/kg/day (0.7 mmol/kg/day); infants fed their own mother's milk or a whey-predominant formula receive about half this amount. The amount of cyst(e)ine supplementation usually recommended for parenteral nutrition is 121 mg (1 mmol)/kg/day. Considering this, it seems reasonable to recommend that parenteral nutrition regimens provide a cyst(e)ine intake of 0.5 to 1.0 mmol/kg/day (or 0.4 to 0.8 mmol/dL, assuming the infusate is delivered at a rate of 125 mL/kg/day). However, a note of caution is in order when using this dose in small infants (<1,250 g). Even infants receiving the lower recommended intake of half the usual dose of cysteine as cysteine hydrochloride should be monitored for acidosis and treated as suggested in this section.

Taurine

Taurine, a β-amino sulfonic acid (2-aminoethane sulfonic acid) is formed endogenously in most animal species, including the human adult, from cysteine. Although not a component of structural proteins, taurine is present in appreciable amounts in both intracellular and extracellular compartments. Its one well-established functional role is in conjugation of bile acids. Taurine also is thought to play a role in osmoregulation, and it may be involved in neurotransmission either as a neurotransmitter per se or as a modulator of neurotransmission.[3,39,40] In vitro, it functions as an antioxidant and as an apparent growth factor.[3,39,40]

The rate-limiting enzyme for endogenous taurine formation is cysteine sulphinic acid decarboxylase (Fig. 17.1). Although the activity of this enzyme is lower in the human than in many other animal species,[39,40] the adult appears to be able to produce sufficient taurine provided the transsulfuration pathway is intact or exogenous cyst(e)ine intake is adequate. However, cysteine sulphinic acid decarboxylase activity is much lower in infants than in adults, and it is not clear that either the LBW or term infant can synthesize adequate taurine endogenously even if exogenous cyst(e)ine intake is generous. Indeed, both LBW and term infants receiving taurine-free but cyst(e)ine-adequate formulas have lower plasma and urinary concentrations of taurine than infants fed human milk, in which taurine is the second most plentiful amino acid of the nonprotein-nitrogen or free–amino-acid fraction.[23,41] Primarily on the basis of this finding, infants are believed to require an exogenous source of taurine, and for the past several years, infant formulas have contained taurine in roughly the same amounts present in human milk. Most pediatric parenteral amino acid mixtures also contain taurine; the amounts present in these mixtures vary from roughly the same amount present in human milk to roughly three times this amount. Recent findings of apparent functional advantages of taurine support its inclusion in these products.

The human species, unlike some other animal species, can conjugate bile acids with glycine as well as taurine; and although taurine appears to be preferred, the human receiving inadequate taurine readily converts to conjugation with glycine. Therefore, it is not surprising that taurine supplementation fails to enhance bile salt synthesis in LBW infants,[42] although it maintains the preponderance of taurine-conjugated bile salts present at birth.[42,43] Infants fed human milk, which contains taurine, have a greater rate of synthesis of bile salts and a larger bile salt pool,[42] and this is thought to be at least partially responsible for the more efficient fat absorption of infants fed human milk versus infants fed the same type of fat as a component of formulas. However, human milk also contains various lipases that formulas do not.[44] Indeed, Okamoto et al.[43] found that taurine supplementation has no effect on the fat absorption of LBW infants. In contrast, Galeano et al.[45] found that taurine supplementation improves the fat absorption of LBW infants. Taurine supplementation also has been shown to improve the fat absorption of children with cystic fibrosis.[46] In addition, there is some evidence that inclusion of taurine in total parenteral nutrition (TPN) regimens may lower the prevalence of cholestasis during prolonged parenteral nutrition.[47]

Studies in a variety of animal species show that the taurine content in the brain and the retinas is very high during development and decreases gradually after birth to reach adult concentrations at about the age of weaning.[39] Recent in vivo proton spectroscopy magnetic resonance studies show that the same general pattern of central nervous system taurine content is true for human infants.[48] The taurine content of the retina is particularly high during development. In kittens a diet deficient in taurine for even a short period results in blindness.[49] However, the fact that cats can conjugate bile acids *only* with taurine may contribute to their peculiar susceptibility to a lack of taurine intake. Nonetheless, ultrastructural changes consistent with the changes likely to occur in the retinas of taurine-deficient kittens also have been observed in the retinas of nonhuman primates raised on taurine-free diets.[50,51] In addition, alterations in visual evoked potentials and in electroretinograms occur in children receiving long-term, taurine-free parenteral nutrition regimens.[52,53] Although similar changes have been observed in infants receiving diets deficient in tocopherol or ω3 polyunsaturated fatty acids,[54] taurine supplementation alone restored the altered electroretinograms and visual evoked potentials to normal. Taurine supplementation also seems to enhance development of auditory evoked potentials.[55]

Toxicity. Toxicity related to taurine supplementation has not been reported; in fact, even very large doses appear to have no adverse effects. Considering this and the abundant circumstantial as well as somewhat more limited definitive evidence that exogenous taurine is beneficial, it is reasonable to recommend that all infants receive dietary taurine.

Suggested Intakes. Suggested intakes for taurine should be at about the same levels as for infants fed human milk—i.e., 40 to 50 μmol/kg/day, or about 20 to 40 μmol/dL of formula. Most currently available infant formulas provide this amount. Some parenteral amino acid mixtures also contain taurine (50 mmol/2.5 g amino acids to 1.71 mmol/2.5 g amino acids). Whether amounts substantially in excess of 50 μmol/kg/day are desirable with one of these available mixtures is not clear. The age at which exogenous taurine intake is no longer required also is unknown. Until more information is available, it seems wise to provide taurine to all pediatric patients (and perhaps adults as well) requiring parenteral nutrition. The suggested parenteral dose is 40 to 120 μmol/dL, the amount provided by conventional use of currently available parenteral amino acid mixtures intended for pediatric use.

Tyrosine

Tyrosine also is usually considered an essential amino acid for infants,[55-60] primarily following Snyderman's observation that removal of tyrosine from the otherwise adequate synthetic diet of infants born prematurely some 2 to 4 months earlier resulted in lower rates of weight gain and nitrogen retention as well as in lower plasma tyrosine concentrations.[14]

The amount of tyrosine required to restore the rates of weight gain and nitrogen retention and the plasma concentration to control values was 50 mg/kg/day.

The basis for a requirement for tyrosine during infancy is not clear. The hepatic activity of phenylalanine hydroxylase, the key enzyme in conversion of phenylalanine to tyrosine, is at or near adult levels from the early weeks of gestation onward.[56] Indeed, the more usual derangement in the plasma amino acid pattern of enterally fed infants is hypertyrosinemia rather than isolated hyperphenylalaninemia as would be expected if the infant were unable to convert phenylalanine to tyrosine.[57] The hypertyrosinemia frequently can be reversed by administration of relatively large amounts of ascorbic acid.[58] Since phenylalanine hydroxylase requires a tetrahydropterin cofactor,[59] a lack of this cofactor may be responsible for the apparent inability of infants to convert phenylalanine to tyrosine. Indeed, neonatal rats have low dihydropterin reductase activity.[60]

Tyrosine is virtually insoluble; hence, no parenteral amino acid mixture contains an appreciable amount of tyrosine. As a result, presumably, plasma tyrosine concentrations of infants receiving parenteral nutrition exclusively are quite low. The evidence that adults also have low plasma tyrosine concentration if dependent exclusively on parenteral nutrition is less convincing than that concerning low plasma cysteine concentrations.[32] Nonetheless, data are sufficient to at least suggest that phenylalanine, like methionine, is metabolized differently when administered parenterally versus enterally. If so, tyrosine is a conditionally essential nutrient for all subjects requiring parenteral nutrition.

The only known soluble salt of tyrosine available for inclusion in parenteral amino acid mixtures is N-acetyl-L-tyrosine, which is present in some of the currently available pediatric parenteral amino acid mixtures. However, whereas an amino acid mixture, which provides 0.25 mmol (or 45 mg)/kg/day of tyrosine, primarily as N-acetyl-L-tyrosine, results in somewhat higher plasma tyrosine concentrations than mixtures without N-acetyl-L-tyrosine,[29,61] this tyrosine derivative does not appear to be an optimal source of tyrosine. For example, N-acetyl-L-tyrosine is found in plasma of both preterm and term infants in roughly the same amounts as tyrosine.[29,61] In addition, Wykes et al.[62] have shown that N-acetyl-L-tyrosine is not nearly as effective as an equimolar amount of dipeptide tyrosine in reversing the poor nitrogen retention and weight gain of piglets receiving tyrosine-free parenteral nutrition regimens.

Currently, N-acetyl-L-tyrosine is the only soluble tyrosine derivative that can be included in parenteral amino acid mixtures. Although it seems to be efficacious with respect to maintaining a near-normal plasma tyrosine concentration, there is no evidence whether it contributes to the apparently greater rate of weight gain and nitrogen retention of infants in whose parenteral nutrition regimens it is included.

Toxicity. Toxicity related to tyrosine or N-acetyl-L-tyrosine has not been described; however, the consequences reported from elevations in plasma are not known. On balance, there is no reason to discourage parenteral nutrition regimens providing N-acetyl-L-tyrosine. There also is no reason currently to advocate inclusion of more N-acetyl-L-tyrosine in parenteral amino acid mixtures. Thus, until further information is available, it seems reasonable to recommend a parenteral tyrosine intake of 0.25 mmol (45 mg)/kg/day, or about 0.2 mmol/dL. Interestingly, this is the recommendation established by Snyderman in enterally fed infants.[14]

Suggested Intakes. Suggested intakes based on human milk content and currently available bovine-milk formulas for LBW and term infants appear to provide generous amounts of tyrosine. The tyrosine content of human milk protein is 47 mg/g. The tyrosine content of the protein in casein-predominant bovine milk is 50 mg/g; in whey-predominant bovine milk the tyrosine content of the protein is 41 mg/g.[15] Thus, infants fed adequate amounts of human milk or any of these formulas receive more than the apparent requirement as defined by Snyderman.[14] Low-birthweight infants fed casein-predominant formulas tend to have higher plasma tyrosine concentrations than infants fed whey-predominant formulas.[22,43,57] Thus, for this population, the whey-predominant formulas which provide 123 to 148 mg (0.68 to 0.82 mmol)/kg/day (at protein intakes of 3 to 3.6 g/kg/day) appear preferable. These amounts equate to 0.6 to 0.7 mmol/100 kcal and 0.4 to 0.46 mmol/dL (for a 20 kcal/oz formula).

Arginine

This basic diamino acid has been traditionally considered nonessential for humans, but it is essential for several rapidly growing mammalian species.[63] Conditional essentiality can be postulated during recovery from injury since arginine supplementation has been shown to enhance nitrogen retention, wound healing, and the immune response in patients recovering from surgery.[63-65] Furthermore, in early life this amino acid plays an important regulatory role in priming the urea cycle and in the activation of the carbamoyl phosphate synthetase (Fig. 17.2). Its role as a precursor for creatinine synthesis is also of potential importance for muscle and brain energy utilization.[63,64]

In pharmacologic doses, arginine stimulates insulin secretion and growth hormone secretion; thus it may play a role in anabolism.[66] Arginine is a precur-

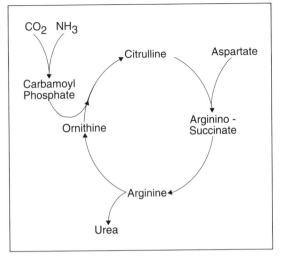

Fig. 17.2. Urea cycle showing arginine.

sor of guanidino nitrogen, which is necessary for the formation of nitric oxide, a potent endothelium relaxing factor.[67] Nitric oxide acts as an intracellular signal that leads to smooth muscle relaxation.

In normal animals, arginine enhances cellular immune mechanisms—in particular, T cell activity. It may also promote an immunopreserving effect in the face of immunosuppression induced in patients by protein energy malnutrition due to cancer. Arginine supplementation in postoperative surgical patients results in enhanced T lymphocyte response and augmented T helper cell number, with a more rapid return to normal T cell function postoperatively compared with control patients.[64,65,68] These data suggest that arginine may stimulate or preserve immune function in high-risk surgical patients and may improve host resistance to infection. However, this putative effect has only been studied in animals using pharmacologic intakes and has not been substantiated in clinical trials.

Toxicity. Toxicity related to arginine has been demonstrated in children receiving 20 to 30 times the customary daily dietary intake. Arginine may be toxic in infants with arginase deficiency, with other defects of urea cycle metabolism such as argininosuccinate lyase deficiency, or with liver failure.[34] Since arginine is a potent stimulator of insulin, excess intake may promote hypoglycemia.

Human milk provides 0.3 mmol/kg/day while infant formulas have up to five times that amount. Infants on TPN will typically receive 1 to 2 mol/kg/day. The current use of arginine salts in antibiotic therapy is based on improved solubility and stability of antibiotics as arginine salts but may provide an additional arginine load of up to 4 mmol of arginine per 100 mg of antibiotic. Thus total arginine supply to preterm

infants, depending on diet and antibiotic usage, may exceed by 5 to 10 times the amount provided by human milk.[69]

Suggested Intakes. No recommendation for arginine supplementation to infant formulas should be made in view of the known toxicity from excessive intakes, the high intakes from TPN and antibiotics, and the lack of demonstrated benefit in human trials.

Glutamine

Interest in glutamine has developed over the last 5 years, subsequent to developments in two areas: (*a*) the understanding of the metabolic importance of glutamine as a fuel for lymphocytes and intestinal epithelial cells[70–73]; (*b*) new knowledge concerning the importance and regulation of the skeletal muscle glutamine pool.[71,72,74] All studies showing positive effects have been performed in animal models or adult humans using doses vastly in excess of that expected from human milk (40% to 60% of the total nitrogen intake).

Toxicity. Toxicity related to high concentrations of glutamine can be expected since its metabolic byproduct γ-aminobutyric acid (GABA) plays an inhibitory role in central nervous system function. Glutamate, a derivative of glutamic acid, used as a flavor enhancer, also serves as a neurotransmitter but at high concentrations has neurotoxic potential; it is one of the classical dietary "excitotoxins."[35]

The instability of glutamine during autoclaving has resulted in its effective omission from parenteral nutrition solutions. For this reason, if glutamine is determined to be an important ingredient for TPN, peptides containing glutamine might represent a reasonable source.[75]

Suggested Intakes. At this time there is no quantitative information about either immune function or gut mucosal function to enable recommendations for enteral or parenteral glutamine supplementation for either term-gestation or preterm infants.

Choline

This quaternary amine (trimethyl-beta-hydroxyethyl-ammonium) contains three methyl groups (Fig. 17.3). The choline metabolite, betaine, acts as a methyl donor to homocysteine to form methionine and the S-adenosylmethionine derivative that serves in a variety of methylation reactions including carnitine synthesis. Choline is an important component of phospholipids such as phosphatidylcholine (PC), choline plasmalogen, and sphingomyelin, which are constituents of all cell membranes.[76] Important membrane properties such as fluidity and transport are largely

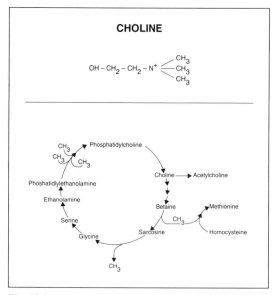

Fig. 17.3. Metabolic interactions of choline and phosphatidyl inositol.

dependent on lipid composition of the bilayer; PC is the main phospholipid in the outer leaflet of cell membranes. Dipalmitoyl PC is also the main component of lung surfactant. Acetylated choline constitutes a small fraction of the choline pool, yet this is crucial since it is required as a neurotransmitter. Acetylcholine synthesis and release are in part dependent on dietary choline and can be augmented by providing free choline or PC.[76,77]

Choline synthesis occurs mainly in the liver (Fig. 17.3) by the sequential trimethylation of phosphatidylethanolamine (PE); synthetic activity has also been reported in the brain, the heart, the lungs, the adrenal glands, and the spleen. Choline formed via this de novo pathway is dependent on folate and vitamin B_{12} since these are responsible for maintaining the one-carbon methyl pool; alternatively, methionine can serve as a methyl donor. Thus choline sufficiency in the absence of dietary choline will be dependent on the interaction of PE, folate, vitamin B_{12}, methionine, etc., and on PE methyltransferase activity.

Under usual conditions, only a fraction of the requirement for choline is derived from de novo synthesis; most of the requirement comes from diet. Choline is present in plant and animal foods as free choline and in phospholipids contained in cell membranes.[76,77] Free choline is absorbed in the small intestine passively at high concentrations but at low concentrations is actively transported by a carrier protein.[78] Choline in phospholipids may be released after pancreatic lipases cleave the fatty acids and deacylation occurs within the enterocyte. Free choline is then transported into the bloodstream and taken up by the tissues. Choline can be oxidized to form betaine, or it can be used for phospholipid synthesis. Betaine cannot be recycled back to choline; glycine is formed after all methyl groups are donated. Excess choline may be lost via the urine as such, although most is excreted as betaine and some is metabolized to glycine.[76,77]

Choline deficiency in humans has not been firmly established as a clinical syndrome, although patients with severely compromised liver function showed improved nitrogen balance following choline supplementation. In animal models, choline-deficient diets are associated with fatty infiltration of the liver. This is reversible by the addition of choline to the diet. Thus, choline is considered essential for several mammalian species including the rat, hamster, dog, and baboon. The syndrome encompasses altered renal function, infertility, hypertension, bone abnormalities, hemorrhages, and abnormal erythropoiesis. The effects of choline-deficient diets are exacerbated by deficiencies in methionine, folate, and vitamin B_{12}. The lack of choline affects the liver phospholipid synthesis necessary for lipoprotein assembly and the extrusion of very low-density liproproteins (VLDL) from the hepatocyte; thus fat accumulates in the hepatocyte. This is the likely mechanism for the observed fatty infiltration and hepatic dysfunction. Recent animal data indicate that early exposure to choline-rich colostrum in the rat may enhance learning ability later on in life.[76,79]

Presently there are no established methods of assessing choline deficiency in humans. Malnourished individuals and patients receiving choline-free TPN solutions decrease their plasma and red cell choline concentrations and lose less betaine in their urine. Patients receiving intravenous lipids that provide choline-containing soy or egg phospholipids will maintain higher plasma and tissue choline concentrations.[80] Choline concentrations in the brain and other tissues can now be measured in vivo using magnetic resonance proton spectroscopy; a postnatal drop in brain choline concentration has been noted when adult and infant brains have been compared. The functional effects of choline supplementation on central nervous system development have not been fully tested in the human; preliminary data from randomized clinical trials on patients with head injury and with degenerative central nervous system conditions indicate that choline supplementation can have demonstrable effects, improving altered central nervous system function.[81]

Human milk and formulas provide varying amounts of free choline and choline-containing phospholipids. The concentration of choline is high (about 150 μmol/dL) in colostrum; in mature breast milk it drops to approximately 75 to 110 μmol/dL. Using newer methods of choline detection, analyses of preterm milk are incomplete. Infant formulas based on bovine milk range from 40 to 150 μmol/dL, depending upon the protein source. The phospholipids in human milk are predominantly phosphatidylcholine, sphingomyelin, and glycerophosphocholine; these are present at concentrations of 20, 20, and 50 μmol/dL, respectively. Bovine milk formulas generally have <10 μmol/dL of each, while soy formulas have higher PC (19 to 24 μmol/dL) but nondetectable sphingomyelin and glycerophosphocholine.[79,82]

Toxicity. Toxicity related to choline has not been reported in infants. Although renal excretion of high intakes is efficient, this amine has neuromodulatory effects; thus, excess supply could have potentially adverse consequences on central nervous system function.

Suggested Intakes. Recommended intakes can only be tentative, based on human milk content and on the plasma and tissue concentration observed in fully breast-fed infants. Intravenous lipid emulsions (Intralipid, Kabi Pharmacia, Inc., Stockholm, Sweden) contain 1.2% egg phospholipid. This provides about 117 mg choline per 100 mL of 10% or 20% Intralipid.[83] The usual dose of Intralipid is 3 g per kg body weight, and at this dose, 165 μmol choline are provided daily using 20% Intralipid. Further human and animal studies supporting conditional essentiality for choline are needed before recommended intakes can be established based on functional effects. Until specific information is available, it is prudent to supply choline in amounts approximating the expected intake based on human milk content of 100 to 150 μmol/dL (S. Zeisel, personal communication). Current bovine milk and soy-based formulas contain about 120 μmol/dL.

Carnitine

Carnitine is discussed in Chapter 5, which covers the fat needs of the preterm infant.

Inositol

Inositol is a six-carbon cyclic polyalcohol sugar derived from inositol 1-phosphate formed by the cyclization of glucose 6-phosphate (Fig. 17.4). It is abundant, mainly as free myo-inositol, in animal and plant biological systems. Other inositols, more notably chiro-inositol, are present but at much lower concentrations. Inositols are readily synthesized by most tissues and act as growth factors for several human cell lines in cultures.[84,85] The evidence accumulated over the past decades indicates that inositol's actions are not like the action of vitamins but are dependent

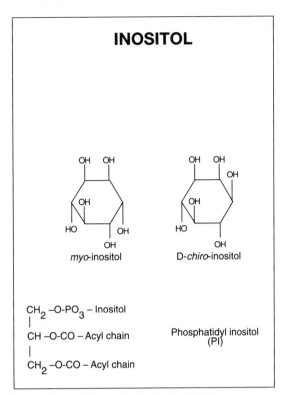

Fig. 17.4. Inositol and phosphatidyl inositol structure.

on the inositol-containing phospholipids known as phosphoinositides. Membrane phosphatidylinositol is the precursor for a series of phosphoinositides that mediate multiple transmembrane signalling processes. The inositol metabolites are part of a second messenger signal transduction system. The relevant effects of inositol are as follows. First, inositide metabolism is linked to the activation of cell surface enzymes (e.g., Na/K ATPase) and receptors (e.g., those responsible for Ca mobilization). Second, the inositol metabolites modulate cell proliferation through release of 1,2-diacylglycerol and activation of protein kinase C and epidermal growth factor. Third, the inositol-containing glycophospholipids are rich in arachidonic acid and thus serve as a readily available pool for eicosanoid synthesis.[84,86] Recently a novel glycoprotein containing inositol has been identified as a recognition molecule for synaptic dendritic growth during development.[87] In addition, it has been hypothesized that chiro-inositol plays an integral role in insulin mediation.[88]

Historically, inositol was shown to prevent a syndrome characterized by fat accumulation in the liver and gut in rats and gerbils. These animals develop severe intestinal lipodystrophy, and if deficiency is prolonged, progressive weight loss, dermatitis, alopecia, inanition, and ultimately death occurs.[89]

The fatty liver is thought to be produced by limited lipoprotein secretion induced by low liver phosphoinositides. No human deficiency syndrome has been described, although diabetic animals have demonstrably lower inositide synthesis and exhibit altered growth, respiratory distress, and renal and nerve function which can be reversed by inositol administration.[90] Primates with non–insulin-dependent diabetes mellitus have shown a reduction in the high circulating glucose concentrations following an acute intravenous injection of chiro-inositol. Studies on the effect of inositide supplementation in diabetic patients have shown higher plasma inositol concentrations and improved nerve conduction.[88,90] The kidney plays a major role in inositol metabolism and excretion. Inositol is excreted mainly as urinary D-glucuronolactone formed via the glucuronic acid pathway. Patients with renal insufficiency have plasma inositol concentrations that are 8 to 10 times normal.[91]

Dietary supply constitutes a significant proportion of body pool, although de novo synthesis from glucose 6-phosphate is sufficient under normal conditions. Adult humans consume about one gram of inositol a day. Inositol hexaphosphate (phytic acid) is the main source of inositol from plants, while myo-inositol is present in animal food products; in addition, milk contains an inositol-derived disaccharide 6-β-galactinol.[85] Inositol is transported by an active transport system in the brush border. Absorbed inositol is taken up by tissues against a concentration gradient by active transport different from that of glucose.[92] The kidney is the main site of inositol biosynthesis; as much as 4 g/day can be made by the adult human kidney.[85,91]

Newborn infants and other mammals are particularly dependent on inositol supplied by the early diet. Colostrum provides 1.5 to 2.5 mmol/L (27 to 47 mg/dL) of inositol, mature human milk 1 to 2 mmol/L (18 to 36 mg/dL), and infant formula 0.2 to 0.8 mmol/L (4 to 15 mg/dL), while parenteral nutrition provides about 0.1 mmol/L (1.8 mg/dL). Correspondingly, serum concentrations are higher in infants fed human milk and fall with advancing postnatal age. Preterm infants have cord blood inositol concentrations twice that of term infants and three times higher than maternal concentrations. The functional significance of these differences remains unknown.[93]

A recent double-blind controlled randomized clinical trial of parenteral inositol supplementation for preterm infants with respiratory distress was reported by Hallman et al.[8] The trial revealed that inositol supplementation at 80 mg per kg of birthweight per day for at least the first 5 days of life was associated with increased survival, a lower incidence of bronchopulmonary dysplasia, and a lower incidence of retinopathy of prematurity. The 221 infants studied were also part of a surfactant-controlled trial; all were <2,000 g and 24 to 32 weeks gestation at birth and required mechanical ventilation with F_{IO_2} >0.4 and parenteral nutrition. Infants receiving no surfactant but inositol supplementation had additional benefits during the course of their respiratory disease; they required less oxygen and lower mean airway pressure. The inositol-treated group maintained higher serum concentrations for the first 2 weeks of life. Since inositol supplementation had an effect on the acute course of infants not receiving surfactant, the authors suggest that inositol may increase surfactant availability through increased synthesis, release, or recycling. The effect on oxygen-induced retinal and lung damage may be related to effects on cell differentiation or on free-radical protection. Overall survival was significantly better in the inositol-supplemented group (91%) than in the control group (76%). Much remains to be learned about this fascinating nonessential nutrient and its effect during early life.[8,85,86]

Toxicity. Toxicity related to inositol appears to be due to its diuretic effect. Thus, excessive intakes which produce large fluid losses could generate dehydration.

Suggested Intakes. Recommended intakes for inositol supplementation at present can be tentatively made based on human milk content and plasma concentrations observed in preterm infants receiving human milk or parenteral inositol supplementation. Formula for preterm infants should contain 1 to 2.5 mmol/L. Similar recommendations can be made for infants on TPN. Additional information on efficacy under diverse conditions is needed before additional inositol supplementation can be recommended for all preterm infants with respiratory distress.

Nucleic Acids and Nucleotides

Nucleotides and their related metabolic products are present in human milk in relatively large amounts: up to 20% of the nonprotein nitrogen consists of free nucleotides. The possibility that exogenous nucleotides play a role in the modulation of normal immune response and in the development of the gastrointestinal tract has been suggested by experimental studies.[7] Rapidly dividing cells such as lymphoid and intestinal epithelial cells are dependent on nucleotide salvage rather than on de novo pathways for nucleic acid synthesis (Fig. 17.5).[94] The functional effects of sparing these tissues from the synthesis of their own nucleotides are presently the object of both animal and clinical research. As Figure 17.5 indicates, de novo synthesis of one molecule of adenine requires

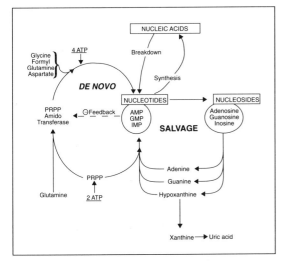

Fig. 17.5. Intracellular purine nucleotide pools are maintained by the salvage pathway or by de novo synthesis. Regulation of de novo synthesis is accomplished by negative feedback of nucleotide concentration on phosphoribosyl pyrophosphate (PRPP) amino transferase. Hypoxanthine guanine phosphoribosyl transferase (HGPRT) and adenine phosphoribosyl transferase (APRT) are the rate-limiting enzymes for the salvage of purine bases. AMP = adenosine monophosphate; IMP = inosine monophosphate; GMP = guanosine monophosphate.

six ATPs, whereas the salvage pathway requires only two. Thus, the salvage pathway is comparatively energy efficient.

Nucleotides contain a nitrogenous base (purine or pyrimidine), a pentose, and one or more phosphate groups. The major purine bases in living organisms are adenine and guanine; the main pyrimidines are cytosine, thymine, and uracil. The metabolism of these bases yields hypoxanthine, xanthine, inosine, and orotate. Purines can be formed de novo from amino acid precursors or salvaged from dietary sources or nucleic acid breakdown. Intracellular nucleotide pools are maintained by the salvage pathway or by de novo synthesis. The pathways are regulated based on availability of preformed bases or nucleosides for salvaging. The product of purine catabolism in the human is uric acid, while β-alanine and aminoisobutyric acid are formed from pyrimidine breakdown.[7] As illustrated in Figure 17.5, the normal end product of purine is hypoxanthine. The conversion of hypoxanthine to uric acid promotes the generation of hydroxyradicals. This reaction may also represent a potential negative effect from excessive nucleotide supplementation.

Laboratory and clinical responses to dietary nucleotides include three investigative areas: immune function, intestinal function, and lipoprotein metabolism. Investigations relating immune function to dietary nucleotides have demonstrated that BALB/c mice maintained on a nucleotide-free diet show increased survival of cardiac allograft as compared to a group receiving nucleic acid supplements.[95] In addition, animals receiving a nucleotide-free diet had significant suppression of lymphoproliferative response to alloantigens.[96] Similarly, delayed cutaneous hypersensitivity response upon challenge with purified protein derivative was diminished in the nucleotide-free group.[97] These experiments suggest that T lymphocyte function is diminished in dietary nucleotide deprivation, yet the mechanism responsible for these effects remains undetermined. Other studies of immune function showed that the lack of nucleotides in the diet decreased the resistance of mice to staphylococcal sepsis and adversely affected host resistance to *Candida albicans*.[98,99] Macrophages from mice receiving nucleotide-free diets also demonstrated diminished phagocytic activity.[100] The addition of nucleotides to a nucleotide-free diet resulted in an increase of the phagocytic capacity of mice macrophages, along with an increase of the natural killer (NK) cell activity of spleen cells.[101] A study in human infants showed that 13 infants fed nucleotide-supplemented formula had NK activity similar to that of 9 breast-fed infants; both groups had significantly higher NK activity than 15 infants receiving nonsupplemented formula.[102] Infants fed nucleotide-supplemented formula had higher percentages of fecal bifidobacteria and lower percentages of gram-negative enterobacteria than formula-fed infants.[103] Thus, it is possible that dietary nucleotides may favor the development of fecal flora with a predominance of bifidobacteria, similar to that of the breast-fed infant. The preliminary human data are supportive, yet it is too early to conclude that all infants will benefit from nucleotide supplementation of formula by showing increased resistance to infections.[104]

Intestinal function has been studied both with in vitro and in vivo techniques. These experiments suggest that de novo synthesis of purines is limited or inactive in the intestinal epithelium. Nucleotide supplementation has been shown to enhance the growth and development of the intestinal mucosa in weaning animals. The protein and DNA content of the upper jejunum of rats fed a nucleotide-free diet was lower than for controls. Maltase activity was also higher throughout the small intestine in the nucleotide-supplemented animals.[105] Improved recovery from radiation-induced injury in nucleotide-supplemented animals has also been demonstrated.[106] The clinical relevance of these findings remains to be established.[7,104,107]

Human milk has a specific content of free nucleotides which differs from bovine milk formulas.[108–110] It has abundant cytidine monophosphate, adenosine monophosphate, and uridine monophosphate, while it is low in orotate. Free nucleotides in human milk range from 5 to 8 mg/dL, while in unsupplemented milk-based formulas they are <1 mg/dL. Total nucleic acids from the cells present in human milk can add up to 30 mg/dL. Thus, assuming that nucleotides and nucleic acids present in human milk are metabolically available, they will contribute 20% to 25% of daily nucleotide needs, which are estimated to be in the order of 160 mg/kg/day.[7]

Toxicity. Toxicity from excessive intake of nucleotides relates primarily to the normal catabolic product, uric acid. Thus, chronic excessive intake could conceivably result in a uric acid nephropathy or increased free-radical generation in the catabolism of xanthinuric acid. No changes in serum uric acid concentrations or evidence of free-radical toxicity have been observed with the use of nucleotide-supplemented formula at levels similar to those found in human milk.

Suggested Intakes. No recommendation for the inclusion of nucleotides in preterm formula or in TPN solutions can be made at this time, although at present some infant formulas in Europe and in the United States are supplemented with the major free nucleotides to mimic human milk content. Further studies documenting efficacy and safety will be required before nucleic acids can be recommended for routine inclusion into formula.

References

1. National Research Council. *Recommended dietary allowances.* 10th ed. Washington, DC: National Academy of Science Press, 1989.
2. Scott ML. *Nutrition of humans and selected animal species.* New York: John Wiley & Sons, 1986.
3. Gaull GE. Taurine in pediatric nutrition: review and update. *Pediatrics* 1989; 83:433–442.
4. Sturman JA, Gaull GE, Räihä NCR. Absence of cystathionase in human fetal liver: is cysteine essential? *Science* 1970; 169:74–76.
5. Rebouche CJ, Panagides DD, Nelson SE. Role of carnitine in utilization of dietary medium-chain triglycerides by term infants. *Am J Clin Nutr* 1990; 52:820–824.
6. Sheard NF, Zeisel SH. Choline: an essential dietary nutrient? *Nutrition* 1989; 5:1–5.
7. Uauy R. Dietary nucleotides and requirements in early life. In: Lebenthal E, ed. *Textbook of gastroenterology and nutrition in infancy.* 2nd ed. New York: Raven Press, 1989; 265–280.
8. Hallman M, Bry K, Hoppu K, Lappi M, Pohjavuori M. Inositol supplementation in premature infants with respiratory distress syndrome. *N Engl J Med* 1992; 326: 1233–1239.
9. World Health Organization. *FAO/WHO/UNU energy & protein requirements.* Technical Report Series No. 724. Geneva, Switzerland: WHO, 1985.
10. Jackson AA. Amino acids: essential and non-essential. *Lancet* 1983; I:1034–1037.
11. Jackson AA. Optimising amino acid and protein supply and utilization in the newborn. *Proc Nutr Soc* 1989; 48: 189–197.
12. Gaull GE, Sturman JA, Räihä NCR. Development of mammalian sulfur metabolism: absence of cystathionase in human fetal tissues. *Pediatr Res* 1972; 6:538–547.
13. Zlotkin SH, Anderson GH. The development of cystathionase activity during the first year of life. *Pediatr Res* 1982; 16:65–68.
14. Snyderman SE. The protein and amino acid requirements of the premature infant. In: Visser HKA, Toreistra JA, eds. *Nutricia symposium: metabolic processes in the foetus and newborn infant.* Leiden, Netherlands: Stenfert Kroese, 1971.
15. Renner E. *Milk and dairy products in human nutrition.* Regensburg, Federal Republic of Germany: Friedrich Pustet, 1983.
16. Barness LA, Omans WB, Rose CS, et al. Progress of premature infants fed a formula containing demineralized whey. *Pediatrics* 1963; 32:52–55.
17. Berger HM, Scott PH, Kenward C, et al. Curd and whey proteins in the nutrition of low-birthweight babies. *Arch Dis Child* 1979; 54:98–104.
18. Darling P, Lepage G, Tremblay P, et al. Protein quality and quantity in preterm infants receiving the same energy intake. *Am J Dis Child* 1985; 139:186–190.
19. Järvenpää AL, Räihä NCR, Rassin DK, et al. Milk protein quantity and quality in the term infant. I. Metabolic responses and effects on growth. *Pediatrics* 1982; 70:214–220.
20. Janas LM, Picciano MF, Hatch TF. Indices of protein metabolism in term infants fed human milk, whey-predominant formula, or cow's milk formula. *Pediatrics* 1985; 75:775–784.
21. Scott PH, Berger HM, Wharton BA. Growth velocity and plasma amino acids in the newborn. *Pediatr Res* 1985; 19: 446–450.
22. Kashyap S, Okamoto E, Kanaya S, et al. Protein quality in feeding low-birthweight infants: a comparison of whey-predominant versus casein-predominant formulas. *Pediatrics* 1987; 79:748–755.
23. Gaull GE, Rassin DK, Räihä NCR, et al. Milk protein quantity and quality in low-birthweight infants. III. Effects of sulphur amino acids in plasma and urine. *J Pediatr* 1977; 90:348–355.
24. Winters RW, Heird WC, Dell RB, et al. Plasma amino acids in infants receiving parenteral nutrition. In: Greene HL, Holliday MA, Munro HN, eds. *Clinical nutrition update: amino acids.* Chicago: American Medical Association, 1977.
25. Zlotkin SH, Bryan MH, Anderson GH. Cysteine supplementation to cysteine-free intravenous feeding regimens in newborn infants. *Am J Clin Nutr* 1981; 34:914–923.
26. Malloy MH, Rassin DK, Richardson CJ. Total parenteral nutrition in sick preterm infants: effects of cysteine supplementation with nitrogen intakes of 240 and 400 mg/kg/d. *J Pediatr Gastroenterol Nutr* 1984; 3: 239–244.
27. Heird WC. Sulfur-containing amino acids in parenteral nutrition. In: Filer LJ, Leathem WD, eds. *Parenteral nutrition in the infant patient.* Chicago: Abbott Laboratories, 1983.
28. Helms RA, Christensen ML, Mauer EC, et al. Comparison of a pediatric versus standard amino acid formulation in preterm neonates requiring parenteral nutrition. *J Pediatr* 1987; 3:466–472.
29. Heird WC, Hay W, Helms RA, Storm MC, Kashyap S, Dell RB. Pediatric parenteral amino acid mixture in low-birthweight infants. *Pediatrics* 1988; 81:41–50.

30. Kashyap S, Abildskov A, Heird WC. Cysteine (CYS) supplementation of very low-birthweight (VLBW) infants receiving parenteral nutrition (TPN). *Pediatr Res* 1992; 31:290A.

31. Steginak LD, Denbesten L. Synthesis of cysteine from methionine in normal adult subjects: effect of route of alimentation. *Science* 1982; 178:514–516.

32. Chawla RK, Berry CJ, Kutner MH, et al. Plasma concentrations of transsulfuration pathway products during nasoenteral and intravenous hyperalimentation of malnourished patients. *Am J Clin Nutr* 1985; 42:577–584.

33. Hansen TN, Smith CV, Martin NE, Smith HW, Elliott SJ. Oxidant stress responses in ventilated newborn infants. *Pediatr Res* 1990; 27:208A.

34. Laine L, Shulman RJ, Pitre D, Lifschitz CH, Adams J. Cysteine usage increases the need for acetate in neonates who receive total parenteral nutrition. *Am J Clin Nutr* 1991; 54:565–567.

35. Malloy MH, Rassin DK, Gaull GE. A method for measurement of free and bound plasma cyst(e)ine. *Anal Biochem* 1981; 113:407–415.

36. Eagle HA, Oyama VI, Piez KA. The reversible binding of half cystine residues to serum protein and its bearing on the cystine requirement of cultured mammalian cells. *J Biol Chem* 1960; 235:1719–1726.

37. Stein WH, Moore S. Free amino acids of human blood plasma. *J Biol Chem* 1954; 211:915–926.

38. Pettei M, Abildoskov A, Heird WC. Instability of cysteine-HC (CYSH) in total parenteral nutrition (TPN) infusates [Abstract]. *J Am Coll Nutr* 1987; 6:83.

39. Gaull G. E. Taurine nutrition in man. *Adv Exp Med Biol* 1982; 139:89–95.

40. Sturman JA. Critical review: taurine in development. *J Nutr* 1988; 118:1169–1176.

41. Järvenpää A-L, Rassin DK, Räihä NCR, et al. Milk protein quantity and quality in the term infant. II. Effects on acidic and neutral amino acids. *Pediatrics* 1982; 70:221–230.

42. Watkins JB, Järvenpää A-L, Szczepanik-VanLeeuwen P, et al. Feeding the low-birthweight infant. V. Effects of taurine, cholesterol, and human milk on bile acid kinetics. *Gastroenterology* 1983; 85:793–800.

43. Okamoto E, Rassin DK, Zucker CL, Salen GS, Heird WC. Role of taurine in feeding the low-birthweight infant. *J Pediatr* 1984; 104:936–940.

44. Watkins JB. Lipid digestion and absorption. *Pediatrics* 1985; 75:151–156.

45. Galeano NF, Darling P, Lepage G, et al. Taurine supplementation of a premature formula improves fat absorption in preterm infants. *Pediatr Res* 1987; 22:67–71.

46. Darling PB, Lepage G, Leroy C, Roy CC. Effect of taurine supplements on fat absorption in cystic fibrosis. *Pediatr Res* 1985; 19:578–582.

47. Zelikovic I, Chesney RW, Friedman AL, Ahlfors CE. Taurine depletion in very low-birthweight infants receiving prolonged total parenteral nutrition: role of renal immaturity. *J Pediatr* 1990; 116:301–306.

48. Huppi PS, Posse S, Lazeyras F, Burri R, Bossi E, Herschkowitz N. Magnetic resonance in preterm and term newborns: 1H-spectroscopy in developing human brain. *Pediatr Res* 1991; 30:574–578.

49. Hayes KC, Carey RE, Schmidt J. Retinal degeneration associated with taurine deficiency in the cat. *Science* 1975; 188:950–951.

50. Sturman JA, Wen GY, Wisniewski HM, et al. Retinal degeneration in primates raised on a synthetic human infant formula. *Int J Dev Neurol Sci* 1984; 2:121–129.

51. Palackal T, Kujawa M, Moretz R, Neuringer M, Sturman J. Laminar analysis of the number of neurons, astrocytes,

52. oligodendrocytes and microglia in the visual cortex (area 17) of 3-month-old rhesus monkeys fed a human infant soy-protein formula with or without taurine supplementation from birth. *Dev Neurosci* 1991; 13:20–33.

52. Geggel HS, Ament ME, Heckenlively JR, Martin DA, Kopple JD. Nutritional requirements for taurine in patients receiving long-term parenteral nutrition. *N Engl J Med* 1985; 312:142–146.

53. Vinton NE, Heckenlively JR, Laidlaw SA, et al. Visual function in patients undergoing long-term total parenteral nutrition. *Am J Clin Nutr* 1990; 52:895–902.

54. Uauy R, Birch EE, Birch DG, Peirano P. Visual and brain function in studies of n-3 fatty acid requirements of infants. *J Pediatr* 1992; 120:S168–180.

55. Tyson JE, Lasky R, Flood D, Mize C, Picone T, Paule CL. Randomized trial of taurine supplementation for infants <1,300 gram birthweight: effect on auditory brainstem responses. *Pediatrics* 1989; 83:406–415.

56. Räihä NCR. Phenylalanine hydroxylase in human liver during development. *Pediatr Res* 1973; 7:1–4.

57. Rassin DK, Gaull GE, Räihä NCR, et al. Milk protein quantity and quality in low-birthweight infants. IV. Effects on tyrosine and phenylalanine in plasma and urine. *J Pediatr* 1977; 90:356–360.

58. Light IJ, Berry HK, Sutherland JM. Amino-acidemia of prematurity. *AJDC* 1966; 112:229–236.

59. Kaufman S. The phenylalanine hydroxylating system from mammalian liver. *Adv Enzymol* 1971; 35:245–319.

60. Brenneman AR, Kaufman S. Characteristics of the hepatic phenylalanine hydroxylating system in newborn rats. *J Biol Chem* 1965; 240:3617–3622.

61. Heird WC, Dell RB, Helms RA, et al. Amino acid mixture designed to maintain normal plasma amino acid patterns in infants and children requiring parenteral nutrition. *Pediatrics* 1987; 80:401–408.

62. Wykes LJ, Ball RO, Pencharz PB. Evaluation of a neonatal piglet model for total parenteral nutrition. *FASEB* 1992; 6:A1089, #888.

63. Laidlaw SA, Kopple JD. Newer concepts of the indispensable amino acids. *Am J Clin Nutr* 1987; 46:593–605.

64. Visek WJ. Arginine needs, physiological state and usual diets: a reevaluation. *J Nutr* 1986; 116:36–46.

65. Dudrick PS, Souba WW. Amino acids in surgical nutrition: principles and practice. *Surg Clin North Am* 1991; 71:459–476.

66. Soliman AT, Hassan AE, Aref MK, Hintz RL, Rosenfeld RG, Rogol AD. Serum insulin-like growth factors I and II concentrations and growth hormone and insulin responses to arginine infusion in children with protein-energy malnutrition before and after nutritional rehabilitation. *Pediatr Res* 1986; 20:1122–1130.

67. Moncada S, Higgs EA, Palmer RMJ. Characterization and biological significance of endothelium-derived relaxing factor. *Biochem Soc Trans* 1988; 16:4–5.

68. Barbul A, Fishel RS, Shimazu S. Intravenous hyperalimentation with high arginine levels improves wound healing and immune function. *J Surg Res* 1985; 38:328–334.

69. Uauy R, Mize CC, Argyle CA, McCracken G. Metabolic tolerance to an arginine load: implications for the safe use of aztreonam in the newborn period. *J Pediatr* 1991; 118:965–970.

70. Newsholme EA, Crabtree B, Ardawi MSM. Glutamine metabolism in lymphocytes: its biochemical, physiological and clinical importance. *Q J Exp Physiol* 1985; 70:473–489.

71. Jepson MM, Bates PC, Broadbent P, Pell JM, Millward DJ. Relationship between glutamine concentration and protein synthesis in rat skeletal muscle. *Am J Physiol* 1988; 255:E166–172.

72. Parry-Billings M, Evans J, Calder PC, Newsholme EA. Does glutamine contribute to immunosuppression after major burns? *Lancet* 1990; 336:523–525.

73. Souba WW, Klimberg VS, Hautamaki RD. Oral glutamine reduces bacterial translocation following abdominal radiation. *J Surg Res* 1990; 48:1–5.

74. Stehle P, Zander J, Mertes N. Effect of parenteral glutamine dipeptide supplement on muscle glutamine loss and nitrogen balance after major surgery. *Lancet* 1989; I: 231–233.

75. Adibi SA, Fekl W, Furst P, Oehmke M, eds. *Dipeptides as new substrates in nutrition therapy.* Munich, Germany: Karger, 1987.

76. Zeisel SH. Dietary choline: biochemistry, physiology and pharmacology. *Annu Rev Nutr* 1981; 1:95–121.

77. Zeisel SH. Dietary influences on neurotransmission. *Adv Pediatr* 1986; 33:23–48.

78. Sheard NF, Zeisel SH. An in vitro study of choline uptake by intestine from neonatal and adult rats. *Pediatr Res* 1986; 20:768–772.

79. Zeisel SH. Requirement for choline: do breast milk and/or infant formulas provide optimal amounts. *J Cell Biochem* 1992; 16B:259A.

80. Sheard NF, Tayek JA, Bistrian BR, Blackburn GL, Zeisel SH. Plasma choline concentrations in humans fed parenterally. *Am J Clin Nutr* 1986; 43:219–224.

81. Calatayud-Maldonado V, Calatayud-Pérez JB, Aso-Escario J. Effects of CDP-choline on the recovery of patients with head injury. *J Neurol Sci* 1991; 103:S15–18.

82. Zeisel SH, Char D, Sheard NF. Choline, phosphatidylcholine and sphingomyelin in human milk, bovine milk and infant formulas. *J Nutr* 1986; 116:50–58.

83. Sotirhos N, Herslöf B, Kenne L. Quantitative Analysis of Phospholipids ^{31}P–NMR. *J Lipid Res* 1986; 27:386–392.

84. Hawthorne JN. Inositol phospholipid and phosphatidic acid metabolism in response to membrane receptor activation. *Proc Roy Nutr Soc* 1985; 44:167–172.

85. Holub BJ. Metabolism and function of *myo*-inositol and inositol phospholipids. *Annu Rev Nutr* 1986; 6:563–597.

86. Berridge MJ, Inositol triphosphate and diacylglycerol: two interacting second messengers. *Annu Rev Biochem* 1987; 56:159–193.

87. Yoshihara Y, Oka S, Watanabe Y, Mori K. Developmentally and spatially regulated expression of HNK-1 carbohydrate antigen on a novel phosphatidylinostol-anchored glycoprotein in rat brain. *J Cell Biol* 1991; 115:731–744.

88. Kennington HS, Hill CR, Craig J. Low urinary chiroinositol in non-insulin-dependent diabetes mellitus. *N Eng J Med* 1990; 323:373–378.

89. Hegsted DM, Gallagher A, Hanford H. Inositol requirements of the gerbil. *J Nutr* 1974; 104:588–592.

90. Greene DA, Lattimer SA, Sima AAF. Sorbitol, phosphoinositides and sodium-potassium-ATPase in the pathogenesis of diabetic complications. *N Eng J Med* 1987; 316:599–606.

91. Clements RS, Dietheim AG. The metabolism of myo-inositol by the human kidney. *J Lab Clin Med* 1979; 93:210–219.

92. Caspari WF, Crane RK. Active transport of myo-inositol and its relation to the sugar transport system in hamster small intestine. *Biochim Biophys Acta* 1970; 203: 308–316.

93. Pereira GR, Baker L, Egler J, Corcoran L, Chiavacci R. Serum myo-inositol concentrations in premature infants fed human milk, formula for infants, and parenteral nutrition. *Am J Clin Nutr* 1990; 51:589–593.

94. Savaiano DA, Clifford AJ. Adenine, the precursor of nucleic acids in intestinal cells unable to synthesize purines de novo. *J Nutr* 1981; 111:1816–1822.

95. Van Buren CT, Kulkarni AD, Schandle VB, et al. The influence of dietary nucleotides on cell mediated immunity. *Transplantation* 1983; 36:350–352.

96. Rudolph FD, Kulkarni AD, Schandle VB, et al. Involvement of dietary nucleotides in T lymphocyte function. *Adv Exp Med Biol* 1984; 165:175–178.

97. Kulkarni AD, Fanslow WC, Rudolph FB, et al. Modulation of delayed hypersensitivity in mice by dietary nucleotide restriction. *Transplantation* 1987; 44:847–848.

98. Kulkarni AD, Fanslow WC, Rudolph FB, et al. Effect of dietary nucleotides in response to bacteria infections. *JPEN* 1982; 10:169–171.

99. Fanslow WC, Kulkarni AD, Van Buren CT, et al. Effect of nucleotide restriction and supplementation on resistance to experimental murine candidiasis. *JPEN* 1988; 12:49–52.

100. Kulkarni AD, Fanslow WC, Drath DB, et al. Influence of dietary nucleotide restriction on bacteria sepsis and phagocytic cell function in mice. *Arch Surg* 1986; 121: 169–172.

101. Carver TD, Cox WI, Barness LA. Dietary nucleotide effect upon murine NK cell activity and macrophage activation. *JPEN* 1990; 14:18–22.

102. Barness LA, Carver J. Nucleotides and immune function. *Semin Pediatr Gastroenterol Nutr* 1991; 2:11–13.

103. Gil A, Coval E, Martinez A, et al. Effects of dietary nucleotides on the microbial pattern of feces of at term newborn infants. *J Clin Nutr Gastroenterol* 1986;1: 34–48.

104. Quan R, Barness LA, Uauy R. Do infants need nucleotide supplemented formula for optimal nutrition? *J Pediatr Gastroenterol Nutr* 1990; 11:429–437.

105. Uauy R, Stringel G, Thomas R, Quan R. Effect of dietary nucleosides on growth and maturation of the developing gut in the rat. *J Pediatr Gastroenterol Nutr* 1990;10: 497–503.

106. Quan R, Gil A, Uauy R. Effect of dietary nucleosides (DN) on intestinal growth and maturation after injury from radiation. *Pediatr Res* 1991; 29:111A.

107. Pizzini RP, Saroj-Kumar BS, Kulkarni AD, Rudolph FB, Van Buren CT. Dietary nucleotides reverse malnutrition and starvation-induced immunosupression. *Arch Surg* 1990; 125:86–90.

108. Janas LM, Picciano MF. The nucleotide profile of human milk. *Pediatr Res* 1982; 16:659–662.

109. Gil A, Sanchez-Medina F. Acid-soluble nucleotides of human milk at different stages of lactation. *J Dairy Res* 1982; 49:301–306.

110. Gil A, Sanchez-Medina F. Effects of thermal industrial processing on acid-soluble nucleotides of milk. *J Dairy Res* 1982; 49:295–300.

18. Regulatory and Public Policy Aspects

Allan L. Forbes

Kenneth J. Falci

Margaret C. Cheney

This text is intended primarily for use as a reference book by practicing neonatologists, residents, fellows, nutritionists in neonatal intensive care units, and researchers concerned with nutritional management of preterm infants. However, it is also of value from the standpoint of regulatory and public policy; and the infant formula industry, domestically and internationally, is keenly interested in its use as a guide to development of new formulas for the preterm infant. Organizations involved in the infrastructure of health care delivery systems—both public and private—will utilize the text. Examples include health insurance carriers; health planners at federal, state and local levels; and groups involved in management of assistance programs, e.g., the Department of Agriculture's Special Supplemental Food Program for Women, Infant and Children (commonly referred to as the WIC Program).

This chapter briefly reviews some of the specifics concerning governmental regulation in the United States and Canada of the products used for nutritional management of the preterm infant. This introduction was written by Dr. Forbes, the section on infant formula regulation in the United States by Dr. Falci, and the section on infant formula regulation in Canada by Dr. Cheney.

In the United States, infant formulas, including those for the preterm infant, are regulated as a food for special dietary use under the provisions of the food portions of the Food, Drug and Cosmetic Act (FDCA), and the regulations promulgated to implement the relevant portions of the Act by the Food and Drug Administration (FDA). More specifically, all infant formulas are regulated under the provisions of the Infant Formula Acts of 1980 and 1986, which are amendments to the FDCA. All "parenterals," including nutrient solutions, and vitamin and mineral preparations administered parenterally, are regulated as prescription drugs under the provisions of the drug portions of the FDCA. Unlike infant formulas, "parenterals" are not governed by specific regulations; they are regulated on an ad-hoc basis as individual situations arise. Hence, enteral feedings are regulated entirely differently from parenteral feeding, under different portions of the law, different regulations, and different staffs at the FDA. Foods are under the general management of the Center for Food Safety and Applied Nutrition of the FDA, while drugs

are under the Center for Drug Evaluation and Research of the FDA. As reviewed below, the regulatory framework in Canada is somewhat similar to the one in the United States, falling under the jurisdiction of the Health Protection Branch of the Department of National Health and Welfare in Ottawa.

It is important to keep in mind that the United Nations develops guidelines and standards (the latter are essentially regulations) pertaining to infant formulas and drugs. All countries are obliged to consider these guidelines and standards in developing their own national regulations. In this regard, the most important UN agency concerned with infant formulas is the Codex Alimentarius Commission (Codex), which is a joint Commission of the World Health Organization and the Food and Agriculture Organization of the United Nations. The Codex Committee on Nutrition and Foods for Special Dietary Uses, chaired by the Federal Republic of Germany, has developed standards for infant formulas for normal babies, and it is reasonable to anticipate that in the future this Committee will take under consideration the special needs of the preterm infant. The World Health Organization develops guidelines and standards for drugs, including products used for total parenteral nutrition. Currently, the European Community is deeply involved in developing standards and guidelines for the Community members, including approaches to products used for infant feeding. It is virtually inevitable that the next few years will see formal standards for infant formulas, including those for the preterm infant.

For the United States, the FDA uses a number of mechanisms for formal advice on matters concerned with infant feeding. These include: (1) the Food and Nutrition Board, Institute of Medicine, National Academy of Sciences, which develops the Recommended Dietary Allowances, including those for infants; (2) the Life Sciences Research Office of the Federation of American Societies for Experimental Biology, which under FDA contract considers many topics in the nutrition area, including issues concerned with inborn errors of metabolism and the need for research and development of orphan food products for rare disorders; (3) the Committee on Nutrition of the American Academy of Pediatrics, which also under FDA contract has performed numerous studies of nutritional aspects of pediatric care, including guidelines for clinical testing of new infant formulas; and (4) the advisory committee system used by the Center for Drug Evaluation and Research for review of each class of drugs, including those used for parenteral feeding.

Internationally, the International Union of Nutritional Sciences (IUNS) is advisory to the various United Nations organizations concerned with human health, especially the Codex. The IUNS is the only international body that represents the entire nutrition scientific community worldwide, and through its committee structure IUNS has provided advice to the UN agencies on innumerable occasions. Through its Committee on Nutritional Aspects of Food Standards, IUNS has recently provided major advice to the Codex on medical foods (i.e., foods administered to patients only under medical supervision). Infant formulas are philosophically a type of "medical food."

Infant Formula Regulation in the United States

A reliable alternative to breast feeding was virtually unheard of until the beginning of the 20th century. At that time, the need for an inexpensive, convenient, nutritionally effective, and safe infant formula was recognized. Growing out of this need came a new industry. Today, the availability of many different specialty formulas attests to the ability of the infant formula industry to respond to the needs of term and preterm infants, and infants with metabolic disorders. The industry continues to seach for "perfect specialty formulas" as it responds to increased scientific knowledge about the nutritional needs of all infants.

The first attempt in the beginning of this century to produce a commercial infant formula resulted in the development and acceptance of sterilized evaporated milk as a substitute for human breast milk. Evaporated milk entered the market without government regulation. Regulation for infant formulas did not take form until 1941, when the FDA published a final order requiring label declarations for nutrients and ingredients of food for special dietary use, as well as minimum requirements for four vitamins and iron.[1] The rapid development of nutrition knowledge at the time was responsible for this modest regulatory beginning.

The need for further regulation was hotly contested and debated over the next 30 years, particularly by pediatricians and nutritionists who were concerned about the appropriate levels of nutrients in formulas. Incidents that occurred over these years involved the manufacture of nutrient-deficient and contaminated formulas. In 1966, the FDA responded with a proposed regulation expanding the number of nutrients, vitamins, and minerals required in infant formulas. In 1971, after many public hearings and a regulatory review conducted by the Committee on Nutrition of the American Academy of Pediatrics (AAPCON), a final rule became law.[2]

On November 1, 1979, the situation changed dramatically. On that date, an infant formula hearing was convened by the Subcommittee on Oversight and Investigations, Committee on Interstate and Foreign Commerce, House of Representatives. In the months before this investigation, 31 cases of metabolic alkalosis in infants had been documented. The documentation on most of these infants indicated that this disorder was associated with the consumption of two popular soy infant formulas. The formulas were critically deficient in chloride, causing more than 100 infants to become afflicted with a rare and potentially fatal disorder known as hypochloremic metabolic alkalosis. This tragic event led to the passage of the Infant Formula Act of 1980. As noted in the *Congressional Record,* Congress passed this Act to subject infant formulas to mandatory ingredient standards, as well as conscientious and periodic testing during their manufacture in order to prevent a repetition of this tragedy.

Congress authorized in the Act the establishment of minimum (and some maximum) nutrient specification requirements; quality factors, quality control procedures, and record keeping for these procedures; notification to the FDA of each new formula or change in formulation or processing; recall requirements whenever a manufacturer initiated a recall; increased inspection authority over records and periodic testing results to confirm compliance with the Act (although not every batch of formula produced would be tested); infant formula labeling; and the terms and conditions of use of infant formulas that were considered exempt from certain requirements of the Act.

In response to the passage of the Act, the FDA published several regulations (Code of Federal Regulations [CFR], Title 21, Parts 106 and 107, Infant Formula) within the next 6 years. The regulation that remained to be completed at the end of this period involved quality factors. Among other things, these factors deal with the development of test procedures for specific nutrients when necessary, and clinical testing requirements for infant formulas, including data supporting the growth and development of infants on a formula.

Congressional authorization of "exempt" infant formulas must be viewed within the bounds of the Infant Formula Act of 1980. The Act defines exempt infant formulas as those that are represented and labeled for use by an infant who has an inborn error of metabolism, low birthweight, or unusual medical or dietary problem. Under the Act, these formulas are currently exempt from (1) the requirements of listing all nutrients required by the Act; (2) meeting quality factor requirements; (3) compliance with good manufacturing practices and quality control procedures; (4) registering the manufacturing company and its manufacturing sites; and (5) a number of other prescribed requirements for formulas for healthy full-term infants.

Although exempt infant formulas must comply with the adulteration (i.e., containing filth, or a deleterious substance, or omission of a valuable constituent) and misbranding (i.e., labeling) provisions of the Act, they may be manufactured without containing all the nutrients required by the Act and still not be considered adulterated. This allowance is considered necessary, because certain nutrients must either be removed from or added to some exempt infant formulas to satisfy particular infant needs. Manufacturers of exempt infant formulas are also subjected to the recall provisions of the Act and must retain records concerning the distribution of the formula in the marketplace.

Congress provided the exemptions in the Act because it recognized the need for a regulatory approach for these formulas that was different from those for healthy full-term infants. In fact, in the Act, Congress also allowed the FDA to define the terms and conditions of the exemptions by regulation. Congress also intended that these formulas be manufactured at the same high standard of quality required for formulas for healthy full-term infants.[3,4]

From 1983 to 1985, the FDA established regulations for exempt infant formulas, providing for two broad categories of these formulas: (1) retail formulas for the dietary management of diseases and conditions not clinically serious, and (2) formulas not available at retail to be used for potentially more serious conditions.[5,6] Because these regulations were published before the 1986 amendments to the 1980 Act, they do not address the aspects of good manufacturing practices or audit requirements in the 1986 amendments to the Infant Formula Act. In addition, although quality factors are applicable to exempt formulas, the quality issue remains to be addressed by the FDA in future regulations.

The FDA established regulations requiring manufacturers of exempt infant formulas to: (1) provide detailed descriptions of the medical conditions for which the infant formula is represented, and scientific, nutritional, and medical rationales to support any deviations in nutrient specifications from standard recommendations; (2) follow the quality control procedures described in Title 21 of the Code of Federal Regulations, Part 106, with the exception that manufacturers of formulas not available for retail use may establish their own procedures; and (3) register

all such formulas with the FDA. In addition, the FDA required that the labeling requirements for nonexempt infant formulas apply to exempt formulas.

After establishing the terms and conditions for exempt infant formulas, the FDA provided for manufacturer deviation from quality control procedures when technological problems in manufacturing the formula are difficult, as well as from labeling when the required labeling information could lead to inappropriate use of the formula. The FDA retained the right, as provided by law, to withdraw the exempt status of a formula if the manufacturer's request for exemption could not be supported by submitted data. Exempt infant formulas account for an increasing percentage of FDA infant formula notifications. They represented approximately 25% of the 90-day premarket notifications received by the FDA in 1990, and 40% of the notifications in 1991.

By September of 1986, Congress expressed concern that mistakes in the processing of formulas could occur and a company's quality control system might fail to catch them. In addition, Congress also noted consumer concern that FDA regulation provided only the periodic analysis (every 3 months) of newly processed formulas.[7] Because manufacturers were not required to test each batch of infant formula for all the nutrients specified in the law before distribution, some defective formulas could still reach consumers. On October 27, 1986, in response to this and other concerns, Congress drafted amendments to the 1980 Infant Formula Act as part of the "Drug Enforcement, Education, and Control Act of 1986" (Pub.L. 99–570).

The infant formula amendments of 1986 generally require manufacturers to: (1) test each batch of infant formula for each mandated nutrient before release and during shelf life; (2) retain records on consumer complaints and on all certificates from premix suppliers; (3) develop internal audit requirements and document and retain audit findings; and (4) retain records on the microbiological quality and purity of raw materials. The FDA, on the other hand, is required to establish guidelines for good manufacturing practices and quality control, as well as update its recall regulations and revise the exempt infant formula regulations to be consistent with the new amendments.

In response to the 1986 amendments, the FDA published a final rule concerning infant formula microbiological testing, consumer complaints, and record retention requirements on December 24, 1991,[8] and a final rule concerning infant formula recall requirements on January 27, 1989.[9] A proposal and a final rule concerning additional quality control and good manufacturing practices, possibly to include a description of quality factors, should be published soon.

Currently, the FDA assists manufacturers before they submit infant formula notifications (i.e., a manufacturer's description of changes made in an infant formula) by: (1) reviewing clinical and nonclinical protocol data for growth and development, as well as nutrient balance studies, and (2) conducting labeling reviews. Manufacturers are advised of the current regulations applicable to infant formulas, including thermally processed infant formulas (i.e., low-acid food regulations) in liquid concentrate and ready-to-use form. A guideline concerning notifications to the FDA and testing of infant formulas is provided, along with the June 1988 recommendations of the AAPCON on the clinical testing of infant formulas with respect to their nutritional suitability for term infants. Also provided are two guidelines produced in August of 1988 by the AAPCON while under FDA contract that concern evaluation of formulas for feeding preterm infants, and the April 1989 clinical evaluation of products used in dietary management of infants, children, and pregnant women with metabolic disorders.

A major change in formulation is defined as any new formulation, or any change of ingredients or processes, where experience or theory predicts a possible significant adverse impact on levels of nutrients or availability of nutrients. A minor change in formulation is defined as a minor reduction or increase in nutrient levels required by the Act or appropriate regulations, or a change where experience or theory would not predict a possible significant adverse impact on nutrient levels or nutrient availability. Such changes are received at the FDA as a notification, and usually only the specific change being brought to the FDA's attention is analyzed. When infant formula notifications for exempt and nonexempt formulas involving a major change are received at the FDA, an analysis is made of: (1) the label and any labeling received; (2) the food-contact surface of the packaging material for the infant formula; (3) the quality control procedures used; (4) the nutrient levels; (5) data supporting infant growth and development (when these data are needed); (6) any claims made by the manufacturer; and (7) the regulatory status of ingredients used in the formulas. The firm is then contacted directly by letter and informed of the results of this analysis within 90 days of the date the notification was received.

In addition to the regulations that will soon be published, future actions potentially include the development of three separate FDA guidelines for manufacturers of infant formulas that address: (1) the clinical testing of infant formulas for term infants; (2) clinical evaluation of formulas for infants with metabolic disorders; and (3) evaluation of labeling claims made for infant formulas. To a large extent, these guidelines will update the previous actions suggested by AAPCON.

The FDA also will need to take a closer look at the ingredients used in infant formulas and decide how to approve new ingredients. As the frontiers of nutrition research for the preterm infant require more flexibility in the formula ingredient mix and as advances in technology demonstrate the positive effect of certain ingredients on the growth of preterm and term infants, the agency must quickly approve uses of these ingredients wherever possible and whenever practicable. To accomplish this, advisory bodies could be formed to assist in the approval process, and a new system of review established within the FDA could be dedicated exclusively to the review and approval of new ingredients in infant formulas.

The area of infant formula claims also needs closer regulatory consideration. Labeling and promotional materials that accompany infant formulas for a particular manufacturer should be routinely reviewed by FDA, and agency opinion and comment on this labeling should be shared with that firm. A closer review would help to prevent any imbalance in claims made by infant formula manufacturers.

Infant Formula Regulation in Canada

In Canada, the safety, nutritional quality, and labeling of infant formulas are regulated under the Food and Drugs Act and Regulations. The regulatory requirements apply to all infant formulas, including those for preterm infants. Unlike the United States, there is no category of exempt infant formulas.

Nutrient Requirements

The nutrient requirements for infant formula are based primarily on the Codex Standard for Infant Formula. As shown in Table 18.1, the regulations set out minimum levels for 28 nutrients. In addition, protein, fat, vitamins A and D, sodium, potassium, and chloride are subject to maximum levels. Except as noted, all formulas, including those for the preterm infant, are required to comply.

Certain limited exceptions to the nutrient requirements exist. For example, formulas for the aminoacidurias are exempt from the minimum protein quantity and quality requirements. At present, there are no exceptions for preterm formulas.

Manufacturers may add nutritive substances present in human milk, such as selenium, inositol, and taurine, to formula, provided that the level in the formula is equal to that in human milk.

An amendment to the Food and Drug Regulations would be required to permit the sale of a formula containing nutrient amounts in excess of maximum levels indicated in Table 18.1. The regulatory process requires that any such amendment be justified on the basis of scientific evidence and clinical need. A Tem-

Table 18.1. Nutrient Requirements for Infant Formula (amount per 100 kcal)

Nutrient	Minimum	Maximum
Protein (g)	1.8*	4.0
Fat (g)	3.3	6.0
Linoleic acid (mg)	500†	—
Vitamin A (IU)	250	500
Vitamin D (IU)	40	80
Alpha-tocopherol (IU)	0.6†	—
Vitamin K (μg)	8	—
Thiamine (μg)	40	—
Riboflavin (μg)	60	—
Niacin (μg)	250	—
Vitamin B_6 (μg)	35‡	—
Folic acid (μg)	4	—
Vitamin B_{12} (μg)	0.15	—
d-Pantothenic acid (μg)	300	—
Biotin (μg)	2	—
Calcium (mg)	50§	—
Phosphorus (mg)	25§	—
Magnesium (mg)	6	—
Iron (mg)	0.15	—
Zinc (mg)	0.5	—
Copper (μg)	60	—
Manganese (μg)	5	—
Sodium (mg)	20	60
Potassium (mg)	80	200
Chloride (mg)	55	150
Choline (mg)	12	—

*Minimum protein quality; 85% of casein; quantity $\times$ quality $\geqslant$1.8.

†Tocopherol:linoleic acid $\geqslant$0.6 IU:1 g.

‡Vitamin B_6:protein $\geqslant$15 μg:1 g.

§Calcium:phosphorus $\geqslant$1.2 g:1 g; $\leqslant$2.0 g:1 g.

porary Marketing Authorization Letter may be issued to permit the sale or distribution of a noncompliant formula, for the purpose of generating information in support of a regulatory amendment.

Premarket Notification

Manufacturers or importers are required to notify the Health Protection Branch (HPB) at least 90 days before the sale or advertisement for sale of a new infant formula or a formula that has undergone a major change in formulation, processing, or packaging. A notification for a new infant formula must contain information on the formulation, ingredients, manufacturing process, quality control procedures, and evidence relied upon to establish that the formula is nutritionally adequate to promote acceptable growth and development in infants when consumed according to directions for use. Notification to the HPB about a major change in formula must contain information on the evidence relied upon to establish nutritional adequacy and to establish that the change has had no adverse effect on the formula.

Good Manufacturing Practice

A good manufacturing practice guideline has been developed by the HPB to provide guidance to industry with respect to systems, conditions, and procedures necessary to ensure that infant formula products meet expected standards for microbial and nutritional quality.

Labeling

The labels of infant formulas are required to carry: (1) a list of ingredients; (2) complete nutrition labeling comprising the energy value and the amounts of protein, fat and carbohydrate, choline, vitamins, minerals (see Table 18.1), and any added nutritive substance expressed per 100 g or 100 mL as sold and per stated quantity when ready-to-serve; (3) directions for preparation, use, and storage; and (4) expiration date.

Regulation of Parenteral Nutrient Products

All parenterals are regulated as drugs in Canada. As new products are proposed or changes are made in existing products, they are handled from a regulatory point of view on a case-by-case basis.

References

1. Food and Drug Administration. Rules and regulations: label statements concerning dietary properties of food purporting to be or represented for special dietary uses. *Fed Reg* 1941; 6:5921.
2. Food and Drug Administration. Rules and regulations: label statements concerning dietary properties of food purporting to be or represented for special dietary uses. *Fed Reg* 1971; 36(238):23553.
3. 96th Congress, 2nd Session. Senate Report No. 96–916. August 26, 1980.
4. 96th Congress, 2nd Session. House Report No. 96–936. May 12, 1980.
5. Food and Drug Administration. Proposed rules: exempt infant formula. *Fed Reg* 1983; 48(134):31875.
6. Food and Drug Administration. Rules and regulations: exempt infant formula. *Fed Reg* 1985; 50(226):48183.
7. 102nd Congress, 2nd Session. Senate Report No. S14044. September 27, 1986.
8. Food and Drug Administration. Infant formula record and record retention requirements. *Fed Reg* 1991; 56:66566.
9. Food and Drug Administration. Infant formula recall requirements. *Fed Reg* 1989; 54:4006.

Appendix

Compiled by James W. Hansen

Knowledge of the unique nutritional needs of premature infants has been evolving since the 1970s. As new information became available, manufacturers developed new products and improved existing ones.

In the early 1980s, recommendations for the premature infant, most noticeably for vitamins and minerals, varied from expert to expert. In 1984, Dr. Reginald Tsang convened a symposium to develop a consensus on the vitamin and mineral requirements of these infants. A book entitled *Vitamin and Mineral Requirements in Preterm Infants* (Tsang RC, ed. New York: Marcel Dekker, 1985) resulted from this meeting. In the following year, the Committee on Nutrition of the American Academy of Pediatrics (AAPCON) published its recommendations on the nutritional needs of premature infants in the *Pediatric Nutrition Handbook* (Forbes GB, Woodruff CW, eds. Elk Grove Village, Ill: American Academy of Pediatrics, 1985:66–86). Then in 1987, the European Society of Paediatric Gastroenterology and Nutrition, through its Committee on Nutrition of the Preterm Infant (ESPGAN-CON), issued a statement on the "Nutrition and Feeding of Preterm Infants" (*Acta Paediatr Scand* 1987;336(suppl):1–14).

As we enter the 1990s, experience, research, and the survival of infants of ever lower birthweights define a number of unique nutritional needs. *Nutritional Needs of the Preterm Infant* addresses the requirements for parenteral and enteral nutrition for premature infants, based on their gestational age and/or weight during three periods—transition, initial growth, and after hospital discharge. Table A.1, following, summarizes the consensus recommendations of the editors and authors of this text. Table A.2 compares the consensus recommendations for stable, growing premature infants to the AAPCON and ESPGAN-CON recommendations.

This rapidly expanding knowledge base has been challenging for formula manufacturers. In some cases, local regulations do not acknowledge the unique needs of the premature versus the term infant. Thus, the variety of commercial products in use worldwide reflects the evolution of our knowledge about nutrition and some adaptation of regulatory requirements over the decade of the 1980s. For example, Tables A.3 and A.4 show the diversity of manufacturers' formulations for current (1992) premature infant products.

This book by a panel of internationally known experts was sponsored by the International Union of Nutrition Sciences. The recommendations made here provide a basis for regulatory agencies to allow marketing of products that manufacturers design to meet the unique needs of premature infants.

Table A.1. Consensus Recommendations

Nutritional Needs of Stable/Growing Preterm Infants — mass units

| | | Preterm <1,000 g | | | Preterm ≥1,000 g | | |
| | | Parenteral | Enteral | | Parenteral | Enteral | |
		per kg/day	per kg/day	per 100 kcal	per kg/day	per kg/day	per 100 kcal
Water	mL	120–150	150–200	125–167	120–150	150–200	125–167
Energy	kcal	80–90+	110–120	100	80–90+	110–120	100
Protein	g	3.6–3.8	3.6–3.8	3.0–3.16	3.0–3.6	3.0–3.6	2.5–3.0
Carbohydrate	g	6–12*	—	—	6–12*	—	—
Lactose	g	—	3.8–11.4	3.16–9.5	—	3.8–11.8	3.16–9.8
Oligomers	g	—	0–8.4	0–7.0	—	0–8.4	0–7.0
Fat	g	0.5–1 up to 3	—	—	0.5–1 up to 3	—	—
Linoleic	g	4–15% cal	4–15% cal	0.44–1.7 g	4–15% cal	4–15% cal	0.44–1.7 g
Linolenic	g	1–4% cal	1–4% cal	0.11–0.44 g	1–4% cal	1–4% cal	0.11–0.44 g
C18:2/C18:3		≥5	≥5	≥5	≥5	≥5	≥5
Vitamin A	IU	700–1,500	700–1,500	583–1,250	700–1,500	700–1,500	583–1,250
lung disease		1,500–2,800	1,500–2,800	1,250–2,333	1,500–2,800	1,500–2,800	1,250–2,333
Vitamin D	IU	40–160†	150–400‡	125–333‡	40–160†	150–400‡	125–333‡
Vitamin E	IU	3.5§	6–12‖	5–10	3.5§	6–12‖	5–10
supplement HM		—	3.5	2.9	—	3.5	2.9
Vitamin K	µg	8–10	8–10	6.66–8.33	8–10	8–10	6.66–8.33
Ascorbate	mg	15–25	18–24	15–20	15–25	18–24	15–20
Thiamin	µg	200–350	180–240	150–200	200–350	180–240	150–200
Riboflavin	µg	150–200	250–360	200–300	150–200	250–360	200–300
Pyridoxine	µg	150–200	150–210	125–175	150–200	150–210	125–175
Niacin	mg	4–6.8	3.6–4.8	3–4	4–6.8	3.6–4.8	3–4

Nutrient	Unit						
Pantothenate	mg	1–2	1.2–1.7	1–1.5	1–2	1.2–1.7	1–1.5
Biotin	µg	5–8	3.6–6	3–5	5–8	3.6–6	3–5
Folate	µg	56	25–50	21–42	56	25–50	21–42
Vitamin B₁₂	µg	.3	.3	0.25	.3	.3	0.25
Sodium	mg	46–69	46–69	38–58	46–69	46–69	38–58
Potassium	mg	78–120	78–120	65–100	78–120	78–120	65–100
Chloride	mg	70–105	70–105	59–89	70–105	70–105	59–89
Calcium	mg	60–90¶	120–230	100–192	60–90¶	120–230	100–192
Phosphorus	mg	47–70¶	60–140	50–117	47–70¶	60–140	50–117
Magnesium	mg	4.3–7.2¶	7.9–15	6.6–12.5	4.3–7.2¶	7.9–15	6.6–12.5
Iron	mg	0.1–0.2	2	1.67	0.1–0.2	2	1.67
Zinc	µg	400	1,000	833	400	1,000	833
Copper	µg	20	120–150	100–125	20	120–150	100–125
Selenium	µg	1.5–2.0	1.3–3.0	1.08–2.5	1.5–2.0	1.3–3.0	1.08–2.5
Chromium	µg	0.05–0.2	0.1–0.5	0.083–0.42	0.05–0.2	0.1–0.5	0.083–0.42
Manganese	µg	1.0	7.5	6.3	1.0	7.5	6.3
Molybdenum	µg	0.25	0.3	0.25	0.25	0.3	0.25
Iodine	µg	1.0	30–60	25–50	1.0	30–60	25–50
Taurine	mg	1.88–3.75	4.5–9.0	3.75–7.5	1.88–3.75	4.5–9.0	3.75–7.5
Carnitine	mg	—	~2.9	~2.4	—	~2.9	~2.4
Inositol	mg	54	32–81	27–67.5	54	32–81	27–67.5
Choline	mg	—	14.4–28	12–23.4	—	14.4–28	12–23.4

*Max = 18 g
†Max = 400 IU/day
‡Aim = 400 IU/day
§Max = 7 IU
‖Max = 25 IU
¶Assuming a fluid intake of 120 to 150 mL/kg/day.

Table A.1. Consensus Recommendations (continued)

Nutritional Needs of Transitional Preterm Infants—mass units

| | | Preterm <1,000 g | | | Preterm ≥1,000 g | | |
| | | Parenteral | Enteral | | Parenteral | Enteral | |
		per kg/day	per kg/day	per 100 kcal	per kg/day	per kg/day	per 100 kcal
Water	mL	<5 days, 90–140 <2 wk, 80–120	<5 days, 90–140 <2 wk, 80–120	125–167 125–167	<5 days, 90–140 <2 wk, 80–120	<5 days, 80–120 <2 wk, 80–100	125–167 125–167
Energy	kcal	35 to 90+ in 7–14 days	110–120	100	35 to 90+ in 4–6 days	110–120	100
Protein	g	0–3.8	3.6–3.8	3.0–3.16	0–3.6	3.0–3.6	2.5–3.0
Carbohydrate	g	6–12*	—	—	6–12*	—	—
Lactose	g	—	3.8–11.2	3.16–9.3	—	3.8–11.8	3.16–9.8
Oligomers	g	—	0–8.4	0–7.0	—	0–8.4	0–7.0
Fat	g	0.5–1 up to 3	—	—	0.5–1 up to 3	—	—
Linoleic	g	4–15% cal	4–15% cal	0.44–1.7 g	4–15% cal	4–15% cal	0.44–1.7 g
Linolenic	g	1–4% cal	1–4% cal	0.11–0.44 g	1–4% cal	1–4% cal	0.11–0.44 g
C18:2/C18:3		≥5	≥5	≥5	≥5	≥5	≥5
Vitamin A lung disease	IU	700–1,500 1,500–2,800	700–1,500 1,500–2,800	583–1,250 1,250–2,333	700 1,500–2,800	700 1,500–2,800	583 1,250–2,333
Vitamin D	IU	40–160†	150–400‡	125–333‡	40–160†	150–400‡	125–333‡
Vitamin E	IU	3.5§	6–12‖	5–10	3.5§	6–12‖	5–10
supplement HM		—	3.5	2.9	—	3.5	2.9
Vitamin K by bolus injection	µg	300	300	—	300	300	—
Ascorbate	mg	15–25	18–24	15–20	15–25	18–24	15–20
Thiamin	µg	200–350	180–240	150–200	200–350	180–240	150–200
Riboflavin	µg	150–200	250–360	200–300	150–200	250–360	200–300
Pyridoxine	µg	150–200	150–210	125–175	150–200	150–210	125–175
Niacin	mg	4–6.8	3.6–4.8	3–4	4–6.8	3.6–4.8	3–4

	Units						
Pantothenate	mg	1–2	1.2–1.7	1–1.5	1–2	1.2–1.7	1–1.5
Biotin	μg	5–8	3.6–6	3–5	5–8	3.6–6	3–5
Folate	μg	56	25–50	21–42	56	25–50	21–42
Vitamin B_{12}	μg	.3	.3	0.25	.3	.3	0.25
Sodium	mg	0–23	0–23	0–20	0–23	0–23	0–20
Potassium	mg	0–39	0–39	0–33	0–39	0–39	0–33
Chloride	mg	0–35	0–35	0–30	0–35	0–35	0–30
Calcium	mg	60–90¶	120–230	100–192	60–90¶	120–230	100–192
Phosphorus	mg	47–70¶	60–140	50–117	47–70¶	60–140	50–117
Magnesium	mg	4.3–7.2¶	7.9–15	6.6–12.5	4.3–7.2¶	7.9–15	6.6–12.5
Iron	mg	0–0.2	0–2	0–1.67	0–0.2	0–2	0–1.67
Zinc	μg	150	500–800	415–670	150	500–800	415–670
Copper	μg	0, 20	120	100	0, 20	120	100
Selenium	μg	0, 1.3	1.3	1.1	0, 1.3	1.3	1.1
Chromium	μg	0, 0.05	0.05	0.04	0, 0.05	0.05	0.04
Manganese	μg	0, 0.75	0.75	0.63	0, 0.75	0.75	0.63
Molybdenum	μg	0, 0	0.3	0.25	0, 0	0.3	0.25
Iodine	μg	0, 1.0	11–27	9.2–22.5	0, 1.0	11–27	9.2–22.5
Taurine	mg	1.88–3.75	4.5–9.0	3.75–7.5	1.88–3.75	4.5–9.0	3.75–7.5
Carnitine	mg	—	—	—	—	—	—
Inositol	mg	54	32–81	27–67.5	54	32–81	27–67.5
Choline	mg	—	14.4–28	12–23.4	—	14.4–28	12–23.4

*Max = 18 g
†Max = 400 IU/day
‡Aim = 400 IU/day
§Max = 7 IU
‖Max = 25 IU
¶Assuming a fluid intake of 120 to 150 mL/kg/day.

Table A.1. Consensus Recommendations (continued)

Nutritional Needs of Stable/Growing Preterm Infants—SI units

		Preterm <1,000 g			Preterm ≥1,000 g		
		Parenteral	Enteral		Parenteral	Enteral	
		per kg/day	per kg/day	per 419 kJ	per kg/day	per kg/day	per 419 kJ
Water	mL	120–150	150–200	125–167	120–150	150–200	125–167
Energy	kJ	335–377+	460–502	419	335–377+	460–502	419
Protein	g	3.6–3.8	3.6–3.8	3.0–3.16	3.0–3.6	3.0–3.6	2.5–3.0
Carbohydrate	g	6–12*	—	—	6–12*	—	—
Lactose	g	—	3.8–11.4	3.16–9.5	—	3.8–11.8	3.16–9.8
Oligomers	g	—	0–8.4	0–7.0	—	0–8.4	0–7.0
Fat	g	0.5–1 up to 3	—	—	0.5–1 up to 3	—	—
Linoleic	g	4–15% cal	4–15% cal	0.44–1.7 g	4–15% cal	4–15% cal	0.44–1.7 g
Linolenic	g	1–4% cal	1–4% cal	0.11–0.44 g	1–4% cal	1–4% cal	0.11–0.44 g
C18:2/C18:3		≥5	≥5	≥5	≥5	≥5	≥5
Vitamin A	IU	700–1,500	700–1,500	583–1,250	700–1,500	700–1,500	583–1,250
lung disease		1,500–2,800	1,500–2,800	1,250–2,333	1,500–2,800	1,500–2,800	1,250–2,333
Vitamin D	IU	40–160†	150–400‡	125–333‡	40–160†	150–400‡	125–333‡
Vitamin E	IU	3.5§	6–12‖	5–10	3.5§	6–12‖	5–10
supplement HM		—	3.5	2.9	—	3.5	2.9
Vitamin K	nmol	18–22	18–22	15–18.5	18–22	18–22	15–18.5
Ascorbate	µmol	85–142	102–136	85–114	85–142	102–136	85–114
Thiamin	µmol	0.59–1.04	0.53–0.71	0.45–0.59	0.59–1.04	0.53–0.71	0.45–0.59
Riboflavin	µmol	0.40–0.53	0.66–0.96	0.53–0.80	0.40–0.53	0.66–0.96	0.53–0.80
Pyridoxine	µmol	0.73–0.96	0.73–1.02	0.61–0.85	0.73–0.96	0.73–1.02	0.61–0.85
Niacin	µmol	33–56	30–39	25–33	33–56	30–39	25–33

Pantothenate	µmol	4.6–9.1	5.5–7.8	4.6–6.8	4.6–9.1	5.5–7.8	4.6–6.8
Biotin	nmol	20–33	15–25	12–20	20–33	15–25	12–20
Folate	nmol	127	56–113	48–95	127	56–113	48–95
Vitamin B_{12}	nmol	0.22	0.22	0.18	0.22	0.22	0.18
Sodium	mEq	2–3	2–3	1.66–2.5	2–3	2–3	1.66–2.5
Potassium	mEq	2–3	2–3	1.66–2.5	2–3	2–3	1.66–2.5
Chloride	mEq	2–3	2–3	1.66–2.5	2–3	2–3	1.66–2.5
Calcium	mmol	1.5–2.25¶	3.0–5.63	2.5–4.69	1.5–2.25¶	3.0–5.63	2.5–4.69
Phosphorus	mmol	1.5–2.25¶	1.94–4.52	1.61–3.77	1.5–2.25¶	1.94–4.52	1.61–3.77
Magnesium	mmol	0.18–0.30¶	0.33–0.63	0.275–0.53	0.18–0.30¶	0.33–0.63	0.275–0.53
Iron	µmol	1.8–3.6	36	30	1.8–3.6	36	30
Zinc	µmol	6.1	15	12.7	6.1	15	12.7
Copper	µmol	0.31	1.9–2.4	1.6–2.0	0.31	1.9–2.4	1.6–2.0
Selenium	nmol	19–25	16–38	14–32	19–25	16–38	14–32
Chromium	nmol	1–3.8	1.9–9.5	1.6–8.1	1–3.8	1.9–9.5	1.6–8.1
Manganese	nmol	18	136	115	18	136	115
Molybdenum	nmol	2.6	3.1	2.6	2.6	3.1	2.6
Iodine	nmol	7.9	236–472	197–394	7.9	236–472	197–394
Taurine	µmol	22.5–45	36–72	30–60	22.5–45	36–72	30–60
Carnitine	µmol	—	~18	~15	—	~18	~15
Inositol	mmol	0.300	0.18–0.45	0.15–0.375	0.300	0.18–0.45	0.15–0.375
Choline	µmol	—	138–270	115–225	—	138–270	115–225

419 kJ = 100 kcal
*Max = 18 g
†Max = 400 IU/day
‡Aim = 400 IU/day
§Max = 7 IU
‖Max = 25 IU
¶Assuming a fluid intake of 120 to 150 mL/kg/day.

293

Table A.1. Consensus Recommendations (continued)

Nutritional Needs of Transitional Preterm Infants—SI units

	Units	Preterm <1,000 g			Preterm ≥1,000 g		
		Parenteral per kg/day	Enteral per kg/day	Enteral per 419 kJ	Parenteral per kg/day	Enteral per kg/day	Enteral per 419 kJ
Water	mL	<5 days, 90–140 <2 wk, 80–120	<5 days, 90–140 <2 wk, 80–120	125–167 125–167	<5 days, 90–140 <2 wk, 80–120	<5 days, 80–120 <2 wk, 80–100	125–167 125–167
Energy	kJ	146–377+ in 7–14 days	460–502 as tolerated	419 as tolerated	146–377+ in 4–6 days	460–502 as tolerated	419 as tolerated
Protein	g	0–3.8	3.6–3.8	3.0–3.16	0–3.6	3.0–3.6	2.5–3.0
Carbohydrate	g	6–12*	—	—	6–12*	—	—
Lactose	g	—	3.8–11.2	3.16–9.3	—	3.8–11.8	3.16–9.8
Oligomers	g	—	0–8.4	0–7.0	—	0–8.4	0–7.0
Fat	g	0.5–1 up to 3	—	—	0.5–1 up to 3	—	—
Linoleic	g	4–15% cal	4–15% cal	0.44–1.7 g	4–15% cal	4–15% cal	0.44–1.7 g
Linolenic	g	1–4% cal	1–4% cal	0.11–0.44 g	1–4% cal	1–4% cal	0.11–0.44 g
C18:2/C18:3	g	>5	>5	>5	>5	>5	>5
Vitamin A lung disease	IU	700–1,500 1,500–2,800	700–1,500 1,500–2,800	583–1,250 1,250–2,333	700 1,500–2,800	700 1,500–2,800	583 1,250–2,333
Vitamin D	IU	40–160†	150–400‡	125–333‡	40–160†	150–400‡	125–333‡
Vitamin E	IU	3.5§	6–12‖	5–10	3.5§	6–12‖	5–10
supplement HM		—	3.5	2.9	—	3.5	2.9
Vitamin K by bolus injection	nmol	666	666		666	666	
Ascorbate	µmol	85–142	102–136	85–114	85–142	102–136	85–114
Thiamin	µmol	0.59–1.04	0.53–0.71	0.45–0.59	0.59–1.04	0.53–0.71	0.45–0.59
Riboflavin	µmol	0.40–0.53	0.66–0.96	0.53–0.80	0.40–0.53	0.66–0.96	0.53–0.80
Pyridoxine	µmol	0.73–0.96	0.73–1.02	0.61–0.85	0.73–0.96	0.73–1.02	0.61–0.85
Niacin	µmol	33–56	30–39	25–33	33–56	30–39	25–33

Pantothenate	µmol	4.6–9.1	5.5–7.8	4.6–6.8	4.6–9.1	5.5–7.8	4.6–6.8
Biotin	nmol	20–33	15–25	12–20	20–33	15–25	12–20
Folate	nmol	127	56–113	48–95	127	56–113	48–95
Vitamin B_{12}	nmol	0.22	0.22	0.18	0.22	0.22	0.18
Sodium	mEq	0–1	0–1	0–0.8	0–1	0–1	0–0.8
Potassium	mEq	0–1	0–1	0–0.8	0–1	0–1	0–0.8
Chloride	mEq	0–1	0–1	0–0.8	0–1	0–1	0–0.8
Calcium	mmol	1.5–2.25‖	3.0–5.63	2.5–4.69	1.5–2.25‖	3.0–5.63	2.5–4.69
Phosphorus	mmol	1.5–2.25‖	1.94–4.52	1.61–3.77	1.5–2.25‖	1.94–4.52	1.61–3.77
Magnesium	mmol	0.18–0.30‖	0.33–0.63	0.275–0.53	0.18–0.30‖	0.33–0.63	0.275–0.53
Iron	µmol	0–3.6	0–36	0–30	0–3.6	0–36	0–30
Zinc	µmol	2.29	7.6–12.2	6.3–10.2	2.29	7.6–12.2	6.3–10.2
Copper	µmol	0, 0.31	1.9	1.6	0, 0.31	1.9	1.6
Selenium	nmol	0, 16	16	14	0, 16	16	14
Chromium	nmol	0, 1	1	0.8	0, 1	1	0.8
Manganese	nmol	0, 14	14	11	0, 14	14	11
Molybdenum	nmol	0, 0	3	2.6	0, 0	3	2.6
Iodine	nmol	0, 7.9	87–213	72–177	0, 7.9	87–213	72–177
Taurine	µmol	22.5–45	36–72	30–60	22.5–45	36–72	30–60
Carnitine	µmol	—	~18	~15	—	~18	~15
Inositol	mmol	0.300	0.18–0.45	0.15–0.375	0.300	0.18–0.45	0.15–0.375
Choline	µmol	—	138–270	115–225	—	138–270	115–225

419 kJ = 100 kcal
*Max = 18 g
†Max = 400 IU/day
‡Aim = 400 IU/day
§Max = 7 IU
‖Max = 25 IU
¶Assuming a fluid intake of 120 to 150 mL/kg/day.

295

Table A.2. Comparison of Enteral Intake Recommendations for Stable/Growing Preterm Infants

Nutrients per 100 kcal*

		Consensus Recommendations by the Authors of This Book		AAPCON[†]	ESPGAN-CON[‡]
		<1,000 g	≥1,000 g		
Water	mL	125–167	125–167	—	115–154
Energy	kcal	100	100	100	100
Protein	g	3.0–3.16	2.5–3.0	2.9–3.3	2.25–3.1
Carbohydrate	g			9–13	7–14
Lactose	g	3.16–9.5	3.16–9.8	—	—
Oligomers	g	0–7.0	0–7.0	—	—
Fat	g			4.5–6.0	3.6–7
Linoleic	g	0.44–1.7	0.44–1.7	0.4+	0.5–1.4
Linolenic	g	0.11–0.44	0.11–0.44	—	>0.055
C18:2/C18:3		>5	>5	—	5–15
Vitamin A	IU	583–1,250	583–1,250	75–225	270–450
lung disease		1,250–2,333	1,250–2,333	—	—
Vitamin D	IU	125–333[§]	125–333[§]	270	800–1,600/day
Vitamin E	IU	5–10	5–10	>1.1	0.6–10
supplement HM		2.9	2.9	—	—
Vitamin K	μg	6.66–8.33	6.66–8.33	4	4–15
Ascorbate	mg	15–20	15–20	35	7–40
Thiamin	μg	150–200	150–200	>40	20–250
Riboflavin	μg	200–300	200–300	>60	60–600
Pyridoxine	μg	125–175	125–175	>35	35–250
Niacin	mg	3–4	3–4	>0.25	0.8–5.0
Pantothenate	mg	1–1.5	1–1.5	>0.30	>0.3
Biotin	μg	3–5	3–5	>1.5	>1.5
Folate	μg	21–42	21–42	33	>60
Vitamin B$_{12}$	μg	0.25	0.25	>0.15	>0.15
Sodium	mg	38–58	38–58	48–67	23–53
Potassium	mg	65–100	65–100	66–98	90–152
Chloride	mg	59–89	59–89	—	57–89
Calcium	mg	100–192	100–192	175	70–140
Phosphorus	mg	50–117	50–117	91.5	50–87
Magnesium	mg	6.6–12.5	6.6–12.5	—	6–12
Iron	mg	1.67	1.67	1.7–2.5	1.5
Zinc	μg	833	833	>500	550–1,100
Copper	μg	100–125	100–125	90	90–120
Selenium	μg	1.08–2.5	1.08–2.5	—	—
Chromium	μg	0.083–0.42	0.083–0.42	—	—
Manganese	μg	6.3	6.3	>5	1.5–7.5
Molybdenum	μg	0.25	0.25	—	—
Iodine	μg	25–50	25–50	5	10–45
Taurine	mg	3.75–7.5	3.75–7.5	—	—
Carnitine	mg	~2.4	~2.4	—	>1.2
Inositol	mg	27–67.5	27–67.5	—	—
Choline	mg	12–23.4	12–23.4	—	—

*120 kcal/kg/day was used where conversion was made from per kg recommendations.
†American Academy of Pediatrics, Committee on Nutrition
‡European Society of Paediatric Gastroenterology and Nutrition, Committee on Nutrition of the Preterm Infant
§Aim = 400 IU/day

Table A.3. Commercial Formulas for Preterm Infants, 1992

Nutrients per 100 kcal

		Enfamil Premature Formula–24 (Mead Johnson USA)	Enfamil Premature Formula + Fe–24 (Mead Johnson USA)	Enfamil Premature Formula (Mead Johnson Canada)	Enfamil Premature Formula Plus (Mead Johnson Canada)	Enfamil Premature Formula Special (Mead Johnson Canada)	Enfalac Premature Formula (Mead Johnson International)
Volume	mL	124	124	147	124	124	—
Water	mL	109	109	134	109	109	—
Energy	kcal	100	100	100	100	100	100
Protein	g	3.0	3.0	3.0	3.0	2.5	3.0
Carbohydrate	g	11.1	11.1	10.7	10.7	11.0	11.0
Lactose	g	4.6	4.6	4.2	4.2	4.0	—
Oligomers	g	6.5	6.5	6.5	6.5	7.0	—
Fat	g	5.1	5.1	5.05	5.05	5.05	5.1
Linoleic	g	1.06	1.06	—	—	—	1.3
Linolenic	g	0.15	0.15	—	—	—	—
C18:2/C18:3		7.1	7.1	—	—	—	—
Vitamin A	IU	1,250	1,250	430	430	370	390
Vitamin D	IU	270	270	68	68	57	62.5
Vitamin E	IU	6.3	6.3	4.6	4.6	3.8	2.5
Vitamin K	µg	8	8	13	13	11	9
Ascorbate	mg	20	20	37	37	31	19
Thiamin	µg	200	200	250	250	210	79
Riboflavin	µg	300	300	620	620	520	160
Pyridoxine	µg	150	150	250	250	210	75
Niacin	mg	4	4	4.9	4.9	4.1	1.2
Pantothenate	mg	1.2	1.2	1.85	1.85	1.54	0.46
Biotin	µg	4	4	3.7	3.7	3.1	3
Folate	µg	35	35	37	37	31	36
Vitamin B_{12}	µg	0.25	0.25	0.56	0.56	0.47	0.5
Sodium	mg	39	39	40	40	34	48
Potassium	mg	103	103	100	100	83	129
Chloride	mg	85	85	86	86	71	85
Calcium	mg	165	165	163	163	135	120
Phosphorus	mg	83	83	81	81	68	66
Magnesium	mg	6.8	6.8	7.4	7.4	6.2	12
Iron	mg	0.25	1.8	0.25	0.25	0.21	0.2
Zinc	µg	1,500	1,500	1,000	1,000	830	1,000
Copper	µg	125	125	120	120	100	120
Selenium	µg	1.8	1.8	—	—	—	—
Chromium	µg	0.4	0.4	—	—	—	—
Manganese	µg	6.3	6.3	12.3	12.3	10.2	37
Molybdenum	µg	0.25	0.25	—	—	—	—
Iodine	µg	25	25	7.4	7.4	6.2	15
Taurine	mg	6	6	5.9	5.9	4.9	5
Carnitine	mg	2	2	2.0	2.0	1.7	—
Inositol	mg	17	17	28.2	25	25	6.0
Choline	mg	12	12	15.7	15.7	13.1	12

Table A.3.   Commercial Formulas for Preterm Infants, 1992 *(continued)*

Nutrients per 100 kcal

		Similac Special Care (Ross)	PM 60/40 (Ross Holland)	"Preemie" SMA 20 (Wyeth USA)	"Preemie" SMA 24 (Wyeth USA)	S–26 LBW (Wyeth)
Volume	mL	124	148	148	125	—
Water	mL	109	134	133	108	—
Energy	kcal	100	100	100	100	100
Protein	g	2.71	2.34	3.0	2.4	2.5
Carbohydrate	g	10.6	10.2	10.5	10.5	10.6
Lactose	g	5.3	—	5.3	5.25	5.3
Oligomers	g	5.3	—	5.3	5.25	5.3
Fat	g	5.43	5.6	5.2	5.4	5.3
Linoleic	g	0.70	1.3	0.485	0.5	0.55
Linolenic	g	—	—	—	—	—
C18:2/C18:3		—	—	—	—	—
Vitamin A	IU	680	300	475	300	300
Vitamin D	IU	150	60	75	60	60
Vitamin E	IU	4.0	3.0	2.2	1.9	1.9
Vitamin K	µg	12	8	10.5	8.6	8.6
Ascorbate	mg	37.0	9.0	10.5	8.6	8.6
Thiamin	µg	250	100	120	100	100
Riboflavin	µg	620	150	190	160	160
Pyridoxine	µg	250	60	75	60	60
Niacin	mg	5	1.05	0.93	0.75	0.80
Pantothenate	mg	1.9	0.45	0.53	0.45	0.45
Biotin	µg	37	4.5	2.5	2.2	2.2
Folate	µg	37	15.0	15	12.5	60
Vitamin B_{12}	µg	0.55	0.25	0.3	0.3	0.3
Sodium	mg	43	24	47	40	40
Potassium	mg	129	86	110	90	90
Chloride	mg	81	59	80	66	66
Calcium	mg	180	56	110	90	100
Phosphorus	mg	90	28	55	50	50
Magnesium	mg	12	6	10.5	8.6	8.6
Iron	mg	0.37	0.22	0.45	0.38	0.38
Zinc	µg	1,500	750	1,200	1,000	1,000
Copper	µg	250	90	105	86	90
Selenium	µg	1.8	1.9	—	—	—
Chromium	µg	—	—	—	—	—
Manganese	µg	12	5.0	30	25	7.5
Molybdenum	µg	—	—	—	—	—
Iodine	µg	20	6.0	12	10	10
Taurine	mg	6.7	6.7	7.0	6.0	5.9
Carnitine	mg	5.9	1.7	—	—	—
Inositol	mg	5.5	24.0	4.4	4	4
Choline	mg	10.0	12.0	19	16	16

Table A.3. Commercial Formulas for Preterm Infants, 1992 *(continued)*

Nutrients per 100 kcal

		PreNan (Nestle)	OsterPrem (Farley)	LBWF (Cow & Gate)	Prematil (Milupa)	Nenatal (Nutricia)	Pregallia (Gallia)
Volume	mL	—	—	—	—	125	—
Water	mL	—	—	—	—	109	—
Energy	kcal	100	100	100	100	100	100
Protein	g	2.9	2.5	2.7	2.9	2.75	2.86
Carbohydrate	g	11.4	8.8	10.6	10.8	10.00*	11.3
Lactose	g	8.7	7.5	5.2	7	5.0	7.85
Oligomers	g	2.7	1.3	5.4	3.8	4.0	3.43
Fat	g	4.9	6.1	5.5	5	5.50	4.86
Linoleic	g	0.63	1.0	1.8	—	0.88	0.78
Linolenic	g	0.057	0.094	0.17	—	0.09	0.092
C18:2/C18:3		11/1	11/1	10/1	22/1	10/1	—
Vitamin A	IU	300	430	413	300	413	300
Vitamin D	IU	100	120	120	120	120	0
Vitamin E	IU	2	19	1.7	2.8	1.63	1.14
Vitamin K	µg	12	9	11	4	11.25	12
Ascorbate	mg	16	35	35	22	35	10
Thiamin	µg	60	120	120	60	125	52.8
Riboflavin	µg	130	230	200	190	200	200
Pyridoxine	µg	75	130	100	130	35	57.2
Niacin	mg	1.0	1.3	1.2	0.8	1.25	0.88
Pantothenate	mg	0.45	0.63	0.6	0.4	0.63	0.38
Biotin	µg	2.2	2.5	4	1.5	3.75	1.72
Folate	µg	60	63	60	61	60.0	70
Vitamin B$_{12}$	µg	0.22	0.25	0.3	0.2	0.25	0.21
Sodium	mg	37	53	40	44	38	46
Potassium	mg	109	90	88	109	87	129
Chloride	mg	57	75	56	57	56	57
Calcium	mg	100	100	134	100	135	100
Phosphorus	mg	65	46.5	67	50	67.5	57.2
Magnesium	mg	11	6	10	8	10	7.42
Iron	mg	1.5	0.05	1.1	0.12	1.13	0.04
Zinc	µg	750	1,100	900	550	875	570
Copper	µg	90	120	100	91	100	100
Selenium	µg	—	20	0.9	—	—	—
Chromium	µg	—	—	—	—	—	—
Manganese	µg	6.9	4	15	14	—	27.2
Molybdenum	µg	—	—	6.3	—	—	—
Iodine	µg	10	10	12	14	12.5	13.8
Taurine	mg	8.0	6.4	6.9	8.3	6.75	—
Carnitine	mg	1.6	1.3	1.9	—	1.88	—
Inositol	mg	4.5	4.0	4	—	3.75	—
Choline	mg	7.5	7.0	8	—	7.50	2.9

*0.25 g glucose; 0.75 g maltose; 5.0 g lactose; 4.0 g oligomers.

Table A.4. Commercial Human Milk Fortifiers for Preterm Infants, 1992

Nutrients per 100 kcal

		Enfamil Human Milk Fortifier		Similac Natural Care		Éoprotein		FM 85		Preterm
		Powder (Mead Johnson)	Mixed as directed	(Ross)	Mixed 1:1	Powder (Milupa)	Mixed as directed	Powder (Nestle)	Mixed as directed	human milk estimate*
Volume	mL	—	124	124	136	—	130	—	125	150†
Water	mL	—	109	109	121	—	112	—	110	136
Energy	kcal	100	100	100	100	100	100	100	100	100
Protein	g	5.0	2.9	2.71	2.6	5.4	2.9	5.0	3.0	2.4†
Carbohydrate	g	19.3	12.5	10.6	10.8	18.8	12.3	20.1	12.9	11†
Lactose	g	4.6	9.1	—	—	0.2	8.6	—	8.0	10
Oligomers	g	10.4	2.6	—	—	18.3	3.7	20.1	5.1	1
Fat	g	0.28	4.4	5.43	5.4	0.4	4.5	—	4.2	5.3†
Linoleic	g	—	—	0.70	—	—	—	—	—	—
Linolenic	g	—	—	—	—	—	—	—	—	—
C18:2/C18:3		—	—	—	—	—	—	—	—	—
Vitamin A	IU	6,800	1,250	680	406	890	198	—	56.7	72‡
Vitamin D	IU	1,500	270	150	88	—	10	—	9.4	12§
Vitamin E	IU	33	6.2	4	2.5	1.8	0.8	—	0.5	0.6‡
Vitamin K	µg	31	8	12	8	1.8	2.8	—	2.4	3.0∥
Ascorbate	mg	83	20	37	23.4	135	26	—	5.3	6.7‡
Thiamin	µg	1,080	200	250	143	—	11	—	10.2	13¶
Riboflavin	µg	1,500	300	620	359	—	35	—	32.3	41¶
Pyridoxine	µg	815	150	250	141	—	7.6	—	7.1	9¶
Niacin	mg	21.4	4.0	5.0	2.88	—	0.25	—	0.2	0.3¶
Pantothenate	mg	5.2	1.2	1.9	1.18	—	0.25	—	0.2	0.3¶
Biotin	µg	19	4.1	37.0	20.7	—	0.68	—	0.6	0.8¶
Folate	µg	180	35	37	22.6	—	4.2	—	3.9	5¶
Vitamin B$_{12}$	µg	1.3	0.25	0.55	0.32	—	0.025	—	0.02	0.03¶
Sodium	mg	50	44	43	43	182	64	150	65	44†
Potassium	mg	111	82	129	104	21	66	63	72	74†

		126	95	81	85	135	96	107	92	89[†]
Chloride	mg	126	95	81	85	135	96	107	92	89[†]
Calcium	mg	640	144	210	133	335	83.6	279	89.2	38[†]
Phosphorus	mg	320	74	105	68	230	54	190	57.6	22[†]
Magnesium	mg	7	5.4	12	8.9	19	7.2	11.1	6.3	5[#]
Iron	mg	—	0.11	0.37	0.26	0.13	0.14	—	0.11	0.14[**]
Zinc	μg	5,100	1,350	1,500	1,077	135	495	—	441	560[††]
Copper	μg	440	125	250	163	27	53	—	44.9	57[‡]
Selenium	μg	—	—	1.8	—	—	—	—	—	—
Chromium	μg	—	—	—	—	—	—	—	—	—
Manganese	μg	34	6.3	12	6.8	27	4.6	—	0.4	0.54[‡‡]
Molybdenum	μg	—	—	—	—	—	—	—	—	—
Iodine	μg	—	22	6.0	15.5	4	23	—	21.3	27[‖]
Taurine	mg	—	—	6.7	—	16	2.5	—	—	—
Carnitine	mg	—	—	—	—	—	—	—	—	—
Inositol	mg	—	—	5.5	—	—	—	—	—	—
Choline	mg	—	—	10.0	—	—	—	—	—	—

*Preterm human milk estimates of 2-4 weeks postpartum.
[†]Gross SJ. N Engl J Med 1983;308(5):237–241 (postpartum week #3).
[‡]Adapted from Moran JR et al. J Ped Gastroenterol Nutr 1983;2:629–634 (21-day sample).
[§]Atkinson SA et al. Nutr Res 1987;7:1005–1011 (14–21 days).
[‖]Tsang RC, ed. Vitamin and mineral requirements in preterm infants. New York: Marcel Dekker, 1985.
[¶]Ford JE et al. Arch Dis Child 1983;58:367–372 (16-196 days).
[#]Adapted from Atkinson SA et al. Early Human Dev 1980;4:5-14 (first 4 weeks).
[**]Adapted from Mendelson RA et al. Early Human Dev 1982;6:145-151 (28-30 days).
[††]Adapted from Ehrenkranz RA. Ped Res 1984;18:195A, abstract #597 (28-day sample).
[‡‡]Personal communication, Atkinson SA et al. FASEB J 1989;3:A1246, abstract #5930 (2-4 weeks).

Index